T0214582

Lecture Notes in Computer Science   11201

Commenced Publication in 1973
Founding and Former Series Editors:
Gerhard Goos, Juris Hartmanis, and Jan van Leeuwen

Taisuke Izumi · Petr Kuznetsov (Eds.)

Stabilization, Safety, and Security of Distributed Systems

20th International Symposium, SSS 2018
Tokyo, Japan, November 4–7, 2018
Proceedings

Springer

Editors
Taisuke Izumi
Nagoya Institute of Technology
Nagoya, Japan

Petr Kuznetsov
Telecom ParisTech
Paris, France

ISSN 0302-9743 ISSN 1611-3349 (electronic)
Lecture Notes in Computer Science
ISBN 978-3-030-03231-9 ISBN 978-3-030-03232-6 (eBook)
https://doi.org/10.1007/978-3-030-03232-6

Library of Congress Control Number: 2018959139

LNCS Sublibrary: SL1 – Theoretical Computer Science and General Issues

This Springer imprint is published by the registered company Springer Nature Switzerland AG
The registered company address is: Gewerbestrasse 11, 6330 Cham, Switzerland

Preface

The papers in this volume were presented at the 20th International Symposium on Stabilization, Safety, and Security of Distributed Systems (SSS), held during November 4–7, 2018, in Tokyo, Japan.

SSS is an international forum for researchers and practitioners in the design and development of distributed systems with a focus on systems that are able to provide guarantees on their correctness, performance, and/or security in the face of an adverse operational environment. Research in distributed systems is now at a crucial point in its evolution, marked by the importance and variety of dynamic distributed systems such as peer-to-peer networks, large-scale sensor networks, mobile ad hoc networks, and cloud computing. Moreover, new applications such as grid and Web services, distributed command and control, and a vast array of decentralized computations in a variety of disciplines have driven the need to ensure that distributed computations are self-stabilizing, safe, secure, and efficient.

SSS started as the Workshop on Self-Stabilizing Systems (WSS), the first two of which were held in Austin in 1989 and in Las Vegas in 1995. Starting in 1995, the workshop was held biennially; it was held in Santa Barbara (1997), Austin (1999), and Lisbon (2001). As interest grew and the community expanded, in 2003 the title of the forum was changed to the Symposium on Self-Stabilizing Systems (SSS). SSS was organized in San Francisco in 2003 and in Barcelona in 2005. As SSS broadened its scope and attracted researchers from other communities, significant changes were made in 2006. It became an annual event, and the name of the conference was changed to the International Symposium on Stabilization, Safety, and Security of Distributed Systems (SSS). From then, SSS conferences were held in Dallas (2006), Paris (2007), Detroit (2008), Lyon (2009), New York (2010), Grenoble (2011), Toronto (2012), Osaka (2013), Paderborn (2014), Edmonton (2015), Lyon (2016), and Boston (2017).

This year the program was organized into three tracks reflecting major trends related to distributed systems: (1) Theoretical and Practical Aspects of Stabilizing Systems, (2) Distributed Networks and Concurrency, and (3) Safety in Malicious Environment. We received 55 submissions from 13 countries. Each submission was reviewed by at least three Program Committee members with the help of external reviewers. Out of the submitted papers, 24 were selected for presentation as regular papers. The symposium also included five brief announcements. Selected papers from the symposium will be published in a special issue of the journal *Information and Computation*. The committee also selected the following papers to be awarded:

- *Best paper:* Keisuke Doi, Yukiko Yamauchi, Shuji Kijima and Masafumi Yamashita, "Exploration of Finite 2D Square Grid by a Metamorphic Robotic System"
- *Best student paper:* Chirag Juyal, Sweta Kumari, Archit Somani, Sathya Peri and Sandeep Kulkarni, "An Innovative Approach to Achieve Compositionality Efficiently Using Multi-Version Object Based Transactional Systems"

On behalf of the Program Committee, we would like to thank all the authors who submitted their work to SSS. Special thanks to the track Program Committee chairs, Shantanu Das, Swan Dubois, and Jared Saia, for the great work that they put in making the symposium a success. We sincerely acknowledge the tremendous time and effort that the Program Committee members invested in the symposium. We are grateful to the external reviewers for their valuable and insightful comments and to EasyChair for tremendously simplifying the reviewing process and the preparation of the proceedings.

We also thank the general chairs, Xavier Defago, Toshimitsu Masuzawa, and Koichi Wada, for their effort in putting together the symposium and their invaluable advice. We gratefully acknowledge the Organizing Committee members, Doina Bein, François Bonnet, Masahiro Shibata, Yuichi Sudo, Yasumasa Tamura, for their time and invaluable effort that greatly contributed to the success of this symposium.

November 2018   Taisuke Izumi
                                                                     Petr Kuznetsov

Organization

General Chairs

Xavier Defago — Tokyo Institute of Technology, Japan
Toshimitsu Masuzawa — Osaka University, Japan
Koichi Wada — Hosei University, Japan

Steering Committee

Anish Arora — Ohio State University, USA
Ajoy K. Datta — University of Nevada, Las Vegas, USA
Shlomi Dolev — Ben-Gurion University, Israel
Sukumar Ghosh — University of Iowa, USA
Mohamed Gouda — UT Austin, USA
Ted Herman — University of Iowa, USA
Toshimitsu Masuzawa — Osaka University, Japan
Franck Petit — UPMC, France
Sébastien Tixeuil — UPMC, France

Program Committee Chairs

Taisuke Izumi — Nagoya Institute of Technology, Japan
Petr Kuznetsov — Telecom ParisTech, France

Local Arrangements Chair

Yasumasa Tamura — Tokyo Institute of Technology, Japan

Publicity Chairs

Doina Bein — California State University, USA
François Bonnet — Tokyo Institute of Technology, Japan
Masahiro Shibata — Kyushu Institute of Technology, Japan

Publication Chair

Yuichi Sudo — Osaka University, Japan

Track A: Theoretical and Practical Aspects of Stabilizing Systems

Track Chair

Swan Dubois — Sorbonne University, France

Program Committee

Leonid Barenboim	Open University of Israel, Israel
Silvia Bonomi	University of Rome La Sapienza, Italy
Sylvie Delaët	Paris-Sud University, France
Colette Johnen	Bordeaux University, France
Sayaka Kamei	Hiroshima University, Japan
Shay Kutten	Technion, Israel
Christoph Lenzen	MPI for Informatics, Germany
Alexandre Maurer	EPFL, Switzerland
Fukuhito Ooshita	NAIST, Japan
Stéphane Rovedakis	CNAM, France
Christian Scheideler	Paderborn University, Germany
Elad Schiller	Chalmers University of Technology, Sweden

Track B: Distributed Networks and Concurrency

Track Chair

Shantanu Das	Aix-Marseille University, France

Program Committee

François Bonnet	Tokyo Institute of Technology, Japan
Armando Castañeda	National Autonomous University of Mexico, Mexico
Antonella Del Pozzo	CEA LIST, France
Leszek Gasieniec	University of Liverpool, UK
Tomasz Jurdzinski	University of Wroclaw, Poland
Evangelos Kranakis	Carleton University, Canada
Flaminia Luccio	Ca' Foscari University of Venice, Italy
Thomas Nowak	Paris-Sud University, France
Lata Narayanan	Concordia University, Canada
Gopal Pandurangan	University of Houston, USA
Giuseppe Prencipe	University of Pisa, Italy
Nicola Santoro	Carleton University, Canada

Track C: Safety in Malicious Environment

Track Chair

Jared Saia	University of New Mexico, USA

Program Committee

James Aspnes	Yale University, USA
John Augustine	IIT Madras, India
Valerie King	University of Victoria, Canada
Seth Pettie	University of Michigan, USA
Cindy Phillips	Sandia National Labs, USA

Peter Robinson	McMaster University, Canada
Amitabh Trehan	Loughborough University, UK
Maxwell Young	Mississippi State University, USA
Mahnush Movahedi	DFINITY, USA
Mahdi Zamani	Visa Research, USA
Chaodong Zheng	Nanjing University, China

Additional Reviewers

Barath Ashok	Jonas Lefèvre
Gary Bennett	Atul Luykx
Janna Burman	Ioannis Marcoullis
Soumyottam Chatterjee	Ali Mashreghi
Stéphane Devismes	William K. Moses Jr.
Giuseppe Antonio Di Luna	Lars Nagel
Reza Fathi	Dominik Pajak
Robert Gmyr	Will Rosenbaum
Thorsten Götte	Negin Salajegheh
Kristian Hinnenthal	Iosif Salem
Hirotsugu Kakugawa	Alexander Setzer
Bruce Kapron	Hossein Shafagh
Ryan Killick	Masahiro Shibata
Anissa Lamani	Ben Wiederhake
Robert Lauko	

Sponsored by

  Springer

Supported by

 Japan Science and Technology Agency    東京工業大学 Tokyo Institute of Technology

Contents

A Self-stabilizing Hashed Patricia Trie.............................. 1
Till Knollmann and Christian Scheideler

Self-stabilizing Overlays for High-Dimensional Monotonic Searchability 16
Michael Feldmann, Christina Kolb, and Christian Scheideler

An Adaptive Logging Framework for Persistent Memories.............. 32
Pavan Poudel and Gokarna Sharma

On Underlay-Aware Self-Stabilizing Overlay Networks 50
Thorsten Götte, Christian Scheideler, and Alexander Setzer

A $O(\log n)$ Distributed Algorithm to Construct Routing Structures
for Pub/Sub Systems: Regular Submission 65
Volker Turau

Self-stabilization and Byzantine Tolerance for Maximal Matching......... 80
Stephan Kunne, Johanne Cohen, and Laurence Pilard

Exploration of Finite 2D Square Grid by a Metamorphic Robotic System ... 96
Keisuke Doi, Yukiko Yamauchi, Shuji Kijima, and Masafumi Yamashita

Physical Zero-Knowledge Proof for Makaro........................ 111
*Xavier Bultel, Jannik Dreier, Jean-Guillaume Dumas,
Pascal Lafourcade, Daiki Miyahara, Takuaki Mizuki, Atsuki Nagao,
Tatsuya Sasaki, Kazumasa Shinagawa, and Hideaki Sone*

Searching with Increasing Speeds 126
Leszek Gąsieniec, Shuji Kijima, and Jie Min

BEE'S STRATEGY AGAINST BYZANTINES Replacing Byzantine Participants
(Extended Abstract)... 139
*Amitay Shaer, Shlomi Dolev, Silvia Bonomi, Michel Raynal,
and Roberto Baldoni*

Simple and Fast Approximate Counting and Leader Election
in Populations.. 154
Othon Michail, Paul G. Spirakis, and Michail Theofilatos

Reliable Broadcast in Dynamic Networks with Locally Bounded
Byzantine Failures... 170
Silvia Bonomi, Giovanni Farina, and Sébastien Tixeuil

Acyclic Strategy for Silent Self-stabilization in Spanning Forests   186
  Karine Altisen, Stéphane Devismes, and Anaïs Durand

On Fast Pattern Formation by Autonomous Robots   203
  Ramachandran Vaidyanathan, Gokarna Sharma, and Jerry L. Trahan

Load Balanced Distributed Directories   221
  Shishir Rai, Gokarna Sharma, Costas Busch, and Maurice Herlihy

Relays: A New Approach for the Finite Departure Problem
in Overlay Networks   239
  Christian Scheideler and Alexander Setzer

Clairvoyant State Machine Replications   254
  Rida Bazzi and Maurice Herlihy

Set Agreement and Renaming in the Presence of Contention-Related
Crash Failures.   269
  Anaïs Durand, Michel Raynal, and Gadi Taubenfeld

An Innovative Approach to Achieve Compositionality Efficiently Using
Multi-version Object Based Transactional Systems   284
  Chirag Juyal, Sandeep Kulkarni, Sweta Kumari, Sathya Peri,
  and Archit Somani

Ring Exploration with Myopic Luminous Robots   301
  Fukuhito Ooshita and Sébastien Tixeuil

Uniform Circle Formation for Swarms of Opaque Robots with Lights   317
  Caterina Feletti, Carlo Mereghetti, and Beatrice Palano

Arbitrary Pattern Formation with Four Robots   333
  Quentin Bramas and Sébastien Tixeuil

Gracefully Degrading Gathering in Dynamic Rings   349
  Marjorie Bournat, Swan Dubois, and Franck Petit

Concurrent Lock-Free Unbounded Priority Queue with Mutable Priorities . . .   365
  Ivan Walulya, Bapi Chatterjee, Ajoy K. Datta, Rashmi Niyolia,
  and Philippas Tsigas

Brief Announcement: Deterministic Leader Election in Self-organizing
Particle Systems   381
  Rida A. Bazzi and Joseph L. Briones

Brief Announcement: Time Efficient Self-stabilizing Stable Marriage   387
  Joffroy Beauquier, Thibault Bernard, Janna Burman, Shay Kutten,
  and Marie Laveau

Brief Announcement: Feasibility of Weak Gathering in
Connected-over-Time Dynamic Rings 393
   Fukuhito Ooshita and Ajoy K. Datta

Brief Announcement: Optimal Self-stabilizing Mobile Byzantine-Tolerant
Regular Register with Bounded Timestamps 398
   Silvia Bonomi, Antonella Del Pozzo, Maria Potop-Butucaru,
   and Sébastien Tixeuil

Brief Announcement Continuous *vs.* Discrete Asynchronous Moves:
A Certified Approach for Mobile Robots 404
   Thibaut Balabonski, Pierre Courtieu, Robin Pelle, Lionel Rieg,
   Sébastien Tixeuil, and Xavier Urbain

Author Index 409

A Self-stabilizing Hashed Patricia Trie

Till Knollmann[1(✉)] and Christian Scheideler[2(✉)]

[1] Heinz Nixdorf Institute, Computer Science Department, Paderborn University,
Paderborn, Germany
tillk@mail.upb.de
[2] Computer Science Department, Paderborn University, Paderborn, Germany
scheideler@upb.de
https://www.hni.uni-paderborn.de/alg/
https://cs.uni-paderborn.de/ti/

Abstract. While a lot of research in distributed computing has covered solutions for self-stabilizing computing and topologies, there is far less work on self-stabilization for distributed data structures. Considering crashing peers in peer-to-peer networks, it should not be taken for granted that a distributed data structure remains intact. In this work, we present a self-stabilizing protocol for a distributed data structure called the *hashed Patricia Trie* (Kniesburges and Scheideler WALCOM'11) that enables efficient prefix search on a set of keys. The data structure has a wide area of applications including string matching problems while offering low overhead and efficient operations when embedded on top of a distributed hash table. Especially, longest prefix matching for x can be done in $\mathcal{O}(\log |x|)$ hash table read accesses. We show how to maintain the structure in a self-stabilizing way. Our protocol assures low overhead in a legal state and a total (asymptotically optimal) memory demand of $\Theta(d)$ bits, where d is the number of bits needed for storing all keys.

Keywords: Self-stabilizing · Prefix search · Distributed data structure

1 Introduction

We consider the problem of maintaining a distributed data structure for efficient *Longest Prefix Matching* in peer-to-peer (P2P) systems. We focus on the *hashed Patricia Trie* (HPT) introduced in [14] and present an algorithm rendering a self-stabilizing version of this data structure when applied on top of any reliable *distributed hash table* (DHT).

Definition 1 (Longest Prefix Matching). *Consider a set of binary strings called* keys *and a binary string x. The task of Longest Prefix Matching is to find a key y sharing the longest common prefix with x. A prefix of a binary string is a substring beginning with the first bit. We denote the longest common prefix of x and y by $lcp(x, y)$.*

This work was partially supported by the German Research Foundation (DFG) within the Collaborative Research Center 'On-The-Fly Computing' (SFB 901).

© Springer Nature Switzerland AG 2018
T. Izumi and P. Kuznetsov (Eds.): SSS 2018, LNCS 11201, pp. 1–15, 2018.
https://doi.org/10.1007/978-3-030-03232-6_1

We denote a prefix p of x by $p \sqsubseteq x$. p is a *proper prefix* of x ($p \sqsubset x$) if p is a prefix of x and $|p| < |x|$, where $|p|$ is the length of p. Longest Prefix Matching is an old problem with applications in various areas including string matching problems and IP lookup in Internet routers. To solve it efficiently in a distributed P2P system, the HPT has been introduced [14]. The HPT is a distributed data structure applied to any common DHT which allows efficient prefix search for x in $\mathcal{O}(\log |x|)$ read accesses to the hash table, i.e., solely based on the length of the search word x. The costs for an insertion of x is in $\mathcal{O}(\log |x|)$ read accesses and $\mathcal{O}(1)$ write accesses, while deletion can be done in $\mathcal{O}(1)$ accesses. The memory space used is asymptotically optimal in $\Theta(\text{sum of all key lengths})$. Moreover, *Suffix Trees* can be implemented efficiently using Patricia Tries and thus also hashed Patrica Tries (called *PAT Trees* [10]). This allows us to efficiently decide if a given string x is a substring of a text in a runtime only depending on the length of x.

The usefulness of Patricia Tries motivates us to investigate how a HPT can be maintained in a P2P system where nodes may enter/leave or even fail. While a lot of research has considered the design of self-stabilizing computation or topologies (see Sect. 1.2), to the best of our knowledge there are far fewer results concerning self-stabilizing distributed data structures. However, failures of peers may affect the correctness of any distributed data structure. Therefore, we consider the problem of finding an efficient distributed protocol to maintain a HPT in a self-stabilizing way.

1.1 Model

We assume the existence of a self-stabilizing *distributed hash table* (DHT) which provides the operations DHT-INSERT(x) to insert data and DHT-SEARCH(x) to retrieve data. These operations are carried out reliably on the stored data, i.e., no operation is ever canceled. We assume the existence of a collision-free hash function which maps binary strings to positions in $[0, 1)$ to store data in the DHT. The function is available locally at every peer. Each peer has a unique identifier, manages local variables and maintains a *channel*. When a peer sends a message m to peer p, it puts m in the channel of p. A channel has unbounded capacity and messages never get lost. If a peer processes a message in its channel, the message is removed from the channel afterwards.

We distinguish between two types of *actions*: The first one is for standard procedures and has the form $\langle label \rangle(\langle parameters \rangle) : \langle command \rangle$ where *label* is the name of the action, *parameters* define the set of parameters and *command* defines the statements that are executed when calling the action. It may be executed locally or remotely. The second type has the form $\langle label \rangle : (\langle guard \rangle) \rightarrow \langle command \rangle$ where *label* and *command* are defined as above and *guard* is a predicate over local variables. An action at peer p can only be executed if its guard is *true* or a message in the channel of p requests to call it. We call such an action *enabled*. The guard of our protocol routine TIMEOUT is always *true*.

A *state* of the system is defined by the assignment of variables at every peer, the data items and their values stored at every peer and all messages in channels of peers. The system can transform from a state s to another state s' by executing an enabled *action* at a peer. An infinite sequence of states $(s_1, s_2, \dots)$ is a *computation* if s_{i+1} can be reached by executing an action enabled in s_i for all $i \geq 1$. The state s_1 is called *initial state*. We assume *fair message receipt*, i.e., every message contained in a channel is eventually processed. Also, we assume *weakly fair action execution* such that any action that is enabled in all but finitely many states is executed infinitely often. This especially applies to the TIMEOUT procedure. We call a protocol *self-stabilizing* if it fulfills *convergence* and *closure*. Convergence means that starting from an arbitrary initial state, the protocol transforms the system to a legal state in finite time. Closure means that starting from a legal state, the protocol only transforms the system to consecutive legal states. Our goal is to provide a self-stabilizing HPT. We define the legal state of a HPT later in Sect. 4.1.

1.2 Related Work

The basic data structure we consider here is the Patricia Trie. This compressed tree structure has been introduced by Morrison in [16]. It was extended to the hashed Patricia Trie by Kniesburges and Scheideler in [14]. In [10], Gonnet et al. presented PAT Trees which are essentially Patricia Tries for special suffixes (*sistrings*) of a text. This widens the applications of Patricia Tries to general string problems such as deciding if a word or sentence is contained in a text [10]. The work on self-stabilization started with the research of Dijkstra in [7] where he analyzed self-stabilization in a token ring scenario. Since then, research has covered wide areas including self-stabilizing computation [3,5] and coordination [1,2,7,9]. Furthermore, with the rise of P2P systems [18,20], self-stabilizing topologies in the sense of overlay networks gained attraction [4,6,8,11–13,19]. We use approaches originally presented for topological self-stabilization. This includes a technique called *Linearization* presented by Onus et al. in [17]. A common approach for storing data in overlay networks is a distributed hash table (DHT) like Chord [20]. Using hashing, data items, as well as network peers, are mapped to the $[0, 1)$ interval such that a mapping between them is established. There are various results on self-stabilizing DHTs in the literature (for example [13]). Further, most (self-stabilizing) overlay networks can easily be extended to a DHT given sortable unique identifiers for the peers which is a common assumption.

1.3 Our Contribution

We present a self-stabilizing protocol called SHPT to maintain a slightly modified version of the HPT as presented in [14]. Whenever we refer to HPT, we implicitly mean the modified version. The HPT and our modification are briefly introduced in Sect. 2. Afterwards, Sect. 3 gives a high-level description of the most important mechanisms of our protocol. We only require for an initial state that the underlying DHT is in a legal state and that a set of unique keys is stored at DHT nodes. In Sect. 4, we show that our protocol stabilizes a HPT in finite time out of any initial state. When the HPT is in a legal state, our protocol guarantees a low overhead of a constant amount of hash table read accesses and messages generated at each DHT node per call of the protocol routine. Furthermore, we can bound the total memory consumption in a legal state to $\Theta(d)$ bits if d is the number of bits needed to store all keys. Due to space limitations, we deferred the Pseudocode and the full proofs concerning correctness and overhead to the full version [15].

2 Hashed Patricia Trie

We consider a data structure called the *hashed Patricia Trie* (HPT) as presented in [14]. The HPT is an extended Patricia Trie that is distributed in a P2P System by using a DHT. We briefly describe the construction. For details, we refer to [14]. The Patricia Trie is a compressed trie which was proposed by Morrison in [16]. Suppose we are given a key set KEYS consisting of strings. A trie is a tree structure that consists of labeled nodes and labeled edges. The root node is labeled by the empty string and every edge is labeled by one character. The label of a node is the concatenation of all edge labels of edges traversed on the unique path from the root to the node. For each $k \in$ KEYS there is a node labeled by k (see Fig. 1). The Patricia Trie introduces compression by allowing edge labels to be strings such that inner nodes with a single child, which do not represent a key, can be avoided. Similar to [14], we restrict ourselves to keys represented by binary strings. We store the Patricia Trie in a DHT by hashing all nodes by their label resulting in the hashed Patricia Trie. Our notation is close to the one of [14] and can be seen in Fig. 2.

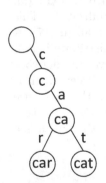

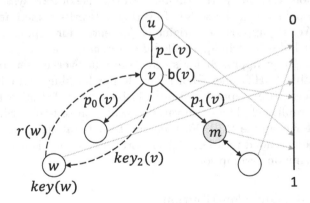

Fig. 1. Example of a classical Trie containing the keys "car" and "cat".

Fig. 2. Values stored at nodes of the HPT from the perspective of v. Nodes are stored by hashing their label to $[0, 1)$ in combination with a DHT. White nodes denote Patricia nodes while Msd nodes are depicted in gray.

Every Patrica node v has a label denoted by $b(v)$ and stores three edges. The *root* node stores the empty string $b(root) = \varepsilon$. $p_-(v)$ is the parent edge of

v pointing to the parent node u such that $b(u) \circ p_-(v) = b(v)$. We denote by $\circ$ the concatenation of strings. By $p_x(v)$ we denote the child edge of v starting with the value x for $x \in \{0, 1\}$. If $b(w) \in$ KEYS for a Patricia node w, we set $key(w) = b(w)$. Additionally, an inner Patricia node stores a $key_2(v) = k$, where k is a key with $b(v) \sqsubseteq k$. For efficient updates, the node w storing k has a field $r(w) = b(v)$. These key_2 values allow returning a valid result for a prefix search when stopping at any Patricia node. It is possible to assure that every inner Patricia node with two children has a key_2 pointing to a leaf node in its subtree.

To allow efficient prefix search, the Patricia Trie has been extended in [14]. Between every pair of directly connected Patricia nodes, Msd nodes (from Most Significant Digit) are added. Their length is chosen in a way that those nodes are hit by a binary search first. More specifically, Msd nodes are inserted between Patricia nodes such that their length is considered first by the binary search before the Patricia nodes around them are considered. We only give a short definition of the calculation of an Msd label in Definition 2. In the special case that an Msd label equals the label of a surrounding Patricia node, no Msd node is needed at that position. For details on how Msd nodes improve the prefix search operation, see [14].

Definition 2 (Msd Label). *Let $a = (a_m, \dots, a_0)$ and $b = (b_m, \dots, b_0)$ be two binary strings of the same length. Possibly, one of them is filled up with leading zeros to have length $m+1$. We define $msd(a, b)$ to be the position j where $a_j \neq b_j$ and $a_i = b_i$ for all $i > j$. That means, $msd(a, b)$ is the most significant bit (digit) at which a and b differ.*

Consider the binary labels $b(u)$ and $b(v)$ of two nodes u, v. Let $\ell_u = |b(u)|$ and $\ell_v = |b(v)|$ and without loss of generality let $\ell_u < \ell_v$. We define the Msd label $b(m)$ between u and v to be the prefix of v of length $\sum_{i=msd(\ell_u, \ell_v)}^{\lfloor \log \ell_v \rfloor + 1} (\ell_v)_i \cdot 2^i$.

For example, consider u, v with $b(u) = 10$ and $b(v) = 100101$, where $\ell_u = |b(u)| = (10)_2$ and $\ell_v = |b(v)| = (110)_2$. Then $msd(\ell_u, \ell_v) = msd((010)_2, (110)_2) = 2$, such that an Msd node m between u and v has label $b(m) = 1001 \sqsubset b(v)$ of length $2^2 = 4$.

The HPT supports operations PREFIXSEARCH(x) and INSERT(x) for a binary string x in $\mathcal{O}(\log |x|)$ read accesses on the hash table. Insertion takes additional $\mathcal{O}(1)$ write accesses and DELETE(x) is supported in constant hash table accesses. Furthermore, the memory space usage is in $\Theta\left(\sum_{k \in \text{KEYS}} |k|\right)$.

Modification. We modify the HPT to simplify the stabilization technique. Consider Fig. 3. The original HPT has a structure as shown on the left side. The Msd node m is in between the Patricia nodes u and w such that u and w point to m and m points to u (parent) and w (child). We modify this structure by having u and w point to each other and not to m. By this, deletions of Msd nodes do not concern the connectivity between Patricia nodes while the advantages of Msd nodes are still present. The crucial property of Msd nodes is that they point to Patricia nodes. Edges towards Msd nodes are not needed for the efficient operations introduced in [14]. For the rest of this paper, when we refer to the HPT, we mean the HPT with this small modification.

Next, we introduce some common terms that are used throughout the paper. HPT is the set of all data nodes of the HPT. This includes PAT as the set of nodes used in the original Patricia Trie and MSD which are the Msd nodes. By definition HPT = PAT ∪ MSD. We denote by KEYS the set of keys stored by the HPT. Let $u, v \in$ HPT with $b(u) \sqsubset b(v)$. In this case we say, u is *above* v while v is *below* u. Let $w \in$ HPT such that $b(u) \sqsubset b(w) \sqsubset b(v)$. Then w is in *between* u and v. If for two $u, v \in$ HPT with $b(u) \sqsubset b(v)$ there is no $w \in$ HPT with $b(u) \sqsubset b(w) \sqsubset b(v)$, then u and

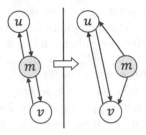

Fig. 3. Modified HPT

v are *closest* to each other. We say a child edge e of $v \in$ HPT is *valid*, if there exists a node $w \in$ HPT with $b(v) \circ e = b(w)$. Similar, a parent edge e of $v \in$ HPT is valid, if there exists a node $w \in$ HPT with $b(w) \circ e = b(v)$. Consider two nodes $v, u \in$ HPT, where u has an edge pointing to v and vice versa. We then speak of a *bidirectional* edge.

3   The SHPT Protocol

In the following, we present SHPT, our self-stabilizing protocol for maintaining a HPT. The corrections of SHPT can be divided into several parts. We present our assumptions concerning the underlying DHT first. Afterwards, we give an intuition on the different types of repairs our protocol performs. We often speak about actions executed by a HPT node v. This translates to actions that are executed by the corresponding DHT node storing v. For detailed Pseudocode, we refer to [15].

3.1   Properties of the DHT

We assume that the underlying DHT is in a legal state, i.e., it provides the actions DHT-SEARCH(x) and DHT-INSERT(x) which are carried out reliably on the stored data. Deletion of data is only done locally by our protocol. Stability of the DHT is crucial as our protocol relies on finding/manipulating nodes of the HPT solely based on their hash value given by their label. There are a lot of different self-stabilizing DHTs presented in the literature. Some of them are mentioned in Sect. 1.2.

Our main demand on the DHT is that at some point nodes are stored such that they can always be retrieved by their labels. HPT nodes are essentially data-items. Every DHT node regularly checks if all its stored data is at the correct peer based on the hashing. If data is stored incorrectly, it is sent towards the correct DHT node. When a data item i is inserted at a DHT node n, n checks if i is already present. If yes, i is only inserted if it does not collide with an already stored Patricia node that stores a key. If a HPT node v has been inserted, a presentation method is triggered for v and v is directly presented to the nodes referred to by $p_-(v)$, $p_0(v)$ and $p_1(v)$. The presentation mechanism is presented later. This assumption assures that keys are preserved while insertion is not blocked and every HPT node is presented at least once.

3.2 Correcting Edge Information

One general problem for self-stabilizing solutions is that every stored information can be corrupted. Thus, our protocol regularly checks information stored in a HPT node. Consider a node $v \in$ HPT. We refer to the information provided by the fields $p_-(v)$, $p_1(v)$ and $p_0(v)$ as well as $key_2(v)$ and $r(v)$ as *edge information*. Edge information can be checked rather simply as it allows reconstruction of a node's label $b(w)$. The label can be used to query the DHT for an (incomplete) copy of w. v can then compare the information stored at w with its own and decide for corrections. Some inconsistencies in the local structure can also be checked without querying the DHT. In general, when checking an edge e at node v, we distinguish three cases (see Fig. 4):

(a) e has a wrong form. For example, if $p_1(v) = (0\ldots)$ or $p_-(v)$ is not a suffix of $b(v)$. In this case, the edge is considered corrupted and is cleared.
(b) The node w that e points to does not exist. Again, e is not correct and is cleared.
(c) The node $w \in$ HPT that e points to does exist, but the edge provided by w which should point to v does not match e. Several sub-cases arise here. The protocol may have to simply present v to w, or a new node may need to be inserted.

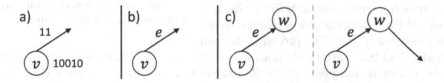

Fig. 4. Examples for the cases of wrong edge information.

Additionally, every node avoids edges pointing to Msd nodes. Such edges are treated as if they pointed to a non-existing node. A node v can check the values of $p_-(v)$, $key_2(v)$ and $r(v)$ by calculating if the prefix relation between itself and the respective nodes fulfills the definition of the hashed Patricia Trie. To prevent the spreading of incorrect information, new edges are only stored if they comply with the definition of the hashed Patricia Trie from the local perspective of v. We will go into detail on the creation of new edges and the insertion of nodes later.

3.3   Maintaining Connections

Our goal to stabilize the Patricia nodes of a HPT can also be formulated using *Branch Sets* as described in Definition 3. A Branch Set consists of all Patricia nodes on a branch from the root to a leaf node (see Fig. 5). When the HPT is in a legal state, there are as many Branch Sets as there are leaf nodes.

Definition 3 (Branch Set). *Consider a set of Patricia nodes with maximum cardinality S such that $u, w \in S$ implies $b(u) \sqsubset b(w)$ or $b(w) \sqsubset b(u)$ and the Patricia node $v \in S$ with maximum label length stores a key k. We call this set the* Branch Set *of k.*

We apply a technique called Linearization [17] to all Patricia nodes to create a list sorted by label length for all Branch Sets in finite time. It is important to exclude Msd nodes from the Linearization. Msd nodes are not presented nor do they delegate presentation messages. Due to deletion of a Patricia node, an Msd node might still be presented accidentally. However, we limit this problem by carefully handling deletions and insertions as described later. For the Linearization to work, we need to make sure that all nodes in a Branch Set are brought into and kept in a weakly connected state.

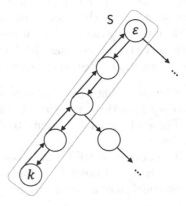

A Patricia node v with an empty parent edge tries to recreate connectivity by doing a modified PREFIXSEARCH($b(v)$) similar to the one presented in [14]. The procedure we call

Fig. 5. Branch Set S from the root (ε) to a leaf node (k) is the set of nodes in a branch of the hashed Patricia Trie in a legal state.

BINARYPREFIXSEARCH($b(v)$) does not search for $b(v)$ itself and only consists of the binary search phase of the PrefixSearch(x) of [14], returning a copy of a Patricia node w with $b(w) \sqsubset b(v)$. If no such node exists, we conclude that the root node is non-existent and trigger a construction of it.

Further, we let every Patricia node present its own label to its parent and its two children using a *presentation message*. A message presenting v is delegated to the Patricia node w closest to v. Delegation happens only by using edges and intermediate nodes sharing a Branch Set with v. All nodes maintain connections to labels which are closest to them while delegating presentations of other labels. This behavior resembles the Linearization approach presented in [17], allowing our protocol to form a sorted list for all branches of the HPT.

There is still an important issue we need to resolve. Consider a Branch Set S of nodes. We can end up in situations where nodes exist that do not contribute to the hashed Patricia Trie. Such nodes can be Patricia nodes not storing a key. To reduce memory demands, we are interested in removing unneeded nodes. In principle, deletion without harming connectivity can be done since the root node is always known implicitly. However, deletion increases distances. In addition, our protocol must provide the ability to create and integrate new Patricia nodes. When inserting and deleting nodes, we need to make sure that no loops are possible in which the system may take forever to stabilize. We will explain how to avoid such loops in the following.

3.4 Removal/Creation of Nodes

Due to the implicitly known root node, deletion is possible and should be considered to reduce memory demands. We distinguish between Msd nodes and Patricia nodes. Our modification allows us to handle Msd nodes in a simple and efficient way. We try to avoid any edges pointing to Msd nodes such that eventually, deletion and creation of Msd nodes does not influence the Patricia nodes and their structure. Only if there are two Patricia nodes u, w connected via a bidirectional edge, an Msd node between them might be inserted. Fortunately, Msd labels can be calculated locally and a corresponding Msd node can easily be accessed by querying the DHT. Any Msd node which is not between such two Patricia nodes, or has an incorrect label, is deleted.

A Patricia node v (except for the root) is *unnecessary* if $key(v) = nil$ and there are no two Patricia nodes u, w, both storing a key, such that $b(v) = \ell cp(b(u), b(w))$, i.e., u should be in a different subtree than w below v. From a global point of view, we can easily decide if v is unnecessary solely based on information about the situation below v. From a local perspective, v cannot decide but only assume to be unnecessary if it lacks child edges. We make the local protocol aggressive by deleting any node that lacks child edges and assumes to be unnecessary. This also introduces deletion of necessary Patricia nodes. Therefore, we always trigger a creation of new HPT nodes by Patricia nodes below the new ones. This avoids loops of creation and deletion of nodes, because newly created nodes inherently have valid children and, thus, do not assume to be unnecessary. Patricia nodes storing a key essentially form a stable starting point, because they are never deleted. The need to insert a Patricia node is detected by comparing a node's parent edge with the corresponding edge provided by the parent.

3.5 Distribution of References to Keys

In addition, SHPT tries to achieve the following. Every inner Patricia node v with two children should store a $key_2(v) = b(w)$ which points to a leaf node w storing a key such that $b(v) \sqsubset b(w)$. The respective leaf node w stores an $r(w)$ value pointing to v. This property is helpful for efficient prefix search. No matter at which Patricia node the prefix search stops, there is a key referenced having the node's label as a prefix. This key is a valid result for the search query. We call all inner Patricia nodes with two children and the root node key_2 *nodes*. Due to the resemblance of the hashed Patricia Trie with a binary tree, Fact 1 holds.

Fact 1. *Let L be the number of leaf nodes. Let I be the number of key_2 nodes. When the HPT is in a legal state, it holds $I \leq L \leq I + 1$. $L = I$, if the root has one child and $L = I + 1$ if it has two.*

To assure that every leaf node is referenced by a key_2 node, we allow the root to store up to two key_2 values. This reduces the number of hash table accesses created by our protocol, when the HPT is in a legal state.

If we naively assign leaf nodes to key_2 nodes, this may lead to situations in which a key_2 node cannot get a key_2 value. For an example, consider Fig. 6. The critical observation is that key_2 nodes with a shorter label, in general, have more possible leaf nodes they can point to than key_2 nodes with a longer label. Therefore, our protocol aims at prioritizing key_2 nodes which are closer to leaf nodes.

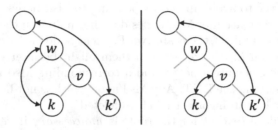

Fig. 6. Example where v cannot get a key_2 (left). The leaf nodes k and k' storing a key are already associated to Patricia nodes above v. The blocking of v is resolved as v takes over the key_2 of w (right).

We divide the protocol into three parts. First, all nodes continuously check if they should store a key_2 or r value and whether such a value points to a leaf node, respectively key_2 node. Second, if a leaf node v does not store a value in $r(v)$, it presents its label upwards in the HPT by sending a message crossing only parent edges. The first key_2 node w without a key_2 receiving the message sets $key_2(w) = b(v)$. Third, a key_2 node v repairs in the following way. If $key_2(v)$ points to leaf node w with $b(v) \sqsubset b(w)$, there are two cases.

(a) $b(v) \sqsubset r(w)$: Then $key_2(v)$ is set to nil since there may already be some key_2 node with longer label pointing at w.
(b) Else, v has either longer label than $r(w)$ or $r(w) = nil$. The protocol sets $r(w) = b(v)$.

If $key_2(v) = nil$, a message is sent upwards in the HPT and the first key_2 node w with $b(v) \sqsubset key_2(w)$ responds to v. Then, $key_2(v)$ is set to $key_2(w)$. Eventually, v takes over the key_2 value of w, because w executes case (a).

Intuitively, key_2 nodes without a key_2 pull values from nodes with shorter label. Simultaneously, leaf nodes without an r value present their label towards the root.

4   Protocol Analysis

In this section, we show that SHPT is self-stabilizing and transforms the HPT in finite time to a legal state. Furthermore, we present results concerning memory usage and the number of hash table accesses and messages when the HPT is in a legal state.

4.1 Correctness

We begin by showing the correctness of our self-stabilizing protocol. We use a commonly known technique introduced by Dijkstra in [7]. Our goal is to show Theorem 1. For that we consider a sequence of intermediate states that are reached consecutively until the HPT is in a legal state. For every state we show *convergence* towards the state and *closure* within it, i.e., the properties of the state are kept by our protocol.

Theorem 1. *The algorithm creates in finite time a hashed Patricia Trie in a legal state out of any initial state in which the DHT is in a legal state and there is a set of unique keys stored at DHT nodes.*

In the following, we briefly sketch the main proof by presenting a sequence of main lemmas that roughly reflect the states the system reaches. Each main lemma thereby consists of multiple properties that are proven by a set of lemmas on its own. The full proof consisting of all lemmas, their respective proofs, and the complete definition of a legal state of the HPT can be found in [15].

To prove the correctness captured in Theorem 1, we first need to formally define a legal state of the HPT. Due to space limitations, we only give an intuitive definition. For the complete definition, see the full version [15]. Intuitively, the HPT is in a legal state if we have as few HPT nodes as possible in the system, all keys are stored correctly, the structure is consistent to the (modified) definition presented in Sect. 2, and the references to keys in key_2 nodes are existing and stored at correct nodes.

Initially, we only assume that a set of unique keys is stored at DHT nodes. The first lemma states that general repair mechanisms assure correctly stored keys and Patricia nodes.

Lemma 1. *In finite time it holds: Every key k is stored in a node $v \in PAT$ with $b(v) = k$. Furthermore, every node is stored at the DHT node responsible for it. Consider any $v \in HPT$ that is deleted. As long as v is not reconstructed, in finite time it holds:*

(a) There is no presentation message for $b(v)$.
(b) There is no edge pointing towards $b(v)$ in the system.

From now on, the proof consists of three phases. In a first phase, all Patricia nodes which are not needed for the final structure are removed. The second phase considers the reconstruction of the binary tree structure of the HPT and corrects the sets of Patricia nodes and Msd nodes. In the third and last phase, information stored in key_2 and r fields is made consistent.

Phase I – Deletion of Patricia Nodes
In this phase, the protocol makes sure that all Patricia nodes which are not needed in the final structure are removed. Initially, information stored at HPT nodes that directly contradicts the definition of the HPT is cleared. This can be information such as a parent edge at $v \in$ HPT that is no suffix of $b(v)$. After that, Patricia nodes and Msd nodes in unnecessary subtrees, i.e., subtrees not containing a key, and unnecessary inner Patricia nodes are gradually removed (Fig. 7). Every leaf node in an unnecessary subtree detects in finite time that it has no valid children and is deleted.

Lemma 2. *In finite time, every unnecessary Patricia node is removed. A Patricia node v is* unnecessary *if there are no two keys k_1 and k_2 with $b(v) = \ell cp(k_1, k_2)$.*

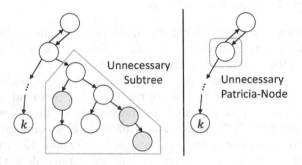

Fig. 7. Node k stores a key. Msd nodes are sketched in grey. First, unnecessary subtrees are deleted (left), then remaining unnecessary Patricia nodes are removed (right).

Patricia nodes which are necessary may still be deleted because of their local perspective. However, this deletion is limited and stops after finitely many deletions. This holds, because Patricia nodes are only deleted due to incorrect child edges. If a new Patricia node with a long label is inserted, its child edges are initially valid and stay valid. There cannot be infinitely many deletions triggered, because the structure stabilizes bottom-up.

Lemma 3. *In finite time, every Patricia node has valid child edges pointing to Patricia nodes and no further Patricia node is deleted.*

Phase II – Reconstruction
In the second phase, SHPT reconstructs the HPT by rebuilding missing Patricia nodes and repairing connections. Since every node tries to create a parent edge pointing to a Patricia node with shorter label, eventually all missing Patricia nodes are detected and can be inserted. The process works in a bottom-up fashion, i.e., Patricia nodes with longer labels reconstruct missing nodes with shorter ones. The Patricia nodes storing a key as well as the root node act as fixed points in this case, because they are never deleted once constructed.

Lemma 4. *In finite time, the root node exists and no Patricia node points to an Msd node. Furthermore, missing Patricia nodes are reconstructed. Also, every Patricia node has valid edges pointing only to existing Patricia nodes, i.e., there is a path from every Patricia node to the root and there is a path from the root to every Patricia node.*

It is crucial that no Patricia node points to an Msd node, because edges to Msd nodes are effectively treated as corrupt ones. This property assures that Msd nodes are eventually excluded from the Linearization procedure. Linearization then allows us to show that every Branch Set (see Definition 3) of Patricia nodes eventually forms a stable sorted list. Incorrect Msd nodes are removed without affecting the rest of the HPT and missing Msd nodes are inserted. Further, correct Msd nodes are not deleted, because the two Patricia nodes closest to a correct Msd node are not deleted and do not change their edges any more. All these properties are reflected in Lemma 5. For completeness, we refer to the definition of incorrect and missing Msd nodes in the full proof in [15].

Lemma 5. *In finite time for every Branch Set S it holds: Between every pair of closest Patricia nodes $u, w \in S$ there is a bidirectional edge. Furthermore, every incorrect Msd node is removed and all missing Msd nodes are inserted.*

Phase III – Consistency

In the final phase the information stored in key_2 and r fields is corrected to be consistent. Due to Fact 1, we know that this can be achieved. The root is allowed to store up to two key_2 values. Therefore, there is always a way to store all keys of leaf nodes in key_2 nodes. First, we show that nodes which should not store a key_2 value remove any such stored value. Further, references in key_2 and r fields are deleted when they contradict the relationship $r(key_2(v)) = b(v)$, where v is a key_2 nodes and $key_2(v)$ references a leaf node.

Lemma 6. *In finite time, only key_2 nodes store a key_2 and only leaf nodes store an r value. Every key_2 value stored at a Patricia node v points to a leaf w with $b(v) \sqsubseteq b(w)$ and every r value stored at a Patricia node w points to a key_2 node v with $b(v) \sqsubseteq b(w)$.*

From now on, key_2 nodes not storing a key_2 try to acquire the key_2 of a key_2 node above them. Leaf nodes lacking a reference in r present themselves to key_2 nodes above them. Therefore, the length of the longest label of a key_2 node not storing a staying key_2 reduces over time. As this length is finite, the process terminates. Thereafter, the r values of leaf nodes are corrected, because the key_2 values do not change any more.

Lemma 7. *In finite time, all key_2 nodes store a stable key_2 and all leaf nodes store a stable r value. For every key_2 node v, the node w with $b(w) = key_2(v)$ is a leaf node with $r(w) = b(v)$.*

Finally, our protocol is correct as all unnecessary nodes are removed, missing nodes are inserted, Patricia nodes are connected by bidirectional edges, and the information stored in key_2 and r fields is consistent such that the HPT is is in a legal state in finite time.

4.2   Overhead

Assume, the HPT is in a legal state. We give results for the complexity in terms of hash table accesses and messages and the memory overhead of our solution. Due to space limitations, we refer to the full version [15] for the proofs of the following theorems. When a DHT node executes SHPT by calling its TIMEOUT Method, exactly one HPT node is checked. Thereby, at most a constant number of other HPT nodes may be partially acquired or notified and Theorem 2 holds.

Theorem 2. *When the HPT is in a legal state, SHPT creates a constant number of hash table (read) accesses and messages per call of* TIMEOUT *at each DHT node.*

Unnecessary Patricia nodes and incorrect Msd nodes are removed by SHPT. Therefore, the HPT nodes are the same as presented in the construction in Sect. 2 and Theorem 3 holds.

Theorem 3. *Let d be the number of bits needed to store all keys. The total memory used by a HPT in a legal state is in $\Theta(d)$ bits.*

References

1. Afek, Y., Kutten, S., Yung, M.: Memory-efficient self stabilizing protocols for general networks. In: van Leeuwen, J., Santoro, N. (eds.) WDAG 1990. LNCS, vol. 486, pp. 15–28. Springer, Heidelberg (1991). https://doi.org/10.1007/3-540-54099-7_2
2. Arora, A., Gouda, M.: Distributed reset. IEEE Trans. Comput. **43**(9), 1026–1038 (1994)
3. Awerbuch, B., Varghese, G.: Distributed program checking: a paradigm for building self-stabilizing distributed protocols. In: Proceedings 32nd Annual Symposium of Foundations of Computer Science, pp. 258–267. IEEE, October 1991
4. Clouser, T., Nesterenko, M., Scheideler, C.: Tiara: a self-stabilizing deterministic skip list and skip graph. Theor. Comput. Sci. **428**, 18–35 (2012)
5. Collin, Z., Dolev, S.: Self-stabilizing depth-first search. Inf. Process. Lett. **49**(6), 297–301 (1994)
6. Cramer, C., Fuhrmann, T.: Self-stabilizing ring networks on connected graphs. Technical report, University of Karlsruhe (2005)
7. Dijkstra, E.W.: Self-stabilizing systems in spite of distributed control. Commun. ACM **17**(11), 643–644 (1974)
8. Dolev, S., Kat, R.I.: HyperTree for self-stabilizing peer-to-peer systems. In: 3rd IEEE International Symposium on Proceedings of the Network Computing and Applications. NCA 2004, pp. 25–32. IEEE Computer Society, Washington, DC (2004)
9. Flatebo, M., Datta, A.K.: Two-state self-stabilizing algorithms for token rings. IEEE Trans. Softw. Eng. **20**(6), 500–504 (1994)
10. Gonnet, G.H., Baeza-Yates, R.A., Snider, T.: New indices for text: PAT Trees and PAT arrays. In: Frakes, W.B., Baeza-Yates, R. (eds.) Information Retrieval, pp. 66–82. Prentice-Hall Inc., Upper Saddle River (1992)

11. Jacob, R., Richa, A., Scheideler, C., Schmid, S., Täubig, H.: SKIP+: a self-stabilizing skip graph. J. ACM **61**(6), 36 (2014)
12. Jacob, R., Ritscher, S., Scheideler, C., Schmid, S.: A self-stabilizing and local Delaunay graph construction. In: Dong, Y., Du, D.-Z., Ibarra, O. (eds.) ISAAC 2009. LNCS, vol. 5878, pp. 771–780. Springer, Heidelberg (2009). https://doi.org/10.1007/978-3-642-10631-6_78
13. Kniesburges, S., Koutsopoulos, A., Scheideler, C.: Re-chord: a self-stabilizing chord overlay network. In: Proceedings of the 23rd Annual ACM Symposium on Parallelism in Algorithms and Architectures. SPAA 2011, pp. 235–244. ACM, New York (2011)
14. Kniesburges, S., Scheideler, C.: Hashed Patricia Trie: efficient longest prefix matching in peer-to-peer systems. In: Katoh, N., Kumar, A. (eds.) WALCOM 2011. LNCS, vol. 6552, pp. 170–181. Springer, Heidelberg (2011). https://doi.org/10.1007/978-3-642-19094-0_18
15. Knollmann, T., Scheideler, C.: A Self-stabilizing hashed Patricia Trie. ArXiv e-prints. http://arxiv.org/abs/1809.04923 (2018)
16. Morrison, D.R.: PATRICIA - practical algorithm to retrieve information coded in alphanumeric. J. ACM **15**(4), 514–534 (1968)
17. Onus, M., Richa, A., Scheideler, C.: Linearization: locally self-stabilizing sorting in graphs. In: Proceedings of the Meeting on Algorithm Engineering & Expermiments, pp. 99–108. Society for Industrial and Applied Mathematics, Philadelphia (2007)
18. Rowstron, A., Druschel, P.: Pastry: scalable, decentralized object location, and routing for large-scale peer-to-peer systems. In: Guerraoui, R. (ed.) Middleware 2001. LNCS, vol. 2218, pp. 329–350. Springer, Heidelberg (2001). https://doi.org/10.1007/3-540-45518-3_18
19. Shaker, A., Reeves, D.S.: Self-stabilizing structured ring topology P2P systems. In: Proceedings of the 5th IEEE International Conference on Peer-to-Peer Computing, pp. 39–46. IEEE, August 2005
20. Stoica, I., Morris, R., Liben-Nowell, D., Karger, D.R., Kaashoek, M.F., Dabek, F., Balakrishnan, H.: Chord: a scalable peer-to-peer lookup protocol for internet applications. IEEE/ACM Trans. Netw. **11**(1), 17–32 (2003)

Self-stabilizing Overlays
for High-Dimensional Monotonic
Searchability

Michael Feldmann[✉], Christina Kolb, and Christian Scheideler

Paderborn University, Fürstenallee 11, 33102 Paderborn, Germany
{michael.feldmann,ckolb,scheideler}@upb.de

Abstract. We extend the concept of monotonic searchability [17,18] for self-stabilizing systems from one to multiple dimensions. A system is self-stabilizing if it can recover to a legitimate state from any initial illegal state. These kind of systems are most often used in distributed applications. Monotonic searchability provides guarantees when searching for nodes while the recovery process is going on. More precisely, if a search request started at some node u succeeds in reaching its destination v, then all future search requests from u to v succeed as well. Although there already exists a self-stabilizing protocol for a two-dimensional topology [10] and an universal approach for monotonic searchability [18], it is not clear how both of these concepts fit together effectively. The latter concept even comes with some restrictive assumptions on messages, which is not the case for our protocol. We propose a simple novel protocol for a self-stabilizing two-dimensional quadtree that satisfies monotonic searchability. Our protocol can easily be extended to higher dimensions and offers routing in $\mathcal{O}(\log n)$ hops for any search request.

Keywords: Distributed systems · Topological self-stabilization
Monotonic searchability · Quadtrees · Octtrees

1 Introduction

Due to the growth and relevance of the Internet, the importance of distributed systems is increasing. Such systems are needed, for instance, in social media networks or multiplayer games and have to support a large number of participants. However, as soon as such a system has become large, the occurrence of changes or faults are not an exception but the rule. In order to recover from an arbitrary state to a legitimate one, distributed protocols are needed that are *self-stabilizing*.

Most of the proposed self-stabilizing protocols only show that the system *eventually* converges to a legitimate state, without considering the *monotonicity*

This work was partially supported by the German Research Foundation (DFG) within the Collaborative Research Center On-The-Fly Computing (SFB 901).

T. Izumi and P. Kuznetsov (Eds.): SSS 2018, LNCS 11201, pp. 16–31, 2018.
https://doi.org/10.1007/978-3-030-03232-6_2

of the actual recovery process. Monotonicity means that the functionality of the system regarding a specific property never gets worse as time progresses, i.e., for two points in time t, t' with $t < t'$, the functionality of the system is better in t' than in t.

In this paper we are interested in *searching*, as this is one of the most important operations in a distributed system. We study systems that satisfy *monotonic searchability*: If a search request for node w starting at node v succeeds at time t, then every search request for w initiated by v at time $t' > t$ succeeds as well.

Previous work on monotonic searchability [17,18] proposed self-stabilizing protocols for one-dimensional topologies (for instance a sorted list). Still, up to this point it is not known how to come up with an efficient self-stabilizing protocol for high-dimensional settings that satisfies monotonic searchability. High-dimensional settings are relevant for example in wireless ad-hoc networks or social networks where processes are defined by multiple parameters.

This paper introduces a novel protocol BUILDQUADTREE for a self-stabilizing quadtree along with a routing protocol SEARCHQUAD that satisfies monotonic searchability and terminates after $\mathcal{O}(\log n)$ hops on any input. To the best of our knowledge, this is the first protocol that combines self-stabilization and monotonic searchability for the two-dimensional case. In addition, one can easily extend our protocols in order to work for multiple dimensions. For the two-dimensional case, we expand the notion of monotonic searchability to an even stronger and more realistic property, which we call *geographic monotonic searchability* and show that SEARCHQUAD satisfies this property as well. Our protocols stand out due to their simplicity and elegance and do not enforce restrictive assumptions on messages, as it has been done for the universal approach [18].

1.1 Model

We consider a two-dimensional square P of unit side length and model the distributed system as a directed graph $G = (V, E)$ with n nodes. Each node $v \in V$ represents a single peer and can be identified via its *unique position* in P given by *coordinates* $(v_x, v_y) \in [0, 1]^2$. We define $\|(u, v)\|$ as the Euclidean distance between two nodes $u, v \in V$, i.e., $\|(u, v)\| = \sqrt{(u_x - v_x)^2 + (u_y - v_y)^2}$. Additionally, each node v maintains local protocol-based variables and has a *channel* $v.Ch$, which is a system-based variable that contains incoming messages. We assume a channel to be able to store any finite number of messages. Messages are never duplicated or get lost in the channel. If a node u knows the coordinates of some other node v, then u can send a message m to v by putting m into $v.Ch$. There is a directed edge $(u, v) \in E$ whenever u stores (v_x, v_y) in its local memory or when there is a message in $u.Ch$ carrying (v_x, v_y). In the former case, we call that edge *explicit* and in the latter case we call that edge *implicit*.

Nodes may execute *actions*: An action is a standard procedure and has the form $\langle label \rangle(\langle parameters \rangle) : \langle command \rangle$, where *label* is the name of that action, *parameters* defines the set of parameters and *command* defines the statements that are executed when calling that action. It may be called locally or remotely, i.e., every message that is sent to a node has the form $\langle label \rangle(\langle parameters \rangle)$.

An action in a process v is *enabled* if there is a request for calling it in $v.Ch$. Once the request is processed, it is removed from $v.Ch$. There is a special action called TIMEOUT that is not triggered via messages but is executed periodically by each node.

We define the *system state* to be an assignment of a value to every node's variables and messages to each channel. A *computation* is an infinite sequence of system states, where the state s_{i+1} can be reached from its previous state s_i by executing an action in s_i. We call the first state of a given computation the *initial state*. We assume *fair message receipt*, meaning that every message of the form $\langle label\rangle(\langle parameters\rangle)$ that is contained in some channel, is eventually processed. We place no bounds on message propagation delay or relative node execution speed, i.e., we allow fully asynchronous computations and non-FIFO message delivery. Our protocol does not manipulate node coordinates and thus only operates on them in *compare-store-send* mode, i.e., we are only allowed to compare node coordinates to each other, store them in a node's local memory or send them in a message.

We assume for simplicity that there are no *corrupted coordinates* in the initial state of the system, i.e., coordinates of unavailable nodes. One could use failure detectors to solve this, but this is not within the scope of this paper, since without them the problem of guaranteeing monotonic searchability is still non-trivial. Having node coordinates to be read-only also makes sense in our setting, as these are usually delivered by an external component that is not in control of our protocol, for instance like GPS. In initial states there may exist *corrupted messages* in node channels, i.e., messages containing false information. We will argue that at a certain point in time, all of these messages will be processed and no more corrupted messages are in the system.

Nodes are able to issue search requests at any point in time: A search request is a message SEARCH$(v, (x, y))$, where v is the sender of the message and $(x, y) \in [0, 1]^2$ are the coordinates we want to search for. A search request is delegated along edges in G according to a given routing protocol, until the request *terminates*, i.e., either the node with coordinates (x, y) is reached or the request cannot be forwarded anymore. Note that (x, y) do not necessarily need to be coordinates of an existing node, i.e., in such a case the routing protocol may just stop at some node that is close to (x, y). Upon termination at node w, the reference of w is returned to the sender v (in the pseudocode we indicate this via a return statement).

1.2 Problem Statement

In this paper we consider the standard definition for self-stabilization:

Definition 1 (Self-stabilization). *A protocol is self-stabilizing w.r.t. a set of legitimate states if it satisfies the following two properties:*

1. *Convergence: Starting from an arbitrary system state, the protocol is guaranteed to arrive at a legitimate state.*

2. *Closure: Starting from a legitimate state, the protocol remains in legitimate states thereafter.*

We are interested in *topological self-stabilization* in this paper, meaning that our self-stabilizing protocol is allowed to perform changes to the overlay network G. In order for our protocol to work, we require the directed graph G containing all explicit and implicit edges to be at least weakly connected initially. Once there are multiple weakly connected components in G, these components cannot be connected to each other anymore as it has been shown in [13] for compare-store-send protocols. For a graph that contains multiple weakly connected components, our protocol converts each of these components to our desired topology.

Consider the following definition of (standard) monotonic searchability:

Definition 2 (Monotonic Searchability). *A self-stabilizing protocol satisfies* monotonic searchability *according to some routing protocol $\mathcal{R}$ if it holds for any pair of nodes v, w that once a search request $\text{SEARCH}(v, (w_x, w_y))$ returns w at time t, any search request $\text{SEARCH}(v, (w_x, w_y))$ initiated at at time $t' > t$ also returns w.*

Realizing monotonic searchability in self-stabilizing systems is a non-trivial problem, because once a $\text{SEARCH}(v, (w_x, w_y))$ request returns w to v, it cannot trivially be guaranteed that w is found again by v at later stages, due to the modification of edges by the self-stabilizing protocol.

The above definition differs in a minor detail compared to the definition stated in [17,18]: The initial search request issued by v terminates at time t, but Scheideler et al. define the time step t to be the one at which the initial search request was generated by v. They use a probing approach to check for a node v whether v is still waiting for the result of a previously issued search request and cache all search requests searching for the same target. The same approach can be applied to our protocol as well to overcome this, but for the sake of simplicitiy we use the slightly modified definition stated above.

In two-dimensional scenarios it is more realistic to search for geographic positions rather than for concrete node addresses. To handle this, we introduce the following definition of geographic monotonic searchability.

Definition 3 (Geographic Monotonic Searchability). *Let $(x, y) \in [0, 1]^2$ be an arbitrary position in P. Let $w \in V$ be the node that would be returned by $\text{SEARCH}(v, (x, y))$ if the system is in a legitimate state. A self-stabilizing protocol satisfies* geographic monotonic searchability *according to some routing protocol $\mathcal{R}$ if in case the system is in an arbitrary state and $\text{SEARCH}(v, (x, y))$ returns w at time t, then any request $\text{SEARCH}(v, (x, y))$ initiated at time $t' > t$ also returns w.*

This definition is even stronger than (standard) monotonic searchability, i.e., a protocol satisfying geographic monotonic searchability also satisfies monotonic searchability. Therefore we focus on geographic monotonic searchability for the rest of this paper.

We aim to solve the following problem: Given a weakly connected graph of n nodes with coordinates in P, construct a self-stabilizing protocol along with a routing protocol such that geographic monotonic searchability is satisfied.

1.3 Our Contribution

In the following we summarize our contributions:

(1) We propose a novel self-stabilizing protocol BUILDQUADTREE that arranges the nodes in a quadtree. BUILDQUADTREE is based on a special kind of subdivision of P into subareas inducing an ordering via a space-filling curve (see Sect. 2) and the BUILDLIST protocol (Sect. 3.1). To the best of our knowledge this is the first self-stabilizing protocol for the quadtree structure.

(2) Along with the self-stabilizing protocol BUILDQUADTREE we propose the routing protocol SEARCHQUAD. When searching for coordinates (x, y), the protocol returns the node w, which lies within the same subarea as (x, y). We show that BUILDQUADTREE along with SEARCHQUAD satisfies geographic monotonic searchability (and thus also standard monotonic searchability).

(3) We get an upper bound of $\mathcal{O}(\log n)$ on the number of hops for a search message (i.e., the amount of times a search message is delegated until it terminates) if we assume that the Euclidean distance $||(u, v)||$ between any pair of nodes $(u, v) \in V$ is at least $1/n$. This is particularly an improvement on the protocols proposed in [17,18] regarding the maximum number of hops for searching a target, even for target addresses that do not exist (see Sect. 1.4 on related work). To reach this bound, the space-filling curve mentioned above is of great help, as it allows nodes to construct shortcut edges based on the subdivision of P.

(4) Finally, one can easily extend BUILDQUADTREE and SEARCHQUAD to work in high-dimensional settings, realizing the first self-stabilizing protocol for octtrees - the high-dimensional equivalent of quadtrees - that even satisfies geographic monotonic searchability. This makes our protocols highly versatile. Due to space reasons we defer the discussion on this to the full version of this paper [5].

The rest of the paper is structured as follows: After stating some related work, we describe our topology for the quadtree in Sect. 2. Then we present our novel protocol BUILDQUADTREE in Sect. 3 along with the routing protocol SEARCHQUAD. We analyze our protocols in Sect. 4. Finally we conclude and give an outlook on future work in Sect. 5. Due to space constraints, the full pseudocode and proofs are deferred to the full version of this paper [5].

1.4 Related Work

Quadtrees have first been introduced in 1974 by R. A. Finkel and J.L. Bentley [6]. Since then quadtrees and octrees are most often used in computational geometry (for surveys consider for example [1,16]). There are also peer-to-peer approaches relying on quadtrees [8,19]. Still, the problem of designing a self-stabilizing protocol that arranges peers in a quadtree is untouched until today.

The concept of self-stabilization has first been introduced by E. W. Dijkstra in 1974 via a self-stabilizing token-based ring [4]. This led to the introduction of various other self-stabilizing protocols for network topologies such as sorted lists [7,14], De Bruijn graphs [15], Chord graphs [11], Skip graphs [3,9] and many more. A universal approach that is able to derive self-stabilizing protocols for several types of topologies was introduced in [2]. Interestingly, topological self-stabilization in two- or high-dimensional settings is barely investigated until now: There exists only a single self-stabilizing protocol that transforms any weakly connected graph into a two-dimensional topology - the Delaunay graph [10]. Unfortunately, it seems non-trivial to extend this such that monotonic searchability is satisfied, without resorting to expensive mechanisms like broadcasting. Also, one cannot guarantee searching in $\mathcal{O}(\log n)$ hops in the Delaunay graph, as its diameter is too large.

Research on monotonic searchability was initiated in [17], where the authors presented a self-stabilizing protocol for the sorted list that satisfies monotonic searchability. They also showed that providing monotonic searchability is impossible in general when the system contains corrupted messages. However, this property is restricted to cases where the desired topology to which the graph should converge is clearly defined, forcing the underlying protocol to eventually remove an explicit edge if it is not part of the desired topology. This is not the case for our topology, because once a specific explicit edge (which we define as *quad edge* later on) is generated by our protocol it is never deleted, so the legitimate state s that we reach is dependent on the specific computation done before reaching s. Therefore we do not need to enforce any restrictions on messages, as routing is done via quad edges only. Building on that research, the same authors presented a universal approach for maintaining monotonic searchability at DISC 2016 along with a generic routing protocol that can be applied to a wide range of topologies [18]. However, adapting their protocol to specific topologies comes at the cost of convergence times and additional message overhead. This is due to the fact that whenever an explicit edge is delegated from node u to v, u has to wait for an acknowledgment from v until it is allowed to remove the explicit edge from its local storage. Furthermore, search request forwarded via their generic routing protocol might travel $\Omega(n)$ hops when searching for non-existing nodes, whereas our routing protocol only needs $\mathcal{O}(\log n)$ hops on any input to terminate, while still satisfying monotonic searchability. In addition to this, our protocol BUILDQUADTREE is simpler and also more lightweight regarding the message overhead. This is mostly due to the simplicity of the quadtree topology.

Closest but different from our notion of monotonic searchability is the notion of *monotonic stabilization* [20]. A self-stabilizing protocol is monotonically stabilizing, if every change done by its nodes is making the system approach a legitimate state and if every node changes its output only once. The authors show that processes have to exchange additional information in order to satisfy monotonic stabilization.

For the computation of an ordering, we use a space-filling curve similar to the Morton-curve [12], as it matches the structure of the quadtree best. Other curves like the Hilbert-curve would also work in principle, however, using them would make the presentation of our ideas way more harder.

2   Topology and Legitimate State

In this section we introduce our desired topology for the quadtree and define what it means for our system to be in a legitimate state. We first provide some intuition: Given a set V of n nodes with coordinates in P, we first cut the area P into two equally sized *subareas*, via a vertical cut. This is done recursively for each subarea, alternating between vertical and horizontal cuts, as long as the subarea contains more than one node. Once this is done, we can define a total order on all nodes in P, that is used to connect the nodes into a (doubly-linked) sorted list. Based on this list and the generated subareas, we establish further edges, which we use for the routing protocol.

More formally, let us consider the recursive algorithm QUADDIVISION having a set of nodes, a (sub-)area and a flag indicating the next cut (vertical or horizontal) as input. Initially we call QUADDIVISION$(V, P, 1)$ and thus perform a vertical cut on P, dividing it into equally sized subareas P_1 and P_2. Then we call QUADDIVISION recursively on P_1 and P_2 as long as they contain more than one node. We say a subarea A *contains* node v (or conversely, node v is contained in the subarea A), denoted by $v \in A$, if v's coordinates (v_x, v_y) lie within A. If a subarea A contains no node from V, we say that A is *empty*. For simplicity, we assume that nodes do not lie on the boundaries of subareas, as this would disturb the presentation of our algorithm, but the problem can easily be resolved in practice. QUADDIVISION$(V, P, 1)$ returns the set S of subareas that contain at most one node. Figure 1 shows an example for a sequence of cuts with 4 nodes $v_1, \ldots, v_4$. Note that upon termination, QUADDIVISION returns 5 subareas (one subarea for each node v_i and the empty subarea on the bottom left).

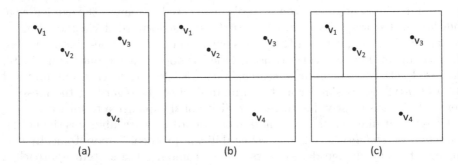

(a)   (b)   (c)

Fig. 1. Illustration of QUADDIVISION performed on nodes $v_1, \ldots, v_4$. (a) illustrates the first vertical cut on P. (b) illustrates the horizontal cuts done to subareas P_1 and P_2. (c) illustrates the final vertical cut before termination.

In the following we want to view the output of QUADDIVISION as a binary tree T: The root node corresponds to the whole square P. An inner node of T corresponding to a (sub-)area P has two child nodes: Cutting P into two subareas P_1 and P_2, the *left child* represents the subarea that lies west of the other (when performing a vertical cut on P) or north of the other (when performing a horizontal cut on P). Similarly, the *right child* represents the subarea that lies east of the other (when performing a vertical cut on P) or south of the other (when performing a horizontal cut on P). The binary tree is the unique minimal such tree having no leaf node $t \in T$ correspond to a subarea of P that contains more than one node $v \in V$. Note that this makes nodes $v \in V$ correspond to leaf nodes in T, but a leaf node $t \in T$ does not necessarily correspond to a node in V, as the subarea represented by t may be empty. Figure 2 shows the corresponding binary tree T to the previous example from Fig. 1.

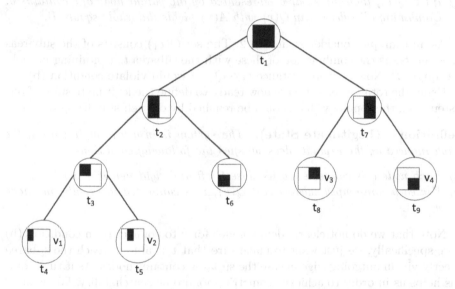

Fig. 2. Corresponding binary tree to the previous example from Fig. 1. The subareas marked in black are the subareas that are represented by the corresponding tree node. Performing a depth-first search on the tree, when always going to the left child first, yields the total order $v_1 \prec v_2 \prec v_3 \prec v_4$.

Using the binary tree notation, we can define a total order on V:

Definition 4 (Two-Dimensional Ordering). *Let T the be tree corresponding to the subareas that are returned by* QUADDIVISION$(V, P, 1)$. *The total order $\prec$ is given by the depth-first search (DFS) traversal of T, always going to the left child first.*

When comparing nodes v and w via $\prec$ we say that v is *left* of w, if $v \prec w$, otherwise v is *right* of w (note that either of the two cases always holds as we assume node coordinates to be unique). In addition we say that v is w's *closest left neighbor* if $v \prec w$ and there is no node u with $v \prec u \prec w$. Analogously we define a node v being the *closest right neighbor* of w.

As nodes in the binary tree T correspond to subareas of P and vice versa, we use them interchangeably for the rest of the paper. We say that a node $t \in T$ *represents* a subarea A, if A is the corresponding subarea to t. The next definition introduces important notation in order to define the legitimate state:

Definition 5. *Let T be the tree representing the subareas that are returned by a* QUADDIVISION$(V, P, 1)$ *call. For a node $v \in V$, denote the leaf node representing the subarea that contains v by $A(v)$. Define the set $Q(v)$ as the set of subareas represented by nodes $t \in T$ such that the following holds:*

(a) If $t \in Q(v)$, then the subarea represented by t does not contain v.
(b) If $t \in Q(v)$, then the subarea represented by the parent node of t contains v.
(c) Combining all subareas in $Q(v)$ with $A(v)$ yields the whole square P.

As an example consider again Fig. 2: The set $Q(v_1)$ consists of the subareas t_5, t_6 and t_7, as the combination of these with the subarea t_4 containing v_1 yield the square P. Note that for instance $t_8 \in Q(v_1)$ would violate condition (b).

Using the total order $\prec$ we are now ready to define the legitimate state of our system, i.e., the topology that should be reached by our self-stabilizing protocol:

Definition 6 (Legitimate State). *The system is in a legitimate state if the graph induced by the explicit edges satisfies the following conditions:*

(a) Each node v is connected to its closest left and right neighbor w.r.t. $\prec$.
(b) For each non-empty subarea $A \in Q(v)$, v is connected to exactly one node $w \in A$.

Note that we do not clearly define nodes for v to connect to in condition (b) more specifically, we just want to make sure that v is able to reach the subarea directly via an outgoing edge in case the subarea contains nodes. As it turns out, this helps us in order to achieve geometric monotonic searchability. We want to emphasize that edges in T are not part of the legitimate state, as we use the binary tree to illustrate our approach and only let nodes compute necessary parts of the tree locally.

3   Protocol Description

In this section we describe the self-stabilizing BUILDQUADTREE protocol and the routing algorithm SEARCHQUAD. We first define the protocol-based variables for each node. We denote by $\perp$ that the variable does not contain any node. Each node $v \in V$ maintains the following variables:

- Variables $v.left, v.right \in V \cup \{\perp\}$ storing v's left and right neighbor.
- A set $v.Q \subset V$ storing a single node $w \in V$ for each non-empty subarea $A \in Q(v)$ such that $w \in A$.

We refer to the edges represented by variables $v.left$ and $v.right$ as *list edges* and to edges (v, w) with $w \in v.Q$ as *quad edges*. Observe that a node w is allowed to be contained in both $v.left$ (resp. $v.right$) and $v.Q$ simultaneously in a legitimate state. The reason for this is that we allow the delegation of search messages only via quad edges (as we will see in Sect. 3.3), so if v wants to delegate a search message to the subarea containing one of its list edges, it has to make sure that there is a node in $v.Q$ for this area.

Before we can describe how we establish the correct list and quad edges, we shortly describe how a node v that knows some node w is able to locally determine whether $v \prec w$ or $w \prec v$ holds: v just calls QUADDIVISION($\{v, w\}, P, 1$) and gets a binary tree with subareas containing v and w as leaf nodes. Performing a DFS on that tree as described earlier yields either $v \prec w$ or $w \prec v$.

It is important to note that using the same approach, v is also able to compute the set $Q(v)$ for the current system state: v just calls QUADDIVISION($\{v, v.left, v.right\}, P, 1$). It is easy to see that the corresponding tree contains all nodes representing subareas in $Q(v)$, so v just has to check each node in the tree for the properties from Definition 5. Obviously, as long as $v.left$ and $v.right$ are still subject to changes, $Q(v)$ also changes, but we will show later that by the way we defined our protocol, $Q(v)$ monotonically increases, s.t. none of the proposed properties are violated.

We now describe how we build the correct list edges at each node and then proceed with the description for quad edges. As we have to perform actions in both parts periodically, we split the TIMEOUT action into subroutines LISTTIMEOUT and QUADTIMEOUT. For list edges, we extend the BUILDLIST protocol that is based on [14] for the one-dimensional case to the two-dimensional case.

3.1 List Edges

The base of our self-stabilizing protocol consists of a sorted list for all nodes $v \in V$ based on the ordering $\prec$ from Definition 4.

The main idea of BUILDLIST is that each node of V keeps its closest left and right neighbor in $v.left$ and $v.right$. More concretely, the protocol consists of two actions called LISTTIMEOUT and LINEARIZE (Algorithm 1). LISTTIMEOUT is periodically executed and LINEARIZE can be called locally or remotely.

Whenever LISTTIMEOUT or LINEARIZE is executed, v first performs a local consistency check on its variables $v.left$ and $v.right$: It might happen that in initial states $v.left \succ v$ (or $v.right \prec v$). If that is the case, v sets $v.left$ (or $v.right$) to $\bot$ and locally calls LINEARIZE(w) for the removed value w. In addition to the above described consistency check, v *introduces* itself to $v.left$ and $v.right$ in LISTTIMEOUT by sending a LINEARIZE(v) message to them.

In case v processes a LINEARIZE(w) request, v does the following: v sets $v.left = w$, if w is left of v and closer to v than $v.left$, i.e., $v.left \prec w \prec v$. In that case, v delegates the value w' that got replaced by w in $v.left$ to w, i.e., v calls LINEARIZE(w') on w. In case $v.left = \bot$, v just sets $v.left = w$. In case w is right of v, v proceeds analogously for $v.right$.

Algorithm 1. The BUILDLIST Protocol (executed at node v)

1: **procedure** LISTTIMEOUT
2:     Consistency check for $v.left$ and $v.right$ w.r.t. $\prec$
3:         $v.left \leftarrow$ LINEARIZE(v)   ▷ Send LINEARIZE(v) message to $v.left$
4:         $v.right \leftarrow$ LINEARIZE(v)

5:
6: **procedure** LINEARIZE(w)
7:     Consistency check for $v.left$ and $v.right$ w.r.t. $\prec$
8:     **if** $w \prec v.left$ **then**   ▷ Analogously for $v.right$
9:         $v.left \leftarrow$ LINEARIZE(w)
10:    **if** $v.left \prec w \prec v$ **then**   ▷ Analogously for $v.right$
11:        $w \leftarrow$ LINEARIZE($v.left$)
12:        $v.left \leftarrow w$

Note that node references are never deleted but delegated until the referenced node arrives at the correct spot in the sorted list. From [14] we derive the following result. The proof works the same as for the one-dimensional setting, we just replace the (one-dimensional) operator $<$ by $\prec$.

Lemma 1. BUILDLIST *is self-stabilizing.*

3.2   Quad Edges

Now we describe the approach for generating quad edges. Note that v can easily check whether there exists a subarea $A \in Q(v)$ for which v does not yet have a quad edge, by assigning each $w \in v.Q$ to the subarea in $Q(v)$ that contains w.

The protocol consists of actions QUADTIMEOUT and QLINEARIZE (see Algorithm 2). Before executing any statement of any of these actions, a node v always checks its set $v.Q$ for consistency, ensuring that no two nodes $w_1, w_2 \in v.Q$ are contained in the same subarea $A \in Q(v)$. In case v finds out that $w_1, \ldots, w_k \in v.Q$ are contained in the same subarea $A \in Q(v)$ (which may happen in an initial state), we only keep one of these nodes (arbitrarily chosen) and delegate all other nodes w_i to BUILDLIST by calling LINEARIZE(w_i).

In QUADTIMEOUT, v chooses a node w from its set $v.Q$ in round-robin fashion and delegates w to BUILDLIST. This has to be done to ensure that the sorted list converges even if the initial weakly connected graph consists of quad edges only. Afterwards v introduces itself to its left and right neighbors $v.left$ and $v.right$ by calling QLINEARIZE on them. As part of the same QLINEARIZE request, v asks these nodes if they know a node $w \in A$, where $A \in Q(v)$ is a subarea, for which v does not have a quad edge yet. If that is the case, then v will receive a QLINEARIZE call containing the desired node w as the answer. The subarea A is chosen in round-robin fashion as well, such that each subarea for which v does not have a quad edge yet is chosen by v eventually. The reason for choosing nodes and subareas in round-robin fashion is that we do not want to overload the network with too many stabilization messages that are generated periodically.

Processing a QLINEARIZE(w, A) request at node v works as follows: We delegate w to BUILDLIST and then check if w is contained in a subarea $A' \in Q(v)$ for which there does not exist a node $w' \in v.Q$ with $w' \in A'$. If that is the case, then v does not have a quad edge to the subarea A' yet, so v includes w into $v.Q$, which corresponds to v generating a new quad edge (v, w). Finally v generates an answer to w as already described above, in case v knows a node (including itself) that is contained in A.

Algorithm 2. Protocol for establishing quad edges (executed at node v)

1: **procedure** QUADTIMEOUT
2:     Consistency check for $v.Q$
3:     Choose $w \in v.Q$ in round-robin fashion and call LINEARIZE(w)
4:     Determine $A(v)$ and $Q(v)$ via QUADDIVISION
5:     Choose $A \in Q(v)$ in round-robin fashion s.t. $\forall w \in v.Q : w \notin A$
6:     $v.left \leftarrow$ QLINEARIZE(v, A)   ▷ $A = \perp$ if no such A exists
7:     $v.right \leftarrow$ QLINEARIZE(v, A)
8:
9: **procedure** QLINEARIZE(w, A)
10:     Consistency check for $v.Q$
11:     LINEARIZE(w)   ▷ Delegation to BUILDLIST
12:     Determine $A(v)$ and $Q(v)$ via QUADDIVISION
13:     **if** $\exists A' \in Q(v) \ \forall w' \in v.Q : w' \notin A'$ **then**
14:         $v.Q \leftarrow v.Q \cup w$ ▷ Generates new quad edge (v, w)
15:     **if** $A \neq \perp \land \exists w' \in v.Q \cup v : w' \in A$ **then**
16:         $w \leftarrow$ QLINEARIZE($w', \perp$) ▷ Answers w so w can generate quad edge (w, w')

3.3 Routing

As the last part of this section, we state the routing protocol SEARCHQUAD for our topology (see Algorithm 3 for pseudocode).

Before a node v processes a search message, it first performs the same consistency checks on its set $v.Q$ as it has been described previously. This makes sure that our routing protocol is well-defined. Now assume node v wants to process a SEARCH($u, (x, y)$) message. Consider the subarea $A(v)$ and the set $Q(v)$ of subareas as defined in Definition 5. Then v determines the subarea $A(x, y)$ out of $Q(v) \cup A(v)$ that contains the position (x, y). If $A(x, y) = A(v)$, then the algorithm terminates and returns v itself to u as the result. Otherwise, v delegates the SEARCH($u, (x, y)$) message to the node $w \in v.Q$ with $w \in A(x, y)$. If no edge to a node in $A(x, y)$ exists in $v.Q$, then the algorithm terminates and returns v itself to u as the result.

Algorithm 3. The SEARCHQUAD Protocol (executed at node v)

1: **procedure** SEARCH($u, (x, y)$)
2:     Consistency check for $v.Q$
3:     Determine $A(v)$ and $Q(v)$ via QUADDIVISION
4:     **if** $(x, y) \in A(v)$ **then**
5:         **return** v ▷ Search terminated - v is returned to u as the result
6:     **else**
7:         Let $A(x, y) \in Q(v)$ with $(x, y) \in A(x, y)$
8:         **if** $\exists w \in v.Q : w \in A(x, y)$ **then**
9:             $w \leftarrow$ SEARCH($u, (x, y)$)   ▷ Delegate request via quad edge (v, w)
10:        **else**
11:            **return** v

---

4   Analysis

4.1   Quadtree

This section is dedicated to show that BUILDQUADTREE is self-stabilizing according to Definition 1, i.e., BUILDQUADTREE satisfies convergence and closure.

Recall that our system initially is given by an arbitrary weakly connected graph $G = (V, E)$. As the graph may consist of both list and quad edges, we denote the set of list edges by E_L and the set of quad edges by E_Q, so $G = (V, E_L \cup E_Q)$. In each action executed by node v, we perform a consistency check for v's variables, such that no inconsistencies appear, like $v \prec v.left$, $v.right \prec v$ or v having multiple quad edges into the same subarea. We show the following theorem:

Theorem 1. BUILDQUADTREE *is self-stabilizing.*

Proof (Sketch). As the first step to show convergence, it is not hard to see that eventually a state s is reached where $G = (V, E_L \cup E_Q)$ is free of corrupted messages, while staying weakly connected. Continuing from state s, we can show that eventually the explicit edges in E_L induce a sorted list w.r.t. $\prec$. The main argument here is that each quad edge is periodically delegated to BUILDLIST, such that the graph induced by edges in E_L becomes weakly connected, triggering Lemma 1. Once the sorted list has formed we can show that all necessary explicit quad edges in E_Q are eventually generated such that a legitimate state is reached. Here the main argument is that each node v that needs a quad edge into a specific area $A \in Q(v)$ will eventually be introduced by its closest list neighbor to a node in A. For closure it is easy to see that edges in E_L and E_Q are preserved at any point in time once a legitimate state is reached.   □

4.2   Geographic Monotonic Searchability

In this section we show that BUILDQUADTREE along with the routing protocol SEARCHQUAD (Algorithm 3) satisfies geographic monotonic searchability (Definition 3) and thus also monotonic searchability (Definition 2). First we need the following technical lemma stating that for each node $v \in V$ the set $Q(v)$ monotonically increases over time:

Lemma 2. *Consider an arbitrary system state at time t and a node $v \in V$. Let $Q(v)$ be the output of QUADDIVISION($\{v, v.left, v.right\}, P, 1$) executed at time t and let $Q(v)'$ be the output of QUADDIVISION($\{v, v.left, v.right\}, P, 1$) executed at any point in time $t' > t$. Then it holds $Q(v) \subseteq Q(v)'$.*

Proof. By definition of our protocols it holds that if node v locally calls QUADDIVISION($\{v, v.left, v.right\}, P, 1$) in order to compute the set $Q(v)$, then any inconsistencies regarding $v.left$ and $v.right$ are already resolved. The lemma then follows from the fact that BUILDLIST does not replace list variables $v.left$ and $v.right$ with nodes that are further away from v than the current entries. More formally, consider w.l.o.g. the variable $v.right$ such that $v \prec v.right$. By the definition of LINEARIZE, v does not replace $v.right$ by a node w for which $v.right \prec w$ holds. This implies that any subsequent QUADDIVISION($\{v, v.left, v.right\}, P, 1$) call only transfers subareas to $Q(v)$ that are obtained by cutting $A(v)$. Therefore, it holds for any subarea $A \in Q(v)$ that $A \in Q(v)'$. $\square$

Theorem 2. BUILDQUADTREE *along with* SEARCHQUAD *satisfies geographic monotonic searchability and monotonic searchability.*

Proof (Sketch). One can formally show that once a SEARCH($v, (x, y)$) request terminated and returned $w \in V$ to v at time t, then any subsequent SEARCH($v, (x, y)$) request initiated by v at time $t' > t$ traverses the exact same path P as before. By Lemma 2, P is preserved at any time $t' > t$ implying geographic monotonic searchability and thus also monotonic searchability. $\square$

Finally, we are able to derive an upper bound on the number of hops for any search message if we assume that the Euclidean distance between any pair $(u, v) \in V$ is at least $||(u, v)|| \geq \frac{1}{n}$.

Theorem 3. *If for the Euclidean distance between any pair $(u, v) \in V$ it holds $||(u, v)|| \geq 1/n$, then any search message is delegated at most $\mathcal{O}(\log n)$ times.*

5 Conclusion and Future Work

In this paper we studied monotonic searchability in high-dimensional settings and came up with a self-stabilizing protocol BUILDQUADTREE along with its routing protocol SEARCHQUAD. We showed that BUILDQUADTREE along with SEARCHQUAD satisfies monotonic searchability, as well as the even stronger variant of geographic monotonic searchability.

For future work, one may consider the dynamic setting, where nodes are able to join or leave the system. Our protocol can be easily extended to include nodes that join the system at an old node, meaning that an implicit edge is generated. We then just let BUILDQUADTREE transform the system to a legitimate state again. The more interesting scenario is to think of a protocol that allows nodes to leave the system without violating geometric monotonic searchability. This is non-trivial, as a leaving node potentially destroys search paths for other nodes.

References

1. Aluru, S.: Quadtrees and octrees. In: Mehta, D.P., Sahni, S. (eds.) Handbook of Data Structures and Applications. Chapman and Hall/CRC, Boca Raton (2004). https://doi.org/10.1201/9781420035179.ch19
2. Berns, A., Ghosh, S., Pemmaraju, S.V.: Building self-stabilizing overlay networks with the transitive closure framework. Theor. Comput. Sci. **512**, 2–14 (2013)
3. Clouser, T., Nesterenko, M., Scheideler, C.: Tiara: a self-stabilizing deterministic skip list and skip graph. Theor. Comput. Sci. **428**, 18–35 (2012)
4. Dijkstra, E.W.: Self-stabilizing systems in spite of distributed control. Commun. ACM **17**(11), 643–644 (1974)
5. Feldmann, M., Kolb, C., Scheideler, C.: Self-stabilizing overlays for high-dimensional monotonic searchability. CoRR abs/1808.10300 (2018). http://arxiv.org/abs/1808.10300
6. Finkel, R.A., Bentley, J.L.: Quad trees: a data structure for retrieval on composite keys. Acta Inf. **4**, 1–9 (1974). https://doi.org/10.1007/BF00288933
7. Gall, D., Jacob, R., Richa, A.W., Scheideler, C., Schmid, S., Täubig, H.: A note on the parallel runtime of self-stabilizing graph linearization. Theory Comput. Syst. **55**(1), 110–135 (2014). https://doi.org/10.1007/s00224-013-9504-x
8. Gao, J., Guibas, L.J., Hershberger, J., Zhang, L.: Fractionally cascaded information in a sensor network. In: IPSN, pp. 311–319 (2004). https://doi.org/10.1145/984622.984668
9. Jacob, R., Richa, A.W., Scheideler, C., Schmid, S., Täubig, H.: A distributed polylogarithmic time algorithm for self-stabilizing skip graphs. In: PODC, pp. 131–140. ACM (2009)
10. Jacob, R., Ritscher, S., Scheideler, C., Schmid, S.: Towards higher-dimensional topological self-stabilization: a distributed algorithm for delaunay graphs. Theor. Comput. Sci. **457**, 137–148 (2012). https://doi.org/10.1016/j.tcs.2012.07.029
11. Kniesburges, S., Koutsopoulos, A., Scheideler, C.: Re-chord: a self-stabilizing chord overlay network. Theory Comput. Syst. **55**(3), 591–612 (2014)
12. Morton, G.: A computer oriented geodetic data base and a new technique in file sequencing. In: International Business Machines Company (1966). https://books.google.de/books?id=9FFdHAAACAAJ
13. Nor, R.M., Nesterenko, M., Scheideler, C.: Corona: a stabilizing deterministic message-passing skip list. Theor. Comput. Sci. **512**, 119–129 (2013)
14. Onus, M., Richa, A.W., Scheideler, C.: Linearization: locally self-stabilizing sorting in graphs. In: ALENEX 2007. SIAM (2007)
15. Richa, A., Scheideler, C., Stevens, P.: Self-stabilizing De Bruijn networks. In: Défago, X., Petit, F., Villain, V. (eds.) SSS 2011. LNCS, vol. 6976, pp. 416–430. Springer, Heidelberg (2011). https://doi.org/10.1007/978-3-642-24550-3_31
16. Samet, H.: Hierarchical spatial data structures. In: Buchmann, A.P., Günther, O., Smith, T.R., Wang, Y.-F. (eds.) SSD 1989. LNCS, vol. 409, pp. 191–212. Springer, Heidelberg (1990). https://doi.org/10.1007/3-540-52208-5_28
17. Scheideler, C., Setzer, A., Strothmann, T.: Towards establishing monotonic searchability in self-stabilizing data structures. In: OPODIS, pp. 24:1–24:17 (2015). https://doi.org/10.4230/LIPIcs.OPODIS.2015.24
18. Scheideler, C., Setzer, A., Strothmann, T.: Towards a universal approach for monotonic searchability in self-stabilizing overlay networks. In: Gavoille, C., Ilcinkas, D. (eds.) DISC 2016. LNCS, vol. 9888, pp. 71–84. Springer, Heidelberg (2016). https://doi.org/10.1007/978-3-662-53426-7_6

19. Tanin, E., Harwood, A., Samet, H.: Using a distributed quadtree index in peer-to-peer networks. VLDB J. **16**(2), 165–178 (2007). https://doi.org/10.1007/s00778-005-0001-y
20. Yamauchi, Y., Tixeuil, S.: Monotonic stabilization. In: Lu, C., Masuzawa, T., Mosbah, M. (eds.) OPODIS 2010. LNCS, vol. 6490, pp. 475–490. Springer, Heidelberg (2010). https://doi.org/10.1007/978-3-642-17653-1_34

An Adaptive Logging Framework
for Persistent Memories

Pavan Poudel and Gokarna Sharma[✉]

Department of Computer Science, Kent State University, Kent, OH 44242, USA
{ppoudel,sharma}@cs.kent.edu

Abstract. Persistent memory is receiving a tremendous amount of attention recently from both academia and industry. Atomic and durable transactions have been studied to ensure *crash consistency* in persistent memory. However, whether to use undo or redo logging to execute those transactions is still a hotly debated topic. *Redo* logging seems appropriate for write-dominated workloads and transactions in high contention scenarios whereas *undo* logging seems appropriate for read-dominated workloads and transactions in low contention scenarios. This necessitates a priori knowledge on the workload and contention scenario to select an appropriate logging method between redo or undo to achieve better performance. In this paper, we argue that we can obtain the best of both worlds without the need of such a priori knowledge. Particularly, we present an *adaptive* logging framework that dynamically switches between redo and undo logging at runtime so that the performance is always better than that is obtained from a priori selection of either undo or redo logging. We formally model our framework, prove its correctness, and provide an extensive evaluation of it through a persistent memory emulation of TinySTM using 5 micro-benchmarks and 8 complex benchmarks from STAMP and STAMPEDE suites that are well-known and widely used in the literature. The results show significant benefits of our logging framework.

1 Introduction

Recent advancements in memory technology (such as phase change memory, STT-RAM, and memristors) suggest the possibility of non-volatile memory (NVM) devices that are fast and byte-addressable as dynamic random access memory (DRAM). Moreover, they are predicted to be more power-efficient than DRAM, yet non-volatile and cheap as hard disk drives (HDDs) [3]. Persistent memory can allow applications to access the data structures through a fast load/store interface, without first performing block I/O and then transferring data into memory based structures [6,20,21]. This feature is quite instrumental to avoid many overheads and drawbacks of block-oriented storage such as HDDs. Therefore, one of the most central issues in persistent memory is programming models that directly leverage persistence of the memory.

The challenge for any programming model designed for persistent memory is how to ensure consistency of the application data in the event of sudden power

© Springer Nature Switzerland AG 2018
T. Izumi and P. Kuznetsov (Eds.): SSS 2018, LNCS 11201, pp. 32–49, 2018.
https://doi.org/10.1007/978-3-030-03232-6_3

failure or system crash. This issue is commonly known as *crash consistency* and the existing research has quite focused on this issue [6,13,16,20,23]. A simply way to achieve crash consistency is to serialize multiple write operations when manipulating data structures. However, this hampers application performance due to inherent serialization. One common technique used in modern processors to avoid this problem is *reordering*, i.e., exploit parallelism through shuffling the execution of multiple write operations. However, if a failure occurs between two reordered writes, it is again difficult to guarantee consistency and the data structure could end up in an inconsistent state.

Further difficulty arises when persistency meets the growing number of cores. On the one hand, as data is already in persistent memory, it seems unnecessary and redundant to allocate another (duplicate) persistent storage for it. On the other hand, when an address is written, the new value must be exposed *atomically* with a new consistent and persistent state to ensure consistency of data. One way of guaranteeing this atomicity is by means of *locks*. However, locking has several drawbacks and bottlenecks when dealing with particularly the ever growing number of cores [10,18]. A method to achieve atomicity (without the use of locking) is through transactions studied heavily recently in the context of hardware/software transactional memory [10,18]. A *transaction* (in the context of persistent memory) is a sequence of operations on persistent memory that either all occur, or nothing occurs with respect to failures. If the execution of a transaction is interrupted, it is guaranteed, after system restart, to restore the consistent state from the moment when the transaction was started. The ideal goal is to maintain consistent persistent states without the use of locking and without duplicating data.

The prior persistent memory designs, e.g., [6,13,16,20,23], provide *atomic* and *durable* transactions to move the data from a consistent state to another consistent state supporting the ideal goal discussed above (i.e., do not allocate another duplicate persistent storage but duplicate *only* the data needed to maintain consistent states, when necessary). This guarantee is provided by requiring the transactions to write data to a log area (usually called *transaction log*) before updating the data in the original persistent memory locations. Notice that this logging only duplicates the data that a transaction is going to update in persistent memory (reducing significantly the overhead of allocating another duplicate persistent storage for whole data). Transaction logs are of two kinds:

- *Undo logs.* In this logging method, a transaction works by first copying the data in persistent memory locations to a log area (called *undo log*) in persistent memory, makes them durable, and then performs updates in-place in the original data locations. In the event the transaction fails, any modifications to original persistent memory locations are *rolled back* using the old data stored in the (undo) log area.
- *Redo logs.* In this logging method, a transaction copies data in each persistent memory location that it is going to read/write to a log area (called *redo log*), appends all its data updates to that log area, and makes them durable in persistent memory (different than original locations) before writing the

Table 1. A comparison of undo and redo logging in persistent memory [12,13,20,21]

Constraint	Undo logging	Redo logging
Memory update	Performs in-place memory update	Updates are written to memory at the commit time
Reading overhead	Allows to read most recent data directly from in-place memory [12,21]	Reads are intercepted and redirected to the redo log area to read recent uncommitted data [12,13,21]
Persist ordering	Requires to ensure persist ordering for each memory write in a transaction [20]	Requires only one persist ordering for each transaction [13,20]
Data movement	Transaction aborts are costly as the memory updates need to be rolled back to consistent state using undo log	Transaction commits are costly as the updates need to be written back to original persistent memory using redo log

data back to original persistent memory locations. If the transaction fails, the updates in log area are simply discarded. Therefore, the writing of data to redo log in persistent memory and back to original persistent memory locations happens only when transaction commits.

Table 1 summarizes the advantages and disadvantages of undo and redo logging methods. Although both undo and redo logging for consistency in persistent memory are studied heavily in the literature [6,13,16,20,23], which logging method is better is still not clear and the previous studies provide contradictory conclusions. For example, consider two prominent previous work NV-HEAPS [6] and MNEMOSYNE [20]. The authors of MNEMOSYNE [20] suggested using redo logging whereas the authors of NV-HEAPS [6] and others [7,16] suggested using undo logging. There is no study that elaborates the performance gap between undo and redo logging with comprehensive practical evaluations, besides [21] which answers this partially. Looking at [21], redo logging seems appropriate for write-dominated workloads and high contention scenarios whereas undo logging seems appropriate for read-dominated workloads and low contention scenarios. However, this necessitates a priori knowledge on the workload and contention scenario to select a logging method to obtain better performance.

Contributions. We argue that we can obtain the best of both worlds without any a priori knowledge on workload and contention scenario. Particularly, we present an adaptive logging framework, which we call ADAPTIVE, that dynamically switches the execution using either undo logging or redo logging at the runtime so that the performance on any workload (and contention scenario) is always better than that is obtained by executing the transactions using either undo logging or redo logging selected a priori. For the experimental evaluation, we incorporate ADAPTIVE in TinySTM [8,9] through appropriate changes and modifications in the TinySTM execution model to emulate persistent memory. TinySTM is a well known software transactional memory (STM) implementation [18] that has been used for experimentation in both persistent and volatile memory settings. TinySTM has already implemented individually both undo and redo logging methods but only for DRAM settings. We extend (open source) TinySTM distribution 1.0.5 [2] to incorporate our ADAPTIVE framework as well as to emulate persistent memory support (as real persistent memory is not yet available [13]). We then run experiments using ADAPTIVE against a diverse set of benchmarks (5 micro-benchmarks and 8 complex benchmarks from STAMP and STAMPEDE benchmark suites [15,17]) widely used in transactional memory (TM) research in the literature [8–10].

We measure the performance of ADAPTIVE in terms of *total number of movement of data* by a transaction to and from persistent memory. The motivation behind this performance metric is as follows. It has been heavily advocated that persistent memories significantly outperform traditional DRAM due to low standby power and fast access speed [22,24]. However, persistent memories suffer from the *write endurance* problem, i.e., every persistent memory unit can sustain a very limited number of writes before it wears-out. The total number of writes to the persistent memory address can also be defined as the total number of movement of data to and from the memory address. To mitigate the endurance problem, the movements of data should be minimized.

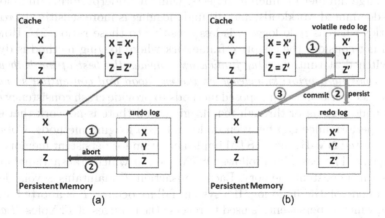

Fig. 1. An illustration of (a) undo and (b) redo logging methods in persistent memory.

Therefore, ADAPTIVE focuses on minimizing the total number of movements of data to and from the persistent memory by incorporating the best of both redo and undo logging frameworks switching dynamically. Specifically, for undo logging, we measure the total number of movement of data between the original persistent memory locations and the undo log area, whereas for redo logging, we measure the total number of movement of data between the original persistent memory, volatile redo log area, and the persistent redo log area. Figure 1 illustrates these moves through ◯ steps for both undo and redo logging methods. The results suggest that, when using an *eager* version of redo logging, ADAPTIVE achieves up to 6× better performance than redo logging and up to 4.6× better performance than undo logging. When a *lazy* version of redo logging is used, ADAPTIVE again achieves up to 6× better performance than redo logging and up to 35× better performance than undo logging. The implication of our results is that switching between undo and redo logging dynamically at runtime provides a way to exploit positive aspects of both the logging methods, minimizing the total number of movements of data using undo or redo logging methods individually. This all is achieved with a minimal increase in total execution time, i.e., the execution time increase in ADAPTIVE is only at most 17% more than the total execution time using either undo or redo logging.

Related Work. The literature on redo and undo logging methods for crash consistency in persistent memory is vast. We discuss here only very closely related works. The most closely related work is due to Wan *et al.* [21], where they empirically evaluated redo and undo logging methods on the open source NVM library (NVML) [1] for some constrained workloads, and suggested that *"one logging method does not fit all workloads"*. Particularly, they reported that (i) redo logging significantly outperforms undo logging for workloads in which a transaction updates large number of different objects, while it underperforms undo logging for read-dominated workloads, and (ii) undo logging is more sensitive to *read-to-write* ratios whereas redo logging is less sensitive to those ratios [21]. However, they did not consider the adaptive framework where logging method is dynamically switched at runtime. *Our framework provides the best of the both worlds without requiring a priori knowledge on the workload and contention scenario.*

The other works mostly proposed methods to provide crash consistency either through undo logging or through redo logging, and there is no work that elaborates the performance gap between undo and redo logging methods. Coburn *et al.* [6] suggested NV-HEAPS, a STM implementation for persistent memory using undo logging. The basic idea follows DSTM [10], in which transactional objects are stored in persistent memory. Each transaction T maintains a volatile read log and a non-volatile undo log. If a system failure occurs, T is aborted and the undo log, which is persistent, is used to reverse the changes of T. Volos *et al.* [20] suggested MNEMOSYNE for persistent memory using redo logging and derived from TinySTM [8,9]. We observed that NV-HEAPS [6] and MNEMOSYNE [20] drew absolutely opposite conclusions on whether undo or redo logging is better for persistent memory. The former prefers to use undo logging, and the latter opts to use redo logging. Our results suggest that a combination of both of them is better than using these methods individually. A salient feature of our method is it does not require any priori knowledge on workload and contention scenarios.

Recently, Avni *et al.* [3] studied hardware transactional memory (HTM) based transactions for consistency in persistent memory through redo logging. DUDETM [13] provided a technique to answer whether to use undo or redo logging through a framework where a transaction first runs in volatile memory using any HTM or STM implementation and produces a redo log for that transaction. The redo log is then flushed to persistent memory satisfying atomicity of data and then modify the original data in persistent memory according to the persistent redo log. Notice that this approach is different than ours and needs a shared shadow memory, besides persistent memory where that data is. The recent several papers, e.g., [4,5,11,12,14,16,19,23], provided techniques to improve the time to log the data (e.g., through coalescing, through persistent cache, through hardware support, through undo+redo logging methods, etc.) for both undo and redo logs. However, our focus is on taking a different approach of dynamically switching between undo and redo logging at runtime to exploit advantages of both the methods and our extensive experimental evaluation (Sect. 4) confirms this exploitation.

Paper Organization. We discuss the memory model in Sect. 2. We outline our adaptive logging framework in Sect. 3 and evaluate it in Sect. 4. Finally, we conclude in Sect. 5. Some experimental results are omitted due to space constraints.

2 Model

We consider a computer system with unlimited persistent memory, many processing cores, and no HDD. All persistent memory is cacheable and caches are volatile and coherent. The system may include limited size DRAM (but we do not assume its necessity). We assume that all the writes of a committed transaction can be accommodated in the volatile cache, i.e., once a transaction commits but before the commit is reflected in original memory locations in persistent memory, all its newly modified data is in volatile cache. The system restarts and resumes its computation after experiencing failures/crashes. Therefore, the task after restart is to bring the data to a consistent state, removing effects of uncommitted transactions and applying the missing effects of the committed ones. We simulate crashes by periodically wiping out the volatile logs, and use the data stored in undo or redo logs in persistent memory to recover consistency. We employ a function that checks and maintains consistency while under execution.

For redo logging, we make sure that all writes that are in volatile cache reach persistent log before a transaction commit, while all transactional writes stay in the cache. Moreover, to make sure that the last committed value is used in the restart process, we attach a version to each logged variable x. Note that the technique of verifying that x is logged only once in the system can also be used for this purpose. For undo logging, the data in persistent undo log is used in the restart process (no versioning required).

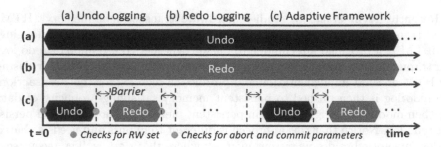

Fig. 2. An illustration of undo logging, redo logging, and adaptive logging methods. The barrier in ADAPTIVE is to let finish executing in-flight transactions before switching.

3   Adaptive Logging Framework

We now describe our adaptive logging framework, ADAPTIVE, that runs transactions using either undo or redo logging, switching between these two logging methods dynamically at runtime. In the existing persistent memory designs, e.g., [6,13,16,20,23], transactions execute using either redo logging or undo logging (without switching) selected a priori. Figure 2 compares ADAPTIVE with undo and redo logging. The pseudocode of ADAPTIVE is given in Algorithm 1.

Let T be a transaction that comes to the system at time $t \geq 0$. We assume that the execution starts at time $t_0 = 0$. In the following, we describe how ADAPTIVE schedules T using either undo logging or redo logging dynamically switching at runtime.

We need the following definitions. Let $N_{ucommit}, N_{rcommit}$ be the number of transaction commits in ADAPTIVE from time $t_0 = 0$ until the current time $t > t_0$ for transactions executed using undo logging and redo logging, respectively. Particularly, $N_{ucommit}$ ($N_{rcommit}$) counts the number of transactions that are committed in ADAPTIVE while running using undo (redo) logging method. Similarly, let N_{uabort}, N_{rabort} be the number of transaction aborts in ADAPTIVE from time $t_0 = 0$ until time $t > t_0$ for transactions executed using undo logging and redo logging, respectively. Furthermore, let N_{commit} and N_{abort} be the total number of commits and aborts in ADAPTIVE, respectively. We have that $N_{commit} = N_{ucommit} + N_{rcommit}$ and $N_{abort} = N_{uabort} + N_{rabort}$, respectively.

The idea in ADAPTIVE is to decide on which logging method to use for executing T based on the parameters $N_{ucommit}, N_{rcommit}, N_{uabort}$, and N_{rabort} learned from the system at runtime. However, if T comes to the system at time $t_0 = 0$, we have all $N_{ucommit}, N_{rcommit}, N_{uabort}$, and N_{rabort} zero. We treat this as a special case and rely on the size of the read and write sets of T to decide on which logging method to use. Let $Wset(T)$ be the *write set* of T which is essentially the persistent memory locations that T would modify while in execution. Similarly, let $Rset(T)$ be the *read set* of T which is essentially the persistent memory locations that T would read (but not modify) while in execution. We have that $RW(T) = Rset(T) + Wset(T)$, where $RW(T)$ denotes

---

Algorithm 1. Adaptive logging framework for a transaction T at any time $t \geq 0$.

---

1 $N_{ucommit} \leftarrow$ number of commits until t for transactions executed using undo logging;

2 $N_{rcommit} \leftarrow$ number of commits until t for transactions executed using redo logging;

3 $N_{uabort} \leftarrow$ number of aborts until t for transactions executed using undo logging;

4 $N_{rabort} \leftarrow$ number of aborts until t for transactions executed using undo logging;

5 $N_{commit} \leftarrow N_{ucommit} + N_{rcommit}$, $N_{abort} \leftarrow N_{uabort} + N_{rabort}$;

6 **if** $N_{commit} + N_{abort} == 0$ **then**

7      $Wset(T) \leftarrow$ write set of transaction T;

8      $Rset(T) \leftarrow$ read set of transaction T;

9   **if** $Wset(T)$ *is greater than* $Rset(T)$ **then** execute T using redo logging;

10   **else** execute T using undo logging;

11 **if** $N_{commit} + N_{abort} > 0$ **then**

12      $AAR \leftarrow \frac{N_{abort}}{N_{commit} + N_{abort}}$, $AAR_{undo} \leftarrow \frac{N_{uabort}}{N_{ucommit} + N_{uabort}}$, $ACR_{undo} \leftarrow \frac{N_{uabort}}{N_{ucommit}}$, $ACR_{redo} \leftarrow \frac{N_{rabort}}{N_{rcommit}}$;

13   **if** $(AAR \geq \frac{2}{3}) \vee ((ACR_{undo} > ACR_{redo}) \wedge (AAR_{undo} \geq \frac{2}{3}))$ **then**

14   execute T using redo logging;

15   **else** execute T using undo logging;

---

the total number of persistent memory locations that T reads and modifies while in execution. Therefore, at $t_0 = 0$, if $Wset(T)$ is greater than $Rset(T)$, then T is executed using redo logging, otherwise using undo logging.

If T comes to the system after at least a transaction finishes executing one time (irrespective of whether that transaction aborts or commits), then it is executed based on the following parameters. $AAR = \frac{N_{abort}}{N_{commit} + N_{abort}}$ denotes the *average abort ratio* of transactions in ADAPTIVE from time $t = 0$ until time t (using both redo and undo logging). $AAR_{undo} = \frac{N_{uabort}}{N_{ucommit} + N_{uabort}}$ denotes the average abort ratio of transactions in ADAPTIVE from time $t = 0$ until time t executed using undo logging. Furthermore, $ACR_{undo} = \frac{N_{uabort}}{N_{ucommit}}$ and $ACR_{redo} = \frac{N_{rabort}}{N_{rcommit}}$ denote the *abort to commit ratio* of transactions in ADAPTIVE from time $t = 0$ until time t using undo logging and redo logging, respectively. At any time $t \geq 0$, $0 \leq AAR \leq 1$ and $0 \leq AAR_{undo} \leq 1$.

At any time $t > t_0$ in ADAPTIVE, T is executed using redo logging if (i) $AAR \geq \frac{2}{3}$ or (ii) $ACR_{undo} > ACR_{redo}$ and $AAR_{undo} \geq \frac{2}{3}$. Otherwise, T is executed using undo logging. We call the value $\frac{2}{3}$ *switching threshold* and we describe later how this switching threshold $\frac{2}{3}$ is computed. The motivation behind using $\frac{2}{3}$ as switching threshold in ADAPTIVE is that it works on all the benchmarks we experimented our framework against. We now discuss how the switching threshold is computed.

Computing the Switching Threshold $\frac{2}{3}$. The idea we employ is to compute the number of data movements for redo and undo logging, separately, and switch between these methods when the data movement increases. Ideally, we would like to use the logging method in ADAPTIVE that gives optimum data movement performance for any specific workload. We use the following notions. Let N be the total number of transactions in any workload. When the workload finishes execution and all transactions commit, we have $N_{commit} = N$ number of commits and $N_{abort} \geq 0$ number of aborts (if each transaction commits without even aborting a single time, then $N_{abort} = 0$, otherwise $N_{abort} > 0$). Suppose each transaction T has read write set $RW(T)$ of size S. Let W_{undo} be the total number of operations of moving data (i) from the original persistent memory locations to the undo log area (again in persistent memory) and (ii) from the undo log area back to the original persistent memory locations. The first kind of moves are shown as ① in Fig. 1(a) and the second kind of moves are shown as ② in Fig. 1(a). The first kind of moves are always done in undo logging and the second kind of moves are done only when the transaction aborts. Therefore,

$$W_{undo} = (N_{commit} + 2N_{abort}) \cdot S. \tag{1}$$

Let W_{redo} be the total number of operations of moving data (i) from the original persistent memory locations to the redo log area (in volatile cache), (ii) from the redo log area (in volatile cache) to persistent memory locations to persist the redo log in the volatile cache, and (iii) finally, writing the data back to the original persistent memory locations either from redo log area in persistent memory after restart or from redo log area in volatile cache. The first kind of moves are shown as ① in Fig. 1(b), and the second and third kind of moves are shown as ② and ③ in Fig. 1(b), respectively. The first kind of moves are always done in redo logging and the second and third kind of moves are done only when the transaction commits. Therefore,

$$W_{redo} = (3N_{commit} + N_{abort}) \cdot S, \tag{2}$$

Notice that a transaction can run using either undo or redo logging when $W_{undo} = W_{redo}$ as the selection of a logging method does not have impact on the total number of movements. Therefore, from Eqs. 1 and 2, we have that

$$(N_{commit} + 2N_{abort}) \cdot S = (3N_{commit} + N_{abort}) \cdot S \tag{3}$$

$$N_{commit} + 2N_{abort} = 3N_{commit} + N_{abort} \tag{4}$$

$$N_{abort} = 2N_{commit} \tag{5}$$

Also, we have that $N \leq N_{abort} + N_{commit}$. This implies that

$$\frac{N_{abort}}{N} + \frac{N_{commit}}{N} \geq 1 \tag{6}$$

$$\frac{2N_{commit}}{N} + \frac{N_{commit}}{N} \geq 1 \tag{7}$$

$$\frac{N_{commit}}{N} \geq \frac{1}{3} \tag{8}$$

Therefore, $\frac{N_{abort}}{N} < \frac{2}{3}$. That is, if the value of N_{abort} is such that $\frac{N_{abort}}{N}$ is higher than $\frac{2}{3}$, then $W_{undo} > W_{redo}$. Thus, ADAPTIVE switches execution to redo logging when $\frac{N_{abort}}{N} \geq \frac{2}{3}$ (Line 13 of Algorithm 1) and stay with undo logging, otherwise.

Time Barrier Requirement and Design. The ideal scenario in ADAPTIVE is to let each transaction T run Algorithm 1 and decide which logging method (redo or undo) to use for it to execute individually based on the parameters it infers at runtime. For several benchmarks we experimented with, this works perfectly fine. However, for some benchmarks, this creates a problem as some transactions are still in progress using one logging method and when T executes using other logging method, the conflict detection and resolution mechanisms interfere, hampering consistency. Therefore, to handle this situation, we introduce a *time barrier* (as shown in Fig. 2) that helps to synchronize the transactions while switching from one logging method to another. Suppose currently transactions are running using undo logging. Let a new transaction T arrives and it decides to run using redo logging. Since there are transactions still running using undo logging, T waits until those transactions finish executing. We show later in the experimental results that the possible increase in total execution time is due to time barriers and this increase is minimal compared to the substantial reductions in the total number of data movements achieved in ADAPTIVE.

Correctness of ADAPTIVE: We provide the correctness proof showing that the algorithm discussed above behaves correctly even under faults, achieving crash consistency.

Theorem 1. *Algorithm 1 provides crash consistency.*

Proof. Consider a transaction T that arrives at time $t \geq 0$. Suppose T runs with undo logging (Line 10 or 15 from Algorithm 1). T maintains the undo log with unique transaction ID in the undo log area in persistent memory where the current records of memory locations accessed by T are stored. T then directly updates on those persistent memory locations. Now, consider any new transaction $T_1 \neq T$ that arrives at time $t_1 > t$. Suppose T_1 also runs with undo logging and at some time $t_2 > t_1$, T and T_1 both conflict. Now, the transaction T aborts and to rollback to the previous consistent state, the records stored in the persistent undo log are written back to the original memory locations accessed by T.

Suppose now that T_1 tries to execute using redo logging. Since T has arrived before T_1, T is already running with undo logging. Since T_1 satisfied for redo logging, T_1 has to wait until T finishes executing (either commit or abort). Since $t_1 > t$ and T_1 runs after T finishes its execution, there is no conflict between T and T_1 and barrier helps to synchronize the execution of T and T_1.

Finally, consider the power failure scenario. Let a transaction T is running using either undo logging or redo logging and suddenly, the power failure occurs. When the system is restarted, the persistent log area is scanned and replayed. With the persistent undo log records, the inconsistent memory locations are rolled back to the previous consistent states. With the persistent redo log records, the memory locations are updated with the latest committed values. Both the log records are discarded after they are replayed. The incomplete log records are also discarded.   □

4   Experimental Evaluation

We now evaluate the performance of ADAPTIVE using 5 micro-benchmarks and 8 complex benchmarks. The evaluation is performed in a STM-based implementation using TinySTM [8,9] modified appropriately to emulate persistent memory model described in Sect. 2. The tests were executed on an Intel Core i7-7700K 4.20 GHz, 64-bit Haswell processor with 4 cores, each with 2 hyper threads. Each core has private L1 and L2 caches, whose sizes are 256 KB and 1 MB, respectively. There is also an 8 MB L3 cache shared by all 4 cores and 32 GB main memory. We first describe in detail how the experimental platform is set up. We then describe how a persistent memory framework is emulated. We finally describe benchmarks and the results achieved. All the results presented in this section are the average of 10 experimental runs. Moreover, the results are for varying number of threads ranging from 1 to 16.

Experimental Setup. We developed a STM-based implementation using TinySTM [8,9]. TinySTM is a word-based STM that uses locks to protect shared memory locations. TinySTM has implemented separately both redo logging and undo logging methods (called *Redo* and *Undo*, respectively) through *Write_Back* and *Write_Through* designs, respectively. With *Write_Through* design, transactions directly write to original memory locations and revert their updates in case the transactions abort. However, with *Write_Back* design, transactions work on a copy of data and delay their updates to original memory locations of data until commit [8,9]. Furthermore, *Write_Back* design has two different implementations: *Write_Back_ETL* (also called *eager or encounter-time locking*) and *Write_Back_CTL* (also called *lazy or commit-time locking*). Encounter-time locking (ETL) detects transaction conflicts early at the time of memory write and acquires the lock on the memory address before it is written. Commit-time locking (CTL) defers conflict detection on memory address until commit, i.e., the lock is acquired on the memory address at the commit time. Therefore, there are two different implementations of *Redo* in TinySTM: one based on *ETL* is called *Redo_ETL* and another based on *CTL* is called *Redo_CTL*.

We use *Redo_ETL* and *Undo* implementations to obtain an adaptive design, which we call *Adaptive_ETL*. Specifically, *Adaptive_ETL* uses *Redo_ETL* design of TinySTM as a redo logging method and *Undo* design of TinySTM as a undo logging method while executing Algorithm 1. Similarly, we use *Redo_CTL* and *Undo* implementations to obtain an adaptive design, which we call *Adaptive_CTL*. Therefore, we run experiments with five different designs *Redo_ETL*, *Redo_CTL*, *Undo*, *Adaptive_ETL*, and *Adaptive_CTL*, and compare, particularly, the results using *Adaptive_ETL* with *Redo_ETL* and *Undo* implementations, and the results using *Adaptive_CTL* with *Redo_CTL* and *Undo* implementations.

Persistent Memory Emulation. Persistent memory is not available yet (even for experimentation purposes) [13]. Therefore, we emulate it using DRAM in our experiments following previous works, e.g., [3]. We separate 500 MB region of DRAM for the persistent memory emulation. We use this region for keeping the persistent undo log when a transaction runs using undo logging and to persist the redo log when transaction runs using redo logging. To emulate the power failure and crash in persistent memory, we leave the power on and wipe out all the volatile log records so that the rollback (in case of abort in undo logging) and update (in case of commit but not yet written to memory in redo logging) operations will be handled by those persistent log records.

Benchmarks. We use both micro and complex benchmarks in the experiments. *Micro − Benchmarks:* We use 5 well-known and widely-used different micro-benchmarks, namely *bank, red black tree, hash set, linked list,* and *skip list* that are available in the TinySTM distribution [8,9] and used for experimentation in several papers, e.g., [10,13,21]. These micro-benchmarks simulate the basic concurrent access scenario for transactions with (relatively) small read/write sets.

STAMP: STAMP is also a well-known and widely-used benchmark suite. It consists of eight applications: *bayes, genome, intruder, kmeans, labyrinth, ssca2, vacation,* and *yada* of varying complexity. These applications span a variety of computing domains as well as runtime transactional characteristics such as varying transaction lengths, read and write set sizes, and amounts of contention [15].

STAMPEDE: Recently, Nguyen *et al.* [17] argued that the programming model and data structures used in STAMP benchmarks introduce performance bottlenecks. They modified them in a way the bottlenecks can be removed. They provided a set of rewritten STAMP benchmarks called STAMPEDE benchmarks. These are the same 8 STAMP benchmarks with the only difference on programming model and data structures.

Results on Micro-benchmarks. Figure 3 provides the experimental results for all 5 different micro-benchmarks. All the transactions in these benchmarks were run with *update rate* of 20%. When transactions were executed with small number of threads, we found that the transaction commit rate is higher than the transaction abort rate and the cost in redo logging is higher than the cost in undo logging. With the increase in number of threads, the abort rate is also increased. We noticed that *Redo_CTL* has consistently better performance than *Redo_ETL* on all the five micro-benchmarks. This is because the early detection of conflict and locking the memory address has increased the abort rate than the detecting conflict and locking the memory address at the commit time. *Adaptive_ETL* achieved up to 3.4× performance improvement compared to *Redo_ETL*. Similarly, *Adaptive_CTL* achieved up to 3× performance improvement compared to the *Redo_CTL*. Compared to *Undo*, *Adaptive_ETL* achieved up to 1.1× performance improvement and *Adaptive_CTL* achieved up to 1.3× performance improvement. Furthermore, *Adaptive_CTL* performed up to 2.5× better than *Adaptive_ETL*. The results show that ADAPTIVE always performs

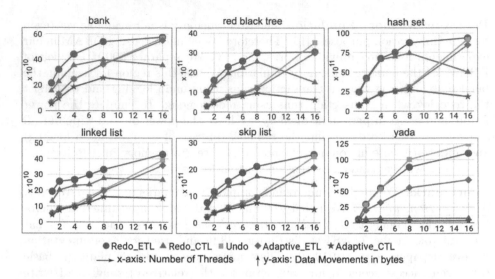

Fig. 3. An illustration of data movements in micro-benchmarks and *yada* from STAMP

better than *Redo* or *Undo*. We also noticed that *Adaptive_CTL* performs better than *Adaptive_ETL* in each micro-benchmark, since *Redo_CTL* performing better than *Redo_ETL*.

Results on STAMP Benchmarks. Figure 4 provides results for STAMP benchmarks. We found that when the transactions are executed with low number of threads, the transaction commit rate is higher and undo performs better than redo. This is due to low contention for memory access with small number of threads. With increasing number of threads, transaction abort rate also increases and undo starts to perform worse due to the frequent requirement of rollback. The results obtained for *genome* and *kmeans-low* show that undo starts to perform worse than redo beyond 8 threads. The same scenario starts beyond 4 threads in *Intruder* and *yada*. Moreover, we noticed that, irrespective of the abort rate change in redo and undo logging, ADAPTIVE always has better performance. Specifically, *Adaptive_ETL* achieved up to 6× performance improvement compared to *Redo_ETL* and up to 2× performance improvement compared to *Undo*. *Adaptive_CTL* achieved up to 3× performance improvement compared to *Redo_CTL* and up to 35× performance improvement (in *yada*) compared to *Undo*.

Results on STAMPEDE Benchmarks. Figure 5 provides the experimental results for STAMPEDE benchmarks. Similar to micro-benchmarks and STAMP benchmarks, ADAPTIVE has better performance compared to *Redo* or *Undo* in STAMPEDE benchmarks. *Adaptive_ETL* performed up to 3.6× better than the *Redo_ETL*. *Adaptive_CTL* performed up to 6× better than the *Redo_CTL*. Compared to *Undo*, *Adaptive_ETL* achieved up to 4.6× better performance and *Adaptive_CTL* achieved up to 3.1× better performance.

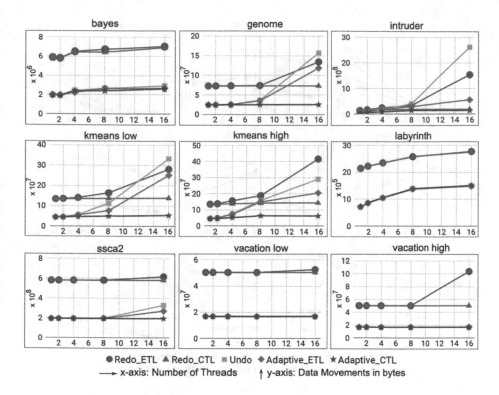

Fig. 4. An illustration of data movements in STAMP benchmarks

Execution Time and Throughput Results. The execution time is impacted in ADAPTIVE due to the switching between undo and redo logging at runtime. In most of the benchmarks, the increase in time is compensated as ADAPTIVE lowers the number of aborts. We were interested in what is the maximum increase on time in any benchmark we used in our experimentation. For micro-benchmarks, we measured *throughput* (instead of execution time) in terms of total number of transactions executed per second. This is because all 5 micro-benchmarks were executed for a fixed time interval of 10,000 ms and throughput is a natural performance parameter to examine the execution characteristic in this interval. All the 5 micro-benchmarks were executed with 5 different logging designs and the total number of transactions for each design were counted. The results obtained are omitted due to space constraints. We noticed that, in some applications, throughput of *Redo_ETL* is at most 16% more than the throughput of *Adaptive_ETL*. Throughput of *Redo_CTL* is at most 13% more than that of *Adaptive_CTL*. Throughput of *Undo* is at most 11% more than the throughput of *Adaptive_ETL* and at most 16% more than the throughput of *Adaptive_CTL*. These results imply that the throughput of ADAPTIVE is slightly decreased (less than 16%) compared to *Undo* or *Redo*. That means, the execution time for

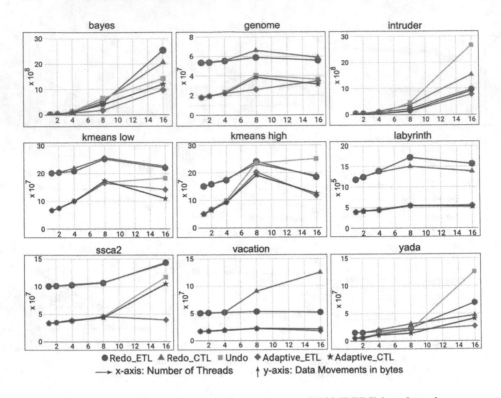

Fig. 5. An illustration of data movements in STAMPEDE benchmarks

the micro-benchmarks may increase by at most 16% in ADAPTIVE compared to *Undo* or *Redo*.

For the STAMP and STAMPEDE benchmarks, we measured the execution time for each of the applications. Figure 6 compares the execution time for STAMP benchmarks (the results for STAMPEDE are omitted due to space constraints). We noticed that the execution time in ADAPTIVE is at most 17% more compared to the execution time of *Undo* or *Redo*. As ADAPTIVE lowers the number of aborts, some applications (e.g. bayes, kmeans high, ssca2 in Fig. 6) have decreased execution time in ADAPTIVE than in *Undo* or *Redo* designs. We claim that the increase in execution time (decrease in throughput accordingly) for some applications is largely dominated by the performance improvement in terms of *total number of data movements*.

To summarize, in all of the cases, ADAPTIVE performs better for number of data movements compared to individual *Undo* and *Redo* designs, without increasing the execution time running using *Undo* and *Redo* designs. In some cases, the execution time increases but that is minimal compared to that of using *Undo* and *Redo* designs.

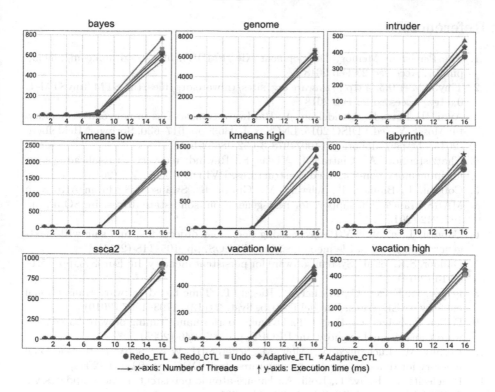

Fig. 6. An illustration of execution time for STAMP benchmarks

5 Concluding Remarks

Persistent memory is gaining much attention recently from both academia and industry. One of the most challenging issues in persistent memory is how to ensure consistency of the application data in the event of sudden power failure or system crash (commonly known as crash consistency). Redo and undo logging methods are the widely used techniques for maintaining crash consistency in persistent memory. However, they were studied separately and whether to use redo or undo logging (and which is in fact better) is still in hot debate. In this paper, we have presented an adaptive logging framework that dynamically switches between undo and redo logging methods at runtime to obtain the best of the both worlds. Our framework is quite simple and achieves significantly better performance (in terms of number of data movements addressing the write endurance problem) compared to undo and redo logging in 5 micro-benchmarks and 8 applications in STAMP and STAMPEDE benchmarks (with a minimal overhead in execution time). We believe our results and techniques will be helpful in choosing proper logging method for future consistency designs for persistent memories.

References

1. The Persistent Memory Development Kit (PMDK). https://github.com/pmem/pmdk/. Accessed 23 Feb 2018
2. TinySTM 1.0.5. http://tmware.org/sites/tmware.org/files/tinySTM/tinySTM-1.0.5.tgz. Accessed 23 Feb 2018
3. Avni, H., Levy, E., Mendelson, A.: Hardware transactions in nonvolatile memory. In: Moses, Y. (ed.) DISC 2015. LNCS, vol. 9363, pp. 617–630. Springer, Heidelberg (2015). https://doi.org/10.1007/978-3-662-48653-5_41
4. Chatzistergiou, A., Cintra, M., Viglas, S.: Rewind: recovery write-ahead system for in-memory non-volatile data-structures. PVLDB **8**, 497–508 (2015)
5. Coburn, J., Bunker, T., Schwarz, M., Gupta, R., Swanson, S.: From ARIES to MARS: transaction support for next-generation, solid-state drives. In: SOSP, pp. 197–212 (2013)
6. Coburn, J., et al.: NV-Heaps: making persistent objects fast and safe with next-generation, non-volatile memories. In: ASPLOS, pp. 105–118 (2011)
7. Dulloor, S.R., et al.: System software for persistent memory. In: EuroSys, pp. 15:1–15:15 (2014)
8. Felber, P., Fetzer, C., Marlier, P., Riegel, T.: Time-based software transactional memory. IEEE Trans. Parallel Distrib. Syst. **21**(12), 1793–1807 (2010)
9. Felber, P., Fetzer, C., Riegel, T.: Dynamic performance tuning of word-based software transactional memory. In: PPOPP, pp. 237–246 (2008)
10. Herlihy, M., Luchangco, V., Moir, M., Scherer III, W.N.: Software transactional memory for dynamic-sized data structures. In: PODC, pp. 92–101 (2003)
11. Izraelevitz, J., Kelly, T., Kolli, A.: Failure-atomic persistent memory updates via JUSTDO logging. ASPLOS **44**, 427–442 (2016)
12. Kolli, A., Pelley, S., Saidi, A., Chen, P.M., Wenisch, T.F.: High-performance transactions for persistent memories. In: ASPLOS, pp. 399–411 (2016)
13. Liu, M., et al.: DudeTM: building durable transactions with decoupling for persistent memory. In: ASPLOS, pp. 329–343 (2017)
14. Lu, Y., Shu, J., Sun, L.: Blurred persistence: efficient transactions in persistent memory. Trans. Storage **12**(1), 3:1–3:29 (2016)
15. Minh, C.C., Chung, J., Kozyrakis, C., Olukotun, K.: STAMP: stanford transactional applications for multi-processing. In: IISWC, pp. 35–46 (2008)
16. Narayanan, D., Hodson, O.: Whole-system persistence. In: ASPLOS, pp. 401–410 (2012)
17. Nguyen, D., Pingali, K.: What scalable programs need from transactional memory. In: ASPLOS, pp. 105–118 (2017)
18. Shavit, N., Touitou, D.: Software transactional memory. In: PODC, pp. 204–213 (1995)
19. Shin, S., Tirukkovalluri, S.K., Tuck, J., Solihin, Y.: Proteus: a flexible and fast software supported hardware logging approach for NVM. In: MICRO, pp. 178–190 (2017)
20. Volos, H., Tack, A.J., Swift, M.M.: Mnemosyne: lightweight persistent memory. In: ASPLOS, pp. 91–104 (2011)
21. Wan, H., Lu, Y., Xu, Y., Shu, J.: Empirical study of redo and undo logging in persistent memory. In: NVMSA, pp. 1–6 (2016)
22. Zhang, Y., Swanson, S.: A study of application performance with non-volatile main memory. In: 2015 31st Symposium on Mass Storage Systems and Technologies (MSST), pp. 1–10 (2015)

23. Zhao, J., Li, S., Yoon, D.H., Xie, Y., Jouppi, N.P.: Kiln: closing the performance gap between systems with and without persistence support. In: MICRO, pp. 421–432 (2013)
24. Zhou, P., Zhao, B., Yang, J., Zhang, Y.: A durable and energy efficient main memory using phase change memory technology. In: SIGARCH Computer Architecture News, vol. 37, no. 3, pp. 14–23 (2009)

On Underlay-Aware Self-Stabilizing Overlay Networks

Thorsten Götte$^{(\boxtimes)}$, Christian Scheideler, and Alexander Setzer

Department of Computer Science, Paderborn University,
Fürstenallee 11, 33102 Paderborn, Germany
{thgoette,scheidel,asetzer}@mail.upb.de

Abstract. We present a self-stabilizing protocol for an overlay network that constructs the Minimum Spanning Tree (MST) for an underlay that is modeled by a weighted tree. The weight of an overlay edge between two nodes is the weighted length of their shortest path in the tree. We rigorously prove that our protocol works correctly under asynchronous and non-FIFO message delivery. Further, the protocol stabilizes after $\mathcal{O}(N^2)$ asynchronous rounds where N is the number of nodes in the overlay.

Keywords: Topological self-stabilization · Overlay networks
Minimum spanning tree

1 Introduction

The Internet is perhaps the world's most popular medium to exchange any kind of information. Common examples are streaming platforms, file sharing services or social media networks. Such applications are often maintained by overlay networks, called overlays for short. An overlay is a computer network that is built atop another network, the so-called underlay. In an overlay, nodes that may not be directly connected in the underlay can create virtual links and exchange messages if they know each others' addresses. The resulting links then represent a path in the underlying network, perhaps through several of its links.

With increasing size of the network, there are several obstacles in designing these overlays. First of all, errors such as node or link failures are inevitable. Thus, there is a need for protocols that let the system recover from these faults. This can be achieved through self-stabilization, which describes a system's ability to reach a desired state from *any* initial configuration. Since its conception by Edsger W. Dijkstra in 1975, self-stabilization has proven to be a suitable paradigm to build resilient and scalable overlays that can quickly recover from changes. There is a plethora of self-stabilizing protocols for the formation and maintenance of overlay networks with a specific topology. These topologies range

This work was partially supported by the German Research Foundation (DFG) within the Collaborative Research Center "On-The-Fly Computing" (SFB 901).

T. Izumi and P. Kuznetsov (Eds.): SSS 2018, LNCS 11201, pp. 50–64, 2018.
https://doi.org/10.1007/978-3-030-03232-6_4

from simple structures like line graphs and rings [23] to more complex overlay networks with useful properties for distributed systems [12,17,22,26]. These overlays usually minimize the diameter while also maintaining a small node degree, usually at most logarithmic in the number of nodes. However, the aforementioned overlay protocols are often not concerned with path lengths in the underlay. This is remarkable, since for many use cases these path lengths and the resulting latency are arguably more important than the diameter.

In this paper, we work towards closing this gap by proposing a self-stabilizing protocol that forms and maintains an overlay that resembles the Minimum Spanning Tree (MST) implied by the distances between nodes in the underlying network. In particular, we model these distances as a tree metric, i.e., as the length of the unique shortest path between two overlay nodes in a weighted tree. We chose this type of metric because one can find weighted trees in many areas of networking. In the simplest case, the physical network that interconnects the overlay nodes resembles a tree. This is often the case in data centers. Here, the servers are the tree's leaves while the switches are the tree's intermediate nodes (cf. [4,6,21]). Therefore, we can define a tree metric directly on the paths in this physical infrastructure. Of course, not all physical networks are strictly structured like trees, and may instead contain cycles. However, for small networks there are practical protocols that explicitly reduce the network graph to a tree for routing purposes [24]. These protocols are executed directly on the network appliances and exclude certain physical connections, such that the remaining connections form a spanning tree. Thus, we can define a tree metric based on this tree. Last, in large-scale networks like the internet neither the physical network nor the routing paths strictly resemble trees. However, there is strong evidence that even these large-scale networks can be closely approximated by or embedded into weighted trees by assigning them virtual coordinates (cf. [2,3,10,28]). Thus, we can define a tree metric based on the shortest paths in such an embedding. In summary, tree metrics promise to be a versatile abstraction for many kinds of real-world networks.

1.1 Model and Definitions

We consider a distributed system based on a fixed set of nodes V. Each node $v \in V$ represents a computational unit, e.g., a computer, that possesses a set of local variables and references to other nodes, e.g., their IP addresses. These references are immutable and cannot be corrupted. If clear from the context, we refer to the reference of some node $w \in V$ simply as w. Further, each node in V has access to a *tree metric* $d_T : V^2 \to \mathbb{R}^+$ that assigns a weight to each possible edge in the overlay. In particular, the function d_T returns the weighted length of the unique shortest path between two nodes in the weighted tree $T := (V_T, E_T, f)$ with $f : V^2 \to \mathbb{R}^+$ and $V_T \supseteq V$. A node $v \in V$ can check the distance $d_T(v, w)$ only if it has a reference to $w \in V$ in its local variables. Furthermore, it can check the distance $d_T(u, w)$ of all nodes $u, w \in V$ in its local variables. Throughout this paper, we refer to the metric space (V, d_T) also as a tree metric for ease of description.

Sending a message from a node u to another node v in the overlay is only possible if u has a reference to v. All messages for a single node are stored in its so-called channel and we assume *fair message receipt*, which means each message will *eventually* be received. In particular, we do *not* assume FIFO-delivery, i.e., the messages may be received and processed in any order.

We assume that each node runs a protocol that can perform computations on the node's local variables and send them within messages to other nodes. To formalize the protocol's execution, we use the notion of *configurations*. A configuration c contains each node's internal state, i.e., its assignment of values to its local variables, its stored references, and all messages in the node's channel. We denote C to be the set of all possible configurations. Further, a *computation* is an infinite series of configurations $(c_t, c_{t+1}, \dots)$, such that c_{i+1} is a succeeding configuration of c_i for $i \geq t$ according to the protocol. In each step from c_i to c_{i+1}, the following happens: One node $v \in V$ is activated and an arbitrary (possibly empty) set of messages from v's channel is delivered to v. Once activated, the node will execute its protocol and processes all messages delivered to it. As we do not specify which node is activated and which messages get delivered, there are maybe several possible succeeding configurations $c' \in C$ for any configuration c. Last, we assume *weakly fair execution*, which means that each node is eventually activated. Other than that, we place no restriction on the activation order.

Given a subset $C' \subseteq C$, we say that the system *reaches* C' from c_t if *every* computation that starts in configuration c_t eventually contains a configuration $c_{t'} \in C'$. Note that this does not imply that any succeeding configuration of $c_{t'}$ is in C' as well.

Based on this notion of configurations, we can now define self-stabilization. A protocol is self-stabilizing concerning a set of legal configurations $L \subseteq C$ if starting from any initial configuration $c_0 \in C$ each computation will eventually reach L (Convergence) and every succeeding configuration is also in L (Closure). Formally:

Definition 1 (Self-Stabilization). *A protocol $\mathcal{P}$ is self-stabilizing if it fulfills the following two properties.*

1. *(Convergence) Let $c_0 \in C$ be any configuration. Then every computation that starts in c_0 will reach L in finitely many steps.*
2. *(Closure) Let $c_t \in L$ be any legal configuration. Then every succeeding configuration of c_t is legal as well.*

Throughout this paper we distinguish between two kinds of edges in each configuration $c \in C$. We call an edge $(v, w) \in V^2$ *explicit* if and only if v has a reference to w stored in its local variables. Otherwise, if the reference is in v's channel, we call the edge *implicit*. Based on this definitions, we define the directed graph $G_c := (V, E_c^X \cup E_c^T)$ where the set $E_c^X \subseteq V^2$ denotes the set of explicit edges and $E_c^T \subseteq V^2$ denotes the set of implicit edges. Further, the undirected graph $G_c^* := (V, E_c^*)$ arises from G_c if we ignore all edges' direction and whether they are implicit or explicit.

1.2   Our Contribution

Our main contribution is BUILDMST, a self-stabilizing protocol that forms and
maintains an overlay representing the MSTs of all connected components of V.
An MST is a set of edges that connects a set of nodes and minimizes the sum of
the edges' weights given by the underlying metric. Because of this minimality,
it can serve as a building block for more elaborate topologies. Note that in our
model it is not always possible to construct the MST of all nodes, even if it is
unique. To exemplify this, consider an initial configuration c_0 where $G_{c_0}^*$ is *not*
connected. Then two nodes from two different connected components of $G_{c_0}^*$ can
never communicate with each other and create edges because they cannot learn
each other's reference. This was remarked in [22]. In this case, it is impossible
to construct an MST for all nodes as no protocol can add the necessary edges.
Instead one can only construct the MST of all initially connected components,
i.e., a Minimum Spanning Forest. Formally an MST is defined as follows.

Definition 2 (Minimum Spanning Tree). *Let $G := (V, E)$ be a graph and
$f : E \to \mathbb{R}^+$ a weight function, then the Minimum Spanning Tree $MST(G, f) \subseteq
E$ is a set of edges, such that:*

1. *$(V, MST(G, f))$ is a connected graph, and*
2. *$\sum_{e \in MST(G,f)} f(e)$ is minimum.*

*For the special case of $E := V^2$, i.e., the MST over all possible edges, we write
$MST(V, f)$ for short.*

In this paper, we will only consider metrics with distinct distances for each
pair of nodes. Otherwise the MST may not be unique for a metric space (V, d_T).
If we had edges with equal distances, we would need to employ some mechanism
of tie-breaking, e.g., via the nodes' identifiers.

In the following, we define the set $\mathcal{L}_{MST} \subset C$ of legal configurations for
BUILDMST. We regard all configurations $c \in \mathcal{L}_{MST}$ as legal in which the explicit
edges form the MST of each connected component in c. Further, a legal configuration may contain arbitrarily many implicit edges as long as they are part of
an MST. Formally:

Definition 3. (Legal Configurations $\mathcal{L}_{MST}$). *Let (V, d_T) be a tree metric
and $c \in C$ be a configuration. Further denote $G_1, \ldots, G_k$ as the connected components of G_c^*. Then the set of legal configurations $\mathcal{L}_{MST}$ is defined by the following
two conditions:*

1. *A configuration $c \in \mathcal{L}_{MST}$ contains an explicit edge $(v, w) \in E_c^X$ if and only
   if there is a component $G_i := (V_i, E_i)$ with $\{v, w\} \in MST(V_i, d_T)$.*
2. *A configuration $c \in \mathcal{L}_{MST}$ contains an implicit edge $(v, w) \in E_c^T$ only if there
   is a component $G_i := (V_i, E_i)$ with $\{v, w\} \in MST(V_i, d_T)$.*

2   Related Work

There are several self-stabilizing protocols for constructing spanning trees in a fixed communication graph, e.g., [5,7–9,16,20]. These works do not consider a model where nodes can create arbitrary overlay edges. Instead, each node has a *fixed* set of neighbors and chooses a subset of these neighbors for the tree. Furthermore, the communication graph in all these works is modeled as an arbitrary weighted graph instead of a tree. The fastest protocol given in [7] constructs an MST in $\mathcal{O}(N^2)$ rounds where N is the number of nodes. Note that [20] proves the existence of a protocol that converges in $\mathcal{O}(N)$ rounds but does not present and rigorously analyze an actual protocol. As stated in the introduction, these protocols can be used in the underlying network to construct a tree metric for our protocol.

In the area of topological self-stabilization of overlay networks, there is a plethora of works that consider different topologies like line graphs [23], De-Bruijn-Graphs [12,26], or Skip-Graphs [17,22]. Besides these results that do not take the underlying network into account, there are also efforts to build a topology based on a given metric. An interesting result in this area is a protocol for building the Delaunay Triangulation of two-dimensional metric space by Jacob et al. [18]. This work bears several similarities with ours. In particular, the Delaunay Triangulation is a superset of the metric's MST and shares some of the properties we present in Sect. 3. Also their protocol D_{STAB} is very similar to our protocol BUILDMST. Recently Gmyr et al. proposed a self-stabilizing protocol for constructing an overlay based on an arbitrary metric [13]. Instead of building a spanning tree, their goal is to build an overlay in which the distance between two nodes is exactly the distance in the underlying metric. In particular, their algorithm is also applicable to a tree metric. However, note that for a tree metric the number of edges in the resulting overlay can be as high as $\Theta(N^2)$.

Last, there are several non-self-stabilizing approaches for creating underlay-aware overlays, e.g., [1,15,25,27]. With their often-cited work in [25], Plaxton et al. introduced these so-called location-aware overlays. The authors present an overlay for an underlay modeled by a growth-bounded two-dimensional metric. This means that the number of nodes within a fixed distance of a node only grows by a factor of $\Delta \in \mathbb{R}^+$ when doubling the distance. Their overlay has a polylogarithmic degree and the length of the routing paths approximate the distances in the underlying metric by a polylogarithmic factor. In [1] Abraham et al. extended on [25] and proposed an overlay for growth-bounded metrics where the latter is reduced to a factor of $1 + \epsilon$. Here, $\epsilon \in \mathbb{R}^+$ is a parameter that can be set to an arbitrarily small value. The resulting overlay's degree depends on ϵ and is not analyzed in detail.

3   Preliminaries

In this section, we present some useful properties of tree metrics and their MSTs that will help us in designing and analyzing our protocol. Therefore, we use the notion of *relative neighbors*. Two nodes $v, w \in V$ are relative neighbors with regard to a metric d_T if there is no third node that is closer to either of them, i.e., it holds $\nexists u \in V : (d_T(u,v) < d_T(v,w)) \wedge (d_T(u,w) < d_T(v,w))$. Throughout this paper we write $u \prec (v,w)$ as shorthand for $(d_T(u,v) < d_T(v,w)) \wedge (d_T(u,w) < d_T(v,w))$. Relative neighbors have been defined and analyzed for a variety of metrics (cf. [19,29,30]), but they prove to be especially useful in the context of tree metrics. In particular, they allow nodes to form and maintain an MST based on local criteria. This fact is stated by the following lemma:

Lemma 1. *Let (V, d_T) be a tree metric, then the following two statements hold:*

1. $\{v,w\} \in MST(V,d_T) \implies \nexists u \in V : u \prec (v,w)$
2. $\{v,w\} \notin MST(V,d_T) \implies \exists u \in V : \big(u \prec (v,w) \wedge \{v,u\} \in MST(V,d_T)\big)$

In the following, we will outline the proof and thereby present some helpful lemmas, which we will reuse in Sect. 5. First, we note that the lemma's first statement is generally true for all metrics (cf. [29]). Thus, it remains to show the second statement. We begin the proof with a useful fact that will be at the core of many proofs in this paper.

Lemma 2. *Let (V, d_T) be a tree metric. Further let $u, v, w, r \in V$ be four nodes, s.t.*

$$d_T(u,r) < d_T(w,r) \wedge d_T(v,r) < d_T(w,r)$$

Then it either holds $u \prec (v,w)$ or $v \prec (u,w)$ (and in particular not $w \prec (u,v)$).

We provide a detailed version of the lemma's proof in the full version [14]. In the proof, we use the fact that there must be a single unique node $\varphi \in V_T$, the so-called median, that lies on the three unique paths between u, v and r in the underlying tree T. The lemma then follows from two facts: First, u and v must be strictly closer to φ than w. Second, either the path from u to w or from v to w must contain φ. Thus, it must either hold $d_T(w,u) > d_T(u,v)$ or $d_T(w,v) > d_T(u,v)$. Since both $d_T(w,u) < d_T(u,v)$ and $d_T(w,v) < d_T(u,v)$ is required for $w \prec (u,v)$, it cannot hold.

Using Lemma 2 we can show the following.

Lemma 3. *Let (V, d_T) be a tree metric and $v, w \in V$ two of its nodes. Further, let $v_0, \ldots, v_k \in V$ be the unique path from $v_0 := v$ to $v_k := w$ in the MST. Then it holds:*

$$d_T(v_i, v) < d_T(v_{i+1}, v) \ \forall v_i \in (v_0, \ldots, v_{k-1})$$

As before, we present a detailed proof in the full version [14] and only sketch it here. The main idea is constructing a simple contradiction: If we assume there is a path where the property does not hold, there must be a first deviator v_i with $d_T(v_i, v) > d_T(v_{i+1}, v)$. Note that we assumed that no two nodes have the same distance to w. Because v_i is the first deviator, it holds $d_T(v_{i-1}, v) < d_T(v_i, v)$ for its direct predecessor v_{i-1}. Also, v_1 cannot be the first deviator because then it would be closer to v than v itself. Now we can use Lemma 2 to show that the MST could be improved by swapping either (v_{i-1}, v_i) or (v_i, v_{i+1}) for (v_{i-1}, v_{i+1}), which is a contradiction.

```
Upon activation a node v ∈ V performs:
       for all w ∈ Nᵥ
          if ∃u ∈ Nᵥ : u ≺ (v,w)
             Nᵤ ⟵ Nᵤ ∪ {w}  #v delegates w to u
             Nᵥ ⟵ Nᵥ \ {w}
          else
             Nᵥ ⟵ Nᵥ ∪ {v}  #v introduces itself
```

Listing 1.1. BUILDMST

In the remainder, we conclude the proof sketch for Lemma 1. Therefore, let $v, w \in V$ be two nodes with $\{v, w\} \notin MST(V, d_T)$. Further, let $u \in V$ be the first node of the path P_{vw} from v to w in the MST. Such a node must exist because there is no direct edge between v and w in the MST. Note that P_{vw} contains the same nodes as a path P_{wv} from w to v but in reverse order. Thus, we can apply Lemma 3 in "both directions". That means, the node u with $\{v, u\} \in MST(V, d_T)$ must be closer to w than v, but also closer to v than its successor in P_{wv}. A simple induction then yields that $u \prec (v, w)$. Since by definition it holds $\{v, u\} \in MST(V, d_T)$, this proves the lemma.

4 Protocol

In this section, we describe our protocol BUILDMST, which forms and constructs an overlay according to Definition 3. Intuitively, the protocol works as follows: Upon activation, a node $v \in V$ checks, which of its current neighbors are relative neighbors. All nodes that fulfill the property are kept in the neighborhood. All others are delegated in a greedy fashion. This idea resembles that of the protocols in [18] and [23], where essentially the same technique is used for different underlying metrics, i.e., the two-dimensional plane and a line.

The pseudocode for this protocol is given in Listing 1.1. Therein, each node $v \in V$ only maintains a single variable $N_v \subseteq V$. This is a set that contains all currently stored references to other nodes. It contains each entry only once and multiple occurrences of the same reference are merged automatically.

With each activation, a node iterates over all nodes in $w \in N_v$ and checks whether to delegate w or to introduce itself. In this context, a delegation means that v sends a reference of w to u and then deletes the reference to w from N_v. The protocol assures that a node v delegates w to u, if and only if it holds $u \prec (v, w)$. Otherwise v introduces itself to w, which means that it sends a reference of itself to w. Note, that the primitives of introduction and delegation preserve the system's connectivity (cf. [22]).

In the pseudocode introductions and delegations are indicated by statements of the form $N_u \longleftarrow N_u \cup \{w\}$. This notation is used for convenience. It describes that the executing node v sends a message containing a reference of w to u. The variable N_u is not directly changed and w is only added in some later configuration when u is activated and the message is delivered to u. A graphical example of the protocol's computations can be seen in Fig. 1.

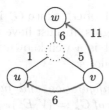 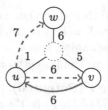

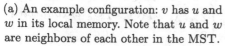

(a) An example configuration: v has u and w in its local memory. Note that u and w are neighbors of each other in the MST.

(b) The succeeding configuration: v has delegated w to u and introduced itself to u.

Fig. 1. An example of the protocol's execution. The black edges are part of the underlying tree. Red edges denote the overlay's edges. The dotted edges are implicit, i.e., the references are still the node's channel. Solid edges are explicit, i.e., the references are in the node's memory. The numbers denote the edges' weights. (Color figure online)

5   Analysis

In this section we rigorously analyze BUILDMST. We prove the protocol's correctness with regard to Definition 1 and the set of configurations given in Definition 3. Furthermore, we bound the protocol's convergence time.

The main result of this section is that BUILDMST is indeed a self-stabilizing protocol as stated by the following theorem:

Theorem 1. *Let (V, d_T) be a tree metric. Then* BUILDMST *is a self-stabilizing protocol that constructs an overlay with regard to $\mathcal{L}_{MST}$.*

In this section, we will concentrate on initial configurations $c_0 \in C$ where $G_{c_0}^*$ is connected. Since two nodes from different components can *never* communicate with each other (cf. [22]), the result can trivially be extended to all initial configurations.

Our proof's structure is as follows. First, we will show that eventually the system will contain all edges of $MST(V, d_T)$ and also keeps them in all subsequent configurations. This will be the major part of this section. Then we show that all remaining edges that are not part of the MST but may still be part of a configuration will eventually vanish. This proves the protocol's convergence. Last, we prove that once the system is in a legal configuration, the set of explicit edges does not change and no more edges that are not part of the MST are added. This shows the protocol's closure. We then conclude the section by analysing the protocol's time complexity.

Over the course of this section we will refer to all edges $e \in MST(V, d_T)$ as *valid* edges. We call all other edges *invalid*. Further note that all omitted proofs can be found in the full version [14].

We begin by showing that the system eventually reaches a configuration that contains all valid edges. For the proof, we assign a potential to each configuration $c \in C$. As the potential, we choose the weight of the minimum spanning tree that can be constructed from all implicit and explicit edges in the configuration if we ignore their direction, i.e., we consider the MST of G_c^*. Since G_c^* is simply an undirected, weighted graph with unique edge weights, it must have a unique minimum spanning tree if it is connected. This fact is a well-known result in graph theory. The potential is formally defined as follows:

Definition 4 (Potential). *Let $c \in C$ be a configuration and further let $\mathcal{M}_c := MST(E_c^*, d_T)$ be the minimum spanning tree of $G_c^* := (V, E_c^*)$. Then the potential $\Phi : C \to \mathbb{R}^+$ is defined as $\Phi(c) := \begin{cases} \sum_{e \in \mathcal{M}_c} d_T(e) & \text{if } G_c^* \text{ is connected} \\ \infty & \text{else} \end{cases}$*

The weight of the globally optimal minimum spanning tree $MST(V, d_T)$ that considers all edges provides a lower bound for the potential. Therefore, it cannot decrease indefinitely. In the following, we show that the potential decreases monotonically and once the system reached a configuration with minimum potential it will eventually contain all valid edges. First, we show that the potential can not increase.

Lemma 4. *Consider an execution of BuildMST and let the system be in configuration $c \in C$. Further, let c' be an arbitrary succeeding configuration of c. Then it holds $\Phi(c') \leq \Phi(c)$.*

Proof. To simplify notation let E and E' be the set of all edges in G_c^* and $G_{c'}^*$, respectively. In the following, we will show that we can only construct equally good or better spanning trees from the edges in E'. Per definition, exactly one node $v \in V$ is activated in the transition from c to c'. This node then executes the for-loop given in the pseudocode in Listing 1.1. Let v be the node that is activated and $\{v, w\} \in E$ be an edge that is delegated removed from E during its activation, i.e., v delegates w to some node u. As a result of the delegation, the configuration c' contains the (implicit) edge $(u, w) \in E_{c'}^T$ and thus E' contains the edge $\{u, w\} \in E'$. This allows us to view the delegation as swapping edge $\{v, w\}$ for $\{u, w\}$.

In the following we observe the swaps $(e_1, e_1'), \ldots, (e_k, e_k')$, such that $e_i \in E$ is swapped for $e_i' \in E'$ in the transition from c to c'. The order in which we observe these swaps must be consistent with the protocol. That means that two delegations must appear in the same order as they could in the for-loop, i.e., v can only delegate to node whose reference's are still in its local memory. Next, we define $E_0, \ldots E_k \subseteq V^2$ with $E_0 := E$ and $E_i := E_{i-1} \setminus \{e_i\} \cup \{e_i'\}$ for $i > 0$ as the edge sets resulting from these swaps.

As the proof's main part we inductively show that each $MST(E_i, d_T)$ with $i \in \{1, \ldots, k\}$ has a lower or equal weight than $MST(E_{i-1}, d_T)$. For this, we distinguish between two cases. First, if $e_i \notin MST(E_{i-1}, d_T)$, the spanning tree is not affected by the swap and thus the weight remains equal. Second, if $e_i \in MST(E_{i-1}, d_T)$, we must show that we can construct an equally good spanning tree in E_i. For this, consider $\mathcal{M}_i := MST(E_{i-1}, d_T) \setminus \{e_i\} \cup \{e_i'\}$. Note $\mathcal{M}_i$ and $MST(E_{i-1}, d_T)$ only differ in the edges $e_i := \{v, w\}$ and $e_i' := \{u, w\}$. For the delegation of w to u it must have held $u \prec (v, w)$ and thus $d_T(u, w) < d_T(v, w)$. Therefore, $\mathcal{M}_i$ has lower weight than $MST(E_{i-1}, d_T)$. It remains to show that $\mathcal{M}_i$ is a connected spanning tree for V. Further denote T_v and T_w as the subtrees of $MST(E_{i-1}, d_T)$ connected by $\{v, w\}$. To prove that $\mathcal{M}_i$ is a spanning tree, we must show that $\{u, w\}$ connects T_v and T_w, i.e., it holds $u \in T_v$. Suppose for contradiction that $u \in T_w$. Then the path from v to u in $MST(E_{i-1}, d_T)$ contains the edge $\{v, w\}$. Further, note that E_{i-1} must have contained the edge $\{v, u\}$ because v cannot delegate any node to u without having a reference to u itself. Therefore, the edges $\{v, w\}$ and $\{v, u\}$ are *both* part of E_i and *both* connect T_v and T_w. Now consider that $\{v, u\}$ is shorter than $\{v, w\}$, because a delegation requires $u \prec (v, w)$ and thus $d_T(v, u) < d_T(v, w)$. Hence $MST(E_{i-1}, d_T)$ could be improved by swapping $\{v, w\}$ for $\{v, u\}$. This is a contradiction because $MST(E_{i-1}, d_T)$ is a minimum spanning tree. Therefore $u \in T_v$ and the edge $\{u, w\}$ connects T_v and T_w.

Thus, $\mathcal{M}_i$ is a spanning tree that can be constructed solely from edges in E_i. Further, it has a lower or equal weight than $MST(E_{i-1}, d_T)$. The lemma then follows by a simple induction.

It remains to show that the potential actually decreases until it reaches the minimum. That means, we need to show that there cannot be a configuration with suboptimal potential where no more delegations that decrease the potential occur. Note that the proof of Lemma 4 tells us that the potential decreases if an edge $\{v, w\} \in \mathcal{M}_c$ is delegated. Therefore, we first show that in each suboptimal spanning tree there is a node that can potentially detect an improvement.

Lemma 5. *Let the system be in configuration $c \in C$, s.t. the potential $\Phi(c)$ is not minimum. Then there must exist nodes $u, v, w \in V$, such that*

$$\big(u \prec (v, w)\big) \wedge \big(\{v, u\} \in \mathcal{M}_c\big) \wedge \big(\{v, w\} \in \mathcal{M}_c\big)$$

Proof. Let $\mathcal{M}_c$ be the minimum spanning tree of a configuration c. Since the potential is suboptimal, there must be two nodes $v, w \in V$ with $\{v, w\} \in MST(V, d_T) \backslash \mathcal{M}_c$. Since $\mathcal{M}_c$ is connected, there is a path $v := v_0, v_1, \ldots, v_k := w$ from v to v_k in $\mathcal{M}_c$.

Now consider v_1. According to Lemma 1 it cannot hold $v_1 \prec (v, w)$ because $\{v, w\} \in MST(V, d_T)$. Thus, it holds $d_T(v, w) < d_T(v_1, w)$ or $d_T(v, w) < d_T(v_1, v)$. In the following, we assume that $d_T(v, w) < d_T(v_1, w)$. For the other case we refer to the full version [14]. Next, consider that it holds $d_T(v_{k-1}, w) > d_T(v_k, w)$ because no node can be closer to $w = v_k$ than w itself. Thus, there must be a first node v_i on the path with $d_T(v_i, w) > d_T(v_{i+1}, w)$. Since $d_T(v, w) < d_T(v_1, w)$ it further holds that $i \geq 1$. Therefore, the node v_{i-1} is well-defined and it must hold $d_T(v_{i-1}, w) < d_T(v_i, w)$ because v_{i+1} is the first node that is closer to w than its successor. Hence, it holds $\big(d_T(v_{i-1}, w) < d_T(v_i, w)\big)$ and $\big(d_T(v_{i+1}, w) < d_T(v_i, w)\big)$ Following Lemma 2 it follows that either $v_{i-1} \prec (v_i, v_{i+1})$ or $v_{i+1} \prec (v_{i-1}, v_i)$. Since in both cases all of the involved edges are part of $\mathcal{M}_c$, the lemma follows.

Lemma 5 only made assumptions about edges in G_c^* and did not consider the actual edges. Since each node only has access to its local references, node v can only perform a delegation if it ever has explicit references to u and w. In the following lemma, we will see that if the potential does not decrease, a node will eventually have the references in local memory.

Lemma 6. *Let the system be in configuration $c \in C$ and let $\mathcal{M}_c$ be the minimum spanning tree of c. If the potential does not decrease, then the following two statements hold:*

1. *Every computation that starts in c will reach a set $C_c \subset C$, such that*

$$\forall c^* \in C_c : (\{v, w\} \in \mathcal{M}_c \Rightarrow (v, w) \in E_{c^*}^X)$$

2. *Every succeeding configuration of $c^* \in C_c$ is in C_c as well*

The idea behind the proof is simple: If no node performs a delegation and reduces the potential, all nodes eventually introduce themselves. Thus, each node which can potentially perform a delegation will eventually be able to do it if the potential does not decrease otherwise. Using this fact we can finally show that the following holds:

Lemma 7 (Convergence I). *The following two statements hold:*

1. *Every computation will reach a set $C_{MST} \subset C$, such that*

$$\forall c' \in C_{MST} : (\{v, w\} \in MST(V, d_T) \Rightarrow (v, w) \in E_{c'}^X)$$

2. *Every succeeding configuration of $c' \in C_{MST}$ is in C_{MST} as well.*

The proof's idea is as follows: Using Lemmas 4, 5 and 6 we show that the system must reach a configuration with minimum potential. Lemma 6 further tells us that eventually all valid edges are added because the potential is fixed. Last, Lemma 1 implies that valid edges can never be removed because they never fulfill the condition for a delegation.

This concludes the first part of the convergence proof. Now we know that the system eventually converges to a superset of the MST. It remains to show that eventually all invalid edges will vanish.

Lemma 8 (Convergence II). *The following two statements hold:*

1. *Eventually each computation will reach a set of configurations $C' \subset C$, such that*
$$\forall c \in C' : (\{v, w\} \notin MST(V, d_T) \Rightarrow \{v, w\} \notin E_c^*)$$

2. *Every succeeding configuration of $c' \in C'$ is in C' as well.*

Proof. For this proof, we will again employ a potential function. The potential of a configuration $c \in C$ is the weight of the longest invalid edge. Formally:

$$\tilde{\Phi}(c) := \begin{cases} \max_{e \in E_c^* \setminus MST(V, d_T)} d_T(e) & \text{if } E_c^* \setminus MST(V, d_T) \neq \emptyset \\ 0 & \text{else} \end{cases}$$

If this potential is 0, there are no invalid edges left. This trivially follows from the fact that all distances are greater than zero. Just as with the other potential, we will show that this potential (1) never increases and (2) will decrease as long as it is not minimum.

1. $\tilde{\Phi}(c)$ *cannot increase.*

   For the proof let $c \in C$ be an arbitrary configuration and $c' \in C$ be any succeeding configuration of c. To prove the assumption, we show that the protocol never adds an invalid edge that is longer than any existing edge. Let $v \in V$ be the node that is activated in the transition from c to c' and let $w \in V$ be an explicit neighbor of v in G_c. Then v performs one of the following two actions that add new edges to the system:

   (a) If v introduces itself to w, it adds the implicit edge $(w, v) \in E_{c'}^T$ to the system. Since the edge $(v, w) \in E_c^X$ with $d_T(v, w) = d_T(w, v)$ is already present, this cannot raise the potential.

   (b) If v delegates w to some node $u \in V$, then it adds the implicit edge $(u, w) \in E_{c'}^T$ to system if it was not already present before. Since for delegation it must hold that $d_T(u, w) < d_T(v, w)$ for the existing edge $(v, w) \in E_c^X$, the new edge cannot raise the potential.

   Thus, it holds $\tilde{\Phi}(c') \leq \tilde{\Phi}(c)$.

2. $\tilde{\Phi}(c)$ *will eventually decrease if* $\tilde{\Phi}(c) > 0$.

   Let $c \in C$ be an arbitrary configuration and $\{v, w\} \in E_c^*$ an invalid edge in c with $\tilde{\Phi}(c) = d_T(v, w)$. Since $\{v, w\}$ is oblivious of the true edge's direction, both (v, w) and (w, v) could be part of the configuration. Since the proof is analogous for both edges, we will only consider (v, w) and show that all instances of this edge will eventually be delegated.

   First, consider the case that v has an explicit edge to w. Since we assume the system is in a configuration that contains all edges in $MST(V, d_T)$, we can use Lemma 1. According to the Lemma, there must be a node $u \in V$ with an explicit edge $(v, u) \in E_c^X$ and $u \prec (v, w)$. Thus, v will delegate w to u upon activation and add the edge (u, w) with $d_T(u, w) < d_T(v, w)$.

   Second, consider the case that $(v, w) \in E_c^T$ is implicit. For the proof, we need to mind that there can be multiple instances of the reference to w in v's channel. The potential will only sink once all of these instances are gone. Therefore let θ_v be the number of references to w in v's channel. In the following, we will show that θ_v decreases to 0. Note that θ_v can only be raised if some node $u \in V$ delegates w to v or w introduces itself. A delegation always implies that some node u has a reference to w and it holds $d_T(u, w) > d_T(v, w)$. In that case, there exists an invalid edge $\{u, w\} \in E_c^*$, which is longer than $\{v, w\}$. This is impossible because $\{v, w\}$ is by assumption the longest invalid edge. Hence, θ_v may only increase if w introduces itself. To do this, there must be an explicit edge (w, v). However, we can apply the same argumentation as above for (v, w) and see that w must delegate its reference of v to some other node $u' \in V$ instead of introducing itself. In summary, the protocol never increases θ_v and thus it can only decrease if a reference is delivered to v. Since this eventually happens to every reference, the system will reach a configuration with no references of w in v's channel.

Hence, the potential will eventually reach 0 and no more invalid edges are left. Furthermore, no more invalid edges can ever be added as this would increase the potential.

Thus, we have shown that starting from any weakly connected initial configuration $c \in C$ the system will converge to a superset of the MST and eventually to a legal configuration. This is the combined result of Lemmas 7 and 8. To complete the proof we must show that the system once it is legal never leaves the set of legal configurations. Formally:

Lemma 9 (Closure). *Let the system be in a legal configuration $c \in \mathcal{L}_{MST}$, then every succeeding configuration $c' \in C$ is also legal.*

However, the lemma is a direct corollary of Lemmas 7 and 8. Hence, BUILDMST is self-stabilizing with regard to Definition 1. This proves Theorem 1 and concludes the analysis of the protocol's correctness.

It remains to analyze how many steps are needed until a legal configuration is reached. Therefore, we adapt the notion of *asynchronous rounds* from [11]. Each computation can be divided into rounds $R_0, \ldots, R_t$ with $t \to \infty$, such that each round R_i consists of a finite sequence of consecutive configurations. Let c_i be the first configuration of R_i, then the rounds in the first configuration, such that:

1. For each $v \in V$, all messages that are in v's channel in configuration c_i have been delivered at any of v's activations in this round.
2. All nodes have been activated at least once.

Since we assume weakly fair action execution and fair message receipt rounds are well-defined. Using this definition, we can show the following.

Theorem 2. BUILDMST *needs $\mathcal{O}(N^2)$ asynchronous rounds to converge to a legal configuration.*

The proof can be found in the full version [14]. Therein we again consider the potential functions from Definition 4 and the proof of Lemma 8. We show that both these functions must decrease after a constant number of rounds. Together with the fact that the functions can only decrease $\mathcal{O}(N^2)$ times respectively, the theorem follows.

6   Conclusion and Outlook

In this work, we focused on designing and analysing self-stabilizing overlay networks that take into account the underlay. For the tree metric we considered, it turns out that there is an extremely simple protocol for MST construction that naturally follows from some general properties of MSTs in such tree metrics (notice the close relation between Lemma 1 and the protocol). Considering different kinds of underlays (such as planar graphs or graphs with bounded growth) as well as other types of overlays than a minimum spanning tree may be possible next steps. Of course, the high upper bound on the running time of our algorithm naturally raises the question whether a better running time can be achieved by a more sophisticated algorithm or a refined analysis. Thus, improving on our results may also be a possible next step.

References

1. Abraham, I., Malkhi, D., Dobzinski, O.: LAND: stretch (1 + epsilon) locality-aware networks for DHTs. In: 15th Annual ACM-SIAM Symposium on Discrete Algorithms, pp. 550–559 (2004)
2. Abu-Ata, M., Dragan, F.F.: Metric tree-like structures in real-world networks: an empirical study. Networks **67**(1), 49–68 (2016)
3. Adcock, A.B., Sullivan, B.D., Mahoney, M.W.: Tree-like structure in large social and information networks. In: 13th International Conference on Data Mining, pp. 1–10 (2013)
4. Al-Fares, M., Loukissas, A., Vahdat, A.: A scalable, commodity data center network architecture. In: ACM 2008 Conference on Data Communication, pp. 63–74 (2008)
5. Antonoiul, G., Srimani, P.K.: Distributed self-stabilizing algorithm for minimum spanning tree construction. In: Lengauer, C., Griebl, M., Gorlatch, S. (eds.) Euro-Par 1997. LNCS, vol. 1300, pp. 480–487. Springer, Heidelberg (1997). https://doi.org/10.1007/BFb0002773
6. Arregoces, M., Portolani, M.: Data Center Fundamentals. Cisco Press, Indianapolis (2003)
7. Blin, L., Dolev, S., Potop-Butucaru, M.G., Rovedakis, S.: Fast self-stabilizing minimum spanning tree construction. In: Lynch, N.A., Shvartsman, A.A. (eds.) DISC 2010. LNCS, vol. 6343, pp. 480–494. Springer, Heidelberg (2010). https://doi.org/10.1007/978-3-642-15763-9_46
8. Blin, L., Potop-Butucaru, M., Rovedakis, S., Tixeuil, S.: A new self-stabilizing minimum spanning tree construction with loop-free property. In: Keidar, I. (ed.) DISC 2009. LNCS, vol. 5805, pp. 407–422. Springer, Heidelberg (2009). https://doi.org/10.1007/978-3-642-04355-0_43
9. Blin, L., Potop-Butucaru, M.G., Rovedakis, S., Tixeuil, S.: Loop-free super-stabilizing spanning tree construction. In: Dolev, S., Cobb, J., Fischer, M., Yung, M. (eds.) SSS 2010. LNCS, vol. 6366, pp. 50–64. Springer, Heidelberg (2010). https://doi.org/10.1007/978-3-642-16023-3_7
10. de Montgolfier, F., Soto, M., Viennot, L.: Treewidth and hyperbolicity of the internet. In: 10th IEEE International Symposium on Networking Computing and Applications, pp. 25–32 (2011)
11. Dolev, S.: Self-Stabilization. MIT Press, Cambridge (2000)
12. Feldmann, M., Scheideler, C.: A self-stabilizing general De Bruijn graph. In: Spirakis, P., Tsigas, P. (eds.) SSS 2017. LNCS, vol. 10616, pp. 250–264. Springer, Cham (2017). https://doi.org/10.1007/978-3-319-69084-1_17
13. Gmyr, R., Lefèvre, J., Scheideler, C.: Self-stabilizing metric graphs. In: Bonakdarpour, B., Petit, F. (eds.) SSS 2016. LNCS, vol. 10083, pp. 248–262. Springer, Cham (2016). https://doi.org/10.1007/978-3-319-49259-9_20

14. Götte, T., Scheideler, C., Setzer, A.: On underlay-aware self-stabilizing overlay networks. ArXiv e-prints (2018). http://arxiv.org/abs/1809.02436
15. Gross, C., Stingl, D., Richerzhagen, B., Hemel, A., Steinmetz, R., Hausheer, D.: Geodemlia: a robust peer-to-peer overlay supporting location-based search. In: 12th IEEE International Conference on Peer-to-Peer Computing, Tarragona, Spain, pp. 25–36 (2012)
16. Higham, L., Liang, Z.: Self-stabilizing minimum spanning tree construction on message-passing networks. In: Welch, J. (ed.) DISC 2001. LNCS, vol. 2180, pp. 194–208. Springer, Heidelberg (2001). https://doi.org/10.1007/3-540-45414-4_14
17. Jacob, R., Richa, A.W., Scheideler, C., Schmid, S., Täubig, H.: A distributed poly-logarithmic time algorithm for self-stabilizing skip graphs. In: 28th Annual ACM Symposium on Principles of Distributed Computing, pp. 131–140 (2009)
18. Jacob, R., Ritscher, S., Scheideler, C., Schmid, S.: A self-stabilizing and local delaunay graph construction. In: Dong, Y., Du, D.-Z., Ibarra, O. (eds.) ISAAC 2009. LNCS, vol. 5878, pp. 771–780. Springer, Heidelberg (2009). https://doi.org/10.1007/978-3-642-10631-6_78
19. Jaromczyk, J.W., Toussaint, G.T.: Relative neighborhood graphs and their relatives. Proc. IEEE **80**(9), 1502–1517 (1992)
20. Korman, A., Kutten, S., Masuzawa, T.: Fast and compact self stabilizing verification, computation, and fault detection of an MST. In: 30th Annual ACM Symposium on Principles of Distributed Computing, pp. 311–320 (2011)
21. Leiserson, C.E.: Fat-trees: universal networks for hardware-efficient supercomputing. IEEE Trans. Comput. **C–34**(10), 892–901 (1985)
22. Nor, R.M., Nesterenko, M., Scheideler, C.: Corona: a stabilizing deterministic message-passing skip list. In: 13th International Symposium Stabilization, Safety, and Security of Distributed Systems, pp. 356–370 (2011)
23. Onus, M., Richa, A.W., Scheideler, C.: Linearization: locally self-stabilizing sorting in graphs. In: 9th Workshop on Algorithm Engineering and Experiments, pp. 99–108 (2007)
24. Perlman, R.J.: An algorithm for distributed computation of a spanningtree in an extended LAN. In: 9th Symposium on Data Communications, pp. 44–53 (1985)
25. Plaxton, C.G., Rajaraman, R., Richa, A.W.: Accessing nearby copies of replicated objects in a distributed environment. In: 9th Annual ACM Symposium on Parallel Algorithms and Architectures, pp. 311–320 (1997)
26. Richa, A., Scheideler, C., Stevens, P.: Self-stabilizing De Bruijn networks. In: Défago, X., Petit, F., Villain, V. (eds.) SSS 2011. LNCS, vol. 6976, pp. 416–430. Springer, Heidelberg (2011). https://doi.org/10.1007/978-3-642-24550-3_31
27. Rowstron, A., Druschel, P.: Pastry: scalable, decentralized object location, and routing for large-scale peer-to-peer systems. In: Guerraoui, R. (ed.) Middleware 2001. LNCS, vol. 2218, pp. 329–350. Springer, Heidelberg (2001). https://doi.org/10.1007/3-540-45518-3_18
28. Shavitt, Y., Tankel, T.: Hyperbolic embedding of internet graph for distance estimation and overlay construction. IEEE/ACM Trans. Netw. **16**(1), 25–36 (2008)
29. Supowit, K.J.: The relative neighborhood graph, with an application to minimum spanning trees. J. ACM **30**(3), 428–448 (1983)
30. Toussaint, G.T.: The relative neighbourhood graph of a finite planar set. Pattern Recognit. **12**(4), 261–268 (1980)

A $O(\log n)$ Distributed Algorithm to Construct Routing Structures for Pub/Sub Systems

Regular Submission

Volker Turau$^{(\boxtimes)}$ (iD)

Institute for Telematics, Hamburg University of Technology,
Am Schwarzenberg-Campus 3, 21073 Hamburg, Germany
turau@tuhh.de

Abstract. The Industrial Internet of Things relies on event-driven services that run on wireless networks using low power protocols. The loose coupling and the inherent scalability make publish/subscribe systems an ideal candidate for such systems. This work introduces a new routing structure for such systems and an efficient distributed algorithm to build this structure. This routing structure supports all features of PSVR, a recently introduced publish/subscribe Middleware for IIoT applications. Provided the density of the underlying communication graph is sufficiently high, each node can be reached using at most $O(\log n)$ hops. The algorithm is analyzed for random graphs and we prove that w.h.p. the data structure can be built in $O(\log n)$ synchronous rounds.

Keywords: Distributed algorithm · Publish/Subscribe
Routing structure · Random graph

1 Introduction

Emerging applications such as the Industrial Internet of Things (IIoT) require dynamic forms of the many-to-many communication paradigm for data dissemination. This communication style is best supported by publish/subscribe systems instead of using request-reply messaging. Pub/Sub is a well-established communication paradigm allowing any number of publishers to communicate with any number of subscribers asynchronously and anonymously. In topic-based pub/sub systems, each publication carries a topic id. The pub/sub paradigm guarantees disseminating all messages to all subscribers that expressed their interest in the topic, a.k.a. subscribing to a topic. The advantage is the loose coupling, publishers are unaware of the subscribers that will receive their messages. Nodes can take the role of publishers, subscribers, or both and can freely change their

This work is supported by the Deutsche Forschungsgemeinschaft (DFG) under grant DFG TU 221/6-3.

© Springer Nature Switzerland AG 2018
T. Izumi and P. Kuznetsov (Eds.): SSS 2018, LNCS 11201, pp. 65–79, 2018.
https://doi.org/10.1007/978-3-030-03232-6_5

role at any time. An overview about existing applications of pub/sub systems in IIoT ranging from virtual power plants to electric vehicles is given in [19].

The main requirement for a pub/sub system is to reliably deliver publications to all current subscribers of the specified topic. The dominating non-functional requirements concern message latency, bandwidth, and local memory usage to store routing tables. Particularly in wireless networks with limited bandwidth, it is crucial to keep the number of message forwards during the delivery process as low as possible. To get along with the restricted memory size of IIoT devices routing tables must be kept small. In addition the time complexity for constructing routing tables is an important criteria for evaluating the quality of routing schemes.

The two main parameters characterizing a routing scheme are the size of its routing tables, and the *path stretch*. The latter is defined as the maximum, taken over all pairs of source-target nodes, of the ratio between the path length from the source to the target achieved by a routing scheme, and the length of a shortest path between these two nodes. There is a fundamental relationship between the size of a routing table and the quality of routes it defines. It is well-known that to accomplish shortest path routing, the routing table of each node needs to grow as $\Omega(n)$, where n denotes the number of nodes. Gavoille and Gengler proved that any protocol that keeps the path stretch strictly below three, requires a $\Omega(n)$ bit state at each node [10]. Hence, in order to significantly reduce the state required for routing (e.g., to $O(\log n)$), algorithms that may inflate the path lengths must be considered. This is even more true for pub/sub systems, because of the many-to-many communication style.

This work proposes an efficient distributed algorithm $\mathcal{A}_{\mathsf{Fiber}}$ for constructing routing structures using a $O(\log n)$ bit state that support pub/sub systems in resource constrained networks. To this effect the paper extends the work of Siegemund et al. [19]. They proposed a distributed self-stabilizing data structure based on a virtual ring that implicitly defines a multicast tree for each node. The advantage of their proposal is that the maintenance of routing tables in case of fluctuations is well supported. A *virtual ring* is a directed closed path of a network involving each node, possibly several times. The basic scheme is to route a publication around the virtual ring, each node with a subscription to the topic grabs the message. Upon returning to the sender a publication is discarded. The key idea of [19] is to dynamically augment the virtual ring with shortcuts such that a hierarchical structure emerges. This allows to concurrently forward publications along disjoint paths to all subscribers. This way the delivery time of a publication is significantly reduced. The routing along shortcuts is dynamically updated as nodes subscribe to and unsubscribe from topics.

There are two determining factors for the time complexity of all pub/sub operations. Firstly, the length of the virtual ring and secondly, the number and the distribution of shortcuts. Turau et al. propose a distributed algorithm to construct short virtual rings in $O(n)$ rounds [23] extending the work of [11]. The shortest possible virtual ring is a Hamiltonian cycle, but this is a rather illusive target. In [19] shortcuts are selected purely based on link quality, their range respectively their coverage is not a selection a criterion.

The main contribution of this paper is a proposal to replace the virtual ring by a considerably shorter ring and attaching the remaining nodes evenly to the nodes on the ring. In particular, while for the algorithm of [23] no statement about the length L of a constructed virtual ring can be made (except $L \geq n$), in our case L is part of the input and can be as small as $\sqrt{n} \log n$.

Secondly, the shortcuts (called fibers) constructed in this work guarantee that each path has length at most $O(\log n)$. No limit about the path length is given in [23]. This shorter ring structure together with the system of fibers still supports the concepts of [19] and thus leads to more efficient pub/sub systems. The proposed distributed algorithm to construct the routing structure works very efficiently. We formally prove that for random graphs, the algorithm terminates in $O(\log n)$ rounds.

The rest of the paper is organized as follows. After a summary of the state of the art, Sect. 2 informally introduces algorithm $\mathcal{A}_{\mathsf{Fiber}}$. A formal description is given in the following section. In Sect. 4 we analyze the behavior of $\mathcal{A}_{\mathsf{Fiber}}$ for random graphs $G(n, p)$ and prove its correctness for the case $p \geq \gamma \log n / \sqrt{n}$ for some constant γ. The last section discusses possible extensions of this work.

1.1   State of the Art

A variety of options for routing in pub/sub systems have been considered. Flooding publications into the entire network does not require routing tables but leads to scaling issues. Flooding can also be performed along a fixed spanning tree. In this case each node needs to store the indices of the addresses of its successors in the tree only. Alon et al. proved that the best achievable upper bound on average path stretch for spanning trees is in $\Omega(\log n)$ [1]. This result only considers point-to-point communication and not the many-to-many style. Obviously, routing structures that incorporate or even dynamically adopt to subscriptions and unsubscriptions will lead to shorter routes.

The majority of recent research on topic-based pub/sub systems has focused on overlay networks. Chockler et al. introduced an optimization problem, called *Topic-Connected Overlay*, capturing the trade-off between the scalability of the overlay and the message forwarding overhead [7]. The task is to select a minimal number of edges of a fully connected network such that for each topic c the selected edges incident to the publishers and subscribers for c form a connected subgraph. Such overlays are called topic-connected. The decision problem whether there exists a topic-connected overlay with at most k edges is NP-hard. Chockler et al. present a centralized algorithm with approximation ratio $O(\log T)$ (T is the number of topics). Topic-connected overlays were recently further researched [5, 6, 15]. The results show that optimal routing structures are illusive and suggest to focus on approximations.

Overlay networks are logical networks on top of real network where links correspond to paths in the underlying topology. The main assumption is that the underlying network routing protocol provides connectivity between all pairs of nodes. Thus, to implement this approach in networks without a network or transport layer requires additional efforts. All these approaches based on peer-to-peer networks have in common that they construct an overlay from a potentially fully connected network instead of constructing an overlay structure from an existing network. Therefore, we consider approaches such as Chord [20] and Pastry [18] not applicable in wireless low power networks. Instead we construct an overlay network by selecting existing edges with high link quality.

Two different types of routing schemes are considered in the literature. The first allows the routing scheme to assign names to nodes, and each target node is then identified by this given name. This allows for example to use techniques such as network address translation (NAT). The other, called *name independent*, assumes that fixed names are given a priori, and the scheme cannot take benefit of naming nodes for facilitating routing. An import name dependent routing scheme was proposed in [21]. This scheme's routing tables have size $\tilde{O}(\sqrt{n})$ bits and stretch 3, in any network. The routing scheme proposed in this work is name-independent. Note that pub/sub systems do not rely on request-reply messaging. The proposed scheme can be extend to also support this style of communication. This requires to assign new names to some of the nodes.

The only work that comes close to our work is that of Banerjee et al. They propose two proximity-aware, on-demand, distributed algorithms for constructing ring-like overlays at the application layer for wireless sensor networks [2]. This approach is rather ad hoc and no formal analysis is given.

Only few distributed algorithms have been analyzed for random graphs. To the best of our knowledge the only work dedicated to the analysis of distributed algorithms for random graphs is [4,12,13,22]. This is rather surprising considering the profound knowledge about the structure of random graphs available since decades [3,9]. While algorithms designed for general graphs obviously can be used for random graphs the specific structure of random graphs often allows to prove asymptotic bounds that are far better. Distributed algorithms to efficiently construct w.h.p. a Hamiltonian cycle in random graphs are given in [4,22].

1.2 Computational Model and Assumptions

This work employs the synchronous $\mathcal{CONGEST}$ model of the *distributed message passing model* [16], i.e., each message contains at most $O(\log n)$ bits. The communication network is represented by an undirected graph $G = (V, E)$, where V is a set of n processors (nodes) and E represents the set of m bidirectional communication links (edges) between them. Each node carries a unique identifier and has only limited local memory, e.g. it is impossible to locally store a copy of the graph. Communication between nodes is performed in synchronous rounds using messages exchanged over the links. Upon reception of a message, a node performs local computations and possibly sends messages to its neighbors. These operations are assumed to take negligible time.

The prerequisite of our algorithms is a distinguished node v_0 which is the starting point to construct a cycle. Also, each node needs to know the total number of nodes. In the analysis we use the classical Erdős and Rényi model for random graphs: A graph $G(n, p)$ is an undirected graph with n nodes where each edge independently exists with probability p [8]. The results proved in this work hold for random graphs *with high probability* (w.h.p.) which means with probability tending to 1 as $n \to \infty$. Note that p will also depend on n and if n goes to infinity p converges to 0.

2 Informal Description of Algorithm $\mathcal{A}_{\mathsf{Fiber}}$

The input to algorithm $\mathcal{A}_{\mathsf{Fiber}}$ is a starting node v_0 and an upper bound L for the size of the constructed cycle C. $\mathcal{A}_{\mathsf{Fiber}}$ operates in sequential phases. The first two phases last $O(\log n)$ rounds. Each subsequent phase requires a constant number of rounds only. Let r be an integer such that $2^r \in O(\log n)$. Phase 0 constructs in $2^r - 2$ rounds a path P of length $2^r - 1$ starting in v_0. In the next $\log n$ rounds Phase 1 closes P into a cycle C of length 2^r. The following $k = \lceil \log L / \log n - r \rceil$ middle phases extend C by integrating nodes outside C into C and construct the system of fibers. The choice of k implies $|C| \leq L$. Note that r is also part of the input. As we show later, the values of r and L influence the density of the fibers as well as the runtime of the algorithm.

The integration of new nodes is achieved by replacing edges (v, w) of C by two edges (v, x) and (x, w), where x is a node outside of C, edge (v, w) becomes a fiber. In the best case, the number of nodes of C double in every phase. We prove that provided the graph has a particular density, C increases in every phase by a constant factor. After the number of nodes of C has reached a predefined limit, the ring and fiber structure is completed. Figure 1(a) shows an example for the fiber structure. In this case the cycle after phase 1 (depicted in red) consists of the four nodes $c_0, c_4.c_8$, and c_{12}, i.e., $r = 2$. The resulting cycle C that emerges after two middle phases is depicted.

In the final phase each node outside C randomly selects a neighbor on C. This node acts as a *proxy* for the node outside C. When the algorithm terminates each node outside C is attached to a single proxy and the number of nodes attached to individual proxy has small variance. Figure 1(b) shows the assignment of nodes outside the circle C to proxies.

We call the constructed subgraph as depicted in Fig. 1 a *sunlet graph with fibers*. It is called *perfect* if the fiber structure is complete, i.e., during the construction the number of nodes of C doubles in every middle phase.

2.1 Relationship to Routing Scheme PSVR

PSVR arranges nodes in a virtual ring and constructs short-cuts, i.e., edges between nodes on the ring in the style of chords. The edges of the ring together with the shortcuts define the *virtual ring graph*, an overlay structure. As nodes subscribe and unsubscribe from topics the pub/sub layer of PSVR dynamically builds a routing structure on top of the virtual ring graph. The advantage of this structure is that it can be efficiently maintained in case of frequent fluctuations of subscribers.

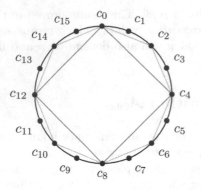

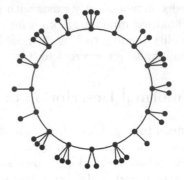

(a) Emerging fiber structure for an initial cycle with 4 nodes after two middle phases.

(b) Nodes outside of C are homogeneously attached to proxies on C (fibers are not depicted).

Fig. 1. Routing structure constructed by algorithm $\mathcal{A}_{\mathsf{Fiber}}$. (Color figure online)

The idea of our work is to replace the virtual ring graph by a new ring based structure, such that the pub/sub layer of PSVR can be executed unaltered. This allows to carry over the efficient adaptability of PSVR with respect to fluctuating subscribers. PSVR dynamically uses the fibers to construct a routing structure that reflects the current set of subscribers (for details see [19]). There are two improvements compared to the original proposal of [19]: The size of the ring is considerably shorter and the selection of fibers (i.e., shortcuts) produces routes of length in $O(\log n)$ for some classes of graphs.

The first improvement is achieved by the proxies. Nodes outside C that are attached to the proxies do no longer participate in the forwarding of messages. Thus, the circle becomes significantly shorter than the virtual ring. The proxies maintain the subscriptions of their attached nodes and upon reception of a publication they deliver it to all subscribed attached nodes. Thus, a proxy subscribes to a topic if at least one attached node or itself has interest in the topic. Hence, subscriptions and unsubscriptions of attached nodes do not entail further messages to be sent along the ring, except for the first subscription of an attached node.

Note that message delivery in pub/sub systems is anonymous, i.e. there is no need for addresses. If the ring structure is to be used for the routing of messages outside the pub/sub system network address translation (NAT) can be used. After a node is attached to a proxy, the proxy assigns a new unique address to the attached node. The address of the proxy is a prefix of the new address.

The second improvement is due to the replacement of shortcuts by the fibers, i.e., PSVR is executed on the subgraph consisting of the nodes on the cycle C and the fibers. This reduces the number of messages and the latency since $|C| \ll n$. Furthermore, the systematic arrangements of fibers as opposed to the rather random procedure of selecting shortcuts in [19] brings considerable performance effects, since the length of the routing paths is bounded (see Lemma 7).

In PSVR the number of shortcuts is bounded by a constant depending on the available memory. This was done to respect the resource-constraint character of devices use in IIoT. For the same reason the number of fibers is limited. This number can be controlled by the number of middle phases. Note that as in [19] the selection of links for the communication graph can still be based on a topology control algorithm.

In contrast to [19] our approach is not self-stabilizing, but the use of the leasing technique to handle faults with respect to subscriptions as described in [19] is still possible. Also the relatively fast construction of the ring in $O(\log n)$ rounds makes a repeated recomputation feasible.

3   Formal Description of Algorithm $\mathcal{A}_{\mathsf{Fiber}}$

Algorithm $\mathcal{A}_{\mathsf{Fiber}}$ operates in synchronous rounds. By counting the rounds a node is always aware in which round and therefore also in which phase it is. Each phase lasts a known fixed number of rounds. If the work is completed earlier, the network is idle for the remaining rounds. This requires each node to know n. Algorithm $\mathcal{A}_{\mathsf{Fiber}}$ gradually builds an oriented cycle C.

3.1   Phase 0

Let $r = \lceil \log(d \log n)/\log 2 \rceil$, for some constant $d > 1$. This yields $2^r \in O(\log n)$. As stated above the value of d resp. r determines the length of the initial cycle. This value allows to tailor the resulting routing structure with respect to the diameter. It has no influence on the analysis.

In phase 0 an oriented path P starting in v_0 of length $2^r - 1$ is constructed in $O(\log n)$ rounds. Initially $P = \{v_0\}$. For $2^r - 2$ rounds the end node v of P sends a message to all neighbors. All neighbors not on P respond to v and v selects a successor among the responding nodes. After completion of phase 0 each node on P knows the id of node v_0.

3.2   Phase 1

In phase 1 one more node is added to P such that P becomes a cycle C with 2^r nodes. The overall idea is as follows: The end node of P sends a message including the id of node v_0 to all neighbors. If a receiving node outside P is connected to v_0 the cycle can be completed. Otherwise, P is extended by a new node and node v_0 is removed, i.e., the successor of v_0 takes over the role of v_0. Thus, the length of P is unchanged. This is repeated $d \log n$ times.

At the beginning of phase 1 each node on P sends its id towards the end node w of P. Thus, after $2^r - 2$ rounds w has a list $L = v_0, v_1, \ldots, v_{v_{2^r-2}}$ with the nodes of P. In the following P is either extended by one node or P is closed into a cycle of 2^r nodes. In parallel node w successively sends the ids of the nodes of

L towards the new end of P. Thus, due to this pipe-lining at any point in time the current end node of P always is aware of the node on P with distance $2^r - 2$. The id of this end node is included in the message sent to all neighbors. After the cycle C is established, the nodes of P that are forerunner of the current end node of P are informed that they are no longer part of C. All these actions can be completed in $O(\log n)$ rounds. After the completion of phase 1 each node knows whether it is on C or not.

We will prove that in random graphs phases 0 and 1 succeed w.h.p. In principle it is not necessary that the size of C is a power of 2. This simplifies the analysis for random graphs.

3.3   Middle Phases

The middle phases are almost identical to those of Algorithm $\mathcal{A}_{HC}$ of [22]. Each middle phase performs the following steps in three rounds (see Fig. 2).

1. Each node node maintains a variable C_u with $C_u = \emptyset$ at the beginning of every phase.
2. Each node c_i on C broadcasts its own id and the id of its predecessor on C using message I_1 (red arrows).
3. If a node u outside C receives a message I_1 from a node c_i such that the predecessor of c_i on C is a neighbor of u, it inserts c_i into a set C_u.
4. Each node u outside C with $C_u \neq \emptyset$ randomly selects a node c_i from C_u and sends an invitation message I_2 to the predecessor of c_i on C (orange arrows).
5. A node $c_i \in C$ that received an invitation I_2 randomly selects a node u from which it received an invitation, sets $c_i.next = u$, and informs u with acceptance message I_3 (blue edge). Thus, edge (c_i, c_{i+1}) is replaced by the edges (c_i, u) and (u, c_{i+1}). Furthermore, nodes c_i and c_{i+1} mark edge (c_i, c_{i+1}) as a fiber.

Individual extensions do not interfere with each other. Each node outside C gets in the last round of a middle phase at most one request for extension and for each edge of C at most one request is sent.

3.4   The Final Phase

In the final phase each node in $v \in V \setminus C$ randomly selects a neighbor u on C and informs it. Node u is the proxy for v. Next, the proxy assigns unique addresses to all attached nodes, e.g. by appending a bit string that is unique in its neighborhood to its own address. These new addresses must then be made public. Note that this is only required if point-to-point communication is desired.

4   Analysis of Algorithm $\mathcal{A}_{Fiber}$ for Random Graphs

In this section we analyze the time complexity of algorithm $\mathcal{A}_{Fiber}$ for a class of random graphs $G(n, p)$. To analyze the time complexity of iterative algorithms

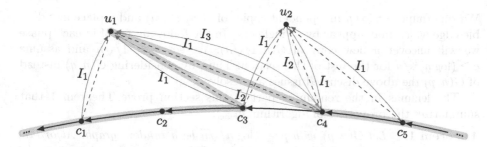

Fig. 2. Integration of nodes during a middle phase. The blue ribbon depicts extended cycle and edge (c_3, c_4) becomes a fiber. (Color figure online)

on random graphs it is necessary to organize the proof such that one only slowly uncovers the random choices in the input graph while constructing the desired structure, i.e., the cycle C. This is done in order to cleanly preserve the needed randomness and independence of events that establish the correctness proof. We achieve this by partitioning the edges of G into disjoint subsets E_i and in phase i the edges E_i are revealed. The idea of the *coupling technique* is to choose E_i such that the graph (V, E_i) is of type $G(n, q)$ for some value q (see [9], p. 5). For $i \geq 0$ let G^i be the union of i independent copies of $G(n, q)$. In middle phase i the constructed cycle C consists of edges belonging to G^i. Note that the probability that any two nodes of V are connected with an edge from $G^{i+1} \setminus G^i$ is q. In each middle phase we only consider the nodes outside C.

For each such node we consider *unused* edges incident to it, each of those exist with probability q independent of the choice of C, because C consist of edges of other copies of $G(n, q)$. Some unused edges may also exist in G^i, but that does not matter. The downside of this technique is that $q > p$. Algorithm $\mathcal{A}_{\mathsf{Fiber}}$ requires $\gamma \log n$ phases ($\gamma \in \mathbb{N}$), γ depends on the desired length of C as specified by the input. Thus, we require $\gamma \log n$ copies of a suitable random graph. Let $\hat{p} = 1 - (1 - p)^{1/\gamma \log n}$. Then $p = 1 - (1 - \hat{p})^{\gamma \log n}$ and $G(n, p)$ is equal to the union of $\gamma \log n$ independent copies of $G(n, \hat{p})$.

Since algorithm $\mathcal{A}_{\mathsf{Fiber}}$ is similar to algorithm $\mathcal{A}_{\mathsf{HC}}$ of [22] (except the final phase) it follows from the analysis of $\mathcal{A}_{\mathsf{HC}}$ that γ is at most 21.

For which value of p does algorithm $\mathcal{A}_{\mathsf{Fiber}}$ construct w.h.p. the described routing structure? Let C be a cycle of length c. What is the minimum value for c such that w.h.p. all nodes can attach to C? The probability of this event is $(1 - (1 - p)^c)^{n-c}$. This converges to 1 if $(1 - p)^c(n - c)$ converges to 0. Thus, if $p = \gamma \log n / \sqrt{n}$ and $c \geq \log n \sqrt{n}$ then w.h.p. each node of $V \setminus C$ has a neighbor on C. Therefore, we consider $p = \gamma \log n / \sqrt{n}$ in the following. Then we have $\hat{p} \geq 1/\sqrt{n}$ and thus,

$$\bigcup_{i=1}^{\gamma \log n} G(n, 1/\sqrt{n}) \subseteq G(n, \gamma \log n / \sqrt{n}).$$

We superimpose $\gamma \log n$ independent copies of $G(n, 1/\sqrt{n})$ and replace any double edge which may appear by a single one. In the following proof in each phase we will uncover a new copy of $G(n, 1/\sqrt{n})$. We set $q = 1/\sqrt{n}$ and assume $c \geq (\log n)^2 \sqrt{n}$ for the rest of this section. Thus, by considering $G(n, q)$ instead of $G(n, p)$ the above discussed issues are resolved.

The lemmas in the remaining part of this section prove Theorem 1 that summarizes the properties of algorithm $\mathcal{A}_{\text{Fiber}}$.

Theorem 1. *Let $G(n, p)$ with $p \geq \gamma \log n/\sqrt{n}$ be a random graph. Algorithm $\mathcal{A}_{\text{Fiber}}$ computes in the synchronous model in $O(\log n)$ rounds w.h.p. a sunlet graph with fibers for G using messages of size $O(\log n)$.*

4.1   Phase 1

Phase 1 sequentially tries to extend P into a cycle C in at most $\log n$ rounds.

Lemma 1. *If $q \geq 1/\sqrt{n}$ phase 1 finds w.h.p. in $\log n$ rounds a cycle with 2^r nodes.*

Proof. By considering only the edges of the fresh copy of $G(n, q)$ we note that the probability that path P cannot be closed into a cycle with 2^r nodes within $d \log n$ rounds is at most

$$(1 - q^2)^{(n - \log n \sqrt{n}) d \log n}.$$

Calculations show that this value converges to 0.   □

4.2   Middle Phases

For $v \in V \setminus C$ let X_v be a random variable that is 1 if v forms a triangle with at least one even numbered edge of C. Denote by c the length of C. The variables $X_{v_1}, \ldots, X_{v_{n-c}}$ are independent Bernoulli-distributed random variables. Define a random variable X as $X = \sum_{v \in V \setminus C} X_v$. Then we have

$$E[X] = (n - c)(1 - (1 - q^2)^{c/2}). \tag{1}$$

Obviously X is a lower bound for the number of nodes that sent a message I_2.

Lemma 2. *Let $n, c \in \mathbb{N}$ and $0 < \theta < 1$. Then $(n-c)(1-(1-\frac{1}{n})^{c/2}) > 0.39(1-\theta)c$ for all $0 \leq c \leq \theta n$.*

Proof. For fixed n let $f_n(c) = 1 - (1 - \frac{1}{n})^{c/2}$. Then f_n is monotonically increasing and concave because $f_n(c)'' < 0$. Note that $f_n(n) = 1 - (1 - \frac{1}{n})^{n/2} = 1 - e^{n \log(1-1/n)/2} > 1 - e^{-1/2}$. Thus, the line segment from $(0, f_n(0))$ to $(n, f_n(n))$ is below f_n. Hence,

$$1 - \left(1 - \frac{1}{n}\right)^{c/2} \geq f_n(n)c/n > (1 - e^{-1/2})c/n \geq 0.39c/n$$

and hence, $(n-c)(1-(1-\frac{1}{n})^{c/2}) \geq 0.39c(1-c/n)$. For $c \leq \theta n$ we have $1 - c/n \geq (1 - \theta)$. Thus, $(n - c)(1 - (1 - \frac{1}{n})^{c/2}) \geq 0.39(1 - \theta)c$.   □

Lemma 3. *Let $n \in \mathbb{N}$ and $0 < \theta < 1$. Let $3 \log n \leq c \leq \theta n$. Then there exists $d > 0$ such that $X > 0.39(1 - \theta)c$ with probability $1 - n^{-0.01887(1-\theta)^3 c / \log n}$.*

Proof. From Eq. (1) and Lemma 2 it follows that

$$E[X] = (n - c)(1 - (1 - \frac{1}{n})^{c/2}) > 0.39(1 - \theta)c \geq 1.17(1 - \theta) \log n.$$

Thus, $1 > 0.39(1 - \theta)c/E[X]$ for $3 \log n \leq c \leq \theta n$. Also, $0.39(1 - \theta)c/E[X]$ is strictly monotonically increasing in this range for fixed n. Furthermore, for fixed n we have

$$\lim_{c \to \theta n} \frac{0.39(1 - \theta)c}{E[X]} \leq \frac{0.39\,\theta}{(1 - e^{-\theta/2})} < 0.22\theta + 0.78.$$

Thus, for c in the specified range

$$\lim_{n \to \infty} (1 - 0.39(1 - \theta)c/E[X])^2 > 0.0484(1 - \theta)^2.$$

Let $\delta = 1 - 0.39(1 - \theta)c/E[X]$. Then $0 < \delta < 1$ and we have

$$E[X]\delta^2 = E[X] \left(1 - 0.39(1 - \theta)c/E[X]\right)^2 \geq 0.01887(1 - \theta)^3 c$$

for $3 \log n \leq c < \theta n$. Hence, $e^{-E[X]\delta^2/2} \leq n^{-0.01887(1-\theta)^3 c / \log n}$. The Chernoff bound yields that

$$X > (1 - \delta)E[X] = \left(1 - 1 + \frac{0.39(1 - \theta)c}{E[X]}\right) E[X] = 0.39(1 - \theta)c$$

with probability at least $1 - n^{-0.01887(1-\theta)^3 c / \log n}$. □

Let Y be a random variable denoting the number of nodes of $V \setminus C$ that receive a message I_3 provided that $X = x$ nodes sent an invitation I_2. The computation of $E[Y|X = x]$ can be reduced to the urns and balls model: The number of balls is x and the number of bins is c. Note that the probability that a node v in C is connected to a node w in $V \setminus C$ is independent of v and w at least q. Thus, Y is equal to the number of nonempty bins and hence

$$E[Y|X = x] = c(1 - (1 - 1/c)^x). \tag{2}$$

Lemma 4. *Let $\beta = 0.92$, $0 < \theta < 1$, and $3 \log n < c \leq \theta n$. Then there exist $d > 0$ such that $Y \geq \beta \left(1 - \frac{1}{e^{0.39(1-\theta)}}\right) c$ with probability $1 - n^{-d}$.*

Proof. From Eq. (2) it follows

$$E[Y|X \geq 0.39(1 - \theta)c] \geq c \left(1 - (1 - \frac{1}{c})^{0.39(1-\theta)c}\right).$$

Let $\delta^2 = 2\alpha \log n/c$ with $\alpha = (3/2)(1 - \beta)^2$. Then $\delta^2 < 1$ and

$$e^{-E[Y|X \geq 0.39(1-\theta)c]\delta^2/2} \leq e^{-2\alpha \log n(1-(1-1/c)^{0.39(1-\theta)c})/2} = \left(\frac{1}{n}\right)^{\alpha(1-(1-1/c)^{0.39(1-\theta)c})}.$$

The Chernoff bound implies that $Y|(X \geq 0.39(1-\theta)c) > (1-\delta)E[Y|X \geq 0.39(1-\theta)c]$ with probability $1 - 1/n^{\alpha(1-(1-1/c)^{0.39(1-\theta)c})}$. Hence, by Lemma 3 there exists $d > 0$ such that

$$Y \geq \left(1 - \sqrt{\frac{2\alpha \log n}{c}}\right) c(1 - (1-\frac{1}{c})^{0.39(1-\theta)c})$$

with probability $1 - n^{-d}$. This gives for any $\theta n \geq c \geq 3 \log n$

$$\frac{Y}{c} \geq \left(1 - \sqrt{\frac{2\alpha \log n}{c}}\right)(1 - (1-\frac{1}{c})^{0.39(1-\theta)c}) \geq \beta(1 - \frac{1}{e^{0.39(1-\theta)}}).$$

$\square$

Lemma 5. *Let $0 < \theta \leq 1/2$ and C be a cycle with $3 \log n < c < n\theta$ nodes. Then after $5i$ phases C has w.h.p. at least $(4(1-\theta))^i c$ nodes. In particular for any constant κ, after at most $4 \log n$ phases C has w.h.p. at least $\kappa \log n \sqrt{n}$ nodes. Similarly after at most $8 \log n$ phases C has at least $n/2$ nodes.*

Proof. Lemma 4 yields that while the circle has less than θn nodes w.h.p. in i phases the number of nodes in C grows from c to $c\left(1 + \left(1 - \frac{1}{e^{0.39(1-\theta)}}\right)\right)^i$. In particular, $c\left(1 + \left(1 - \frac{1}{e^{0.39(1-\theta)}}\right)\right)^5 \geq 4c(1-\theta) \geq 2c$. Thus, it doubles at least every five phases, provided $\theta \leq 1/2$. Hence, starting with $c = 3 \log n$, after at i phases C has at least $2^{i/5} 3 \log n$ nodes.

Note that $2^{i_0/5} 3 \log n \geq \kappa \log n \sqrt{n}$ for $i_0 = 5/\log 2 (\log(\kappa/3) + \log n/2)$. Hence, $4 \log n \geq i_0$ for larger values of n. Therefore, the union bound implies that after at most $4 \log n$ phases w.h.p. the circle has at least $\kappa \log n \sqrt{n}$ nodes. $\square$

The last lemma gives a lower bound for the number of nodes on C for a given number of phases. Trivially the following upper bound also holds.

Lemma 6. *After k phases, C has at most 2^{k+r} nodes.*

We call a middle phase *perfect* if the number of nodes of C doubles. The following lemma states an upper bound for the diameter of the resulting sunlet graph with fibers in the optimal case. Depending on the density of the graph not all fibers will exist and therefore, the diameter may be larger.

Lemma 7. *Let $|C| = 2^r$ after phase 1. Then after k perfect middle phases any two nodes of the fiber graph have distance at most $2k + 2^r \in O(\log n)$.*

Proof. Denote the merging cycles by C_i for $i = 0, \ldots, k$, where C_0 is the initial cycle. Then $|C_i| = 2^{r+i}$. A node from cycle C_i can reach in one hop a node on cycle C_{i+1} and vice versa. Thus, an upper bound for the distance between two nodes is given by the following simple routing procedure: The route goes first from a starting node to a node on cycle C_0. Then it continues along cycle C_0 to the node that is nearest to the target node and finally from there to the target node. Clearly this path has length at most $2k + 2^r$. Since $n \geq 2^{r+k}$ we have $\log n \geq (r + k) \log 2$. Thus, $k \in O(\log n)$. Since $2^r \in O(\log n)$ we have $2k + 2^r \in O(\log n)$. $\square$

4.3   The Final Phase

The probability that w.h.p. all nodes can attach to C is $(1 - (1 - q)^c)^{n-c}$. This converges to 1 if $(1 - q)^c(n - c)$ converges to 0. Thus, if $q = 1/\sqrt{n}$ and $c \geq (\log n)^2 \sqrt{n}$ then w.h.p. each node of $V \setminus C$ has a neighbor on C.

The following lemma shows that the load of the proxies is rather equally spread.

Lemma 8. *The maximum number of nodes attached to a single proxy is less than $e(n/c - 1)$ with probability $1 - 1/c$.*

Proof. The probability that a node $v \in V \setminus C$ has no neighbor in C is equal to $(1 - q)^c$. Thus, for $c \in \omega(\sqrt{n})$ (e.g., $c = \log n \sqrt{n}$) w.h.p. each node $v \in V \setminus C$ has a neighbor in C. The probability that $w \in C$ becomes a proxy for $v \in V \setminus C$ is independent of v and w at least q. Hence, this phase can be described using the balls and bins model: $n - c$ balls are thrown independently and uniformly at random into c bins. The probability that a node of C is not attached to a node outside C (i.e., is not a proxy) is at most $c(1 - 1/c)^{n-c}$. If $n \in \omega(c)$ then this value is 0 w.h.p. If $n \geq c(1 + \log c)$ (e.g., $c \leq n/\log n$) the maximum number of nodes attached to a single proxy is less than $e(n/c - 1)$ with probability $1 - 1/c$. Even better bounds can be found in [17].   □

This analysis heavily relies on the properties of random graphs. It can only be conjectured that the properties of the algorithm still hold in general graphs with similar densities.

5   Extensions

There are several variations of the proposed routing structure. In the following two such options are discussed. One option is to connect nodes outside C indirectly to their proxies, e.g., via path of length 2 (see Fig. 3(a)). To equally

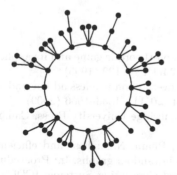
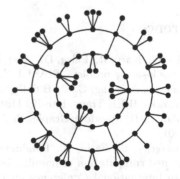

(a) Nodes outside the ring need not to be connected directly to the proxies. This allows to have even shorter rings.

(b) The double ring structure allows PSVR to send more messages concurrently.

Fig. 3. Routing structures that can be build with a variation of algorithm $\mathcal{A}_{\text{Fiber}}$. Note, that in both cases the fibers are not depicted.

spread the load we first compute a maximal matching for the graph induced by the nodes outside C. This can be achieved in $O(\log n)$ time, see [12,14]. The final phase is then executed for the unmatched nodes and the nodes with the smaller id of each edge contained in the matching. The addresses of the nodes can easily adopted to work with the PSVR system.

A second option is to randomly partition the nodes in two subsets and to run Algorithm $\mathcal{A}_{\mathsf{Fiber}}$ in each partition. In a final phase a maximal matching is constructed for the bipartite graph formed by the sets of nodes of the two cycles (see Fig. 3(b)). These edges form a set of spokes for the two cycles. This structure requires some small changes of PSVR. Subscriptions and publications are forwarded into both rings.

6   Conclusion

This work introduces a new routing structure for pub/sub systems in wireless networks and an efficient distributed algorithm to build this structure. The kernel of the routing structure is a ring that contains a fraction of the nodes of the network, e.g., $O(\sqrt{n}\log n)$. The nodes on the ring have the role of a proxy. Nodes outside attached to a single proxy, which administers the subscriptions of the attached nodes. This structure can be used for the lower layer of PSVR, a recently introduced publish/subscribe Middleware for IIoT applications. Provided the density of the underlying communication graph is sufficiently high, each node can be reached using at most $O(\log n)$ hops. The algorithm is analyzed for random graphs and we prove that w.h.p. the data structure can be build in $O(\log n)$ rounds.

We leave it as future work to formally analyze the variations of algorithm $\mathcal{A}_{\mathsf{Fiber}}$ discussed in Sect. 5. Another open problem is determine the expected value for the diameter of the constructed sunlet graph with fibers for $p = \log n/\sqrt{n}$.

References

1. Alon, N., Karp, R., Peleg, D., West, D.: A graph-theoretic game and its application to the k-server problem. SIAM J. Comput. **24**(1), 78–100 (1995)
2. Banerjee, A., King, C.-T.: Building ring-like overlays on wireless ad hoc and sensor networks. IEEE Trans. Parallel Distrib. Syst. **20**(11), 1553–1566 (2009)
3. Bollobás, B.: Random Graphs, 2nd edn. Cambridge University Press, Cambridge (2001)
4. Chatterjee, S., Fathi, R., Pandurangan, G., Pham, N.D.: Fast and efficient distributed computation of hamiltonian cycles in random graphs. In: Proceedings of 38th International Conference on Distributed Computing Systems, ICDCS 2018 (2018)
5. Chen, C., Jacobsen, H.-A., Vitenberg, R.: Algorithms based on divide and conquer for topic-based publish/subscribe overlay design. IEEE Trans. Netw. **24**(1), 422–436 (2016)

6. Chen, C., Vitenberg, R., Jacobsen, H.-A.: A generalized algorithm for publish/subscribe overlay design and its fast implementation. In: Aguilera, M.K. (ed.) DISC 2012. LNCS, vol. 7611, pp. 76–90. Springer, Heidelberg (2012). https://doi.org/10.1007/978-3-642-33651-5_6

7. Chockler, G., Melamed, R., Tock, Y., Vitenberg, R.: Constructing scalable overlays for Pub-Sub with many topics. In: Proceedings of 22nd Annual ACM Symposium Principles of Distributed Computing, pp. 109–118 (2007)

8. Erdős, P., Rényi, A.: On random graphs I. Publ. Math. (Debr.) **6**, 290–297 (1959)

9. Frieze, A., Karoński, M.: Introduction to Random Graphs. Cambridge University Press, Cambridge (2015)

10. Gavoille, C., Gengler, M.: Space-efficiency for routing schemes of stretch factor three. J. Parallel Distrib. Comput. **61**(5), 679–687 (2001)

11. Hélary, J., Raynal, M.: Depth-first traversal and virtual ring construction in distributed systems. Research Report RR-0704, IRISA-Institut de Recherche en Informatique et Systèmes Aléatoires, INRIA Rennes (1987)

12. Krzywdziński, K., Rybarczyk, K.: Distributed algorithms for random graphs. Theor. Comput. Sci. **605**, 95–105 (2015)

13. Levy, E., Louchard, G., Petit, J.: A distributed algorithm to find hamiltonian cycles in $\mathcal{G}(n, p)$ random graphs. In: López-Ortiz, A., Hamel, A.M. (eds.) CAAN 2004. LNCS, vol. 3405, pp. 63–74. Springer, Heidelberg (2005). https://doi.org/10.1007/11527954_7

14. Lotker, Z., Patt-Shamir, B., Pettie, S.: Improved distributed approximate matching. J. ACM **62**(5), 38:1–38:17 (2015)

15. Onus, M., Richa, A.W.: Parameterized maximum and average degree approximation in topic-based publish-subscribe overlay network design. Comput. Netw. **94**, 307–317 (2016)

16. Peleg, D.: Distributed Computing: A Locality-Sensitive Approach. Monographs on Discrete Mathematics and Applications. Society for Industrial and Applied Mathematics, Philadelphia (2000)

17. Raab, M., Steger, A.: "Balls into Bins" — a simple and tight analysis. In: Luby, M., Rolim, J.D.P., Serna, M. (eds.) RANDOM 1998. LNCS, vol. 1518, pp. 159–170. Springer, Heidelberg (1998). https://doi.org/10.1007/3-540-49543-6_13

18. Rowstron, A., Druschel, P.: Pastry: scalable, decentralized object location, and routing for large-scale peer-to-peer systems. In: Guerraoui, R. (ed.) Middleware 2001. LNCS, vol. 2218, pp. 329–350. Springer, Heidelberg (2001). https://doi.org/10.1007/3-540-45518-3_18

19. Siegemund, G., Turau, V.: A self-stabilizing publish/subscribe middleware for IoT applications. ACM Trans. Cyber-Phys. Syst. (TCPS) **2**(2), 12:1–12:26 (2018)

20. Stoica, I., Morris, R., Karger, D., Kaashoek, M.F., Balakrishnan, H.: Chord: a scalable peer-to-peer lookup service for internet applications. SIGCOMM Comput. Commun. Rev. **31**(4), 149–160 (2001)

21. Thorup, M., Zwick, U.: Compact routing schemes. In: Proceedings of the Thirteenth Annual ACM Symposium on Parallel Algorithms and Architectures, SPAA 2001, pp. 1–10. ACM, New York (2001)

22. Turau, V.: A distributed algorithm for finding hamiltonian cycles in random graphs in $O(\log n)$ time. In: Lotker, Z., Patt-Shamir, B. (eds.) SIROCCO 2018. LNCS, vol. 11085. Springer, Cham (2018). https://doi.org/10.1007/978-3-030-01325-7_11

23. Turau, V., Siegemund, G.: Scalable routing for topic-based publish/subscribe systems under fluctuations. In: Proceedings of 37th International Conference on Distributed Computing Systems, ICDCS 2017 (2017)

Self-stabilization and Byzantine Tolerance for Maximal Matching

Stephan Kunne[1], Johanne Cohen[1(✉)] [iD], and Laurence Pilard[2] [iD]

[1] LRI-CNRS, Université Paris-Sud, Université Paris Saclay, Orsay, France
{kunne,jcohen}@lri.fr
[2] LI-PaRAD, Université Versailles-St. Quentin, Université Paris Saclay,
Versailles, France
laurence.pilard@uvsq.fr

Abstract. We analyse the impact of transient and Byzantine faults on the construction of a maximal matching in a general network. We consider the self-stabilizing algorithm called *AnonyMatch* presented by Cohen *et al.* [3] for computing such a matching. Since self-stabilization is transient fault tolerant, we prove that this algorithm still works under the more difficult context of arbitrary Byzantine faults. Byzantine nodes can prevent nodes close to them from taking part in the matching for an arbitrarily long time. We give bounds on their impact depending on the distance between a non-Byzantine node and the closest Byzantine, called the *containment radius*. We present the first algorithm tolerating both transient and Byzantine faults under the fair distributed daemon while keeping the best known containment radius. We prove this algorithm converges in $O(\max(\Delta n, \Delta^2 \log n))$ rounds w.h.p., where n and Δ are the size and the maximum degree of the network, resp.. Additionally, we improve the best known complexity as well as the best containment radius for this problem under the fair central daemon.

Keywords: Matching · Self-stabilization · Byzantine faults
Randomized algorithm

1 Introduction and State of the Arts

A *matching* M in a graph G is a subset of the edges of G without common nodes. A matching is *maximal* if no proper superset of M is also a matching. A *maximum* matching is a maximal matching with the highest cardinality among all possible maximal matchings. Computing a matching is one of the important tasks in distributed computing. Matchings are often used as building blocks in complex distributed algorithms such as the implementation of load balancing [2, 9,22]. In the wireless network context, the wireless resource management problem can be viewed as a matching problem between resources and users. Computing

---

S. Kunne—This work is eligible for best student paper.

T. Izumi and P. Kuznetsov (Eds.): SSS 2018, LNCS 11201, pp. 80–95, 2018.
https://doi.org/10.1007/978-3-030-03232-6_6

the maximal matching is the basic fundamental problem in matching theory (see [12] for a survey).

In this paper, we focus on the construction of a maximal matching handling both transient and Byzantine faults. On one side, transient faults can appear in the whole system, possibly impacting all nodes. However, these faults are not permanent, thus they stop at some point of the execution. Self-stabilization [5] is the classical paradigm to handle transient faults. Starting from any arbitrary configuration, a self-stabilizing algorithm eventually resumes a correct behavior without any external intervention. On the other side, (permanent) Byzantine faults [17] are located on some faulty nodes and so the faults only occur from them. However, these faults can be permanent, *i.e.*, they could never stop during the whole execution.

In this work, we assume the fair distributed daemon, and we deal with randomized and anonymous algorithm. Indeed, on one side, it is well known that some mechanism is required to break symmetry under the distributed daemon. This can be done either relying on identifiers or using random trial. Breaking symmetry using identifiers allows Byzantine nodes to use this mechanism at their advantage by always choosing the most convenient identifier. However, this is not the case using random trial. This is why we focus on randomized distributed algorithm in anonymous network. On the other side, because of the presence of Byzantines with the unfair daemon, it is impossible to bound the number of transitions before a correct behavior is reached; indeed, for an arbitrarily high number of transitions, the daemon could choose to activate Byzantine nodes and their neighbours only. Thus the fairness of the daemon is needed since it guarantees that eventually, all activable nodes will be activated.

Self-stabilizing algorithms for computing a maximal matching have been designed in various models (anonymous network [1,3,14] or not [13,14,18,23], weighted or unweighted, see [11] for a survey, 1-maximal[1] [1,15]). Hsu and Huang's algorithm [14] is the first one working in an anonymous network. This algorithm operates under the central daemon, which guarantees symmetry breaking. Manne *et al.* [18] proved that in an anonymous general network there exists no deterministic self-stabilizing solution to the maximal matching problem under the distributed daemon. This is a general result that holds whatever the communication and atomicity model. Cohen *et al.* [3] extends this previous result by presenting a randomized self-stabilizing algorithm in anonymous networks that converges in $O(n^2)$ moves w.h.p. under the distributed unfair daemon. Observe that self-stabilizing algorithms for optimization problems in anonymous networks can sometimes be solved by a deterministic algorithm, provided the algorithm only uses the distance-2 unique identifier property. This can be achieved by a distance-2 coloring algorithm that builds a coloring of the graph in which each node has a distinct color among colors used by any other node within distance 2. But creating identifiers, even if there are only unique at distance 2, would give more power to the Byzantine nodes. We avoid this technique.

---

[1] A matching M is 1-maximal if it is not possible to build a matching by removing one edge and adding two edges to M.

Making a distributed system tolerant to both transient and Byzantine faults is challenging. Since 1982, it is known that the classical consensus problem is impossible to solve in the presence of at least one third of Byzantine nodes in the system [17]. Many other impossible results came, *e.g.*, for some matching [8], or asynchronous unison [7]. However, for some locally checkable problems such as edge or link coloring, maximal independent set, or matching, the *fault containment technique* can be used. Nesterenko and Arora [20] define the *strict stabilization* property that guarantees a *containment radius* exists such that no node outside this radius can be affected by the Byzantine nodes once the stabilization is reached: see [8] for matchings and [19, 21] for colorings.

Dubois *et al.* [8] present an anonymous self-stabilizing maximal matching algorithm resilient to Byzantine faults under the strongly-fair central daemon, which converges in a finite number of moves. In this work, we analyse algorithm *AnonyMatch* [3] under the more general weakly-fair distributed daemon (Definition 1). We prove its resilience to Byzantine faults and its convergence in $O(\Delta n \log n)$ rounds w.h.p, with the same containment radius as [8]. We reduce the previous best known containment radius by 1 under the fair central daemon.

Organization of the Document: We present the model in Sect. 2. The algorithm *AnonyMatch* and its specification are given in Sect. 3. In Sect. 4, the algorithm is proven to be self-stabilizing using a containment radius equal to 2 under the distributed daemon. This is a generalization of the result from Dubois *et al.* [8] to a more general daemon and of the result from Cohen *et al.*[3] to Byzantine fault tolerance. In Sect. 5, *AnonyMatch* is proven to be self-stabilizing using a containment radius equal to 1 under the central daemon, improving the result from Dubois *et al.* [8] by reducing the containment radius. In Sect. 6, a counterexample shows that *AnonyMatch* is not self-stabilizing using a containment radius equal to 1 under the distributed daemon.

2 Model

The system consists of a set of processes, or nodes, where two adjacent nodes can communicate with each other. The communication relation is represented by an undirected graph $G = (V, E)$, where $|V| = n$, V is the set of nodes, E of edges. The set of neighbours of a node u is N_u. The maximum degree of the graph is Δ. The network is *anonymous*: nodes are not assumed to have unique identifiers. It is assumed that each node u may distinguish its neighbours by locally labelling them; each neighbour $v \in N_u$ will recognize itself if its label is used in an internal variable of u. This is a classical assumption; for instance, Hsu and Huang [14] make it implicitly; Goddard *et al.* [10] explicitly assume that every two adjacent nodes share a private register containing an incorruptible link number. Each node maintains a set of internal variables. The variables of a node u make up the *local state* of that node. The product of all local states make up the *configuration* of the system. We assume the *state model*, meaning each node can read from the variables of its neighbours, and read and write to its own variables. The nodes of V execute the same distributed algorithm, which is a set of *rules* denoted by *name* :: ⟨*guard*⟩ → ⟨*action*⟩. A *guard* is a predicate on the variables of the node and of its neighbours. An *action* is a modification of the variables of the node. A rule is *enabled* if its predicate is *true*. A node is *enabled* if one of its rules is enabled. Starting from an arbitrary initial configuration, *i.e.*, from arbitrary values for all internal variables, at each step, a subset $S \subseteq V$ is chosen, and the nodes of S are activated. The chosen nodes must be enabled.[2] Then, all activated nodes simultaneously execute the action of the rule they were activated for. We assume *rule atomicity*, meaning that a node can execute a rule in an atomic step, *i.e.*, without being interrupted by another node action. An *execution* is a sequence of configurations $\gamma_0, \gamma_1, \ldots$ such that for every pair (γ_t, γ_{t+1}) of consecutive configurations, there exists a set $S_t \subseteq V$ such that:

- all nodes in S_t are enabled in γ_t, and $S_t \neq \emptyset$;
- $\forall u \in V \setminus S_t$, u has the same local state in γ_t and γ_{t+1};
- $\forall u \in S_t$, the local state of u in γ_{t+1} is the result of u's local state in γ_t and the execution of the rule u was enabled for.

A pair of consecutive configurations is called a *transition*. An execution is said to be *maximal* if it is infinite, or if it is finite and no nodes are enabled in the final configuration. The set $S \subseteq V$ of nodes to be activated during a transition is chosen by a virtual entity called the *daemon*. The daemon is *central* if it guarantees that only one node will be activated at a time, and *distributed* in the general case. In Sect. 4, the daemon is *distributed*, and in Sect. 5, it is *central*. We use the weakest fairness property [4,16]:

Definition 1. *The daemon is* weakly fair *if it guarantees that in any execution, no node may be continuously enabled while never activated. It is* strongly fair *if it guarantees that no node may be infinitely often enabled while never activated. The daemon is* unfair *if it is not assumed to be fair.*

A *self-stabilizing* algorithm ensures a *legitimate*, or desired, configuration is eventually reached, from any arbitrary initial configuration and despite the choices made by the daemon; and that the set of legitimate configurations is closed, *i.e.*, an execution starting in a legitimate configuration may not contain any non-legitimate configuration. A *silent* self-stabilizing algorithm further ensures that legitimate configurations are *stable*, *i.e.*, in any legitimate configuration, no node is enabled; and thus no node may be activated or change states. The algorithm is to be executed in the presence of Byzantine nodes; that is, there is a subset $B \subseteq V$ of adversarial nodes that are not bound by the algorithm. Byzantine nodes are always enabled. An activated Byzantine node is free to update or not its internal variables. Without loss of generality, we assume that the distributed daemon activates all Byzantine nodes in every transition.

---

[2] Alternatively, the daemon could specify a set of pairs (enabled node, rule for which that node is enabled). In our algorithm, all guards are mutually exclusive; that is, at any time, a given node can be enabled for one rule at most. Therefore, that distinction does not matter.

We make no assumption for the central daemon. Finally, because of the Byzantine nodes, observe that all maximal executions are infinite. In the presence of Byzantines, the concept of stability has to be relaxed: Byzantines can always be activated, and their activation might result in a change of states of neighbouring nodes. Thus, a definition of silence or stability should ignore the possible activation or change of states of nodes that are very close to the Byzantines. These definitions will be given along with the definitions of legitimate configurations, in Subsect. 3.1. The time complexity of an algorithm that assumes the fair daemon is calculated in number of *rounds*. The concept of round was introduced by Dolev *et al.* [6], and reworded by Cournier *et al.* [4] to take into account enabled nodes. We quote the two following definitions from Cournier *et al.* [4]:

Definition 2. *"We consider that a node u executes a* disabling action *in the transition* $\gamma_1 \mapsto \gamma_2$ *if u (i) is enabled in* γ_1, *(ii) does not execute any rule in* $\gamma_1 \mapsto \gamma_2$ *and (iii) is not enabled in* γ_2. *The disabling action represents the situation where at least one neighbour of u changes its state in* $\gamma_1 \mapsto \gamma_2$, *and this change effectively made the guard of all rules of u false in* γ_2. *The definition of round [6] captures the speed of the slowest node in any execution: Given an execution* $\mathcal{E}$, *the first* round *of* $\mathcal{E}$ *(let us call it* $\mathcal{R}_1$) *is the minimal prefix of* $\mathcal{E}$ *containing the execution of one action (the execution of a rule or a* disabling action*) of every enabled processor from the initial configuration. Let* $\mathcal{E}'$ *be the suffix of* $\mathcal{E}$ *such that* $\mathcal{E} = \mathcal{R}_1\mathcal{E}'$. *The second round of* $\mathcal{E}$ *is the first round of* $\mathcal{E}'$, *and so on."*

Observe that Definition 2 is equivalent to Definition 3, which is simpler in the sense that it does not refer back to the set of enabled nodes from the initial configuration of the round.

Definition 3. *Let* $\mathcal{E}$ *be an execution. A* round *is a sequence of consecutive steps in* $\mathcal{E}$. *The first round begins at the beginning of* $\mathcal{E}$; *successive rounds begin immediately after the previous round has ended. The current round ends once every node* $u \in V$ *satisfies at least one of the following two properties:*

- *u has been activated in at least one transition during the current round;*
- *u has been non-enabled in at least one configuration during the current round.*

When studying a configuration γ, it is convenient to ignore what might have happened before γ, and consider that γ is the initial configuration in an execution $\mathcal{E}_0$. If the results of this study were then to be applied to an execution $\mathcal{E}_1$ in which configuration γ appears, it should be noted that the rounds in $\mathcal{E}_0$ do not necessarily align exactly with the rounds in $\mathcal{E}_1$. However, not all hope is lost:

Lemma 1. *Let* $\mathcal{E}_1$ *be an execution, and* γ *a configuration appearing in* $\mathcal{E}_1$. *Let* $\mathcal{E}_0$ *be the suffix of* $\mathcal{E}_1$ *starting with* γ. *Let* R_0 *be the first round of* $\mathcal{E}_0$, *and* R_1 *the first round of* $\mathcal{E}_1$ *after* γ. *Then* R_0 *ends before or at the same time as* R_1.

3   Maximal Matchings

The algorithm studied in this paper, called *AnonyMatch*, was introduced in [3]. Each node $u \in V$ has an internal variable p_u whose possible values are the elements of the set $N_u \cup \{\bot\}$. Hence, the space complexity of this algorithm is $O(\log n)$ per node. If two adjacent nodes u and v are such that $p_u = v \land p_v = u$, then these two nodes are married. Algorithm *AnonyMatch* builds a matching:

Definition 4. *Every configuration γ induces a matching $M(\gamma)$:*

$$M(\gamma) = \{(u, v) \in E \; : \; p_u = v \land p_v = u\}.$$

In any configuration, a given node u is in exactly one of the following six classes[3]:
if $p_u = \bot$:

- undecided: $\exists v \in N_u, \; p_v = u$;
- single : $\forall v \in N_u, \; p_v \neq u \land \exists v \in N_u, \; p_v = \bot$;
- alone : $\forall v \in N_u, \; p_v \notin \{u, \bot\}$;

if $p_u \neq \bot$:

- married : $p_{p_u} = u$;
- proposing : $p_{p_u} = \bot$;
- doomed : $p_{p_u} \notin \{u, \bot\}$.

Algorithm *AnonyMatch* has three rules. Their three guards are equivalent to the three classes single, undecided and doomed, respectively. A node in one of the other three classes is not enabled. It is well known that under the distributed daemon, algorithms need some way of symmetry-breaking; *AnonyMatch* is a random algorithm. The random element appears in the form of function choose(S), which chooses an element uniformly at random in finite set S. A single node u executes rule Seduction to try and initiate a marriage with one of its neighbours. This attempt is successful if neighbour v later responds by executing rule Marriage so that u and v become married, or fails if v updates its own variable to show its preference for a third node w (either by executing rule Marriage, or by coincidentally executing rule Seduction in the same transition as u). If the attempt fails, node u then executes rule Abandonment to reset its variable. When a node executes rule Marriage, it becomes married to one of its neighbours, and this marriage is definitive unless one of the two nodes is a Byzantine.

Algorithm 1. *(AnonyMatch)*

Seduction :: $(p_u = \bot) \land (\forall v \in N_u, \; p_v \neq u) \land (\exists v \in N_u, \; p_v = \bot)$
$\quad\quad\quad \rightarrow \quad$ if $choose(\{0, 1\}) = 1$ then $p_u := choose(\{v \in N_u : p_v = \bot\})$

Marriage :: $(p_u = \bot) \land (\exists v \in N_u, \; p_v = u) \rightarrow p_u := choose(\{v \in N_u : p_v = u\})$

Abandonment :: $(p_u \neq \bot) \land (p_{p_u} \notin \{u, \bot\}) \quad \rightarrow p_u := \bot$

---

[3] The names and definitions of the six classes are inspired by similar definitions in [3,8], but were adapted to form a partition and to depend on the states of node u and its direct neighbours' internal variables only.

The Marriage rule is a particular instance of that rule in the original algorithm [3]: in the original algorithm, the action does not specify how to choose which node to get married to among all proposing nodes $v \in N_u : p_v = u$. Because of Byzantines, we need to guarantee that a node u will not be tricked into repeatedly becoming married to a Byzantine neighbour while a non-Byzantine node is also proposing to u. For this reason, we introduce a random choice in rule Marriage. Note that a node u's variable p_u can take a value outside the set $N_u \cup \{\bot\}$ as the result of a transient fault. In this situation, we decide that u is enabled for rule Abandonment. Thus, at the end of the first round of execution, all variables of non-Byzantine nodes hold a value inside their domain of definition. Similarly, a Byzantine node b may choose a value outside $N_b \cup \{\bot\}$. However, the proofs below make no hypotheses on the possible states of Byzantine nodes, therefore this has no impact on the correctness and time complexity of the algorithm.

3.1   Problem Specification

The aim of the algorithm is to reach a matching as large as possible. Because of the presence of Byzantines, however, it is unreasonable to define the specification as a maximal matching on V. Instead, we should define the specification as a maximal matching on a subset $S \subseteq V$. This set should only contain nodes sufficiently far from Byzantines. We use the following definitions from Dubois *et al.* [8], where $d(u, B)$ is the distance from node u to the closest Byzantine:

Definition 5.

$$\forall k \geq 0, \ V_k = \{u \in V \ : \ d(u, B) > k\};$$
$$V_k' = V_k \cup \{u \in V \setminus V_k \ : \ \exists v \in V_k, \ p_u = v \wedge p_v = u\}.$$

In words, V_k is the set of nodes at a distance at least $k + 1$ away from the nearest Byzantine. In particular, V_0 is the set of all non-Byzantine nodes; $V_0 \setminus V_1$ is the set of non-Byzantine nodes neighbour to Byzantines; and a close attention will be given to V_2, the set of nodes at a distance at least 3 from the Byzantines. V_k' is the set of nodes that are either in V_k themselves, or married to a node in V_k. Based on this definition, we give the specification of the problem:

Definition 6. k-Spec: *Build a maximal matching on a superset of* V_k.

Figure 1 depicts a network. An arrow starting from a node represents the internal variable of that node. No arrow means the variable is set to $\bot$. Two arrows on the same edge form a marriage. Byzantine nodes are shown with a square. The greyness of a non-Byzantine node and the thickness of its border represent its distance to the nearest Byzantine: nodes x, y, v are at distance 1, 2, 3, respectively. Set V_k is the set of nodes at distance greater than k from the Byzantines; for instance, nodes x, y, v are all in V_0; y and v are both in V_1; and v is in V_2. z is not in V_1, but is in V_1' because it is married to node $t \in V_1$.

Taking $k = 2$: In this paper, we prove that algorithm *AnonyMatch* is self-stabilizing and silent for 2-Spec under the weakly-fair distributed daemon, using the legitimate configuration and silence properties defined below.

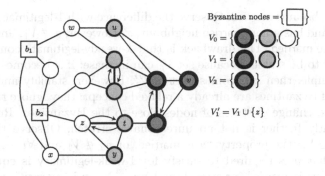

Fig. 1. Illustration of our notations V_k and V_k'.

Definition 7. *A configuration γ is k-legitimate if, for every node $u \in V_k$, either u is married, or $p_u = \perp$ and all of its neighbours $v \in N_u$ are married. A k-legitimate configuration induces a maximal matching on V_k'.*

Definition 8. *A configuration γ is k-stable if no node in V_k' is enabled in γ, and in any execution starting in configuration γ, the state of every node in V_k' remains constant. A self-stabilizing algorithm is said to be k-silent if all legitimate configurations are k-stable.*

The configuration in Fig. 1 is not 2-legitimate. Indeed, node v is in V_2, but it is not married, and its neighbour u is not married either. The configuration would become 2-legitimate if v became married to u (in which case all nodes in V_2 would be married, and u would be part of V_2'), or if u became married to w (in which case v would be alone, and all of its neighbours would be married).

Taking $k = 1$: Observe that the set V_2' is constant in any execution starting from a 2-legitimate configuration. However, in an execution starting from a 1-legitimate configuration, it is not true that set V_1' remains constant. Indeed, in a k-legitimate configuration, if $u \in V_k$ and $p_u = \perp$, then all neighbours of u are required to be married. When $k = 2$, these marriages are final, since they only involve V_0 nodes. However, when $k = 1$, these marriages can be destroyed since they could involve Byzantines. Hence, the definition of 1-legitimacy is not suited to prove that algorithm *AnonyMatch* is self-stabilizing for 1-Spec. We give a relaxed definition for legitimate configurations. In this paper, we prove that *AnonyMatch* is self-stabilizing for 1-Spec under the weakly-fair central daemon, using this definition:

Definition 9. *A configuration is k-weakly-legitimate if, for every node $u \in V_k$, either u is married, or $p_u \notin V_k$ and all of its neighbours $v \in N_u \cap V_k$ are married. A k-weakly-legitimate configuration induces a maximal matching on V_k'.*

The main difference with the definition of k-legitimacy is that if a node $u \in V_k$ is not married, only its neighbours in V_k are required to be married. The configuration in Fig. 1 is not 1-weakly-legitimate; but it would be if nodes u and

v, or u and w, became married. Observe the difference with 1-legitimacy: node y is not married, and has a non-married neighbour, x. However, $x \notin V_1$, and all nodes in $N_y \cap V_1$ are married. The drawback is that k-weakly-legitimate configurations are not likely to be stable, because set V'_k can increase: if x becomes married to y in the example, then x becomes part of V'_1. However, stability and silence in the context of Byzantines are already a relaxed concept: they ignore the possible activation and change of states of nodes close to the Byzantines. Relaxing the concept slightly further is not an unreasonable stretch. Observe that for all $u \in V_2$, $N_u \subset V_1$; the property "u is married, or $p_u \notin V_1$ and $\forall v \in N_u \cap V_1$, v is married" that u is required to satisfy for 1-weak-legitimacy is equivalent to the property "u is married, or $p_u = \perp$ and $\forall v \in N_u$, v is married" required for 2-legitimacy, provided $u \in V_2$. Hence, 1-weakly-legitimacy is strictly stronger than 2-legitimacy. Moreover, a maximal matching on V'_1 induces a maximal matching on V'_2. In addition, although each 1-weakly-legitimate configuration might not be stable in itself, the set of 1-weakly-legitimate configurations is closed:

Proposition 1. *The set $\mathcal{LC}_2$ of 2-legitimate configurations is closed. Every 2-legitimate configuration is 2-stable: if $\mathcal{E}$ is an execution starting in configuration $\gamma \in \mathcal{LC}_2$, then set V'_2 remains constant throughout $\mathcal{E}$, and no node $u \in V'_2$ is ever enabled during $\mathcal{E}$. The set $w\mathcal{LC}_1$ of 1-weakly-legitimate configurations is closed.*

Finally, a given 1-weakly-legitimate configuration can only evolve into a "better" 1-weakly-legitimate configuration, in the sense that set V'_1 can only increase during a transition.

3.2   From legitimacy to weakly-legitimacy

Dubois *et al.* [8] study the same problem, but limit themselves to the strongly-fair central daemon. The legitimate configuration considered in their paper is the same as 2-legitimate from Definition 7. They motivate the need to stay at distance at least 3 away from Byzantines with a counterexample for which the set of 1-legitimate configurations cannot be closed, regardless of the algorithm.

Fig. 2. Example of a 1-legitimate configuration given by Dubois *et al.* [8]. Node b is the only Byzantine. $V_1 = \{u_2, u_3, u_4\}$.

The configuration in Fig. 2 is indeed 1-legitimate; every node in V_1 is either married (u_3 and u_4) or all of its neighbours are married (u_2 is neighbour only to u_1 and u_3, which are both married). However, no algorithm can ensure that the next configuration is 1-legitimate: if the daemon activates only Byzantine node b in the next transition, and node b sets its variable p_b to $\perp$, then node u_1 becomes proposing instead of married; hence u_2 is no longer neighbour only to married nodes, and the next configuration is not 1-legitimate.

That counterexample is specific to the definition of 1-legitimacy, and does not exclude that for another, well-chosen, definition of legitimacy, an algorithm might be self-stabilizing, with legitimate configurations inducing a maximal matching on a superset of V_1. In Fig. 2, although the configuration ceases to be 1-legitimate, it does so because u_1 ceases to be married; but $u_1 \notin V_1'$, and the configuration still induces a maximal matching on V_1' after the activation of b. The only way u_1 can perturbate V_1' is to become married to u_2. Then set V_1' would actually increase with the addition of u_1; the configuration would be 1-legitimate once again, stable this time; and the induced matching on V_1' would be greater than it was before. The argument against 1-legitimate configurations thus amounts to saying that they are unstable because good situations are susceptible to become even better. This is quite unsatisfying, which is why we gave the relaxed Definition 9 of k-weakly-legitimate configurations.

4   2-Spec under the Distributed Daemon

We give in this section a sketch of the proof of our main result: algorithm *Anony-Match* is self-stabilizing for 2-Spec [Theorem 1]. The proof consists in the study of a potential function, the edge set of marriages between two non-Byzantine nodes in a configuration γ:

$$\alpha(\gamma) = \{(u, v) \in E : u \in V_0 \wedge v \in V_0 \wedge p_u = v \wedge p_v = u\}.$$

Every node in V can contribute to at most one edge in $\alpha(\gamma)$, and each edge in $\alpha(\gamma)$ requires two nodes: $|\alpha(\gamma)| \leq n/2$. Observe that for any transition $\gamma_1 \mapsto \gamma_2$, $\alpha(\gamma_1) \subseteq \alpha(\gamma_2)$. Indeed, married non-Byzantine nodes are never enabled, thus can never break their marriage. We show that until a 2-legitimate configuration is reached, α keeps increasing with some positive probability; this implies that the algorithm eventually converges to a 2-legitimate configuration, with high probability bound on the convergence time. The driving force behind α's increase are the non-doomed nodes in V_2 (either undecided or single). In a first step, we show that their activation directly or indirectly causes α to increase. To understand the indirect link between activations of nodes in V_2 and α, we study a second edge set, called $\beta(\gamma)$, and then give more attention to a specific kind of undecided nodes, called dangerously-undecided. $\beta(\gamma)$ is the set of edges proposing-to-undecided between two non-Byzantine nodes:

$$\beta(\gamma) = \{(u, v) \in E : u \in V_0 \wedge v \in V_0 \wedge p_u = v \wedge p_v = \bot\}.$$

We show that if a non-doomed node $u \in V_2$ is activated in a transition $\gamma_1 \mapsto \gamma_2$, then with probability at least $1/4$, either α increases or $\beta(\gamma_2) \neq \emptyset$:

Proposition 2. *Let $\gamma_1 \mapsto \gamma_2$ be a transition in which a node $u \in V_2$ is activated.*

1. *if u is undecided in γ_1, then u executes rule Marriage, and $\alpha(\gamma_1) \subsetneq \alpha(\gamma_2)$;*
2. *if u is single in γ_1, then u executes rule Seduction, and with probability at least $1/4$, u seduces a neighbour $v \in N_u$ in such a way that either $\alpha(\gamma_1) \subsetneq \alpha(\gamma_2)$, or $\beta(\gamma_2) \neq \emptyset$;*
3. *otherwise, u is doomed in γ_1.*

The second case eventually leads to α increasing as well. To prove this, we first give a definition: a dangerously-undecided node is a node that is undecided, has been proposed to by a non-Byzantine neighbour, and is neighbour to a Byzantine. Second, we show the two following propositions:

Proposition 3. *Consider a round $\mathcal{R}$ starting in a configuration γ_1 such that $\beta(\gamma_1) \neq \emptyset$, and ending in a configuration γ_2. Then either a dangerously-undecided node is activated during $\mathcal{R}$, or $\alpha(\gamma_1) \subsetneq \alpha(\gamma_2)$.*

Indeed, $\beta \neq \emptyset$ means there exist two neighbours u and v such that u is proposing to v, and v is undecided. When v executes rule Marriage, if v is not dangerously-undecided, then its marriage is added to α.

Proposition 4. *Let $\mathcal{E}$ be an execution. The number n_{danger} of activations of dangerously-undecided nodes in $\mathcal{E}$ is finite with probability 1, and $\forall 0 < p < 1$, $n_{danger} = O(\max(\Delta n, -\Delta^2 \log p))$ with probability at least $1 - p$.*

Whenever a dangerously-undecided node u is activated, it becomes married to a non-Byzantine with probability at least $1/\Delta$. Such a marriage is impossible to break, and in particular u can never be dangerously-undecided again. The number of distinct nodes that can be dangerously-undecided is of course bounded by n. The exact high probability bound is derived using Hoeffding's inequality.

We still need to take care of the third case of Proposition 2: doomed nodes in V_2. Nodes that are already doomed in the initial configuration are not an issue, since the fairness of the daemon ensures that they either execute rule Abandonment, or cease being doomed for another reason, within one round. We prove in Lemma 2 that if a non-doomed node $u \in V_2$ becomes doomed during a transition, then α increases or β becomes nonempty with probability at least $1/2$, or a dangerously-undecided node is activated, during that transition. Indeed, for a node $u \in V_2$ to become doomed, one of its neighbours $v \in N_u$ needs to execute rule Marriage or Seduction and update its variable p_v to a neighbour $w \neq u$, with consequences on α and β depending on the action of w.

Lemma 2. *Consider a transition $\gamma_1 \mapsto \gamma_2$, and a node $u \in V_2$ which is doomed in γ_2 but not doomed in γ_1. Then one of the following three scenarii happens:*
- *a dangerously-undecided node is activated in $\gamma_1 \mapsto \gamma_2$;*
- *$\alpha(\gamma_1) \subsetneq \alpha(\gamma_2)$;*
- *$\beta(\gamma_2) \neq \emptyset$ with probability at least $1/2$.*

So far, we have proven that activating a node in V_2 eventually gets the system closer to a 2-legitimate configuration, either by increasing the potential function, or by depleting the reserve of potentially dangerously-undecided nodes. It remains to be shown that nodes in V_2 are, in fact, activated.

Lemma 3. *Consider a sequence $\mathcal{S}$ of four consecutive rounds $\mathcal{R}_1, \mathcal{R}_2, \mathcal{R}_3, \mathcal{R}_4$, ending with configuration γ. Assume γ is not 2-legitimate. Then at least one of the three following scenarii happens:*

- *a node in V_2 is activated during $\mathcal{R}_1, \mathcal{R}_2$ or $\mathcal{R}_3$;*

– a *dangerously-undecided* node is activated during $\mathcal{R}_1$, $\mathcal{R}_2$, or $\mathcal{R}_3$;
– α increases during S with probability at least $1/(2\Delta)$.

Proof. Assume that no node in V_2 is activated during $\mathcal{R}_1, \mathcal{R}_2$ or $\mathcal{R}_3$. Then, by definition of a round, every node $u \in V_2$ has been non-enabled in at least one configuration γ^u in $\mathcal{R}_1$; *i.e.*, has been one of married, proposing, or alone. Note that since configuration γ is not 2-legitimate, no previous configuration can be 2-legitimate, according to the contrapositive of Proposition 1. All V_2 nodes which are married will remain so. Since γ is not 2-legitimate, at least one node in V_2 is not married. If a node $u \in V_2$ is proposing in a configuration in $\mathcal{R}_1$, then according to Proposition 3 and Lemma 1, either α increases, or a dangerously-undecided node is activated, during $\mathcal{R}_1$ or $\mathcal{R}_2$. Assume now that there is no proposing V_2 node in any configuration in $\mathcal{R}_1$. Therefore, at least one node in V_2 is alone in at least a configuration in $\mathcal{R}_1$. Furthermore, since all configurations in $\mathcal{R}_1$ are non-2-legitimate, there exists a node $u \in V_2$ and a configuration γ^u in $\mathcal{R}_1$, such that u is alone and has a non-married neighbour $v_0 \in N_u \subset V_1$ in configuration γ^u. Since u is alone, $p_{v_0} = v_1 \notin \{u, \bot\}$. Consider the chain $p_{v_0} = v_1$, $p_{v_1} = v_2$, $p_{v_2} = v_3$, ..., $p_{v_{k-1}} = v_k$, where v_k is the first node in the chain whose variable p_{v_k} is either $\bot$, a Byzantine, or a previous node in the chain.

Case 1. If $p_{v_k} = \bot$, since $v_k \in V_0$ by definition, Proposition 3 can be applied: either a dangerously-undecided node is activated, or α increases, during $\mathcal{R}_1$ or $\mathcal{R}_2$.

Case 2. If p_{v_k} is a Byzantine, then all nodes $v_0, ..., v_{k-1}$ will remain continuously enabled for rule Abandonment, until either one of them executes Abandonment, or v_k executes Abandonment. This will happen within one round. Among the one or more nodes in the chain that execute Abandonment first, consider the node v_i which is closest in the chain to u. There are two cases: $i > 0$, and $i = 0$.

Case 2.1. If $i > 0$, then the situation becomes that of Case 1 (after a delay of up to one round). Either a dangerously-undecided node is activated, or α increases, during $\mathcal{R}_1, \mathcal{R}_2$, or $\mathcal{R}_3$.

Case 2.2. If $i = 0$, then u and v_0 are both single or undecided, and in V_1. In particular, none of them is alone, since they are neighbours. They will remain continuously single or undecided, until one of them is activated during $\mathcal{R}_1, \mathcal{R}_2$ or $\mathcal{R}_3$. In the best case, u executes rule Marriage or Seduction, or v_0 executes rule Marriage. In the worst case, v_0 executes rule Seduction; then v_0 has probability at least $1/(2\Delta)$ of seducing u. If that happens, u will remain continuously enabled for rule Marriage, until it is activated during $\mathcal{R}_1, \mathcal{R}_2, \mathcal{R}_3$ or $\mathcal{R}_4$, and α increases.

Case 3. If p_{v_k} is a previous node in the chain, then all nodes $v_0, ..., v_k$ are continuously enabled for rule Abandonment, and at least one of them will execute it within one round: the situation is exactly the same as Case 2.

Proposition 2 and Lemma 2 combine to refine Lemma 3:

Proposition 5. *Consider a sequence S of 6 consecutive rounds $\mathcal{R}_1, \mathcal{R}_2, \mathcal{R}_3, \mathcal{R}_4$, $\mathcal{R}_5, \mathcal{R}_6$. Assume $\mathcal{R}_6$ ends in a non-2-legitimate configuration. Then at least one of the following two scenarii happens:*
– a *dangerously-undecided* node is activated during S;
– α increases during S with probability at least $1/(2\Delta)$.

Finally, we apply Hoeffding's inequality to get Theorem 1. Then, taking $p = 1/n$ in this theorem, we obtain Corollary 1.

Theorem 1. *Under the weakly-fair distributed daemon, algorithm* AnonyMatch *is self-stabilizing for 2-Spec: in any execution, a 2-legitimate configuration is eventually reached with probability 1; this takes less than $12\Delta n$ rounds in expectation; furthermore, for any $0 < p < 1$, a 2-legitimate configuration is reached within $24\max(\Delta n, -\Delta^2 \log p)$ rounds with probability at least $(1-p)$.*

Corollary 1. *Under the weakly-fair distributed daemon, algorithm* AnonyMatch *is self-stabilizing for 2-Spec, with time complexity $O(\max(\Delta n, \Delta^2 \log n))$ rounds with probability $1 - \frac{1}{n}$.*

5   1-Spec Under the Central Daemon

The structure of the proof that *AnonyMatch* is self-stabilising for 1-Spec under the central daemon is very similar to that of 2-Spec under the distributed daemon. However, the study of what happens in a given transition is different: previously, things worked out well because the nodes involved were far from the Byzantines. In what follows, the nodes which are required to become married are closer to the Byzantines, but only one node can be activated at a time. In particular, the only way for a node $u \in V_1$ to become doomed is if a neighbour $v \in V_0$ executes rule Marriage; immediately increasing α if v is not dangerously-undecided. This time, the lead role is played by nodes in V_1. We adapt the results of Propositions 2 and 5 to take advantage of the central daemon. Note that the bound on the number of activations of dangerously-undecided nodes (Proposition 4) still applies under the central daemon, which is a specific instance of the distributed daemon. Finally, we apply Hoeffding's inequality to get Theorem 2. Then, taking $p = 1/n$ in this theorem, we obtain Corollary 2.

Theorem 2. *Under the weakly-fair central daemon, algorithm AnonyMatch is self-stabilising for 1-Spec: in any execution, a 1-weakly-legitimate configuration is eventually reached with probability 1; this takes less than $6n(\Delta+1)$ rounds in expectation; furthermore, for any $0 < p < 1$, a 1-weakly-legitimate configuration is reached within $24\max(\Delta n, -\Delta^2 \log p)$ rounds of execution with probability at least $(1-p)$.*

Corollary 2. *Under the weakly-fair central daemon, algorithm* AnonyMatch *is self-stabilising for 1-Spec, with time complexity $O(\max(\Delta n, \Delta^2 \log n))$ rounds with probability $1 - \frac{1}{n}$.*

6   About 1-Spec and the Distributed Daemon

According to previous sections, algorithm *AnonyMatch* ensures that a maximal matching is found on a superset of V_2 under the distributed daemon, and on a superset of V_1 under the more forgiving central daemon. A natural question to ask is whether a maximal matching can always be found by *AnonyMatch* on a superset of V_1 under the distributed daemon. Unfortunately, the answer is no, even with just one Byzantine node in the network. Consider the configuration in Fig. 3(a).

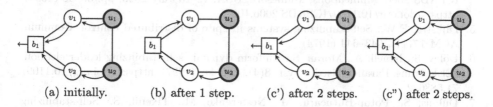

(a) initially.   (b) after 1 step.   (c') after 2 steps.   (c") after 2 steps.

Fig. 3. Node b is a Byzantine node. $V_1 = \{u_1, u_2\}$.

Whatever the definition of legitimacy, if the algorithm is self-stabilizing for 1-Spec, the configuration should eventually induce a maximal matching on a superset of V_1, *i.e.*, a set containing u_1 and u_2. Unfortunately, the daemon and the Byzantine node have a colluding strategy to prevent u_1 and u_2 from ever proposing to one another, and to prevent v_1 and v_2 from ever accepting u_1 and u_2's proposals. Consider the following execution of algorithm *AnonyMatch*, which is consistent with the strongly-fair distributed daemon (and thus also with any less fair distributed daemon). In the first step, the daemon activates v_1 (Abandonment), and u_1 (Abandonment), while b sets $p_b := v_1$, leading to Fig. 3(b). In the second step, the daemon activates v_1 (Marriage), and u_1 (Seduction), while b sets $p_b := w \notin \{v_1, \perp\}$. Node u_1 randomly decides whether to set $p_{u_1} := \perp$, leading to Fig. 3(c'), or $p_{u_1} := v_1$, leading to Fig. 3(c"). If u_1 chooses $p_{u_1} := \perp$, the daemon activates v_1 (Abandonment), while b sets $p_b := v_1$, leading back to Fig. 3(b). Since u_1 has probability $1/2$ of choosing $p_{u_1} := v_1$ every time it executes rule Seduction, this cycle will eventually be broken, leading to Fig. 3(c"). The configuration is now the same as the initial configuration. The daemon is assumed to be fair, so nodes v_2 and u_2 need to be activated before the execution can be called an infinite loop. However, the configuration is obviously symmetric, so the daemon and the Byzantine node can apply the strategy of steps 1 and 2 to v_2 and u_2, eventually leading back to the initial configuration. Algorithm *AnonyMatch* is indeed stuck in a infinite loop, and there will be no maximal matching on a set containing V_1.

References

1. Asada, Y., Inoue, M.: An efficient silent self-stabilizing algorithm for 1-maximal matching in anonymous networks. In: Rahman, M.S., Tomita, E. (eds.) WALCOM 2015. LNCS, vol. 8973, pp. 187–198. Springer, Cham (2015). https://doi.org/10.1007/978-3-319-15612-5_17
2. Berenbrink, P., Friedetzky, T., Martin, R.A.: On the stability of dynamic diffusion load balancing. Algorithmica **50**(3), 329–350 (2008)

3. Cohen, J., Lefèvre, J., Maâmra, K., Pilard, L., Sohier, D.: A self-stabilizing algorithm for maximal matching in anonymous networks. Parallel Process. Lett. **26**(4), 1–17 (2016). https://doi.org/10.1142/S012962641650016X
4. Cournier, A., Devismes, S., Villain, V.: Snap-stabilizing PIF and useless computations. In: 12th International Conference on Parallel and Distributed Systems, ICPADS 2006, Minneapolis, Minnesota, USA, 12–15 July 2006, pp. 39–48 (2006). https://doi.org/10.1109/ICPADS.2006.100
5. Dijkstra, E.W.: Self-stabilizing systems in spite of distributed control. Commun. ACM **17**(11), 643–644 (1974)
6. Dolev, S., Israeli, A., Moran, S.: Uniform dynamic self-stabilizing leader election. IEEE Trans. Parallel Distrib. Syst. **8**(4), 424–440 (1997). https://doi.org/10.1109/71.588622
7. Dubois, S., Potop-Butucaru, M., Nesterenko, M., Tixeuil, S.: Self-stabilizing Byzantine asynchronous unison. J. Parallel Distrib. Comput. **72**(7), 917–923 (2012). https://doi.org/10.1016/j.jpdc.2012.04.001
8. Dubois, S., Tixeuil, S., Zhu, N.: The Byzantine brides problem. In: Kranakis, E., Krizanc, D., Luccio, F. (eds.) FUN 2012. LNCS, vol. 7288, pp. 107–118. Springer, Heidelberg (2012). https://doi.org/10.1007/978-3-642-30347-0_13
9. Ghosh, B., Muthukrishnan, S.: Dynamic load balancing by random matchings. J. Comput. Syst. Sci. **53**(3), 357–370 (1996)
10. Goddard, W., Hedetniemi, S.T., Shi, Z.: An anonymous self-stabilizing algorithm for 1-maximal matching in trees. In: Proceedings of the International Conference on Parallel and Distributed Processing Techniques and Applications and Conference on Real-Time Computing Systems and Applications, PDPTA, vol. 2, pp. 797–803 (2006)
11. Guellati, N., Kheddouci, H.: A survey on self-stabilizing algorithms for independence, domination, coloring, and matching in graphs. J. Parallel Distrib. Comput. **70**(4), 406–415 (2010)
12. Han, Z., Gu, Y., Saad, W.: Matching Theory for Wireless Networks. WN. Springer, Cham (2017). https://doi.org/10.1007/978-3-319-56252-0
13. Hedetniemi, S.T., Jacobs, D.P., Srimani, P.K.: Maximal matching stabilizes in time O(m). Inf. Process. Lett. **80**(5), 221–223 (2001)
14. Hsu, S.C., Huang, S.T.: A self-stabilizing algorithm for maximal matching. Inf. Process. Lett. **43**(2), 77–81 (1992)
15. Inoue, M., Ooshita, F., Tixeuil, S.: An efficient silent self-stabilizing 1-maximal matching algorithm under distributed daemon for arbitrary networks. In: Spirakis, P., Tsigas, P. (eds.) SSS 2017. LNCS, vol. 10616, pp. 93–108. Springer, Cham (2017). https://doi.org/10.1007/978-3-319-69084-1_7
16. Karaata, M.H.: Self-stabilizing strong fairness under weak fairness. IEEE Trans. Parallel Distrib. Syst. **12**(4), 337–345 (2001). https://doi.org/10.1109/71.920585
17. Lamport, L., Shostak, R., Pease, M.: The Byzantine generals problem. ACM Trans. Program. Lang. Syst. (TOPLAS) **4**(3), 382–401 (1982)
18. Manne, F., Mjelde, M., Pilard, L., Tixeuil, S.: A new self-stabilizing maximal matching algorithm. Theor. Comput. Sci. (TCS) **410**(14), 1336–1345 (2009)
19. Masuzawa, T., Tixeuil, S.: Stabilizing link-coloration of arbitrary networks with unbounded Byzantine faults. Int. J. Princ. Appl. Inf. Sci. Technol. (PAIST) **1**(1), 1–13 (2007)
20. Nesterenko, M., Arora, A.: Tolerance to unbounded Byzantine faults. In: Proceedings 21st IEEE Symposium on Reliable Distributed Systems 2002, pp. 22–29. IEEE (2002)

21. Sakurai, Y., Ooshita, F., Masuzawa, T.: A self-stabilizing link-coloring protocol resilient to Byzantine faults in tree networks. In: Higashino, T. (ed.) OPODIS 2004. LNCS, vol. 3544, pp. 283–298. Springer, Heidelberg (2005). https://doi.org/10.1007/11516798_21
22. Sauerwald, T., Sun, H.: Tight bounds for randomized load balancing on arbitrary network topologies. In: 2012 IEEE 53rd Annual Symposium on Foundations of Computer Science (FOCS), pp. 341–350. IEEE (2012)
23. Turau, V., Hauck, B.: A new analysis of a self-stabilizing maximum weight matching algorithm with approximation ratio 2. Theor. Comput. Sci. (TCS) 412(40), 5527–5540 (2011)

Exploration of Finite 2D Square Grid by a Metamorphic Robotic System

Keisuke Doi, Yukiko Yamauchi$^{(\boxtimes)}$, Shuji Kijima, and Masafumi Yamashita

Graduate School of Information Science and Electrical Engineering,
Kyushu University, 744 Motooka, Nishi-ku, Fukuoka 819-0395, Japan
doi@tcslab.csce.kyushu-u.ac.jp,
{yamauchi,kijima,mak}@inf.kyushu-u.ac.jp

Abstract. We consider exploration of a finite 2D square grid by a metamorphic robotic system consisting of anonymous oblivious modules. The number of possible shapes of the metamorphic robotic system grows as the number of modules increases. The shapes of the system serve as its memory and show its functionality. We consider the effect of global compass on the minimum number of modules for exploration of a finite 2D square grid. We show that if the modules agree on the directions (north, south, east, and west), three modules are necessary and sufficient for exploration from an arbitrary initial configuration, otherwise five modules are necessary and sufficient for limited initial configurations.

Keywords: Metamorphic robotic system · Autonomous modules Exploration

1 Introduction

Distributed systems consisting of mobile computing entities, often called robots, agents, or particles have gathered much attention in these twenty years as computational models for mobile networks, biological systems, chemical reactions, etc. Each computing entity is often assumed to have very weak capabilities, i.e., it is *anonymous* and *oblivious* (memory-less), and does not have any communication capability or any access to the global coordinate system. Most existing papers focus on *shape formation* that requires mobile computing entities to form a specified shape. Suzuki and Yamashita investigated the *pattern formation problem* by anonymous autonomous *mobile robots*, each of which moves in continuous 2D space by sensing the positions of other robots and computing its next position with a common (deterministic) algorithm. They pointed out that the pattern formation problem is essentially related to the *agreement problem* because once the robots agree on a common coordinate system, they can form an arbitrary pattern [17]. Derakhshandeh et al. first presented a shape formation algorithm

---

This work is partially supported by JST SICORP and JSPS KAKENHI Grant Number JP17K19982.

T. Izumi and P. Kuznetsov (Eds.): SSS 2018, LNCS 11201, pp. 96–110, 2018.
https://doi.org/10.1007/978-3-030-03232-6_7

for the *amoebot model* [6]. The system consists of programmable particles moving in the 2D triangular grid by repeating an extension and a contraction. Each vertex of a triangular grid is occupied by at most one particle, which is equipped with constant-size memory and communication capability with other particles in its neighboring vertex. Their algorithm is based on a randomized *leader election*, which allows formation of an arbitrary shape. Dumitrescu et al. considered the *metamorphic robotic system model*, which consists of autonomous modules moving in the 2D square grid [10,11]. Each module can perform two types of local movements, called a rotation and a sliding, with maintaining their connectivity. They showed a canonical shape, to which any shape can be transformed. The reversibility of movements guarantees transformation between any pair of shapes via the canonical shape. The goal of all these studies is the structure of shapes. Reachability among shapes decomposes the system's configuration space into subspaces, which indicate the degree of global agreement and coordination, in other words, distributed computing ability of the system. However, when we take a closer look at existing shape formation algorithms, we find that intermediate shapes are used to guarantee the progress of distributed coordination. That is, geometric configuration of the system is used as global memory though each computing entity is memory-less or equipped with constant-size memory.

In this paper, we investigate the functionality of shapes of a distributed system consisting of mobile computing entities. We focus on the *exploration problem* in the metamorphic robotic system model. The problem requires the system to find a target put in one cell of a given field, which is a finite rectangular subspace of the 2D square grid. Clearly, as the number of modules increases, the number of possible shapes increases and the system can memorize more information with its shape. We present the minimum number of modules to accomplish exploration and investigate the effect of the global compass, which allows the modules to agree on north, south, east, and west.

Our Results. In this paper, we consider the exploration problem by a metamorphic robotic system. Although shape formation [10,16] and locomotion [2,11] by the metamorphic robotic system have been discussed, to the best of our knowledge, this is the first time the exploration problem is discussed for the model. We demonstrate the effect of the global compass on the minimum number of modules for exploration. We first show when the modules are equipped with the global compass, three modules are necessary and sufficient for exploration from an arbitrary initial configuration. Then, we show that when the modules lack the global compass, five modules are necessary and sufficient for exploration; however, there are initial shapes from which the metamorphic robotic system cannot accomplish exploration.

Related Works. Computational power of a distributed system consisting of mobile computing entities with very weak capabilities is currently one of the most active topics in distributed computing theory. The quest also reveals the minimum capabilities to accomplish a given task. The results serve as a design guideline for robotic systems with cheap hardware and are expected to give a clue to understanding complex behavior of natural systems. There are a variety of indicator tasks such as gathering, shape formation, leader election, computing a function, exploration, and decomposition. Regarding the autonomous mobile robot model, formable patterns have discussed by considering various aspects, such as obliviousness [17], asynchrony [14,18], limited visibility [20], and randomness [21]. These papers showed that symmetry of initial positions of the robots determines formable shapes, i.e., obliviousness and asynchrony generally have no effect. Randomness allows probabilistic symmetry breaking and realizes universal pattern formation. Yamauchi et al. introduced the *plane formation problem* in 3D space and used the rotation group to measure the symmetry of the robots [19].

Distributed shape formation in the amoebot model is investigated for shapes consisting of triangles [6] and arbitrary shapes [9]. Di Luna et al. considered the limit of deterministic leader election and characterized formable shapes by the symmetry of an initial configuration [9]. Derakhshandeh et al. proposed the *universal coating problem* of a given obstacle [5].

Shape formation in the metamorphic robotic system model is investigated in a distributed setting and in a centralized setting. Dumitrescu et al. considered distributed transformability of an initial (horizontally) convex shape to a line (also called a chain) shape with the global compass [10]. Dumitrescu et al. considered *locomotion* of a metamorphic robotic system and showed the shape that realizes fastest locomotion [11]. While these two papers assume unlimited visibility, Chen et al. considered locomotion with limited visibility [2]. When the movement is limited to rotations, there are pairs of shapes that are not transformable. Michail et al. considered the complexity of deciding transformability of a pair of shapes only by rotations [16].

Michail and Spirakis proposed the *network constructor model* that considers finite-state agents under passive movement [15]. The communication model is based on the *population protocol model* [1], while the agents can construct an edge when they interact. They discussed distributed transformation of shapes in the network constructor model.

All these papers consider reachability and classification of shapes. Little is known about the functionality of shapes. Das et al. investigated the formation of a sequence of patterns, which also serves as finite memory formed by oblivious mobile robots [3]. Simulating a Turing machine by a line shape of computing entities has been separately discussed for the metamorphic robotic system model [10], the network constructor model [15], and the amoebot model [9]. Di Luna et al. showed a constant number of oblivious mobile robots can simulate a robot with memory [8]. In this paper, we focus on the fact that geometric configuration of a metamorphic robotic system functions as memory and processor, and we investigate how a small number of oblivious modules accomplish exploration of a given field. Note that exploration by a single metamorphic robotic system is different from exploration by ants [12], mobile agents [4], or mobile robots [7,13] because a metamorphic robotic system cannot separate into several small fragments.

2 Preliminary

We consider the rectangular metamorphic robotic system introduced in [2,10,11, 16]. Consider a two dimensional (2D) square grid where each square cell $c_{i,j}$ is labeled by the underlying x-y coordinate system. We consider a finite subspace of width w and height h and call it the *field*. Without loss of generality, we assume that $c_{0,0}$ is the southwesternmost cell and $c_{w-1,h-1}$ is the northeasternmost cell (Fig. 1). Each cell $c_{i,j}$ has eight *adjacent* cells; (E)ast $c_{i+1,j}$, (N)orth(E)ast $c_{i+1,j+1}$, (N)orth $c_{i,j+1}$, (N)orth(W)est $c_{i-1,j+1}$, (W)est $c_{i-1,j}$, (S)outh(W)est $c_{i-1,j-1}$, (S)outh $c_{i,j-1}$, and (S)outh(E)ast $c_{i+1,j-1}$. The four cells N, S, E, and W are said to be *side-adjacent* to $c_{i,j}$. An infinite sequence of cells with the same x coordinate is called a *column* and an infinite sequence of cells with the same y coordinate is called a *row*. The field is surrounded by walls, the (-1)th column (the west wall), the wth column (the east wall), the (-1)th row (the south wall), and the hth row (the north wall). These cell labels are used just for description and there is no way to distinguish the cells.

A metamorphic robotic system R consists of n anonymous modules, each of which occupies a distinct cell in the grid at discrete time steps $t = 0, 1, 2, \ldots$. The *configuration* C_t of R at time t is the set of cells occupied by the modules at time t. An *execution* is an evolution of configurations $C_0, C_1, C_2, \ldots$.

The evolution is generated by movements of modules. Let M_t be the set of modules that move at time t. We call the modules in $B_t = C_t \setminus M_t$ a *backbone*, that does not move at time t. There are two types of movements, a *rotation* and a *sliding*, guided by backbone modules (Fig. 2). A rotation of a moving module m side-adjacent to a backbone module b is a rotation around b by an angle of $\pi/2$ either clockwise or counter-clockwise. A 1-sliding of a moving module m is a sliding to a side-adjacent cell. In this case, there must be two backbone modules; one is b_1 that is side-adjacent to m and the other is b_2 that is side-adjacent to b_1 and the target cell of m. A k-sliding $(k \geq 2, 3, \ldots)$ is defined in the same way; however, it requires $(k + 1)$ backbone modules along the track.[1] In a rotation and a sliding, the cells that m passes must not contain any module.

The connectivity of configuration C_t is represented by a connectivity graph $G_t = (C_t, E_t)$. The edge set E_t contains an edge (c, c') for $c, c' \in C_t$ if and only if cells c and c' are side-adjacent. When G_t is connected, we say C_t is *connected*. Any execution $C_0, C_1, C_2, \ldots$ must satisfy the following three conditions:

1. Connectivity: For any $t = 0, 1, 2, \ldots$, C_t is connected.
2. Single backbone: For any $t = 0, 1, 2 \ldots$, B_t is connected.
3. No interference: For any $t = 0, 1, 2, \ldots$, the trajectories of two moving modules m and m' never overlap.

The modules are *uniform*, i.e, they are anonymous and execute a common deterministic distributed algorithm. At each time step, each module observes the modules in its neighborhood and decides its movement. Thus, the modules

---

[1] The original metamorphic robotic system model in [2,10,11,16] allows rotations and 1-slidings. We extended the original model by allowing k-slidings for $k = 2, 3, \ldots$.

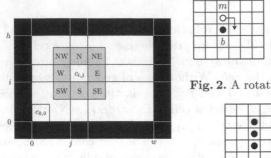

Fig. 1. A field and walls.

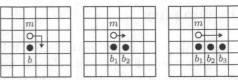

Fig. 2. A rotation, a 1-sliding, and a 2-sliding

Fig. 3. Symmetry Fig. 4. A deadlock

are *synchronous*. A cell $c_{i',j'}$ is a *k-neighborhood* of cell $c_{i,j}$ if $|i' - i| \le k$ and $|j' - j| \le k$. A distributed algorithm of neighborhood size k is a total function that maps a $(2k + 1) \times (2k + 1)$ square grid to one cell. Thus, the modules are *oblivious*. We assume that k is constant regarding w and h, and a module can observe whether each cell in its k-neighborhood is occupied by a module or a target and whether the cell is a part of the walls or not. When the modules are equipped with the *global compass*, they share common north, south, east, and west directions. When the modules are not equipped with the global compass, they do not know directions and their observations may be inconsistent. However, we assume that the modules agree on the clockwise direction, i.e., they share a common handedness.

The *state* of R in C_t is the local shape of R. We often describe a state of n modules as S^n. If the modules are equipped with global compass, the state of R contains global directions; otherwise, it does not contain any direction because the modules cannot recognize any rotation on their state.

The *exploration problem* requires the metamorphic robotic system to find the target put in one cell in a given field without any a priori information (i.e., the size of the field and the target cell). We say that the metamorphic robotic system *finds* the target from a given initial configuration C_0, if, in any execution from C_0, some module reaches the cell with the target and the metamorphic robotic system stops thereafter. We say that the metamorphic robotic system accomplishes exploration if, for any given field and a target, it can find the target from any initial configuration.

When the modules are equipped with the global compass, the execution is uniquely determined by C_0 because the modules are synchronous. On the other hand, when the modules have no access to the global compass, there exist multiple executions from C_0 depending on the local compass of each module. For example, if one endpoint module in Fig. 3 performs a rotation, the other endpoint module may also perform a rotation when they have symmetric local compasses. More precisely, due to symmetry, the two modules cannot distinguish themselves. Another example is shown in Fig. 4. In this case, the only possible movements are rotations; however, the four modules cannot move because if one of them moves, then others may also move. Then, the backbone requirement is not satisfied. Consequently, without global compass, exploration is generally impossible from an arbitrary initial configuration.

3   Exploration with Global Compass

In this section, we consider the metamorphic robotic system consisting of modules with the global compass. We show the following theorem.

Theorem 1. *Three modules are necessary and sufficient for a metamorphic robotic system with the global compass to accomplish exploration.*

The necessity is shown by the impossibility with less than three modules. Due to space limitation, we omit the proof.

To show the sufficiency, we present an exploration algorithm. Our basic method is to make the metamorphic robotic system R visit all cells of the field, i.e., R moves to the south with sweeping each row. However, since the initial configuration is arbitrary, when it reaches the southernmost (0th) row, it moves to the northernmost $((w-1)\text{st})$ row along either the east wall or the west wall and it explores unvisited cells. Figure 5 shows examples of "tracks" of R. Depending on the number of rows and an initial configuration, R moves along one of such tracks. We demonstrate the progress of exploration using a reference point of R defined by its *spine* and *frontier* that will be defined later. The tracks in Fig. 5 show the tracks of reference points. Note that the reference point does not refer to some specific module. Rather, different modules serve as reference points during an evolution of configurations.

The proposed algorithm consists of the following basic moves;

- A move to the east and a move to the west.
- A turn on the east wall and a turn on the west wall.
- A turn on the southwest corner and a turn on the southeast corner.
- A move to the north wall along the east wall and that along the west wall.
- A turn on the northeast corner and a turn on the northwest corner.

Figure 6 shows all possible states of R. We assume that each module can observe the cells in its 2-neighborhood. When one module of R reaches a cell with the target, R stops. More precisely, because of the sufficient visibility, each module can detect the target and never perform any movement thereafter.

Moves along a Row. Figures 7 and 8 show the move to the east and the move to the west, respectively. By repeating one of the two moves, R moves to one direction. Each module can observe the state of R and the two sets of configurations used in the two moves are disjoint. Thus, the modules can consistently agree on the direction to which R is moving.

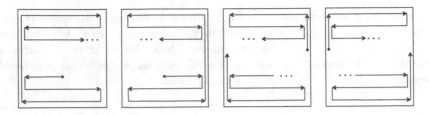

Fig. 5. Example of tracks. Each track starts from the black circle.

In the first state of the unit move to the east, the spine is the ith row and the frontier is the jth column (Fig. 7). At the end of a unit move, the frontier reaches $(j + 1)$st column. During the move, the modules do not care whether $(i + 1)$st row, $(i − 2)$nd row and $(j − 3)$rd column are walls or not.

In the first state of the unit move to the west, the spine is the ith row and the frontier is the jth column (Fig. 8). The modules do not care whether $(i − 2)$nd row, $(i + 1)$st row and $(j + 1)$st column are walls or not.

Turns on the Walls. Figures 9 and 10 show a turn on the east wall and a turn on the west wall, respectively. On the east wall and the west wall, R changes its spine and starts a new move to the west and to the east, respectively.

Turns on the South Corners and Moves to the North Wall. By repeating the above four moves, R eventually reaches the south wall. Then, it turns and moves along either the east wall or the west wall until it reaches the north wall. Figures 11 and 12 show these turns. Figures 13 and 14 show the moves to the north wall. When R moves along the east wall or the west wall, its spine is the $(w − 1)$th column and the 0th column, respectively. The frontier is the northernmost module in both cases. By repeating one of the two moves, the reference point of R moves to the north.

Turns on the North Corners. By repeating either the moves in Fig. 13 or Fig. 14, R eventually reaches the north wall. Then, it turns in the corner (Figs. 15 and 16) and starts moving along a row with the moves shown in Figs. 7 and 8.

We finally add exceptional movements. When R is in the center of the field, all states appear in the above moves and any move can be executed. However, when R is on a wall or in a corner, moves for some states are not defined or impossible. Figure 17 shows additional movements to avoid deadlocks in these states.

The reference point of R visits all cells in each row except the southernmost row and the northern most row. The cells of the southernmost row are visited by the modules under the spine when R moves along the first row. The cells of the northernmost row are visited by the modules over the spine when R moves along the $(h − 2)$nd row. Thus, we have Theorem 1.

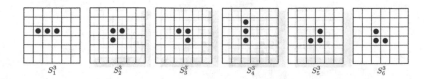

Fig. 6. States of R consisting of three modules

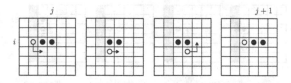

Fig. 7. Move to the east $(S_1^3 \rightarrow S_2^3 \rightarrow S_3^3 \rightarrow S_1^3)$

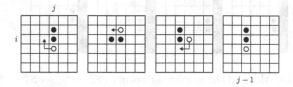

Fig. 8. Move to the west $(S_4^3 \rightarrow S_5^3 \rightarrow S_6^3 \rightarrow S_4^3)$

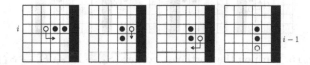

Fig. 9. Turn on the east wall $(S_1^3 \rightarrow S_2^3 \rightarrow S_6^3 \rightarrow S_1^3)$

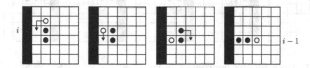

Fig. 10. Turn on the west wall $(S_4^3 \rightarrow S_3^3 \rightarrow S_5^3 \rightarrow S_1^3)$

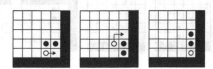

Fig. 11. Turn on the southeast corner $(S_2^3 \rightarrow S_3^3 \rightarrow S_4^3)$

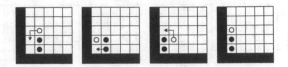

Fig. 12. Turn on the southwest corner ($S_4^3 \to S_3^3 \to S_2^3 \to S_4^3$)

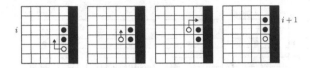

Fig. 13. Move to the northeast corner ($S_4^3 \to S_5^3 \to S_3^3 \to S_4^3$)

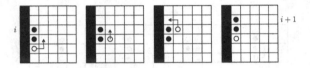

Fig. 14. Move to the northwest corner ($S_4^3 \to S_6^3 \to S_2^3 \to S_4^3$)

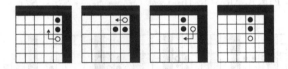

Fig. 15. Turn on the northeast corner ($S_4^3 \to S_5^3 \to S_6^3 \to S_4^3$)

Fig. 16. Turn on the northwest corner ($S_4^3 \to S_6^3 \to S_2^3 \to S_3^3 \to S_1^3$)

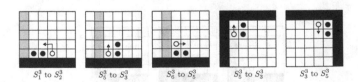

Fig. 17. Exceptions. A gray column is either a wall or non-wall cells.

4   Exploration Without Global Compass

In this section, we consider the metamorphic robotic system consisting of modules without the global compass. We show the following theorem.

Theorem 2. *Five modules are necessary and sufficient for a metamorphic robotic system without the global compass to accomplish exploration from allowed initial configurations.*

When the metamorphic robotic system R consists of five modules, there is a state from which no module can move. Additionally, there are three states from which R may transit to the deadlock state. These three states also form a cycle. More precisely, we consider the transition diagram of the four states in Fig. 18, where each arc represents the fact that there are possible movements that translates its starting state to its endpoint state. In S_1^5, no module can move. The three states S_2^5, S_3^5, and S_4^5 form a cycle and from these states, R can transit to themselves and S_1^5. For example, in S_4^5, possible movements are rotations of the two endpoint modules. However, when one of them moves, the other may also move. Then, possible next states are S_2^5 and S_3^5. In the same manner, when two endpoint modules move in S_2^5 and S_3^5, possible next states are S_1^5 (by 1-slidings), S_2^5 (by 2-slidings), S_3^5 (by 2-slidings), and S_4^5 (by rotations). During these transitions, R cannot move forward to any direction. Hence, from these states, R cannot accomplish exploration and these states cannot be used in an exploration algorithm.

The necessity of Theorem 2 is shown by the impossibility with less than five modules. Due to space limitation, we omit the proof.

To show the sufficiency, we present an exploration algorithm. In the following, we consider initial configurations where the state of R is none of the four states. Figure 19 shows all the other possible states of R. Note that since the modules lack the global compass, they cannot recognize a rotation of a state. We assume that each module can observe the cells in its 4-neighborhood. In addition, we use 2-slidings and 3-slidings, which are not used in Sect. 3.

We adopt the same method as Sect. 3, i.e., R visits every cell in the field. However, the modules cannot use the global compass, and even with five modules it is not easy to realize all the ten moves in Sect. 3. Instead, R uses a single track that checks the rows from north to south with visiting each cell of a row from west to east (Fig. 20). R rotates the track by $\pi/2$ at the southwest corner in order to visit all cells. It repeats the moves until it finds the target. We explain the basic case where the directions are identical to the global compass.

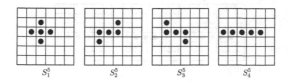

Fig. 18. Forbidden states.

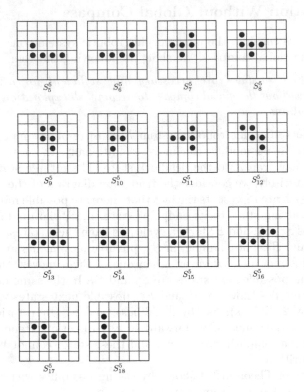

Fig. 19. States of R consisting of five modules

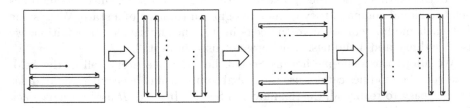

Fig. 20. Track of the metamorphic robotic system consisting of five modules.

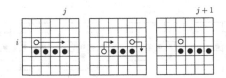

Fig. 21. Move to the east ($S_5^5 \rightarrow S_6^5 \rightarrow S_5^5$)

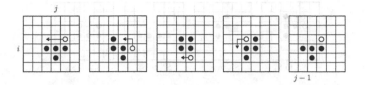

Fig. 22. Move to the west $(S_7^5 \rightarrow S_8^5 \rightarrow S_9^5 \rightarrow S_{10}^5 \rightarrow S_7^5)$

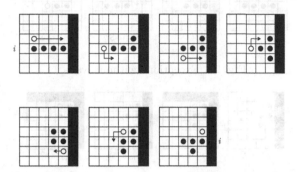

Fig. 23. Turn on the east wall $(S_5^5 \rightarrow S_6^5 \rightarrow S_2^5 \rightarrow S_{11}^5 \rightarrow S_9^5 \rightarrow S_{10}^5 \rightarrow S_7^5)$

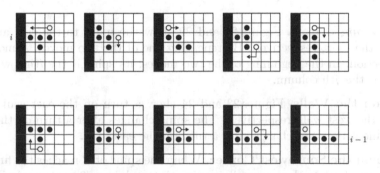

Fig. 24. Turn on the west wall $(S_7^5 \rightarrow S_8^5 \rightarrow S_{12}^5 \rightarrow S_7^5 \rightarrow S_{13}^5 \rightarrow S_{11}^5 \rightarrow S_9^5 \rightarrow S_{10}^5 \rightarrow S_{14}^5 \rightarrow S_5^5)$

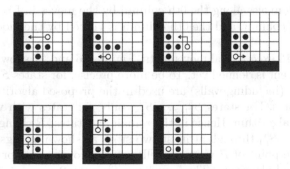

Fig. 25. Turn on the southeast corner $(S_7^5 \rightarrow S_8^5 \rightarrow S_{11}^5 \rightarrow S_{10}^5 \rightarrow S_9^5 \rightarrow S_{14}^5 \rightarrow S_5^5)$

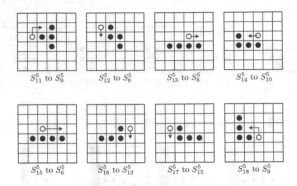

Fig. 26. Exceptions without walls

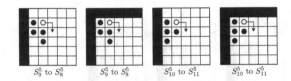

Fig. 27. Exceptions with walls

Moves along a Row. Figures 21 and 22 show the move to the east and the move to the west, respectively. By repeating one of the two moves, R moves to one direction. In the beginning of the two moves, its spine is the ith row an its frontier is the jth column.

Turns on the Walls. Figures 23 and 24 show a turn on the east wall and a turn on the west wall, respectively. The spine changes after a turn on the west wall, while it does not change after a turn on the east wall.

A Turn on the Southwest Corner. When the spine of R reaches the first row and it comes back to the west wall, it turns the track by $\pi/2$ as shown in Fig. 25. Note that the cells of the 0th row have been visited by the modules under the spine when R moves from the east wall to the west wall. The final state of the turn is S_5^5 and R moves along the 0th column by the moves in Fig. 21. Here, the spine is the first column, and the 0th column is visited by the modules over the spine.

We finally add exceptional movements. Figures 26 and 27 show all states, for which no movement is defined yet. To be more precise, for states $S_1^5, S_2^5, \ldots, S_{10}^5$, almost all states (including walls) are used in the proposed algorithm except S_9^5 and S_{10}^5 with walls. For states $S_{11}^5, \ldots, S_{18}^5$, only six states with walls are used in the proposed algorithm. Hence in the remaining states, R changes its state to one of $S_1^5, S_2^5, \ldots, S_{10}^5$ through at most two steps as shown in Figs. 26 and 27.

The reference point of R visits all cells in each row and its progress is clear from the proposed algorithm. Thus, we have Theorem 2.

5 Conclusion and Future Work

We proposed the exploration problem of a finite 2D square grid by a metamorphic robotic system. We demonstrated the effect of global compass on the necessary and sufficient number of modules to accomplish exploration and presented exploration algorithms that make the metamorphic robotic system visit all cells. One of the most important research directions is to consider other fields, for example, a convex field in the 2D square grid, a finite 3D square grid, torus, graphs, sphere, and generalization to continuous space.

References

1. Angluin, D., Aspnes, J., Diamadi, Z., Fischer, M.J., Peralta, R.: Computation in networks of passively mobile finite-state sensors. Distrib. Comput. **18**(4), 235–253 (2006)
2. Chen, F., Yamauchi, Y., Kijima, S., Yamashita, M.: Locomotion of metamorphic robotic systems based on local information (extended abstract), In: Proceedings of SRDS Workshops 2014, pp. 40–45 (2014)
3. Das, S., Flocchini, P., Santoro, N., Yamashita, M.: Forming sequences of geometric patterns with oblivious mobile robots. Distrib. Comput. **28**(2), 131–145 (2015)
4. Das, S., Flocchini, P., Kutten, S., Nayak, A., Santoro, N.: Map construction of unknown graphs by multiple agents. Theor. Comput. Sci. **385**(1–3), 34–48 (2007)
5. Derakhshandeh, Z., Gmyr, R., Richa, A.W., Scheideler, C., Strothmann, T.: Universal coating for programmable matter. Theor. Comput. Sci. **671**, 56–68 (2017)
6. Derakhshandeh, Z., Gmyr, R., Richa, A.W., Scheideler, C., Strothmann, T.: Universal shape formation for programmable matter. In: Proceedings of SPAA 2016, pp. 289–299 (2016)
7. Devismes, S., Lamani, A., Petit, F., Raymond, P., Tixeuil, S.: Optimal grid exploration by asynchronous oblivious robots. In: Richa, A.W., Scheideler, C. (eds.) SSS 2012. LNCS, vol. 7596, pp. 64–76. Springer, Heidelberg (2012). https://doi.org/10.1007/978-3-642-33536-5_7
8. Di Luna, G.A., Flocchini, P., Santoro, N., Viglietta, G.: TuringMobile: a turing machine of oblivious mobile robots with limited visibility and its applications. In: Proceedings of DISC 2018 (to appear)
9. Di Luna, G.A., Flocchini, P., Santoro, N., Viglietta, G., Yamauchi, Y.: Shape formation by programmable particles. In: Proceedings of OPODIS 2017, pp. 31:1–31:16 (2017)
10. Dumitrescu, A., Suzuki, I., Yamashita, M.: Motion planning for metamorphic systems: feasibility, decidability, and distributed reconfiguration. IEEE Trans. Robots Autom. **20**(3), 409–418 (2004)
11. Dumitrescu, A., Suzuki, I., Yamashita, M.: Formation for fast locomotion of metamorphic robotic systems. Int. J. Robot. Res. **23**(6), 583–593 (2004)
12. Emek, Y., Langner, T., Stolz, D., Uitto, J., Wattenhofer, R.: How many ants does it take to find the food? Theor. Comput. Sci. **608**, 255–267 (2015)
13. Flocchini, P., Ilcinkas, D., Pelc, A., Santoro, N.: Computing without communicating: ring exploration by asynchronous oblivious robots. Algorithmica **65**(3), 562–583 (2013)
14. Fujinaga, N., Yamauchi, Y., Ono, H., Kijima, S., Yamashita, M.: Pattern formation by oblivious asynchronous mobile robots. SIAM J. Comput. **44**(3), 740–785 (2015)

15. Michail, O., Spirakis, P.G.: Connectivity preserving network transformers. Theor. Comput. Sci. **671**, 36–55 (2017)
16. Michail, O., Skretas, G., Spirakis, P.G.: On the transformation capability of feasible mechanisms for programmable matter. In: Proceedings of ICALP 2017, pp. 136:1–136:15 (2017)
17. Suzuki, I., Yamashita, M.: Distributed anonymous mobile robots: formation of geometric patterns. SIAM J. Comput. **28**(4), 1347–1363 (1999)
18. Yamashita, M., Suzuki, I.: Characterizing geometric patterns formable by oblivious anonymous mobile robots. Theor. Comput. Sci. **411**(26–28), 2433–2453 (2010)
19. Yamauchi, Y., Uehara, T., Kijima, S., Yamashita, M.: Plane formation by synchronous mobile robots in the three-dimensional euclidean space. J. ACM **64**(3), 16:1–16:43 (2017)
20. Yamauchi, Y., Yamashita, M.: Pattern formation by mobile robots with limited visibility. In: Moscibroda, T., Rescigno, A.A. (eds.) SIROCCO 2013. LNCS, vol. 8179, pp. 201–212. Springer, Cham (2013). https://doi.org/10.1007/978-3-319-03578-9_17
21. Yamauchi, Y., Yamashita, M.: Randomized pattern formation algorithm for asynchronous oblivious mobile robots. In: Proceedings of DISC 2014, pp. 137–151 (2014)

Physical Zero-Knowledge Proof for Makaro

Xavier Bultel[1], Jannik Dreier[2], Jean-Guillaume Dumas[3], Pascal Lafourcade[4],
Daiki Miyahara[5,6], Takaaki Mizuki[5], Atsuki Nagao[7], Tatsuya Sasaki[5],
Kazumasa Shinagawa[6,8(✉)], and Hideaki Sone[5]

[1] University of Rennes 1, IRISA, Rennes, France
[2] Université de Lorraine, CNRS, Inria, LORIA, 54000 Nancy, France
[3] Université Grenoble Alpes, IMAG-LJK, CNRS UMR 5224,
700 avenue centrale, 38058 Grenoble, France
[4] University Clermont Auvergne, LIMOS, CNRS UMR 6158,
Campus des Cézeaux, Aubière, France
[5] Tohoku University, Sendai, Japan
[6] National Institute of Advanced Industrial Science and Technology,
Kōtō, Japan
shinagawakazumasa@gmail.com
[7] Ochanomizu University, Bunkyō, Japan
[8] Tokyo Institute of Technology, Meguro, Japan

Abstract. Makaro is a logic game similar to Sudoku. In Makaro, a grid
has to be filled with numbers such that: given areas contain all the numbers up to the number of cells in the area, no adjacent numbers are
equal and some cells provide restrictions on the largest adjacent number.
We propose a proven secure physical algorithm, only relying on cards,
to realize a zero-knowledge proof of knowledge for Makaro. It allows a
player to show that he knows a solution without revealing it.

Keywords: Zero-knowledge proofs
Card-based secure two-party protocols · Puzzle · Makaro · Privacy

1 Introduction

To maintain safety in malicious environment, implementing cryptographic technologies such as secure multi-party computations and zero-knowledge proofs are
indispensable. While these technologies must be useful, usefulness alone is not
always sufficient for technology diffusion, as Hanaoka pointed out [13]. In other
words, we need to convince not only researchers but also everyone from engineers
to non-experts of the importance of such techniques.

To understand the concept of zero-knowledge proof, games and puzzles can
serve as powerful models of computation. Indeed, in game-theoretic terms, the
P vs NP asks whether an optimal puzzle player can be simulated efficiently by a
Turing machine [15]. The NP class is that of problems for which a given solution

© Springer Nature Switzerland AG 2018
T. Izumi and P. Kuznetsov (Eds.): SSS 2018, LNCS 11201, pp. 111–125, 2018.
https://doi.org/10.1007/978-3-030-03232-6_8

correctness is easy to verify. There, a zero-knowledge proof is such a verification procedure, but which prevents the verifier from gaining any knowledge about the solution other than its correctness. For instance, there exist generic cryptographic zero-knowledge proofs for all problems in NP [10], via a reduction to an NP-Complete problem with a known zero-knowledge proof.

More precisely, a *Zero Knowledge Proof of knowledge (ZKP)* is a secure two-party protocol that allows a prover P to convince a verifier V that he knows a solution s to the instance $\mathcal{I}$ of a problem $\mathcal{P}$, without revealing any information about s. In fact, when both randomization and interaction are allowed, the proofs that can be verified in polynomial time are exactly those proofs that can be generated within polynomial space [36]. More than the mere existence of a cryptographic interactive protocol, it is interesting to obtain *direct* (rather than via a reduction) and *physical* (rather than computer-aided) proofs in order to improve on their understandability. Further, sometimes, an interplay of physical and cryptographic protocols can improve efficiency or practicality due to the reduced cryptographic overhead [33]. With this in mind, finding direct physical proofs for puzzles actually augments the number of constraints that can be very efficiently proven in zero knowledge. For instance, we know how to guarantee the presence of all numbers in some set without revealing their order [12], or how to guarantee that two numbers are distinct without revealing their respective values [2]. In this paper, via providing a complete physical zero-knowledge proof for the Nikoli puzzle Makaro, we will show in particular that it is possible to physically prove that a number is the largest in a list, without revealing any value in the list.

Formally, for a solution s to any instance $\mathcal{I}$ of a problem P, a convincing interactive zero-knowledge protocol between P and V must then satisfy the three following properties[1]:

Completeness: If P knows s, then he is able to convince V.

Extractability[2]**:** If P does not know s, then he is not able to convince V except with some *small* probability. More precisely, we want a negligible probability, *i.e.*, the probability should be a function f of a security parameter λ (for example the number of repetitions of the protocol) such that f is negligible, that is for every polynomial Q, there exists $n_0 > 0$ such that $\forall\, x > n_0, f(x) < 1/Q(x)$.

Zero-Knowledge: V learns *nothing* about s except $\mathcal{I}$, *i.e.* there exists a probabilistic polynomial time algorithm $\mathtt{Sim}(\mathcal{I})$ (called the simulator) such that outputs of the real protocol and outputs of $\mathtt{Sim}(\mathcal{I})$ follow the same probability distribution.

---

[1] Moreover, if $\mathcal{P}$ is NP-complete, then the ZKP should be run in a polynomial time [11]. Otherwise it might be easier to find a solution than proving that a solution is a correct solution, making the proof pointless.

[2] This implies the standard soundness property, which ensures that if there exists no solution of the puzzle, then the prover is not able to convince the verifier regardless of the prover's behavior.

As already mentioned, there exist two kinds of ZKP: *interactive* and *non-interactive*. In an interactive ZKP the prover can exchange messages with verifier in order to convince him, while in the non-interactive case the prover can just create the proof in order to convince the verifier.

ZKPs are usually executed by computers. They are often used in electronic voting to prove that some parties correctly mix some ballots without cheating, or in multi-party computation [4,6,34].

In this paper, we consider *physical ZKPs*, such proofs only rely on physical objects such as cards or envelopes and are executed by humans.

Contributions: In this paper we construct a secure physical ZKP for Makaro. This provides in particular a physical zero-knowledge proof of knowledge of the largest element in a list. Our construction uses only $2k - 1 + n + (k-1)(n+4)$ cards where n is the number of empty cells and k is the maximum room size of the Makaro's grid. The salient feature of our protocol is to use efficient zero knowledge shuffle and shift operations together with a positional encoding in order to obtain an efficient implementation of zero-knowledge proof. Our construction physically proves that a number is the largest in a list, without revealing any value in the list.

As mentioned above, our protocol uses a deck of physical cards, and such *card-based cryptography* has attracted many people from researchers to non-experts, and many *card-based protocols* have been published in top-tier conferences in cryptography such as Crypto, Eurocrypt, and Asiacrypt [5,8,20,22,26]. Thus, card-based cryptography has contributed to increasing the number of people who have strong interest in cryptography and information security. We hope that the protocol in this paper also will motivate potential users to understand and use zero-knowledge proof to attain safety in malicious environment.

Related Work: Secure computation without computers have been widely studied and constructed based on various objects: a deck of cards [8] (including polarizing plates [37], polygon cards [38], and the standard deck of playing cards [23]), a PEZ dispenser [1], tamper-evident seals [28], a dial lock [24], and a 15 puzzle [25], Among them, secure computations with cards, referred to as card-based protocols, especially has been studied recently, due to its simplicity and applicability. Indeed, card-based protocols can be used to compute many boolean functions as shown in [5], later improved in terms of efficiency by [22,27,30,39], or to perform specific computations [14,17,29,32].

Sudoku, introduced under this name in 1986 by the Japanese puzzle company Nikoli, and similar games such as Akari, Takuzu, Ken-Ken or Makaro have gained immense popularity in recent years. Many of them have been proved to be NP-complete [7,19,21], and, in 2007, Gradwohl, Naor, Pinkas, and Rothblum proposed the first physical zero-knowledge proof protocols for Sudoku [12]. A novel protocol for Sudoku using fewer cards and with no soundness error was then proposed [35]. Physical protocols for other games, such as Hanjie, Akari, Kakuro, KenKen and Takuzu have then extended the physically verifiable set of functions [2,3].

Outline: We first present the rules of the game, Makaro, in Sect. 2. We construct our zero-knowledge proof in Sect. 3. We start with some notations in Subsect. 3.1, then we describe the shuffling and shifting subroutines in Subsect. 3.2 as well as our construction in Subsect. 3.3. Finally we prove the security of our protocol in Sect. 4. We also propose some optimizations and conclude in the last section.

2   Rules of Makaro

Makaro is a pencil puzzle published in the famous puzzle magazine *Nikoli*. The puzzle instance is a rectangular grid of cells. All cells are colored either white or black. All white cells are divided into *rooms* enclosed by bold lines. Some white cells already contain numbers while most white cells are empty. The former is called a *(white) filled cell* and the latter is called a *(white) empty cell*. Some black cells contain an arrow and they are called *(black) arrow cells*. The goal of the puzzle is to fill in all empty white cells with numbers according to the following rules [31]:

1. *Room condition*: Each room contains all the numbers from 1 up to the number of cells in the room.
2. *Neighbor condition*: A number can not be next (adjacent) to the same number in another room.
3. *Arrow condition*: Every black arrow cell must point at the largest number among the numbers in the adjacent cells of the black cell (possibly the fours cells: right, left, above, and bottom).

In Fig. 1, we give a simple example of a Makaro game, where all black cells are arrow cells and all white cells are empty cells except for one filled cell with three. It is easy to verify that the three constraints are satisfied in the solution on the right part of the figure. We remark that in a solution all white cells are filled with numbers between 1 and k, where k is the maximum size of all the rooms of the grid.

Solving Makaro was shown to be NP-complete via a reduction from 3-SAT in [19].

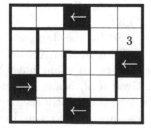

Fig. 1. Example of a Makaro grid and its solution.

3   Zero-Knowledge Proof for Makaro

In this section, we construct our protocol of zero-knowledge proof for Makaro. We first introduce some notations in order to properly give our encoding of the values of a Makaro's solution using some cards. We also describe a few tricks that we use in our construction in order to obtain the extractability and the zero-knowledgeness.

3.1   Notations

Card. We use the following cards:

$$\clubsuit \quad \heartsuit \quad 1 \quad 2 \quad 3 \quad 4 \quad 5 \quad \cdots$$

We call $\clubsuit$ $\heartsuit$ *binary cards* and the others *number cards*. We note that binary cards are not necessary when 1 2 are regarded as binary cards. However, we believe that the use of binary cards makes it easier to understand our protocol. In our construction, binary cards are used to encode the value of a cell, while number cards are used for rearrangement.

All the back sides of the cards are assumed to be indistinguishable. Our protocol also works when all back sides of binary cards are indistinguishable and all back sides of number cards are indistinguishable, but these back sides of the former and the latter are *distinguishable*. For ease of explanation, we assume that all of them are indistinguishable and denote them by $?$.

Encoding. Let k be an integer. For a number $x \in \{1, 2, \cdots, k\}$, we use the following encoding:

$$E_k(x) = \underbrace{\clubsuit \cdots \clubsuit}_{x-1} \heartsuit \underbrace{\clubsuit \cdots \clubsuit}_{k-x}$$

The position of the $\heartsuit$ corresponds to the value of x. Note that in our actual construction, encodings are placed *face-down* in order not to reveal encoded values.

Matrix. In our construction, we often place a sequence of cards as a *matrix*. The following is an example of a 4×6 matrix (of face-down cards).

$$
\begin{array}{c c c c c c}
 & 1 & 2 & 3 & 4 & 5 & 6 \\
1 & ? & ? & ? & ? & ? & ? \\
2 & ? & ? & ? & ? & ? & ? \\
3 & ? & ? & ? & ? & ? & ? \\
4 & ? & ? & ? & ? & ? & ? \\
\end{array}
$$

It contains four rows and six columns. We refer to the leftmost column as the 1st column and to the topmost row as the 1st row.

Pile-Shifting Shuffle. Given an $\ell \times k$ matrix M, a *Pile-shifting shuffle*, which is first used in [38], generates a new "randomly shifted" $\ell \times k$ matrix M': a random number r is uniformly chosen in $\{0, 1, \cdots, k-1\}$; and then, each column of M is cyclically shifted by r. Here, the shifting number r is hidden from all parties. This operation is performed on cards face-down. For example if we consider the following 4×6 matrix with a shift of $r = 2$.

$$
\begin{array}{c|cccccc}
 & 1 & 2 & 3 & 4 & 5 & 6 \\
\hline
1 & ? & ? & ? & ? & ? & ? \\
2 & ? & ? & ? & ? & ? & ? \\
3 & ? & ? & ? & ? & ? & ? \\
4 & ? & ? & ? & ? & ? & ? \\
\end{array}
$$

We obtain the following matrix, where columns have been shifted by to position on the right side.

$$
\begin{array}{c|cccccc}
 & 5 & 6 & 1 & 2 & 3 & 4 \\
\hline
1 & ? & ? & ? & ? & ? & ? \\
2 & ? & ? & ? & ? & ? & ? \\
3 & ? & ? & ? & ? & ? & ? \\
4 & ? & ? & ? & ? & ? & ? \\
\end{array}
$$

In order to implement a pile-shifting shuffle, we first put each columns of cards in an envelope; and then, we cyclically shuffle them by applying a *Hindu cut* to the sequence of envelopes, which is widely used in games of playing cards (see, e.g., [40] for the implementation of random shifting by the Hindu cut).

Pile-Scramble Shuffle. Given an $\ell \times k$ matrix M, a *Pile-scramble shuffle*, which is first used in [17], generates a new "randomly scrambled" $\ell \times k$ matrix M': a random permutation π is uniformly chosen in S_k, the set of all possible permutations of length k; and then, the i-th column of M is moved to the $\pi(i)$-th column of M'. Here, the random permutation π is hidden from all parties. This operation is performed on cards face-down. For example if we consider the following 4×6 matrix with the following permutation $\pi = (13652)$.

$$
\begin{array}{c|cccccc}
 & 1 & 2 & 3 & 4 & 5 & 6 \\
\hline
1 & ? & ? & ? & ? & ? & ? \\
2 & ? & ? & ? & ? & ? & ? \\
3 & ? & ? & ? & ? & ? & ? \\
4 & ? & ? & ? & ? & ? & ? \\
\end{array}
$$

We obtain the following matrix, where columns have been mixed according to π.

$$
\begin{array}{c|cccccc}
 & 2 & 5 & 1 & 4 & 6 & 3 \\
\hline
1 & ? & ? & ? & ? & ? & ? \\
2 & ? & ? & ? & ? & ? & ? \\
3 & ? & ? & ? & ? & ? & ? \\
4 & ? & ? & ? & ? & ? & ? \\
\end{array}
$$

In order to implement a pile-scramble shuffle, similar to the pile-shifting shuffle, we first put each columns of cards in an envelope; and then, we mix them completely randomly.

Miscellaneous Definitions. We define two sequences of cards as follows:

$$\mathbf{e}_k = \boxed{1}\boxed{2}\boxed{3}\boxed{4}\cdots\boxed{k}$$

$$\beta_k = \underbrace{\boxed{\clubsuit}\boxed{\clubsuit}\boxed{\clubsuit}\boxed{\clubsuit}\cdots\boxed{\clubsuit}}_{k}$$

Moreover, we call the former the *identity commitment of degree* k. Again, we note that they are placed face-down in our actual construction. We define "∘" as a concatenation of sequences. For example, $\mathsf{E}_3(2) \circ \beta_3$ is a concatenation of $\mathsf{E}_3(2)$ and β_3 as shown in the following:

$$\mathsf{E}_3(2) \circ \beta_3 = \boxed{\clubsuit}\boxed{\heartsuit}\boxed{\clubsuit}\boxed{\clubsuit}\boxed{\clubsuit}\boxed{\clubsuit}$$

This results in $\mathsf{E}_6(2)$. In general, it holds that $\mathsf{E}_k(x) \circ \beta_\ell = \mathsf{E}_{k+\ell}(x)$.

3.2 Rearrangement Protocol

In this section, we present the Rearrangement Protocol which is invoked by our main construction as a subroutine. This protocol is implicitly used in some previous works of *card-based protocols with permutations* (e.g., Ibaraki et al. [16], Hashimoto et al. [14], and Sasaki et al. [35]).

The input of our Rearrangement Protocol is an $\ell \times k$ matrix whose first row consists of number cards $\boxed{1}\boxed{2}\cdots\boxed{k}$ in an arbitrary order. It outputs an $\ell \times k$ matrix such that the i-th column of the resultant matrix is the column of the input matrix containing the number card $\boxed{i}$ (without revealing the original order). It proceeds as follows:

1. Apply a pile-scramble shuffle to the matrix .
2. Turn over the first row. Suppose that the opened cards are $\boxed{v_1}\boxed{v_2}\ldots\boxed{v_k}$ such that $\{v_1, v_2, \cdots, v_k\} = \{1, \cdots, k\}$.
3. Sort the columns of the matrix so that the v_i-th column of the new matrix is the i-th column of the old matrix.

3.3 Our Construction

In this section, we present our construction of zero-knowledge proof for Makaro. Suppose that a puzzled instance M has n empty cells and the maximum room-size is k. The protocol is played with two players, a *verifier* V and a *prover* P, where only P has a solution of M. It requires $2k - 1$ numbered cards (from 1 up to $2k - 1$) and $n + (k - 1)(n + 4)$ binary cards (n cards of type $\boxed{\heartsuit}$ and $(k - 1)(n + 4)$ cards of type $\boxed{\clubsuit}$). Our protocol proceeds as follows.

Setup. In the setup phase, the prover P places an encoding of the number x on each empty cell, where x is the value of the cell according to the solution. Note that they are placed *face-down* in order to hide the solution. Similarly, the prover P and the verifier V (cooperatively) place k face-down cards on each filled cell according to the value given by the Makaro grid, in the same way.

Verification. The verification proceeds as follows:

1. The prover P convinces the verifier V of the validity of the *room condition* by performing the following for each room: Let k' be the room-size of the room and let $\alpha_1, \cdots, \alpha_{k'}$ be the sequence of cards on each cell in the room. The prover P and the verifier V interact as follows:
   (a) Arrange a $k \times k'$ matrix A such that the i-th *column* is α_i.

   $$A = [\alpha_1^{\mathrm{T}} \; \alpha_2^{\mathrm{T}} \cdots \alpha_{k'}^{\mathrm{T}}]$$

   (b) Append $\mathbf{e}_{k'}$ to the topmost row of A. The following is an example when $k = 4$, $k' = 3$, $\alpha_1 = \mathsf{E}_4(2)$, $\alpha_2 = \mathsf{E}_4(3)$, and $\alpha_3 = \mathsf{E}_4(1)$:

   $$\begin{bmatrix} \mathbf{e}_{k'} \\ A \end{bmatrix} = \begin{bmatrix} 1 & 2 & 3 \\ \alpha_1^{\mathrm{T}} & \alpha_2^{\mathrm{T}} & \alpha_3^{\mathrm{T}} \end{bmatrix} =$$

1	2	3
♣	♣	♡
♡	♣	♣
♣	♡	♣
♣	♣	♣

   Note that all cards are face-down in an actual execution.
   (c) Apply a pile-scramble shuffle to the matrix.
   (d) Turn over all cards except for the topmost row. If the columns do not contain the encodings $\mathsf{E}_k(1), \mathsf{E}_k(2), \cdots, \mathsf{E}_k(k')$, then the verifier outputs 0 and the protocol terminates.
   (e) Turn over all face-up cards so that all cards are face-down; then, apply the Rearrangement Protocol explained in Sect. 3.2; finally, put back $\alpha_1, \cdots, \alpha_{k'}$ to their original cells.
2. The prover P convinces the verifier V of the validity of the *neighbor condition* by performing the following verification for each two adjacent cells that are in different rooms: Let α_1 and α_2 be two sequences on these two adjacent cells. The prover P and the verifier V interact as follows:
   (a) Arrange the following $3 \times k$ matrix:

   $$\begin{bmatrix} \mathbf{e}_k \\ \alpha_1 \\ \alpha_2 \end{bmatrix}$$

   The following is an example when $k = 4$ and $\alpha_1 = \mathsf{E}_4(2)$ and $\alpha_2 = \mathsf{E}_4(1)$.

   $$\begin{bmatrix} \mathbf{e}_k \\ \alpha_1 \\ \alpha_2 \end{bmatrix} = \begin{bmatrix} \mathbf{e}_4 \\ \mathsf{E}_4(2) \\ \mathsf{E}_4(1) \end{bmatrix} =$$

1	2	3	4
♣	♡	♣	♣
♡	♣	♣	♣

   Note that all cards are face-down in an actual execution.

(b) Apply a pile-scramble shuffle to the matrix.

(c) Turn over the second and third rows. If two ♡ s are in distinct columns, it proceeds to Step 2-(d). Otherwise, the verifier outputs 0 and the protocol terminates. The following is an example when the turning result is valid.

?	?	?	?
♡	♣	♣	♣
♣	♣	♡	♣

(d) Turn over all face-up cards so that all cards are face-down; then, apply the Rearrangement Protocol; finally, put back α_1 and α_2 to their original cells.

3. The prover P convinces the verifier V of the validity of the *arrow condition* by performing the following verification for each black arrow cell: Suppose that the black cell has four adjacent white cells and that the arrow of the cell points to the above cell. We note that three-neighbors case and two-neighbors case can be performed in the same way. Let $\alpha_a, \alpha_b, \alpha_r$, and α_l be sequences of k cards placed respectively on the above, bottom, right, and left cells of the black cell. The prover P and the verifier V interact as follows:

(a) Arrange the following $5 \times (2k-1)$ matrix:

$$\begin{bmatrix} \mathbf{e}_{2k-1} \\ \alpha_a \circ \beta_{k-1} \\ \alpha_b \circ \beta_{k-1} \\ \alpha_r \circ \beta_{k-1} \\ \alpha_l \circ \beta_{k-1} \end{bmatrix}$$

The following is an example when $k = 4$ and $\alpha_a = \mathsf{E}_4(4), \alpha_b = \mathsf{E}_4(2), \alpha_r = \mathsf{E}_4(3)$, and $\alpha_l = \mathsf{E}_4(2)$.

$$\begin{bmatrix} \mathbf{e}_{2k-1} \\ \alpha_a \circ \beta_{k-1} \\ \alpha_b \circ \beta_{k-1} \\ \alpha_r \circ \beta_{k-1} \\ \alpha_l \circ \beta_{k-1} \end{bmatrix} = \begin{bmatrix} \mathbf{e}_7 \\ \mathsf{E}_7(4) \\ \mathsf{E}_7(2) \\ \mathsf{E}_7(3) \\ \mathsf{E}_7(2) \end{bmatrix} =$$

1	2	3	4	5	6	7
♣	♣	♣	♡	♣	♣	♣
♣	♡	♣	♣	♣	♣	♣
♣	♣	♡	♣	♣	♣	♣
♣	♡	♣	♣	♣	♣	♣

Note that all cards are face-down in an actual execution.

(b) Apply a pile-shifting shuffle to the matrix.

(c) Turn over the second row. Let $v \in \{1, \cdots, 2k-1\}$ be the position of ♡ . The following is an example when $v = 3$ and other parameters are the same as in the previous example.

?	?	?	?	?	?	?
♣	♣	♡	♣	♣	♣	♣
?	?	?	?	?	?	?
?	?	?	?	?	?	?
?	?	?	?	?	?	?

(d) Turn over $k-1$ columns, $v+1, v+2, \cdots, v+k-1$ columns in a cyclic sense, of the third, fourth, and fifth rows of the matrix. If they are not $3(k-1)$ ♣s, the verifier outputs 0 and the protocol terminates. The following is an example when the parameters are the same as in the previous example. In this example, three columns, $v+1, v+2$, and $v+3$ columns, are turned over.

?	?	?	?	?	?	?
♣	♣	♡	♣	♣	♣	♣
?	?	?	♣	♣	♣	?
?	?	?	♣	♣	♣	?
?	?	?	♣	♣	♣	?

(e) Turn over all face-up cards so that all cards are face-down; then, apply the Rearrangement Protocol; finally, put back $\alpha_a, \alpha_b, \alpha_r$, and α_l to their original cells (unless these cells are not used in the next verification of the Arrow condition).
4. The verifier accepts by outputting 1.

4   Security Proofs for Our Construction

In this section, we prove the completeness, the extractability, and the zero-knowledge property of our construction.

Lemma 1 (Completeness). *If the prover P has a solution for the Makaro puzzle, then P can always convince the verifier V (i.e., V outputs 1).*

Proof. We show that for prover P with a solution, the verifier never outputs 0.

- First, let us consider Step 1. Due to the room condition, for each room of room-size k', all cells in the room have distinct numbers from 1 up to k'. Thus, the $k \times k'$ matrix A in Step 1-(a) contains all encodings $\mathsf{E}_k(1), \cdots, \mathsf{E}_k(k')$. Therefore, the verifier never outputs 0 after the turning over in Step 1-(d).
- Let us move to Step 2. Due to the Neighbor condition, for each pair of cells between different rooms, they have different numbers. Thus, the turning over in Step 2-(c) brings one $(\heartsuit, \clubsuit)$ column, one $(\clubsuit, \heartsuit)$ column, and $k-2$ $(\clubsuit, \clubsuit)$ columns. Therefore, the verifier never outputs 0 in Step 2-(c).
- Let us consider Step 3. Due to the Arrow condition, for each black arrow cell, the arrow points to the largest number in adjacent cells. Let $x_a, x_b, x_r, x_l \in \{1, 2, \cdots, k\}$ be numbers in adjacent cells and suppose that x_a is the largest number pointed by the arrow. Then, the position of $\boxed{\heartsuit}$ of $\mathsf{E}_k(x_a)$ is also the largest number among other encodings $\mathsf{E}_k(x_b), \mathsf{E}_k(x_r)$, and $\mathsf{E}_k(x_l)$. Therefore, the turning over in Step 3-(d) brings $3(k-1)$ ♣ cards which never causes the verifier to output 0.

Therefore, the protocol always proceeds to Step 4 and the verifier outputs 1. □

Lemma 2 (Extractability). *If the prover does not know a solution for the Makaro puzzle, then the verifier V always rejects (i.e., V outputs 0) regardless of the prover P's behavior.*

Proof. If some of encodings are invalid, i.e., do not form the encoding format, then this fact is always exposed in Step 1-(d). Thus, we can assume that all encodings are valid. Because the verifier does not know a solution, at least one condition among three conditions must be violated. The following three cases occur:

- Suppose that room condition is violated for some room. In this case, the turning over in Step 1-(d) does not bring $E_k(1), \cdots, E_k(k')$, which causes the verifier to output 0.
- Suppose that Neighbor condition is violated for some pair of cells. In this case, the turning over in Step 2-(c) brings two $(\heartsuit, \heartsuit)$ in one column, which causes the verifier to output 0.
- Suppose that Arrow condition is violated for some black cell with an arrow. Let $\alpha_a, \alpha_b, \alpha_r$, and α_l be encodings on the adjacent cells of such a black cell such that $\alpha_a = E_k(x_a), \alpha_b = E_k(x_b), \alpha_r = E_k(x_r)$, and $\alpha_l = E_k(x_l)$ for some $x_a, x_b, x_r, x_l \in \{1, 2, \cdots, k\}$. Due to the violation of Arrow condition, one of x_b, x_r, and x_l is larger than x_a while the arrow points to the above cell. In this case, the turning over in Step 3-(d) brings at least one $\boxed{\heartsuit}$, which causes the verifier to output 0.

In any case, the verifier always outputs 0. □

Lemma 3 (Zero-knowledge). *During an execution of our protocol, the verifier V learns nothing about P's solution.*

Proof. In order to prove this, it is sufficient to show that all distributions of opening values are simulated without knowing the prover's solution.

- In Step 1, the "turning over" appears only in Step 1-(d) and 1-(e). The opening in Step 1-(d) brings a set of encodings $E_k(1), \cdots, E_k(k')$, where k' is the room-size. Their order is uniformly distributed among $S_{k'}$ due to the pile-scramble shuffle. Thus, it can be simulated without knowing the solution. The opening in Step 1-(e), specifically the Rearrangement Protocol, brings number cards from 1 up to k'. Their order is uniformly distributed among $S_{k'}$ due to the pile-scramble shuffle. Thus, it can be simulated without knowing the solution.
- In Step 2, there are two steps with a "turning over": Steps 2-(c) and 2-(d). The opening in Step 2-(c) brings one $(\heartsuit, \clubsuit)$ column, one $(\clubsuit, \heartsuit)$ column, and $k - 2$ $(\clubsuit, \clubsuit)$ columns. The position of the former two columns are uniformly distributed due to the pile-scramble shuffle. Thus, it can be simulated without knowing the solution. The opening in Step 2-(d), specifically the Rearrangement Protocol, brings number cards from 1 up to k. Their order is uniformly distributed among S_k due to the pile-scramble shuffle. Thus, it can be simulated without knowing the solution.

- In Step 3, there are three steps containing a "turning over": Steps 3-(c), 3-(d), and 3-(e). The opening in Step 3-(c) brings one $\boxed{\heartsuit}$ and $k-1$ $\boxed{\clubsuit}$ cards. The position of $\boxed{\heartsuit}$ is uniformly distributed among $\{1, 2, \cdots, 2k-1\}$ due to the pile-shifting shuffle. Thus, it can be simulated without knowing the solution. The opening in Step 3-(d) brings $3(k-1)$ $\boxed{\clubsuit}$ cards. Thus, it can be trivially simulated without knowing the solution. The opening in Step 3-(e), specifically the Rearrangement Protocol, brings number cards from 1 up to $2k-1$. Their order is uniformly distributed among S_{2k-1} due to the pile-scramble shuffle. Thus, it can be simulated without knowing the solution.

Therefore, the verifier V learns nothing about the solution.   □

5   Conclusion

In this paper we construct the first physical zero-knowledge proof for Makaro. Our construction uses a special encoding of the values of a Makaro solution. This allows us to design a physical zero-knowledge proof that uses a reasonable number of cards and hence, our proposed protocol is efficient. This number can even be further reduced via the following two optimizations:

Optimization 1. For each room, use encodings $E_{k'}(x)$ for the room-size k' instead of $E_k(x)$, where k is the maximum room-size. When encodings in different rooms appear in Steps 1 and 2, append additional $\boxed{\clubsuit}$ cards. This idea reduces the number of cards.

Optimization 2. Do not place cards in the *initially (white) filled* cells although other cards on empty cells are still placed. Instead, make an encoding of filled cells only when it is needed. Indeed those numbers are part of the input problem and are thus known to the verifier, so no secrecy is required there. This idea also reduces the overall number of cards.

We finally note that our technique especially for the Arrow condition can also be reused for other interesting problems including zero-knowledge proofs for other games or real-world problems related to auctions, stock markets, and so on. We leave it as an open problem to find such interesting applications.

Acknowledgments. This work was supported in part by JSPS KAKENHI Grant Numbers 17J01169 and 17K00001. It was conducted with the support of the FEDER program of 2014-2020, the region council of Auvergne-Rhône-Alpes, the Indo-French Centre for the Promotion of Advanced Research (IFCPAR) and the Center Franco-Indien Pour La Promotion De La Recherche Avancée (CEFIPRA) through the project DST/CNRS 2015-03 under DST-INRIA-CNRS Targeted Programme.

References

1. Balogh, J., Csirik, J.A., Ishai, Y., Kushilevitz, E.: Private computation using a PEZ dispenser. Theor. Comput. Sci. **306**(1–3), 69–84 (2003)
2. Bultel, X., Dreier, J., Dumas, J.-G., Lafourcade, P.: Physical zero-knowledge proofs for Akari, Takuzu, Kakuro and KenKen. In: Demaine, E.D., Grandoni, F. (eds.) 8th International Conference on Fun with Algorithms, FUN 2016. LIPIcs, La Maddalena, Italy, 8–10 June 2016, vol. 49, pp. 8:1–8:20 (2016)
3. Chien, Y.-F., Hon, W.-K.: Cryptographic and physical zero-knowledge proof: from Sudoku to Nonogram. In: Boldi, P., Gargano, L. (eds.) FUN 2010. LNCS, vol. 6099, pp. 102–112. Springer, Heidelberg (2010). https://doi.org/10.1007/978-3-642-13122-6_12
4. Cramer, R., Damgård, I., Nielsen, J.B.: Multiparty computation from threshold homomorphic encryption. In: Pfitzmann, B. (ed.) EUROCRYPT 2001. LNCS, vol. 2045, pp. 280–300. Springer, Heidelberg (2001). https://doi.org/10.1007/3-540-44987-6_18
5. Crépeau, C., Kilian, J.: Discreet solitary games. In: Stinson, D.R. (ed.) CRYPTO 1993. LNCS, vol. 773, pp. 319–330. Springer, Heidelberg (1994). https://doi.org/10.1007/3-540-48329-2_27
6. Damgård, I., Faust, S., Hazay, C.: Secure two-party computation with low communication. In: Cramer, R. (ed.) TCC 2012. LNCS, vol. 7194, pp. 54–74. Springer, Heidelberg (2012). https://doi.org/10.1007/978-3-642-28914-9_4
7. Demaine, E.D.: Playing games with algorithms: algorithmic combinatorial game theory. In: Sgall, J., Pultr, A., Kolman, P. (eds.) MFCS 2001. LNCS, vol. 2136, pp. 18–33. Springer, Heidelberg (2001). https://doi.org/10.1007/3-540-44683-4_3
8. Boer, B.: More efficient match-making and satisfiability *the five card trick*. In: Quisquater, J.-J., Vandewalle, J. (eds.) EUROCRYPT 1989. LNCS, vol. 434, pp. 208–217. Springer, Heidelberg (1990). https://doi.org/10.1007/3-540-46885-4_23
9. Foresti, S., Persiano, G. (eds.): Cryptology and Network Security - 15th International Conference, CANS 2016, Milan, Italy, 14–16 November 2016, Proceedings. LNCS, vol. 10052. Springer, Cham (2016). https://doi.org/10.1007/978-3-319-48965-0
10. Goldreich, O., Micali, S., Wigderson, A.: Proofs that yield nothing but their validity and a methodology of cryptographic protocol design. In: 27th Annual Symposium on Foundations of Computer Science (SFCS 1986), pp. 174–187, October 1986
11. Goldreich, O., Micali, S., Wigderson, A.: How to prove all NP statements in zero-knowledge and a methodology of cryptographic protocol design (extended abstract). In: Odlyzko, A.M. (ed.) CRYPTO 1986. LNCS, vol. 263, pp. 171–185. Springer, Heidelberg (1987). https://doi.org/10.1007/3-540-47721-7_11
12. Gradwohl, R., Naor, M., Pinkas, B., Rothblum, G.N.: Cryptographic and physical zero-knowledge proof systems for solutions of Sudoku puzzles. In: Crescenzi, P., Prencipe, G., Pucci, G. (eds.) FUN 2007. LNCS, vol. 4475, pp. 166–182. Springer, Heidelberg (2007). https://doi.org/10.1007/978-3-540-72914-3_16
13. Hanaoka, G.: Towards user-friendly cryptography. In: Phan, R.C.-W., Yung, M. (eds.) Mycrypt 2016. LNCS, vol. 10311, pp. 481–484. Springer, Cham (2017). https://doi.org/10.1007/978-3-319-61273-7_24
14. Hashimoto, Y., Shinagawa, K., Nuida, K., Inamura, M., Hanaoka, G.: Secure grouping protocol using a deck of cards. In: Shikata, J. (ed.) ICITS 2017. LNCS, vol. 10681, pp. 135–152. Springer, Cham (2017). https://doi.org/10.1007/978-3-319-72089-0_8

15. Hearn, R.A., Demaine, E.D.: Games, Puzzles, and Computation. A. K. Peters Ltd., Natick (2009)
16. Ibaraki, T., Manabe, Y.: A more efficient card-based protocol for generating a random permutation without fixed points. In: 2016 Third International Conference on Mathematics and Computers in Sciences and in Industry (MCSI), pp. 252–257, August 2016
17. Ishikawa, R., Chida, E., Mizuki, T.: Efficient card-based protocols for generating a hidden random permutation without fixed points. In: Calude, C.S., Dinneen, M.J. (eds.) UCNC 2015. LNCS, vol. 9252, pp. 215–226. Springer, Cham (2015). https://doi.org/10.1007/978-3-319-21819-9_16
18. Ito, H., Leonardi, S., Pagli, L., Prencipe, G. (eds.) 9th International Conference on Fun with Algorithms, FUN 2018. LIPIcs, La Maddalena, Italy, vol. 100. Schloss Dagstuhl - Leibniz-Zentrum fuer Informatik, June 2018
19. Iwamoto, C., Haruishi, M., Ibusuki, T.: Herugolf and Makaro are NP-complete. In: Ito et al. [18], pp. 24:1–24:11
20. Kastner, J., et al.: The minimum number of cards in practical card-based protocols. In: Takagi, T., Peyrin, T. (eds.) ASIACRYPT 2017. LNCS, vol. 10626, pp. 126–155. Springer, Cham (2017). https://doi.org/10.1007/978-3-319-70700-6_5
21. Kendall, G., Parkes, A.J., Spoerer, K.: A survey of NP-complete puzzles. ICGA J. 31(1), 13–34 (2008)
22. Koch, A., Walzer, S., Härtel, K.: Card-based cryptographic protocols using a minimal number of cards. In: Iwata, T., Cheon, J.H. (eds.) ASIACRYPT 2015. LNCS, vol. 9452, pp. 783–807. Springer, Heidelberg (2015). https://doi.org/10.1007/978-3-662-48797-6_32
23. Mizuki, T.: Efficient and secure multiparty computations using a standard deck of playing cards. In: Foresti and Persiano [9], pp. 484–499
24. Mizuki, T., Kugimoto, Y., Sone, H.: Secure multiparty computations using a dial lock. In: Cai, J.-Y., Cooper, S.B., Zhu, H. (eds.) TAMC 2007. LNCS, vol. 4484, pp. 499–510. Springer, Heidelberg (2007). https://doi.org/10.1007/978-3-540-72504-6_45
25. Mizuki, T., Kugimoto, Y., Sone, H.: Secure multiparty computations using the 15 puzzle. In: Dress, A., Xu, Y., Zhu, B. (eds.) COCOA 2007. LNCS, vol. 4616, pp. 255–266. Springer, Heidelberg (2007). https://doi.org/10.1007/978-3-540-73556-4_28
26. Mizuki, T., Kumamoto, M., Sone, H.: The five-card trick can be done with four cards. In: Wang, X., Sako, K. (eds.) ASIACRYPT 2012. LNCS, vol. 7658, pp. 598–606. Springer, Heidelberg (2012). https://doi.org/10.1007/978-3-642-34961-4_36
27. Mizuki, T., Sone, H.: Six-card secure AND and four-card secure XOR. In: Deng, X., Hopcroft, J.E., Xue, J. (eds.) FAW 2009. LNCS, vol. 5598, pp. 358–369. Springer, Heidelberg (2009). https://doi.org/10.1007/978-3-642-02270-8_36
28. Moran, T., Naor, M.: Basing cryptographic protocols on tamper-evident seals. In: Caires, L., Italiano, G.F., Monteiro, L., Palamidessi, C., Yung, M. (eds.) ICALP 2005. LNCS, vol. 3580, pp. 285–297. Springer, Heidelberg (2005). https://doi.org/10.1007/11523468_24
29. Nakai, T., Tokushige, Y., Misawa, Y., Iwamoto, M., Ohta, K.: Efficient card-based cryptographic protocols for millionaires' problem utilizing private permutations. In: Foresti and Persiano [9], pp. 500–517
30. Niemi, V., Renvall, A.: Secure multiparty computations without computers. Theor. Comput. Sci. 191(1), 173–183 (1998)
31. Nikoli: Makaro. https://www.nikoli.co.jp/en/puzzles/makaro.html

32. Nishida, T., Mizuki, T., Sone, H.: Securely computing the three-input majority function with eight cards. In: Dediu, A.-H., Martín-Vide, C., Truthe, B., Vega-Rodríguez, M.A. (eds.) TPNC 2013. LNCS, vol. 8273, pp. 193–204. Springer, Heidelberg (2013). https://doi.org/10.1007/978-3-642-45008-2_16

33. Ramzy, I., Arora, A.: Using zero knowledge to share a little knowledge: bootstrapping trust in device networks. In: Défago, X., Petit, F., Villain, V. (eds.) SSS 2011. LNCS, vol. 6976, pp. 371–385. Springer, Heidelberg (2011). https://doi.org/10.1007/978-3-642-24550-3_28

34. Romero-Tris, C., Castellà-Roca, J., Viejo, A.: Multi-party private web search with untrusted partners. In: Rajarajan, M., Piper, F., Wang, H., Kesidis, G. (eds.) SecureComm 2011. LNICST, vol. 96, pp. 261–280. Springer, Heidelberg (2012). https://doi.org/10.1007/978-3-642-31909-9_15

35. Sasaki, T., Mizuki, T., Sone, H.: Card-based zero-knowledge proof for Sudoku. In: Ito et al. [18], pp. 29:1–29:10

36. Shamir, A.: IP = PSPACE. J. ACM 39(4), 869–877 (1992)

37. Shinagawa, K., et al.: Secure computation protocols using polarizing cards. IEICE Trans. 99-A(6), 1122–1131 (2016)

38. Shinagawa, K., et al.: Card-based protocols using regular polygon cards. IEICE Trans. 100-A(9), 1900–1909 (2017)

39. Stiglic, A.: Computations with a deck of cards. Theor. Comput. Sci. 259(1), 671–678 (2001)

40. Ueda, I., Nishimura, A., Hayashi, Y., Mizuki, T., Sone, H.: How to implement a random bisection cut. In: Martín-Vide, C., Mizuki, T., Vega-Rodríguez, M.A. (eds.) TPNC 2016. LNCS, vol. 10071, pp. 58–69. Springer, Cham (2016). https://doi.org/10.1007/978-3-319-49001-4_5

Searching with Increasing Speeds

Leszek Gąsieniec[1(✉)], Shuji Kijima[2,3], and Jie Min[1]

[1] Department of Computer Science, University of Liverpool, Liverpool, UK
lechu@liverpool.ac.uk
[2] Department of Informatics, Kyushu University, Fukuoka, Japan
[3] JST PRESTO, Tokyo, Japan

Abstract. In the classical search problem on the line or in higher dimension one is asked to find the shortest (and often the fastest) route to be adopted by a robot R from the starting point s towards the target point t located at unknown location and distance D. It is usually assumed that robot R moves with a fixed unit speed 1. It is well known that one can adopt a "zig-zag" strategy based on the exponential expansion, which allows to reach the target located on the line in time $\leq 9D$, and this bound is tight. The problem was also studied in two dimensions where the competitive factor is known to be $O(D)$.

In this paper we study an alteration of the search problem in which robot R starts moving with the initial speed 1. However, during search it can encounter a point or a sequence of points enabling faster and faster movement. The main goal is to adopt the route which allows R to reach the target t as quickly as possible. We study two variants of the considered search problem: (1) with the *global knowledge* and (2) with the *local knowledge*. In variant (1) robot R knows *a priori* the location of all intermediate points as well as their expulsion speeds. In this variant we study the complexity of computing optimal search trajectories. In variant (2) the relevant information about points in P is acquired by R gradually, i.e., while moving along the adopted trajectory. Here the focus is on the competitive factor of the solution, i.e., the ratio between the solutions computed in variants (2) and (1). We also consider two types of search spaces with points distributed on the line and subsequently with points distributed in two-dimensional space.

Keywords: Search problem · Line · 2d space · Increasing speeds

1 Introduction

Search problems refer to frequently considered combinatorial (structural or algorithmic) problems within and across multiple fields including operations research, computing, mathematics and others. The search problem in the form studied in

This work was initiated while the first author visited Kyushu University. The work is partly supported by JST PRESTO Grant Number JPMJPR16E4 and Networks Sciences and Technologies (NeST) EEECS School initiative, University of Liverpool.

T. Izumi and P. Kuznetsov (Eds.): SSS 2018, LNCS 11201, pp. 126–138, 2018.
https://doi.org/10.1007/978-3-030-03232-6_9

this paper was originally posed more than a half-century ago by Bellman [6] who asked: *"A hiker is lost in a forest which size is not known to her. What is the best path to adopt to escape the forest?"*

In more general terms, search problems deal with either single or multiple searchers looking for a hidden object referred to as *target*, with the ultimate goal of minimising the time required to accomplish the task. Numerous variants of the problem have been considered reflecting on different search spaces (e.g., a geometric setting vs. a graph), whether the target is fixed or mobile, whether the search space is stable, or if the target is a point or a collection of points, a curve or a closed non-zero volume region. Another separation line refers to deterministic versus randomized search strategies, and whether the searchers have access to extra tools supporting navigation, see [2–4, 7, 8, 14, 16, 21, 22].

The search on the line has been analysed in detail by Baeza-Yates et al. in [2] under the name of the *cow-path problem*. This seminal work prompted further work on on different variants of the search problem including extensions [3, 4, 14, 17, 18, 22, 24]. In addition to the line, Baeza-Yates et al. [2, 3] studied the cow-path problem on co-centred w infinite rays, and proposed a deterministic algorithm with the name *linear spiral search*. The case with $w = 1$ is trivial, and for $w = 2$ (the case with infinite line) the algorithm always finds the target in time at most $9D$, where D is the time needed to move from the starting point s to the target t. They also provided the lower bound argument showing optimality of their solution up to lower order terms. In the same work, the authors considered also a system of rays with $w > 2$ showing an optimal (up to lower order terms) result of $\left(1 + 2\frac{w^w}{(w-1)^{w-1}}\right) \cdot D$ time bound to find the target using a deterministic search strategy.

In [4] Baeza-Yates and Schott examined also other variants of the cow-path problem. They observed that if D is known in advance, the search on the line requires time $3D$ in the worst case. They also studied scenarios with two or more robots having uniform speeds. They show that if robots are able to communicate at arbitrary distance, the total distance $2D$ must be travelled to find the destination, and $4D$ if the two robots must reach the destination. Baeza-Yates and Schott showed also that the total distance travelled when no communication is present, and both robots must reach the target is also $9D$, the same time it would take a single robot. A similar study, however with an arbitrary number of robots can be found in [9] where the authors study also the case with different speeds. More tight analysis for two robots with different speeds was subsequently published in [5]. The case with multiple speeds was also studied in the context of patrolling linear environments first by Czyzowicz *et al.* in [11] and in the follow up work of Kawamura and Kobayashi in [19]. Another interesting study on robots with different speeds can be found in [10] where the authors distinguish between moving and searching speeds.

In terms of probabilistic approach Kao et al. [18] examined the first randomized algorithm for the cow-path problem and, for the case of $w = 2$ rays, he obtained an optimal randomized $4.59112 \cdot D$ bound for the search time. They also provided a bound for $w > 2$ paths, where they conjecture their this approach to be an optimal randomized strategy.

In this paper we consider the search problem in which the robot can increase its speed by visiting specific points in space. This work apart from having an intrinsic combinatorial value can be also seen as a simplification of the *gravity assist* concept [23] used in space exploration. Also there is some parallel to sharing schemes with different vehicle types, e.g., city bikes combined with electric cars and others.

1.1   The Model and the Search Problem

In this work we consider search by a single robot R either on the infinite line or in two-dimensional (Euclidean) space. The robot has a zero-visibility radius, moves freely and starts the exploration with the uniform speed 1. The search space is populated by n points from set $P = \{p_1, \ldots, p_n\}$, with the starting point $s = p_\sigma$ and the target $t = p_\tau$, for some integer $1 \leq \sigma \neq \tau \leq n$. Similarly to the past work in this area we assume that the points in P have integer coordinates. This is to avoid dealing with infinitesimal moves and the assumption about non-zero visibility radius of R. Each point $p_i \in P$ has the associated *expulsion speed* v_i. More precisely, robot R always leaves p_i with the speed v_i if the speed it entered p_i was smaller or equal. Please note that R can only go faster, i.e., visiting a node with a smaller expulsion speed does not affect the current speed of R. For the completeness we also assume that $v_\sigma = 1$ and $v_\tau = +\infty$.

The *main task* for robot R is to compute (and subsequently adopt) the fastest route from the starting point s to the target/destination point t taking advantage of the increasing expulsion speeds of points in P visited on the way to t. We study two variants of the considered search problem: (1) with the *global knowledge* and (2) with the *local knowledge*. In variant (1) robot R knows a priori the location of all points in P as well as their expulsion speeds. In this variant we study the complexity of computing optimal search trajectories. In variant (2) the relevant information about points in P is acquired by R gradually, i.e., while moving along the adopted trajectory. Here the focus is on the competitive ratio of the solution, i.e., the ratio between the solution computed in variant (2) and the optimal solution from (1). We also consider two types of search spaces with points distributed on the line and subsequently with points distributed in two-dimensional space.

1.2   Our Contribution

The following results constitute the contribution of this paper.

On the Line. In *variant (1)* with full knowledge we show that the line of points can be processed in time $O(n)$ to find the fastest route from any point in P to t. The algorithm is based on the known solution for the range queries. In fact after $O(n)$–time preprocessing one can query any point on the line for the shortest route to t in time $O(\log n)$. In *variant (2)* with local knowledge we show that the trajectory based on the classical "zig-zag" strategy always admits a competitive factor 9. I.e., consistently with the classical version of the search problem where it is known that one cannot reduce this constant in the worst case.

In 2D Space. In *variant (1)* we observe that one can process P with Dijkstra's algorithm in time $O(n^2)$ to compute the fastest route from any point in P to target t. After this preprocessing one can query any point on the plane for the shortest route to t in time $Q(n)$, where $Q(n) = \text{polylog}(n)$ refers to query time for the nearest point in additively weighted Voronoi diagrams of size n. Using this result we show that if there are at most k different expulsion speeds one can process the points in P in time $O(k \cdot n \cdot \text{polylog}(n))$. In *variant (2)* we show that the spiral strategy admits the asymptotically optimal competitive ratio $O(D)$.

2 Search on the Line

In this section we assume that the moves of robot R are limited to an infinite (integer) line $\mathcal{L}$ which contains all points in P offering different expulsion speeds. In Sect. 2.1 we consider the search problem in the *full-knowledge* model where we show how to find the fastest route to from the starting point s to the target t in the optimal time $O(n)$. We also comment on querying arbitrary points on the line. Later in Sect. 2.2 we show that the classical zig-zag strategy [3] provides 9-competitive solution also when R is allowed to increase its speed throughout the searching process.

2.1 Variant (1) - with Full Knowledge

Recall that in this variant robot R is fully aware of its own starting position s, the content of P including offered speeds and the location of target t.

Example. In order to build some intuition we first consider a simple informal example, see Fig. 1, where $s = p_4$ is the starting point with the initial speed $v_4 = 1$, each point p_i offers the relevant expulsion speed v_i, and the arcs indicate the consecutive steps (during which R moves with strictly increasing expulsion speeds) on the optimal (fastest) path towards target $t = p_8$.

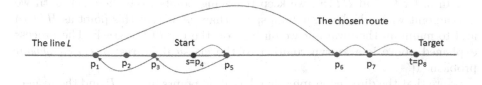

The chosen route

The line $\mathcal{L}$ Start   Target

p_1 p_2 p_3 $s=p_4$ p_5 p_6 p_7 $t=p_8$

The chosen speeds

$$1 = v_4 < v_5 \ll v_3 \ll v_1 < v_6 < v_7 < v_8 = +\infty$$

Fig. 1. Solution example

In the example above the robot must have a very good reason to turn back (as it is initially moving towards the target) after visiting p_5. In other words it must be more beneficial for the robot to visit (and to adopt the expulsion speeds of) points p_3 and p_1, rather than going directly from p_5 to p_6. This can happen when points p_1, p_3, and p_5 are relatively close to each other and $v_5 \ll v_3 \ll v_1$. And the total time needed to move with speed v_5 from p_5 to p_3, then with speed v_3 from p_3 to p_1, and finally with speed v_1 towards p_6 is smaller than going directly from p_5 to p_6 with speed v_5. The adopted route has to be faster also from a more direct route $p_5 \rightarrow p_3 \rightarrow p_6$. This example indicates also that robot R changes the direction on its walk only in points with higher expulsion speeds.

Motivated by this example one can summarise the properties of the optimal (fastest) walk to be adopted by the robot as follows.

1. While visiting point p_i robot R adopts the expulsion speed v_i iff v_i is higher than the current speed of R. This reflects the assumption that at any time R moves with the highest possible speed encountered so far.
2. Robot R changes the direction on its walk only at points with higher speeds. I.e., changing direction without increasing speed always results in suboptimal solution as one could construct a faster route by turning a bit earlier.
3. It is enough to compute for each point $p_i \in P$ the closest to the left and to the right points $HL(p_i)$ and $HR(p_i)$ with higher expulsion speeds than v_i. According to properties 1 and 2 these are the only points in which the speed and possibly the direction of the walk change.

Let a *walk* be a direct move from $p_i \in P$ to $p_j \in P$ with the expulsion speed v_i (walks are denoted by arcs in the example). Thanks to property 3 one can conclude that in search for the optimal solution (from any point in P to t) instead of dealing with a quadratic number of walks, it is enough to consider at most $2n$ walks connecting any $p_i \in P$ with the corresponding $HL(p_i)$ and $HR(p_i)$.

Nearest Larger Neighbour. Note that all these walks can be determined in time $O(n)$ by swiping (with the help of a single stack) the line of points once in each direction. During each swipe, e.g., from left to right, while processing each point p_i we assume inductively that on the top of the stack we have the expulsion speeds of p_{i-1}, and below of $HL(p_{i-1})$, and below of $HL(HL(p_{i-1}))$, etc. In order to find $HL(p_i)$ we keep removing points from the stack until we find a point with a higher expulsion speed than v_i. We set this point as $HL(p_i)$ and to maintain the invariant we push p_i on the top of the stack. The process explained above is a known solution to the classical *nearest larger neighbour* problem [1].

Note that the directed graph solely based on points in $p_i \in P$ and the respective walks p_i to $HL(p_i)$ and to $HL(p_i)$ is acyclic, I.e., the walks always lead towards higher speeds. Thus the points in P can be sorted topologically (starting from the target t) in time $O(n)$. Finally, one can visit these points one by one in the computed order to determine the fastest route between any point $p_i \in P$ and target t. Such route is computed instantly on the basis of the fastest routes already computed for $HL(p_i)$ and $HR(p_i)$ as the fastest route from p_i to t has to visit first one of these points. The following theorem holds.

Theorem 1. *For the collection P of n points on the line one can compute the fastest route between any point p_i and target t in the optimal time $O(n)$.*

Having computed optimal routes towards t for all points in P one can also compute for any point $p \in \mathcal{L}$ the closest point (to the left and to the right) in P by simple binary search in time $O(\log n)$. This allows to compute the fastest route from any point p to target t in time $O(\log n)$.

2.2   Variant (2) - with Local Knowledge

Recall that in this case, the robot only knows its initial speed 1 and is not aware of neither the location of other points nor the expulsion speeds available in them. In what follows we show that the classical "zig-zag" strategy $Z_{\mathcal{L}}$ can be adopted here with the same 9-competitive guarantee as in the cow-path problem.

Given an instance I of the considered search problem. Let the route $S \equiv (s = p_\sigma \xrightarrow{v_\sigma = 1} p_{i_2} \xrightarrow{v_{i_2}} \ldots p_{i_l} \xrightarrow{v_{i_l}} t = p_\tau)$ be the optimal solution of I. The points chosen to this solution are called *critical points*. This solution is based on l potentially overlapping segments on the line L. The first segment defined by critical points p_σ, p_{i_2} is traversed with the speed $v_\sigma = 1$. The next $l - 2$ segments based on points $p_{i_j}, p_{i_{j+1}}$ are traversed with the speeds v_{i_j} respectively, for all $j = 2, \ldots, l - 1$. The last segment based on points p_{i_l}, p_τ is traversed with the speed v_{i_l}. Let d_j be the total distance traversed from p_σ to p_{i_j}, for all $j = 2, \ldots, l$, and d_{l+1} referring to the total distance traversed on the way to target $t = p_\tau$. In addition let D_j be the absolute (Euclidean) distance between p_σ and all critical points included in the optimal solution S. Note that the lengths of l segments defined above can be expressed as $d_j - d_{j-1}$, for all $j = 2, \ldots, l$, where $d_1 = 0$. And finally, the respective traversal times on the considered segments are: $\frac{d_2}{v_\sigma}$ on segment (p_σ, p_{i_2}), $\frac{d_{j+1} - d_j}{v_{i_j}}$ on segments $(p_{i_j}, p_{i_{j+1}})$, for all $j = 2, \ldots, l$, including $\frac{d_{l+1} - d_l}{v_{i_l}}$ on segment (p_{i_l}, p_τ).

Lemma 1. *Given a traversal path $U = (p_{i_1} \xrightarrow{v_{i_1}} p_{i_2} \xrightarrow{v_{i_2}} \ldots \xrightarrow{v_{i_{k-1}}} p_{i_k})$ with strictly increasing expulsion speeds and the traversal time $T(U)$. And another traversal path with the same points $U' = (p_{i_1} \xrightarrow{v'_{i_1}} p_{i_2} \xrightarrow{v'_{i_2}} \ldots \xrightarrow{v'_{i_{k-1}}} p_{i_k})$ with the traversal time $T(U')$, where $v_{i_j} \le v'_{i_j}$, for all $j = 1, \ldots, k$. Then $T(U') \le T(U)$.*

Proof. The thesis of the lemma follows directly from the fact that all segments are shared by U and U', and each of them is traversed not slower in U'.

Lemma 2. *If the order of critical points used in the optimal solution $S \equiv (s = p_\sigma \xrightarrow{v_\sigma = 1} p_{i_2} \xrightarrow{v_{i_2}} \ldots p_{i_l} \xrightarrow{v_{i_l}} t = p_\tau)$ corresponds to the first occurrences of these points on the zigzag path $Z_{\mathcal{L}}$, the traversal time admitted by $Z_{\mathcal{L}}$ is 9-competitive.*

Proof. Let P_Z be the actual path that robot R adopted on the way to target t, i.e., the relevant prefix of $Z_\mathcal{L}$. Also, let d'_{i_j} be the length of prefix of P_Z until the first encounter of p_{i_j} and v'_{i_j} be the expulsion speed associated with the segment of P_Z connecting p_{i_j} and $p_{i_{j+1}}$. This segment is of length $d'_{i_{j+1}} - d'_{i_j}$. Thus the total traversal time to target t along consecutive segments of $Z_\mathcal{L}$ is

$$T(P_Z) = \sum_{j=1}^{l} \frac{d'_{i_{j+1}} - d'_{i_j}}{v'_{i_j}}$$

Note that the speed used by robot R between consecutive critical points can be the same as in the optimal solution, or it may be faster as due to taking wider swings (on $Z_\mathcal{L}$) robot R can pick some faster expulsion speeds earlier at non-critical points visited on the way. Thus the (average) speeds adopted between critical points satisfy $v_{i_j} \leq v'_{i_j}$. And, the competitive ratio of the "zig-zag" strategy can be expressed as:

$$r = \frac{T(P_Z)}{T(S)} = \frac{\sum_{j=1}^{l} \frac{d'_{i_{j+1}} - d'_{i_j}}{v'_{i_j}}}{\sum_{j=1}^{l} \frac{d_{i_{j+1}} - d_{i_j}}{v_{i_j}}} \leq \frac{\sum_{j=1}^{l} \frac{d'_{i_{j+1}} - d'_{i_j}}{v_{i_j}}}{\sum_{j=1}^{l} \frac{d_{i_{j+1}} - d_{i_j}}{v_{i_j}}}$$

$$= \frac{\frac{d'_{i_l}}{v_{i_l}} + \sum_{j=1}^{l-1} d'_{i_j} \left(\frac{1}{v_{i_{j-1}}} - \frac{1}{v_{i_j}} \right)}{\frac{d_{i_l}}{v_{i_l}} + \sum_{j=1}^{l-1} d_{i_j} \left(\frac{1}{v_{i_{j-1}}} - \frac{1}{v_{i_j}} \right)}.$$

Now knowing that $d'_{i_j} \geq D_{i_j}$ and using the fact from [3] that the distance walked along $Z_\mathcal{L}$ towards each critical point p_{i_j} is $d'_{i_j} \leq 9D_{i_j}$, for each $j = 1, \ldots, l$, we can estimate the competitive ratio

$$r \leq \frac{\frac{9D_{i_l}}{v_{i_l}} + \sum_{j=1}^{l-1} 9D_{i_j} \left(\frac{1}{v_{i_{j-1}}} - \frac{1}{v_{i_j}} \right)}{\frac{D_{i_l}}{v_{i_l}} + \sum_{j=1}^{l-1} D_{i_j} \left(\frac{1}{v_{i_{j-1}}} - \frac{1}{v_{i_j}} \right)} = 9$$

We conclude with the following theorem.

Theorem 2. *The traversal time admitted by $Z_\mathcal{L}$ is 9-competitive.*

Proof. We already know, see Lemma 2, that the 9-competitive ratio is secured if the order in which the critical points are visited in the optimal solution is the same as their first occurrences in $Z_\mathcal{L}$. However, if this order is altered certain critical points will be approached (and segments in between traversed) with faster speeds than in the optimal solution S. This observation combined with Lemma 1 admit the thesis of the theorem.

3   Search on 2d Plane

In this section we consider the search problem in 2d Euclidean plane Π. Similarly to the case on the line we study first the variant with the full knowledge and later focus on the case where robot R has only local knowledge. Also in this section we assume that the points in P have integer coordinates.

3.1   Variant (1) - with Global Knowledge

The task of finding the optimal route in 2d-plane is to some extent similar to the case on the line. Namely, one can construct a $DAG = (P, A)$ with a collection A of directed edges (arcs) $p_i \to p_j$, for all $p_i, p_j \in P$ with $v_i < v_j$. Each arc $p_i \to p_j$ has the associated weight representing the time needed to traverse from p_i to p_j with the expulsion speed v_i available in p_i. The size of DAG is quadratic in $|P| = n$, thus one can solve the search problem by finding all shortest (fastest) paths from points in P to target t in time $O(n^2)$.

While in the case on the line we managed to reduce the size of such DAG to $O(n)$, in 2d-plane the challenge is steeper due to greater freedom of movement of robot R. In addition, after computing all shortest paths in DAG further queries on arbitrary points (outside of P) for the fastest routes towards target t remain non-trivial. To counterpart, one can use the concept of *additively weighted Voronoi diagrams*, see, e.g., [13], based on points in P where each $p_i \in P$ has weight w_i which reflects the time required to move from p_i to t in DAG. This type of diagram partitions the whole plane into n cells $C_1, \ldots, C_n$, where cell C_i contains all points p for which the value $|(p, p_i)| + w_i$ is minimised w.r.t. all $i = 1, \ldots, n$. It is known, that one can compute additively weighted Voronoi diagrams on n points in time $O(n \log n)$ [13]. One can also enhance such diagrams in time $O(n \cdot \text{polylog} n)$ to enable a (randomised) algorithm finding the closest (among n) weighted point in time $\mathcal{Q}(n) = \text{polylog}(n)$, see the work of Karavelas and Yvinec [15] based on the ideas from [12]. While this complexity is not as good as the basic query time $O(\log n)$ available for unweighed points, see the classical algorithm of Kirkpatrick for planar point location [20], it still allows us to construct a faster solution to the search problem if there is a relatively small number $k \ll n$ of distinct expulsion speeds $v_1^* \geq \cdots \geq v_k^*$ present in the system.

The Invariant. The improved construction of all fastest paths (to target t) operates in k rounds and is based on the following invariant. On the conclusion of round i we compute the fastest routes to t for any point with the expulsion speed at least as fast as v_i^*. Let $P_i = \{p_{i_1}, \ldots, p_{i_m}\} \subset P$ be the set of all such points with the traversal times $T_{i_1}, \ldots, T_{i_m}$ respectively. Note that these times are computed for good, i.e., they never change, as in further rounds we only add points with strictly smaller expulsion speeds. During round $i + 1$ for each point $p \in P_{i+1} \setminus P_i$ we need to determine whether robot should go directly to t or should be relayed via some point in P_i with a higher expulsion speed. The time of moving directly to target t can be computed easily, however, choosing the right relay point in P_i is more complex.

The Best Relay Node. In the solution we use additively weighted Voronoi diagrams in which times $T_{i_1}, \ldots, T_{i_m}$ will determine (after proper rescaling) the weights of points in P_i. Recall that in additively weighted Voronoi diagrams the closest point is chosen according to the (Euclidean) distance to the point added to its weight. In our problem we try to minimise the sum of times needed to walk from p to a point $p_{i_j} \in P_i$ and its weight T_{i_j} which is $\dfrac{dist(p, p_{i_j})}{v_{i+1}^*} + T_{i_j}$. Since the first term is not referring to the Euclidean distance we can multiply both terms by v_{i+1}^* to obtain $dist(p, p_{i_j}) + T_{i_j} \cdot v_{i+1}^*$. This rescaling applied for each point in P_i does not change the selection of the fastest route to t via points in P_i, while it allows to use additively weighted Voronoi diagrams to speed up the search for the best relay node in P_i. Thus if we construct an additively weighted Voronoi diagram for points in P_i with weights $T_{i_1} \cdot v_{i+1}^*, \ldots, T_{i_m} \cdot v_{i+1}^*$, we can find for any $p \in P_{i+1} \setminus P_i$ the best relay node in P_i in polylogarithmic time.

The following theorem holds.

Theorem 3. *If the number of distinct speeds is limited to $k \ll n$ one can find all fastest routes to target t in time $O(n \cdot k \cdot \text{polylog}(n))$.*

Proof. The algorithm works in k rounds. During each round one needs to construct an additively weighted Voronoi diagram which is enhanced to answer the closest point queries. The total cost of such construction is $k \cdot O(n \cdot \text{polylog}(n))$. In addition, every point in P is queried exactly once during the search for the best relay node. This give the total complexity $k \cdot O(n \cdot \text{polylog}(n)) + O(n \cdot \text{polylog}(n)) = O(n \cdot k \cdot \text{polylog}(n))$.

After computing all fastest paths from points in P to target t one can compute one more (enhanced) additively weighted Voronoi diagram to provide the fastest route queries for any point in Π in time $Q(n) = \text{polylog}(n)$.

Search on a 2d-Grid. In the last part of this section we show that if all points in P are located on a relatively small grid with at least one dimension limited to size $g \ll n$ (e.g., the grid has g rows) and the robot is allowed to use only edges of the grid one can find all fastest routes to target t in time $O(g \cdot n \log n)$.

Dynamic Nearest Larger Neighbour. In this model we also use the solution to the *nearest larger neighbour* problem on the line. However this time we adopt the dynamic version in which one can ask queries at arbitrary points, remove and add values in time $O(\log n)$, where n is the cap on the number of values currently stored. The three operations can be implemented with the help of a balanced binary search tree, in which all values are kept in the leaves and each internal node contains the largest value stored in the respective subtree.

Also here the construction is done by considering distinct expulsion speeds in decreasing order $v_1^* \geq \cdots \geq v_k^*$, for some $k \leq n$. In fact we use the same notation, division into rounds and a similar invariant. In particular, we assume that on the conclusion of round i the fastest routes from all points in P_i to t are already computed and they never change. In addition we assume that the points from P_i are processed in the relevant rows for the nearest larger neighbour queries according to their expulsion speeds.

During round $i + 1$ we consider points from $P_{i+1} \setminus P_i$ in an arbitrary order. Let $p \in P_{i+1} \setminus P_i$ where p belongs to some column c in the grid. In order to compute the fastest route from p to t we first compute the fastest direct route (without relay nodes) in constant time. This route needs to be compared with the best route via some relay node in P_i. In order to find the best relay node we query each row at column c for the nearest largest value, i.e., to find the closest points p_l and p_r, to the left and right respectively, with larger expulsion speeds for which the fastest routes are already computed in earlier rounds. These are the only relay points in this row which need to be considered as going directly (i.e., not visiting any other relay points in this or some other rows which are considered separately) to any other relay point in this row will always result in slower solution. Thus the fastest route from p to target t can be computed by examining at most $2g$ nodes which can be done in time $O(g \cdot \log n)$. And when the fastest route from p is finally computed, we insert p to the *nearest larger neighbour* solution in the relevant row in time $O(\log n)$.

Finally, since the cost of inclusion (finding the fastest route) of each node in P is bounded by time $O(g \cdot \log n)$ we conclude with the following theorem.

Theorem 4. *If the points from P are distributed in a grid with one dimension limited to $g \ll n$ and robot R can move only along edges of the grid, all fastest routes towards target t can be computed in time $O(g \cdot n \log n)$.*

3.2   Variant (2) - with Local Knowledge

It is well known that in the classical search problem in 2d space the competitive ratio of search process is $\Omega(D)$ as on the way to target t located at an unspecified distance D robot R needs to visit all (discrete, with integer coordinates) points within a ball of radius D centred in s. Since there are $\Omega(D^2)$ integral points in such ball and the fastest route is of length D the competitive ratio follows.

In this section we show that analogously to the classical search the spiral strategy admits also in this case $O(D)$-competitive solution w.r.t. the fastest route from the starting point s to target t. Since we adopted the model with the integral points we will use a simplification of the spiral shape formed of borders b_i of increasing in size boxes B_i, where $B_0 = \{s\}$ with $s = (x_\sigma, y_\sigma)$, and for $i \geq 1$ box B_i contains all points $u = (x, y)$, such that $|x - x_\sigma|, |y - y_\sigma| \leq i$. The border b_i is defined as $B_i \backslash B_{i-1}$, it has a square shape and it contains exactly $8 \cdot i$ integral points, for any $i \geq 0$. The spiral strategy instructs robot R to search through the consecutive (with increasing i) borders b_i, and to adopt faster expulsion speeds as soon as they are encountered.

The proof of $O(D)$-competitiveness is done in two steps. We first relocate points in set P such that the fastest solution S' for the new locations of points is at least as fast as S, which is the fastest solution for the original location of points in P. We later show that the spiral based solution is $O(D)$-competitive with respect to S', so in turn it is also $O(D)$-competitive with respect to S.

Let $D' \leq D$ be the index of the border to which target t belongs to, i.e., $t \in b_{D'}$ and let $S \equiv (s = p_{i_1} \xrightarrow{v_\sigma = 1} p_{i_2} \xrightarrow{v_{i_2}} \ldots p_{i_l} \xrightarrow{v_{i_l}} t)$ be the fastest route from s to t. We construct a different arrangement (with alternative locations) of points in the solution S in which if $p_{i_j} \in S$ belongs to border b_j, for any $j < D'$, it is moved to the location $(x_\sigma, y_{\sigma+j})$ on the vertical line originating in s. All other points in S including target t are moved to the location $(x_\sigma, y_{\sigma+D'})$.

Let $S' \equiv (s = p_{i'_1} \xrightarrow{v_{i'_1} = 1} p_{i'_2} \xrightarrow{v_{i'_2}} \ldots p_{i'_{m-1}} \xrightarrow{v_{i'_{m-1}}} p_{i'_m} = t)$ be the fastest route from s to t on the newly formed line. We point out here that the time complexity $T(S')$ of the solution S' is not worse than the time complexity $T(S)$, in other words $T(S') \leq T(S)$. And this happens because the distance between any pair of points in S can be only reduced during the relocation process.

Finally, we show that the time complexity T_s of our spiral strategy applied to points in P (before rearrangement) is only $O(D)$ multiplicative factor away from $T(S')$. In the analysis, we bound T_s from above by T_s^* referring to the time complexity of a "lazy" strategy in which while searching border b_i robot R uses the fastest expulsion speed $v^*(i-1)$ encountered earlier in box B_{i-1}, and the fastest expulsion speed found in b_i (if larger than $v^*(i-1)$) will be used only in border b_{i+1} and later (until finally substituted by a higher expulsion speed).

In what follows we show that $\frac{T_s^*}{T(S')} = O(D')$. Note that $T(S') = \sum_{j=2}^{m} \frac{i'_j - i'_{j-1}}{v_{i'_{j-1}}}$. On the other hand in the lazy strategy robot R will search $i'_2 - i'_1 + 1$ the most central borders with the speed $v_{i'_1}$, then it will search through $i'_j - i'_{j-1}$ borders with speed $v_{i'_{j-s}}$, for any $j = 3, \ldots m$, and finally the last $i'_m - i'_{m-1}$ borders with speed $v_{i'_{m-1}}$. The size of each border is not larger than $8 \cdot D$, thus we can estimate T_s^* from above by $\sum_{j=2}^{m} \frac{(i'_j - i'_{j-1}) \cdot 8D'}{v_{i'_{j-1}}} + \frac{8}{v_{i'_1}}$. Comparing the two complexities we note that in the summations every term in T_s^* is larger at most $8D'$ times, where $D' \leq D$. The only extra (positive) cost in T_s^* refers to the term $\frac{8}{v_{i'_1}}$. However, since robot R has to walk at least distance 1 along P with the speed $v_s = v_{i'_1}$ we obtain a good amortisation and finally conclude with the following theorem.

Theorem 5. *The spiral search strategy admits asymptotically optimal solution with $O(D)$-competitive factor.*

4   Conclusion

In this paper we considered the search problem with increasing speeds for models with local and global knowledge. Several problems remain open. This includes computation of more accurate asymptotic bound (beyond *Big-O*) notation of the competitive factor in the solution based on the spiral strategy. Another unanswered question refers to faster computation of the best routes from points in P to target t when the number of distinct expulsion speeds can be linear in n. Finally, one could also consider the case with points in P moving along known or unknown trajectories.

Acknowledgements. The authors would like to thank Jurek Czyzowicz for early discussions on the studied problem and the anonymous reviewers for a number of corrections and suggestions which helped us to improve the presentation.

References

1. Asano, T., Bereg, S., Kirkpatrick, D.: Finding nearest larger neighbors. In: Albers, S., Alt, H., Näher, S. (eds.) Efficient Algorithms. LNCS, vol. 5760, pp. 249–260. Springer, Heidelberg (2009). https://doi.org/10.1007/978-3-642-03456-5_17
2. Baeza-Yates, R.A., Culberson, J.C., Rawlins, G.J.E.: Searching with uncertainty extended abstract. In: Karlsson, R., Lingas, A. (eds.) SWAT 1988. LNCS, vol. 318, pp. 176–189. Springer, Heidelberg (1988). https://doi.org/10.1007/3-540-19487-8_20
3. Baeza-Yates, R.A., Culberson, J.C., Rawlins, G.J.E.: Searching in the plane. Inf. Comput. **106**(2), 234–252 (1993)
4. Baeza-Yates, R.A., Schott, R.: Parallel searching in the plane. Comput. Geom. Theory Appl. **5**(3), 143–154 (1995)
5. Bampas, E., et al.: Linear search by a pair of distinct-speed robots. In: Suomela, J. (ed.) SIROCCO 2016. LNCS, vol. 9988, pp. 195–211. Springer, Cham (2016). https://doi.org/10.1007/978-3-319-48314-6_13
6. Bellman, R.: Minimization problem. Bull. AMS **62**(3), 270 (1956)
7. Bender, M.A., Fernández, A., Ron, D., Sahai, A., Vadhan, S.P.: The power of a pebble: exploring and mapping directed graphs. In: STOC 1998, pp. 269–278 (1998)
8. Bose, P., De Carufel, J.-L., Durocher, S.: Revisiting the problem of searching on a line. In: Bodlaender, H.L., Italiano, G.F. (eds.) ESA 2013. LNCS, vol. 8125, pp. 205–216. Springer, Heidelberg (2013). https://doi.org/10.1007/978-3-642-40450-4_18
9. Chrobak, M., Gąsieniec, L., Gorry, T., Martin, R.: Group search on the line. In: Italiano, G.F., Margaria-Steffen, T., Pokorný, J., Quisquater, J.-J., Wattenhofer, R. (eds.) SOFSEM 2015. LNCS, vol. 8939, pp. 164–176. Springer, Heidelberg (2015). https://doi.org/10.1007/978-3-662-46078-8_14
10. Czyzowicz, J., Gąsieniec, L., Georgiou, K., Kranakis, E., MacQuarrie, F.: The beachcombers' problem: walking and searching with mobile robots. Theor. Comput. Sci. **608**, 201–218 (2015)
11. Czyzowicz, J., Gąsieniec, L., Kosowski, A., Kranakis, E.: Boundary patrolling by mobile agents with distinct maximal speeds. In: Demetrescu, C., Halldórsson, M.M. (eds.) ESA 2011. LNCS, vol. 6942, pp. 701–712. Springer, Heidelberg (2011). https://doi.org/10.1007/978-3-642-23719-5_59
12. Devillers, O.: Improved incremental randomized Delaunay triangulation. In: Symposium on Computational Geometry, pp. 106–115 (1998)
13. Fortune, S.: A sweepline algorithm for Voronoi diagrams. Algorithmica **2**, 153–174 (1987)
14. Ghosh, S.K., Klein, R.: Online algorithms for searching and exploration in the plane. Comput. Sci. Rev. **4**(4), 189–201 (2010)
15. Karavelas, M.I., Yvinec, M.: Dynamic additively weighted Voronoi diagrams in 2D. In: Möhring, R., Raman, R. (eds.) ESA 2002. LNCS, vol. 2461, pp. 586–598. Springer, Heidelberg (2002). https://doi.org/10.1007/3-540-45749-6_52
16. Hammar, M., Nilsson, B.J., Schuierer, S.: Parallel searching on m rays. Comput. Geom. **18**(3), 125–139 (2001)
17. Jeż, A., Łopuszański, J.: On the two-dimensional cow search problem. Inf. Process. Lett. **131**(11), 543–547 (2009)
18. Kao, M.Y., Reif, J.H., Tate, S.R.: Searching in an unknown environment: an optimal randomized algorithm for the cow-path problem. Inf. Comput. **109**(1), 63–79 (1996)

19. Kawamura, A., Kobayashi, Y.: Fence patrolling by mobile agents with distinct speeds. Distrib. Comput. **28**(2), 147–154 (2015)
20. Kirkpatrick, D.G.: Optimal search in planar subdivisions. SIAM J. Comput. **12**(1), 28–35 (1983)
21. Koutsoupias, E., Papadimitriou, C., Yannakakis, M.: Searching a fixed graph. In: Meyer, F., Monien, B. (eds.) ICALP 1996. LNCS, vol. 1099, pp. 280–289. Springer, Heidelberg (1996). https://doi.org/10.1007/3-540-61440-0_135
22. Li, H., Chong, K.P.: Search on lines and graphs. In: Proceedings of 48th IEEE Conference on Decision and Control, 2009 held jointly with the 2009 28th Chinese Control Conference (CDC/CCC 2009), vol. 109, no. 11, pp. 5780–5785 (2009)
23. Shortt, D.: Gravity assist, 27 September 2013. www.planetary.org
24. Temple, T., Frazzoli, E.: Whittle-indexability of the cow path problem. In: American Control Conference (ACC), pp. 4152–4158 (2010)

Bee's Strategy Against Byzantines
Replacing Byzantine Participants
(Extended Abstract)

Amitay Shaer[1], Shlomi Dolev[1(✉)], Silvia Bonomi[2], Michel Raynal[3],
and Roberto Baldoni[2]

[1] Department of Computer Science, Ben-Gurion University of the Negev,
Beer-Sheva, Israel
{shaera,dolev}@cs.bgu.ac.il
[2] Research Center of Cyber Intelligence and Information Security (CIS),
Department of Computer, Control, and Management Engineering "A. Ruberti",
Sapienza Università di Roma, Via Ariosto 25, 00185 Roma, Italy
{bonomi,baldoni}@diag.uniroma1.it
[3] IRISA, Université de Rennes, 35042 Rennes, France
michel.raynal@irisa.fr

Abstract. Schemes for the identification and replacement of two-faced Byzantine processes are presented. The detection is based on the comparison of the (blackbox) decision result of a Byzantine consensus on input consisting of the inputs of each of the processes, in a system containing n processes $p_1, \ldots, p_n$. Process p_i that received a gossiped message from p_j with the input of another process p_k, that differs from p_k's input value as received from p_k by p_i, reports on p_k and p_j being two-faced. If enough processes (where enough means at least $t+1$, $t < n$ is a threshold on the number of Byzantine participants) report on the same participant p_j to be two-faced, participant p_j is replaced. If less than the required $t+1$ processes threshold report on a participant p_j, both the reporting processes and the reported process are replaced. If one of them is not Byzantine, its replacement is the price to pay to cope with the uncertainty created by Byzantine processes. The scheme ensures that any two-faced Byzantine participant that prevents fast termination is eliminated and replaced. Such replacement may serve as a preparation for the next invocations of Byzantine agreement possibly used to implement a replicated state machine.

Keywords: Distributed algorithms · Consensus · Byzantine failures
Detection

The research was partially supported by the Rita Altura Trust Chair in Computer Sciences; the Lynne and William Frankel Center for Computer Science; the Ministry of Foreign Affairs, Italy; the grant from the Ministry of Science, Technology and Space, Israel, and the National Science Council (NSC) of Taiwan; the Ministry of Science, Technology and Space, Infrastructure Research in the Field of Advanced Computing and Cyber Security; and the Israel National Cyber Bureau. Michel Raynal visited BGU with the support of the Dozor foundation. Contact author: Shlomi Dolev.

T. Izumi and P. Kuznetsov (Eds.): SSS 2018, LNCS 11201, pp. 139–153, 2018.
https://doi.org/10.1007/978-3-030-03232-6_10

1   Introduction

The Byzantine Agreement (BA) problem, introduced by Pease, Shostak, and Lamport in [7], is known as a fundamental problem in fault-tolerant distributed computing. The problem has received a lot of attention in the literature and has become the essence of a variety of schemes in distributed computing.

Solving the Byzantine agreement problem is not necessarily tied to the detection of the Byzantine processes, the only success criterion of the agreement is whether all correct processes agree on the same value. In this work, we focus on detecting a sub-class of Byzantine behavior (i.e., namely *two-faced* Byzantine processes) for the sake of replacing them in the next Byzantine agreement invocation. The detection and replacement procedure can be plugged in any other algorithm using a Byzantine Agreement e.g., possibly as part of the implementation of a replicated state machine. The final goal is to prepare for the future invocations of the agreement, trying to ensure that the next invocation of the Byzantine agreement will cope with a smaller number of two-faced Byzantine processes.

The Byzantine Agreement Problem. In the Byzantine Agreement Problem, there are n processes, $\Pi = \{p_1, \ldots, p_n\}$ with unique names over $N = \{1, \ldots, n\}$ and at most $t < n$ of the processes can be Byzantine. Each process starts with an input value v from a set of values V^1. The goal is to ensure that all non-faulty processes eventually output the same value. The output of a non-faulty process is called the *decision value*.

More formally, an algorithm solves the Byzantine Agreement if the following conditions hold:

- **Agreement.** All non-faulty processes agreed on the same value (i.e., there are no two non-faulty processes that decide different values).
- **Validity.**[2] If all non-faulty processes start with the same value v, the decision value of all non-faulty participants is v.
- **Termination.** Eventually, all non-faulty processes decide a value.

Reaching agreement in presence of Byzantine processes is expensive as the number of messages grows quadratically with the number of participants n and the number of rounds (time) grows linearly with the number of Byzantine participants t (with $n > 3t$).

Applications may repeatedly invoke agreement instances (e.g., as part of implementing a replicated state machine). Typically, the presence of Byzantine activity is rare, and it is desirable that the overhead in handling Byzantine activity will be tuned to the actual situation. Hence, we want to adjust the time it takes for each consensus invocation to run according to the actual situation at the time. In addition, when the system is interactive and never stops (as in the case of a replicated state machine) the number of Byzantine participants may be

---

[1] Binary Agreement is defined with the set $V = \{0, 1\}$.

[2] There is an alternative, stronger property for *Validity* [6]. The decision value v has to be an input value of at least one non-faulty process.

accumulated to exceed any threshold. To avoid the accumulation of Byzantine participants over time, we suggest a detection and replacements of Byzantine participants. Thus, we suggest to couple the consensus algorithm with a detection mechanism. As soon as a Byzantine activity is detected, the suspected Byzantine process will be eliminated and replaced.

The rest of the paper is organized as follows: in Sect. 2, we describe shortly our system settings. In Sect. 3, we introduce our approach of the detection process as a combination of two algorithms, *fast* and *slow* presented in Sects. 4 and 5 respectively. Due to space limitations, proofs and details are omitted from this extended abstract and can be found in [8].

2   System Settings

We consider a distributed system composed of n processes, each having a unique identifier $p_1, p_2, \ldots, p_n$. We assume that up to t processes can be Byzantine with $n > 3t$. A process is said to be *Byzantine* if it deviates from the protocol, otherwise it is said to be *correct*. Processes communicate trough message exchanges. A reliable communication is assumed, where a point-to-point channel exists for every pair of processes. More precisely, if a correct process p_i sends a message m to a process p_j, then m will be delivered by process p_j. Channels are authenticated, i.e., when a process p_j receives a message m from a process p_i, p_j knows that m has been generated by p_i.

We consider a particular sub-class of Byzantine failures called *two-faced Byzantine*. A process is said to be *two-faced Byzantine* if it is supposed to send a broadcast message to all processes in the system but it is sending different messages to different processes. In the sequel, we use the term *process acting as Byzantine* to refer to a process that exhibits two-faced behaviour.

The system is synchronous and evolves in sequential synchronous rounds $r_1, r_2, \ldots r_i \ldots$ Every round is divided into three steps: (i) *send step* where the processes send all the messages for the current round, (ii) *receive step* where the processes receive all the messages sent at the beginning of the current round[3] and (iii) *computation step* where the processes process the received messages and prepare new messages to be sent in the next round. The processes have the ability to make speculative execution when needed, meaning an execution is made, but all states are saved until a condition holds, sometimes forcing the system rolling back to the previous state (see e.g., [5]).

We assume the existence of a trusted entity component (or components), called *hypervisor*. The *hypervisor* can only receive messages from the processes but cannot send them messages. The *hypervisor* can eliminate or replace a process with a different process instance. The *hypervisor* is assumed to be correct all the time. We consider two different types in which the hypervisor integrated into the system:

---

[3] Let us note, that in round-based computations, all deliver() events happen during the receive step.

- **Global hypervisor.** There exists just one global hypervisor that controls all the processes in the system.
- **Local hypervisor.** There is a hypervisor that controls p for each process p. Each local hypervisor can communicate with the other local hypervisors.

3   Byzantine Detection and Replacement

Many various algorithms exist for solving different problems given Byzantine processes (some of the algorithms require a restriction on the number of Byzantine participants). In order to detect Byzantine processes, it is necessary that participants running the distributed algorithm report and audit activities performed by each other. Let us observe that given $t + 1$ or more testimonies for process p_j as faulty, p_j is Byzantine as there exists at least one correct process suspecting p_j with correct evidences (i.e., there exists at least one correct process that observed a misbehavior from p_j). On the other hand, in case there are at least one and less than $t + 1$ testimonies on p_j being Byzantine, then at least one process is Byzantine among the reporting processes and p_j. Unfortunately, in this case it is not possible to detect who is the Byzantine process but it is possible to identify a group of processes that collectively exhibits a bad behavior and that for sure contains the Byzantine process.

In the heart of the detection, we expect two main parts: fast and slow. The fast part is run by the processes as long as there is no Byzantine activity. When Byzantine activity is discovered the slow part takes place and replaces the Byzantine processes that acted in a two faced fashion, enforcing the system to continue beyond the fast part. We use the term *fast termination* for a scenario in which the fast part is successfully completed.

Thus, our problem can be summarized by adding the following properties to the specification of the original Byzantine agreement problem:

- **Completeness.** A process p_i acting two-faced in a manner that eliminates fast termination is suspected by some correct process p_j.
- **Sacrifice.** If process p_i is suspected by at least $t + 1$ processes, p_i is the only one to be replaced. Otherwise, p_i and the processes that suspect p_i are replaced.

Note, that the *completeness* above somewhat resembles game theory consideration, enforcing Byzantine process that would like to survive to allow the system to terminate fast, and the best global utility is achieved.

4   Byzantine Free Fast Termination

We suggest a Byzantine agreement protocol composed of *fast* and *slow* parts. As long as there is no indication of a Byzantine activity, such that is causing the slow algorithm to be executed, only the fast algorithm takes place (Algorithm 1). Combined with the capability of speculative execution and roll back, the actual execution is only two rounds (rounds 1 and 2 of Phase 1). Contrarily, when a testimony of Byzantine activity has been discovered, processes start to execute the slow algorithm (Algorithms 3 or 4).

Optimistically, all processes are assumed to be correct and start with the fast algorithm. When a Byzantine activity is detected by a correct process, the correct process notifies other processes, essentially, invoking the slow algorithm.

Preliminaries. In our schemes, a process p is replaced whenever enough testimonies of a two-faced behavior of p are collected. When there is no sufficient number of testimonies for a two-faced behavior of a particular process p, several replacements may take place. A replacement may be scheduled for the processes that provide the testimonies (possibly as a sacrifice action), and also for the process that is blamed to be two-faced.

A *consensus vector* of n inputs is required for maintaining the replicated state machine as described, for example in [3]. We are interested in providing a *consensus vector* solution with Byzantine detection, as we define next. The properties of the consensus vector task are defined in terms of n inputs. In a more formal way:

- **Agreement.** All non-faulty processes agreed on the same vector. There are not two non-faulty processes that decide on different vectors.
- **Validity.** Let V be the decision vector. $\forall i \in N$, if p_i is correct then $vector[i]$ is the input value of p_i.

As for the detection properties, the following are defined:

- **Completeness.** A process p_i acting in a two-faced manner that causes the system not to decide in a *fast termination* fashion is suspected by some correct process p_j (and eventually replaced by the hypervisor).
- **Sacrifice.** If process p_i is suspected by at least $t + 1$ processes, p_i is the only one to be replaced. Otherwise, p_i and the processes that suspect p_i are replaced.

The Fast Algorithm (Algorithm 1). The fast algorithm takes place in the first three rounds following a consensus invocation. In the first round (lines 1–2), each process sends its input value while in the second round (lines 3–5) each process sends the values it received in the previous round. After these two rounds, each process looks for conflicting messages as an indication for Byzantine activity and extracts a suspect list. In the third round, a process sends a bit (an indication bit) with value of 1 (*suspect message*) as an indication for Byzantine activity if such activity is detected. Then, processes start a new binary consensus invocation (phase 2 line 9). The input value is determined as follows: if a process receives suspect messages, the process uses 1 as an input value and uses 0 otherwise.

Either way, starting from this point, the processes make a speculative execution of the consensus. The processes use the consensus vector of the first two rounds as a decision value, save the state before the consensus execution and concurrently, start the consensus and a new fast algorithm. If the decision value is 0, then the speculative execution appears to be the right execution and the saved state is discarded. Otherwise, the decision value equals 1, meaning a Byzantine activity occurred. The processes roll back to the state before making the consensus and start the slow algorithm that will replace the Byzantine processes that cause disagreement on the input vectors. The relevant suspect lists that have been recorded in the corresponding incarnation of the fast algorithm is used by the slow one.

An *early stopping* Byzantine agreement is used to agree on the indication bit. For example, one may use the algorithm suggested in [1,4]. Such an *early stopping* algorithm terminates in $min\{t+1, f+1\}$ rounds, where t is the maximum number of Byzantine and f is the actual Byzantine processes.

Algorithm 1. Fast Algorithm for process p_i, Denote by N the group of processes' identities, by v_i, the input value of process p_i:

Process fields (initialized with each invocation):
$vector = [\perp, \dots, \perp]$
$vectors = [\perp, \dots, \perp]$
$slow = 0$, $suspects = \emptyset$
Phase 1:
   Round 1:
1:    $\forall j \in N$: send v_i to p_j
2:    on **receive** of v_j from p_j: $vector[j] = v_j$
   Round 2:
3:    $\forall j \in N$: send $vector$ to p_j
4:    on **receive** of $vector_j$ from p_j: $vectors[j] = vector_j$
                        ▷ Concurrently decides $vector$ and speculatively executes the rest
   Round 3:
5:    $suspects = getSuspects(vectors)$ ▷ check for conflicts
6:    **if** $(|suspects| \geq 1)$ **then** $\forall j \in N$: send $'1'$ to p_j ▷ indication for suspicion
7:    on **receive** of $'1'$ from p_j: $slow = 1$

Phase 2:
8:    **if** $BA.decide(slow) = 1$ **then**   ▷ BA - optimal early stopping Agreement
9:       role back state and apply *SLOW algorithm* with *suspects* list

---

The *getSuspected* function is used in the third round of the first phase. This function is used to detect Byzantine processes based on the received messages of the first two rounds. The function input is $vectors_i$, a vector of vectors that represents all the received messages of the two rounds. The value of $vectors_i[k][j]$, $k, j \in N$, represents the value of p_j as received by p_k in the first round. The value of $vectors_i[k][j]$ has been sent to p_i by p_k during the second round (if $k = i$ then $vectors_i[i][j]$ is known after the first round).

At the beginning, the function finds Byzantine processes and removes their values from $vectors_i$. Then the function searches for suspected processes. By analysing the vector it is possible to use a voting approach for each value proposed on the basis of the value received during the exchanges in the first two rounds. Majority of process p_j is the most frequent value in $\{vectors[i][j] : i \in N\}$, where N is the unique processes' identifier.

In order to find faulty processes based on $vectors_i$, the $getSuspects$ function checks, for each process p_k, if there are at least $n - t$ processes that sent the same value in the second round, otherwise p_k is faulty. This check is done by examining the k-th entry of each vector in $vectors_i$. Then, the function counts how many times p_k provides a value v for p_j (given by $vectors_i[k][j]$), such that v and the majority value for p_j are different. If it counts more than t occurrences, p_k is faulty. The function then checks, that the value received from p_k in the first round equals the majority value for p_k. After finding faulty process (or processes), their value is removed from $vectors_i$. However, when at least one faulty process had been found, less than $t + 1$ testimonies are required to discover additional faulty processes. Finally, when no more faulty processes can be discovered, the remaining processes' conflicts are considered to be the *suspected* processes only. The function returns a union of the faulty and suspect groups.

Algorithm 2. Description of the function **getSuspects**(vectors) for process p_i

---

1: **procedure** $getSuspects(vectors)$
2:     $maxFaults = t$
3:     $faulty = \emptyset$
4:     **repeat**
5:         $newFaulty = \emptyset$
6:         **for** $k \in N \setminus faulty$ **do**
7:             $majorityDiff = \{j \in N \setminus faulty : vectors[k][j] \neq majority(j)\}$
8:             **if** $(majority(k) = \bot)$ **OR** $(vectors[i][k] \neq majority(k))$
                        OR $(|majorityDiff| \geq maxFaults + 1)$ **then**
9:                 $newFaulty = newFaulty \cup \{k\}$
10:         **for** $k \in newFaulty$ **do**
11:             $vectors[k] = [\bot, ..., \bot]$
12:             $\forall j \in N : vectors[j][k] = \bot$
13:         $maxFaults = t - |faulty|$
14:         $faulty = faulty \cup newFaulty$
15:     **until** $(newFaulty = \emptyset$ **OR** $|faulty| = t)$
16:     $suspects = \{k : k \in \{i, j\}$ s.t. $\exists_{j,i \in N \setminus faulty}\ vectors[j][i] \neq majority(i)\}$
17:     **return** $faulty \cup suspects$

18: **procedure** $majority(k)$
19:     **if** $vectors[i][k] = \bot$ **then**
20:         **return** $\bot$
21:     **return** v s.t. $|\{j \in N : vectors[j][k] = v\}| \geq n - t$, $\bot$ otherwise

---

The first two rounds of the algorithm are based on the exponential information gathering (EIG) Byzantine agreement algorithm introduced in [2]. In the first round, each process sends its own input value. In round $r > 1$, each process sends all the messages it receives in round $r - 1$.

The following definitions and proofs are used to explain the detection process of the fast algorithm. The main detection process is done by the function *getSuspects* (Algorithm 2) after collecting messages of two rounds. The function starts with identification of the Byzantine processes, then the function finds suspect processes using p_i messages (i.e., from p_i's point of view). The definitions *c-order lie with respect to* p_i and *A c-discoverable with respect to* p_i are used to explain the detection of Byzantine process and the definition p_i *co-suspects* p_j and p_k is used for explaining the detection of suspected processes. Then lemmas are used, based on those definitions, to prove the correctness of the detection algorithm. First, *getSuspects* function tries to identify Byzantine processes by finding *A c-discoverable with respect to* p_i processes. Then, identifies the suspects process by looking for processes p_j, p_k such that p_i *co-suspects* p_j and p_k.

Definition 1. p_i **co-suspects** p_j **and** p_k. *Let $r > 1$, process p_i co-suspects p_j and p_k if in round r, p_j has sent to p_i value v, which supposed to be the value that p_k sent in round $r - 1$, while a majority of processes have sent value $v' \neq v$ to p_i as the value sent by p_k in round $r - 1$.*

Definition 2. *c-order lie with respect to* p_i. *Let $c \geq 1$, C - a correct processes group of size c, called the lied group, $p_i \in C$. There are two kinds of c-order lie:*

- **Two-faced.** *Process $p_j, j \in N/C$ sends value v to all processes in C and a different value (or values) to others not in C.*
- **Anomalous.** *$\forall p_i \in C$, p_i co-suspects p_j and p_k, $k \in N$.*

A better understanding of the difference between two-faced and anomalous requires a look in Algorithm 1. In the first round only one value, the input value, is sent. In the second round, n values are sent (as a single message). A two-faced lie can be made in the first round and be discovered in the second round. In that case, in the first round, the process may send v as its initial value to $0 < c < n$ processes and value v', $v \neq v'$, to others, but it can only lie concerning a single value in its message. On the other hand, an anomalous lie can be made in the second round, where there are n possibilities to lie for each one of the n values.

c-order lie leads to the *c-discoverable* definition. Usually, given $t + 1$ testimonies for process p to be Byzantine, process p is doomed to be Byzantine. However, if we already count x Byzantine processes, then only $t + 1 - x$ testimonies are required to discover another Byzantine process. Using this fact, the algorithm starts looking for Byzantine processes using $t + 1$ testimonies to find x Byzantine processes, then uses $t - x + 1$ testimonies, and so on, as long as new Byzantine processes are found. Note, that both lies are two-faced, but the way of detecting those lies is different.

Definition 3. *A c-discoverable with respect to* p_i *process. Let $1 \leq c \leq t + 1$, a process p_j is c-discoverable with respect to p_i if $i \neq j$, and p_j made a c-order lie to the lied group C, $p_i \in C$ and:*

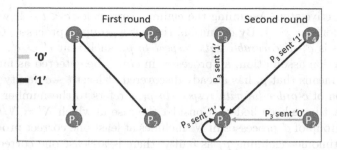

Fig. 1. We focus only on messages regarding process p_3. p_1 co-suspects p_2 and p_3. Three processes (including p_1) notify p_1 that p_3 sent '1' at the first round and p_2 tells p_1 that p_3 sent '0' at the first round.

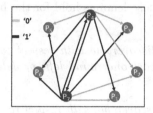

Fig. 2. p_4 sends different values to different processes. p_4 is 3-discoverable ($C = \{5, 3, 2\}$) and P_7 is 2-discoverable ($C = \{1, 2\}$). p_4 and p_7 will cause the processes to run the slow algorithm. p_4 and p_7 will be replaced by the hypervisor then.

- $c = t + 1$ *or*
- $c < t + 1$, *and there is a group* $G = \{k \in N : p_k$ *is a c'-discoverable with respect to* p_i, $c' > c\}$, *such that* $|G| > t - c$

In Fig. 1, we focused only on messages involving p_3, even though other messages are sent as well. In the first round p_1, p_2 and p_4 receive the value 1 from p_3. In the second round, p_4 and p_1 notify p_1 (p_1 sends the message to itself), that p_3 sent 1 in the first round, while p_2 claims that the value 0 had been sent by p_3. In that case, p_1 has two processes, including itself, that report 1, and one process that reports 0. p_1 cannot identify whether p_3 or p_2 are faulty and p_1 suspects them both. p_1 *co-suspects* p_2 and p_3. Figure 2 depicts the case in which p_4 and p_7 are 4 and 3-discoverable, respectively. The algorithm first detects p_4 and only then can detect p_3.

Lemma 1. *If p is a c-discoverable with respect to p_i, then p is detected as Byzantine by p_i.*

Proof Sketch. The proof is given by decreasing induction on the value of c, $1 \leq c \leq t + 1$, starting with $c = t + 1$ as the base case. Let $c = t + 1$, p_i has $t + 1$ testimonies claiming p_j as faulty. Since there are at most t faulty processes, at least one of them is correct. Thus p_j is faulty.

The inductive step. Assuming the claim is correct for $c < t + 1$, we show its correctness for $c' = c - 1$. By definition, there is a group of processes G wherein, each process is c''-*discoverable with respect to* p_j, such that $c'' > c'$. Therefore, by the induction assumption, all processes in G will be detected as faulty by p_i. $|G| > t - c'$ means that p_i has already discovered at least $t - c'$ faulty processes. By definition of c-*order lie with respect to* p_i, c refers to the number of correct processes that have been lied to. Consider the case in which $N' = N/G$, in such a case any group of c' processes in N' includes at least one correct process. Now, given c' testimonies claiming p_j as faulty, there is at least one correct process, therefore p_j is faulty and discovered by p_i.

The following lemmas can be used for the exponential information gathering (EIG) Byzantine agreement algorithm [2] where the algorithm terminates in $t + 1$ rounds. In our algorithm, these lemmas hold for the first two rounds of the fast algorithm.

Lemma 2. *Let p_j be a c-discoverable with respect to p_i in round $r \geq 1$. If p_j is two-faced, assuming at least one round left, p_i detects p_j as faulty in round $r + 1$.*

Lemma 3. *Let p_j be a c-discoverable with respect to p_i in round $r \geq 1$. If $r > 1$ and p_j is anomalous, p_i detects p_j as faulty in round r.*

Remark 1. Lines 5–9 in Algorithm 2 are searching for $two - faced$ or $anomalous$ processes with $maxFaults$ testimonies.

Remark 2. Line 16 in Algorithm 2 when applied with $vectors_i$ is searching for p_j, p_k such that p_i co-suspects p_j and p_k.

Lemma 4. *Let p_j a c-discoverable with respect to p_i, then $getSuspects(vectors_i)$ for p_i will return p_j as faulty.*

Lemma 5. *Let p_j be a c-discoverable with respect to p_i, with $two - faced$ in round 1 or anomalous in round 2, where p_i is a correct process. Then all processes moved to the slow algorithm, where at least one process has non-empty suspect list.*

Claim 1. After applying $getSuspects(vectors_i)$ for each correct process p_i the following holds:

- Let p_j be a Byzantine process that exhibits Byzantine behavior. If p_j is a c-discoverable with respect to p_i, p_j will be included in p_i's faulty list, where p_i is a correct process. Otherwise, if p_i co-suspects p_j and $p_k, k \in N$, p_j will be included in p_i's suspect list, where p_i is correct process.

Proof Sketch. Suppose p_j acts in a Byzantine two-faced fashion in the first two round of the *fast algorithm*. In case p_j acts in a c-*discoverable* fashion, then by Lemma 4 p_j will be discovered as faulty. Otherwise, suppose p_i co-suspects p_j and $p_k, k \in N$, by Remark 2 it will be discovered as suspected.

Lemma 6. *If there is no Byzantine activity, while running the fast algorithm, the algorithm satisfies Agreement, validity, and termination.*

Theorem 1. *The fast algorithm satisfies completeness.*

Proof Sketch. Suppose there is a Byzantine behavior of c-order lie (either two-faces or anomalous) occurs by process p_k while running the Fast algorithm. suppose the Byzantine activity occurs at phase 1, by Claim 1 there is a correct process p_i that the return value of applying *getSuspects* function will return process p_k either as faulty or suspect. Thus, p_i will let the other correct processes know about the Byzantine activity and the Slow algorithm will be scheduled. Otherwise, suppose that Byzantine activity occurs at phase 2 only, by the speculative execution method, the fast algorithm keeps running and if the decision value equals 1, a rollback is scheduled, and the slow algorithm is scheduled to replace the faulty process that has been detected before running the consensus.

Sacrifice property will be dealt with later in the Slow algorithm.

5 Using Byzantine Agreement Objects

5.1 Global Hypervisor

The Slow Algorithm (Algorithm 3). The algorithm consists of n stages that run one after another, one for each process. The stage computation steps are presented in Algorithm 3 and composed of 3 phases. The first 2 phases are done by the processes, and the third phase is done by the *global hypervisor*, a single hypervisor for controlling all the processes as defined earlier. In stage s, phase 1 (lines 1–7), process p_i, such that $(s \bmod n) + 1 = i$, is the sender. The sender sends its input value, v_i, to all the other processes. Then the processes invoke an initialized version of a Byzantine consensus on v_i. Process p_j sets the *suspect* variable to 1 (line 7) if an agreement is reached, but the decision value is differed from the received value, or p_j had suspect p_i in the *fast algorithm* already. In that cases, p_j suspects p_i. In phase 2 (lines 8–10) each process, with *suspect* variable set to 1, sends a suspect message to the *global hypervisor* (line 10).

The hypervisor can decide to eliminate or replace a process based on the testimonies of other processes. In phase 3 (lines 11–14), if the hypervisor receives at least $t + 1$ testimonies claiming that process p_i is faulty, p_i is doomed to be a Byzantine process since at least one non-faulty process's testimony exists. If the number of testimonies is less than $t + 1$, it is unclear whether p_i is Byzantine or not. Either the testimonies are correct and p_i is Byzantine, or the t Byzantine processes worked together to incriminate p_i. Thus, in this case, the hypervisor has to replace them all, i.e., p_i and the other processes that sent the testimonies.

By this approach, once Byzantine activity occurs by sender process p_i, it will be replaced by the hypervisor. Still, sometimes some correct processes would be replaced along with p_i. As a conclusion, the addition of third party (the hypervisor) cannot identify Byzantine process p_i unless there are at least $t + 1$

Algorithm 3. Code for process p_i and hypervisor in stage s, each process starts with suspect list it discovered in the fast algorithm:

Process fields: $in_i[1 \ldots n]$ initially [null, ... ,null],
   $suspect = 0$
   $suspects$ = initialized from *fast algorithm*
   $BA[1 \ldots n]$ initially [null, ... ,null]

Phase 1 of stage s:
```
1:     if s (mod n)+1 = i then
2:         send v_i to all processes
3:     else                                            ▷ upon receiving v_j from p_j
4:         in_i[j] = v_j
5:         dec_i[j] = BA[j].decide(v_j)           ▷ BA - Byzantine Agreement object
6:         if dec_i[j] ≠ in_i[j] OR j ∈ suspects then
7:             turn on hypervisor ; suspect = 1
```

Phase 2 of stage s:
```
8:     if s (mod n)+1 ≠ i AND suspect = 1 then
9:         j = s (mod n)+1
10:        send suspect(j) to hypervisor
```

Hypervisor code:

Phase 3 of stage s: ▷ Let $P = \{i_1, \ldots , i_k\}$ group of processes that send $suspect(i)$ messages.
```
11:    if (k > t) then
12:        replace p_i
13:    else
14:        ∀j ∈ P ∪ {i}: replace p_j
```

processes that claim p_i is Byzantine. Otherwise, in the worst case scenario, the only possibility left is to suspect all the $t + 1$ processes. That way, in all cases Byzantine process p_i that has been discovered in the fast part is doomed to be replaced at stage s', such that $(s' \bmod n) + 1 = i$. At the end of the n stages, each Byzantine process that has been discovered in the fast algorithm will be replaced and each non-faulty process will have the same vector of values. The next theorem summarizes the above observations.

Theorem 2. *Algorithm 3 satisfies agreement, validity, and termination.*

Proof Sketch. **Agreement.** The algorithm consists of n stages, at each stage, all the correct processes agree on the same value for process p_i with $s(\bmod n)+1 = i$ through a Byzantine consensus (line 5). Eventually, after n stages, all correct processes received the same n values representing the vector of size n.

Validity. For each entry i in the vector a consensus had been made at stage s, such that $i(\bmod n) + 1 = i$. *Validity*, by definition, concerns only the input value of correct processes. If the sender is correct, it sent the same value, v to

Algorithm 4. Code for separated hypervisors and process p_i in stage s, each process starts with suspect list it discovered in the fast algorithm:

---

local hypervisor turned off except for p_i, such that s *(mod n)*+1 = i
Process fields:
  $in_i[1\ldots n]$ initially [null, $\ldots$,null],
  $BA[1\ldots n]$ initially [null, $\ldots$,null]   ▷ BA - Byzantine Agreement object
  suspects = initialized from *fast algorithm*

Phase 1 of stage s:
1:    **if** s *(mod n)*+1 = i **then**
2:        send $val(v_i)$ to all processes
3:    **else**   ▷ *upon receiving v_j from p_j*
4:        $in_i[j] = v_j$
5:        $dec_i[j] = BA[j].decide(v_j)$ ▷ BA - Byzantine Agreement object
6:        **if** $dec_i[j] \neq in_i[j]$ **OR** $j \in$ *suspects* **then**
7:            turn on *local hypervisor*

Hypervisor code (for p_i's turned on (active) local hypervisor):

Phase 2 of stage s:
8:    **if** s *(mod n)*+1 $\neq$ i **then**
9:        $j = s$ *(mod n)*+1
10:       send $suspect(j)$ to all active *hypervisors*
11:   **else**   ▷ *counter-testimony for all active hypervisors*
12:       $\forall j \in N$ s.t. p_j's *hypervisor* is active: send $suspect(j)$ to p_j's *local hypervisor*

Phase 3 of stage s: ▷ k - amount of received $suspect(i)$ messages.
13:   **if** s *(mod n)*+1 = i **AND** $k > 0$ **then**
14:       replace p_i
15:   **else if** $k \leq t$ **then**   ▷ *upon receiving k **suspect(j)** messages*
16:       replace p_i

---

all processes in phase 1 (line 2). Then Byzantine agreement is invoked and all correct processes hold the same input value v. By validity property of Byzantine consensus, the decision value is v.

Termination. The algorithms consist of n stages. Each stage composed of three phases. The first phase contains one round and Byzantine agreement execution (lines 1–7), which is finite due to the Byzantine agreement termination property. The second phase lasts for one round (lines 8–10) and finally, the third phase (lines 11–14) contains the hypervisor part which requires one round. Given that stage is finite, n stages are also finite, thus the algorithm terminates.

5.2   Local Hypervisor

In this part, we assume a different hypervisor, namely, a *local hypervisor* for each process. The *local hypervisor* can be turned on by its process and assumed to be correct all the time. The local hypervisors can send and receive suspects messages (as explained in the sequel) but cannot send messages to the processes. The *hypervisor* can replace the process based on the suspect messages.

Algorithm 4. The algorithm starts the same as Algorithm 3, in phase 1 there is a sender process sending its own input value to all processes, following by Byzantine consensus invocation for the received value, and suspect if the decision value is different from the received value or if the sender had already suspected in the *fast algorithm*. Algorithm 4 differs from Algorithm 3 following the detection part. A process that suspects the sender turns on its local hypervisor as an indication for the detection. In phase 2, the *local hypervisor* sends suspect messages to all other hypervisors. During phase 3, after all suspects messages of phase 2 have been received, the local hypervisor that controls the sender replaces the sender as a consequence of receiving at least one suspect message. The local hypervisor of the other processes, different from the sender, replaces their hosted process only when there are less than $t + 1$ suspect messages.

Theorem 3. *Algorithm 4 satisfies agreement, validity, and termination.*

Proof Sketch. **Agreement.** The algorithm consists of n stages, at each stage, all the correct processes agree on the same value for process p_i with $s(mod\ n) + 1 = i$ through a Byzantine consensus (line 5). Eventually, after n stages, all correct processes receive the same n values representing the vector of size n.

Validity. For each entry i in the vector a consensus had been made at stage s, such that $i(mod\ n) + 1 = i$. *Validity*, by definition, concerns only the input value of correct processes. If the sender is correct, it sent the same value, v, to all processes in phase 1 (line 2). Then Byzantine agreement is invoked and all correct processes hold the same input value v. By validity property of Byzantine consensus, the decision value is v.

Termination. The algorithms consist of n stages. Each stage composed of three phases. The first phase contains one round and Byzantine agreement execution (lines 1–7), which is finite due to the Byzantine agreement termination property. The second phase lasts for one round (lines 8–12) and finally, the third phase (lines 13–16) which requires one round. Given that stage is finite, n stages are also finite, thus the algorithm terminates.

Theorem 4. *The slow algorithm satisfies completeness and sacrifice.*

Proof Sketch. **Completeness.** As seen in the algorithm, a process can lie either as the sender (line 2) and make up to processes to be restarted, or as a receiver (line 7) and it will make itself and the sender be restarted. Either way the faulty process will pay for it.

Sacrifice. Following lines 13–16, if there is not enough, e.g. at least $t + 1$, receivers that claims the sender (process i with $s\ (mod\ n) + 1 = i$) for being faulty, the sender and the reporting receivers will be restarted as an act of sacrifice. Otherwise, the sender alone will be restarted.

Theorem 5. *The combinations of Algorithm 4 and Algorithm 1 satisfies Completeness and sacrifice.*

Proof Sketch. **Completeness.** As already mentions, the fast algorithm satisfy completeness (Theorem 1) by recording and delivering the faulty and suspects process list to the slow algorithm. Then the slow algorithm continues satisfies Completeness (Theorem 4) collect more evidences (if there is any) for Byzantine behavioral.

Sacrifice. Restart of processes is done only in the slow part. As seen earlier (Theorem 4), the slow algorithm satisfies sacrifice.

6   Conclusion

This paper presented an approach to detect and remove Byzantine processes from consensus-based computation. Long-lived computation relying on consensus (e.g., state machine replication) may benefit from our solution as it allows to continuously monitor the computation and inhibits Byzantine processes to act, if they wants to remain in the computation.

References

1. Abraham, I., Dolev, D.: Byzantine agreement with optimal early stopping, optimal resilience and polynomial complexity. In: Proceedings of the 47th Annual on Symposium on Theory of Computing (STOC) (2015)
2. Bar-Noy, A., Dolev, D., Dwork, C., Strong, H.R.: Shifting gears: changing algorithms on the fly to expedite Byzantine agreement. Inf. Comput. **97**(2), 205–233 (1992)
3. Binun, A., et al.: Self-stabilizing Byzantine-tolerant distributed replicated state machine. In: Bonakdarpour, B., Petit, F. (eds.) SSS 2016. LNCS, vol. 10083, pp. 36–53. Springer, Cham (2016). https://doi.org/10.1007/978-3-319-49259-9_4
4. Dolev, D., Reischuk, R., Strong, H.R.: Early stopping in Byzantine agreement. J. ACM **37**(4), 720–741 (1990)
5. Kung, H.T., Robinson, J.T.: On optimistic methods for concurrency control. ACM Trans. Database Syst. **6**(2), 213–226 (1981)
6. Mostfaoui, A., Raynal, M.: Intrusion-tolerant broadcast and agreement abstractions in the presence of Byzantine processes. IEEE Trans. Parallel Distrib. Syst. **27**(4), 1085–1098 (2016)
7. Pease, M., Shostak, R., Lamport, L.: Reaching agreement in the presence of faults. J. ACM **27**(2), 228–234 (1980)
8. Shaer, A., Dolev, S., Bonomi S., Raynal, M., Baldoni, R.: Bee's strategy against Byzantines, replacing Byzantine participant. Technical report #18-05, Department of Computer Science, Ben-Gurion University of the Negev (2018)

Simple and Fast Approximate Counting and Leader Election in Populations

Othon Michail[1(✉)], Paul G. Spirakis[1,2(✉)], and Michail Theofilatos[1(✉)]

[1] Department of Computer Science, University of Liverpool, Liverpool, UK
[2] Computer Engineering and Informatics Department, University of Patras, Patras, Greece
{Othon.Michail,P.Spirakis,Michail.Theofilatos}@liverpool.ac.uk

Abstract. We study the problems of leader election and population size counting for *population protocols*: networks of finite-state anonymous agents that interact randomly under a uniform random scheduler. We provide simple protocols for approximate counting of the size of the population and for leader election. We show a protocol for leader election that terminates in $O(\frac{\log^2 n}{\log m})$ parallel time, where $1 \leq m \leq n$ is a parameter, using $O(\max\{m, \log n\})$ states. By adjusting the parameter m between a constant and n, we obtain a single leader election protocol whose time and space can be smoothly traded off between $O(\log^2 n)$ to $O(\log n)$ time and $O(\log n)$ to $O(n)$ states. We also give a protocol which provides an upper bound $\hat{n}$ of the size n of the population, where $\hat{n}$ is at most n^a for some constant $a > 1$. This protocol assumes the existence of a unique leader in the population and stabilizes in $\Theta(\log n)$ parallel time, using constant number of states in every node, except from the unique leader which is required to use $\Theta(\log^2 n)$ states.

Keywords: Population protocol · Epidemic · Leader election
Counting · Approximate counting · Polylogarithmic time protocol

1 Introduction

Population protocols [1] are networks that consist of very weak computational entities (also called *nodes* or *agents*), regarding their individual capabilities. These networks have been shown that are able to construct complex shapes [2] and perform complex computational tasks when they work collectively. Leader Election, which is a fundamental problem in distributed computing, is the process of designating a single agent as the coordinator of some task distributed among several nodes. The nodes communicate among themselves in order to

All authors were supported by the EEE/CS initiative NeST. The last author was also supported by the Leverhulme Research Centre for Functional Materials Design. This work was partially supported by the EPSRC Grant EP/P02002X/1 on Algorithmic Aspects of Temporal Graphs.

T. Izumi and P. Kuznetsov (Eds.): SSS 2018, LNCS 11201, pp. 154–169, 2018.
https://doi.org/10.1007/978-3-030-03232-6_11

decide which of them will get into the *leader* state. *Counting* is also a funda-mental problem in distributed computing, where nodes must determine the size n of the population. Finally, we call *Approximate Counting* the problem in which nodes must determine an estimation k of the population size n. Counting can be then considered as a special case of population size estimation, where $k = n$.

Many distributed tasks require the existence of a leader prior to the execution of the protocol and, furthermore, some knowledge about the system (for instance the size of the population) can also help to solve these tasks more efficiently with respect both to time and space.

Consider the setting in which an agent is in an initial state a, the rest $n - 1$ agents are in state b and the only existing transition is $(a, b) \rightarrow (a, a)$. This is the *one-way epidemic* process and it can be shown that the expected time to conver-gence under the uniform random scheduler is $\Theta(n \log n)$ (e.g., [3]), thus $\Theta(\log n)$ *parallel time*. Here, parallel time is the total number of interactions divided by n. In this work, we make an extensive use of epidemics, which means that infor-mation is being spread throughout the population, thus all nodes will obtain this information in $O(\log n)$ expected parallel time. We use this property to construct an algorithm that solves the *Leader Election* problem. In addition, by observing the rate of the epidemic spreading under the uniform random scheduler, we can extract valuable information about the population. This is the key idea of our *Approximate Counting* algorithm.

1.1   Related Work

The framework of population protocols was first introduced by Angluin et al. [1] in order to model the interactions in networks between small resource-limited mobile agents. When operating under a uniform random scheduler, population protocols are formally equivalent to a restricted version of stochastic Chemical Reaction Networks (CRNs), which model chemistry in a well-mixed solution [4]. "CRNs are widely used to describe information processing occurring in natural cellular regulatory networks, and with upcoming advances in synthetic biology, CRNs are a promising programming language for the design of artificial molecu-lar control circuitry" [5,6]. Results in both population protocols and CRNs can be transfered to each other, owing to a formal equivalence between these models.

Angluin et al. [7] showed that all predicates stably computable in popula-tion protocols (and certain generalizations of it) are semilinear. Semilinearity persists up to $o(\log \log n)$ local space but not more than this [8]. Moreover, the computational power of population protocols can be increased to the commu-tative subclass of **NSPACE**(n^2), if we allow the processes to form connections between each other that can hold a state from a finite domain [9], or by equip-ping them with unique identifiers, as in [10]. For introductory texts to population protocols the interested reader is encouraged to consult [9,11] and [12] (the lat-ter discusses population protocols and related developments as part of a more general overview of the emerging theory of dynamic networks).

Optimal algorithms, regarding the time complexity of fundamental tasks in distributed networks, for example leader election and majority, is the key for many distributed problems. For instance, the help of a central coordinator can lead to simpler and more efficient protocols [3]. There are many solutions to the problem of leader election, such as in networks with nodes having distinct labels or anonymous networks [13–17].

Although the availability of an initial leader does not increase the computational power of standard population protocols (in contrast, it does in some settings where faults can occur [18]), still it may allow faster computation. Specifically, the fastest known population protocols for semilinear predicates without a leader take as long as linear parallel time to converge ($\Theta(n)$). On the other hand, when the process is coordinated by a unique leader, it is known that any semilinear predicate can be stably computed with polylogarithmic expected convergence time ($O(\log^5 n)$) [19].

For several years, the best known algorithm for leader election in population protocols was the pairwise-elimination protocol of Angluin et al. [1], in which all nodes are leaders in state l initially and the only effective transition is $(l, l) \rightarrow (l, f)$. This protocol always stabilizes to a configuration with unique leader, but this takes on average linear time. Recently, Doty and Soloveichik [20] proved that not only this, but any standard population protocol requires linear time to solve leader election. This immediately led the research community to look into ways of strengthening the population protocol model in order to enable the development of sub-linear time protocols for leader election and other problems (note that Belleville, Doty, and Soloveichik [21] recently showed that such linear time lower bounds hold for a larger family of problems and not just for leader election). Fortunately, in the same way that increasing the local space of agents led to a substantial increase of the class of computable predicates [8], it has started to become evident that it can also be exploited to substantially speed-up computations. Alistarh and Gelashvili [15] proposed the first sub-linear leader election protocol, which stabilizes in $O(\log^3 n)$ parallel time, assuming $O(\log^3 n)$ states at each agent. In a very nice work, Gasieniec and Stachowiak [16] designed a space optimal ($O(\log \log n)$ states) leader election protocol, which stabilises in $O(\log^2 n)$ parallel time. They use the concept of phase clocks (introduced in [3] for population protocols), which is a synchronization and coordination tool in distributed computing. General characterizations, including upper and lower bounds, of the trade-offs between time and space in population protocols were recently achieved in [22]. Moreover, some papers [23,24] have studied leader election in the mediated population protocol model.

For counting, the most studied case is that of *self-stabilization*, which makes the strong adversarial assumption that arbitrary corruption of memory is possible in any agent at any time, and promises only that eventually it will stop. Thus, the protocol must be designed to work from any possible configuration of the memory of each agent. It can be shown that counting is *impossible* without having one agent (the "base station") that is protected from corruption [25]. In this scenario $\Theta(n \log n)$ time is sufficient [26] and necessary [27] for self-stabilizing counting.

In the less restrictive setting in which all nodes start from the same state (apart possibly from a unique leader and/or unique ids), not much is known. In a recent work, Michail [28] proposed a terminating protocol in which a pre-elected leader equipped with two n-counters computes an approximate count between $n/2$ and n in $O(n \log n)$ parallel time with high probability. The idea is to have the leader implement two competing processes, running in parallel. The first process counts the number of nodes that have been encountered once, the second process counts the number of nodes that have been encountered twice, and the leader terminates when the second counter catches up the first. In the same paper, also a version assuming unique ids instead of a leader was given.

A uniform protocol for exact population counting, but much more complicated than here is provided by our team and other co-authors in [29].

The task of counting has also been studied in the related context of worst-case dynamic networks [30–34].

1.2 Contribution

In this work we employ the use of simple epidemics in order to provide efficient solutions to approximate counting the size of a population of agents and also to leader election in populations. Our model is that of population protocols. Our goal for both problems is to get polylogarithmic parallel time and to also use small memory per agent. First, we show how to approximately count a population fast (with a leader) and then we show how to elect a leader (very fast) if we have a crude population estimate.

(a) We start by providing a protocol which provides an upper bound $\hat{n}$ of the size n of the population, where $\hat{n}$ is at most n^a for some $a > 1$. This protocol assumes the existence of a unique leader in the population. The runtime of the protocol until stabilization is $\Theta(\log n)$ parallel time. Each node except from the unique leader uses only a constant number of states. However, the leader is required to use $\Theta(\log^2 n)$ states.
(b) We then look into the problem of electing a leader. We assume an approximate knowledge of the size of the population (i.e., an estimate $\hat{n}$ of at most n^a, where n is the population size) and provide a protocol (parameterized by the size m of a counter for drawing local random numbers) that elects a unique leader w.h.p. in $O(\frac{\log^2 n}{\log m})$ parallel time, with number of states $O(\max\{m, \log n\})$ per node.
(c) Finally, we combine our two protocols in order to provide a *size oblivious* protocol which elects a leader in $O(\frac{\log^2 n}{\log m})$ parallel time.

2 The Model

In this work, the system consists of a population V of n distributed and anonymous (i.e., do not have unique IDs) *processes*, also called *nodes* or *agents*, that are capable to perform local computations. Each of them is executing as a deterministic state machine from a finite set of states Q according to a transition function $\delta : Q \times Q \to Q \times Q$. Their interaction is based on the probabilistic (uniform random) scheduler, which picks in every discrete step a random edge from the complete graph G on n vertices. When two agents interact, they mutually access their local states, updating them according to the transition function δ. The transition function is a part of the population protocol which all nodes store and execute locally.

The time is measured as the number of steps until stabilization, divided by n (parallel time). The protocols that we propose do not enable or disable connections between nodes, in contrast with [2], where Michail and Spirakis considered a model where a (virtual or physical) connection between two processes can be in one of a finite number of possible states. The transition function that we present throughout this paper, follows the notation $(x, y) \to (z, w)$, which refers to the process states before *(x and y)* and after *(z and w)* the interaction, that is, the transition function maps pairs of states to pairs of states.

The Leader Election Problem. The problem of leader election in distributed computing is for each node eventually to decide whether it is a leader or not subject to only one node decides that it is the leader. An algorithm A solves the leader election problem if eventually the states of agents are divided into *leader* and *follower*, a leader remains elected and a follower can never become a leader. In every execution, exactly one agent becomes leader and the rest determine that they are not leaders. All agents start in the same initial state q and the output is $O = \{leader, follower\}$. A randomized algorithm R solves the leader election problem if eventually only one leader remains in the system w.h.p.

Approximate Counting Problem. We define as *Approximate Counting* the problem in which a leader must determine an estimation $\hat{n}$ of the population size, where $\frac{\hat{n}}{a} < n < \hat{n}$. We call the constant a the estimation parameter.

3   Fast Counting with a Unique Leader

In this section we present our *Approximate Counting* protocol. The protocol is presented in Sect. 3.1. In Sect. 3.2 we prove the correctness of our protocol and finally, in Sect. 5, experiments that support our analysis can be found.

3.1   Abstract Description and Protocol

In this section, we construct a protocol which solves the problem of approximate counting. Our probabilistic algorithm for solving the approximate counting problem requires a unique leader who is responsible to give an estimation on the number of nodes. It uses the epidemic spreading technique and it stabilizes in $O(\log n)$ parallel time. There is initially a unique leader l and all other nodes are in state q. The leader l stores two counters in its local memory, initially both set to 0. We use the notation $l_{(c_q, c_a)}$, where c_q is the value of the first counter and c_a is the value of the second one. The leader, after the first interaction starts an epidemic by turning a q node into an a node. Whenever a q node interacts with an a node, its state becomes a $((a, q) \rightarrow (a, a))$. The first counter c_q is being used for counting the q nodes and the second counter c_a for the a nodes, that is, whenever the leader l interacts with a q node, the value of the counter c_q is increased by one and whenever l interacts with an a node, c_a is increased by one. The termination condition is $c_q = c_a$ and then the leader holds a constant-factor approximation of $\log n$, which we prove that with high probability is $2^{c_q+1} = 2^{c_a+1}$.

We first describe a simple terminating protocol that guarantee with high probability $n^{-a} \leq n_e \leq n^a$, for a constant a, i.e., the population size estimation is polynomially close to the actual size. Chernoff bounds then imply that repeating this protocol a constant number of times suffices to obtain $n/2 \leq n_e \leq 2n$ with high probability.

Protocol 1. Approximate Counting (APC)

$Q = \{q, a, l_{(c_q,c_a)}\}$
$\delta :$

$(l_{(0,0)}, q) \rightarrow (l_{(1,0)}, a)$
$(a, q) \rightarrow (a, a)$
$(l_{(c_q,c_a)}, q) \rightarrow (l_{(c_q+1,c_a)}, q),$ if $c_q > c_a$
$(l_{(c_q,c_a)}, a) \rightarrow (l_{(c_q,c_a+1)}, a),$ if $c_q > c_a$
$(l_{(c_q,c_a)}, \cdot) \rightarrow (halt, \cdot),$ if $c_q = c_a$

3.2   Analysis

Lemma 1. *When half or less of the population has been infected, with high probability $c_q > c_a$. In fact, $c_q - c_a \approx \ln(n/2) - \sqrt{\log n} > 0$.*

The previous results show that the counter c_q is a function of n and with high probability greater than c_a until half of the population becomes infected. Chernoff bounds show that w.h.p. $c_q \approx \ln(n/2)$, while $c_a \approx \ln 2$ and w.h.p. $c_a < \sqrt{\log n}$.

Corollary 1. *APC does not terminate w.h.p. until more than half of the population becomes infected.*

When the infected agents are in the majority, c_q is increased by a small constant number, while c_a eventually catches up the first counter. The termination condition $(c_q = c_a)$ is satisfied and the leader gives a constant-factor approximation of $\log n$. A proof can be found in the full version of the paper.

Lemma 2. *Our Approximate Counting protocol terminates after $\Theta(\log n)$ parallel time w.h.p.*

It takes $\Theta(\log n)$ parallel time for half agents to become infected. At that point, it holds that $|c_a - c_q| = O(\log n)$. When the a nodes are in the majority, this difference reaches zero after $\Theta(\log n)$ leader interactions. Thus, the total parallel time to termination is $\Theta(\log n)$. A proof can be found in the full version of the paper.

Lemma 3. *When half or less of the population has been infected, with high probability $c_q < \log(n/2) + \epsilon$ and $c_q > \log(n/2) - \epsilon$. When more than half of the population is infected, c_q is expected to increase by $\log 2$ and w.h.p. less than $\log n$.*

Corollary 2. *When $c_q = c_a$, w.h.p. 2^{c_q+1} is an upper bound on n.*

4 Leader Election with Approximate Knowledge of n

The existence of a *unique leader agent* is a key requirement for many population protocols [3] and generally in distributed computing, thus, having a fast protocol that elects a unique leader is of high significance. In this section, we present our *Leader Election* protocol, giving, at first, an abstract description Sect. 4.1, the algorithm Sect. 4.2 and then, we present the analysis of it Sect. 4.3. Finally, we have measured the stabilization time of this protocol for different population sizes and the results can be found in Sect. 5.

4.1 Abstract Description

We assume that the nodes know *an upper bound on the population size n^b, where n is the number of nodes and b is any big constant number*.

All nodes store three variables; the round e, a random number r and a counter c and they are able to compute random numbers within a predefined range $[1, m]$. We define two types of states; the leaders (l) and the followers (f). Initially, all nodes are in state l, indicating that they are all potential leaders. The protocol operates in rounds and in every round, the leaders compete with each other trying to survive (i.e., do not become followers). The followers just copy the *tuple* (r, e) from the leaders and try to spread it throughout the population. During the first interaction of two l nodes, one of them becomes follower, a random number between 1 and m is being generated, the leader enters the first round and the follower copies the round e and the random number r from the leader to its local memory. The followers are only being used for information spreading purposes among the potential leaders and they cannot become leaders again. Throughout this paper, n denotes the *population size* and m the *maximum number that nodes can generate*.

Information Spreading. It has been shown that the epidemic spreading of information can accelerate the convergence time of a population protocol. In this work, we adopt this notion and we use the followers as the means of competition and communication among the potential leaders. All leaders try to spread their information (i.e., their round and random number) throughout the population, but w.h.p. all of them except one eventually become followers. We say that a node x wins during an interaction if one of the following holds:

- Node x is in a bigger round e.
- If they are both in the same round, node x has bigger random number r.

One or more leaders L are in the *dominant state* if their tuple (r_1, e_1) wins every other tuple in the population. Then, the tuple (r_1, e_1) is being spread as an epidemic throughout the population, independently of the other leaders' tuples (all leaders or followers with the tuple (r_1, e_1) always win their competitors). We also call leaders L the *dominant leaders*.

Transition to Next Round. After the first interaction, a leader l enters the first round. We can group all the other nodes that l can interact with into three independent sets.

- The first group contains the nodes that are in a bigger round or have a bigger random number, being in the same round as l. If the leader l interacts with such a node, it becomes follower.
- The second group contains the nodes that are in a smaller round or have a smaller random number, being in the same round as l. After an interaction with a node in this group, the other node becomes a follower and the leader increases its counter c by one.
- The third group contains the followers that have the same tuple (r, e) as l. After an interaction with a node in this group, l increases its counter c by one.

As long as the leader l survives (i.e., does not become a follower), it increases or resets its counter c, according to the transition function δ. When the counter c reaches $b \log n$, where n^b is the upper bound on the population size, it resets it and round r is increased by one. The followers can never increase their round or generate random numbers.

Stabilization. The protocol that we present stabilizes, as the whole population will eventually reach in a final configuration of states. To achieve this, when the round of a leader l reaches $\lceil \frac{2b \log n - \log(b \log^2 n)}{\log m} \rceil$, l stops increasing its round r, unless it interacts with another leader. This rule guarantees the stabilization of our protocol.

4.2   The Protocol

In this section, we present our *Leader Election* protocol. We use the notation $p_{r,e}$ to indicate that node p has the random number r and is in the round e. Also, we say that $(r_1, e_1) > (r_2, e_2)$ if the tuple (r_1, e_1) wins the tuple (r_2, e_2). A tuple (r_1, e_1) wins the tuple (r_2, e_2) if $e_1 > e_2$ or if they are in the same round $(e_1 = e_2)$, it holds that $r_1 > r_2$.

4.3   Analysis

The leader election algorithm that we propose, elects a unique leader after $O(\frac{\log^2 n}{\log m})$ parallel time w.h.p.. To achieve this, the algorithm works in stages, called *epochs* throughout this paper and the number of potential leaders decreases exponentially between the epochs. An epoch i starts when any leader enters the ith round ($r = i$) and ends when any leader enters the $(i+1)$th round ($r = i+1$). Here we do the exact analysis for $m = \log n$. This can be generalized to any m between a constant and n.

Lemma 4. *During the execution of the protocol, at least one leader will always exist in the population.*

Protocol 2. Leader Election
$Q = \{l, f_{r,e}, l_{r,e}\} : r \in [1, m]$
δ :

#First interaction between two nodes. One of them becomes follower and the other remains leader. The leader generates a random number r and enters the first round ($e = 1$).
$(l, l) \rightarrow (l_{r,1}, f_{r,1})$

#A leader in round 0 always loses (i.e., becomes a follower) against a node in a higher round.
$(f_{r,e}, l) \rightarrow (f_{r,e}, f_{r,e})$
$(l_{r,e}, l) \rightarrow (l_{r,e}, f_{r,e})$, $l_{counter} = l_{counter} + 1$

#The winning node propagates its tuple. If a leader loses, it becomes follower.
$(f_{r,i}, f_{s,j}) \rightarrow (f_{k,l}, f_{k,l})$, if $(r, i) > (s, j)$ then $(k, l) = (r, i)$ else $(k, l) = (s, j)$
$(l_{r,i}, l_{s,j}) \rightarrow (l_{k,l}, f_{k,l})$, $l_{counter} = l_{counter} + 1$, if $(r, i) \geq (s, j)$ then $(k, l) = (r, i)$ else $(k, l) = (s, j)$
$(l_{r,i}, f_{s,j}) \rightarrow (f_{s,j}, f_{s,j})$, if $(s, j) > (r, i)$
$(l_{r,i}, f_{s,j}) \rightarrow (l_{r,i}, f_{r,i})$, $l_{counter} = l_{counter} + 1$, if $(r, i) > (s, j)$
$(l_{r,e}, f_{r,e}) \rightarrow (l_{k,j}, f_{k,j})$, $l_{counter} = l_{counter} + 1$

#When a leader increases its counter, the following code is being executed. It checks whether it has reached $c \log n$. If yes, it moves to the next round, generates a new random number and checks if it has reached the final round in order to terminate.
if $(l_{counter} = b \log n)$ **then**{
      Increase round;
      Generate a new random number between 1 and m;
      Reset counter to zero;
      if $(Round = \lceil \frac{2b \log n - \log(b \log^2 n)}{\log m} \rceil)$ **Stop increasing the round, unless you interact with a leader;**
}

Our protocol does not allow all nodes to become followers. A proof is in the full version of the paper.

Lemma 5. *Assume an epoch e and k leaders with the dominant tuple (r, e) in this epoch. The expected parallel time to convergence of their epidemic in epoch e is $\Theta(\log n)$.*

Lemma 6. *If a counter c of a leader l reaches $b \log n$, its epidemic will have already been spread throughout the whole population w.h.p.*

The previous lemma implies that no leader enters the next round if the epidemic has not been spread throughout the whole population before. This is important as we need to ensure that a non-dominant leader becomes follower by the end of an epoch, otherwise, the number of leaders would not be decreased exponentially between successive epochs. A proof can be found in the full version of the paper.

Theorem 1. *After $O(\frac{\log n}{\log m})$ epochs, there is a unique leader in the population w.h.p.*

The number of potential leaders decreases exponentially between the epochs, and after $O(\frac{\log n}{\log m})$, a unique leader exists in the population. A proof can be found in the full version of the paper.

Theorem 2. *Our Leader Election protocol elects a unique leader in $O(\frac{\log^2 n}{\log \log n})$ parallel time w.h.p.*

Proof. There are initially n leaders in the population. During an epoch e, by Lemma 5 the dominant tuple spreads throughout the population in $\Theta(\log n)$ parallel time, by Lemma 6 no (dominant) leader can enter to the next epoch if their epidemic has not been spread throughout the whole population before and by Theorem 1, there will exist a unique leader after $O(\frac{\log n}{\log m})$ epochs w.h.p., thus, for $m = b \log n$ the overall parallel time is $O(\frac{\log^2 n}{\log \log n})$. Finally, by Lemma 4, the unique leader can never become follower and according to the transition function in Protocol 2, a follower can never become leader again.

The rule which says the leaders stop increasing their rounds if $r \geq \frac{2b \log n - \log (b \log^2 n)}{\log m}$, unless they interact with another leader, implies that the population stabilizes in $O(\frac{\log^2 n}{\log \log n})$ parallel time w.h.p. and when this happens, there will exist only one leader in the population and eventually, our protocol always elects a unique leader.

Remark 1. By adjusting m to be any number between a constant and n and conducting a very similar analysis we may obtain a single leader election protocol whose time and space can be smoothly traded off between $O(\log^2 n)$ to $O(\log n)$ time and $O(\log n)$ to $O(n)$ space.

4.4   Dropping the Assumption of Knowing $\log n$

Call a population protocol *size-oblivious* if its transition function does not depend on the population size. Our leader election protocol requires a rough estimate on the size of the population in order to elect a leader in polylogarithmic time, while our approximate counting protocol requires a unique leader who initiates the epidemic process and then gives an upper bound on the population size. In this section, we combine our Approximate Counting and Leader Election protocols in order to construct a size-oblivious protocol that elects a unique leader in $O(\frac{\log^2 n}{\log m})$ parallel time and can be executed in any uniform model of population protocols.

To combine our protocols, in the our new *Leader Election* algorithm, the nodes instead of using the c counter, as described in Sect. 4.1, they use two counters c_q and c_a. The first counter is being used in order to count the non-followers and the latter to count the followers. Initially, $c_q = 1$ and $c_a = 0$. Let l be a leader with the tuple (r_1, e_1). As in Sect. 4, a tuple (r_1, e_1) is bigger that the tuple (r_2, e_2) if $r_1 > r_2$ or if $r_1 = r_2$ and $e_1 > e_2$. We can group all the other nodes that l can interact with into three independent sets.

- $(r_1, e_1) > (r_2, e_2)$. l increases its c_q counter by one.
- $(r_1, e_1) = (r_2, e_2)$. l increases its c_a counter by one.
- $(r_1, e_1) < (r_2, e_2)$. l becomes follower and resets its counters to zero.

When $c_q = c_a$ holds, l increases its round e_1 by one and resets c_q to one and c_a to zero. This process simulates the behavior of our *Approximate Counting* protocol, meaning that when $c_q = c_a$ holds, the epidemic of the dominant leaders will have been spread throughout the whole population. Regarding the termination condition, where $\log n$ is needed, the nodes store a variable s which contains the average value of c_q. To this end, whenever a leader enters from round e_1 to $e_1 + 1$, it updates the value of s as follows:

$$s = \frac{s(e_1 - 1) + c_q}{e_1} \tag{1}$$

where s is initially zero. When $e_1 = \lceil \frac{as}{\log m} \rceil$ holds ($a \geq 1$ is a small constant number), the leader stops increasing it's round and the population stabilizes in a configuration with a unique leader. Finally, we show that the variable s of the unique leader is a function of $\log n$. Even though we do not provide any proof of correctness of this protocol, in Sect. 5 we provide experiments that confirm this behavior.

5   Experiments

We have also measured the stabilization time of all of our protocols for different network sizes. We have executed them 100 times for each population size n, where $n = 2^i$ and $i = [4, 14]$. Regarding the *Leader Election* algorithm which assumes some knowledge on the population size, the results (Fig. 1) support our analysis and confirm its logarithmic behavior. In these experiments, the maximum number that the nodes could generate was $m = 100$. Finally, all executions elected a unique leader in $a\frac{\log^2 n}{\log m}$ parallel time.

The stabilization time of our *Approximate Counting with a unique leader* protocol is shown in Fig. 2a. The algorithm always gives a constant factor approximation of $\log n$, as shown in Fig. 2b. Moreover, in Fig. 3, we show the values of the counters c_q and c_a, when half of the population has been infected by the

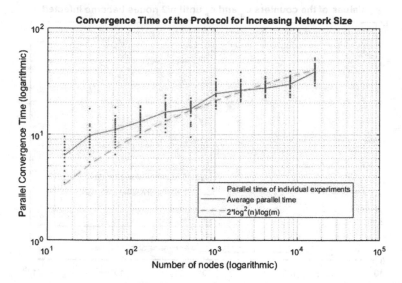

Fig. 1. Leader election with approximate knowledge of n. Both axes are logarithmic. The dots represent the results of individual experiments and the line represents the average values for each network size.

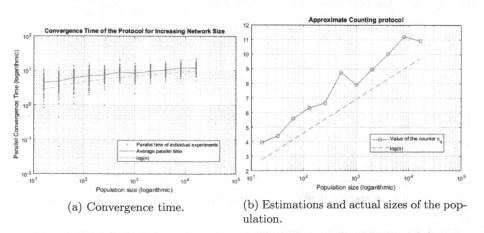

(a) Convergence time.

(b) Estimations and actual sizes of the population.

Fig. 2. Approximate counting with a unique leader.

epidemic. These experiments support our analysis, while the counter of infected nodes reaches a constant number and the counter of non-infected nodes reaches a value close to $\log n$.

Regarding our protocol for leader election with no knowledge of $\log n$, the results are shown in Fig. 4. All executions elected a unique leader after $a\frac{\log^2 n}{\log m}$ parallel time, as shown in Fig. 4a. Finally, as shown in Fig. 4b, the unique leader holds a constant factor upper bound on $\log n$ after $a\frac{\log^2 n}{\log m}$ parallel time.

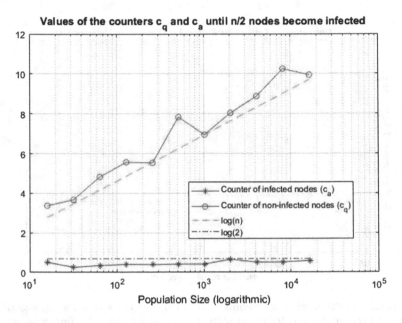

Fig. 3. Approximate counting with a unique leader. Counters c_q and c_a when half of the population has been infected by the epidemic.

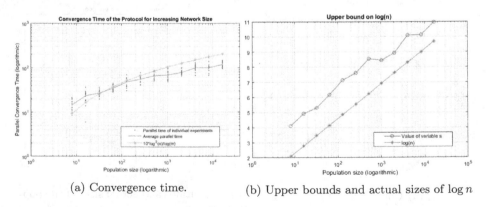

(a) Convergence time. (b) Upper bounds and actual sizes of $\log n$

Fig. 4. Composition of our approximate counting and leader election protocols.

6 Open Problems

In our leader election protocol, when two nodes interact with each other, the amount of data which is transfered is $O(max\{\log \log n, \log m\})$ bits. In certain applications of population protocols, the processes are not able to transfer arbitrarily large amount of data during an interaction. Can we design a polylogarithmic time population protocol for the problem of leader election that satisfies this requirement?

Acknowledgments. We would like to thank David Doty and Mahsa Eftekhari for their valuable comments and suggestions during the development of this research work.

References

1. Angluin, D., Aspnes, J., Diamadi, Z., Fischer, M.J., Peralta, R.: Computation in networks of passively mobile finite-state sensors. Distrib. Comput. **18**(4), 235–253 (2006)
2. Michail, O., Spirakis, P.G.: Simple and efficient local codes for distributed stable network construction. Distrib. Comput. **29**(3), 207–237 (2016)
3. Angluin, D., Aspnes, J., Eisenstat, D.: Fast computation by population protocols with a leader. Distrib. Comput. **21**(3), 183–199 (2008)
4. Soloveichik, D., Cook, M., Winfree, E., Bruck, J.: Computation with finite stochastic chemical reaction networks. Nat. Comput. **7**, 615–633 (2008)
5. Chen, H.-L., Doty, D., Soloveichik, D.: Deterministic function computation with chemical reaction networks. Nat. Comput. **7**, 517–534 (2014)
6. Doty, D.: Timing in chemical reaction networks. In: Proceedings of the 25th Annual ACM-SIAM Symposium on Discrete Algorithms (SODA), pp. 772–784 (2014)
7. Angluin, D., Aspnes, J., Eisenstat, D., Ruppert, E.: The computational power of population protocols. Distrib. Comput. **20**(4), 279–304 (2007)
8. Chatzigiannakis, I., Michail, O., Nikolaou, S., Pavlogiannis, A., Spirakis, P.G.: Passively mobile communicating machines that use restricted space. Theor. Comput. Sci. **412**(46), 6469–6483 (2011)
9. Michail, O., Chatzigiannakis, I., Spirakis, P.G.: New models for population protocols. In: Lynch, N.A. (ed.) Synthesis Lectures on Distributed Computing Theory. Morgan & Claypool (2011)
10. Guerraoui, R., Ruppert, E.: Names trump malice: tiny mobile agents can tolerate byzantine failures. In: Albers, S., Marchetti-Spaccamela, A., Matias, Y., Nikoletseas, S., Thomas, W. (eds.) ICALP 2009. LNCS, vol. 5556, pp. 484–495. Springer, Heidelberg (2009). https://doi.org/10.1007/978-3-642-02930-1_40
11. Aspnes, J., Ruppert, E.: An introduction to population protocols. In: Garbinato, B., Miranda, H., Rodrigues, L. (eds.) Middleware for Network Eccentric and Mobile Applications. Springer, Heidelberg (2009). https://doi.org/10.1007/978-3-540-89707-1_5
12. Michail, O., Spirakis, P.G.: Elements of the theory of dynamic networks. Commun. ACM **61**(2), 72 (2018)
13. Angluin, D.: Local and global properties in networks of processors. In: Proceedings of the 12th Annual ACM Symposium on Theory of Computing (STOC). ACM (1980)

14. Attiya, C., Snir, M., Warmuth, M: Computing on an anonymous ring. In: PODC 1985. ACM (1985)
15. Alistarh, D., Gelashvili, R.: Polylogarithmic-time leader election in population protocols. In: Halldórsson, M.M., Iwama, K., Kobayashi, N., Speckmann, B. (eds.) ICALP 2015. LNCS, vol. 9135, pp. 479–491. Springer, Heidelberg (2015). https://doi.org/10.1007/978-3-662-47666-6_38
16. Gasieniec, L., Stachowiak, G.: Fast space optimal leader election in population protocols. In: SODA 2018, ACM-SIAM Symposium on Discrete Algorithms (2018, to appear)
17. Fischer, M., Jiang, H.: Self-stabilizing leader election in networks of finite-state anonymous agents. In: Shvartsman, M.M.A.A. (ed.) OPODIS 2006. LNCS, vol. 4305, pp. 395–409. Springer, Heidelberg (2006). https://doi.org/10.1007/11945529_28
18. Di Luna, G.A., Flocchini, P., Izumi, T., Izumi, T., Santoro, N., Viglietta, G.: Population protocols with faulty interactions: the impact of a leader. In: Fotakis, D., Pagourtzis, A., Paschos, V.T. (eds.) CIAC 2017. LNCS, vol. 10236, pp. 454–466. Springer, Cham (2017). https://doi.org/10.1007/978-3-319-57586-5_38
19. Angluin, D., Aspnes, J., Eisenstat, D.: Stably computable predicates are semilinear. In: PODC 2006, New York. ACM Press (2006)
20. Doty, D., Soloveichik, D.: Stable leader election in population protocols requires linear time. In: Moses, Y. (ed.) DISC 2015. LNCS, vol. 9363, pp. 602–616. Springer, Heidelberg (2015). https://doi.org/10.1007/978-3-662-48653-5_40
21. Belleville, A., Doty, D., Soloveichik, D.: Hardness of computing and approximating predicates and functions with leaderless population protocols. In: ICALP 2017, Leibniz International Proceedings in Informatics (LIPIcs), vol. 80. Schloss Dagstuhl-Leibniz-Zentrum fuer Informatik (2017)
22. Alistarh, D., Aspnes, J., Eisenstat, D., Gelashvili, R., Rivest, R.L.: Time-space trade-offs in population protocols. In: Proceedings of the 28th Annual ACM-SIAM Symposium on Discrete Algorithms (SODA), pp. 2560–2579. SIAM (2017)
23. Mizoguchi, R., Ono, H., Kijima, S., Yamashita, M.: On space complexity of self-stabilizing leader election in mediated population protocol. Distrib. Comput. **25**(6), 451–460 (2012)
24. Das, S., Di Luna, G.A., Flocchini, P., Santoro, N., Viglietta, G.: Mediated population protocols: leader election and applications. In: Gopal, T.V., Jäger, G., Steila, S. (eds.) TAMC 2017. LNCS, vol. 10185, pp. 172–186. Springer, Cham (2017). https://doi.org/10.1007/978-3-319-55911-7_13
25. Beauquier, J., Clement, J., Messika, S., Rosaz, L., Rozoy, B.: Self-stabilizing counting in mobile sensor networks with a base station. In: Pelc, A. (ed.) DISC 2007. LNCS, vol. 4731, pp. 63–76. Springer, Heidelberg (2007). https://doi.org/10.1007/978-3-540-75142-7_8
26. Beauquier, J., Burman, J., Clavière, S., Sohier, D.: Space-optimal counting in population protocols. In: Moses, Y. (ed.) DISC 2015. LNCS, vol. 9363, pp. 631–646. Springer, Heidelberg (2015). https://doi.org/10.1007/978-3-662-48653-5_42
27. Aspnes, J., Beauquier, J., Burman, J., Sohier, D.: Time and space optimal counting in population protocols. In: OPODIS 2016, vol. 70 (2017)
28. Michail, O.: Terminating distributed construction of shapes and patterns in a fair solution of automata. In: Proceedings of the 2015 ACM Symposium on Principles of Distributed Computing, pp. 37–46 (2015). Also in Distributed Computing (2017)
29. Doty, D., Eftekhari, M., Michail, O., Spirakis, P.G., Theofilatos, M.: Exact size counting in uniform population protocols in nearly logarithmic time. CoRR, abs/1805.04832 (2018)

30. Izumi, T., Kinpara, K., Izumi, T., Wada, K.: Space-efficient self-stabilizing counting population protocols on mobile sensor networks. Theor. Comput. Sci. **552**, 99–108 (2014)
31. Kuhn, F., Lynch, N., Oshman, R.: Distributed computation in dynamic networks. In: Proceedings of the 42nd ACM Symposium on Theory of computing (STOC), pp. 513–522. ACM (2010)
32. Michail, O., Chatzigiannakis, I., Spirakis, P.G.: Naming and counting in anonymous unknown dynamic networks. In: Higashino, T., Katayama, Y., Masuzawa, T., Potop-Butucaru, M., Yamashita, M. (eds.) SSS 2013. LNCS, vol. 8255, pp. 281–295. Springer, Cham (2013). https://doi.org/10.1007/978-3-319-03089-0_20
33. Di Luna, G.A., Baldoni, R., Bonomi, S., Chatzigiannakis, I.: Counting in anonymous dynamic networks under worst-case adversary. In: IEEE 34th International Conference on Distributed Computing Systems (ICDCS) (2014)
34. Casteigts, A., Flocchini, P., Quattrociocchi, W., Santoro, N.: Time-varying graphs and dynamic networks. Int. J. Parallel Emerg. Distrib. Syst. **27**(5), 387–408 (2012)

Reliable Broadcast in Dynamic Networks with Locally Bounded Byzantine Failures

Silvia Bonomi[1], Giovanni Farina[1,2(✉)], and Sébastien Tixeuil[2]

[1] Dipartimento di Ingegneria Informatica Automatica e Gestionale Antonio Ruberti,
Sapienza Università di Roma, Rome, Italy
`bonomi@diag.uniroma1.it`
[2] Sorbonne Université, CNRS, Laboratoire d'Informatique de Paris 6, LIP6,
75005 Paris, France
`{giovanni.farina,sebastien.tixeuil}@lip6.fr`

Abstract. Ensuring reliable communication despite possibly malicious participants is a primary objective in any distributed system or network. In this paper, we investigate the possibility of reliable broadcast in a dynamic network whose topology may evolve while the broadcast is in progress. In particular, we adapt the Certified Propagation Algorithm (CPA) to make it work on dynamic networks and we present conditions (on the underlying dynamic graph) to enable safety and liveness properties of the reliable broadcast. We furthermore explore the complexity of assessing these conditions for various classes of dynamic networks.

Keywords: Byzantine reliable broadcast · Locally bounded failures
Dynamic networks

1 Introduction

Designing dependable and secure systems and networks that are able to cope with various types of adversaries, ranging from simple errors to internal or external attackers, requires to integrate those risks from the very early design stages. The most general attack model in a distributed setting is the Byzantine model, where a subset of nodes participating in the system may behave arbitrarily (including in a malicious manner), while the rest of processes remain correct. Also, reliable communication primitives are a core building block of any distributed software. Finally, as current applications are run for extended periods of time with expected high availability, it becomes mandatory to integrate dynamic

This work was performed within Project ESTATE (Ref. ANR-16-CE25-0009-03), supported by French state funds managed by the ANR (Agence Nationale de la Recherche), and it has has been partially supported by the INOCS Sapienza Ateneo 2017 Project (protocol number RM11715C816CE4CB). Giovanni Farina thanks the *Université Franco-Italienne/Universitá Italo-Francese* (UFI/UIF) for supporting his mobility through the Vinci grant 2018.

© Springer Nature Switzerland AG 2018
T. Izumi and P. Kuznetsov (Eds.): SSS 2018, LNCS 11201, pp. 170–185, 2018.
https://doi.org/10.1007/978-3-030-03232-6_12

changes in the underlying network while the application is running. In this paper, we address the reliable *broadcast* problem (where a *source* node must send data to every other node) in the context of dynamic networks (whose topology may change while the broadcast is in progress) that are subject to Byzantine failures (a subset of the nodes may act arbitrarily). The reliable broadcast primitive is expected to provide two guarantees: *(i)* *safety*, namely if a message m is delivered by a correct process, then m was sent by the source and *(ii)* *liveness*, namely if a message m is sent by the source, it is eventually delivered by every correct process.

Related Works. In static multi-hop networks (in which the topology remains fixed during the entire execution of the protocol) the necessary and sufficient condition enabling reliable broadcast while the maximum number of Byzantine failure is bounded by f has been identified by Dolev [5], stating that this problem can be solved if and only if the network is $2f + 1$-connected. Subsequently, the reliable broadcast problem has been analyzed assuming a local condition on the number of Byzantine neighbors a node may have [10,16]. All aforementioned works require high network connectivity. Indeed, extending a reliable broadcast service to sparse networks required to weaken the achieved guarantees [12–14]: *(i)* accepting that a small minority of correct nodes may accept invalid messages (thus compromising safety), or accepting that a small minority of correct nodes may not deliver genuine messages (thus compromising liveness).

Adapting to dynamic networks proved difficult, as the topology assumptions made by the mentioned proposals may no longer hold: the network changes during the execution. Some core problems of distributed computing have been considered in the context of dynamic networks subject to Byzantine failures [1,8] but, to the best of our knowledge, there exists a single contribution for the reliable communication problem, due to Maurer *et al.* [15]. Their work can be seen as the dynamic network extension of the Dolev [5] solution for static networks, and assumes that no more than f Byzantine processes are present in the network. Also, the protocol to be executed spreads an exponential number of messages with respect to the size of the network and requires each node to compute the minimal cut over the set of paths traversed by each received message, making the protocol unpractical for real applications.

The Byzantine tolerant reliable broadcast can also be solved by employing cryptography (e.g., digital signatures) [4,6] that enable all nodes to exchange messages guaranteeing authentication and integrity. The main advantage of cryptographic protocols is that they allow solving the problem with simpler solutions and weaker conditions (in terms of connectivity requirements). However, on the negative side, the safety of the protocols is bounded to the crypto-system.

Contributions. In this paper, we investigate the possibility of reliable broadcast in a dynamic network that is subject to Byzantine faults. More precisely, we address the possibility of a local criterion on the number of Byzantine (as opposed to a global criterion as in Maurer *et al.* [15]) in the hope that a practically efficient protocol can be derived in case the criterion is satisfied. Our starting point is the CPA protocol [2,10,16,18], that was originally designed for static networks. In particular, our contributions can be summarized as follows: *(i)* we extend the CPA algorithm to make it work in dynamic networks; *(ii)* we prove that the original safety property of CPA naturally extends to dynamic networks and we define new liveness conditions specifically suited for the dynamic networks and *(iii)* we investigate the impact of nodes awareness about the dynamic network on reliable broadcast possibility and efficiency.

Due to lack of space, part of the proofs of lemmas and theorems are omitted. They can be found inside the full version paper https://hal.archives-ouvertes. fr/hal-01712277

2   System Model & Problem Statement

We consider a distributed system composed by a set of n processes $\Pi = \{p_1, p_2, \ldots p_n\}$, each one having a unique integer identifier. The passage of time is measured according to a fictional global clock spanning over natural numbers $\mathbb{N}$. The processes are arranged in a multi-hop communication network. The network can be seen as an undirected graph where each node represents a process $p_i \in \Pi$ and each edge represents a communication channel between two elements $p_i, p_j \in \Pi$ such that p_i and p_j can communicate.

Dynamic Network Model. The communication network is *dynamic* i.e., the set of edges (or available communication channels) changes over time. More formally, we model the network as a *Time Varying Graph* (TVG) [3] i.e., a graph $\mathcal{G} = (V, E, \rho, \zeta)$ where:

- V is the set of processes (in our case $V = \Pi$);
- $E \subseteq V \times V$ is the set of edges (i.e., communication channels);
- $\rho : E \times \mathbb{N} \to \{0, 1\}$ is the *presence* function. Given an edge $e_{i,j}$ between two nodes p_i and p_j, $\rho(e_{i,j}, t) = 1$ indicates that edge $e_{i,j}$ is present at time t;
- $\zeta : E \times \mathbb{N} \to \mathbb{N}$ is the *latency* function that indicates how much time is needed to cross an edge starting from a given time t. In particular, $\zeta(e_{i,j}, t) = \delta_{i,j,t}$ indicates that a message m sent at time t from p_i to p_j takes $\delta_{i,j,t}$ time units to cross edge $e_{i,j}$.

The evolution of $\mathcal{G}$ can also be described as a sequence of static graphs $S_{\mathcal{G}} = G_0, G_1, \ldots G_T$ where G_i corresponds to the *snapshot* of $\mathcal{G}$ at time t_i (i.e. $G_i = (V, E_i)$ where $E_i = \{e \in E \mid \rho(e, t_i) = 1\}$). No further assumptions on the evolution of the dynamic network are made. The static graph $G = (V, E)$ that considers all the processes and all the possible existing edges is called *underlying graph* of $\mathcal{G}$ and it flattens the time dimension indicating only the pairs of nodes that have been connected at some time t'. In the following, we interchangeably use terms *process* and *node* and we will refer to *edges* and *communication channels* interchangeably. Let us note that the TVG model is one among the most general available and it is able to abstract and characterize several real dynamic networks [3].

Communication Model and Timing Assumption. Processes communicate through message exchanges. Every message has (i) a *source*, which is the id of the process that has created the message and (ii) a *sender*, that is the id of the process that is relaying the message. The source and the sender may coincide. The sender is always a neighbor in the communication network. The ID of the source is included inside the message, i.e. any message is composed by its content and the source ID. We refer with m_s to a message m with p_s as source.

We assume *authenticated* and *reliable* point-to-point channels where (a) *authenticated* ensures that the identity of the sender cannot be forged; (b) *reliable* guarantees that the channel delivers a message m if and only if (i) m was previously sent by its sender and (ii) the channel has been up long enough to allow the reception (i.e. given a message m sent at time t from p_i to p_j and having latency $\delta_{i,j,t}$, we will have reliable delivery if $\rho(e_{i,j}, \tau) = 1$ for each $\tau \in [t, t + \delta_{i,j,t}]$). Notice that these channel assumptions are implicitly made also on analysis of CPA on static networks and that they are both essential to guarantees the reliable broadcast properties.

At every time unit t each process takes the following actions: (i) *send* where processes send all the messages for the current time unit (potentially none), (ii) *receive* where processes receive and store all the messages for the current time unit (potentially none) and (iii) *computation* where processes process the buffer of received messages and compute the messages to be sent during the next time unit according to the deterministic distributed protocol $\mathcal{P}$ that they are executing. Thus, the system is assumed to be synchronous in the sense that (i) every channel has a latency function that is bounded and the overall message delivery time is bounded by the maximum channel latency and (ii) computation steps are bounded by a constant that is negligible with respect to the overall message delivery time and we consider it equal to 0. We discuss the implications and consequences of lack of synchrony inside the full version paper.

Failure Model. We assume an omniscient adversary able to control several processes of the network allowing them to behave arbitrarily (including corrupting/dropping messages or simply crashing). We call them *Byzantine* processes. Processes that are not Byzantine faulty are said to be *correct*. Correct processes do not a priori know which processes are Byzantine. Specifically to reliable broadcast protocols, a Byzantine process can spread messages carrying a fake source ID and/or content or it can drop any received message preventing its propagation.

We considered the *f-locally bounded* failure model [10] as all CPA related works, i.e., along time every process p_i can be connected with at most f Byzantine processes. In other words, given the underlying static graph $G = (V, E)$, every process $p_i \in V$ has at most f Byzantine neighbors in G.

Problem Statement. In this paper, we consider the problem of *Reliable Broadcast over dynamic networks* assuming a f-locally bounded Byzantine failure model from a given *correct*[1] source p_s. We say that a protocol $\mathcal{P}$ satisfies *reliable broadcast*, if a message m broadcast by a correct process $p_s \in \Pi$ (also called *source* or *author*) is eventually delivered (i.e., accepted as a valid message) by every correct process $p_j \in \Pi$. Said differently, a protocol $\mathcal{P}$ satisfies *reliable broadcast*, if the following conditions are met:

- **Safety:** if a message m is delivered by a correct process, then such message has been sent by the source p_s;
- **Liveness:** if a message m is broadcast by the source p_s, it is eventually delivered by every correct process.

In other words, a reliable broadcast protocol extends the guarantees provided by the communication channels to the message exchanges between a node and any correct process not directly connected to it.

3   The Certified Propagation Algorithm (CPA)

The Certified Propagation Algorithm (CPA) [10,16] is a protocol enforcing reliable broadcast, from a correct source p_s, in *static* multi-hop networks with a f-locally bounded Byzantine adversary model, where nodes have no knowledge on the global network topology. Given a message m to be broadcast, CPA starts the propagation of m_s from p_s and applies three acceptance policies (denoted by AC) to decide if m_s should be accepted and forwarded (*i.e.*, transmitted also by nodes different from the source) by a process p_j. Specifically:

- p_s delivers m_s (**AC1**), forwards it to all of its neighbors, and stops;
- when receiving m_s from p_i, if p_i is the source then p_j delivers m_s (**AC2**), forwards m_s to all of its neighbors and stops; otherwise the message is buffered.
- upon receiving $f + 1$ copies of m_s from distinct neighbors, p_j delivers m_s (**AC3**), then forwards it to all its neighbors and stops.

The correctness of CPA on static networks has been proved to be dependent on the network topology. In particular, Litsas *et al.* [11] provided topological conditions based on the concept of k-*level ordering*. Informally, given a graph $G = (V, E)$ and considering a node p_s as the source, we can define a k-level ordering as a partition of nodes into *ordered levels* such that: (*i*) p_s belongs to level L_0, (*ii*) all the neighbors of p_s belong to level L_1, and (*iii*) each node in a level L_i has at least k neighbors over levels L_j, with $j < i$. A k-level ordering is *minimum* if every node appears in the minimum level possible.

Definition 1 (MKLO). *Let $G = (V, E)$ be a graph and let p_s be a node of G called* source. *The* minimum k-level ordering (MKLO) *of G from p_s is the*

---

[1] Note the assumption of a possibly faulty source leads to a more general problem, the *Byzantine Agreement* [5].

partition P_k of nodes into disjoint subsets called levels L_i defined as follows:

$$\begin{cases} p \in L_0 & \textit{if } p = p_s \\ p \in L_1 & \textit{if } p \in N_s \\ p \in L_{i>1} & \textit{if } p \in V \setminus (\bigcup\limits_{j=0}^{i-1} L_j) \textit{ and } |N_p \cap (\bigcup\limits_{j=0}^{i-1} L_j)| \geq k \end{cases}$$

For CPA to ensure reliable broadcast from p_s, a sufficient condition is that a k-level ordering from p_s exists, with $k \geq 2f + 1$. Conversely, the necessary condition demands a k-level ordering from p_s with $k \geq f + 1$ (see [11]). Those conditions can be verified with an algorithm whose time complexity is polynomial in the size of the network, specifically with a modified Breadth-First-Search. In the case that a graph $G = (V, E)$ satisfies the necessary condition from p_s but not the sufficient one, then further analysis must be carried out. In particular, in order to verify whether G enables reliable broadcast from p_s, one should check whether a k-level ordering from p_s exists (with $k = f + 1$) in every sub-graph G' obtained from G by removing all nodes corresponding to possible Byzantine placement in the f-locally bounded assumption. The verification of the strict condition has been proven to be NP-Hard [9].

4   The Certified Propagation Algorithm on Dynamic Networks

In this section, we analyze how CPA behaves on dynamic networks, *i.e.* networks whose topology may evolve over time, and how it needs to be extended to work in such settings.

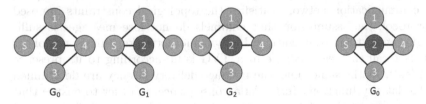

(a) A Time Varying Graph $\mathcal{G} = (V, E, \rho, \varsigma)$.   (b) Underlying graph $G = (V, E)$.

Fig. 1. Example of a simple TVG and its underlying static graph.

Let us consider the TVG shown in Fig. 1 and suppose process p_2 is Byzantine. If we consider the static underlying graph $G = (V, E)$ shown in Fig. 1b, it is easy to verify that running CPA from the source node p_s is possible to achieve reliable broadcast in a 1-locally bounded adversary. However, if we consider snapshots of the TVG at different times[2] as shown in Fig. 1a, one can verify that nodes p_3 and p_4 remain unable to deliver the message forever. In fact, p_3 is not a neighbor of the source p_s when the message is broadcast by p_s (*i.e.*, at time t_0), and even if it had happened ($e_{s,3}$ at time t_0) the edge connecting p_4 with its correct neighbor p_3 appears only before the message would have been delivered and accepted by p_3, and thus it is not available for the retransmission. From this simple example its easy to see that the temporal dimension plays a fundamental role in the definition of topological constraints that a TVG must satisfy to enable reliable broadcast.

4.1 CPA Safety in Dynamic Networks

In the following, we show that the authenticated and reliable channels are necessary to ensure the reliable broadcast through CPA.

Lemma 1. *The CPA algorithm does not ensure safety of reliable broadcast when channels are not both authenticated and reliable (even on static graphs).*

The same channel assumptions are sufficient for ensuring safety also on dynamic networks.

Theorem 1. *Let $\mathcal{G} = (V, E, \rho, \zeta)$ be the TVG of a network with f-locally bounded Byzantine adversary. If every correct process p_i runs CPA on top of reliable authenticated channels, then if a message m_s is delivered by p_i, m_s was previously sent by the correct source p_s.*

4.2 CPA Liveness in Dynamic Networks

The CPA liveness in static networks is based on the availability of a certain topology that supports the message propagation. Indeed every edge is always up so, once the communication network satisfies the topological constraints imposed by the protocol, the assumption that channels do not lose messages is sufficient to guarantee their propagation. In dynamic networks, this is no longer true. Let us recall that each edge e in a TVG is up according to its presence function $\rho(e, t)$. At the same time, the message delivery latency are determined by the edge latency function $\zeta(e, t)$. As a consequence, in order to ensure that a message m sent at time t from p_i to p_j is delivered, we need that (p_i, p_j) remains up until time $t + \zeta(e, t)$. Contrarily, there could exist a communication channel where every message sent has no guarantee to be delivered as the edge disappears while the message is still traveling. Thus, in addition to topological constraints, moving to dynamic networks we need to set up other constraints on when edges appear and for how long they remain up. Considering that processes have no information about the network evolution, they do not know if and when a given transmitted message will reach its receiver. Hence, without assuming extra knowledge, a correct process must re-send messages infinitely often.

---

[2] For the sake of simplicity, we consider the channel delay always equal to 1 in the example.

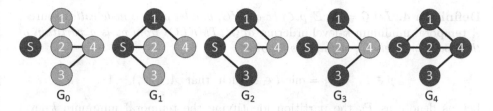

Fig. 2. TVG example.

As a consequence, CPA must be extended to the dynamic context incorporating the following additional steps:

– if process p_i delivers a message m, it forwards m to all of its neighbors infinitely often, at every time unit.

As a consequence, each time that the neighbors of p_i changes, p_i attempts to propagate the message. Let us notice that such an infinite retransmission can be avoided/stopped only if a process get the acknowledgments about the delivery of the communication channels. This issue has been analyzed by considering further assumptions on the dynamic network [7,17]. To ease of explanation, we will refer to this extended version of CPA as Dynamic CPA (DCPA).

We now characterize the conditions enabling a communication channel to deliver messages in order to argue about liveness. For this purpose, we define a boolean predicate whose value is true if and only if the TVG allows the reliable delivery of a message m sent from p_i to p_j at time t.

Definition 2. *Let $\mathcal{G} = (V, E, \rho, \zeta)$ be a TVG. We define the predicate Reliable Channel Delivery at time t', RCD(p_i, p_j, t') as follows:*

$$\text{RCD}(p_i, p_j, t') = \begin{cases} \text{true} & \text{if } \rho(<p_i, p_j>, \tau) = 1, \ \forall \tau \in [t', t' + \zeta(e_{i,j}, t')]. \\ \text{false} & \text{otherwise.} \end{cases}$$

The communication channels do not usually have memory, thus we consider any message sent while the RCD() predicate is false as dropped.

Now that we are able to express constraints on each edge through the RCD() predicate, we need to define those RCD() that enable liveness of reliable broadcast. Let us define the *k-acceptance function*, that encapsulates temporal aspects for the three acceptance conditions of CPA.

Definition 3. *Let $p_s \in \Pi$ be a process that starts a reliable broadcast at time t_{br}. The k-acceptance function $\mathcal{A}_k(p, t)$ over the time $t \in \mathbb{N}$ is defined as follows:*

$$\mathcal{A}_k(p_j, t) = \begin{cases} 1 & \text{if } p_j = p_s \text{ with } t \geq t_{br} & (AK1) \\ 1 & \text{if } \exists\, t' \geq t_{br} \ : \ \text{RCD}(p_s, p_j, t') = \text{true with } t \geq t' + \zeta(e_{s,j}, t') & (AK2) \\ 1 & \text{if } \exists\, p_1, \ldots, p_k \ : \ \forall i \in [1, k], \ \mathcal{A}_k(p_i, t_i) = 1 \text{ and} \\ & \quad \exists\, t_i' \geq t_i \ : \ \text{RCD}(p_j, p_i, t_i') = \text{true with } t \geq t_i' + \zeta(e_{i,j}, t_i') & (AK3) \\ 0 & \text{otherwise} \end{cases}$$

Definition 4. *Let* $\mathcal{G} = (V, E, \rho, \zeta)$ *be a TVG, and let* p_s *be a node called* source. *A* temporal minimum k-level ordering *of* $\mathcal{G}$ *(TMKLO) from* p_s *is a partition of the nodes in levels* L_{t_i} *defined as follows:*

$$p \in L_{t_i} \text{ iff } t_i = \min t \in \mathbb{N} \text{ such that } \mathcal{A}_k(p, t_i) = 1$$

Let us denote as P_k the partition identifying the temporal minimum k-level ordering.

As an example, let us consider the TVG presented in Fig. 2: it evolves in five discrete time instants (*i.e.*, $t_0, t_1, \ldots, t_4$), its latency function $\zeta(e, t)$ is equal to 1 for every edge e at any time t. Now, let us consider process p_s as a source node that broadcasts m at time $t_{br} = 0$, and let us assume that $k = 2$. Such a TVG admits a temporal minimum 2-level ordering $P_2 = \{L_{t_0} = \{p_s\}, L_{t_1} = \{p_1\}, L_{t_2} = \{p_3\}, L_{t_4} = \{p_2, p_4\}\}$. Indeed:

- The 2-acceptance function $\mathcal{A}_2(p_s, t)$ is equal to 1 for $t \geq t_{br} = t_0$ according to *AK1*.
- The acceptance function evaluated on process p_1 is equal to 1 for $t \geq 1$ according to *AK2* (*i.e.*, $t' = 0$ and $RCD(p_s, p_1, 0) = true$ due to the presence function $\rho(<p_s, p_1>, \tau) = 1$, $\forall \tau \in [0, 1])$.
- On processes p_3 and p_2, the acceptance function evaluates to 1 respectively for $t \geq 2$ and for $t \geq 4$, for the same reasons as p_1.
- The acceptance function on p_4 evaluates to 1 for $t \geq 4$ according to *AK3* (*i.e.*, $RCD(p_i, p_4, t'_i) = true$ for $p_i = p_1$, $t'_i = 1$, and for $p_i = p_3$, $t'_i = 3$).

We now present a sufficient condition (Theorem 2) and a necessary condition (Theorem 3) for the liveness of reliable broadcast based on the TMKLO.

Theorem 2 (DCPA liveness sufficient condition). *Let* $\mathcal{G} = (V, E, \rho, \zeta)$ *be a TVG, let* p_s *be the* source *which broadcasts* m *at time* t_{br}, *and let us assume* f-locally bounded Byzantine failures. *If there exists a partition* $P_k = \{L_{t_{br}}, L_{t_1} \ldots L_{t_x}\}$ *of the nodes in* V *representing a TMKLO of* $\mathcal{G}$ *associated to* m *with* $k > 2f$, *then the message* m *spread using DCPA is eventually delivered by every correct process in* $\mathcal{G}$.

Proof. We need to prove that if there exist a TMKLO with $k > 2f$ associated to message m, then any correct process eventually satisfies one of the CPA acceptance policies. A *TMKLO* with $k > 2f$ implies that there exist a time t such that the $2f + 1$-acceptance function $\mathcal{A}_k(p, t)$ is equal to 1 for every node of the network.

The process p_s belongs to any TMKLO due to AK1: as the source of the broadcast, p_s delivers the message according to AC1. Remind that the correct processes running DCPA spread the delivered messages over their neighborhood infinitely often. Then, the other nodes belong to the TMKLO due to the occurrence of AK2 or AK3.

If *AK2* is satisfied by a node p_j from time t_j, then m: *(i)* can be delivered by the channel interconnecting p_s with p_j by definition of RCD(), and *(ii)* it is transmitted by p_s, because t_j is greater than t_{br}. It follows that p_j delivers m according to $AC2$: indeed, p_j has received m directly from the source.

If $AK3$ is satisfied on a node p_j, it is possible to identify two scenarios:

- **Case 1**: RCD() is satisfied between p_j and $2f + 1$ nodes p_i where $AK2$ is already satisfied. We have shown that the processes satisfying $AK2$ accept m, and so they retransmit m. Assuming the f-locally bounded failure model, at most f nodes among the neighbors of p_i can be Byzantine and may not propagate m. Thus, p_j receives at least $f + 1$ copies of m from distinct neighbors. According to $AC3$ of DCPA p_j delivers m.
- **Case 2**: RCD() is satisfied between p_j and $2f + 1$ nodes p_i where $AK2$ or $AK3$ is already satisfied. Inductively, as the nodes considered in **Case 1** deliver m, it follows that the nodes p_j satisfying $AK3$ due to at least $2f + 1$ nodes p_i where $AK2$ or $AK3$ already holds also deliver m.

Theorem 3 (DCPA liveness necessary condition). *Let $\mathcal{G} = (V, E, \rho, \zeta)$ be a TVG, let p_s be the source that starts to broadcast m at time t_{br}, and let us assume f-locally bounded Byzantine failures. The message m can be delivered by every correct process in $\mathcal{G}$ only if a partition $P_k = \{L_{t_{br}}, L_{t_1} \ldots L_{t_x}\}$ of nodes in V representing a TMKLO of $\mathcal{G}$ associated to m with $k > f$ exists.*

Proof. Let us assume for the purpose of contradiction that: *(i)* every correct process in $\mathcal{G}$ delivers m, *(ii)* the Byzantine failures are f-locally bounded, and *(iii)* there does not exist a TMKLO associated to m with $k > f$. The latter implies that the TMKLO with $k = f + 1$ does not include all the nodes, *i.e.* $\exists p \in \Pi \mid \forall t \in \mathbb{N}, \mathcal{A}_{f+1}(p, t) = 0$.

The process p_s is always included in a *TMKLO* of any k. Thus, p_s is included in P_{f+1}. The nodes that deliver m according to $AC2$ have received m from p_s. Thus, the RCD() predicate evaluated between p_s and p_i was true at least once after the delivery of m by p_s. It follows that the condition defined in $AK2$ is eventually satisfied, and that those nodes are included in P_{f+1}.

The remaining nodes that deliver according to $AC3$ have received the message from $f + 1$ distinct neighbors. Let us initially assume that such neighbors have delivered the message by $AC2$. Again, the RCD predicate evaluated between the receiving node p_j and the distinct $f + 1$ neighbors p_i has been true at least once after the respective deliveries of m. We already proved that such neighbors of p_i are included in P_{f+1}, therefore the condition defined in $AK2$ is satisfied by those p_j and they are included in P_{f+1}.

It naturally follows that the remaining nodes (the ones that have received the message from neighbors satisfying $AC2$ or $AC3$) are included in P_{f+1}. This is in contradiction with the assumptions we made, because eventually every process satisfies one of the conditions AK1, AK2 or AK3, and the claim follows.

5   On the Detection of DCPA Liveness

In Sect. 4, we proved that DCPA always ensure the reliable broadcast safety, and we provided the necessary and sufficient conditions about the dynamic network to enforce the reliable broadcast liveness. In this section, we are investigating the ability of individual processes to detect whether the reliable broadcast liveness is actually achieved in the current network. In more detail, we seek answers to the following questions:

- **(Conscious Termination)**: Given a message m_s sent by a source p_s on TVG $\mathcal{G}$, is p_s able to detect if m_s will eventually be delivered by every correct process?
- **(Bounded Broadcast Latency)**: Given a message m_s sent by a source p_s on TVG $\mathcal{G}$, is p_s able to compute upper and lower bounds for reliable broadcast completion?

Obviously, if p_s has no knowledge about $\mathcal{G}$, nothing about termination can be detected. As a consequence, some knowledge about $\mathcal{G}$ is required to enable Conscious Termination and Bounded Broadcast Latency. We now formalize the notion of *Broadcast Latency*, and introduce oracles that abstract the knowledge a process may have about $\mathcal{G}$.

Definition 5 (Broadcast Latency (BL)). *Let $\mathcal{G} = (V, E, \rho, \zeta)$ be a TVG and let p_s be a node called* source *that broadcasts a message m at time t_{br}. We define as* Broadcast Latency *BL the period between t_{br} and the time of the last delivery of m by a correct process.*

We define the following knowledge oracles (from more powerful to least powerful):

- *Full knowledge Oracle (FKO)*: FKO provides full knowledge about the TVG, *i.e.*, it provides $\mathcal{G} = (V, E, \rho, \zeta)$;
- *Partial knowledge Oracle (PKO)*: given a TVG $\mathcal{G} = (V, E, \rho, \zeta)$, PKO provides the underlying static graph $G = (V, E)$ of $\mathcal{G}$;
- *Size knowledge Oracle (SKO)*: given a TVG $\mathcal{G} = (V, E, \rho, \zeta)$, SKO provides the size of $\mathcal{G}$, that is $|V|$.

5.1   Detecting DCPA Liveness on Generic TVGs

In Sect. 4 we showed that the conditions guaranteeing the liveness property of reliable broadcast are strictly bounded to the network evolution. It follows that the knowledge provided by an FKO, in particular about the network evolution starting from the broadcast time t_{br}, is necessary to argue on liveness, unless further assumptions are taken into account. In the following, we clarify how a process can employs an FKO to detect Conscious Termination and Bounded Broadcast Latency.

Lemma 2. *Let $\mathcal{G} = (V, E, \rho, \zeta)$ be a TVG, let p_s be a node called* source *that broadcasts a message m at time t_{br} and let us assume f-locally bounded Byzantine failures. If p_s has access to an FKO then it is able to verify if there exists a TMKLO for the current broadcast on $\mathcal{G}$.*

Proof. In order to prove the claim it is enough to show an algorithm that verifies if a TMKLO exists, given the full knowledge of the TVG provided by FKO.

Such algorithm works as follow: initially, the source p_s is placed in level $L_{t_{br}}$ of the TMKLO. Then, the snapshots characterizing the TVG have to be analyzed, starting from $G_{t_{br}}$ and following their order. In particular, for each snapshot G_{t_i}, $t_i \geq t_{br}$, we need to verify that:

1. edges with only one endpoint already included in some level of the TMKLO are up enough to satisfy RCD() and
2. whenever RCD() is satisfied for a given edge $e_{i,j}$, we need to check if it allows p_j to be part of the TMKLO as it satisfies one condition among AK2 and AK3.

The algorithm ends when a TMKLO is found or when all the snapshots have been analyzed (and in the latter case we can infer that no TMKLO exists for the considered message on the given TVG). Assuming that G spans over T time instants, the complexity of this algorithm is:

$$O(|T||E|) + O(|V| + |E|) = O(|V| + |T||E|)$$

A more detailed description of the algorithm is delegated to the full version paper.

Theorem 4. *Let $G = (V, E, \rho, \zeta)$ be a TVG, let p_s be a node called* source *that broadcasts a message m at time t_{br} and let us assume f-locally bounded Byzantine failures. If p_s has access to an FKO then it is able to detect if eventually every correct process will deliver m.*

Let us note that if a process has the capability of computing the *TMKLO* for a message m sent at time t_{br}, then it can also establish a lower bound and an upper bound on the time needed by every correct process to deliver m simply evaluating the maximum level of the TMKLO that satisfy respectively the necessary and the sufficient condition for DCPA.

Theorem 5. *Let $G = (V, E, \rho, \zeta)$ be a TVG and let p_s be a node called* source *that broadcasts a message m at time t_{br} and let us assume f-locally bounded Byzantine failures. Let $P_{f+1} = \{L_{t_0}, L_{t_1} \ldots L_{t_x}\}$ be the TMKLO with $k = f + 1$ associated to m and let t_{max}^{f+1} be the time associated to the last level of P_{f+1}. Let assume the existence of the TMKLO with $k = 2f + 1$ associated to m, $P_{2f+1} = \{L_{t_0}, L_{t_1} \ldots L_{t_x}\}$, and let t_{max}^{2f+1} be the time associated to the last level of P_{2f+1}. The computed TMKLOs provide respectively a lower bound and an upper bound for BL such that:*

$$t_{max}^{f+1} - t_{br} \leq BL \leq t_{max}^{2f+1} - t_{br}$$

Remind that, as the sufficient condition we provided is not strict, a TMKLO with $k = 2f + 1$ could not exist even if the reliable broadcast is achievable. It is also possible to provide a stricter upper bound for BL as we explained inside the proof of Theorem 4, but is not practical to compute. Finally, let us remark that the knowledge on the underlying topology is not enough on dynamic networks to argue on liveness.

Remark 1. Let $\mathcal{G} = (V, E, \rho, \zeta)$ be a TVG and let p_s be a node called *source* that broadcasts a message m at time t_{br} and let us assume f-locally bounded Byzantine failures. If a process p_s has access only to a PKO (and not to an FKO) then it is not able to detect either Conscious Termination and Bounded Broadcast Latency. Indeed, as we highlighted in Sect. 4.2, moving on dynamic network the knowledge on the underlying graph is not enough, because specific sequences of edge appearances are required in order to guarantee the message propagation (let us take again Fig. 1 as clarifying example). Thus, a PKO is not enough in arguing on liveness. The same can be said about Bounded Broadcast Latency as PKO provides no information about the time instants when the edges will appear.

5.2   Detecting DCPA Liveness on Restricted TVGs

Casteigts *et al.* [3] defined a hierarchy of TVG classes based on the strength of the assumptions made about appearance of edges. So far, we considered the most general TVG[3]. In the following, we consider two more specific classes of the hierarchy where we show that liveness can be detected using oracles weaker than FKO. In particular, we consider the following classes that are suited to model recurring networks:

- **Class recurrence of edges, ER**: if an edge e appears once, it appears infinitively often[4].
- **Class time bounded recurrences, TBER**: if an edge e appears once, it appears infinitively often and there exist an upper bound Δ between two consecutive appearances of e[5].

Let us recall that assuming predicate $\mathsf{RCD}(e_{i,j}, t) = \mathsf{true}$ for every edge $e_{i,j}$ at some time t is necessary to guarantee liveness. While considering classes ER and TBER, such condition must be satisfied infinitely often, otherwise it is easy to show that the results presented in the previous section still apply. Let us also note that the conditions we defined in Sect. 4.2 are related to a single broadcast generated by a specific source p_s i.e., for a source p_s broadcasting a message at time t_{br} the conditions must hold from t_{br} on. Contrarily, exploiting the recurrence of edges it is possible to define different conditions that are valid for every broadcast from the same source p_s, independently from when it starts.

Detecting DCPA Liveness in ER TVG. In this section, we prove that considering TVG of class ER, we can get the following results: *(i)* PKO (an oracle

---

[3] Class 1 TVG according to Casteigts *et al.* [3].
[4] Class 6 TVG in Casteigts *et al.* [3].
[5] Class 7 TVG in Casteigts *et al.* [3].

weaker than FKO) is enough to enable Conscious Termination, *(ii)* despite the more specific TVG considered, FKO is still required to establish upper bounds for *BL*. Intuitively, this results follows from the fact that PKO allows to determine whether a MKLO exists on the static underlying graph, and this is enough to detect if eventually every correct process will be able to deliver the message. However, given the absence of information on when each edge is going to appear, it is impossible to compute an upper bound on the time required to accomplish the broadcast.

Theorem 6. *Let $\mathcal{G} = (V, E, \rho, \zeta)$ be a TVG of class ER that ensures* RCD() *infinitively often, and let p_s be a node called* source *that broadcasts m at time t_{br}, and let us assume f-locally bounded Byzantine failures. If p_s has access to a PKO, then it is able to detect if eventually every correct process delivers m.*

Detecting DCPA Liveness in TBER TVG. The liveness condition enabling CPA to enforce reliable broadcast relays on the network topology, therefore an oracle weaker that FKO cannot enable Conscious Termination unless further assumptions are made. On the other hand, the weaker oracle SKO allows a process to compute Bounded Broadcast Latency.

Theorem 7. *Let $\mathcal{G} = (V, E, \rho, \zeta)$ be a TVG of class TBER where each edge $e_{i,j}$ reappears in at most Δ time instants satisfying* RCD($e_{i,j}, t$). *Let $\delta_{max} = max(\zeta(e, t))$. Let p_s be a node called* source *that broadcasts m at time t_{br}, and let us assume f-locally bounded Byzantine failures. Let $P_{2f+1} = \{L_{t_0}, L_{t_1} \ldots L_{t_x}\}$ be the MKLO with $k = 2f + 1$ associated to m and computed on the underlying graph $G = (V, E)$ (if exists) and let S_{2f+1} be size of P_{2f+1}. If p_s uses SKO or PKO, then p_s is able to compute an upper bound for BL. Specifically:*

$$BL \leq |V|(\delta_{max} + \Delta) using\ SKO$$

$$BL \leq S_{2f+1}(\delta_{max} + \Delta) using\ PKO$$

6 Conclusion

We considered the reliable broadcast problem in dynamic networks represented by TVG. We analyzed the porting conditions enabling CPA to be correctly employed on dynamic networks. The analysis of this simple algorithm is important as it works exploiting only local knowledge. This contrasts to the best result so far in the same setting [15], that demands an exponential costs to check when a message can be delivered. Moreover, we presented necessary and sufficient conditions to ensure safety and liveness DCPA. We analyzed how much knowledge of the TVG is needed to detect whether the liveness condition is satisfied, and its cost. Our work is a starting point to identify more general parameters of dynamic networks that guarantees the fulfillment of the conditions we provided, both in a deterministic and probabilistic way. Other interesting points to address in future works are: (i) the definition of a more realistic locally bounded failure model that takes also the time dimension into account, (ii) the research of conditions on the dynamic network enabling nodes to conscious termination with just local information.

References

1. Augustine, J., Pandurangan, G., Robinson, P.: Fast Byzantine agreement in dynamic networks. In: Fatourou, P., Taubenfeld, G. (eds.) ACM Symposium on Principles of Distributed Computing, PODC 2013, 22–24 July 2013, Montreal, QC, Canada, pp. 74–83. ACM (2013)
2. Bhandari, V., Vaidya, N.H.: Reliable broadcast in radio networks with locally bounded failures. IEEE Trans. Parallel Distrib. Syst. **21**(6), 801–811 (2010)
3. Casteigts, A., Flocchini, P., Quattrociocchi, W., Santoro, N.: Time-varying graphs and dynamic networks. Int. J. Parallel Emergent Distrib. Syst. **27**(5), 387–408 (2012)
4. Castro, M., Liskov, B., et al.: Practical Byzantine fault tolerance. In: OSDI, vol. 99, pp. 173–186 (1999)
5. Dolev, D.: Unanimity in an unknown and unreliable environment. In: 1981 22nd Annual Symposium on Foundations of Computer Science, SFCS 1981, pp. 159–168. IEEE (1981)
6. Drabkin, V., Friedman, R., Segal, M.: Efficient Byzantine broadcast in wireless ad-hoc networks. In: 2005 Proceedings of International Conference on Dependable Systems and Networks, DSN 2005, pp. 160–169. IEEE (2005)
7. Gómez-Calzado, C., Casteigts, A., Lafuente, A., Larrea, M.: A connectivity model for agreement in dynamic systems. In: Träff, J.L., Hunold, S., Versaci, F. (eds.) Euro-Par 2015. LNCS, vol. 9233, pp. 333–345. Springer, Heidelberg (2015). https://doi.org/10.1007/978-3-662-48096-0_26
8. Guerraoui, R., Huc, F., Kermarrec, A.: Highly dynamic distributed computing with Byzantine failures. In: Fatourou, P., Taubenfeld, G. (eds.) ACM Symposium on Principles of Distributed Computing, PODC 2013, 22–24 July 2013, Montreal, QC, Canada, pp. 176–183. ACM (2013)
9. Ichimura, A., Shigeno, M.: A new parameter for a broadcast algorithm with locally bounded Byzantine faults. Inf. Process. Lett. **110**(12–13), 514–517 (2010)
10. Koo, C.Y.: Broadcast in radio networks tolerating Byzantine adversarial behavior. In: Proceedings of the Twenty-Third Annual ACM Symposium on Principles of Distributed Computing, pp. 275–282. ACM (2004)
11. Litsas, C., Pagourtzis, A., Sakavalas, D.: A graph parameter that matches the resilience of the certified propagation algorithm. In: Cichoń, J., Gębala, M., Klonowski, M. (eds.) ADHOC-NOW 2013. LNCS, vol. 7960, pp. 269–280. Springer, Heidelberg (2013). https://doi.org/10.1007/978-3-642-39247-4_23
12. Maurer, A., Tixeuil, S.: Byzantine broadcast with fixed disjoint paths. J. Parallel Distrib. Comput. **74**(11), 3153–3160 (2014)
13. Maurer, A., Tixeuil, S.: Containing Byzantine failures with control zones. IEEE Trans. Parallel Distrib. Syst. **26**(2), 362–370 (2015)
14. Maurer, A., Tixeuil, S.: Tolerating random Byzantine failures in an unbounded network. Parallel Process. Lett. **26**(1) (2016)
15. Maurer, A., Tixeuil, S., Defago, X.: Communicating reliably in multihop dynamic networks despite Byzantine failures. In: 2015 IEEE 34th Symposium on Reliable Distributed Systems (SRDS), pp. 238–245. IEEE (2015)

16. Pelc, A., Peleg, D.: Broadcasting with locally bounded Byzantine faults. Inf. Process. Lett. **93**(3), 109–115 (2005)
17. Raynal, M., Stainer, J., Cao, J., Wu, W.: A simple broadcast algorithm for recurrent dynamic systems. In: 28th IEEE International Conference on Advanced Information Networking and Applications, AINA 2014, 13–16 May 2014, Victoria, BC, Canada, pp. 933–939 (2014)
18. Tseng, L., Vaidya, N.H., Bhandari, V.: Broadcast using certified propagation algorithm in presence of Byzantine faults. Inf. Process. Lett. **115**(4), 512–514 (2015)

Acyclic Strategy for Silent Self-stabilization in Spanning Forests

Karine Altisen[1], Stéphane Devismes[1], and Anaïs Durand[2(✉)]

[1] Univ. Grenoble Alpes, CNRS, Grenoble INP, VERIMAG, 38000 Grenoble, France
{Karine.Altisen,Stephane.Devismes}@univ-grenoble-alpes.fr
[2] IRISA, Université de Rennes, 35042 Rennes, France
Anais.Durand@inria.fr

Abstract. We formalize design patterns, commonly used in self-stabilization, to obtain general statements regarding both correctness and time complexity. Precisely, we study a class of algorithms devoted to networks endowed with a sense of direction describing a spanning forest whose characterization is a simple (*i.e.*, quasi-syntactic) condition. We show that any algorithm of this class is (1) silent and self-stabilizing under the distributed unfair daemon, and (2) has a stabilization time polynomial in moves and asymptotically optimal in rounds. To illustrate the versatility of our method, we review several works where our results apply.

1 Introduction

Numerous self-stabilizing algorithms have been proposed so far to solve various tasks. Those works also consider a large taxonomy of topologies: rings [5], (directed) trees [9,26], planar graphs [19], arbitrary connected graphs [1], *etc.* Among those topologies, the class of directed (in-)trees is of particular interest. Indeed, such topologies often appear, at an intermediate level, in self-stabilizing composite algorithms. *Composition* is a popular way to design self-stabilizing algorithms [25] since it allows to simplify both the design and the proofs. Numerous self-stabilizing algorithms [2,4,11] are actually made as a composition of a spanning directed treelike (*e.g.*, tree or forest) construction and some other algorithms specifically designed for directed tree/forest topologies. Notice that, even though not mandatory, most of these constructions additionally achieve *silence* [17]: a silent algorithm converges within finite time to a configuration from which the values of the communication registers used by the algorithm remain fixed. Silence is a desirable property, as it usually implies more simplicity in the design, and so allows to write simpler proofs; moreover, a silent algorithm may utilize fewer communication operations and communication bandwidth. We consider here the locally shared memory model with composite atomicity, where

This study has been partially supported by the ANR projects DESCARTES (ANR-16-CE40-0023) and ESTATE (ANR-16-CE25-0009), and by the Franco-German DFG-ANR project 40300781 DISCMAT.

T. Izumi and P. Kuznetsov (Eds.): SSS 2018, LNCS 11201, pp. 186–202, 2018.
https://doi.org/10.1007/978-3-030-03232-6_13

executions proceed in atomic steps and the asynchrony is captured by the notion of *daemon*. The most general daemon is the *distributed unfair daemon*. Hence, solutions stabilizing under such an assumption are highly desirable, because they work under any other daemon assumption. The daemon assumption and time complexity are closely related. The *stabilization time* (the main time complexity measure to compare self-stabilizing algorithms) is usually evaluated in terms of rounds, which capture the execution time according to the speed of the slowest processes. But, another crucial issue is the number of local state updates, called *moves*. Indeed, the stabilization time in moves captures the amount of computations an algorithm needs to recover a correct behavior. Now, this complexity can be bounded only if the algorithm works under an unfair daemon. If an algorithm requires a stronger daemon to stabilize, *e.g.*, a *weakly fair* daemon, then it is possible to construct executions whose convergence is arbitrarily long in terms of atomic steps (and so in moves), meaning that, in such executions, there are processes whose moves do not make the system progress towards the convergence. In other words, these latter processes waste computation power and so energy. Such a situation should be therefore prevented, making solutions working under the unfair daemon more desirable. There are many self-stabilizing algorithms proven under the distributed unfair daemon, *e.g.*, [1,12,20]. However, analyses of the stabilization time in moves is rather unusual and this may be an important issue. Indeed, recently, several self-stabilizing algorithms which work under a distributed unfair daemon have been shown to have an exponential stabilization time in moves in the worst case, *e.g.*, the silent leader election algorithms from [12] (see [1]), the Breadth-First Search (BFS) algorithm of Huang and Chen [21] (see [16]).

Contribution. We formalize design patterns, commonly used in self-stabilization, to obtain general statements regarding both correctness and time complexity. Precisely, we study a class of algorithms for networks endowed with a sense of direction describing a spanning forest (*e.g.*, a directed tree, or a network equipped with a spanning tree) whose characterization is a simple (*i.e.*, quasi-syntactic) condition. We show that any algorithm of this class is (1) silent and self-stabilizing under the distributed unfair daemon, and (2) has a stabilization time which is polynomial in moves and asymptotically optimal in rounds. Our condition mainly uses the concept of *acyclic strategy*, which is based on the notions of *top-down* and *bottom-up* actions. Our first goal has been to formally define these two paradigms. We have combined this formalization together with a notion of acyclic causality between actions and a last criteria called *correct-alone* (*n.b.*, only this criteria is not syntactic) to obtain the notion of *acyclic strategy*. We show that any algorithm following an acyclic strategy reaches a terminal configuration in a polynomial number of moves, assuming a distributed unfair daemon. Hence, if its terminal configurations satisfy the specification, the algorithm is both silent and self-stabilizing. Unfortunately, we show that this condition is not sufficient to obtain an asymptotically optimal stabilization time in rounds. So, we enforce the acyclic strategy with the property of *local mutual* *exclusivity* to have an asymptotically optimal round complexity. We also propose a simple method to make any algorithm, that follows an acyclic strategy, locally mutually exclusive. This method has no overhead in moves. Finally, to show the versatility of our approach, we review works where our results apply.

Related Work. General schemes and efficiency are usually understood as orthogonal issues. For example, the general scheme proposed in [23] transforms almost any algorithm working on an asynchronous message-passing identified system of arbitrary topology into its corresponding self-stabilizing version. Such a universal transformer is, by essence, inefficient in space and time complexities: its purpose is only to demonstrate the feasibility of the transformation. However, few works [3,13,18] target both general self-stabilizing algorithm patterns and efficiency in rounds. In [13,18], authors propose a method to design silent self-stabilizing algorithms for a class of fix-point problems. Their solution works in non-bidirectional networks using bounded memory per process. In [18], they consider the locally shared memory model with composite atomicity assuming a distributed unfair daemon, while in [13], they bring their approach to asynchronous message-passing systems. In both papers, they establish a stabilization time in $O(D)$ rounds, where D is the network diameter, that holds for the synchronous case only. Moreover, move complexity is not considered. The rest of the related work only concerns the locally shared memory model with composite atomicity assuming a distributed unfair daemon. In [3], labeling schemes [24] are used to show that every static task has a silent self-stabilizing algorithm which converges within a linear number of rounds in an arbitrary identified network, however no move complexity is given. To our knowledge, until now, only two works [10,15] conciliate general schemes for stabilization and efficiency in both moves and rounds. In [10], Cournier *et al.* propose a general scheme for snap-stabilizing wave, henceforth non-silent, algorithms in arbitrary connected and rooted networks. Using their approach, one can obtain snap-stabilizing algorithms that execute each wave in polynomial number of rounds and moves. In [15], authors propose a general scheme to compute, in a linear number of rounds, spanning directed treelike data structures on arbitrary networks. They also show polynomial upper bounds on its stabilization time in moves holding for several instantiations of their scheme. Our approach is then complementary to [15].

Roadmap. In Sect. 2, we define the model. In Sect. 3, we define the *acyclic strategy* and propose a toy example. In Sect. 4, we study the move complexity of algorithms that follow an acyclic strategy. In Sect. 5, we analyze our case study regarding our results. In Sect. 6, we consider the round complexity issue. In Sect. 7, we review several existing works where our method applies. We conclude in Sect. 8.

2 Preliminaries

A *network* is made of a set of n interconnected *processes*. Communications are bidirectional. Hence, the topology of the network is a simple undirected graph $G = (V, E)$, where V is a set of processes and E is a set of edges that represents communication links, *i.e.*, $\{p, q\} \in E$ means that p and q can directly exchange information. In this latter case, p and q are said to be *neighbors*. For any process p, we denote by $p.\Gamma$ the set of its neighbors. We also note Δ the degree of G. A *distributed algorithm* $\mathcal{A}$ is a collection of $n = |V|$ *local algorithms*, each one operating on a single process: $\mathcal{A} = \{\mathcal{A}(p) \ : \ p \in V\}$ where each process p is equipped with a local algorithm $\mathcal{A}(p) = (Var_p, Actions_p)$: Var_p is the finite set of variables of p, and $Actions_p$ is the finite set of *actions*. Notice that $\mathcal{A}$ may not be uniform. We identify each variable involved in Algorithm $\mathcal{A}$ by the notation $p.x \in Var_p$, where x is the *name* of the variable and p the process that holds it. Each process p runs its local algorithm $\mathcal{A}(p)$ by atomically executing actions. If executed, an action of p consists of reading all variables of p and its neighbors, and then writing into a part of the *writable* variables of p. For any process p, each action in $Actions_p$ is written as follows: $L(p) :: G(p) \ \rightarrow \ S(p)$. $L(p)$ is a *label* used to identify the action in the discussion. The *guard* $G(p)$ is a Boolean predicate involving variables of p and its neighbors. The *statement* $S(p)$ is a sequence of assignments on writable variables of p. A variable $q.x$ is said to be *G-read* by $L(p)$ if $q.x$ is involved in predicate $G(p)$ (in this case, q is either p or one of its neighbors). Let $G\text{-}Read(L(p))$ be the set of variables that are G-read by $L(p)$. A variable $p.x$ is said to be *written* by $L(p)$ if $p.x$ appears as the left operand in an assignment of $S(p)$. Let $Write(L(p))$ be the set of variables written by $L(p)$. An action can be executed by a process p only if it is *enabled, i.e.*, its guard evaluates to true. By extension, a process is *enabled* when at least one of its actions is enabled. The *state* of a process p is a vector of valuations of its variables. A *configuration* of an algorithm $\mathcal{A}$ is a vector made of a state of each process in V. For any configuration γ, we denote by $\gamma(p)$ (*resp.* $\gamma(p).x$) the state of process p (resp. the value of the variable x of process p) in γ.

The asynchrony of the system is modeled by the *daemon*. Assume that the current configuration of the system is γ. If the set of enabled processes in γ is empty, then γ is said to be *terminal*. Otherwise, a *step of* $\mathcal{A}$ is performed as follows: the daemon selects a non-empty subset S of enabled processes in γ, and every process p in S *atomically* executes the statement of one of its actions enabled in γ, leading the system to a new configuration γ'. The step (of $\mathcal{A}$) from γ to γ' is noted $\gamma \mapsto \gamma'$: $\mapsto$ is the binary relation over configurations defining all possible steps of $\mathcal{A}$ in G. An *execution* of $\mathcal{A}$ is a maximal sequence $\gamma_0 \gamma_1 \ldots \gamma_i \ldots$ of configurations such that $\gamma_{i-1} \mapsto \gamma_i$ for all $i > 0$. The term "maximal" means that the execution is either infinite, or ends at a *terminal* configuration. We define a daemon $\mathcal{D}$ as a predicate over executions. An execution e is then said to be an *execution under the daemon* $\mathcal{D}$ if e satisfies $\mathcal{D}$. Here, we assume that the daemon is *distributed* and *unfair*. "Distributed" means that, unless the configuration is terminal, the daemon selects at least one enabled process (maybe more) at each step. "Unfair" means that there is no fairness constraint, *i.e.*, the daemon might never select a process unless it is the only enabled one.

We measure the time complexity using two notions: *rounds* and *moves*. A process *moves* in $\gamma_i \mapsto \gamma_{i+1}$ when it executes an action in $\gamma_i \mapsto \gamma_{i+1}$. The definition of round uses the concept of *neutralization*: a process v is *neutralized* during a step $\gamma_i \mapsto \gamma_{i+1}$, if v is enabled in γ_i but not in configuration γ_{i+1}, and it is not activated in the step $\gamma_i \mapsto \gamma_{i+1}$. The first round of an execution $e = \gamma_0 \gamma_1 \ldots$ is its minimal prefix e' such that every process that is enabled in γ_0 either executes an action or is neutralized during a step of e'. If e' is finite, then the second round of e is the first round of the suffix $\gamma_t \gamma_{t+1} \ldots$ of e starting from the last configuration γ_t of e', and so forth.

Let $\mathcal{A}$ be a distributed algorithm for a network G, SP a predicate over the configurations of $\mathcal{A}$, and $\mathcal{D}$ a daemon. $\mathcal{A}$ is *silent and self-stabilizing for SP in G under $\mathcal{D}$* if the following two conditions hold: (1) every execution of $\mathcal{A}$ under $\mathcal{D}$ is finite, and (2) every terminal configuration of $\mathcal{A}$ satisfies SP. In this case, every terminal (resp. non-terminal) configuration is said to be *legitimate w.r.t. SP* (resp. *illegitimate w.r.t. SP*). The *stabilization time* in rounds (resp. moves) of a silent self-stabilizing algorithm is the maximum number of rounds (resp. moves) over every execution possible under the considered daemon to reach a terminal (legitimate) configuration.

3   Algorithm with Acyclic Strategy

Let $\mathcal{A}$ be a distributed algorithm running on some network $G = (V, E)$.

Variable Names. We assume that every process is endowed with the same set of variables and we denote by *Names* the set of names of those variables, namely: $Names = \{x \ : \ p \in V \wedge p.x \in Var_p\}$. We also assume that for every name $x \in Names$, for all processes p and q, variables $p.x$ and $q.x$ have the same definition domain. The set of names is partitioned into two subsets: *ConstNames*, the set of constant names, and $VarNames = Names \setminus ConstNames$, the set of writable variable names. A name x is in *VarNames* as soon as there exists a process p such that $p.x \in Var_p$ and $p.x$ is written by an action of its local algorithm $\mathcal{A}(p)$. For every $c \in ConstNames$ and every process $p \in V$, $p.c$ is never written by any action and it has a pre-defined constant value (which may differ from one process to another, *e.g.*, Γ, the name of the neighborhood).

We assume that $\mathcal{A}$ is *well-formed*, *i.e.*, *VarNames* is partitioned into k sets $Var_1, \ldots, Var_k$ such that $\forall p \in V$, $\mathcal{A}(p)$ consists of exactly k actions $A_1(p), \ldots, A_k(p)$ where $Write(A_i(p)) = \{p.v \ : \ v \in Var_i\}$, for all $i \in \{1, \ldots, k\}$. Let $A_i = \{A_i(p) \ : \ p \in V\}$, for all $i \in \{1, \ldots, k\}$. Every A_i is called a *family (of actions)*. By definition, $A_1, \ldots, A_k$ is a partition over all actions of $\mathcal{A}$, henceforth called a *families' partition*.

Remark 1. *Since $\mathcal{A}$ is assumed to be* well-formed, *there is exactly one action of $\mathcal{A}(p)$ where $p.v$ is written, for every process p and every writable variable $p.v$ (of p).*

Spanning Forest. We assume that every process is endowed with constants that define a spanning forest over the graph G: we assume the constant names *par* and *chldrn* such that for every process $p \in V$, $p.par$ and $p.chldrn$ are preset as follows.

- $p.par \in p.\Gamma \cup \{\bot\}$: $p.par$ is either a neighbor of p (its *parent* in the forest), or $\bot$. In this latter case, p is called a *(tree) root*. Hence, the graph made of vertices V and edges $\{(p, p.par) \; : \; p \in V \wedge p.par \neq \bot\}$ is assumed to be a spanning forest of G.
- $p.chldrn \subseteq p.\Gamma$: $p.chldrn$ contains the neighbors of p which are the *children* of p in the forest, *i.e.*, for every $p, q \in V$, $p.par = q \iff p \in q.chldrn$. If $p.chldrn = \emptyset$, p is called a *leaf*.

Notice that $p.\Gamma \setminus (\{p.par\} \cup p.chldrn)$ may not be empty. The set of p's *ancestors*, $Anc(p)$, is recursively defined as follows: $Anc(p) = \{p\}$ **if** p is a root, $Anc(p) = \{p\} \cup Anc(p.par)$ **otherwise**. Similarly, the set of p's *descendants*, $Desc(p)$, can be recursively defined as follows: $Desc(p) = \{p\}$ **if** p is a leaf, $Desc(p) = \{p\} \cup \bigcup_{q \in p.chldrn} Desc(q)$ **otherwise**.

Acyclic Strategy. Let $A_1, \ldots, A_k$ be the families' partition of $\mathcal{A}$. A_i, with $i \in \{1, \ldots, k\}$, is said to be *correct-alone* if for every process p and every step $\gamma \mapsto \gamma'$ such that $A_i(p)$ is executed in $\gamma \mapsto \gamma'$, if no variable in $G\text{-}Read(A_i(p)) \setminus Write(A_i(p))$ is modified in $\gamma \mapsto \gamma'$, then $A_i(p)$ is disabled in γ'. Notice that if a variable in $Write(A_i(p))$ is modified in $\gamma \mapsto \gamma'$, then it is necessarily modified by $A_i(p)$, by Remark 1.

Let $\prec_{\mathcal{A}}$ be a binary relation over the families of actions of $\mathcal{A}$ such that for $i, j \in \{1, \ldots, k\}$, $A_j \prec_{\mathcal{A}} A_i$ if and only if $i \neq j$ and there exist two processes p and q such that $q \in p.\Gamma \cup \{p\}$ and $Write(A_j(p)) \cap G\text{-}Read(A_i(q)) \neq \emptyset$. We conveniently represent the relation $\prec_{\mathcal{A}}$ by a directed graph **GC** called *Graph of actions' Causality* and defined as follows: $\mathbf{GC} = (\{A_1, \ldots, A_k\}, \{(A_j, A_i), A_j \prec_{\mathcal{A}} A_i\})$.

Intuitively, a family of actions A_i is top-down if activations of its corresponding actions are only propagated down in the forest, *i.e.*, when some process q executes action $A_i(q)$, $A_i(q)$ can only activate A_i at some of its children p, if any. In this case, $A_i(q)$ writes to some variables G-read by $A_i(p)$, these latter are usually G-read to be compared to variables written by $A_i(p)$ itself. In other words, a variable G-read by $A_i(p)$ can be written by $A_i(q)$ only if $q = p$ or $q = p.par$. Formally, a family of actions A_i is *top-down* if for every process p and every $q.v \in G\text{-}Read(A_i(p))$, we have $q.v \in Write(A_i(q)) \Rightarrow q \in \{p, p.par\}$. Bottom-up families are defined similarly: a family A_i is *bottom-up* if for every process p and every $q.v \in G\text{-}Read(A_i(p))$, we have $q.v \in Write(A_i(q)) \Rightarrow q \in p.chldrn \cup \{p\}$.

A distributed algorithm $\mathcal{A}$ follows an *acyclic strategy* if it is well-formed, its graph of actions' causality **GC** is *(directed) acyclic*, and for every A_i in its families' partition, A_i is correct-alone and either bottom-up or top-down.

Toy Example. We now propose a simple example of an algorithm, called $\mathcal{TE}$, that follows an acyclic strategy. $\mathcal{TE}$ assumes a constant integer input $p.in \in \mathbb{N}$

at each process. $\mathcal{TE}$ computes the sum of all inputs and then spreads this result everywhere in the network. $\mathcal{TE}$ assumes that the network $T = (V, E)$ is a tree with a sense of direction (given by par and $chldrn$) which orientates T as an in-tree rooted at process r. Apart from those constant variables, every process p haconsecutive executionss two variables: $p.sub \in \mathbb{N}$ (which is used to compute the sum of input values in the subtree of p) and $p.res \in \mathbb{N}$ (which stabilizes to the result of the computation). $\mathcal{TE}$ consists of two families of actions S and R. S computes variables sub and is defined as follows. For every process p,

$$S(p) :: p.sub \neq (\sum_{q \in p.chldrn} q.sub) + p.in \rightarrow p.sub \leftarrow (\sum_{q \in p.chldrn} q.sub) + p.in$$

R computes variables res and is defined as follows.

$$R(r) :: r.res \neq r.sub \rightarrow r.res \leftarrow r.sub$$

For every process $p \neq r$,

$$R(p) :: p.res \neq \max(p.par.res, p.sub) \rightarrow p.res \leftarrow \max(p.par.res, p.sub)$$

S is bottom-up and correct-alone, while R is top-down and correct-alone. Moreover, the graph of actions' causality is simply $S \longrightarrow R$. So, $\mathcal{TE}$ follows an acyclic strategy.

4   Move Complexity of Algorithms with Acyclic Strategy

We now exhibit a polynomial upper bound on the move complexity of any algorithm that follows an acyclic strategy. To that goal, we consider a distributed algorithm $\mathcal{A}$ which follows an *acyclic strategy* and runs on the network $G = (V, E)$. We use the same notation as in Sect. 3, e.g., we let $A_1, \ldots, A_k$ be the families' partition of $\mathcal{A}$.

For a process p and a family of actions A_i, $i \in \{1, \ldots, k\}$, we define the *impacting zone* of p and A_i, denoted $Z(p, A_i)$, as follows: $Z(p, A_i)$ is the set of p's ancestors **if** A_i is top-down, $Z(p, A_i)$ is the set of p's descendants **otherwise** (*i.e.*, A_i is bottom-up). Roughly speaking, a process q belongs to $Z(p, A_i)$ if the execution of $A_i(q)$ may cause an execution of $A_i(p)$ in the future.

Remark 2. *By definition, we have $1 \leq |Z(p, A_i)| \leq n$. Moreover, if A_i is top-down, then we have $1 \leq |Z(p, A_i)| \leq H + 1 \leq n$, where H is the height of G, i.e., the maximum among the heights trees of the forest.*

We also define the quantity $M(A_i, p)$ as the *level*[1] of p in G **if** A_i is top-down, the *height* of p in G **otherwise** (*i.e.*, A_i is bottom-up).

Remark 3. *By definition, we have $0 \leq M(A_i, p) \leq H$, where H is the height of G.*

---

[1] The level of p in G is the distance from p to the root of its tree in G (0 if p is the root itself).

We define $Others(A_i, p) = \{q \in p.\Gamma : \exists A_j, i \neq j \land Write(A_j(q)) \cap G\text{-}Read(A_i(p)) \neq \emptyset\}$ to be the set of neighbors q of p that have actions other than $A_i(q)$ which write variables that are G-read by $A_i(p)$. Let

$$maxO(A_i) = \max(\{|Others(A_i, p)| : p \in V\} \cup \{maxO(A_j) : A_j \prec_{\mathcal{A}} A_i)\})$$

Remark 4. *By definition, we have $maxO(A_i) \leq \Delta$. Moreover, if $\forall p \in V, \forall i \in \{1, ..., k\}$, $Others(A_i, p)$ is empty, then $\forall j \in \{1, ..., k\}$, $maxO(A_j) = 0$.*

Lemma 1. *Let A_i be a family of actions and p be a process. For every execution e of the algorithm $\mathcal{A}$ on G, $\#m(e, A_i, p) \leq \left(n \cdot \left(1 + \mathbf{d} \cdot \left(1 + maxO(A_i)\right)\right)\right)^{\mathfrak{H}(A_i)} \cdot |Z(p, A_i)|$, where $\#m(e, A_i, p)$ is the number of times p executes $A_i(p)$ in e, $\mathbf{d}$ is the in-degree of $\mathbf{GC}$, and $\mathfrak{H}(A_i)$ is the height of A_i in $\mathbf{GC}$.[2]*

Proof. Let $e = \gamma_0...\gamma_x...$ be any execution of $\mathcal{A}$ on G. Let $K(A_i, p) = M(A_i, p) + (H + 1) \cdot \mathfrak{H}(A_i)$. We proceed by induction on $K(A_i, p)$.

Base Case: Assume $K(A_i, p) = 0$ for some family A_i and some process p. By definition, $H \geq 0$, $\mathfrak{H}(A_i) \geq 0$ and $M(A_i, p) \geq 0$. Hence, $K(A_i, p) = 0$ implies that $\mathfrak{H}(A_i) = 0$ and $M(A_i, p) = 0$. Since $M(A_i, p) = 0$, $Z(p, A_i) = \{p\}$. A_i is top-down or bottom-up so, for every $q.v \in G\text{-}Read(A_i(p))$, $q.v \in Write(A_i(q)) \Rightarrow q = p$. Moreover, since $\mathfrak{H}(A_i) = 0$, $\forall j \neq i$, $A_j \not\prec_{\mathcal{A}} A_i$. So, for every $j \neq i$ and every $q \in p.\Gamma \cup \{p\}$, $Write(A_j(p)) \cap G\text{-}Read(A_i(q)) = \emptyset$. Hence, no action except $A_i(p)$ can modify a variable in $G\text{-}Read(A_i(p))$. Thus, $\#m(e, A_i, p) \leq 1$ since A_i is correct-alone.

Induction Hypothesis: Let $K \geq 0$. Assume that for every family A_j and every process q such that $K(A_j, q) \leq K$, we have

$$\#m(e, A_j, q) \leq \left(n \cdot \left(1 + \mathbf{d} \cdot \left(1 + maxO(A_j)\right)\right)\right)^{\mathfrak{H}(A_j)} \cdot |Z(q, A_j)|$$

Induction Step: Assume that for some family A_i and some process p, $K(A_i, p) = K + 1$. If $\#m(e, A_i, p)$ equals 0 or 1, then the result trivially holds. Assume now that $\#m(e, A_i, p) > 1$ and consider two consecutive executions of $A_i(p)$ in e, i.e., there exist x, y such that $0 \leq x < y$, $A_i(p)$ is executed in both $\gamma_x \mapsto \gamma_{x+1}$ and $\gamma_y \mapsto \gamma_{y+1}$, but not in steps $\gamma_z \mapsto \gamma_{z+1}$ with $z \in \{x+1, ..., y-1\}$. Then, since A_i is correct-alone, at least one variable in $G\text{-}Read(A_i(p))$ has to be modified by an action other than $A_i(p)$ in a step $\gamma_z \mapsto \gamma_{z+1}$ with $z \in \{x, ..., y-1\}$ so that $A_i(p)$ becomes enabled again. Namely, there are $j \in \{1, ..., k\}$ and $q \in V$ such that *(a)* $j \neq i$ or $q \neq p$, $A_j(q)$ is executed in a step $\gamma_z \mapsto \gamma_{z+1}$, and $Write(A_j(q)) \cap G\text{-}Read(A_i(p)) \neq \emptyset$. Note also that, by definition, *(b)* $q \in p.\Gamma \cup \{p\}$. Finally, by definitions of top-down and bottom-up, *(a)*, and *(b)*, $A_j(q)$ satisfies: (1) $j \neq i \land q = p$, (2) $j = i \land q \in p.\Gamma \cap Z(p, A_i)$, or (3) $j \neq i \land q \in p.\Gamma$. In other words, at least one of the three following cases occurs:

---

[2] The height of A_i in $\mathbf{GC}$ is 0 if the in-degree of A_i in $\mathbf{GC}$ is 0. Otherwise, it is equal to one plus the maximum of the heights of the A_i's predecessors *w.r.t.* $\prec_{\mathcal{A}}$.

(1) p executes $A_j(p)$ in step $\gamma_z \mapsto \gamma_{z+1}$ with $j \neq i$ and $Write(A_j(p)) \cap$ $G\text{-}Read(A_i(p)) \neq \emptyset$. Consequently, $A_j \prec_{\mathcal{A}} A_i$ and, so, $\mathfrak{H}(A_j) < \mathfrak{H}(A_i)$. Moreover, $M(A_j, p) - M(A_i, p) \leq H$ and $\mathfrak{H}(A_j) < \mathfrak{H}(A_i)$ imply $K(A_j, p) <$ $K(A_i, p) = K + 1$. Hence, by induction hypothesis, we have

$$\#m(e, A_j, p) \leq \left(n \cdot \left(1 + \mathbf{d} \cdot \left(1 + maxO(A_j) \right) \right) \right)^{\mathfrak{H}(A_j)} \cdot |Z(p, A_j)|.$$

(2) There is $q \in p.\Gamma \cap Z(p, A_i)$ such that q executes $A_i(q)$ in step $\gamma_z \mapsto \gamma_{z+1}$ and $Write(A_i(q)) \cap G\text{-}Read(A_i(p)) \neq \emptyset$. Then, $M(A_i, q) < M(A_i, p)$. Since $M(A_i, q) < M(A_i, p)$, $K(A_i, q) < K(A_i, p) = K + 1$ and, by induction hypothesis, we have

$$\#m(e, A_i, q) \leq \left(n \cdot \left(1 + \mathbf{d} \cdot \left(1 + maxO(A_i) \right) \right) \right)^{\mathfrak{H}(A_i)} \cdot |Z(q, A_i)|.$$

(3) A neighbor q of p executes an action $A_j(q)$ in step $\gamma_z \mapsto \gamma_{z+1}$, with $j \neq i$ and $Write(A_j(q)) \cap G\text{-}Read(A_i(p)) \neq \emptyset$. Consequently, $A_j \prec_{\mathcal{A}} A_i$ and, so, $\mathfrak{H}(A_j) < \mathfrak{H}(A_i)$. Moreover, $M(A_j, q) - M(A_i, p) \leq H$ and $\mathfrak{H}(A_j) < \mathfrak{H}(A_i)$ imply $K(A_j, q) < K(A_i, p) = K + 1$. Hence, by induction hypothesis, we have

$$\#m(e, A_j, q) \leq \left(n \cdot \left(1 + \mathbf{d} \cdot \left(1 + maxO(A_j) \right) \right) \right)^{\mathfrak{H}(A_j)} \cdot |Z(q, A_j)|.$$

(Notice that Cases 1 and 3 can only occur when $\mathfrak{H}(A_i) > 0$.) We now bound the number of times each of the three above cases occur in the execution e.

Case 1: By definition, there exist at most $\mathbf{d}$ predecessors A_j of A_i in $\mathbf{GC}$ (*i.e.*, such that $A_j \prec_{\mathcal{A}} A_i$). For each of them, we have $\mathfrak{H}(A_j) < \mathfrak{H}(A_i)$, $|Z(p, A_j)| \leq n$ (Remark 2) and $maxO(A_j) \leq maxO(A_i)$. Hence, overall, Case 1 appears at most $m_1 = \sum_{\{A_j\ :\ A_j \prec_{\mathcal{A}} A_i\}} \#m(e, A_j, p)$ times and

$$m_1 \leq \sum_{\{A_j\ :\ A_j \prec_{\mathcal{A}} A_i\}} \left(n \cdot \left(1 + \mathbf{d} \cdot \left(1 + maxO(A_j) \right) \right) \right)^{\mathfrak{H}(A_j)} \cdot |Z(p, A_j)|$$

$$\leq \mathbf{d} \cdot n^{\mathfrak{H}(A_i)} \cdot \left(1 + \mathbf{d} \cdot \left(1 + maxO(A_i) \right) \right)^{\mathfrak{H}(A_i)-1}$$

Case 2: By definition, $Z(p, A_i) = \{p\} \uplus \biguplus_{q \in p.\Gamma \cap Z(p,A_i)} Z(q, A_i)$ Hence, overall, this case appears at most $m_2 = \sum_{q \in p.\Gamma \cap Z(p,A_i)} \#m(e, A_i, q)$ times and

$$m_2 \leq \sum_{q \in p.\Gamma \cap Z(p,A_i)} \left(n \cdot \left(1 + \mathbf{d} \cdot \left(1 + maxO(A_i) \right) \right) \right)^{\mathfrak{H}(A_i)} \cdot |Z(q, A_i)|$$

$$\leq n^{\mathfrak{H}(A_i)} \cdot \left(1 + \mathbf{d} \cdot \left(1 + maxO(A_i) \right) \right)^{\mathfrak{H}(A_i)} \cdot \left(|Z(p, A_i)| - 1 \right)$$

Case 3: $q \in Others(A_i, p)$ since $i \neq j$ and $q \in p.\Gamma$. Then, for every $A_j \prec_{\mathcal{A}} A_i$, we have $\mathfrak{H}(A_j) < \mathfrak{H}(A_i)$, $maxO(A_j) \leq maxO(A_i)$, and $Z(q, A_j) \leq n$ (Remark 2). By definition, there are at most $\mathbf{d}$ families A_j such that $A_j \prec_{\mathcal{A}} A_i$. Finally,

$|Others(A_i,p)| \leq maxO(A_i)$, by definition. Hence, overall, this case appears at most $m_3 = \sum_{\{A_j \,:\, A_j \prec_{\mathcal{A}} A_i\}} \sum_{\{q \in Others(A_i,p)\}} \#m(e, A_j, q)$ times and

$$m_3 \leq \sum_{\{A_j \,:\, A_j \prec_{\mathcal{A}} A_i\}} \sum_{\{q \in Others(A_i,p)\}} \left(n \cdot \left(1 + \mathbf{d} \cdot \left(1 + maxO(A_j)\right)\right) \right)^{\mathfrak{H}(A_j)} \cdot |Z(q, A_j)|$$

$$\leq \mathbf{d} \cdot maxO(A_i) \cdot n^{\mathfrak{H}(A_i)} \cdot \left(1 + \mathbf{d} \cdot \left(1 + maxO(A_i)\right)\right)^{\mathfrak{H}(A_i)-1}$$

Hence, overall, we have

$$\#m(e, A_i, p) \leq 1 + m_1 + m_2 + m_3$$

$$\leq n^{\mathfrak{H}(A_i)} \cdot \left(1 + \mathbf{d} \cdot \left(1 + maxO(A_i)\right)\right)^{\mathfrak{H}(A_i)} \cdot |Z(p, A_i)|$$

$\square$

Since $maxO(A_i) \leq \Delta$ (Remark 4) and $|Z(p, A_i)| \leq n$ (Remark 2), we can deduce the following theorem from Lemma 1 and the definition of silent self-stabilization.

Theorem 5. *If $\mathcal{A}$ follows an acyclic strategy and every terminal configuration of $\mathcal{A}$ satisfies SP, then (1) $\mathcal{A}$ is silent and self-stabilizing for SP in G under the distributed unfair daemon, and (2) its stabilization time is at most $\left(1 + \mathbf{d} \cdot (1 + \Delta)\right)^{\mathfrak{H}} \cdot k \cdot n^{\mathfrak{H}+2}$ moves, where k is the number of families of $\mathcal{A}$, $\mathbf{d}$ is the in-degree of $\mathbf{GC}$, and $\mathfrak{H}$ the height of $\mathbf{GC}$.*

5   Analysis of $\mathcal{TE}$

We now analyze $\mathcal{TE}$ using our results. The aim is to show that: (1) correctness and move complexity of $\mathcal{TE}$ can be easily deduced from our general results, (2) our upper bound on stabilization time in moves is tight for this example, and (3) our definition of acyclic strategy does not preclude the design of solutions (like $\mathcal{TE}$) that are inefficient in terms of rounds. We will see how to circumvent this latter negative result in Sect. 6.

First, we already saw that $\mathcal{TE}$ follows an acyclic strategy and that the graph of actions' causality is simply $S \longrightarrow R$. Then, by induction on the tree T, we can show that every terminal configuration of $\mathcal{TE}$ is legitimate. Hence, by Theorem 5, we conclude that $\mathcal{TE}$ is silent and self-stabilizing for computing the sum of the inputs assuming a distributed unfair daemon. Moreover, its stabilization time is at most $2 \cdot (2 + \Delta) \cdot n^3$ moves. Now, using Lemma 1, the move complexity of $\mathcal{TE}$ can be further refined. Let e be any execution and H be the height of T. First, note that $maxO(S) = maxO(R) = 0$ by Remark 4. Since S is bottom-up, $|Z(p, S)| \leq n$, for every process p. Moreover, the height of S is 0 in the graph of actions' causality. Hence, by Lemma 1, we have $\#m(e, S, p) \leq n$, for all processes p. Thus, e contains at most n^2 moves of S. Similarly, since R is top-down, $|Z(p, R)| \leq H + 1$, for every process p. Moreover, the height of R is 1 in the graph of actions' causality. Hence, by Lemma 1, we have $\#m(e, R, p) \leq 2 \cdot n \cdot (H + 1)$, for all processes p. Thus, e contains at most $2 \cdot n^2 \cdot (H + 1)$ moves of R. Overall, the stabilization time of $\mathcal{TE}$ is actually at most $n^2(3 + 2H)$ moves.

Lower Bound in Moves. We now show that the stabilization time of $\mathcal{TE}$ is $\Omega(H \cdot n^2)$ moves, meaning that the previous upper bound (obtained by Lemma 1) is asymptotically reachable. To that goal, we consider a directed line of n processes, with $n \geq 4$, noted $p_1, \ldots, p_n$: p_1 is the root and for every $i \in \{2, \ldots, n\}$, there is a link between p_{i-1} and p_i, moreover, $p_i.par = p_{i-1}$ (note that $H = n$). We build a possible execution of $\mathcal{TE}$ running on this line that contains $\Omega(H \cdot n^2)$ moves. We assume a central unfair daemon: at each step exactly one process executes an action. In this execution, we fix that $p_i.in = 1$, for every $i \in \{1, \ldots, n\}$. We consider two classes of configurations: Configurations X_{2i+1} (with $3 \leq 2i + 1 \leq n$) and Configurations Y_{2i+2} (with $4 \leq 2i + 2 \leq n$), see Fig. 1. The initial configuration of the execution is X_3. Then, we proceed as follows: the system converges from configuration X_{2i+1} to configuration Y_{2i+2} in $\Omega(i^2)$ moves using Schedule 1 and then from Y_{2i+2} to X_{2i+3} in $\Omega(i)$ moves using Schedule 2, back and forth, until reaching a terminal configuration (X_n if n is odd, Y_n otherwise).

Configuration X_{2i+1}, $3 \leq 2i + 1 \leq n$:

	p_1	$\cdots$	p_{2i-2}	p_{2i-1}	p_{2i}	p_{2i+1}	p_{2i+2}	p_{2i+3}	p_{2i+4}	p_{2i+5}	$\cdots$
in	1	$\cdots$	1	1	1	1	1	1	1	1	$\cdots$
sub	$2i$	$\cdots$	3	2	1	0	$2i$	0	$2i + 2$	0	$\cdots$
res	$2i$	$\cdots$	$2i$	$2i$	$2i$	0	0	0	0	0	$\cdots$

Configuration Y_{2i+2}, $4 \leq 2i + 2 \leq n$:

	p_1	$\cdots$	p_{2i-2}	p_{2i-1}	p_{2i}	p_{2i+1}	p_{2i+2}	p_{2i+3}	p_{2i+4}	p_{2i+5}	$\cdots$
in	1	$\cdots$	1	1	1	1	1	1	1	1	$\cdots$
sub	$4i + 1$	$\cdots$	$2i + 4$	$2i + 3$	$2i + 2$	$2i + 1$	$2i$	0	$2i + 2$	0	$\cdots$
res	$4i + 1$	$\cdots$	$4i + 1$	$4i + 1$	$4i + 1$	$4i + 1$	0	0	0	0	$\cdots$

Fig. 1. Configurations X_{2i+1} and Y_{2i+2}

Hence, following this scheduling of actions, the execution that starts in configuration X_3 converges to X_n (resp. Y_n) if n is odd (resp. even) and contains $\Omega(n^3)$ moves, precisely, $\Omega(H \cdot n^2)$ since the network is a line ($H = n - 1$).

Remark that in this execution, for every process p, when $R(p)$ is activated, $S(p)$ is disabled: this means that if the algorithm is modified so that $S(p)$ has local priority over $R(p)$ for every process p (like in the method proposed in Sect. 6), the proposed execution is still possible keeping a move complexity in $\Omega(H \cdot n^2)$ even for such a prioritized algorithm.

Schedule 1. From X_{2i+1} to Y_{2i+2}	**Schedule 2.** From Y_{2i+2} to X_{2i+3}
1: **for** $j = 2i + 1$ **down to** 1 **do**	1: **for** $j = 2i + 2$ **down to** 1 **do**
2: p_j executes $S(p_j)$	2: p_j executes $S(p_j)$
3: **for** $k = j$ **to** $2i + 1$ **do**	3: **for** $j = 1$ **to** $2i + 1$ **do**
4: p_k executes $R(p_k)$	4: p_j executes $R(p_j)$

Lower Bound in Rounds. We now show that $\mathcal{TE}$ has a stabilization time in $\Omega(n)$ rounds in any tree of height $H = 1$, $i.e.$, a star network. This negative result is due to the fact that families R and S are not locally mutually exclusive. In the next section, we will propose a transformation to obtain a stabilization time in $O(H)$ rounds, so $O(1)$ rounds in the case of a star network, without affecting the move complexity.

We now construct a possible execution that terminates in $n + 2$ rounds in a star network of n processes ($n \geq 2$): p_1 is the root of the tree and $p_2, \ldots, p_n$ are the leaves (namely links are $\{\{p_1, p_i\}, i = 2, \ldots, n\}$). We note C_i, $i \in \{1, \ldots, n\}$, the configuration satisfying the following three conditions:

(1) $\forall i \in \{1, \ldots, n\}$, $p_i.in = 1$;
(2) $p_1.sub = i$, $\forall j \in \{2, \ldots, i\}$, $p_j.sub = 1$, and $\forall j \in \{i + 1, \ldots, n\}$, $p_j.sub = 0$;
(3) $\forall i \in \{1, \ldots, n\}$, $p_i.res = i$.

In every configuration C_i, processes $p_1, \ldots,$ p_i are disabled and processes $p_{i+1}, \ldots, p_n$ are enabled for S. We now build a possible execution that starts from C_1 and successively converges to configurations $C_2, \ldots, C_n$ (C_n is a terminal configuration). To converge from C_i to

Schedule 3. From C_i to C_{i+1}
1:   p_{i+1} executes $S(p_{i+1})$
2:   p_1 executes $S(p_1)$
3:   p_1 executes $R(p_1)$
4:   **for** $j = 2$ **to** n **do**
5:      p_j executes $R(p_j)$

C_{i+1}, $i \in \{1, \ldots, n - 1\}$, the daemon applies Schedule 3. The convergence from C_1 to C_{n-1} last $n - 2$ rounds since for $i \in \{1, \ldots, n - 2\}$, the convergence from C_i to C_{i+1} lasts exactly one round. Indeed, each process executes at least one action between C_i and C_{i+1} and process p_n is enabled in configuration C_i and remains continuously enabled until being activated as the last process to execute in the round. The convergence from C_{n-1} to C_n lasts 4 rounds: in C_{n-1}, only p_n is enabled to execute $S(p_n)$ hence the round terminates in one step where only $S(p_n)$ is executed. Similarly, p_1 then sequentially executes $S(p_1)$ and $R(p_1)$ in two rounds. Finally, $p_2, \ldots, p_n$ execute R in one round and then the system is in the terminal configuration C_n. Hence the execution lasts $n + 2$ rounds.

6   Round Complexity of Algorithms with Acyclic Strategy

We now propose an extra condition that is sufficient for any algorithm following an acyclic strategy to stabilize in $O(H)$ rounds. We then propose a simple method to add this property to any algorithm that follows an acyclic strategy, without affecting the move complexity. Throughout this section, we consider a distributed well-formed algorithm $\mathcal{A}$ designed for a network G endowed with a spanning forest. Let $A_1, \ldots, A_k$ be the families' partition of $\mathcal{A}$.

A Condition for a Stabilization Time in $O(H)$ Rounds. We say that families A_i and A_j are *locally mutually exclusive* if for every process p, there is no configuration γ where both $A_i(p)$ and $A_j(p)$ are enabled. By extension, we say $\mathcal{A}$ is *locally mutually exclusive* if $\forall i, j \in \{1, \ldots, k\}$, $i \neq j$ implies that A_i and A_j are *locally mutually exclusive*. Below, note that $\mathfrak{H} < k$ and, in usual cases, the number of families k is a constant.

Theorem 6. *If $\mathcal{A}$ follows an acyclic strategy and is locally mutually exclusive, then every execution of $\mathcal{A}$ reaches a terminal configuration within at most $(\mathfrak{H} + 1) \cdot (H + 1)$ rounds, where $\mathfrak{H}$ is the height of the graph of actions' causality of $\mathcal{A}$ and H is the height of the spanning forest.*

Proof Outline. Let A_i be a family of actions of $\mathcal{A}$ and p be a process. We note $R(A_i, p) = \mathfrak{H}(A_i) \cdot (H + 1) + M(A_i, p) + 1$. We first show, by induction, that for every family A_i and every process p, after $R(A_i, p)$ rounds, $A_i(p)$ is disabled forever. Then, since for every family A_i and every process p, $\mathfrak{H}(A_i) \le \mathfrak{H}$ and $M(A_i, p) \le H$, we have $R(A_i, p) \le (\mathfrak{H} + 1) \cdot (H + 1)$, and the theorem holds. □

A Transformer. We know that there exist algorithms that follow an acyclic strategy, are not locally mutually exclusive, and stabilize in $\Omega(n)$ rounds (see Sect. 5). We now formalize a method, based on priorities over actions, to transform such algorithms into locally mutually exclusive ones. This ensures a complexity in $O(H)$ rounds, without degrading the move complexity.

In the following, for every process p and every family A_i, we identify the guard and the statement of Action $A_i(p)$ by $G_i(p)$ and $S_i(p)$, respectively. Let $\lhd_{\mathcal{A}}$ be any strict total order on families of $\mathcal{A}$ compatible with $\prec_{\mathcal{A}}$, i.e., $\lhd_{\mathcal{A}}$ is a binary relation on families of $\mathcal{A}$ that satisfies:

Strict Order: $\lhd_{\mathcal{A}}$ is irreflexive and transitive;

Total: for every two families A_i, A_j, we have either $A_i \lhd_{\mathcal{A}} A_j$, $A_j \lhd_{\mathcal{A}} A_i$, or $i = j$; and

Compatibility: for every two families A_i, A_j, if $A_i \prec_{\mathcal{A}} A_j$, then $A_i \lhd_{\mathcal{A}} A_j$.

Let $\mathrm{T}(\mathcal{A})$ be the following algorithm:

(1) $\mathrm{T}(\mathcal{A})$ and $\mathcal{A}$ have the same set of variables.
(2) Every process $p \in V$ holds k actions (recall that k is the number of families of $\mathcal{A}$): for every $i \in \{1, \ldots, k\}$, $A_i^{\mathrm{T}}(p) :: G_i^{\mathrm{T}}(p) \rightarrow S_i^{\mathrm{T}}(p)$

where $G_i^{\mathrm{T}}(p) = \left(\bigwedge_{A_j \lhd_{\mathcal{A}} A_i} \neg G_j(p) \right) \wedge G_i(p)$ and $S_i^{\mathrm{T}}(p) = S_i(p)$.

$G_i(p)$ (resp. the set $\{G_j(p) \ : \ A_j \lhd_{\mathcal{A}} A_i\}$) is called the *positive part* (resp. *negative part*) of $G_i^{\mathrm{T}}(p)$. By definition, $\prec_{\mathcal{A}}$ is irreflexive and the graph of actions' causality induced by $\prec_{\mathcal{A}}$ is acyclic. So, there always exists a strict total order compatible with $\prec_{\mathcal{A}}$, i.e., the above transformation is always possible for any algorithm $\mathcal{A}$ which follows an acyclic strategy. Moreover, by construction, we have the two following remarks:

Remark 7. *(1) $\mathrm{T}(\mathcal{A})$ is well-formed, (2) $A_1^{\mathrm{T}}, \ldots, A_k^{\mathrm{T}}$ is the families' partition of $\mathrm{T}(\mathcal{A})$, where $A_i^{\mathrm{T}} = \{A_i^{\mathrm{T}}(p) \ : \ p \in V\}$, for every $i \in \{1, \ldots, k\}$, and (3) $\mathrm{T}(\mathcal{A})$ is locally mutually exclusive.*

Remark 8. *For every $i, j \in \{1, \ldots, k\}$ such that $i \ne j$, and every process p, the positive part of $G_j^{\mathrm{T}}(p)$ belongs to the negative part in $G_i^{\mathrm{T}}(p)$ if and only if $A_j \lhd_{\mathcal{A}} A_i$.*

Lemma 2. *For every $i, j \in \{1, \ldots, k\}$, if $A_j^{\mathrm{T}} \prec_{\mathrm{T}(\mathcal{A})} A_i^{\mathrm{T}}$, then $A_j \lhd_{\mathcal{A}} A_i$.*

Proof. Let A_i^T and A_j^T be two families such that $A_j^\mathsf{T} \prec_{\mathsf{T}(\mathcal{A})} A_i^\mathsf{T}$. Then, $i \neq j$ and there exist two processes p and q such that $q \in p.\Gamma \cup \{p\}$ and $Write(A_j^\mathsf{T}(p)) \cap G\text{-}Read(A_i^\mathsf{T}(q)) \neq \emptyset$. Then, $Write(A_j^\mathsf{T}(p)) = Write(A_j(p))$, and either $Write(A_j(p)) \cap G\text{-}Read(A_i(q)) \neq \emptyset$, or $Write(A_j(p)) \cap G\text{-}Read(A_\ell(q)) \neq \emptyset$ where $G_\ell(q)$ belongs to the negative part of $G_i^\mathsf{T}(q)$. In the former case, we have $A_j \prec_\mathcal{A} A_i$, which implies that $A_j \lhd_\mathcal{A} A_i$ ($\lhd_\mathcal{A}$ is compatible with $\prec_\mathcal{A}$). In the latter case, $A_j \prec_\mathcal{A} A_\ell$ (by definition) and $A_\ell \lhd_\mathcal{A} A_i$ (by Remark 8). Since, $A_j \prec_\mathcal{A} A_\ell$ implies $A_j \lhd_\mathcal{A} A_\ell$ ($\lhd_\mathcal{A}$ is compatible with $\prec_\mathcal{A}$), by transitivity we have $A_j \lhd_\mathcal{A} A_i$. Hence, for every $i, j \in \{1, \dots, k\}$, $A_j^\mathsf{T} \prec_{\mathsf{T}(\mathcal{A})} A_i^\mathsf{T}$ implies $A_j \lhd_\mathcal{A} A_i$, and we are done.   □

Lemma 3. $\mathsf{T}(\mathcal{A})$ *follows an acyclic strategy.*

Proof. Let A_i^T be a family of $\mathsf{T}(\mathcal{A})$. The lemma is proven by the following three claims.

(1) A_i^T *is correct-alone.* Indeed, as A_i is correct-alone and for every process p, $S_i^\mathsf{T}(p) = S_i(p)$ and $\neg G_i(p) \Rightarrow \neg G_i^\mathsf{T}(p)$, we have that A_i^T is also correct-alone.

(2) A_i^T *is either bottom-up or top-down.* Since $\mathcal{A}$ follows an acyclic strategy, A_i is either bottom-up or top-down. Assume A_i is bottom-up. By construction, for every process q, $S_i^\mathsf{T}(q) = S_i(q)$ so $Write(A_i^\mathsf{T}(q)) = Write(A_i(q))$. Let $q.v \in G\text{-}Read(A_i^\mathsf{T}(p))$.

- Assume $q.v \in G\text{-}Read(A_i(p))$. Then $q.v \in Write(A_i(q)) \Rightarrow q \in p.chldrn \cup \{p\}$ (since A_i is bottom-up), *i.e.*, $q.v \in Write(A_i^\mathsf{T}(q)) \Rightarrow q \in p.chldrn \cup \{p\}$.
- Assume that $q.v \notin G\text{-}Read(A_i(p))$. Then $q.v \in G\text{-}Read(A_j(p))$ such that $G_j(p)$ belongs to the negative part of $G_i^\mathsf{T}(p)$, *i.e.*, $A_j \lhd_\mathcal{A} A_i$ (Remark 8). Assume, by the contradiction, that $q.v \in Write(A_i^\mathsf{T}(q))$. Then $q.v \in Write(A_i(q))$, and since $p \in q.\Gamma \cup \{q\}$ (indeed, $q.v \in G\text{-}Read(A_j(p))$), we have $A_i \prec_\mathcal{A} A_j$. Now, as $\lhd_\mathcal{A}$ is compatible with $\prec_\mathcal{A}$, we have $A_i \lhd_\mathcal{A} A_j$. Hence, $A_j \lhd_\mathcal{A} A_i$ and $A_i \lhd_\mathcal{A} A_j$, a contradiction. Thus, $q.v \notin Write(A_i^\mathsf{T}(q))$ which implies that $q.v \in Write(A_i^\mathsf{T}(q)) \Rightarrow q \in p.chldrn \cup \{p\}$ holds in this case.

Hence, A_i^T is bottom-up. By a similar reasoning, if A_i is top-down, A_i^T is top-down too.

(3) *The graph of actions' causality of* $\mathsf{T}(\mathcal{A})$ *is acyclic.* Indeed, by Lemma 2, for every $i, j \in \{1, \dots, k\}$, $A_j^\mathsf{T} \prec_{\mathsf{T}(\mathcal{A})} A_i^\mathsf{T} \Rightarrow A_j \lhd_\mathcal{A} A_i$. Now, $\lhd_\mathcal{A}$ is a strict total order. So, the graph of actions' causality of $\mathsf{T}(\mathcal{A})$ is acyclic.   □

Lemma 4. *Every execution of* $\mathsf{T}(\mathcal{A})$ *is an execution of* $\mathcal{A}$.

Proof. $\mathcal{A}$ and $\mathsf{T}(\mathcal{A})$ have the same set of configurations; every step of $\mathsf{T}(\mathcal{A})$ is a step of $\mathcal{A}$; and a configuration γ is terminal *w.r.t.* $\mathsf{T}(\mathcal{A})$ iff γ is terminal *w.r.t.* $\mathcal{A}$.   □

Theorem 9. *If* $\mathcal{A}$ *follows an acyclic strategy, and is silent and self-stabilizing for* SP *in* G *under the distributed unfair daemon, then*

(1) $\mathsf{T}(\mathcal{A})$ *is silent and self-stabilizing for* SP *in* G *under the distributed unfair daemon,*

(2) its stabilization time is at most $(\mathfrak{H}+1) \cdot (H+1)$ rounds, and
(3) its stabilization time in moves is less than or equal to the one of $\mathcal{A}$.

where $\mathfrak{H}$ is the height of the graph of actions' causality of $\mathcal{A}$ and H is the height of the spanning forest.

Proof. By Remark 7, Lemmas 3 and 4, and Theorems 5 and 6.   □

Using the above theorem, we can apply the transformer on our toy example: $T(\mathcal{TE})$ stabilizes in at most $2(H+1)$ rounds and $\Theta(H \cdot n^2)$ moves in the worst case.

7   Related Work and Applications

There are many works [6–9,14,22,26] where we can apply our generic results. These works propose silent self-stabilizing algorithms for directed trees or network where a directed spanning tree is available. These algorithms are, or can be easily translated into, well-formed algorithms that follow an acyclic strategy. Hence, their correctness and time complexities (in moves and rounds) are directly deduced from our results. Below, we only present a few of them.

Turau and Köhler [26] proposes three algorithms for directed trees. Each algorithm is given with its proof of correctness and round complexity, however move complexity is not considered. These three algorithms can be trivially translated in our model, and our results allow to obtain the same round complexities, and additionally provide move complexities. Among those three algorithms, the third one is the most interesting since it uses 5 families of actions, while the two first use 1 and 2 families respectively. So, we only detail this latter. The algorithm computes a minimum connected distance-k dominating set using:

$$
\begin{aligned}
A_1(p) &:: p.L \neq \mathcal{L}(p) & &\rightarrow p.L \leftarrow \mathcal{L}(p) \\
A_2(p) &:: p.level \neq level(p) & &\rightarrow p.level \leftarrow level(p) \\
A_3(p) &:: p.cds \neq cds'(p) & &\rightarrow p.cds \leftarrow cds'(p) \\
A_4(p) &:: p.cds \wedge p.dist_l \neq dist_l(p) & &\rightarrow p.dist_l \leftarrow dist_l(p) \\
A_5(p) &:: p.minc \neq minc(p) & &\rightarrow p.minc \leftarrow minc(p)
\end{aligned}
$$

We do not explain here the role of the variables nor their computation using macros, please refer to the original paper [26]. But from their definition in [26], we can observe that: (1) $\mathcal{L}(p)$ depends on $q.L$ for $q \in p.chldrn$; (2) $level(p)$ depends on $p.par.level$; (3) $cds'(p)$ that depend on $p.L$ and $q.cds$ for $q \in p.chldrn$; (4) $dist_l(p)$ depends on $q.L$ and $q.cds$ for $q \in p.chldrn$, and $p.par.dist_l$; finally (5) $minc(p)$ depends on $p.level$, $q.cds$ and $q.minc$ for $q \in p.chldrn$. So, A_1, A_3, A_5 are bottom-up and correct-alone and A_2, A_4 are top-down and correct-alone. The graph of actions' causality is acyclic since $A_1 \prec A_3$, $A_1 \prec A_4$, $A_2 \prec A_5$, $A_3 \prec A_4$, and $A_3 \prec A_5$; and its height is $\mathfrak{H} = 2$. Thus, as in [26], we have a round complexity in $O(H)$. Moreover, by Theorem 5, the move complexity is in $O(\Delta^2.n^4)$, where Δ is the degree of the tree.

The silent algorithm given in [22] finds articulation points in a network endowed with a breadth-first spanning tree, assuming a central unfair daemon.

The algorithm computes for each node p the variable $p.e$ which contains every non-tree edges incident on p and some non-tree edges incident on descendants of p once a terminal configuration is reached. Precisely, a non-tree edge $\{p, q\}$ is propagated up in the tree starting from p and q until the first common ancestor of p and q. Based on $p.e$, the node p can decide whether or not it is an articulation point. The algorithm can be translated as a single family of actions which is correct-alone and bottom-up. So, it follows that this algorithm is silent and self-stabilizing even assuming a distributed unfair daemon. Moreover, its stabilization time is in $O(n^2)$ moves and $O(H)$ rounds.

The algorithm in [14] computes cut-nodes and bridges on connected graph endowed with a depth-first spanning tree. It is silent and self-stabilizing under a distributed unfair distributed daemon and converges within $O(n^2)$ moves and $O(H)$ rounds. Indeed, the algorithm contains a single family of actions which is correct-alone and bottom-up.

8   Conclusion

We have presented a general scheme to prove and analyze silent self-stabilizing algorithms executing on networks endowed with a sense of direction describing a spanning forest. Our results allow to easily (*i.e.* quasi-syntactically) deduce correctness and upper bounds on both move and round complexities of such algorithms. We have identified a number of algorithms [6–9,14,22,26] where our method applies. In several of those works, the assumption about the existence of a directed spanning tree has to be considered as an intermediate assumption, since this structure has to be built by an underlying algorithm. Now, several silent self-stabilizing spanning tree constructions are efficient in both rounds and moves, *e.g.*, [15]. Thus, both algorithms, *i.e.*, the one that builds the tree and the one that computes on this tree, have to be carefully composed to obtain a general composite algorithm where the stabilization time is kept both asymptotically optimal in rounds and polynomial in moves.

References

1. Altisen, K., Cournier, A., Devismes, S., Durand, A., Petit, F.: Self-stabilizing leader election in polynomial steps. Inf. Comput. **254**, 330–366 (2017)
2. Arora, A., Gouda, M., Herman, T.: Composite routing protocols. In: SPDP 1990, pp. 70–78 (1990)
3. Blin, L., Fraigniaud, P., Patt-Shamir, B.: On proof-labeling schemes versus silent self-stabilizing algorithms. In: Felber, P., Garg, V. (eds.) SSS 2014. LNCS, vol. 8756, pp. 18–32. Springer, Cham (2014). https://doi.org/10.1007/978-3-319-11764-5_2
4. Blin, L., Potop-Butucaru, M.G., Rovedakis, S., Tixeuil, S.: Loop-free super-stabilizing spanning tree construction. In: Dolev, S., Cobb, J., Fischer, M., Yung, M. (eds.) SSS 2010. LNCS, vol. 6366, pp. 50–64. Springer, Heidelberg (2010). https://doi.org/10.1007/978-3-642-16023-3_7

5. Blin, L., Tixeuil, S.: Compact deterministic self-stabilizing leader election on a ring: the exponential advantage of being talkative. Dist. Comp. **31**(2), 139–166 (2018)
6. Chaudhuri, P.: An $O(n^2)$ self-stabilizing algorithm for computing bridge-connected components. Computing **62**(1), 55–67 (1999)
7. Chaudhuri, P.: A note on self-stabilizing articulation point detection. J. Syst. Arch. **45**(14), 1249–1252 (1999)
8. Chaudhuri, P., Thompson, H.: Self-stabilizing tree ranking. Int. J. Comput. Math. **82**(5), 529–539 (2005)
9. Chaudhuri, P., Thompson, H.: Improved self-stabilizing algorithms for l(2, 1)-labeling tree networks. Math. Comput. Sci. **5**(1), 27–39 (2011)
10. Cournier, A., Devismes, S., Villain, V.: Light enabling snap-stabilization of fundamental protocols. TAAS **4**(1), 6:1–6:27 (2009)
11. Datta, A.K., Devismes, S., Heurtefeux, K., Larmore, L.L., Rivierre, Y.: Competitive self-stabilizing k-clustering. TCS **626**, 110–133 (2016)
12. Datta, A.K., Larmore, L.L., Vemula, P.: An $O(N)$-time self-stabilizing leader election algorithm. JPDC **71**(11), 1532–1544 (2011)
13. Delaët, S., Ducourthial, B., Tixeuil, S.: Self-stabilization with r-operators revisited. JACIC **3**(10), 498–514 (2006)
14. Devismes, S.: A silent self-stabilizing algorithm for finding cut-nodes and bridges. Parallel Process. Lett. **15**(1–2), 183–198 (2005)
15. Devismes, S., Ilcinkas, D., Johnen, C.: Silent self-stabilizing scheme for spanning-tree-like constructions. Technical report, HAL (2018)
16. Devismes, S., Johnen, C.: Silent self-stabilizing BFS tree algorithms revisited. JPDC **97**, 11–23 (2016)
17. Dolev, S., Gouda, M.G., Schneider, M.: Memory requirements for silent stabilization. Acta Inf. **36**(6), 447–462 (1999)
18. Ducourthial, B., Tixeuil, S.: Self-stabilization with r-operators. Dist. Comp. **14**(3), 147–162 (2001)
19. Ghosh, S., Karaata, M.H.: A self-stabilizing algorithm for coloring planar graphs. Dist. Comp. **7**(1), 55–59 (1993)
20. Christian, G., Nicolas, H., David, I., Colette, J.: Disconnected components detection and rooted shortest-path tree maintenance in networks. In: Felber, P., Garg, V. (eds.) SSS 2014. LNCS, vol. 8756, pp. 120–134. Springer, Cham (2014). https://doi.org/10.1007/978-3-319-11764-5_9
21. Huang, S.-T., Chen, N.-S.: A self-stabilizing algorithm for constructing breadth-first trees. IPL **41**(2), 109–117 (1992)
22. Karaata, M.H.: A self-stabilizing algorithm for finding articulation points. Int. J. Found. Comput. Sci. **10**(1), 33–46 (1999)
23. Katz, S., Perry, K.J.: Self-stabilizing extensions for message-passing systems. Dist. Comp. **7**(1), 17–26 (1993)
24. Korman, A., Kutten, S., Peleg, D.: Proof labeling schemes. Dist. Comp. **22**(4), 215–233 (2010)
25. Tel, G.: Introduction to Distributed Algorithms, 2nd edn. Cambridge University Press, Cambridge (2001)
26. Turau, V., Köhler, S.: A distributed algorithm for minimum distance-k domination in trees. J. Graph Algorithms Appl. **19**(1), 223–242 (2015)

On Fast Pattern Formation
by Autonomous Robots

Ramachandran Vaidyanathan[1], Gokarna Sharma[2(✉)], and Jerry L. Trahan[1]

[1] Louisiana State University, Baton Rouge, LA 70803, USA
{vaidy,jtrahan}@lsu.edu
[2] Kent State University, Kent, OH 44242, USA
sharma@cs.kent.edu

Abstract. We consider the fundamental problem of arranging a set of n autonomous robots (points) on a plane according to a given pattern. Each robot operates in a, largely oblivious, look-compute-move step. In this paper, we present a framework for the pattern formation problem. Leader election is key to this framework. For a given leader election time of T_{LE} (that could be deterministic or randomized), we show that the pattern formation problem can be solved in $O(T_{LE})$ time on the semi-synchronous model using robots that either are transparent (i.e., the classical oblivious robots model where complete visibility is guaranteed at all times) or have lights with a constant number of colors (i.e., the robots with lights model where robots are not transparent but the colors of the lights are persistent between steps). We also prove that, for some cases, the $O(T_{LE})$ time is optimal for pattern formation on the semi-synchronous model. These are the first sublinear-time results on pattern formation by autonomous robots in the look-compute-move framework. Furthermore, our results on the semi-synchronous model indicate that transparency and lights compensate for each other in the pattern formation problem. The proposed method also runs in $O(T_{LE} + \log n)$ time on the asynchronous model of robots with lights.

1 Introduction

The classical model of distributed computing by mobile robots abstracts each robot as a point in the plane [6]. The robots are *autonomous* (no external control), *anonymous* (no unique identifiers), *indistinguishable* (no external identifiers), and *disoriented* (no agreement on coordinate systems and units of distance). They execute the same algorithm and proceed in *Look-Compute-Move* (LCM) cycles: When a robot becomes active, it first gets a snapshot of its surroundings (*Look*), then computes a destination based on the snapshot (*Compute*), and finally moves to the destination (*Move*). Moreover, the robots are *oblivious*, i.e., a robot has no memory of its past LCM cycles [6]. Further, robots are *silent* because they do not communicate directly, and only vision and mobility enable them to coordinate their actions.

© Springer Nature Switzerland AG 2018
T. Izumi and P. Kuznetsov (Eds.): SSS 2018, LNCS 11201, pp. 203–220, 2018.
https://doi.org/10.1007/978-3-030-03232-6_14

Another model that incorporates direct communication is the *robots with lights* model [4,6,9], where each robot has an externally visible light that can assume colors from a constant sized set; robots explicitly communicate with each other using these colors. The colors are *persistent*; i.e., the color is not erased at the end of a cycle. Except lights, the robots are oblivious as in the classical model.

Pattern Formation: We study the fundamental problem of arranging a set of n autonomous robots on a plane according to a pattern given by a set of n points (the PATTERN FORMATION problem) [2,5,7,8,14–17]. The points are given in a global coordinate system that is not necessarily the same as the local coordinate system of any robot. The pattern can be arbitrary, as long as the points are distinct. We say a configuration matches the pattern if rotation, translation, and scaling of the configuration points can produce the pattern points. An algorithm solves PATTERN FORMATION if given any initial configuration of n robots located at distinct points on a plane, they reach a configuration that matches the given pattern and remain stationary thereafter.

We study the PATTERN FORMATION problem in both the classical oblivious robots model and the robots with lights model. To the best of our knowledge, our study is the first for PATTERN FORMATION in the robots with lights model. This problem has been studied extensively in the literature in the classical oblivious robot model, e.g., [2,5,7,8,14–17], in fully synchronous, semi-synchronous, and asynchronous models. Although runtime is a crucial parameter, these previous results provide no runtime analysis (except for a proof of finite time termination). Runtime is in fact largely unexplored in the distributed robotics literature. It seems that all previous algorithms for PATTERN FORMATION need linear $O(n)$ runtime. The goal of this paper is to develop a fast runtime framework for PATTERN FORMATION on both the classical oblivious robots model and the robots with lights model. This is the continuation of our recent research on designing algorithms with guaranteed time bounds for fundamental robot coordination problems [10–13]. We believe that the techniques developed for optimizing runtime may provide insights on the difficulty of and approaches to faster robot coordination.

We consider the classical oblivious robots model of [6] and the robots with lights model of [4,9]. Both models are the same except for the following two differences:

- Robots in the robots with lights model are equipped with a persistent light that can assume a constant number of colors.
- Robots are *transparent* in the classical model, i.e., a robot sees all other robots in the system at all times and hence, for example, the swarm size n is known to robots. Robots *obstruct* visibility in the robots with lights model, i.e., the endpoint robots among three collinear robots do not see each other and here robots do not know n.

Contributions: In this paper, we have the following three contributions:

1. For both the classical and lights models of robots, the time needed to solve PATTERN FORMATION is $\Omega\left(T_{LE}\right)$ on the semi-synchronous model, where T_{LE} is the time needed to solve a form of leader election (Sect. 7).
2. For both the classical and lights models of robots, PATTERN FORMATION can be solved in $O\left(T_{LE}\right)$ time on the semi-synchronous model (Sects. 4 and 6), which is optimal (under certain conditions).
3. For the lights model of robots, PATTERN FORMATION can be solved in $O\left(T_{LE} + \log n\right)$ time on the asynchronous model (Sect. 5).
4. For the PATTERN FORMATION problem, the ability to see all robots (unobstructed visibility) can be traded-off with the ability to broadcast light (within obstructed visibility), with no time penalty on the semi-synchronous or fully synchronous model.

To the best of our knowledge, these are the first results with provable sublinear runtime bounds for PATTERN FORMATION. Our results on the semisynchronous model are tight for the lights model, and conditionally optimal for the classical model. They indicate that, for the semi-synchronous model, transparency (in the classical model with no lights) and lights (in the lights model with obstructed visibility) can trade-off with each other for PATTERN FORMATION. For the asynchronous classical model, it is open to provide similar runtime bounds. One prominent property of our algorithms is that they are collision-free. Our algorithms for the lights model have four phases:

- Phase 0 - *Complete Visibility*, which brings any initial configuration of robots to a mutually visible configuration in which each robot sees all others,
- Phase 1 - *Forming an Oriented Circle*, which positions robots on a circle with three of the robots designated as special to impart an orientation to the circle,
- Phase 2 - *Repositioning on an Oriented Circle*, which relocates the robots that are already on the oriented circle to specific positions, and
- Phase 3 - *Positioning on a Given Pattern*, which moves the robots on the specific positions on an oriented circle to points on the given pattern.

We employ our previous $O(1)$ time, $O(1)$ color technique [12] to execute the Phase 0 on the asynchronous model. Phase 3 also runs in constant time. The remaining two phases use a LEADER ELECTION algorithm to select "special robots." They introduce an $O(T_{LE})$ time, and $O(\log n)$ additional time on the asynchronous model ($O(T_{LE})$ time suffices on the semi-synchronous model). A key component of Phase 2 is a beacon-directed curve positioning procedure [12] that recursively puts robots on the specific positions on the oriented circle. Our algorithm for the classical model has Phases 1–3, as all robots are visible by the nature of the model.

2   Preliminaries

Robots with Lights: We consider a distributed setting of n robots $\mathcal{Q} = \{i : 0 \leq i < n\}$. Each robot is a (dimensionless) point that can move in an infinite 2-dimensional real space $\mathbb{R}^2$. We use a point to refer to a robot as well as its position. A robot i can see, and be visible to, another robot j if and only if (iff) there is no third robot k in the line segment joining i, j (i.e., obstructed visibility). Each robot has a light that can assume one color at a time from a constant number of different colors. The moves of the robots are *rigid* – a robot in motion cannot be stopped (by an adversary) before it reaches its destination point. We assume that two robots cannot head to the same destination point and their paths cannot cross; this would constitute a *collision*.

Look-Compute-Move: At any time a robot $i \in \mathcal{Q}$ could be active (participating in an LCM cycle) or inactive. When a robot i becomes active, it performs the "Look-Compute-Move" cycle as follows.

Look: For each robot j that is visible to it, i can observe the position of j on the plane and the color of the light of j. Robot i can also know its own color and position. Each robot observes position on its own frame of reference, i.e., two different robots observing the position of the same point may produce different coordinates. However a robot observes the positions of points accurately within its own reference frame.

Compute: In any LCM cycle, i may perform an arbitrary computation using only the colors and positions observed during the "look" portion of that cycle. This includes determination of a (possibly) new position and color for i for the start of the next LCM cycle. Robot i maintains this new color from that LCM cycle to the next LCM cycle.

Move: At the end of the LCM cycle, i changes its light to the new color and moves to its new position.

Classical Oblivious Robots: The difference compared to the robots with lights (presented above) is that robots in $\mathcal{Q}$ have no lights in the classical model. Therefore, the color part can be discarded while performing an LCM cycle. Furthermore, it is assumed that a robot i can see, and be visible to, every other robot j of $\mathcal{Q}$ (i.e., transparency or unobstructed visibility).

Robot Activation Models and Synchronization: In the fully synchronous model (FSYNC), every robot is active in every LCM cycle and all LCM cycles begin and end at the same time. In the semi-synchronous model (SSYNC) too all LCM cycles begin and end at the same time. However, not all robots may be active at a given LCM cycle. At least one robot is active in each LCM cycle, and over an infinite number of LCM cycles, every robot is active infinitely often. In the asynchronous model (ASYNC), there is no common notion of time and no assumption is made on the number and frequency of LCM cycles in which a robot can be active. The only guarantee is that every robot is active infinitely often. Complying with the ASYNC setting, we assume that a robot performs its *Look* phase at an instant of time. We also assume that a robot moves at some (not necessarily constant) non-zero speed in a straight line until it reaches its destination.

Measuring Runtime: For the FSYNC model, we measure time in rounds, where one round is one LCM cycle. As a robot in the SSYNC and ASYNC models could stay inactive for an indeterminate amount of time, we use the notion of an *epoch* to measure runtime [3]. Let t_0 denote the starting time of the computation. Epoch i is time period from t_{i-1} to t_i where t_i is the earliest time after t_{i-1} when all robots have executed a complete LCM cycle at least once. In the FSYNC model, an epoch is one round (one LCM cycle). We will use the term "time" generically to mean rounds for the FSYNC model and epochs for the SSYNC and ASYNC models. Note that our time bounds for the SSYNC and ASYNC models hold regardless of the activation schedule. Moreover, the bounds for the SSYNC model apply directly to the FSYNC model as well.

Complete Visibility: Given a set of n robots with lights (and obstructed visibility) at arbitrary positions on a plane, the COMPLETE VISIBILITY problem is to position them so that no three robots are collinear.

Theorem 1 [12]. COMPLETE VISIBILITY *can be solved in* $O(1)$ *time on a set of robots with lights operating in the* ASYNC *model.*

Leader Election: The LEADER ELECTION problem is as follows: Given a set of n robots, select exactly one of the robots as leader such that the leader robot knows that it is the leader and non-leader robots know that they are not the leader [1]. In the context of this paper, LEADER ELECTION is used in various forms, In general, we will use T_{LE} to denote leader election time. Several solutions are possible. For this paper, the following results (based on a slotted Aloha algorithm) provide a bound on T_{LE}; for brevity we omit proofs.

Theorem 2. *For any* $\sigma > 0$, LEADER ELECTION *can be solved for the* ASYNC *robots with lights in* $O(\sigma \log n)$ *time with probability at least* $1 - \Theta(n^{-\sigma})$.

Theorem 3. *For any* $\sigma > 0$, LEADER ELECTION *can be solved for the classical* SSYNC *robots in* $O(\sigma \log n)$ *time with probability at least* $1 - \Theta(n^{-\sigma})$.

Remark: In Theorems 2 and 3 if $\sigma \geq 1$ is a constant, then LEADER ELECTION can be solved in $O(\log n)$ time with high probability (whp). On the other hand if $\sigma \log n$ is a constant, then LEADER ELECTION can be solved in $O(1)$ time with a constant probability of success (which, in this case, translates to $O(1)$ average time).

3   A Pattern Formation Framework

We will call a pattern $\{(\ell_i, \theta_i) : 0 \leq i < n\}$, expressed in polar coordinates, to be in *standard form* iff it includes $(0,0)$ and $(1,0)$ as pattern points and the distance $d_{i,j} = \sqrt{r_i^2 + r_j^2 - 2r_i r_j \cos(\theta_i - \theta_j)}$ between any pair of points (ℓ_i, θ_i) and (ℓ_j, θ_j) is at least 1. Clearly given the pattern, one could select a pair of points with minimum distance between them and transform the coordinate system to place these points at $(0,0)$ and $(1,0)$. From this point on, we will assume the given pattern to be in standard form.

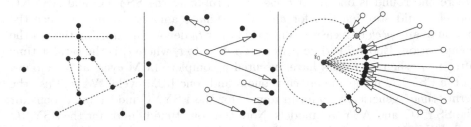

Fig. 1. Left: An initial configuration of $n = 15$ robots; Center: a configuration of complete visibility; Right: An oriented circle for the example with $n = 15$ points. The polar reference and orientation robots are colored blue, red and green, respectively. It should be noted that robots are points on a real plane and are placed on distinct points on the circle. The polar robot has been left at the center for clarity. (Color figure online)

We now present a framework to solve PATTERN FORMATION. The framework has three phases (four for robots with lights). We assume that $n \geq 6$ robots are available.

As we proceed through these phases, we will use the initial (arbitrary) configuration of robots as shown in Fig. 1 as a running example. Though these figures depict robots with lights, the underlying ideas also translate to the classical model.

Phase 0 (Complete Visibility – for Robots with Lights): Position robots such that each robot has unobstructed visibility of all other robots.

Phase 1 (Forming an Oriented Circle): Position all robots on a circle except robots designated as "special robots" and assigned distinct colors or positions to indicate their status. The first of these is the *polar robot* that is placed at the center of the circle. The next one, the *reference robot*, marks a reference point on the circle. On a polar coordinate system with the center of the circle as the pole (origin), the position of the reference robot has an angular coordinate of 0. This robot can be on or within the circle (Fig. 1 shows it on the circle). The third special robot is the *orientation robot*. It is located on or in the circle such that the line connecting it to the reference robot does not traverse the center of the circle. The orientation robot defines the direction in which the angular coordinate increases; specifically, we will assume that the angular coordinate of the orientation robot is strictly smaller than 180°. Figure 1 shows the oriented circle for our example. The polar robot is finally also moved to the circumference of the circle. At this point, each robot i on the circle can also determine the angle θ_i that it makes with the center of the circle. In other words for a circle of radius ℓ, the polar coordinates of robot i on the circle are (ℓ, θ_i). Since each robot on the circle has a distinct position, $\theta_i \neq \theta_j$, for distinct i, j.

The radius ℓ of the oriented circle will also be used as the unit distance for subsequent steps. To comport with a conventional depiction of a polar coordinate system, we will redraw the figure so that the reference robot, which is at the $(1, 0)$ point, is placed to the right of the origin and the angle increases in counterclockwise direction (see Fig. 2).

Phase 2 (Repositioning on an Oriented Circle): Given a set of robots initially positioned on an oriented circle, this phase repositions them on the circle. More specifically, the robots determine a set of destinations on the circle, called target points (as dictated by a common algorithm). These target points are such that robots can move radially outward from these points to the pattern points. Each robot then moves to one of these destinations, without collision.

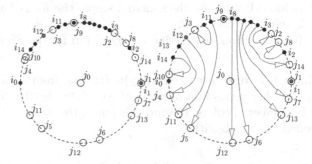

Fig. 2. On the left is Fig. 1(right) redrawn in standard orientation. Small solid circles represent robot positions after they have formed an oriented circle. Slightly larger unfilled circles represent the target positions. The polar robot has been moved off-center to the circumference and its ultimate position at the center is shown. For clarity, the figure on the right slightly repositions the points of the figure on the left, as only the relative positions are important for the illustration. Robot paths are shown curved only for clarity.

The special robots do not move in this phase. Figure 2(right) illustrates the movement of robots for our example.

Phase 3 (Positioning on Given Pattern): Given a set of robots positioned at target points on an oriented circle, this phase moves the robots to pattern points. At this phase the polar robot moves to the origin and the reference robot remains at point $(1, 0)$.

Every pattern point (x_i, y_i) can be expressed in polar coordinates (ℓ_i, θ_i). For an oriented circle of radius 1, the previous phase positions robot i at target point $(1, \theta_i)$. In the current phase, robot i moves along the radius of the oriented circle from distance 1 to distance r_i. Further, the scale is fixed so that the shortest distance of any point in the pattern to the origin is 1. Thus, each $r_i \geq 1$ and there is no robot inside the oriented circle while the non-special robots move. The special robots move last as explained later.

This approach has assumed that all robots to have different angle coordinates θ_i. We will briefly address the case where θ_i is not distinct later.

4   Pattern Formation on SSYNC Robots with Lights

We first make some observations that will enable us to express our algorithms tersely. If an algorithm has a constant number of steps (or phases), then one can enforce explicit synchronization between steps by using a different (but constant sized) set of colors for each step. Although the number of colors used can be reduced by reusing them across steps, the focus here is on the main ideas underlying our approach.

In this section we describe an algorithm for the SSYNC model with lights.

Phase 0 (Complete Visibility): Starting from an arbitrary position robots arrange themselves in a position of complete visibility in $O(1)$ time and with a $O(1)$ number of colors. Beyond this point, the robots will maintain the visibility needed for the algorithm.

Phase 1 (Forming an Oriented Circle): First pick a leader (Theorem 2), say robot i_0, and color it `center`. This robot will (ultimately) be the center of the oriented circle. Let d be the distance of the closest robot to i_0 (other than i_0 itself). Then d will be the radius of the oriented circle. Now each robot, except the center i_0, moves towards i_0 (if needed) to place itself on the circle and assumes a color `on_circle`. We will call robots with color `on_circle` as "circle robots."

To orient the circle, use LEADER ELECTION (Theorem 2) to select two other leaders. The first (reference robot) is any one of the robots on the circumference of the circle. The second leader (orientation robot) could be any robot except one that is diametrically opposite to the first leader. (Assuming $n > 3$ guarantees the existence of such a robot; if $n = 3$, then an orientation is not needed.) Further, as the last step, the polar robot moves to the circumference of the oriented circle. The point selected by the polar robot to move to on the circumference must not be occupied by any robot currently, or be the destination of any robot in Phase 3. (The polar robot can determine all destinations of Phase 3 from the input information.)

At this point, every robot is on the circumference of a circle (a position of complete visibility) and because $n \geq 3$, every robot can determine the center (and radius) of this circle. Thus even though the polar robot is not at the center, the circle is still oriented.

Lemma 4. *For any $\sigma > 0$, given a set of robots in a position of complete visibility, they can form an oriented circle in $O(T_{LE}) = O(\sigma \log n)$ time with probability $1 - \Theta(n^{-\sigma})$.*

Phase 2 (Repositioning Robots on Oriented Circle): At the start of this phase, all robots are positioned on the circumference of an oriented circle. The target points to which robots need to be repositioned are derived from the pattern points in the input/program. (The overview of Phase 3 (Sect. 3) explains how to compute target points on the circle.) All robots except the reference and the polar robots are now repositioned on the circle. Recall also that the reference robot is already at its final position at $(1, 0)$ and that the polar robot (ultimately) needs to move to the pole (origin). The orientation robot will be the last to relocate in this phase and the polar robot will remain on the circumference, moving to the pole in the next phase. Consequently, when all robots are on the circle, they will have the special robots, and hence the oriented circle, in their view.

Let $m = n - 3$. This phase essentially solves the following "Circle Repositioning" problem. Given a set of m (non-special) robots on an oriented circle, the task is to relocate these points to a set of target points on the circle. We will initially leave the special robots out of the discussion, with the understanding that they will be available for use of the remaining m non-special robots to relocate themselves. In Sect. 5 we give solutions to the above problem that run on the ASYNC model.

Coming back to the Circle Repositioning problem on the SSYNC model, we have an oriented circle (with three special robots) and m non-special robots that are to be relocated to m possibly new target positions on the circle. Assume that all of the m robots move to a new position; otherwise we can ignore those robots that are already at a destination position and reduce the value of m. Thus we have a set of $2m$ distinct points, m of which are sources and m are destinations. In the following, sources and destinations are analogous to left and right parentheses and the solution to the problem corresponds to a parenthesis matching. (It can be shown that if sources and destinations are paired by parenthesis matching, then paths will not cross within the circle (for brevity we omit a proof).)

The first task of this phase is to determine a source, starting from which and proceeding along the circle (as dictated by its orientation) one gets a proper parenthesis matching between the sources and destinations. For the example of Fig. 2(right), the orientation is counterclockwise. Here a proper parenthesis matching can start from robot i_3, but not from i_2 (as we encounter more destinations than sources at some point on our way). Since all source and destination positions are visible to all m robots, those that are eligible to start the parenthesis sequence flag themselves in constant time. Next, exactly one of them is selected as the starting point using LEADER ELECTION; this robot is colored appropriately.

Each source (robot) i has a unique destination j_i in this parenthesis sequence. A key point is that removal of a source destination pair, say $i', j_{i'}$, from the parenthesis sequence does not change the mapping of another robot i to j_i.

Consider any source i that wakes at the start of a round. In the SSYNC model, it does not see any robots in the interior of the circle. Every robot it sees has either moved to a destination (this is the same as the source-destination pair not participating in the parenthesis matching) or is waiting to move at the current or future round. From our earlier observation, source i correctly identifies its destination j_i and moves to it, based only on what it sees at the current round (regardless of which robot has already moved in a previous round).

Lemma 5. *For any $\sigma > 0$, the Circle Repositioning problem on n robots can be solved in $O(T_{LE}) = O(\sigma \log n)$ time with probability $1 - \Theta(n^{-\sigma})$ on the SSYNC robots with lights model.*

Phase 3 (Positioning Robots on a Pattern): The reference robot is in its final position $(1, 0)$ on the oriented circle and the polar robot is at some position on the circumference of the oriented circle. Every other robot i, including the orientation robot (that is placed at $(1, \theta_i)$ at some distinct angle θ_i on the circumference of the unit oriented circle) is in a position of complete visibility before its move. Since $r_i \geq 1$ (no robot moves into the unit circle), complete visibility is ensured for robots that are still on the unit oriented circle until the polar robot moves to the pole.

First each non-special robot i moves independently to its final position (ℓ_i, θ_i). For this it only needs the special robots and this step runs in one epoch.

Now that all non-special robots have been moved to the correct positions on the pattern, we turn to the three special robots. Of these, the reference robot is already in its final position. We first move the polar robot to the center of the circle. This is simple as the positions of the reference robot, orientation robot, and polar robot on the circle fully define the circle and its center.

Since the reference robot is not placed diametrically opposite to the orientation robot, and the polar robot is at the center of the circle, both the polar and reference robots are visible to the orientation robot. Along with its own position, the orientation robot can fully determine the oriented circle and move to its destination. At this point all robots are at their final destinations.

For brevity, we omit some details here, including the offset procedure (in Appendix) by which robots with the same angular coordinate for pattern points spread themselves in an arc of the oriented circle to be able to reach their pattern points without collision.

Theorem 6. *For any $\sigma > 0$, PATTERN FORMATION can be solved on the SSYNC robots with lights model with n robots in $O(T_{LE}) = O(\sigma \log n)$ time with probability $1 - \Theta(n^{-\sigma})$.*

5   Pattern Formation on ASYNC Robots with Lights

A robot in transit in the ASYNC model can assume a different (set of) color(s) to indicate that it is in transit. This will only involve replacing a step by two steps, one to change color to a transit color and move and the other to change color to a destination color.

On the SSYNC model, all active robots wake and look at the same time, so they do not see robots in motion. In the ASYNC model, a waking robot can see a robot in motion that blocks its view of a circle robot; recall that robots in motion are so colored. Coping with the positions of robots in motion is a major challenge in moving from SSYNC to ASYNC.

For SSYNC circle formation (Phase 1), since the all robots that have moved from the initial complete visibility position are now circle robots, at least one circle robot is visible to every waking robot. Thus, all robots move to the circle within one epoch.

For ASYNC circle formation, consider any epoch starting with $m \geq 1$ circle robots, and one (i_0) at the center, and the remaining $n - 1 - m$ at distinct angles from i_0. Since every robot moves radially towards the center, a moving robot cannot block the view of the center from any robot. Consider a waking robot i that is unable to see any circle robot. As argued for the SSYNC case each blocking robot must be in motion and will became a circle robot at the next epoch. If all m circle robots are blocked from a single waking robot (at a single instant of time) then there must be at least m robots in motion and the next epoch has at least $2m$ circle robots. Since the number of circle robots at least doubles at each epoch, $O(\log n)$ epochs suffice to move all robots to the circle.

We provide an overview of the ASYNC algorithm for Circle Repositioning (Phase 2). Phases 0, 1, and 3 are easily executed extending the respective phases in Sect. 4. We denote the oriented circle by $\mathcal{OC}$. We assume that the polar robot is on $\mathcal{OC}$.

The algorithm works for Phase 2 in stages as follows. Stages 1 is executed only one time in the beginning of Phase 2 and Stages 2–4 are executed repeatedly until all robots are positioned on their target points on $\mathcal{OC}$. The reference robot is already on its target point and hence it does not move. We also do not move polar and orientation robots. They will be moved to their target points later. Figure 3 illustrates the stages with 15 robots on the circle initially (including the polar robot).

– **Stage 1:** This stage picks a set $\mathcal{X}$ of robots (we fix size 4 and denote as $|\mathcal{X}| = 4$; in fact any constant ≥ 3 should be sufficient) on $\mathcal{OC}$ and places them on their target points on $\mathcal{OC}$. We do not move the reference robot, and we include this robot to be a robot in $\mathcal{X}$. Note that we still have m robots to move to the target points; if some robots are already on their target points, they pick appropriate colors and remain stationary. The stage is done sequentially for each of the $|\mathcal{X}|$ arcs and robots in $\mathcal{X}$ are positioned in such a way that in the arc of $\mathcal{OC}$ between two consecutive robots of $\mathcal{X}$, there are exactly $m' = \frac{m-|\mathcal{X}|-1}{|\mathcal{X}|}$ target points for the robots on $\mathcal{OC}$ to move to (discounting the reference robot). The boundary cases of m' not being an integer can be handled with a simple modification. Let $\overline{ij}$ be a straight line connecting any two consecutive robots i, j of $\mathcal{X}$ and $arc(ij)$ be an arc of $\mathcal{OC}$ between i, j. The robots on $arc(ij)$ are then repositioned on $\overline{ij}$. If less than m' robots are on $arc(ij)$, the robots on the other $|\mathcal{X}| - 1$ arcs will move to $arc(ij)$ to make sure that there are m' robots.

- **Stage 2:** All robots on $\mathcal{OC}$ that are not on their target points are now positioned on $|\mathcal{X}|$ straight lines connecting the consecutive robots of $\mathcal{X}$. This stage forms an arc $arc_{in}(ij)$, bent inward rather than outward like $arc(ij)$, that passes through the endpoints i, j of $\overline{ij}$ and places all the robots on $\overline{ij}$ to the positions on $arc_{in}(ij)$. The relocation is done in such a way that, at the end of this stage, each robot on $arc_{in}(ij)$ sees all other robots on $arc_{in}(ij)$ including i, j and the remaining robots of $\mathcal{X}$. The robots in $\mathcal{X}$, except i, j, may not be visible after the relocation. However, we ask robots on $arc_{in}(.)$ to nudge a bit on the arc itself that they are on if they are collinear with any two robots of $\mathcal{X}$.
- **Stage 3:** Let k be a robot in the middle among the robots on $arc_{in}(ij)$. Since each robot on $arc_{in}(ij)$ sees all other robots on $arc_{in}(ij)$, k can easily compute whether it is a middle robot or not. Robot k moves to its target point on $arc(ij)$ and the other robots of $arc_{in}(ij)$ do not move at this stage. After k is positioned on $arc(ij)$, $arc(ij)$ is divided into two arcs $arc(ik)$ and $arc(kj)$. Represent the straight line connecting i with k by $\overline{ik}$ and the line connecting k with j by $\overline{kj}$.
- **Stage 4:** Let $\mathcal{X}_{left}$ and $\mathcal{X}_{right}$ be the robots on $arc_{in}(ij)$ such that the robots between i and k (before it moved to $arc(ij)$) are in $\mathcal{X}_{left}$ and the remaining robots of $arc_{in}(ij)$ are in $\mathcal{X}_{right}$. The goal in this stage is to move the robots in $\mathcal{X}_{left}$ to position them on $\overline{ik}$ and in $\mathcal{X}_{right}$ to position them on $\overline{kj}$. The robots on $\overline{ik}$ and $\overline{kj}$ then execute Stages 2–4 one after another. This process repeats until all robots on $\mathcal{OC}$ are positioned on the target points on $\mathcal{OC}$.

To achieve our objectives, synchronize through colors the execution in each stage and between subsequent stages. We show that $O(1)$ colors suffice. Each stage runs in $O(1)$ time for each iteration. Stages 2–4 execute at most $O(\log n)$ times during Phase 2. Combining all these results, we have $O(\log n)$ time for Phase 2 in the ASYNC model.

Lemma 7. *The Circle Repositioning problem on n robots can be solved in $O(\log n)$ time on the ASYNC model.*

Combining the results of Lemma 7 with Theorem 2 (leader election in the ASYNC model), we obtain the following theorem for ASYNC robots with lights.

Theorem 8. *For any $\sigma > 0$,* PATTERN FORMATION *can be solved on the ASYNC robots with lights model with n robots in $O(T_{LE} + \log n)$ time with probability $1 - \Theta(n^{-\sigma})$.*

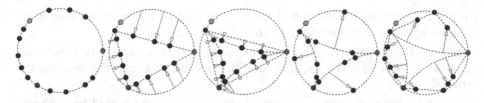

Fig. 3. An illustration of the stages of the asynchronous algorithm for Phase 2. Given n robots on an oriented circle (left), Stage 1 moves them appropriately to the lines connecting a constant number of selected robots. Stage 2 then forms an arc each on those lines and moves all robots on those lines to their arcs. Stage 3 then moves a middle robot on each arc to its target point on the oriented circle. Stage 4 then moves the remaining robots of those arcs to two straight lines formed due to the move of the middle robot on the oriented circle in Stage 3. Stages 2–4 execute repeatedly until all robots on the circle are relocated to their target points.

6 Pattern Formation on SSYNC Classical Robots

Here we consider robots without lights, but with unobstructed visibility (every robot is visible to every other robot, including itself, regardless of the robot positions on the plane). We describe pattern formation on the SSYNC classical robots model, focusing mostly on the differences from the robots with lights model. We will use positional information to indicate robot states (rather than lights), without having to moderate this positioning to account for visibility.

Additionally we will use two constants $0 < \alpha < \beta < 1$ and a non-zero angle ϕ that serve, among other things, to separate configurations at different steps. The values of α, β, ϕ can be determined at compile time, given the destination points.

Lemma 9. *Consider a pattern $P = \{(\ell_i, \theta_i) : 0 \leq i < n\}$ in standard form. Let $Q = \{(1, \phi_i) : 0 \leq i < m\}$ be a set of $m \leq n^2$ points on a unit circle centered at $(0,0)$. Consider a configuration $\mathcal{C}$ in which the polar robot, r_0, the reference robot, r_1, and the orientation robot, r_2, are placed at points $(0,0)$, $(\alpha, 0)$ and (β, ϕ), respectively, and all other robots are placed on $n-3$ of the points of $P \cup Q$. Then the constants α, β, ϕ can be selected (at compile time) so that in configuration $\mathcal{C}$, robots r_0, r_1, r_2 can be uniquely identified.* ◀

We now outline the algorithm for the classical robot model, focusing in the differences from the model with lights (Sect. 4). For brevity (and clarity), we will also omit some details that could entail adding additional condition-action pairs in fairly simple ways.

Because visibility is not a concern, Phase 0 is not needed and we begin with Phase 1.

Phase 1 (Forming an Oriented Circle): This phase is performed in four sub-phases, Phase 1.1–1.4.

PHASE 1.1 (POLAR ROBOT SELECTION): The goal is to select the robot to be at the origin of a coordinate system that we are defining.

Condition 1.1: Always (the first step has to work with an arbitrary input configuration). Because oblivious, this condition means that no other condition is satisfied.

Action 1.1: Find a leader from among all the robots (using Leader Election) and move this leader robot far enough away from the rest so that its angle of view[1] is less than $60°$ (this is needed in Phase 2).

The above leader is the polar robot.

PHASE 1.2 (CIRCLE FORMATION): Here, all robots, except the polar robot, arrange themselves in a circle C. The polar robot will be at the center of this circle.

Condition 1.2: There is only one robot r_0 (with the largest global distance), the angle of view of r_0 is less than $60°$, and not all robots other than r_0 are on a circle centered at r_0.

Action 1.2: Let d be the distance of the furthest robot from r_0. Move each robot along the line connecting it to r_0 to a distance d from r_0. Robots that are collinear with r_0 use an offset procedure (omitted due to space constraints).

Clearly, this algorithm runs in $O(1)$ time on the FSYNC model. However it also runs on the SSYNC model as discussed below. Recall that the angle of view of the polar robot, r_0, is $< 60°$. This ensures that as robots $r_i \neq r_0$ move to circle C, the distance between them will not exceed their distance from r_0. Therefore, robots that have already moved to the circle will wait until the end of the epoch when all robots (other than r_0) have moved to the circle.

At this point the polar robot r_0 is at the center of a circle C and all other robots are on the circumference of the circle. From here, robots treat the radius of the circle as distance 1.

PHASE 1.3 (REFERENCE ROBOT DETERMINATION): We will designate one robot r_1 as the reference robot that will be ultimately located at point $(1, 0)$.

Condition 1.3: All robots, except one, are on the circumference of a circle, C. The last robot is at the center of this circle.

Action 1.3: Use Leader Election to pick one robot r_y on the circumference and move it inward radially to a distance β (for constant $0 < \beta < 1$ consistent with Lemma 9).

PHASE 1.4 (ORIENTATION ROBOT DETERMINATION): We designate another robot r_z, whose position relative to r_y will indicate which way the angle increases. This step proceeds exactly as the previous one except in relocating the orientation robot.

---

[1] The *angle of view* [12] of a robot in a given configuration is the smallest angle subtended at the robot's position within which all robots are included. For example, if all robots are in a straight line, the angle of view is $0°$ for the robots at the ends and $180°$ for all others.

Condition 1.4: All robots, except two, are on the circumference of a circle, C. One of the remaining robots is at the center of this circle and the last robot is at distance β from the center.

Action 1.4: Use Leader Election to pick one robot r_y on the circumference of C and move it inward to point (α, ϕ).

Phase 2 (Repositioning on Oriented Circle): Except for moving the special robots (polar, reference and orientation robots) out of the way, this phase is identical to that of robots with lights. The portions requiring lights to indicate a leader can be effected by moving the leader marginally out of the circle so as not to obstruct movement of robots within the circle.

Condition 2.1: The special robots are within the circle and the remaining robots are on circle, but not all at the correct angles.

Action 2.1: Move the polar, reference and orientation robots from $(0,0)$, $(\beta, 0)$ and (α, ϕ) radially to points (γ_0, ϕ_0), $(\gamma_1, 0)$ and (γ_2, ϕ), respectively, where $1 < \gamma_0 < \gamma_1 < \gamma_2$ and points (γ_0, ϕ_0), $(\gamma_1, 0)$ and (γ_2, ϕ) are not in the pattern.

The points (γ_0, ϕ_0), $(\gamma_1, 0)$ and (γ_2, ϕ) can be computed with the knowledge of n, the pattern to be formed and the current configuration. At this point, the inside of the circle is free for robot relocation. This subphase runs in constant time.

Condition 2.2: Three special robots are outside the circle at non-pattern points and there is at least one non-relocated non-special robot on the circle.

Action 2.2: Relocate robots as indicated earlier.

We now get the special robots back inside the unit circle.

Condition 2.3: Three robots are outside a (unit) circle at non-pattern points (γ_0, ϕ_0), $(\gamma_1, 0)$ and (γ_2, ϕ), with $1 < \gamma_0 < \gamma_1 < \gamma_2$ and the remaining robots are placed at the correct angles (to within offset points) on the circle.

Action 2.3: Move the robot at (γ_0, ϕ_0) to the center of the circle. Move the robot at (γ_0, ϕ_0) to $(\beta, 0)$ and the robot at (γ_2, ϕ) to $(\alpha, 0)$.

Phase 3 (Positioning on Given Pattern): Again this phase is as in the lights case. It is here that we use Lemma 9 to ensure that all robots can identify the special robots as they move to their final positions across multiple SSYNC rounds. We omit additional details.

Theorem 10. *For any $\sigma > 0$,* Pattern Formation *can be solved on the classical* SSYNC *robots model with n robots in $O(T_{LE}) = O(\sigma \log n)$ time with probability $1 - \Theta(n^{-\sigma})$.*

7 Lower Bound, Time-Optimality and Trade-Offs

Consider a set of n robots (under some robot model $\mathcal{M}$). For any integer $1 \leq k \leq n$, the k-RANKING problem selects a set of k robots and assigns a unique rank from 1 to k to each of the selected robots. Each robot knows its rank (or lack of one if it is not selected). Robots start at arbitrary positions. Because a lower bound is sought, we make the k-RANKING as easy as possible and place no requirements on the final robot configuration. It should be noted that the 1-RANKING is a version of LEADER ELECTION.

Theorem 11. PATTERN FORMATION *on any autonomous robot model* $\mathcal{M}(n)$ *with* n *robots requires* $\Omega(T_k(n))$ *time, where* $T_k(n)$ *is the time to solve* k-RANKING *on* $\mathcal{M}(n)$.

We now place this lower bound in the context of the algorithms in Sects. 4 and 6. Clearly LEADER ELECTION is no easier to solve than k-RANKING. Cast in terms of leader election time, the algorithms of Theorems 6 and 10 run in $O(T_{LE})$ time, where $O(T_{LE})$ is the time to solve leader election on the given model. This application of LEADER ELECTION in our algorithm differs from 1-RANKING, as defined, in two ways: (a) robots are expected to maintain certain positional configurations at the end of leader election, and (b) the leader may have to be selected from a subset of robots.

For the robots with lights model, performing LEADER ELECTION on a subset of robots is straightforward using a dedicated (palette of) color(s). Similarly, saving the robot ranks, while rearranging the robots into any desired positions is also a matter of increasing the number of colors used by a constant factor. Therefore, we have:

Theorem 12. *For any* $\mathcal{M} \in$ {FSYNC, SSYNC} *robots with lights model, given a time-optimal algorithm for* LEADER ELECTION *on* $\mathcal{M}$, PATTERN FORMATION *can be solved time-optimally on* $\mathcal{M}$. ◀

For the classical model, such a broad assurance is not possible without specifics of the leader election algorithm.

Theorem 13. *For any* $\mathcal{M} \in$ {FSYNC, SSYNC} *classical robots, if slotted-Aloha-based leader election algorithms are time-optimal on* $\mathcal{M}$, *then* PATTERN FORMATION *can be solved time-optimally on* $\mathcal{M}$. ◀

We close this section with an observation about two (seemingly unrelated) abilities of autonomous robots in the SSYNC model: unobstructed visibility and the availability of lights. Lights allow robots to store and broadcast a constant number of states. In a similar, but less flexible way, unobstructed visibility allows robots to use relative positions to broadcast state information. Our results seem to bear this out since Theorems 6 and 10 show that for the PATTERN FORMATION problem and to within optimality of LEADER ELECTION, unobstructed visibility and lights compensate for each other.

8 Concluding Remarks

We have presented the first, to our knowledge, sublinear-time algorithmic framework for PATTERN FORMATION in the classical model as well as the lights model. Our algorithms for both the models run in $O(T_{LE})$ time on the SSYNC model, where T_{LE} is the time for leader election on the given model. For the lights model, this time is optimal as we also show that $\Omega(T_{LE})$ time is necessary; for the classical model this time is conditionally optimal. We further show that PATTERN FORMATION can be solved for robots with lights on the ASYNC model in $O(T_{LE} + \log n)$ time. All these algorithms are collision-free.

Can other algorithms trade the state information of robots with lights for the position information available due to transparency in the classical robots model? Can the $O(T_{LE} + \log n)$ time be achieved on the ASYNC model for classical oblivious robots? How far is the $O(T_{LE} + \log n)$ ASYNC upper bound from the lower bound? Are algorithms tolerating faults possible? Will these approaches work for fat robots?

References

1. Attiya, H., Welch, J.: Distributed Computing: Fundamentals, Simulations and Advanced Topics. Wiley, Hoboken (2004)
2. Bramas, Q., Tixeuil, S.: Probabilistic asynchronous arbitrary pattern formation (short paper). In: Bonakdarpour, B., Petit, F. (eds.) SSS 2016. LNCS, vol. 10083, pp. 88–93. Springer, Cham (2016). https://doi.org/10.1007/978-3-319-49259-9_7
3. Cord-Landwehr, A., et al.: A new approach for analyzing convergence algorithms for mobile robots. In: Aceto, L., Henzinger, M., Sgall, J. (eds.) ICALP 2011. LNCS, vol. 6756, pp. 650–661. Springer, Heidelberg (2011). https://doi.org/10.1007/978-3-642-22012-8_52
4. Das, S., Flocchini, P., Prencipe, G., Santoro, N., Yamashita, M.: Autonomous mobile robots with lights. Theor. Comput. Sci. **609**(P1), 171–184 (2016)
5. Dieudonné, Y., Petit, F., Villain, V.: Leader election problem versus pattern formation problem. In: Lynch, N.A., Shvartsman, A.A. (eds.) DISC 2010. LNCS, vol. 6343, pp. 267–281. Springer, Heidelberg (2010). https://doi.org/10.1007/978-3-642-15763-9_26
6. Flocchini, P., Prencipe, G., Santoro, N.: Distributed Computing by Oblivious Mobile Robots. Synthesis Lectures on Distributed Computing Theory. Morgan & Claypool Publishers, San Rafael (2012)
7. Flocchini, P., Prencipe, G., Santoro, N., Widmayer, P.: Arbitrary pattern formation by asynchronous, anonymous, oblivious robots. Theor. Comput. Sci. **407**(1-3), 412–447 (2008)
8. Fujinaga, N., Yamauchi, Y., Ono, H., Kijima, S., Yamashita, M.: Pattern formation by oblivious asynchronous mobile robots. SIAM J. Comput. **44**(3), 740–785 (2015)
9. Peleg, D.: Distributed coordination algorithms for mobile robot swarms: new directions and challenges. In: Pal, A., Kshemkalyani, A.D., Kumar, R., Gupta, A. (eds.) IWDC 2005. LNCS, vol. 3741, pp. 1–12. Springer, Heidelberg (2005). https://doi.org/10.1007/11603771_1
10. Poudel, P., Sharma, G.: Universally optimal gathering under limited visibility. In: Spirakis, P., Tsigas, P. (eds.) SSS 2017. LNCS, vol. 10616, pp. 323–340. Springer, Cham (2017). https://doi.org/10.1007/978-3-319-69084-1_23

11. Sharma, G., Busch, C., Mukhopadhyay, S.: Brief announcement: complete visibility for oblivious robots in linear time. In: SPAA, pp. 325–327 (2017)
12. Sharma, G., Vaidyanathan, R., Trahan, J.L.: Constant-time complete visibility for asynchronous robots with lights. In: Spirakis, P., Tsigas, P. (eds.) SSS 2017. LNCS, vol. 10616, pp. 265–281. Springer, Cham (2017). https://doi.org/10.1007/978-3-319-69084-1_18
13. Sharma, G., Vaidyanathan, R., Trahan, J.L., Busch, C., Rai, S.: Logarithmic-time complete visibility for asynchronous robots with lights. In: IPDPS, pp. 513–522 (2017)
14. Suzuki, I., Yamashita, M.: Distributed anonymous mobile robots: formation of geometric patterns. SIAM J. Comput. **28**(4), 1347–1363 (1999)
15. Yamashita, M., Suzuki, I.: Characterizing geometric patterns formable by oblivious anonymous mobile robots. Theor. Comput. Sci. **411**(26–28), 2433–2453 (2010)
16. Yamauchi, Y., Yamashita, M.: Pattern formation by mobile robots with limited visibility. In: Moscibroda, T., Rescigno, A.A. (eds.) SIROCCO 2013. LNCS, vol. 8179, pp. 201–212. Springer, Cham (2013). https://doi.org/10.1007/978-3-319-03578-9_17
17. Yamauchi, Y., Yamashita, M.: Randomized pattern formation algorithm for asynchronous oblivious mobile robots. In: Kuhn, F. (ed.) DISC 2014. LNCS, vol. 8784, pp. 137–151. Springer, Heidelberg (2014). https://doi.org/10.1007/978-3-662-45174-8_10

Load Balanced Distributed Directories

Shishir Rai[1], Gokarna Sharma[1(✉)], Costas Busch[2], and Maurice Herlihy[3]

[1] Kent State University, Kent, OH 44242, USA
srai@kent.edu, sharma@cs.kent.edu
[2] Louisiana State University, Baton Rouge, LA 70803, USA
busch@csc.lsu.edu
[3] Brown University, Providence, RI 02912, USA
mph@cs.brown.edu

Abstract. We present LB-SPIRAL, a novel distributed directory protocol for shared objects, suitable for large-scale distributed shared memory systems. Each shared object has an owner node that can modify its
value. The ownership may change by moving the object from one node
to another in response to *move* requests. The value of an object can
be read by other nodes with *lookup* requests. The distinctive feature of
LB-SPIRAL is that it balances the processing load on nodes in addition
to minimizing the communication cost in general network topologies.
In contrast, the existing distributed directory protocols for general network topologies only minimize the communication cost. In particular,
LB-SPIRAL achieves poly-log approximation for both load and communication cost in general networks with respect to the problem parameters.

1 Introduction

Distributed directories are data structures that enable access to shared objects
in a network. They support three basic operations: (i) *publish*, allowing a shared
object to be inserted in the directory so that other nodes can find it; (ii) *lookup*,
providing a read-only copy of the object to the requesting node; and (iii) *move*,
allowing the requesting node to write the object locally after getting it.

Distributed directories are suitable for distributed systems where shared
objects are moved to those nodes that need them [14]. Tasks operate on local
shared objects and if remote shared objects are required, a task must communicate through the directory to the remote nodes. In the distributed setting *cache-
coherence* for the shared objects ensures that writing to an object automatically
locates and *invalidates* other cached copies of that object. A *distributed directory
protocol* (DDPs) [7] is a distributed directory implementation which realizes a
coherence mechanism. Any DDP guarantees each *lookup* and *move* operation to
the shared object in a distributed directory is individually atomic.

DDPs have a long history of research. They have widely been used in distributed shared memory implementations in multi-cache systems [1, 6, 7]. DDPs
have also been used to implement fundamental problems in distributed systems, including distributed queues [8], mobile object tracking [4], and distributed

© Springer Nature Switzerland AG 2018
T. Izumi and P. Kuznetsov (Eds.): SSS 2018, LNCS 11201, pp. 221–238, 2018.
https://doi.org/10.1007/978-3-030-03232-6_15

mutual exclusion [20]. Very recently, DDPs have been studied for implementing transactional memory [13,27] in large-scale distributed systems [3,14,23,25,30].

In the literature, the performance of a DDP has been typically evaluated with respect to the *communication cost*, the total distance traversed by all the messages in the network. The ratio of the actual communication cost to the optimal cost provides an approximation ratio known as *stretch*. Existing DDPs such as ARROW [8], RELAY [30], COMBINE [3], BALLISTIC [14], and SPIRAL [23] focus only on minimizing the stretch, while several other proposed DDPs [1,6,7] do not have stretch analysis.

Processing load can also significantly affect the DDP performance. *Load* is measured as the worst node utilization, namely, the maximum number of times that operations for objects use a node in the distributed directory. Load minimization is very important because it allows to evenly utilize available network resources (processing power, energy, etc.), avoiding the chance to create bottlenecks due to some "hotspot" resources. Here, we present a novel DDP for general network topologies which simultaneously balances the load (minimizes maximum load) and minimizes the communication cost (minimizes stretch). The only previously known DDP that controls simultaneously the load and stretch is MULTIBEND [25], which however is only suitable for the restricted case of mesh (grid) topologies.

Problem Statement. We describe the problem with respect to a single shared object, since for each object we can apply the same DDP solution. Consider a network and a set $\mathcal{E} = \{r_0, r_1, \ldots, r_\ell\}$ of operations to the shared object (ℓ does not need to be known). The initial operation r_0 is to *publish* the shared object in the directory while the remaining, $r_1, r_2, \ldots r_\ell$, are *move* operations for the object. The objective is to design a DDP that arranges the operations r_i, $i > 0$, in a total order (or a "distributed queue") [8]. Each operation r_i, $i > 0$, has a source node s_i, denoting the previous owner node, and a destination node t_i that issues r_i which will become the new object owner. The destination node of an operation r_{i_1} is the source node of another operation r_{i_2} in the total order, where the total order is a permutation of the requests in $\mathcal{E}$ that preserves the real time ordering. For every request r_i, the directory provides a path p_i from s_i to t_i along which the object is transferred. Ideally, the collection of the paths minimize the load and the stretch. Formally,

– *Load balancing:* Minimize the maximum node *processing load* $PL = \max_v |\{i : v \in p_i\}|$. The processing load PL can be compared to the optimal processing load PL^* that is attainable by any DDP to provide an approximation ratio.
– *Stretch:* Minimize total communication cost $A(\mathcal{E}) = \sum_{i=1}^{\ell} |p_i|$, where $|p_i|$ is the total length of the path p_i. $A(\mathcal{E})$ can be compared to the optimal cost $A^*(\mathcal{E})$ from the optimal algorithm OPT that has complete knowledge about $\mathcal{E}$ to provide a request ordering with minimal stretch $A(\mathcal{E})/A^*(\mathcal{E})$. We are interested to minimize $\max_{\mathcal{E}} A(\mathcal{E})/A^*(\mathcal{E})$.

Contributions. Let G be a network and $\mathcal{Z}$ a distributed directory on it. Previously known DDPs, such as ARROW [8] and RELAY [30], run on top of a spanning tree, while BALLISTIC [14] and COMBINE [3] run on top of an overlay tree, and further, SPIRAL [23] and MULTIBEND [25] use a hierarchy of clusters built on top of G. Therefore, a node *participates* on the directory $\mathcal{Z}$ if it is one of the nodes on the spanning tree, overlay tree, or a leader node of a cluster. It is easy to see that the processing load of a node in all the aforementioned DDPs is $O(\ell)$ in the worst-case, with the exception of MULTIBEND [25] which minimizes simultaneously both stretch and processing load but only on mesh network topologies.

We present LB-SPIRAL, a new DDP for shared objects, that is suitable for general networks, and is load balanced and at the same time maintains low stretch. LB-SPIRAL is based on a hierarchy of clusters $\mathcal{Z}$, which builds upon our previous DDP, SPIRAL [23]. SPIRAL minimizes only the stretch, while LB-SPIRAL minimizes both the stretch and the processing load of participating nodes in $\mathcal{Z}$. We prove the following result.

Theorem 1. LB-SPIRAL *guarantees* $O(\log^3 n \cdot \log D)$ *amortized stretch and* $O(\log n \cdot \log D)$ *approximation of the processing load on any node in any general network G and arbitrary execution, where n is the number of nodes and D is the diameter of G.*

Theorem 1 states that the processing load approximation is independent of the number of operations ℓ. This is in sharp contrast to the existing DDPs in general networks where processing load of a node is linearly dependent on ℓ. At the same time, the stretch approximation is also independent of ℓ. To our knowledge, this is the first DDP which achieves this simultaneous dual performance characteristic.

The stretch of LB-SPIRAL is optimal within a poly-log factor compared to the $\Omega(\log n / \log \log n)$ lower bound of Alon *et al.* [2] for the sequential execution scenario of *move* operations. The universal TSP lower bounds, such as $\Omega(\sqrt{\log n / \log \log n})$ by Jia *et al.* [15] for Euclidean metrics, $\Omega(\sqrt[6]{\log n / \log \log n})$ by Hajiaghayi *et al.* [12] for $n \times n$ grid, and $\Omega(\log n)$ by Gorodezky *et al.* [10] for Ramanujan graphs, apply to the communication cost of concurrent execution scenarios of *move* operations.

LB-SPIRAL provides also guarantees for *lookup* operations. For any individual *lookup* operation, it guarantees $O(\log^5 n)$ stretch, which is in contrast to the *move* stretch that is obtained combining the costs of a set of *move* operations. This *lookup* stretch guarantee is particularly useful for read-dominated workloads. In the analysis, we do not consider the processing load for *lookup* operations as they do not update the directory $\mathcal{Z}$. However, if needed, for balancing processing load for *lookup* accesses we can use the same techniques as for *move* operations. The *publish* cost in LB-SPIRAL is proportional to the diameter of the network and it is a fixed initial cost which is only considered once and compensated by the costs of the *move* operations issued thereafter.

For special network topologies that satisfy bounded doubling dimension properties [14,26] we obtain improved theoretical bounds, where we can show that

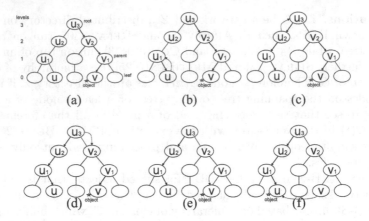

Fig. 1. An illustration of LB-SPIRAL for a *move* request issued by node u. Only leader nodes at respective clusters are shown. **a:** the creator node v issues a *publish* operation forming the initial downward directory path (based on the spiral path from v); **b:** node u issues a *move* request which follows a spiral path from u to the root, adjusting the pointers in subsequent levels to point towards u; **c:** the *move* request finds the downward directory path; **d:** the *move* request starts its down phase, deleting the old pointers of the directory path; **e:** the *move* request reaches previous owner node v; **f:** the object is moved from v to u making u the new owner node.

LB-SPIRAL has both amortized *move* stretch and processing load of $O(\log D)$ in arbitrary executions. Furthermore, the stretch for a *lookup* operation is only $O(1)$.

Techniques. The idea in LB-SPIRAL is to use an overlay structure based on a hierarchy of clusters $\mathcal{Z}$ as in SPIRAL [23], but in a novel way so that processing load is minimized as well. There are $h + 1 = O(\log D)$ levels such that cluster diameters increase exponentially with respect to the level. In each cluster, one node is chosen to act as a leader which is used to communicate with different level clusters. The leader is changed appropriately while serving a request to balance the processing load. Each node participates at all levels of the hierarchy. At the bottom level 0 each cluster consists of an individual node in G which is by default a leader. At the top level h there is a single cluster for the whole graph G with a special leader node called *root*. At any intermediate level a node may belong to several clusters of that level. Only the bottom level nodes can issue *publish*, *lookup*, or *move* requests.

Figure 1 depicts how LB-SPIRAL works for a *move* operation. LB-SPIRAL maintains at all times a *directory path* which is directed from the root to the bottom-level node that *owns* the shared object. The directory path is initialized by the first *publish* operation. After that, the directory path is updated whenever the object moves (changes ownership) from one node to another. To access the object, each bottom level node uses a *spiral path* to find and intersect the directory path. The spiral path visits upward the leader nodes in all the clusters that the node belongs to. (The spiral path in G grows outwards from the origin as the level increases which gives the perception of a *spiral* formation.) It is guaranteed that a spiral path and the directory path intersect at some level. Once they meet, a *move* operation force the directory path to divert at the intersection point toward the new owner node (the origin of the spiral path). A *lookup* operation is served similar to *move* without modifying the existing directory path.

For balancing the processing load, a node that initiates a *move* operation will become the leader of all the clusters it visits in the hierarchy until it intersects the directory path. Each affected cluster requires to inform children and parent clusters, in lower and higher levels, respectively, about the change on the leader node in the cluster and also transferring the directory path information from old the old leader to the new leader, which we call *update overhead*. To bound the update overhead (which can be as much as $O(n)$ in the worst-case), the hierarchical clustering in the original SPIRAL protocol is modified appropriately so that in LB-SPIRAL a binary tree of clusters is formed between two subsequent levels of the hierarchy $\mathcal{Z}$. This helps to control the number of cluster leaders that need to be updated about the change on the cluster leader at any level. The new ideas on load balancing together with the approach of SPIRAL for stretch makes LB-SPIRAL to satisfy Theorem 1.

Related Work. As mentioned earlier, the closest related works to ours are the previously known DDPs such as ARROW [8], RELAY [30], COMBINE [3], BALLISTIC [14], SPIRAL [23], MULTIBEND [25], and other directory algorithms [1,6,7]. Although these DDPs use some kind of overlay structure, their constructions, except MULTIBEND, are useful to minimize just the stretch. Although MULTIBEND simultaneously controls congestion and stretch, it is only tailored for mesh topologies.

Minimizing processing load is along the lines of research on *distributed hash table* protocols (DHTs) [19,22,28,31], where the load is minimized only for the nodes of G that participate as DHT protocol nodes. However, DHTs are different since they store key-value pairs by statically assigning keys (or objects) to nodes, whereas in DDPs objects are mobile.

The concept of LB-SPIRAL (also of BALLISTIC [14] and SPIRAL [23]) is similar to the approaches to locate nearest neighbors, tracking mobile users, compact routing, and related problems (e.g., [4,16–18,29]). However, these approaches provide efficient techniques only to locate copies and when the objects move autonomously (without being requested). The DDPs provide mechanisms that can make moving, looking up, and republishing of objects efficient and also avoid *race conditions* that might occur while synchronizing concurrent requests in distributed shared memory systems [14,23].

Finally, our study of minimizing processing load is different from existing studies where local *memory overhead* is considered for minimization in addition to stretch [18]. The memory overhead is minimized by distributing the storage of objects from the leader node to the other nodes in the cluster and later search them through embedding a De Bruijn graph in each cluster. It was shown [18] that the memory overhead can be just $polylog(n)$ times the optimal. However, in these techniques, the worst processing load of a node (i.e., leader) is still linearly dependent on the total number of operations.

Paper Organization. We describe the network model in Sect. 2. We describe the hierarchical clustering we use for LB-SPIRAL in Sect. 3. We then detail LB-SPIRAL algorithm in Sect. 4 and analyze it in Sect. 5. We omit some proofs and the pseudocode of the algorithm from this paper due to space constraints.

2   Network Model

We represent a distributed network as a weighted graph $G = (V, E, \mathfrak{w})$, with nodes (network machines) V, where $|V| = n$, edges (interconnection links between machines) $E \subseteq V \times V$, and edge weight function $\mathfrak{w} : E \to \mathbb{R}^+$. We assume that $\mathfrak{w}(u, u) = 0$ for any $u \in V$. A path p in G is a sequence of nodes, with respective sequence of edges connecting the nodes, such that $|p| = \sum_{e \in p} \mathfrak{w}(e)$. For convenience, we will treat paths as walks which may consist of a single node or nodes may be repeated. A *sub-path* of p is any any subsequence of consecutive nodes in p; we may also refer to a sub-path as a *fragment* of p. We assume that G is connected, i.e., there is a path in G between any pair of nodes. Let $\text{dist}(u, v)$ denote the shortest path length (distance) between nodes u and v. The *k-neighborhood* of a node v is the set of nodes which are within distance at most k from v (including v). The *diameter D* is the maximum shortest path distance over all pairs of nodes in G.

We assume that G represents a network in which nodes do not crash, it implements FIFO communication between nodes (i.e. no overtaking of messages occurs), and messages are not lost. The previous DDPs [8, 14, 23, 23, 30] (except COMBINE [3]) have the FIFO assumption. We also assume that, upon receiving a message, a node is able to perform a local computation and send a message in a single atomic step. LB-SPIRAL can be extended to accommodate non-FIFO communication and tolerate unreliable communication links (i.e., message losses) by adapting techniques used in COMBINE [3].

3   Hierarchical Clustering

We describe a hierarchy of clusters built on top of G to run our load balanced DDP LB-SPIRAL which we present in Sect. 4. We will then define spiral and directory paths that will be useful in LB-SPIRAL. Some of these definitions are adapted from [23].

Labeled Cover Hierarchy. A *node cluster* is any set of nodes $X \subseteq V$. The diameter of a cluster X is the maximum distance between any of its nodes, i.e., $\text{diam}(X) = \max_{u,v \in X} \text{dist}(u, v)$, where distances are w.r.t. G. A *cover* is any set of clusters $Z = \{X_1, X_2, \ldots, X_k\}$ such that each node in $u \in V$ belongs to at least one cluster in Z. Let $Z(u)$ denote the set of clusters that u belongs to in Z. The diameter of cover Z is the maximum diameter of its clusters: $\text{diam}(Z) = \max_{X \in Z} \text{diam}(X)$. We say that Z has *locality* γ if for a node u there is some cluster $X \in Z$ such that it contains the γ-neighborhood of u. A χ-*labeling* of Z, for some positive integer χ, is an assignment of integer labels to its clusters, $\lambda(X_i) \in \{1, 2, \ldots, \chi\}$. A χ-labeling is *valid* if for each node $u \in V$ every cluster that contains u has a different label, that is, if $X_i, X_j \in Z(u)$, $i \neq j$, then $\lambda(X_i) \neq \lambda(X_j)$. Labels are used to avoid races.

Definition 1 (labeled cover). Z is a (σ, χ, γ)-*labeled cover* if Z is a cover with locality γ, $\text{diam}(Z) \leq \sigma\gamma$, and accepts a valid χ-labeling.

Definition 2 (labeled cover hierarchy). $\mathcal{Z} = \{Z_0, Z_1, \ldots, Z_h\}$ is a (σ, χ)-*labeled cover hierarchy* for G when each Z_i, $1 \leq i \leq h$, is a (σ, χ, γ_i)-labeled cover with locality $\gamma_i = 2^{i-1}$, where $Z_0 = V$ (each node in V is a cluster) and $h = \lceil \log D \rceil + 1$. We say that $Z_i \in \mathcal{Z}$ is the *level i cover*, and any cluster $X \in Z_i$ is a *level i cluster*.

We presented in [23] a $(O(\log n), O(\log n))$-labeled cover hierarchy $\mathcal{Z}$. The structure was based on well-known ideas for clustering the graph to approximate graph distance metrics by distributions over tree metrics [5,9]. Specifically, we borrowed the clustering technique used by Gupta, Hajiaghayi, and Räcke [11]. The labeled cover hierarchy $\mathcal{Z}$ in [23] is computed in polynomial time and has the following properties.

1. At level 0 each node in V belongs to exactly one cluster consisting of only itself.
2. Cover Z_h (highest level) consists of one cluster that contains all nodes V.
3. In any level i, $1 \leq i \leq h - 1$, of $\mathcal{Z}$ each node $u \in V$ belongs to exactly $\chi = O(\log n)$ clusters that is, $|Z_i(u)| = \chi$. (Some clusters could be identical.)
4. Each cluster at level i, $0 \leq i < h$, is completely contained by a cluster at level $i+1$. (Due to the laminar decomposition property of the technique by Gupta *et al.* [11].)

In LB-SPIRAL we need to bound the number of clusters at level $i-1$ that are completely contained inside each cluster at level i. Otherwise, we may not be able to bound the processing load of a node due to high overhead coming from informing leader nodes of the parent and child clusters of the current cluster on the hierarchy in the load balancing process. Let CL_i be a cluster at level i in $\mathcal{Z}$. The $(O(\log n), O(\log n))$-labeled cover hierarchy $\mathcal{Z}$ given in [23] does not bound the number of clusters at level $i-1$ completely contained inside CL_i. Therefore, we modify $\mathcal{Z}$ as follows (see Fig. 2). Let CL_i be a cluster and let $W = \{CL_{i-1}^1, CL_{i-1}^2, \ldots, CL_{i-1}^w\}$ be the level $i-1$ clusters so that each cluster

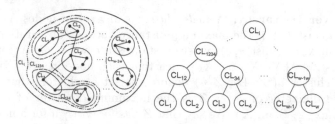

Fig. 2. An illustration of a binary tree embedded between a cluster CL_i at level i and the clusters at level $i-1$ that are completely contained inside CL_i.

$CL_{i-1}^j, 1 \leq j \leq w$, is completely contained inside CL_i. We organize the clusters in W in a "dummy" *binary tree* T of clusters as follows. CL_i acts as the root cluster of T. Each cluster in $CL_{i-1}^j \in W$ acts as a leaf cluster of T, i.e., there will be w leaf clusters in T. In every level $l \geq 1$ of T merge two children clusters at level $l-1$ to obtain the parent cluster at level l. According to this construction, if there are Δ clusters at any level l of T, then at level $l+1$ of T, there will be at most $\lceil \Delta/2 \rceil$ clusters. Figure 2 illustrates the binary tree T construction of clusters at level $i-1$ of $\mathcal{Z}$ that are completely contained inside a cluster at level i.

Lemma 1. *If there are w clusters at level $i-1$ of $\mathcal{Z}$ completely contained inside a cluster CL_i at level i, then a binary tree T is embedded between levels $i-1$ and i with root of T being the cluster CL_i such that T has $O(\log w)$ levels.*

Spiral Paths. Let $\mathcal{Z} = \{Z_0, Z_1, \ldots, Z_h\}$ be a (σ, χ)-labeled cover hierarchy. The spiral path $p(u)$ for each node $u \in V$ is built by visiting designated leader nodes in all the clusters that u belongs to starting from level 0 up to h in $\mathcal{Z}$. Within each level, the clusters are visited according to the order of their labels. Between the levels, the clusters are visited based on the clusters in the binary tree, starting from leaf level going to the root (this requirement was not there for spiral paths used in [23]).

Let $X_{i,j}(u) \in Z_i(u)$ denote the cluster at level i, $1 \leq i \leq h-1$, that u belongs to and has label j. We will refer to level i, label j, as the *sub-level* (i, j). Note that level i consists of χ sub-levels $(i, 1), (i, 2), \ldots, (i, \chi)$, for $1 \leq i \leq h-1$. Levels 0 and h are special cases which consist of a single sub-level each which for convenience we denote as $(0, \chi)$ and $(h, 1)$, respectively. We can order the sub-levels lexicographically so that $(i, j) < (i', j')$ if $i < i'$, or $i = i'$ and $j < j'$. We define the function $\text{next}(i, j)$ (resp. $\text{prev}(i, j)$) to return the sub-level immediately higher (resp. lower) than (i, j).

This ordering can be extended also to the clusters that are organized in a binary tree T (Lemma 1) between two subsequent levels i and $i+1$. Let $X_{i,\chi}(u) \in Z_i(u)$ be a cluster at level i that u belongs to and has label χ and let $X_{i+1,1}(u) \in Z_i(u)$ be a cluster at level $i+1$ that u belongs to and has label 1. We assign levels to the clusters in the respective binary tree T in a path from

$X_{i,\chi}(u)$ (a leaf of T) to $X_{i+1,1}(u)$ (the root of T) from $(i, \chi + 1)$ to $(i, \chi + \delta - 1)$, where $\delta \leq \lceil \log n \rceil$ is the maximum height of T. Therefore, there will be $\chi + \delta - 1$ sub-levels in a level i, summing the sub-levels of level i and the new levels of the tree T. We can normalize all such binary trees in the hierarchy $\mathcal{Z}$ to have the same height δ by repeating the root cluster if necessary.

In every cluster X we choose a designated *leader* node $\ell(X)$ which is chosen arbitrary initially and changed later appropriately to balance the processing load. Denote the leader of cluster $X_{i,j}(u)$ as $\ell_{i,j}(u) = \ell(X_{i,j}(u))$. Since Z_h consists of a single sub-level it has a unique leader which we denote $\ell_{h,1}(u) = r$. Trivially, every node $u \in V$ is a leader of its own cluster at level 0, $\ell_{0,\chi}(u) = u$. For any pair of nodes $u, v \in V$, let $s(u, v)$ denote a shortest path from u to v. For any set of nodes $u_1, u_2, \ldots, u_k \in V$, let $s(u_1, u_2, \ldots, u_k)$ denote the concatenation of shortest paths $s(u_1, u_2)$, $s(u_2, u_3), \ldots$, $s(u_{k-1}, u_k)$. The spiral path $p(u)$ is formed by taking the concatenation of the shortest paths that connect the ascending sequence of leaders starting from node u (sub-level $(0, \chi)$) up to node r (sub-level $(h, 1)$).

Definition 3 (spiral path). *The spiral path of node u is:*

$$p(u) = s(u, \underbrace{\ell_{1,1}(u), \ldots, \ell_{1,\chi}(u)}_{level\ 1}, \underbrace{\ell_{1,\chi+1}(u), \ldots, \ell_{1,\chi+\delta-1}(u)}_{between\ level\ 1\ and\ 2}, \underbrace{\ell_{2,1}(u), \ldots, \ell_{2,\chi}(u)}_{level\ 2}, \ldots,$$

$$\underbrace{\ell_{h-1,1}(u), \ldots, \ell_{h-1,\chi}(u)}_{level\ h-1}, \underbrace{\ell_{h-1,\chi+1}(u), \ldots, \ell_{h,\chi+\delta-1}(u)}_{between\ level\ h-1\ and\ h}, r).$$

We say that two paths *intersect* if they have a common node. We also say that two spiral paths intersect at level i if they visit the same leader at level i.

Lemma 2 ([23]). *For any two nodes $u, v \in V$, their spiral paths $p(u)$ and $p(v)$ intersect at level $\min\{h, \lceil \log(\text{dist}(u, v)) \rceil + 1\}$.*

In the analysis of LB-SPIRAL, the directory path is obtained from fragments of spiral paths obtained from *move* operations. Such a fragmented path is actually a concatenation of shortest paths connecting leaders at successive sub-levels whose clusters share a common node. We will refer to such kind of path as *canonical*.

Definition 4 (canonical path). *A canonical path q up to sub-level $(k, \iota) \leq (h, 1)$ is:*

$$q = s(x_{0,\chi}, \underbrace{x_{1,1}, \ldots, x_{1,\chi}}_{level\ 1}, \underbrace{x_{1,\chi+1}, \ldots, x_{1,\chi+\delta-1}}_{between\ level\ 1\ and\ 2}, \underbrace{x_{2,1}, \ldots, x_{2,\chi}}_{level\ 2},$$

$$\underbrace{x_{2,\chi+1}, \ldots, x_{2,\chi+\delta-1}}_{between\ level\ 2\ and\ 3}, \ldots, \underbrace{x_{k,1}, \ldots, x_{k,\iota}}_{level\ k}),$$

such that for any two consecutive nodes $x_{i,j}$ and $x_{\text{next}(i,j)}$, where $(0, \chi) \leq (i, j) < (k, \iota)$, there is a node $y \in V$ with $x_{i,j} = \ell_{i,j}(y)$ and $x_{\text{next}(i,j)} = \ell_{\text{next}(i,j)}(y)$.

We will refer to $x_{0,\chi}$ and $x_{k,\iota}$ as the *bottom* and *top* nodes of q, respectively. The bottom node is always at level 0. A canonical path can be either *partial* when the top node is below level h (the root level), or *full* when the top node is the root r. A spiral path $p(u)$ is a full canonical path, and any prefix of it is a partial canonical path.

Lemma 3. *For any canonical path q up to level k (and any sub-level (k, ι)) in $\mathcal{Z}$, length$(q) \leq c_3 2^{k+2} \log^3 n$, for some constant c_3.*

4   LB-SPIRAL **Algorithm**

We now present LB-SPIRAL (the pseudocode is omitted), which is a load balanced DDP. We describe LB-SPIRAL for one shared object as it is typical in the DDP literature; multiple objects can be supported replicating the hierarchy for each object.

Overview of LB-SPIRAL. Consider some shared object ξ. LB-SPIRAL guarantees that at any time only one node holds the shared object ξ which is the *owner* of the object. The owner is the only node that can modify (i.e., write) the object; the other nodes can only access the object for read.

LB-SPIRAL is implemented on the $(O(\log n), O(\log n))$-labeled cover hierarchy $\mathcal{Z}$ discussed in Sect. 3. Only the bottom level nodes of $\mathcal{Z}$ can issue requests (*publish*, *lookup*, and *move*) for ξ, while nodes in higher levels of $\mathcal{Z}$ are used to propagate the requests in G. The basic objective of LB-SPIRAL is to maintain a *directory path* in $\mathcal{Z}$ which is directed from the root node r to the bottom-level node that is the current owner of ξ. The directory path is updated whenever · ξ moves from one node to another. Initially, the directory path is formed from the spiral path $p(v)$ of the object creator node v. As soon as the object ξ is created, v publishes ξ by visiting the leaders in its spiral path $p(v)$ towards the root r, making each parent leader node pointing to its child leader (Fig. 1(a)). These leader downward pointers correspond to path segments between consecutive leaders and the concatenation of these path segments from the root r down to v form the initial directory path.

A *move* request from a node u of G for the object ξ at the owner node v of G is served by following upwards leader ancestors in its spiral path $p(u)$ (up phase), setting downward links towards v until $p(u)$ intersects at x the directory path to the owner node v (Fig. 1(b) and (c), where $x = u_3$). Then the *move* request follows a downward trajectory (down phase) deleting the links of the directory path while descending towards the owner node v (Fig. 1(d) and (e)); the directory path now points to the requesting node u. As soon as the *move* request reaches the owner node v, the object is forwarded from the previous owner node along some (shortest) path in the graph G (Fig. 1(f)). This process has resulted to a canonical directory path that consists of two spiral path fragments, a fragment of v's spiral path $p(v)$ between r and the intersection point x, and a fragment of u's spiral path $p(u)$ between x and u. Subsequent *move* operations may further fragment the directory path into multiple spiral path segments, but at all times a canonical directory path is maintained.

A *lookup* operation is served similar to a *move* operation but without modifying (adding or removing pointers) the directory path. A *lookup* operation fetches a copy of the shared ξ object from the current owner v to u. If a *move* operation later invalidates ξ from v, then the local copy of ξ at u is also invalidated.

The processing load is balanced by changing the leader of the clusters that the *move* request visits while it is in its up phase. Specifically, the originating node of the *move* request is selected as a leader in all the clusters it visits in its up phase. For the down phase, this is done only for *lookup* requests. Since the source node of a *lookup* request may not be in the clusters of the directory path in the down phase of a *lookup* request, we choose a node uniformly in random among the nodes in the cluster to act as a leader.

Concurrent *lookup* and *move* requests may be served through partial downward paths instead of the directory path. These requests are queued while the new directory path is being formed. For example, consider the scenario where a *lookup* operation is issued by a node w concurrently with the *move* operation of v. Suppose also that the *lookup* and *move* requests intersect in their up phase paths before their requests reach the directory path to u. Then the *lookup* request will descend down to v through a partial downward path while the *move* request ascends to x. The *lookup* will request the read-only copy of the object ξ from v. However, v may not have the copy of ξ yet. In this case, w's request is queued in v and it will be served when v receives ξ.

In the scenario where w's operation was a *move*, then two partial downward paths would coexist at the same time with the directory path until the up phases of u and v intersect. After that again two partial paths can coexist until the down phase of w reaches v and before the up phase of v reaches x. The result is that the *move* request from w will be queued after v. Similarly, multiple concurrent *move* operations temporarily lead to the formation of multiple partial downward paths to the origins of the requests. The *move* operations get queued in the origin nodes forming a distributed queue of *move* operations. Eventually, every move operation will be served by passing the object from the current owner at the head of the queue to the next node in the queue.

Balancing the Processing Load in LB-SPIRAL. The description of LB-SPIRAL so far does not consider balancing the processing load of the nodes in G, i.e., the technique discussed above only minimizes the communication cost. We use the following technique to balance the processing load on the nodes of G. We describe separately below how we use the balancing technique to serve *publish*, *lookup*, and *move* requests.

Publish: The *publish*(ξ) operation issued by the creator node v sets v as a leader in all the clusters in its spiral path $p(v)$ while going to the root cluster (including the root cluster) in $\mathcal{Z}$. In each cluster in the spiral path $p(v)$, the downward pointers point from leader v in sub-level (i, j) cluster to leader v in sub-level prev(i, j) cluster.

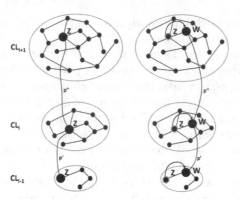

Fig. 3. An illustration of how a leader is selected in each cluster to balance the processing load. A *move* request from node w makes w the leader in each cluster it visits in its up phase and transfers the information from the old leader z to w.

Move: The *move*(ξ) operation issued by a node u is served as follows. The node u sets itself as the leader in all the clusters in its spiral path $p(u)$ in its up phase until $p(u)$ intersects the directory path pointing to the owner v. In other words, the downward pointers point toward u in all the levels. Figure 3 illustrates these ideas. The down phase needs no change.

Lookup: The *lookup*(ξ) operation needs no leader change as it does not add or remove information in the directory $\mathcal{Z}$. However, if balancing is needed, then a *lookup* issued by a node u can set u as the leader in all the clusters similar as of *move*(ξ) in the up phase. In the down phase, it can pick a node uniformly at random in each cluster it visits in its down phase. Our analysis in Sect. 5 focuses on proving the processing load of the nodes of G considering only the *move* operations.

The use of leader selection procedure incurs extra cost to the actual cost of the *move* and *lookup* operations. This is because this procedure requires message exchanges between the old leader and the new leader within a cluster, and also with the parent and child clusters of the old leader to inform them about the new leader. We argue that the pointer update cost is low in comparison to the cost of serving the requests because only the information in the nearby region needs to be updated due to the new leader. This step facilitates to control the processing load, since the processing load on a leader node is always proportional to the number of requests that visit that leader.

A leader selection approach we use in the spiral path plays major role in controlling processing load because it minimizes the overutilization of a node in serving the requests. Through our approach, a node in a cluster becomes a leader of that cluster if and only if the request (*move*, *lookup*, or *publish*) is issued by that node.

Moreover, we observe that at any time a request needs to lock at most three nodes, at levels prev(i, j), (i, j), and next(i, j), along the spiral path (or a directory path for the *lookup* operation). In concurrent situations this might be a problem. This is because we need to lock more than one node (at most three nodes) in the spiral (or directory) path to do the leader change, otherwise directory information necessary for generating a new path may get lost. Therefore, in the concurrent execution of *move* requests, we need to make sure that the nodes that are affected by the leader change should be kept locked until a new path is between subsequent clusters. We can use the notion of a *conflict graph* for each level such that neighbors in the conflict graph cannot perform the leader change at the same time (that is, the leader change process is sequentialized in a cluster). But the non-neighbors can be in the critical section at any time. This sequentialization process does not hamper the stretch and processing load bounds (Sect. 5).

Bounding the *lookup* Cost in LB-SPIRAL. A *lookup* request from any node $w \in G$ for the object ξ at the owner node $v \in G$ may not find the directory path to v at level $\log\lceil(\text{dist}(w,v))\rceil + 1$ leader node X of $\mathcal{Z}$ where their spiral paths $p(w)$ and $p(v)$ intersect. This is because, after several *move* operations, the directory path may become highly fragmented and hence the directory path does not pass through the leader node X where $p(w)$ and $p(v)$ intersect. The notion of a *special-parent* node helps to avoid this situation and guarantees efficient lookups, such that whenever a downward link is formed at a node z the special parent of z is also informed about z holding a downward pointer. The pointer information is stored in (removed from) a special-parent node in the up (down) phase of a *move* operation.

Definition 5 (special-parent [23]**).** A *special-parent* node of y, denoted as $\text{sparent}_{(i,j)}(y)$, at sub-level (i,j) in the spiral path $p(u)$ is the leader node of one of the cluster $X(u) \in \mathcal{Z}_\eta$ at level η, where $\eta = i + 4 + 2\log\log n + \log c_3$, i.e., $\text{sparent}_{(i,j)}(y)$ is some ancestor leader node of y at level η in the spiral path $p(u)$.

Every leader node in any cluster of $\mathcal{Z}$ knows its special parent and has a special downward pointer, *slink* (except the root node which has no special parent). We maintain a list of *slink* pointers if one node is the special parent for the leaders of several clusters which, according to our construction, can happen. These special downward pointers are set (removed) when *move* operations are in the up (down) phase.

5   Analysis of LB-SPIRAL

We give both the stretch and processing load analysis of LB-SPIRAL for sequential, concurrent (one-shot), and dynamic executions. However, the correctness proof of LB-SPIRAL is omitted as it can be easily proven by extending the correctness proofs of DDPs BALLISTIC [14], COMBINE [3], SPIRAL [23], and MULTI-BEND [25].

Performance in Sequential Executions. In a sequential execution scenario the next request is initiated only after the current request completes. We first provide performance bounds for the communication costs of *publish, lookup* and *move* operations, and then we give the approximation of processing load of any node of G.

Theorem 2 (publish cost). *The publish operation in* LB-SPIRAL *has communication cost* $O(D \cdot \log^3 n)$.

Theorem 3 (lookup stretch). *The lookup stretch in* LB-SPIRAL *is* $O(\log^5 n)$ *in sequential executions.*

We now give an amortized stretch analysis of LB-SPIRAL for *move* operations in sequential executions. As *move* requests are non-overlapping in sequential executions, the system attains *quiescent* configuration after a *move* request is served and until a next *move* request is issued. Define a sequential execution of a set $\mathcal{E}$ of $\ell + 1$ requests $\mathcal{E} = \{r_0, r_1, \ldots, r_\ell\}$ for the object ξ, where r_0 is the initial *publish* request and the rest are the subsequent *move* requests (we do not include *lookups* in $\mathcal{E}$ since they do not add or remove links in the directory $\mathcal{Z}$, and hence do not impact the performance of other *move* or *lookup* operations).

Similar as in [23], for the amortized stretch analysis define a two-dimensional array B of size $(k + 1) \times (\ell + 1)$, where $k + 1$ and $\ell + 1$ are the number of rows and columns of B, respectively. The $(k + 1)$ rows of B can be denoted as $\{row_0, row_1, \ldots, row_k\}$, and the $\ell + 1$ columns of B can be denoted as $\{col_0, col_1, \ldots, col_\ell\}$. Each location $[i, j]$ of the array B is initially $\perp$. We fix that $[0, 0]$ be the lower left corner element and $[k, \ell]$ be the upper right corner element in B. The levels visited by each request r_i in the hierarchy $\mathcal{Z}$ while searching for the object ξ are registered in the rows of column col_i. The maximum level reached by r_i before it finds the downward pointer in $\mathcal{Z}$ is called the *peak level* for r_i. We have that $h = k$. The peak level reached by r_0 (the *publish* request) is always h, the maximum level in $\mathcal{Z}$. Notice that r_0 is registered in all the locations of col_0 from 0 to k.

Our goal is to bound the stretch $\max_{\mathcal{E}} A(\mathcal{E})/A^*(\mathcal{E})$, where $A(\mathcal{E})$ denotes the total communication cost of serving requests in $\mathcal{E}$ using LB-SPIRAL and $A^*(\mathcal{E})$ denotes the optimal cost for serving requests in $\mathcal{E}$ through an optimal offline algorithm. We prove the following theorem for stretch $\max_{\mathcal{E}} A(\mathcal{E})/A^*(\mathcal{E})$ using array B.

Theorem 4 (move stretch). *The move stretch in* LB-SPIRAL *is* $O(\log^3 n \cdot \log D)$ *in sequential executions.*

We now analyze the processing load of a node in LB-SPIRAL in sequential executions. We relate the processing load $PL(x)$ of a node $x \in G$ in LB-SPIRAL to the optimal load $PL^*(x)$ of that node to provide the approximation ratio. We prove the following theorem for processing load of any node of G for the sequential execution of *move* operations; we omit the *lookup* operations while computing processing load as they do not add or remove pointer information on the directory hierarchy $\mathcal{Z}$.

Theorem 5 (processing load). *The processing load approximation in* LB-SPIRAL *is* $O(\log n \cdot \log D)$ *for any node of* G.

Performance in One-Shot Executions. The performance analysis of LB-SPIRAL given in Sect. 5 does not apply to concurrent executions because the adversary is not allowed to gain by ordering the requests in a smarter way, i.e., the orderings provided by both LB-SPIRAL and OPT are the same. Concurrent executions can change the order of the requests in execution and hence affect the overall performance of LB-SPIRAL. In one-shot executions, all requests come concurrently (at the same time) in the system. We study the following one-shot instance of concurrent execution. At time t as soon as a *publish* operation finished execution, $R \subseteq V$ nodes issue a *move* request each concurrently and no further requests occur. We divide the time into *periods* and *rounds* such that a level i round has i non-overlapping aligned periods, and we assume that all requests proceed in rounds. When two or more *move* requests reach to level i one is forwarded towards level $i + 1$ and others are "deflected" down following the directory path set by the previously upward forwarded *move* request in the hierarchy $\mathcal{Z}$. Defining total and optimal cost for one-shot execution similar to sequential execution, the optimal cost for any level i of the hierarchy $\mathcal{Z}$ is given by the Steiner tree [21] of the *move* requests that reach that level. The total cost analysis is similar as of sequential execution, and also the analysis for approximation on processing load, and *lookup* and *publish* bounds. Therefore, we summarize the bounds in the theorem below.

Theorem 6. *The* move *stretch in* LB-SPIRAL *is* $O(\log^3 n \cdot \log D)$ *in concurrent (one-shot) executions. It achieves* $O(\log n \cdot \log D)$ *approximation on processing load on any node of* G. *Moreover, the publish operation has* $O(D \cdot \log^3 n)$ *cost and any lookup operation in* LB-SPIRAL *has* $O(\log^5 n)$ *stretch.*

Performance in Dynamic Executions. The performance of LB-SPIRAL can also be analyzed for requests that are initiated in arbitrary moments of time (i.e., dynamic executions). This analysis can capture the execution scenarios where requests are neither completely sequential as considered in Sect. 5 nor completely concurrent as considered in Sect. 5. The idea here is to use the analysis framework presented in [24]. The analysis framework of [24] captures both the time and the distance restrictions in ordering the dynamic requests in DDPs through a notion of *time windows*. All the nodes proceed in time windows; in a window, each node might initiate new requests and each node can exchange a message with each of its neighbors in the hierarchy $\mathcal{Z}$ at the end of the window. Considering a synchronous execution where time is divided into windows of appropriate duration for each level, an upper bound can be obtained. Given an optimal ordering of the requests, the lower bound can be obtained by considering the communication cost provided by a *Hamiltonian path* that visits each request node exactly once according to their order.

In this setting, the idea is to perform the analysis level by level. The time window notion combined with a Hamiltonian path allows us to analyze the competitive ratio for the requests that reach some level. After combining the competitive ratio of all the levels, we obtain the overall competitive ratio. Therefore, we summarize below the guarantees of LB-SPIRAL in dynamic executions.

Theorem 7. *The move stretch in* LB-SPIRAL *is* $O(\log^3 n \cdot \log D)$ *in dynamic executions. The processing load on any node of G is* $O(\log n \cdot \log D)$. *Moreover, the publish operation has* $O(D \cdot \log^3 n)$ *cost and any lookup operation has* $O(\log^5 n)$ *stretch.*

PROOF OF THEOREM 1. Theorems 2, 3, 4, 5, 6, and 7 collectively prove Theorem 1 for LB-SPIRAL in arbitrary executions. ☐

Improved Results for Constant Doubling Dimension Graphs. If the metric on the underlying graph G has a constant doubling dimension (see [14, 26]), we can improve both stretch and processing load for LB-SPIRAL. The idea is to use the hierarchy of clusters suitable for doubling graphs. It was shown in [11,15] that $(O(1), O(1))$-partition scheme is possible for small doubling graphs. We can obtain $(O(1), O(1))$-labeled cover hierarchy extending the technique of [11,15] using our labeled cover construction given in Sect. 3. The spiral and directory paths can be defined similarly and the operations of LB-SPIRAL can also be executed analogously to Sect. 4. Therefore, adapting the analysis of Sect. 5 to the small doubling graph G, we obtain:

Theorem 8. *If the underlying topology G is a small doubling graph, the move stretch in* LB-SPIRAL *is* $O(\log D)$ *in arbitrary executions. It achieves* $O(\log D)$ *approximation on processing load on any node of G. Moreover, the publish operation has* $O(D)$ *cost and any lookup operation in* LB-SPIRAL *has* $O(1)$ *stretch.*

References

1. Agarwal, A., et al.: The MIT alewife machine: a large-scale distributed-memory multiprocessor. In: Dubois, M., Thakkar, S. (eds.) Workshop on Scalable Shared Memory Multiprocessors, pp. 239–261. Springer, Boston (1991). https://doi.org/10.1007/978-1-4615-3604-8_13
2. Alon, N., Kalai, G., Ricklin, M., Stockmeyer, L.J.: Lower bounds on the competitive ratio for mobile user tracking and distributed job scheduling. Theor. Comput. Sci. **130**(1), 175–201 (1994)
3. Attiya, H., Gramoli, V., Milani, A.: Directory protocols for distributed transactional memory. In: Guerraoui, R., Romano, P. (eds.) Transactional Memory. Foundations, Algorithms, Tools, and Applications. LNCS, vol. 8913, pp. 367–391. Springer, Cham (2015). https://doi.org/10.1007/978-3-319-14720-8_17
4. Awerbuch, B., Peleg, D.: Concurrent online tracking of mobile users. SIGCOMM Comput. Commun. Rev. **21**(4), 221–233 (1991)
5. Bartal, Y.: Probabilistic approximation of metric spaces and its algorithmic applications. In: FOCS, pp. 184–193 (1996)

6. Censier, L.M., Feautrier, P.: A new solution to coherence problems in multicache systems. IEEE Trans. Comput. **27**(12), 1112–1118 (1978)
7. Chaiken, D., Fields, C., Kurihara, K., Agarwal, A.: Directory-based cache coherence in large-scale multiprocessors. Computer **23**(6), 49–58 (1990)
8. Demmer, M.J., Herlihy, M.P.: The arrow distributed directory protocol. In: Kutten, S. (ed.) DISC 1998. LNCS, vol. 1499, pp. 119–133. Springer, Heidelberg (1998). https://doi.org/10.1007/BFb0056478
9. Fakcharoenphol, J., Rao, S., Talwar, K.: A tight bound on approximating arbitrary metrics by tree metrics. In: STOC, pp. 448–455 (2003)
10. Gorodezky, I., Kleinberg, R.D., Shmoys, D.B., Spencer, G.: Improved lower bounds for the universal and a *priori* TSP. In: Serna, M., Shaltiel, R., Jansen, K., Rolim, J. (eds.) RANDOM 2010, APPROX 2010. LNCS, vol. 6302, pp. 178–191. Springer, Heidelberg (2010). https://doi.org/10.1007/978-3-642-15369-3_14
11. Gupta, A., Hajiaghayi, M.T., Räcke, H.: Oblivious network design. In: SODA, pp. 970–979 (2006)
12. Hajiaghayi, M.T., Kleinberg, R., Leighton, T.: Improved lower and upper bounds for universal TSP in planar metrics. In: SODA, pp. 649–658 (2006)
13. Herlihy, M., Moss, J.E.B.: Transactional memory: architectural support for lock-free data structures. In: ISCA, pp. 289–300 (1993)
14. Herlihy, M., Sun, Y.: Distributed transactional memory for metric-space networks. Distrib. Comput. **20**(3), 195–208 (2007)
15. Jia, L., Lin, G., Noubir, G., Rajaraman, R., Sundaram, R.: Universal approximations for TSP, steiner tree, and set cover. In: STOC, pp. 386–395 (2005)
16. Krauthgamer, R., Lee, J.R.: Navigating nets: simple algorithms for proximity search. In: SODA, pp. 798–807 (2004)
17. Plaxton, C.G., Rajaraman, R., Richa, A.W.: Accessing nearby copies of replicated objects in a distributed environment. In: SPAA, pp. 311–320 (1997)
18. Rajaraman, R., Richa, A.W., Vöcking, B., Vuppuluri, G.: A data tracking scheme for general networks. In: SPAA, pp. 247–254 (2001)
19. Ratnasamy, S., Francis, P., Handley, M., Karp, R., Shenker, S.: A scalable content-addressable network. SIGCOMM Comput. Commun. Rev. **31**(4), 161–172 (2001)
20. Raymond, K.: A tree-based algorithm for distributed mutual exclusion. ACM Trans. Comput. Syst. **7**(1), 61–77 (1989)
21. Robins, G., Zelikovsky, A.: Improved steiner tree approximation in graphs. In: SODA, pp. 770–779 (2000)
22. Rowstron, A., Druschel, P.: Pastry: scalable, decentralized object location, and routing for large-scale peer-to-peer systems. In: Guerraoui, R. (ed.) Middleware 2001. LNCS, vol. 2218, pp. 329–350. Springer, Heidelberg (2001). https://doi.org/10.1007/3-540-45518-3_18
23. Sharma, G., Busch, C.: Distributed transactional memory for general networks. Distrib. Comput. **27**(5), 329–362 (2014)
24. Sharma, G., Busch, C.: An analysis framework for distributed hierarchical directories. Algorithmica **71**(2), 377–408 (2015)
25. Sharma, G., Busch, C.: A load balanced directory for distributed shared memory objects. J. Parallel Distrib. Comput. **78**, 6–24 (2015)
26. Sharma, G., Busch, C.: Optimal nearest neighbor queries in sensor networks. Theor. Comput. Sci. **608**, 146–165 (2015)
27. Shavit, N., Touitou, D.: Software transactional memory. Distrib. Comput. **10**(2), 99–116 (1997)

28. Stoica, I., Morris, R., Karger, D., Kaashoek, M.F., Balakrishnan, H.: Chord: a scalable peer-to-peer lookup service for internet applications. SIGCOMM Comput. Commun. Rev. **31**(4), 149–160 (2001)
29. Talwar, K.: Bypassing the embedding: algorithms for low dimensional metrics. In: STOC, pp. 281–290 (2004)
30. Zhang, B., Ravindran, B.: Brief announcement: Relay: a cache-coherence protocol for distributed transactional memory. In: Abdelzaher, T., Raynal, M., Santoro, N. (eds.) OPODIS 2009. LNCS, vol. 5923, pp. 48–53. Springer, Heidelberg (2009). https://doi.org/10.1007/978-3-642-10877-8_6
31. Zhao, B.Y., Huang, L., Stribling, J., Rhea, S.C., Joseph, A.D., Kubiatowicz, J.D.: Tapestry: a resilient global-scale overlay for service deployment. IEEE J. Sel. Areas Commun. **22**(1), 41–53 (2006)

Relays: A New Approach for the Finite Departure Problem in Overlay Networks

Christian Scheideler and Alexander Setzer[✉]

Paderborn University, Paderborn, Germany
{scheideler,alexander.setzer}@upb.de
https://cs.uni-paderborn.de/en/ti/

Abstract. A fundamental problem for overlay networks is to *safely* exclude leaving nodes, i.e., the nodes requesting to leave the overlay network are excluded from it without affecting its connectivity. To rigorously study self-stabilizing solutions to this problem, the *Finite Departure Problem* (FDP) has been proposed [9]. In the FDP we are given a network of processes in an arbitrary state, and the goal is to eventually arrive at (and stay in) a state in which all leaving processes irrevocably decided to leave the system while for all weakly-connected components in the initial overlay network, all staying processes in that component will still form a weakly connected component. In the standard interconnection model, the FDP is known to be unsolvable by local control protocols, so oracles have been investigated that allow the problem to be solved [9]. To avoid the use of oracles, we introduce a new interconnection model based on relays. Despite the relay model appearing to be rather restrictive, we show that it is universal, i.e., it is possible to transform any weakly-connected topology into any other weakly-connected topology, which is important for being a useful interconnection model for overlay networks. Apart from this, our model allows processes to grant and revoke access rights, which is why we believe it to be of interest beyond the scope of this paper. We show how to implement the relay layer in a self-stabilizing way and identify properties protocols need to satisfy so that the relay layer can recover while serving protocol requests.

1 Introduction

Once distributed systems become large enough, membership changes in these systems are not an exception but the norm. This particularly holds for peer-to-peer systems but is also true for large server-based systems as servers may need to be taken offline for some maintenance or new servers need to be included in the system to improve or maintain the service quality. So protocols need to be in place to allow members of a distributed system to join and leave it without disrupting its functionality. The most basic requirement for maintaining the

This work was partially supported by the German Research Foundation (DFG) within the Collaborative Research Center "On-The-Fly Computing" (SFB 901).

T. Izumi and P. Kuznetsov (Eds.): SSS 2018, LNCS 11201, pp. 239–253, 2018.
https://doi.org/10.1007/978-3-030-03232-6_16

functionality of a system is that it stays weakly connected. While this is easy to guarantee when new members join a system, it is not so easy to guarantee when members leave the system, in particular, if multiple members want to leave the system at the same time. In the literature on peer-to-peer systems, many proposals for leave protocols have already been made (see, e.g., [2,8,11,15,17, 18]). However, most of these solutions cannot give any guarantees if the system is not in some well-defined state. Distributed systems can easily be pushed into a non-well-defined state if there are network partitions or faulty members, so it would be desirable to have leave protocols that do not need any assumptions on the system state.

In order to rigorously study the problem of guaranteeing weak connectivity for any situation in which a collection of members (henceforth also simply called *processes*) wants to leave the system, Foreback et al. [9] introduced the *Finite Departure Problem (FDP)*. In the FDP the leaving processes have to irrevocably decide in finite time when it is safe to leave the network, i.e., their departure does not cause the network to get disconnected. Foreback et al. showed that there is no self-stabilizing local-control protocol for the FDP. At the heart of the proof are two serious problems: The standard assumption used in overlay networks research that a process may freely pass knowledge about its neighbors to any one of its neighbors has the effect that a process v cannot locally decide whether v is critical for the connectivity of the network or not, simply because it does not have any control on and thereby potentially incomplete knowledge about its incoming connections (i.e., the set of processes knowing its address). Also, when assuming asynchronous communication, where message may have arbitrary finite delays, a process v may not know whether messages carrying critical connectivity information are still on their way to v. This caused Foreback et al. to introduce the NIDEC oracle, which gives a process v the power to determine whether its address is still known somewhere in the system (NID is a short form of "no ID") and whether there are still messages on their way to v (EC is a short form of "empty channel").

Is it possible to avoid the use of oracles by using a different link layer model? We show that this is indeed the case. In fact, we need two layers: a self-stabilizing link layer and, on top of that, a self-stabilizing relay layer, which is our main innovation. On top of the relay layer, a self-stabilizing local-control protocol can then be designed to solve the FDP problem without the use of an oracle. While the link layer ensures that a process is aware of the messages that are still in transit along its outgoing connections, the relay layer gives the processes the power to rigorously control who is allowed to send messages to it. Despite appearing to be rather restrictive, we show that the relay concept is universal in a sense that one can get from any weakly connected topology to any other weakly connected topology while staying weakly connected throughout the transformation process. Because the relay layer now allows the rigorous study of access control problems in overlay networks, which opens up new directions like rigorous studies on the DoS-resistance of overlay networks (given that messages can only be sent via relay connections), we expect it to be of interest beyond this paper.

1.1   System Model

We consider a distributed system consisting of a set of processes that are interconnected to each other (with more details on the type of interconnections once we introduce relays in the next section). The processes are controlled by a local-control protocol that specifies the variables and actions that are available in each process. We assume that there is a reliable link layer that transmits messages from processes to other processes based on an ID of the target process contained in the message. More specifically, each process specifies a set of variables, called *buffers* containing messages to be sent to other processes and the ID of the respective target process is stored along with the buffer or inside the message. We assume that the link layer may take an arbitrary but finite amount of time to process a message that was put into one of these variables, but messages never get lost. We assume the link layer makes sure that every transmitted message will eventually be removed from the buffer it was taken from after it has been processed by the receiver. There are no resources available beyond the processes and the link layer as specified above (such as shared storage or a gateway), so the processes entirely rely on themselves and the link layer in order to handle certain tasks. This implies that there is no way for two disconnected components of processes to connect to each other.

There are two types of *actions* that a protocol can execute. The first type has the form of a standard procedure $\langle label \rangle (\langle parameters \rangle)) \rightarrow \langle commands \rangle$, where *label* is the unique name of that action, *parameters* specifies the parameter list of the action, and *commands* specifies the commands to be executed when calling that action. Such actions can be called locally (which causes their immediate execution) or remotely. In fact, we assume that every message must be of the form $\langle label \rangle (\langle parameters \rangle)$, where *label* specifies the action to be called in the receiving process and *parameters* contains the parameters to be passed to that action call. All other messages are ignored by the processes. The second type has the form $\langle label \rangle : \langle guard \rangle \rightarrow \langle commands \rangle$, where *label* and *commands* are defined as above and *guard* is a predicate over local variables. We call an action whose guard is simply **true** a *timeout* action.

The *system state* is an assignment of values to every variable of each process (including its buffers). An action in some process v is *enabled* in some system state if its guard evaluates to **true**, or if there is a message requesting to call it that was transmitted to the process by the link layer and has not been processed yet.

A *computation* is an infinite fair sequence of system states such that for each state S_i, the next state S_{i+1} is obtained by executing an action that is enabled in S_i. This disallows the overlap of action executions, i.e., action executions are *atomic*. We assume *weakly fair action execution*, meaning that if an action is enabled in all but finitely many states of a computation, then this action is executed infinitely often. Note that a timeout action of a process is executed infinitely often. Besides this, we place no bounds on process execution speeds, and no restrictions on the execution order of enabled actions, i.e., we allow fully asynchronous computations and non-FIFO message delivery.

1.2 Problem Statement

A protocol is *self-stabilizing* with respect to a set of legitimate states if it satisfies the following two properties:

Convergence: starting from an arbitrary system state, the protocol is guaranteed to eventually arrive at a legitimate state.

Closure: starting from a legitimate state the protocol remains in legitimate states thereafter.

A self-stabilizing protocol is thus able to recover from transient faults regardless of their nature. Moreover, a self-stabilizing protocol does not have to be initialized as it eventually starts to behave correctly regardless of its initial state. A formal definition of the FDP can be found in [9] (which is also briefly recapped in the full version of this paper [19]).

1.3 Related Work

The idea of self-stabilization in distributed computing was introduced in a classical paper by Dijkstra in 1974 [4], in which he investigated the problem of self-stabilization in a token ring. In the past 10 years, several self-stabilizing local-control protocols have been proposed for various overlay networks (e.g., [1,3,7,12,13,16]), but none of them has considered the leaving of nodes as an individual problem until the work of Foreback et al. [9]. In that work, two problems are considered: the Finite Departure Problem (FDP) and the Finite Sleep Problem (FSP). The authors show that there is no self-stabilizing local-control protocol for the FDP, so oracles are investigated that allow the FDP to be solved. In the FSP, the leaving processes do not have to make an irrevocable decision when to leave the network. They just fall asleep whenever they think it is safe to do so, but they will be woken up again as long as there are still messages in their channel. So the goal of the FSP is just to ensure that eventually a state is reached where all leaving nodes are permanently asleep. Foreback et al. show that for the FSP problem, a self-stabilizing local-control protocol does exist. While their protocol only works together with a self-stabilizing protocol for arranging nodes in a sorted list, more universal protocols for the FSP were presented in [14]. Another extension of the results in [9] was presented in [10]. In that paper, the authors study churn in general (including join and leave requests) and consider the case that neither the number of churn requests in total, nor the number of concurrent churn requests can be bounded by a constant. They prove that a solution to this problem is possible if and only if not every request needs to be satisfied.

Aside from these results, there has been research on self-stabilizing link layers [5,6] which even guarantee FIFO-delivery, thus giving stronger guarantees than required for the relay layer. More related work concerning relays is discussed in the full version [19].

1.4 Our Contributions

We present a novel approach for interconnecting processes which is based on so-called *relays*. For this we introduce a novel relay layer that acts between the application and the link layer and show that depending on the way an application uses this layer, this relay layer can self-stabilize to a legal state in which a transfer of messages is guaranteed. After that, we show that our relay approach is universal in a sense that one can get from any weakly connected network to any other weakly connected network while maintaining weak connectivity in the transformation process. In the full version [19] we show that existing solutions for the FDP can be transformed for our relay layer such that they solve the FDP without the use of an oracle (assuming a reliable link layer instead). Our relay concept also has some interesting connections to the access control domain as we point out in the full version [19].

2 The Relay Layer

We assume that all connections between processes happen through relays which are managed by a so-called *relay layer*. Each process v is assumed to interact with its own, separate relay layer $RL(v)$ (so that it is clear which relay is owned by which process), and $RL(v)$ is required to reside at the same machine as v so that interactions between v and $RL(v)$ are local. Whenever a message needs to be sent to v, it has to go through $RL(v)$. Each $RL(v)$ has a globally unique address, or short RID, that depends on the address of its machine, so that messages can be sent to it from any other relay layer that knows its RID. Furthermore, every relay layer $RL(v)$ has a local buffer $RL(v).Buf$ that is used for the internal communication between relay layers: Every $RL(v).Buf$ is expected to consist of pairs $(targetRID, message)$ in which $targetRID$ is the RID of the relay layer $message$ is sent to by the link layer. Here $message$ must be an internal message (any other type of message will be ignored). The relay layer of the entire system is the set of relay layers over all of its processes.

2.1 Relays

A relay is basically a socket that is non-transferably owned by exactly one process v, and that can have both incoming connections from other relays as well as an outgoing connection to some relay. More precisely, $RL(v)$ maintains the following variables for each relay r:

- $r.ID$: globally-unique identifier of relay r (containing the RID of its relay layer so that messages can be sent to r when knowing its ID)
- $r.state$: is either *alive* or *dead*
- $r.out$: stores a (Key, ID) pair where Key is a set keys, and ID is the ID of the target of the outgoing connection (if $ID = \perp$ then r is a *sink*, i.e., messages are forwarded to the process owning it)

- $r.level \in \mathbb{N}_0$: stores the distance of r (in hops) to the sink relay reached via its outgoing connection (there is always a unique such one, see below)
- $r.sinkRID$: stores the RID of the *sink* of r, i.e., the RID of the relay layer of the process that will receive messages sent via r
- $r.In$: set of triples of the form $(key, RID, \perp)$ or $(key, \perp, r')$ for some relay r', where *key* is a globally unique key (depending on the RID of r's relay layer), RID specifies the address of the relay layer that can send messages to r via *key*, and r' is a relay via which *key* was supposed to be forwarded; depending on the form, *key* is a *confirmed* or *unconfirmed* key
- $r.Buf$: stores all messages that the link layer should send to the relay layer with RID $r.out.ID$ if $r.out.ID \neq \perp$ or to v if $r.out.ID = \perp$

Note that we assume all buffers (i.e., $RL(v).Buf$ and $r.Buf$ for every relay r) to be insert-only, i.e., only the link-layer can remove a message from them. Furthermore, we assume all IDs in the system to be valid, i.e., for every ID in the system the corresponding RID belongs to an existing process (it would be possible to lift this assumption by introducing another oracle or by giving more power to the underlying link layer, but this is beyond the scope of this paper).

The relay connections can be represented by a so-called relay graph.

Definition 1. *Given any system state S, the* relay graph $G = (V, E)$ *of S is a directed graph that is defined as follows: $V = R \cup P$, where R is the set of relays and P is the set of active processes. $E = E_P \cup E_{Ch}$ where E_P is the set of all explicit edges and E_{Ch} is the set of implicit edges. E_P contains an edge (v, w) whenever*

1. *$v \in P$ and $w \in R$ and w is owned by process v,*
2. *$v \in R$ and $w \in R$ and relay v has an outgoing connection to relay w (i.e., $v.out.ID = w.ID$), or*
3. *$v \in R$ and $w \in P$, and relay v is a sink relay of process w (i.e., $v.out.ID = \perp$).*

E_{Ch} contains an edge (v, w) whenever $v \in R, w \in R$ and a reference to w is contained in the parameter list of a message in $v.Buf$. Thus, while explicit edges can be used to send messages, implicit edges cannot be used to send messages yet.

Observe that the third requirement on a legitimate state implies that every relay graph is cycle-free.

2.2   Relay Layer Primitives

Whenever a process holds a reference to a relay r, which we denote by $\hat{r}$, we assume that it is a "dark" reference, i.e., the variables of the relay cannot be accessed by the process. However, the reference can be used by the processes to call a number of primitives offered by the relay layer (in the following, we assume that all relays mentioned below are *owned* by the calling process, i.e., they are or have been created for it by its relay layer—relays not owned by the calling process will be ignored):

1. **new Relay:** returns a reference to a new sink relay r with a globally unique identifier $r.ID$, $r.state = alive$, $r.In = \{\}$, $r.out = (\{\}, \perp)$, and $r.level = 0$.
2. **delete** $\hat{r}$: prepares the relay referenced by $\hat{r}$ for deletion, in a sense that the relay layer sets $r.In = \{\}$ and $r.state = dead$. This has the effect that r will not accept any further messages, but r still continues to deliver the messages in $r.Buf$. r is deleted by the relay layer once $r.Buf$ is empty and all relay relay keys sent via r have been confirmed or deleted.
3. **merge(R):** if for all relays $r \in R$, $r.state = alive$, $r.out.ID$ is equal to some common ID, $r.level$ is equal to some common ℓ, $r.sinkRID$ is equal to some common $sinkRID$ and $r.In = \{\}$, the relay layer creates a new relay r' with new $r'.ID$, $r'.state = alive$, and $r'.out = (Key, ID)$ with $Key = \bigcup_{r \in R} r.out.Key$, $r'.level = \ell$, $r'.sinkRID = sinkRID$, $r'.In = \{\}$, and $r'.Buf = \bigcup_{r \in R} r.Buf$. Also, all relays in R are deleted. A reference to r' is returned back to the process. (If one of the conditions above is not satisfied, merge does nothing.)
4. **getRelays:** returns (references to) the current set of all relays owned by v that are still alive.
5. **incoming($\hat{r}$):** returns $|r.In|$
6. **direct($\hat{r}$):** returns true iff $r.level \leq 1$
7. **is-sink($\hat{r}$):** returns true iff $r.level = 0$
8. **dead($\hat{r}$):** returns true iff r does not exist anymore or $r.state = dead$
9. **same-target($\hat{r_1}, \hat{r_2}$):** returns true iff $r_1.out.ID = r_2.out.ID$
10. **send($\hat{r}, action(parameters)$):** if r is still alive, adds a message of the form $((key, r.ID, r.out.ID), action(parameters'))$ to $r.Buf$ for some arbitrary key $key \in r.out.Key$ (where $parameters'$ is an adapted form of $parameters$ explained below), where $(key, r.ID, r.out.ID)$ is called the *header* of the message.

Figure 1 gives examples of the uses of these primitives.

If a process v executes **stop**, v becomes inactive, and $RL(v)$ immediately deletes all sink relays and from then on periodically deletes all relays r with $r.In = \emptyset$ and $r.Buf = \emptyset$. $RL(v)$ continues to exist until all relays have been deleted, after which it shuts down. We hightlight that protocols can prevent relay layers from existing forever by making sure that all indirect relay connections (i.e., relay connections where none of the endpoints is a sink) are closed eventually as we will prove.

Note that the fact that **merge** can be used to merge relays is the reason for why the variable $r.out.Key$ of a relay r has to be a set instead of a single value only: The merge could occur in an illegitimate state at which one of the merged relays may store a correct key while another one does not. At this point it is not clear which one to choose.

For convenience, in the following we will use $RL(r)$ to denote the relay layer that owns a relay r, $RID(ID)$ to denote the RID contained in ID, $RID(u)$ to denote the RID of $RL(u)$ and $RID(r)$ to denote the RID of $RL(r)$.

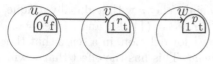

Initial situation. u owns relay q, v owns relay r and w owns relay p. By definition, r and p are direct relays, whereas q is not.

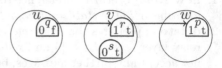

Situation after v has executed **new Relay**, v has an additional (sink) relay s. By definition, s is a direct relay.

Situation after v has executed SEND($\hat{r}, action(\hat{s})$) for some action $action$, $RL(w)$ (w is the so-called sink of r) has created a new relay s' with an outgoing connection to s.

Situation after w has executed **delete** $\hat{s}'$, s' is marked as dead, $s.In$ has been updated (as s no longer has an incoming connection), and the connection from s' to s has been removed.

Fig. 1. Example with three processes u, v, and w. The characters inside a relay r denote (from left to right), $|r.In|$, the ID of r, and whether r is a direct relay. The arrows indicate outgoing connections of relays.

2.3   Message Processing and Action Handling

All messages that can be sent by a process v are required to be remote method invocations of the form $action(parameters)$ (otherwise, they will be ignored by $RL(v)$). More precisely, a process v calls $send(\hat{r}, action(parameters))$ to ask $RL(v)$ to send out a message via r. For simplicity, we assume $parameters$ to consist of a sequence of objects, some of which are relay references, and all other objects do not contain any relay reference at all. We assume that each action has a fixed number of parameters and specifies which of its parameters are relay references. The pseudocodes of the actions described in this section can be found in the full version [19].

When $send(\hat{r}, action(parameters))$ is called for an alive relay r, there are two possibilities: If r is a sink, i.e., $r.out.ID = \bot$, then $action(parameters)$ is put into $r.Buf$ such that the process owning r will receive $action(parameters)$. Otherwise, $RL(r)$ for every relay reference $\hat{s}$ contained in $parameters$ creates a new globally unique key key, inserts $(key, \bot, r)$ into $s.In$ and replaces $\hat{s}$ by the quadruple $(key, s.ID, s.level + 1, s.sinkRID)$. We refer to these quadruples by the term $relay\ parameter$, the first entry of which is called its key, the second is called its id, the third is called its $level$, and the fourth its $sinkRID$. Furthermore we assume that there is a part of each generated key that depends on the generating process and can be used to check whether a key key was generated by a process u, in which case we say $key\ belongs\ to\ u$. Let the list of parameters resulting from the replacements be $parameters'$. Then, $RL(r)$ puts

a TRANSMIT$(((key, r.ID, r.out.ID), action(parameters')))$ message into $r.Buf$
where key is an arbitrary element from $r.out.Key$.

We assume that the link layer for every relay r eventually processes every
message in $r.Buf$ without changing its contents. The link layer makes sure that
every message $m' \in r.Buf$ for a relay r is either processed by the process v
owning r, in case that $outID = \bot$, or successfully delivered to the process whose
relay layer has the RID contained in $r.out.ID$. After the link layer has processed
a message m' in $r.Buf$ for a relay r, it removes m from $r.Buf$.

Definition 2 (Valid message header). *A message m of the form
$((key, inID, outID), action(parameters))$ is said to have a valid header for relay
r if $r.ID = outID$, and either $(key, RID, \bot) \in r.In$ with $RID = RID(inID)$,
or $(key, \bot, r') \in r.In$ and $r'.sinkRID = RID(inID)$.*

When a message $m = ((key, inID, outID), action(parameters))$ is received
by a process w, $RL(w)$ acts according to the Pseudocode given in Listing 1.1.
We assume that PROBE$(controlKeys, keySequence)$ is a dedicated action type
used for the relay layers only, in which $controlKeys$ is a set and $keySequence$ is
a sequence of keys.

Listing 1.1. Pseudocode executed by $RL(w)$ when a message m is received by w

```
1   TRANSMIT(m = ((key, inID, outID), action(parameters))) →
2   if there is a relay r' such that r'.ID = outID and r'.state = alive
3   and m has a valid header for r' then
4      if (key, ⊥, r'') ∈ r'.In for some relay r'' owned by this process
5      and r''.sinkRID = RID(inID) then
6         // first message received via this connection, activate it
7         r.In := r.In \ {(key, ⊥, r'')}
8         r.In := r.In ∪ {(key, RID, ⊥)}
9      if r'.out.ID = ⊥ then // r' is a sink relay
10        if action(parameters) = PROBE(controlKeys, keySequence) then
11           for every key' ∈ controlKeys do
12              if there is no relay r'' such that key' ∈ r''.out.Key then
13                 let (key₁,...,keyₖ) = keySequence
14                 if there is an RID such that (keyₖ, RID, ⊥) ∈ r'.In then
15                    RL.Buf := RL.Buf ∪ {(RID, PROBEFAIL(key', (key₁,...,keyₖ)))}
16        else if all ids of relay parameters of m belong to the
17        same RID senderRID then
18           // (otherwise, the message is obviously corrupted)
19           r'.Buf := r'.Buf ∪ {action(parameters)}
20           for each relay param (key', ID', level', sRID') in parameters do
21              if ∄ relay r'' with key' ∈ r''.out.Key in RL(w) then
22                 create a new relay s with:
23                    s.ID := newID, where newID is a new, globally
24                       unique ID containing the RID of RL(w)
25                    s.state := alive,
26                    s.out := ({key'}, ID'),
27                    s.level := level', and
28                    s.sinkRID := sRID', and
29                    s.In := {}, and
30                    s.Buf := {(((key', s.ID, ID'), PROBE({}, key'))}
31                 replace (key', ID', level', sRID') in parameters by ŝ
```

```
32              else
33                 replace (key', ID', level', sRID') in parameters by ⊥
34          else // m needs to be forwarded
35            r'.Buf := r'.Buf ∪ {TRANSMIT(m)}
36            replace key by an arbitrary key' ∈ r'.out.Key
37            replace inID by r'.ID
38            replace outID by r'.out.ID
39            if action(parameters) = PROBE(controlKeys, keySequence) then
40               append key' to keySequence
41               for every key'' ∈ controlKeys do
42                  if there is a message m' ∈ r'.Buf that contains a relay
43                     parameter with key key'' then
44                     remove key'' from controlKeys
45      else if ∃ a relay r' s.t. r'.ID = outID and r'.state = alive then
46         // m does not have a valid header for r'
47         RL.Buf := RL.Buf ∪ {(RID(inID), NOT_AUTHORIZED(m))}
48      else if outID contains the RID of RL(w)
49         // there is no relay r' s.t. r'.ID = outID and r'.state = alive
50         RL.Buf := RL.Buf ∪ {(RID(inID), OUT-RELAY-CLOSED(outID))}
```

Recall that when a process v calls SEND($\hat{r}, m$), and m contains references to relays, $RL(v)$ replaces these references by relay parameters containing the necessary information to establish a connection to these relays. Additionally $RL(v)$ inserts $(key, \perp, r)$ to $r'.In$ for every relay r' that was contained in this message. These will be replaced by $(key, RID, \perp)$ after the message has been received by a process. To prevent $(key, \perp, r)$ entries in $.In$ sets for which no corresponding messages in the system exist (which would prevent $.In$ from becoming empty after all other relays have been closed), a probing is done via the PROBE() messages to check whether such a message m with a relay parameter with key key exists: On the path from r to the sink relay, it is checked whether m is contained in the buffer of the next relay on the path. If this is not the case and the sink does not have a relay with that key, a PROBEFAIL() message will be sent in return to inform r' about this. Note that the PROBEFAIL() message type contains two parameters: the key that was not found and the sequence of keys that were used to get from the initiator of the PROBE() message to the sink. The latter is used to find the way back to the initiator via the same path (in reverse order) that the PROBE() message took. Details of this are described in the full version [19].

When a NOT_AUTHORIZED(m) control message is received and there is a non-sink relay r such that m could have been sent by this, the relay layer removes the key contained in m from $r.out.Key$. If there is still at least one key left in $r.out.Key$, the message is resent with another key. Otherwise, all elements $(key, \perp, r)$ are removed from $r'.In$ for every relay r', and r is deleted.

The TIMEOUT action mainly detects and corrects all values that are obviously corrupted and contradict to the definition of a legal state that will be given later. In addition, for each relay r it serves the following purposes: First, it periodically sends a PING($r.ID, r.level, r.sinkRID, key$) message to every relay layer whose RID is contained as the second parameter of a triple $(key, RID, \perp)$ in $r.In$. This is to give connected relays r' with $r'.out.ID = ID$ and $key \in r'.out.Key$ the opportunity to correct their level or sinkRID information and also to determine if there are relays in $r.In$ that do not exist. Second, it detects and fully removes deleted relays r that do not need to be kept any more (e.g. because all of their messages have been transmitted) and it also shuts down the relay layer if the process is dead and all relays of it have been deleted. In case r is not a sink, it additionally sends out an IN-RELAY-CLOSED($r.out.Key, RID(r), r.out.ID$) message as to inform the relay layer of the relay with ID $r.out.ID$ that r has been closed. Third, its sends out the aforementioned PROBE() messages.

When a relay layer receives a PING($ID, level, sinkRID, key$) message it checks whether there is a corresponding relay r with $r.out.ID = ID$ and $key \in r.out.Key$. If there is no such relay, it responds to the relay layer owning the relay with id ID with an IN-RELAY-CLOSED() message indicating that there is no such relay with such a key. Otherwise, if $r.level \geq level + 1$, it updates $r.level$ to $level$ and $r.sinkRID$ to $sinkRID$. If $r.level < level + 1$, it deletes r (in this case correcting the value would be dangerous as this would allow for cycles in the relay graph). The IN-RELAY-CLOSED($Keys, senderRID, ID$) basically removes every entry $(key, RID, \bot)$ from all $.In$ sets such that $key \in Keys$.

When **delete** $\hat{r}$ is called, $RL(r)$ sets $r.state$ to $dead$ and sends an OUT-RELAY-CLOSED($r.ID$) message to every relay layer whose RID is the second parameter of a triple in $r.In$. Afterwards, it empties $r.In$ so that no message can be received via r from that point in time. Note that a relay r is not closed immediately during the execution of **delete** $\hat{r}$. This is to allow all messages still in $r.Buf$ to be delivered first. Once this has happened, the relay will be removed completely upon the execution of TIMEOUT.

When a relay layer receives an OUT-RELAY-CLOSED(ID) message and owns a relay r with $r.out.ID = ID$, it removes all triples $(key, \bot, r)$ from $r'.In$ for every relay r' owned by it, empties $r.out.Key$, sets $r.out.ID$ to $\bot$, and calls delete afterwards.

2.4   Properties of the Relay Layer

In order to define legal states for the relay layer, we introduce the following notion of a *valid relay*:

Definition 3 (Valid Relay). *A relay r is* valid *iff*

1. *$r.state = alive$, and*
2. *$r.ID$ is globally unique, and*
3. *$r.out$ stores a pair (Key, ID) such that Key is a set, and*
4. *$r.In$ only consists of triples $(key, RID, \bot)$ with $RID \neq \bot$ or $(key, \bot, r'')$ for a valid relay r'' owned by $RL(r)$, and*
5. *every key key used as a first parameter of a triple in $r.In$ is locally unique (i.e., it does not appear in any other triple in $r.In$ or $r''.In$ for any relay $r'' \neq r$) and belongs to $RID(r)$, and*
6. *there is no PING($r.ID, level, snkRID, key$) message in the system s.t. $level \neq r.level$ or $snkRID \neq r.sinkRID$ or $(key, \bot, r'') \in r.In$ for a relay r'', and*

7. there is no OUT-RELAY-CLOSED($r.ID$) message in the system, and
8. for each $(key, RID, \perp) \in r.In$ there is no NOT_AUTHORIZED$(((key, inID,)$ $r.ID, level), action(parameters))$ message in the system for any level and any $inID$ such that $RID(inID) = RID$, and for each $(key, \perp, r'') \in r.In$ there is no NOT_AUTHORIZED$(((key, inID, r.ID, level), action(parameters)))$ message in the system for any level and any $inID$ such that $RID(inID) = r''.sinkRID$, and
9. for every $(key, \perp, r'') \in r.In$, there is no PROBEFAIL$(key, (key_1, \ldots))$ message in the system such that $key_1 \in r''.out.Key$, and, let $(r_1 = r'', r_2, \ldots, r_k)$ be the sequence of relays such that $r_{i+1}.ID = r_i.out.ID$ for all $1 \le i < k$ and $r_k.out.ID = \perp$, then either for a relay r' owned by the process with RID $r''.sinkRID$ such that $r'.out.ID = r, key \in r'.out.Key$, $r'.level = r.level + 1$, there is a PROBE$(\{\}, key)$ message with a valid header in transit to r and there is no PROBE$(controlKeys, (key_1, \ldots))$ message such that $key \in controlKeys$ and $key_1 \in r''.out.Key$ in $r'''.Buf$ for any relay $r''' \notin \{r_1, \ldots, r_{k-1}\}$, or there is a message m with a valid header for r_{j+1} in $r_j.Buf$ for some $1 \le j < k$ containing a relay parameter with key key, and there is no PROBE$(controlKeys, (key_1, \ldots))$ message such that $key \in controlKeys$ and $key_1 \in r''.out.Key$ in $r'''.Buf$ for any relay $r''' \notin \{r_1, \ldots, r_j\}$, and **either**
10. r is a sink, i.e., $r.out = (\{\}, \perp), r.level = 0$, and $r.sinkRID = RID(r)$, **or**
11. (a) $r.out.ID \ne \perp$, and
    (b) there is a valid relay r' with $r'.ID = r.out.ID$, and
    (c) $r.level = r'.level + 1$, and $r.sinkRID = r'.sinkRID$, and
    (d) there is a key $\in r.out.Key$ such that $(key, RID, \perp) \in r'.In$ and $RID = RID(r)$, or $(key, \perp, r'') \in r'.In$ for a relay r'' and $r''.sinkRID = RID(r)$ and $((key, r.ID, r.out.ID), PROBE(\{\}, key)) \in r.Buf$, and
    (e) for every key $\in r.out.Key$, there is no relay $r''' \ne r$ owned by the same process such that $key \in r'''.out.Key$
    (f) there is no IN-RELAY-CLOSED$(Keys, RID(r), r.out.ID)$ message in transit to $RL(r')$ such that $key \in r.out.Key$ for a $key \in Keys$

Using this definition, we can define a *valid relay graph* as follows:

Definition 4 (Valid relay graph). A valid relay graph of a system state S is the subgraph of the relay graph $G = (R \cup P, E_P \cup E_{Ch})$ of S such that every $r \in R$ is valid and every $(v, w) \in E_{Ch}$ is due to a valid relay parameter.

Note that every valid relay graph is cycle-free due to Property 11(c) of a valid relay. We say a state S is *legal* if the relay graph of S equals its valid relay graph. Furthermore, we say an application is *deliberate* if it does not delete a relay r' if $r'.In \ne \emptyset$ (note that this includes that it does not call **stop** as long as there are sink relays with incoming connections). Given the above definitions, we obtain the following results whose proofs can be found in the full version [19]:

Theorem 1. If the application is deliberate, every message sent via a valid relay r will be received by the process u with $RID(u) = r.sinkRID$.

Thus the process u is also called the *sink process* of r. Observe that in the valid relay graph, every relay r is connected via a directed path to some process v, which is the sink process of r.

Theorem 2. *If the application is deliberate, for every computation that starts in a legal state every state is legal.*

Theorem 3. *If the application is deliberate, and does not send the reference of an indirect relay (i.e., a relay r such that $direct(r) = false$) and does not send any reference via a relay that is not valid, every computation will reach a legal state.*

Corollary 1. *If the application does not issue any commands, starting from any initial state S the system will reach a state S' such S' and every subsequent state are legal.*

Note that this resembles the classical definition of self-stabilization in which it is assumed that starting from the initial state no change occurs to the system other than by the self-stabilizing protocol.

Since the relay layer of a process that issues **stop** is not always shutdown immediately, the following is important as well:

Theorem 4. *If the application does not keep an indirect relay for an infinite time, all relay layers of inactive processes will eventually be shut down.*

3   Universality of the Relay Approach

We introduce three rules for the manipulation of edges of a relay graph and show that they are universal, i.e., using them it is possible to get from any arbitrary weakly connected valid relay graph to any other weakly connected valid relay graph involving the same set of processes. For simplicity, in this section any relay graphs we consider are assumed to be valid relay graphs. The rules we present are an adaptation of known rules introduced by Koutsopoulos et al. [14] (more on this can be found in the full version [19]) to our relay model. In that work, the authors proved these rules to be universal in the common model, which we will rely on in our proofs. For convenience, in the following, for a relay r, we denote the process that stores the sink relay of r as the *sink process of* r. Furthermore, we say a process u has a *relay r to* another process v if v is the sink process of r, and u stores $\hat{r}$ in one of its variables or there is a message in transit to u that will cause such a reference to be created upon receipt. Additionally, a relay r is called a *direct relay* if and only if $direct(r)$ evaluates to true. Otherwise, r is called *indirect*. The set $\mathcal{IFR}$ of relay rules consists of the following rules:

Relay Introduction Assume a process u has a relay r to a process v and another relay s to a process w. Then u may send $\hat{s}$ to v (via r).

Relay Fusion Assume a process u has two relays r and r' with same-target$(\hat{r}, \hat{r}')$. Then u may merge the two relays.

Relay Reversal Assume a process u has two relays r and s such that $r \neq s$ and incoming$(r) = 0$. Then u may send $\hat{s}$ via r and subsequently delete r.

Examples of these rules are presented in the full version [19]. The following is easy to show:

Theorem 5. $\mathcal{IFR}$ preserves weak connectivity, i.e., if any of the rules is applied to a weakly connected relay graph G, then the resulting graph G' is also weakly connected.

The idea of the proof is as follows: Relay Introduction does not delete any relay, thus its application cannot harm the connectivity of the relay graph. Relay Fusion only merges redundant relays. Last, Relay Reversal preserves weak connectivity because although u deletes a connection to the sink process of r, the message sent causes an edge from r to s (and thus there is an undirected path from u to the sink process of r).

The universality of the three relay rules is given by the following theorem, whose proof is deferred the full version [19] due to space constraints:

Theorem 6. The rules in $\mathcal{IFR}$ are universal in a sense that one can get from any weakly connected relay graph $G = (V, E)$ to any other weakly connected relay graph $G' = (V, E')$, where w.l.o.g. E and E' consist solely of explicit edges.

Recall that we dealt with valid relay graphs in this section. Luckily, by Theorem 3 one can show: For every protocol that uses only the primitives in $\mathcal{IFR}$ for the manipulation of edges in the relay graph and only uses references of direct relays in introductions, the underlying relay layer will self-stabilize, i.e., it will reach a state S such the relay graph of S is equal to the valid relay graph of S and starting from any such state for every subsequent state S' the relay graph of S' will be equal to the valid relay graph of S'.

References

1. Aspnes, J., Wu, Y.: $O(logn)$-time overlay network construction from graphs with out-degree 1. In: Tovar, E., Tsigas, P., Fouchal, H. (eds.) OPODIS 2007. LNCS, vol. 4878, pp. 286–300. Springer, Heidelberg (2007). https://doi.org/10.1007/978-3-540-77096-1_21
2. Augustine, J., Pandurangan, G., Robinson, P., Roche, S.T., Upfal, E.: Enabling robust and efficient distributed computation in dynamic peer-to-peer networks. In: Proceedings of the 56th IEEE Annual Symposium on Foundations of Computer Science (FOCS 2015), pp. 350–369 (2015). https://doi.org/10.1109/FOCS.2015.29
3. Berns, A., Ghosh, S., Pemmaraju, S.V.: Building self-stabilizing overlay networks with the transitive closure framework. Theor. Comput. Sci. **512**, 2–14 (2013)
4. Dijkstra, E.W.: Self-stabilizing systems in spite of distributed control. Commun. ACM **17**(11), 643–644 (1974)
5. Dolev, S., Dubois, S., Potop-Butucaru, M., Tixeuil, S.: Stabilizing data-link over non-FIFO channels with optimal fault-resilience. Inf. Process. Lett. **111**(18), 912–920 (2011). https://doi.org/10.1016/j.ipl.2011.06.010

6. Dolev, S., Hanemann, A., Schiller, E.M., Sharma, S.: Self-stabilizing end-to-end communication in (bounded capacity, omitting, duplicating and non-FIFO) dynamic networks. In: Richa, A.W., Scheideler, C. (eds.) SSS 2012. LNCS, vol. 7596, pp. 133–147. Springer, Heidelberg (2012). https://doi.org/10.1007/978-3-642-33536-5_14

7. Dolev, S., Kat, R.I.: Hypertree for self-stabilizing peer-to-peer systems. Distrib. Comput. **20**(5), 375–388 (2008)

8. Drees, M., Gmyr, R., Scheideler, C.: Churn- and DoS-resistant overlay networks based on network reconfiguration. In: Proc. of the 28th ACM Symposium on Parallelism in Algorithms and Architectures (SPAA 2016), pp. 417–427 (2016). https://doi.org/10.1145/2935764.2935783

9. Foreback, D., Koutsopoulos, A., Nesterenko, M., Scheideler, C., Strothmann, T.: On stabilizing departures in overlay networks. In: Felber, P., Garg, V. (eds.) SSS 2014. LNCS, vol. 8756, pp. 48–62. Springer, Cham (2014). https://doi.org/10.1007/978-3-319-11764-5_4

10. Foreback, D., Nesterenko, M., Tixeuil, S.: Infinite unlimited churn (short paper). In: Bonakdarpour, B., Petit, F. (eds.) SSS 2016. LNCS, vol. 10083, pp. 148–153. Springer, Cham (2016). https://doi.org/10.1007/978-3-319-49259-9_12

11. Hayes, T.P., Saia, J., Trehan, A.: The forgiving graph: a distributed data structure for low stretch under adversarial attack. Distrib. Comput. **25**(4), 261–278 (2012)

12. Jacob, R., Richa, A.W., Scheideler, C., Schmid, S., Täubig, H.: Skip$^+$: a self-stabilizing skip graph. J. ACM **61**(6), 36:1–36:26 (2014). https://doi.org/10.1145/2629695

13. Jacob, R., Ritscher, S., Scheideler, C., Schmid, S.: Towards higher-dimensional topological self-stabilization: a distributed algorithm for delaunay graphs. Theor. Comput. Sci. **457**, 137–148 (2012)

14. Koutsopoulos, A., Scheideler, C., Strothmann, T.: Towards a universal approach for the finite departure problem in overlay networks. In: Pelc, A., Schwarzmann, A.A. (eds.) SSS 2015. LNCS, vol. 9212, pp. 201–216. Springer, Cham (2015). https://doi.org/10.1007/978-3-319-21741-3_14

15. Kuhn, F., Schmid, S., Wattenhofer, R.: Towards worst-case churn resistant peer-to-peer systems. Distrib. Comput. **22**(4), 249–267 (2010)

16. Nor, R.M., Nesterenko, M., Scheideler, C.: Corona: a stabilizing deterministic message-passing skip list. Theor. Comput. Sci. **512**, 119–129 (2013). https://doi.org/10.1016/j.tcs.2012.08.029

17. Pandurangan, G., Robinson, P., Trehan, A.: DEX: self-healing expanders. In: Proceedings of the 28th IEEE International Parallel and Distributed Processing Symposium (IPDPS 2014), pp. 702–711 (2014). https://doi.org/10.1109/IPDPS.2014.78

18. Saia, J., Trehan, A.: Picking up the pieces: self-healing in reconfigurable networks. In: Proceedings of the 22nd IEEE International Symposium on Parallel and Distributed Processing (IPDPS 2008), pp. 1–12 (2008)

19. Scheideler, C., Setzer, A.: Relays: a new approach for the finite departure problem in overlay networks (full version). CoRR (2018). http://arxiv.org/abs/1809.05013

Clairvoyant State Machine Replications

Rida Bazzi[1]($\boxtimes$) and Maurice Herlihy[2]

[1] Arizona State University, Tempe, AZ, USA
bazzi@asu.edu
[2] Brown University, Providence, RI, USA
mph@cs.brown.edu

Abstract. We propose a new protocol for the generalized consensus problem in asynchronous systems subject to Byzantine server failures. The protocol solves the consensus problem in a setting in which information about conflict between transactions is available (such information can be in the form of transaction read and write sets). The use of non-skipping timestamps permits servers to commit transactions as soon as they know that no conflicting transaction can be ordered earlier. Unlike most prior proposals (for generalized or classical consensus), which use a leader to order transactions, this protocol is leaderless, and relies on non-skipping timestamps for transaction ordering. Being leaderless, the protocol does not need to pause for leader elections. For n servers of which f may be faulty, this protocol requires $n > 4f$.

1 Introduction

A *distributed ledger* is a distributed data structure, replicated across multiple *nodes*, where *transactions* from clients are published in an agreed-upon total order. Today, Bitcoin [25] is perhaps the best-known distributed ledger protocol.

There are two kinds of distributed ledgers. In *permissionless* ledgers, such as Bitcoin, any node can participate in the common protocol by proposing transactions, and helping to order them. In *permissioned* implementations, by contrast, a node must be authorized before it can participate. Permissionless ledgers make sense for cryptocurrencies which seek to ensure that nobody can control who can participate. Permissioned ledgers make sense for structured marketplaces, such as financial exchanges, where parties do not necessarily trust one another, but where openness and anonymity are not goals. State machine replication [32] is the most common way to implement permissioned ledgers.

In state machine replication, a total order is agreed upon for all transactions and every server replica executes the transactions in the same order. If two successive transactions commute, the two transactions can be executed in different orders by different servers. To determine if two transactions commute, we can check if the state variables accessed for reading or writing (*read* and *write* sets) by one transaction are written to by the other transactions and vice-versa. Existing state machine replication protocols are limited in their ability to exploit transaction commutativity. Protocols that exploit general transaction

© Springer Nature Switzerland AG 2018
T. Izumi and P. Kuznetsov (Eds.): SSS 2018, LNCS 11201, pp. 254–268, 2018.
https://doi.org/10.1007/978-3-030-03232-6_17

commutativity solve what is called the *generalized consensus* problem in which a dependency structure is assumed on the transactions [18,28]. Published work on generalized consensus, [18,28,29,33] with few exceptions, is limited to systems with servers subject to crash failures. Pires et al. [30] propose a leader-based generalized state machine replication algorithm and Abd-El-Malek et al. [1] propose a client-driven quorum-based protocol called Q/U that is very efficient under low contention, but that requires $n > 5f$ and can suffer from livelock due to contention even in synchronous periods.

The contribution of this paper is a novel permissioned ledger algorithm, which we call *Byblos*. Byblos has three properties of interest.

- **Generalized**. Byblos exploits *semantic* knowledge about client requests to reduce transaction latency. Client transactions include statically-declared read and write sets. The technical key to effectively exploiting semantic knowledge is a novel use of *non-skipping timestamp* [5] to bound the set of in-flight transactions that might end up ordered before a particular transaction. If an otherwise-complete transaction does not conflict with any of its potential predecessors, that transaction can be committed without further delay. For loads with few conflicts, solution for generalized consensus can be much more efficient than solutions for traditional consensus [18].
- **Leaderless**. Byblos is *leaderless*. With some exceptions [1,9,21], prior replicated state machine algorithms use a *leader* to order client requests. Leader-based algorithms typically have two kinds of phases: a relatively simple normal phase where the leaders send and receive messages to the others, and a complicated reconciliation phase [11,16,20,34] used to detect and replace faulty leaders. Leader election comes at a cost: client requests are typically blocked during leader election even in periods of synchrony. Such delays are especially problematic if valuable periods of synchrony are spent electing leaders instead of making progress. (Other leaderless protocols, such as EPaxos [23], make similar observations.)
  In Byblos, transactions are guaranteed to terminate in periods of synchrony. Technically, Byblos does not need a leader because it is centered around a leaderless non-skipping timestamp algorithm.
- **Simple**. Byblos is simple to explain and understand. While simplicity is subjective, readers who are familiar with other protocols for Byzantine fault tolerance will note that the full protocol is described in this paper.

In Byblos, transactions are ordered by timestamp, with ties broken canonically. For a given timestamp value t, Byblos can determine an upper bound on the set of in-flight *pending* transactions that *might* have assigned timestamp t. This ability to bound the set of potentially conflicting pending transactions makes Byblos clairvoyant. If a transaction T with timestamp t is the next one to be executed by a replica among those transactions with timestamp t, and T does not conflict with any of the *pending* transactions, then T can be executed without waiting for the status of the pending transactions to be resolved. Byblos guarantees progress using an "off-the-shelf" underlying asynchronous Byzantine agreement algorithm, preferably early deciding [7,35], to CANCEL or COMMIT pending transactions[1].

Byblos tolerates $f < n/4$ faulty servers, assuming the underlying consensus algorithm does the same. If there are no conflicts between pending transactions and transactions waiting for execution, Byblos can make progress even in periods of complete asynchrony. This does not contradict the FLP impossibility [15].

The rest of the paper is organized as follows. Section 2 discusses related work. Section 3 introduces the problem and the system model. Section 4 gives a detailed description of Byblos and Sect. 5 states the theorems for correctness. Section 6 describes how the protocol can be optimized to eliminate the exchange of whole pending sets and Sect. 7 describes how Byzantine clients can be tolerated. Section 8 discusses the performance.

2   Related Work

Leader-based distributed ledgers such as Paxos [17] and Raft [27] do not exploit knowledge of read-write sets to reduce latency and increase throughput. Distributed ledgers that do exploit such information include Generalized Paxos [18], Egalitarian Paxos [23], Hyperledger Fabric [10], NEO [26], and Bitcoin itself [25].

There is a large body of literature on state machine replication, most of which is leader-based. Clement *et al.* [12] observe that many Byzantine fault-tolerant (BFT) protocols can perform poorly in the presence of Byzantine failures. They define the notion of a *fragile optimization*, where a single misbehaving party can knock the system off an optimized path. They also define *gracious* (synchronous, non-faulty) and *uncivil* (synchronous, limited Byzantine faults) executions. They argue that while most BFT protocols are optimized for *gracious* executions, it is also important that protocols perform well in uncivil executions. They propose *Aardvark*, a BFT protocol designed to perform well under uncivil executions. Aardvark uses a leader, with regularly-scheduled view changes. The protocol includes safeguards against censorship by the leader. Amir *et al.* [2] introduce *bounded delay* as a performance goal for BFT protocols. They introduced *Prime*, a BFT protocol that uses a leader that is monitored by other servers to provide bounded delay in the presence of limited Byzantine failures.

Paxos [17] and *Raft* [27] are perhaps the best-known non-Byzantine replication protocols. Other Paxos-related non-Byzantine protocols include *Mencius* [19] and *EPaxos* [23]. These protocols, with the exception of EPaxos [23], use some form of leader (or leaders) and view changes. Milosevic *et al.* [22] proposed a *BFT-Mencius* which also uses performance monitoring and view changes to limit the effects of slow servers. Byblos does not use view changes or performance monitoring and hence allows unbounded variance below the timeout threshold.

Existing protocols that perform relatively well under uncivil executions, perform less well in civil executions, compared to protocols optimized only for civil executions. Byblos is different. Its latency, measured in the number of message

---

[1] Asynchronous consensus algorithms are those that guarantee safety at all times, and progress under eventual synchrony.

round trips, is comparable to protocols optimized for civil execution. In the absence of slow or faulty clients, its latency in uncivil executions is also comparable to that of protocol optimized for civil executions. On the down side, Byblos uses signatures, whereas some protocols use faster message authentication codes.

Many BFT protocols that do not exploit commutativity. BFT protocols that do not use leaders or view changes include *HoneyBadgerBFT* [21]. Unlike most BFT protocols, HoneyBadgerBFT does not assume eventual (or partial) synchrony, but relies on a randomized atomic broadcast protocol with a cryptographic shared coin. HoneyBadgerBFT ensures censorship resistance through a cryptographic subprotocol. Unlike Byblos, HoneyBadgerBFT does not exploit transaction semantics. The *RBFT* BFT protocol [4] uses multiple leaders, who track one another, and provide censorship resistance. It is designed for systems in which clients can have multiple parallel pending requests. Aublin *et al.* [3] describe a family of protocols, some of which have low (2-message) latency in synchronous executions.

As noted, the protocols discussed, with the exception of EPaxos [23] which only tolerates crash failures, do not solve the generalized consensus problem [18, 28]. Abd-El-Malek et al. [1] propose a client-driven quorum-based protocol called Q/U that is very efficient under low contention, but that requires $n > 5f$ and can suffer from livelock due to contention even in synchronous periods. The algorithm is leaderless and uses exponential backoff in the presence of contention. Other work that aims at improving Q/U reverts to using a leader [13]. Recently Pires et al. [30] proposed a leader-based Byzantine version of generalized Paxos.

In general, faulty clients in Byblos can force servers to revert to an "off-the-shelf" binary Byzantine consensus protocol to resolve the outcome of "stuck" transactions. Triggering the agreement protocol might incur a timeout which can be significantly larger than typical communication delay even for fast protocols (for example, Ben-Or *et al.* [8] or Mostefaoui *et al.* [24]). It might seem that Byblos replaces one source of delay (faulty leader) with another (faulty clients), but this replacement allows us to exploit transaction semantics which can be a significant improvement in some settings. In systems in which faulty servers can delay the processing of transactions (which is almost all systems), everyone is delayed. (These issues are discussed in Sect. 8.)

3 Problem and System Model

A *ledger* (Fig. 1) can be thought of as an automaton consisting of a set of *states* (for example, clients' account balances), a set of deterministic state transitions called *transactions* (for example, deposits, withdrawals, and transfers), and a *log* recording the sequence of transactions. The state is needed to efficiently compute transactions' return values (for example, your account is overdrawn). The log provides an audit trail: one can reconstruct any prior state of the ledger, and trace who was responsible for each transaction.

Our solution encompasses the following components. There are n *servers* that maintain the ledger's long-lived state via a set of replicated tamper-proof logs.

```
1    state = initialState
2    log = []
3    while true:
4        on receive T from c:
5            log.append(T)
6            state, result = apply(T, state)
7            send result to c
```

Fig. 1. Ledger abstraction

Up to f of $n = 4f + 1$ servers may be Byzantine (capable of departing from the protocol). The rest of the servers are *honest*. The logs of honest servers are only modified by appending new transactions. The servers satisfy the following safety property: for any pair of honest servers, one server's log is a prefix of the other's. It follows that honest servers execute all transactions in the same order.

There is a potentially unbounded number of *clients* who originate transactions. It is the servers' job to accept transactions from clients, order them, and publish this order. We assume that the clients are not Byzantine; in Sect. 7 we explain how to handle Byzantine clients.

Communication is handled by an underlying message-diffusion system. Clients broadcast messages, which are eventually delivered to all honest servers. All messages are signed, and cannot be forged. Servers communicate with one another though the same diffusion infrastructure.

The ledger state is a key-value store. Each client transaction declares a *read set*, the set of keys it might possibly read, and a *write set*, the set of keys it might possibly write. Any transaction that violates its declaration is rejected. (Systems such as Generalized Paxos [18], Egalitarian Paxos [23], and NEO [26] all make use of similar conflict declarations.)

4   Byblos Description

In Byblos, transactions are assigned integer *timestamps*, which partially determine the order in which they are applied. If two transactions do not overlap in time, the later one will be assigned the later timestamp, but overlapping transactions may be assigned the same timestamp. The timestamps assigned to transactions are non-skipping [5]. This means that if a timestamp t is assigned to a transaction, then every timestamp whose value is less than t must have been previously assigned to some other transaction.

The non-skipping timestamp protocol [5] at the heart of the algorithm is simple. A client broadcasts a timestamp request to the servers, and collects at least $n - f$ timestamps in response. The client selects the $(f + 1)^{st}$ latest timestamp, which is guaranteed to be less than or equal to the latest timestamp assigned to any transaction. The client increments that timestamp by one, and later broadcasts it to the servers. It can be shown [5] that this way of choosing timestamps ensures that no timestamp values are skipped.

The properties of non-skipping timestamps suggest a simple way for servers to execute transactions in a deterministic order in the absence of client failures. For each timestamp value t, starting with 0, execute all transactions whose timestamp is t in a deterministic order. Once all transactions with timestamp t are executed, transactions with timestamp $t + 1$ can be executed and so on. This seems too simple (even in the absence of client failures) and indeed it is. The catch is that servers will need to be able to determine when all transactions with a given timestamp value have been received.

To determine when all transactions with timestamp t have been received, Byblos calculates for each transaction T a set of *pending* transactions: transactions that were detected to be concurrent with T. The set of pending transactions contains transactions, but not their assigned timestamps, because those timestamps might not be determined at the time a transaction is added to a pending set. The crucial property is the following: if a transaction T has timestamp t, then its set of pending transactions is guaranteed to contain all transactions whose assigned timestamp will be t. However, it may also include transactions whose assigned timestamp will be larger than t. With the set of pending transaction, in the absence of client failures, servers can execute all transactions in a deterministic order as follows. If there are no pending transactions that conflict either with T or with any transaction with the same timestamp ordered before T, then T can be executed. Eventually, T will be executed when the timestamps of all conflicting transactions in T's pending set become known.

The description so far assumes no client failures. If clients can fail, some transactions in the pending set might never complete and the servers will be stuck, unable to determine when all potentially conflicting transactions with timestamp t have been received. We resolve this situation by executing a binary consensus algorithm, over the values COMMIT and CANCEL, to resolve the fates of orphaned transactions. Each client tries to commit its own transaction using the consensus algorithm, and servers try to cancel pending set transactions that are slow to arrive (with their timestamp). We can use any "off-the-shelf" consensus algorithm guaranteed to terminate if the system is eventually synchronous, including known algorithms that terminate in one round if the system is well-behaved [35]. Transaction execution proceeds as follows. Once all conflicting transactions in the pending set of some transaction with timestamp t are either cancelled or committed, the set of transactions with timestamp t is also known. The execution can then proceed as outlined above for all transactions that have not been cancelled.

The protocol guarantees safety at all times and liveness under eventual synchrony [11]. The rest of this section describes the client and server code in details.

4.1   Client Code

The client code (Fig. 2) proceeds in three stages. In the first stage (Lines 6–12), the client sends a Propose message to all servers, and collects at least $n - f$ ProposeAck responses. The client calculates $\hat{t}$ which is equal to 1 plus the $(f+1)^{st}$ largest amongst the timestamps it received and assigns it to its transaction. It

```
1     received = ∅ // messages from servers
2     ∀ s in Servers timestamp[s] = 0
3     ∀ s in Servers proposed[s] = ∅
4
5     // get valid timestamp
6     broadcast Propose(T) to Servers
7     repeat
8        on receive m: received = received ∪ {m}
9     until ProposeAck(T, t) received from ≥ n − f servers
10    ∀ s in Servers: if ∃ t : ProposeAck(T, t) received from s
11       timestamp[s] = t
12    t̂ = ((f + 1)ˢᵗ largest value in timestamp[∗]) + 1
13
14    // broadcast timestamp, get set of pending Txns
15    broadcast Confirm(T,t̂) to Servers
16    repeat
17       on receive m: received = received ∪ {m}
18    until ConfirmAck messages received from ≥ n − f servers
19    ∀ s ∈ Servers: if ConfirmAck(T, txns) received from s
20       pending = pending ∪ txns
21
22    // broadcast pending set, get transaction result
23    broadcast Resolve(T, t̂, pending) to Servers
24    repeat
25       on receive m: received = received ∪ {m}
26    until ≥ f + 1 identical ResolveAck(T,code, result) messages received
27    if code == COMMIT (in ≥ f + 1 messages) then
28       return result
29    else :
30       return ⊥
```

Fig. 2. Client code

is important to note that this particular way of choosing timestamps is what guarantees timestamps to be non-skipping. In the second stage (Line 15–20), the client broadcasts a Confirm message with $\hat{t}$, waits for at least $n - f$ responses, each containing a set txn of transactions that have been proposed at a server, and calculates the set pending, which is the union of these sets. The set pending is guaranteed to contain every transactions whose timestamp is less than or equal to $\hat{t}$. We implicitly assume that the client verifies responses for well-formedness, and for authenticity by checking signatures. In the third stage (Line 23–30), the client broadcasts a Resolve message with the set pending, and waits to receive $f + 1$ identical ResolveAck responses to determine the transaction's outcome. A ResolveAck message has three fields: (1) the transaction, (2) a code, either COMMIT or CANCEL, and (3) a result. If the return code is COMMIT, the call was successful, and the result is returned, otherwise a failure indication is returned.

```
state = initialState
clock = 0
proposed = ∅          // Set transaction
pending[*] = ∅        // timestamp ↦ Set transaction
confirmed[*] = ∅      // timestamp ↦ Set transaction
committed = ∅         // timestamp ↦ Set transaction
cancelled = ∅         // Set transaction
resolving = ∅         // Set transaction
log = []              // Sequence transaction
timer[*] = ∞          // timestamp ↦ real time timer
time : real time clock value at a server
```

Fig. 3. Server state with initializations

4.2   Server Code

Server State. The server state (Fig. 3) is composed of the following fields.

- state is the ledger state. A transaction is applied to state when it commits.
- clock is an integer counter that tracks the latest timestamp assigned to a transaction. We assume this counter does not overflow.
  Since timestamps are non-skipping, a 128-bit counter should be more than sufficient in practice.
- proposed is set of transactions that have been proposed. When a transaction is added to proposed, its timestamp might not be known.
- pending is a map from timestamps to sets of transactions. For timestamp t, pending[t] is the set of transactions that might be assigned timestamp t.
- confirmed is a map from timestamps to sets of transactions. For timestamp t, confirmed[t] is the set of known transactions that will either commit with timestamp t or will be cancelled.
- committed is set of transactions known to have committed.
- cancelled is the set of transactions known to be cancelled.
- log is the sequence of committed transactions.
- timer is an array of timers used to timeout pending transactions.
- time is a local clock at the server to measure real time for timeouts. The local clocks of servers are independent and need not be synchronized.

Server Actions. The server continually receives messages (Fig. 4). When it receives a message from client c, it does the following. For Propose(T) (Lines 2–4), it adds T to proposed, and returns the current clock value to the client.

For Confirm(T,$\hat{t}$) (Line 6–12), the server advances clock to the maximum of $\hat{t}$ and its current value, and adds the transaction to the set of confirmed transactions. The server also launches a consensus protocol with the other servers to try to to COMMIT T. Then, it returns the current proposed set to the client.

For Resolve(T,$\hat{t}$, txns) (Lines 14–29), the server adds the set of concurrent transactions, txns, to the pending set. If this is a Resolve for a new transaction,

```
1   repeat
2       if Propose received from c:
3           proposed = proposed ∪ {T}
4           send ProposeAck(T, clock) to c
5
6       if Confirm(T, t̂) received from c:
7           clock = max(clock, t̂)
8           confirmed[t̂] = confirmed[t̂] ∪ {T}
9           if T ∉ resolving :
10              resolving = resolving ∪ {T}
11              fork ResolveThread(T, COMMIT)        // try to commit this transaction
12          send ConfirmAck(T, proposed) to c
13
14      if Resolve(T, t̂, txns) received from c or s:
15          if pending[t̂] = ∅:
16              pending[t̂] = txns
17              send Resolve(T, t̂, txns) to all servers
18              timer[t̂] = time+δ
19
20      if StartResolution (T, code) received from s:  // join another consensus
21          if T ∉ resolving :                          // code is either COMMIT or CANCEL
22              resolving = resolving ∪ {T}
23              fork ResolveThread(T, code);
24
25      if timer[t] expired for some t:                // if timer expired, try to cancel
26          for each txn in pending[t]:
    // any obstructing transactions for
27              if txn ∉ resolving :
28                  resolving = resolving ∪ {txn}
29                  fork ResolveThread(txn, CANCEL)
30
31      ApplyResolvedTransaction()                     // attempt apply transactions
32   until false
```

Fig. 4. Server code

the server propagates the resolve message in case other servers do not hear directly from the client. At this point, at least $2f + 1$ servers must have initiated a consensus protocol to commit T (a client does not send a resolve message until it has received $n - f$ confirm messages). The only remaining point that can obstruct T's execution are pending transactions. So, the server sets a timer to give pending transaction the chance to arrive without being timed out. If the timer expires and a transaction in the pending set is not confirmed, the transaction is considered obstructing and an attempt is made to CANCEL it. In practice the delay can be increased dynamically to guarantee that eventually it reaches a value that works for periods of synchrony [20].

We assume that the consensus protocol executed by a server adds T to the set committed if the server decides to COMMIT and adds T to the set cancelled if it decides to CANCEL the transaction. We also assume that the first message sent by the consensus protocol is a StartResolution (T,code) message which lets

```
1    OrderBefore(T,T') =
2          T ∈ confirmed[t] ∧
3          ((T' ∈ confirmed[t'] ∧ t < t') ∨ (T' ∈ confirmed[t] ∧ T < T') ∨
4           (T' ∈ pending[t'] ∧ ∀t'' < t : T' ∉ pending[t''] ∧  t < t') ∨
5           (T' ∈ pending[t] ∧ ∀t'' < t : T' ∉ pending[t'']  ∧ T < T'))
6        ∨
7          T ∈ cancelled ∧
8          ((T' ∉ cancelled ) ∨ (T' ∈ cancelled ∧ T < T'))
9        ∨
10         (T ∈ pending[t] ∧ ∀t' < t : T' ∉ pending[t']) ∧
11         ((T' ∈ confirmed[t] ∧  conflict (T,T') ∧ T < T') ∨
12          (T' ∈ confirmed[t'] ∧  conflict (T,T') ∧ t < t'))
13
14   ApplyResolvedTransaction()
15       if ∃ T: T ∈ committed ∧ ∀ T': OrderBefore(T',T) ⇒ T' ∈ cancelled ∨ T' ∈ log
16           log.append(T)
17           state, result = apply(T, state )
18           send ResolveAck(T,COMMIT,result) to T sender
19       if ∃ T: T ∈ cancelled ∧ T ∉ log
20           log.append(T)
21           send ResolveAck(T,CANCEL,⊥) to T sender
```

Fig. 5. Applying resolved transactions

a server that has not heard directly from a client join the consensus for a given transaction (Lines 20–23).

Finally, a server attempts to apply transactions (Fig. 5). For every timestamp t, we have three groups of transactions: (1) those that have been committed, (2) those that have been cancelled, and (3) those that are pending. For a pending transaction we assign it to the timestamp t for which it first appeared in a pending set. Note that it is possible that pending transactions might appear in groups with different timestamps at different honest servers, but if they become committed, they will have the same timestamp at all honest servers, and if they are cancelled, they will be cancelled by all honest servers. Servers order all transactions according to their timestamp and for a given timestamp, the transaction (in all three groups) are ordered by taking a hash of the transaction request. The OrderBefore() predicate is used to determine the order of transactions at a given time. A transaction that is confirmed is ordered before another confirmed transaction if it has a smaller timestamp or the same timestamp but $T < T'$ in the canonical order (Line 3). A transaction that is confirmed with timestamp t is ordered before another pending transaction whose first appearance in a pending set is for timestamp t' if $t < t'$ or $t = t'$ but $T < T'$ in the canonical order (Lines 4–5). A transaction that is cancelled is ordered before any other transaction because such transactions do not conflict with other transactions (Lines 6–7). A transaction T that is pending is ordered before another confirmed transaction T' if the first timestamp for which T is pending is the same as the timestamp for T', the two transactions conflict and either T appears before T' in the canonical order or the timestamp of T is smaller than that of T'.

5   Correctness

Safety and progress are established by the following lemmas and theorems. Proofs are omitted for lack of space.

Lemma 1 (Same order for applied transaction). *If two honest servers apply two non-cancelled transactions T_1 and T_2 to the log, they apply them in the same order.*

Lemma 2 (Agreement on committed transaction). *If an honest server decides to commit or cancel a transaction, then every honest server eventually makes the same decision.*

Theorem 1 (Linearizability). *The implementation is linearizable.*

Theorem 2 (Progress in periods of synchrony). *In periods of synchrony, all transactions of correct clients are applied.*

6   Eliminating Pending Sets

For ease of exposition, the protocol as presented so far requires clients and servers to exchange proposed and pending sets that can grow without bounds. We explain how the protocol can be modified to eliminate the exchange of these sets.

At a given correct server, the pending set of a confirmed transaction T with timestamp $\hat{t}$ is the set of all previously proposed transactions received by the time the server receives the Confirm message for T. This is the txns set that the client receives from the server then propagates as part of the pending set.

Instead of sending pending sets to clients, every server sends to every other server confirmed transactions (with their timestamps) and proposed transactions that it receives in the order in which they are received together with the clock value at the time they are received. This is done once for every proposed and confirmed transaction. The pending set for T can be given by the formula

$$\text{pending}_T = \bigcup_{s:s\in S \wedge |S| \geq n-f} \text{previous}(s, T)$$

where $\text{previous}(s, T)$ is the set of proposed transactions received before receiving the Confirm message for T. In the original protocol, the client itself collects $n - f$ previous, which are simply the proposed sets. In the modified protocol, the servers can only be guaranteed to receive $n - 2f$ previous sets because f correct servers might not have heard from the client and another f faulty servers might deny having received the Confirm message for T. This can be easily fixed by requiring every server to treat a Confirm message forwarded by another server as a Confirm received from the client (if it has not previously received it). This way, we guarantee that every server can calculate a pending set for every timestamp.

7   Byzantine Clients

The solution as presented assumes clients fail by crashing. Also, it assumes that some implicit checks are done by clients. For instance, it is possible for a Byzantine server to send some fake pending transactions. We assume that the server provides proof that all transactions in a pending set were indeed received by the server. Conversely, when the client send a pending set to the servers, it can be required to provide proof in the form of signatures that every transaction in the set was indeed received by a server. Similarly, the client should provide proof at the calculated hash is justified based on the individual timestamp received from servers. Avoiding replay attacks is straightforward by having the servers sign a cryptographic hash of the messages they send to the clients. These messages include the transaction identifiers.

8   Performance

To evaluate the performance of our solution, we adopt the definitions of *gracious* and *uncivil* executions from Clement et al. [12].

Definition 1 (Gracious execution [12]). *An execution is gracious if and only if (a) the execution is synchronous with some implementation-dependent short bound on message delay and (b) all clients and servers behave correctly.*

Definition 2 (Uncivil execution [12]). *An execution is uncivil if and only if (a) the execution is synchronous with some implementation-dependent short bound on message delay, (b) up to f servers and an arbitrary number of clients are Byzantine, and (c) all remaining clients and servers are correct.*

8.1   Performance in Gracious Executions

In gracious execution, and in the *absence of contention*, the protocol requires 3 round-trip message delay from the time a client makes a request to the time it gets the result. It takes one round-trip delay to receive the first response and calculate the timestamp $\hat{t}$. It takes $1/2$ round-trip delay for the servers to receive $\hat{t}$. At that time correct servers initiate a consensus protocol to commit the transaction and another one round-trip delay is needed to decide to COMMIT the transaction (this is possible because all correct servers will be proposing the same COMMIT value). The client replies to the confirm message after two round-trip delays and gets a response to its resolve message after 3 round-trip delays (there is no need to wait for the result of the consensus which will arrive at the same time as the resolve message).

In the presence of contention, the processing can be delayed by conflicting transactions that have the same timestamp. The latest a transaction started after T can get the same timestamp as T is just short of 1.5 round-trip delay from the time T started (we assume that previous transactions that are not concurrent with T have already been cleared). In fact, a transaction that starts 1.5 round-trip delay after T cannot reach the servers before the time T's timestamp is propagated and will get a later timestamp (we are assuming that the Propose message for the contending transaction will propagate instantaneously in the worst case). So, in the presence of contention, a response might not arrive before 4.5 round-trip delays.

We expect that a closer integration of the solution with a particular consensus protocol will further reduce the delay by another one half of a round-trip which would make it more competitive in terms of latency (PBFT [11] achieves 2 round-trip delay with a number of optimizations including speculative execution, but PBFT does not perform well in uncivil executions).

8.2   Performance in Uncivil Executions

In uncivil executions, the delay depends on the level of contention. If a transaction is initiated and is not overlapping with any other conflicting transaction, its delay will be the same as in gracious executions.

In the presence of contention, a transaction can be delayed further. As in the gracious execution case, we consider the latest time a transaction can be added to the pending set of transaction T. As in the case of gracious executions, the time is 1.5 round-trip delay after T is initiated. If the client of the contending transaction fails, the full timeout would need to be incurred and a consensus protocol would need to be executed. So, the delay in this case would be the timeout value δ plus the consensus time. The client will get a response by 0.5 round-trip delay after the consensus has ended (because the other message exchanges of the client overlap with the timeout time).

8.3   Other Performance Considerations

It is important to note that the delays are not additive. If we have transactions with different timestamps and for each timestamp there is a pending transaction that is slow, no transaction incurs more than one timeout plus consensus delay because the timers are started in a pipelined fashion. This ensures that Byblos average throughput under client delays is minimally affected by slow clients. Also, recall that this delay is only incurred by conflicting transactions whereas in systems in which faulty servers are the source of the delay, all transactions are affected by server delays.

Another potential performance improvement that we did not consider is *transaction batching* [11]. In our solution, servers communicate information about individual transactions. On the positive side, in Byblos, in the presence of contention, more transactions will get the same timestamp and the delay incurred for that timestamp is one for all transactions. This should improve throughput.

As described, Byblos uses public-key signatures [14,31], which can add significant overhead. Replacing signatures with message authentication codes [6] is a subject for future work. Finally, the message complexity of our solution is rather high: $O(n^2)$ messages per transaction. Such high message complexity is not unusual for protocols that aim to achieve bounded delay ([2,4,12,22] for example).

References

1. Abd-El-Malek, M., Ganger, G.R., Goodson, G.R., Reiter, M.K., Wylie, J.J.: Fault-scalable Byzantine fault-tolerant services. ACM SIGOPS Oper. Syst. Rev. **39**(5), 59–74 (2005)
2. Amir, Y., Coan, B., Kirsch, J., Lane, J.: Prime: Byzantine replication under attack. IEEE Trans. Dependable Secur. Comput. **8**(4), 564–577 (2011)
3. Aublin, P.L., Guerraoui, R., Knežević, N., Quéma, V., Vukolić, M.: The next 700 BFT protocols. ACM Trans. Comput. Syst. **32**(4), 12:1–12:45 (2015)
4. Aublin, P.L., Mokhtar, S.B., Quéma, V.: RBFT: redundant Byzantine fault tolerance. In: Proceedings of the 2013 IEEE 33rd International Conference on Distributed Computing Systems, pp. 297–306 (2013)
5. Bazzi, R.A., Ding, Y.: Non-skipping timestamps for Byzantine data storage systems. In: Guerraoui, R. (ed.) DISC 2004. LNCS, vol. 3274, pp. 405–419. Springer, Heidelberg (2004). https://doi.org/10.1007/978-3-540-30186-8_29
6. Bellare, M., Canetti, R., Krawczyk, H.: Keying hash functions for message authentication. In: Koblitz, N. (ed.) CRYPTO 1996. LNCS, vol. 1109, pp. 1–15. Springer, Heidelberg (1996). https://doi.org/10.1007/3-540-68697-5_1
7. Ben-Or, M.: Another advantage of free choice (extended abstract): completely asynchronous agreement protocols. In: Proceedings of the Second Annual ACM Symposium on Principles of Distributed Computing, pp. 27–30. ACM (1983)
8. Ben-Or, M., Kelmer, B., Rabin, T.: Asynchronous secure computations with optimal resilience (extended abstract). In: Proceedings of the Thirteenth Annual ACM Symposium on Principles of Distributed Computing, pp. 183–192. ACM, New York (1994)
9. Borran, F., Schiper, A.: A leader-free Byzantine consensus algorithm. In: Kant, K., Pemmaraju, S.V., Sivalingam, K.M., Wu, J. (eds.) ICDCN 2010. LNCS, vol. 5935, pp. 67–78. Springer, Heidelberg (2010). https://doi.org/10.1007/978-3-642-11322-2_11
10. Cachin, C.: Architecture of the hyperledger blockchain fabric. In: Workshop on Distributed Cryptocurrencies and Consensus Ledgers (2016)
11. Castro, M., Liskov, B.: Practical Byzantine fault tolerance and proactive recovery. ACM Trans. Comput. Syst. **20**(4), 398–461 (2002)
12. Clement, A., Wong, E., Alvisi, L., Dahlin, M., Marchetti, M.: Making Byzantine fault tolerant systems tolerate Byzantine faults. In: Proceedings of the 6th USENIX Symposium on Networked Systems Design and Implementation, pp. 153–168 (2009)
13. Cowling, J., Myers, D., Liskov, B., Rodrigues, R., Shrira, L.: HQ replication: a hybrid quorum protocol for byzantine fault tolerance. In: Proceedings of the 7th Symposium on Operating Systems Design and Implementation, pp. 177–190 (2006)
14. ElGamal, T.: A public key cryptosystem and a signature scheme based on discrete logarithms. IEEE Trans. Inf. Theory **31**(4), 469–472 (1985)
15. Fischer, M.J., Lynch, N.A., Paterson, M.S.: Impossibility of distributed consensus with one faulty process. J. ACM (JACM) **32**(2), 374–382 (1985)
16. Kotla, R., Alvisi, L., Dahlin, M., Clement, A., Wong, E.: Zyzzyva: speculative byzantine fault tolerance. In: ACM SIGOPS Operating Systems Review, vol. 41, pp. 45–58. ACM (2007)

17. Lamport, L.: The part-time parliament. ACM Trans. Comput. Syst. **16**(2), 133–169 (1998)
18. Lamport, L.: Generalized consensus and paxos. Technical report, Microsoft, March 2005
19. Mao, Y., Junqueira, F.P., Marzullo, K.: Mencius: building efficient replicated state machines for WANs. In: Proceedings of the 8th OSDI Conference, pp. 369–384 (2008)
20. Martin, J.P., Alvisi, L.: Fast Byzantine consensus. IEEE Trans. Dependable Secur. Comput. **3**(3), 202–215 (2006)
21. Miller, A., Xia, Y., Croman, K., Shi, E., Song, D.: The honey badger of BFT protocols. In: ACM CCS, pp. 31–42 (2016)
22. Milosevic, Z., Biely, M., Schiper, A.: Bounded delay in Byzantine-tolerant state machine replication. In: 2013 IEEE 32nd International Symposium on Reliable Distributed Systems, pp. 61–70, September 2013
23. Moraru, I., Andersen, D.G., Kaminsky, M.: There is more consensus in Egalitarian parliaments. In: Proceedings of the Twenty-Fourth ACM Symposium on Operating Systems Principles, pp. 358–372. ACM, New York (2013)
24. Mostefaoui, A., Moumen, H., Raynal, M.: Signature-free asynchronous byzantine consensus with $t < n/3$, $O(n^2)$ messages and $O(1)$ expected time. In: 2014 Proceedings of the 2014 ACM Symposium on Principles of Distributed Computing, pp. 2–9. ACM (2014)
25. Nakamoto, S.: Bitcoin: a peer-to-peer electronic cash system (2008)
26. NEO: Neo contract whitepaper. http://docs.neo.org/en-us/basic/neocontract.html. Accessed 6 May 2018
27. Ongaro, D., Ousterhout, J.: In search of an understandable consensus algorithm. In: Proceedings of the USENIX Annual Technical Conference, pp. 305–320 (2014)
28. Pedone, F., Schiper, A.: Handling message semantics with generic broadcast protocols. Distrib. Comput. **15**(2), 97–107 (2002)
29. Peluso, S., Turcu, A., Palmieri, R., Losa, G., Ravindran, B.: Making fast consensus generally faster. In: 2016 46th Annual IEEE/IFIP International Conference on Dependable Systems and Networks (DSN), pp. 156–167. IEEE (2016)
30. Pires, M., Ravi, S., Rodrigues, R.: Generalized paxos made Byzantine (and less complex). In: Spirakis, P., Tsigas, P. (eds.) SSS 2017. LNCS, vol. 10616, pp. 203–218. Springer, Cham (2017). https://doi.org/10.1007/978-3-319-69084-1_14
31. Rivest, R.L., Shamir, A., Adleman, L.: A method for obtaining digital signatures and public-key cryptosystems. Commun. ACM **21**(2), 120–126 (1978)
32. Schneider, F.B.: Implementing fault-tolerant services using the state machine approach: a tutorial. ACM Comput. Surv. (CSUR) **22**(4), 299–319 (1990)
33. Sutra, P., Shapiro, M.: Fast genuine generalized consensus. In: 2011 30th IEEE Symposium on Reliable Distributed Systems (SRDS), pp. 255–264. IEEE (2011)
34. Van Renesse, R., Altinbuken, D.: Paxos made moderately complex. ACM Comput. Surv. (CSUR) **47**(3), 42 (2015)
35. Zielinski, P.: Optimistically terminating consensus: all asynchronous consensus protocols in one framework. In: 2006 The Fifth International Symposium on Parallel and Distributed Computing, ISPDC 2006, pp. 24–33. IEEE (2006)

Set Agreement and Renaming in the Presence of Contention-Related Crash Failures

Anaïs Durand[1](✉), Michel Raynal[1,2], and Gadi Taubenfeld[3]

[1] IRISA, Université de Rennes, 35042 Rennes, France
anais.durand@inria.fr
[2] Department of Computing, Polytechnic University, Kowloon, Hong Kong
[3] The Interdisciplinary Center, 46150 Herzliya, Israel

Abstract. A new notion of process failure explicitly related to contention has recently been introduced by one of the authors (NETYS 2018). More precisely, given a predefined contention threshold λ, this notion considers the executions in which process crashes are restricted to occur only when process contention is smaller than or equal to λ. If crashes occur after contention bypassed λ, there are no correctness guarantees (e.g., termination is not guaranteed). It was shown that, when $\lambda = n - 1$, consensus can be solved in an n-process asynchronous read/write system despite the crash of one process, thereby circumventing the well-known FLP impossibility result. Furthermore, it was shown that when $\lambda = n - k$ and $k \geq 2$, k-set agreement can be solved despite the crash of $2k - 2$ processes.

This paper considers two types of process crash failures: "λ-constrained" crash failures (as previously defined), and classical crash failures (that we call "any time" failures). It presents two algorithms suited to these types of failures. The first algorithm solves k-set agreement, where $k = m + f$, in the presence of $t = 2m + f - 1$ crash failures, $2m$ of them being $(n-k)$-constrained failures, and $(f-1)$ being any time failures. The second algorithm solves $(n + f)$-renaming in the presence of $t = m + f$ crash failures, m of them being $(n - t - 1)$-constrained failures, and f being any time failures. It follows that the differentiation between λ-constrained crash failures and any time crash failures enlarges the space of executions in which the impossibility of k-set agreement and renaming in the presence of asynchrony and process crashes can be circumvented. In addition to its behavioral properties, both algorithms have a noteworthy first class property, namely, their simplicity.

Keywords: Agreement algorithm · Asynchronous system
Atomic register · Concurrency · Contention · ℓ-mutual exclusion
Participating process · Process crash failure · Read/write register
Renaming · k-set agreement

© Springer Nature Switzerland AG 2018
T. Izumi and P. Kuznetsov (Eds.): SSS 2018, LNCS 11201, pp. 269–283, 2018.
https://doi.org/10.1007/978-3-030-03232-6_18

1   Definitions and Motivation

1.1   Processes, Failures, Communication

The system is composed of n asynchronous sequential processes, denoted $p_1, \ldots, p_n$, which communicate by reading and writing atomic registers. The model parameter t denotes the maximal number of processes that may crash during a run. A process crash is a premature definitive halting. A process that crashes is called *faulty*, otherwise it is *correct*.

It is assumed that all correct processes participate, i.e., execute their local algorithm. (Let us notice that this assumption is a classical –very often left implicit– assumption encountered in message-passing distributed algorithms [17].)

Let us call *contention* the current number of processes that started executing. The model parameter λ denotes a predefined contention threshold. So, an execution can be divided into two parts: a prefix in which the contention is $\leq \lambda$ and a suffix in which contention is $> \lambda$. Hence, we consider a failure model in which there are two types of crashes: the ones that can occur only when contention is $\leq \lambda$ that we call "λ-constrained", and the ones that can appear at "any time"; λ-constrained crashes were introduced in [20] under the name "weak failures".

1.2   Motivation for Considering λ-Constrained Failures

As discussed in [20], the new type of λ-constrained failures enables us to design algorithms that can tolerate several traditional "any time" failures plus several additional λ-constrained failures (i.e., weak failures). More precisely, assume that a problem can be solved in the presence of t traditional failures, but cannot be solved in the presence of $t + 1$ such failures. Yet, the problem might be solvable in the presence of $t_1 \leq t$ "any time" failures plus t_2 λ-constrained failures, where $t_1 + t_2 > t$.

Adding the ability to tolerate λ-constrained failures to algorithms that are already designed to circumvent various impossibility results, such as the Paxos algorithm [14] and indulgent algorithms in general [11,12], would make such algorithms even more robust against possible failures. An indulgent algorithm never violates its safety property, and eventually satisfies its liveness property when the synchrony assumptions it relies on are satisfied. An indulgent algorithm which in addition (to being indulgent) tolerates λ-constrained failures may, in many cases, satisfy its liveness property even before the synchrony assumptions it relies on are satisfied.

When facing a failure related impossibility result, such as the impossibility of consensus in the presence of a single faulty process [10], one is often tempted to use a solution which guarantees no resiliency at all. We point out that there is a middle ground: tolerating λ-constrained (weak) failures enables to tolerate failures some of the time. Also, traditional t-resilient algorithms tolerate failures only some of the time (i.e., as long as the number of failures is at most t). After all, something is better than nothing.

The type of λ-constrained failures which are assumed to occur only *before* a specific predefined threshold on the level of contention is reached, is in particular useful in systems in which contention is usually low. Another possible type of weak failures, also defined in [20], in which failures are assumed to occur only *after* a specific predefined threshold on the level of contention is reached, may correspond to a situation where, when there is high contention, processes are slowed down and as a result give up and abort.

Finally, the new failure model establishes a link between contention and failures, which enables us to better understand various known impossibility results, like the impossibility result for consensus [10] and its generalizations [6,13,18].

1.3   High Level Objects

To make the presentation of the proposed algorithms easier, the basic read/write system is enriched with two types of objects, namely ℓ-mutual exclusion and snapshot. Both can be built on top of a crash-prone asynchronous read/write system.

Deadlock-Free ℓ-Mutual Exclusion. Such an object, which provides the processes with the operations acquire() and release(), allows up to ℓ of them to simultaneously execute their critical section. It is defined by the following properties.

– *Mutual exclusion.* No more than ℓ processes can simultaneously be in their critical section.
– *Deadlock-freedom.* If less than ℓ processes crash, and processes are invoking the operation acquire(), at least one of them will terminate its invocation.

It is shown in [2,9,19] that ℓ-mutual exclusion can be built on top of an asynchronous crash-prone read/write system. In the *one-shot* version, a process invokes acquire() and release() at most once.

Snapshot. A snapshot object provides two operations denoted write() and snapshot() [1,3]. Such an object can be seen as an array of single-writer multi-reader atomic register $SN[1..n]$ such that:

(a) when p_i invokes write(v), it writes v into $SN[i]$; and
(b) when p_i invokes snapshot(), it obtains the value of the array $SN[1..n]$ as if it read simultaneously and instantaneously all its entries.

Said another way, the operations write() and snapshot() are atomic. Snapshot objects can be implemented on top of asynchronous crash-prone read/write systems [1,3,16].

2 k-Set Agreement and M-Renaming

2.1 k-Set Agreement

A k-set agreement (k-SA) object is a one-shot object introduced by Chaudhuri [8] to study the relation linking the number of failures and the agreement degree attainable in a set of crash-prone asynchronous processes. Such an object provides a single operation denoted propose(), which allows the invoking process to propose a value and obtain a result (called *decided* value). Assuming each correct process proposes a value, each process must decide on a value such that the following properties are satisfied.

- *Validity.* A decided value is a proposed value.
- *Agreement.* At most k different values are decided.
- *Termination.* Every correct process decides a value.

When $k = 1$, k-set agreement boils down to consensus, whose impossibility in the presence of asynchrony and a single process crashed was proved in [10] for message-passing systems, and in [15] for read/write systems. It was later shown in [6,13,18] that it is impossible to solve k-set agreement in crash-prone asynchronous read/write systems where $t \geq k$. Hence, as the k-set agreement read/write-based algorithm presented in [20] works despite up to $t = 2k - 2$ λ-constrained failures (where $\lambda = n - k$), the introduction of contention-related failures in [20], is a noteworthy advance in fault-tolerance, which enlarges the space of executions in which k-set agreement can be solved.

2.2 M-Renaming

The renaming object was introduced in the context of message-passing system [4]. An introductory survey to renaming in crash-prone asynchronous read/write systems is presented in [7].

An M-renaming object allows n processes with initially distinct names from a large name space to acquire distinct new names from a smaller name space $\{1, \ldots, M\}$, where M is a predefined value known by the processes. A one-shot renaming object allows each process to acquire a distinct new name just once. A long-lived renaming object allows processes to repeatedly acquire distinct names and release them. In this paper, we consider only one-shot renaming objects.

A process p_i accesses an M-renaming object R using the operation $R.\mathsf{rename}(id_i)$, where id_i is its original name, which returns a new name. A process p_i knows neither its index i, nor the original names of the other processes. The properties defining such an object are the following.

- *Validity.* A new name belongs to the set $\{1, \ldots, M\}$.
- *Agreement.* No two processes obtain the same new name.
- *Termination.* If a process invokes $R.\mathsf{rename}(id)$ and does not crash, it returns from its invocation.

In the classical n-process model (i.e., a model where only any time crash failures are considered), it is known that with t any time failures, there is a tight $(n + t)$ bound on the size of new name space for renaming for infinitely many values of n. We will show how this result can be circumvented. The interested reader will find renaming algorithms in textbooks such as [5,16,19].

3   The Results of the Paper at a Glance

As announced in the abstract, this paper is on k-set agreement and M-renaming in an asynchronous read/write model in which there are two kinds of process crashes:

- the "usual" ones, which are allowed to occur at any time, called "any time" failures in the following;
- the ones (introduced in [20]) that are restricted to occur only while the contention has not bypassed a predefined threshold λ, called "λ-constrained" failures in the following.

As announced in the Introduction, let us recall that all the algorithms presented in the paper assume that all correct processes participate.

3.1   Results Concerning k-Set Agreement

The paper presents a general k-set agreement algorithm that, in addition to the model and problem parameters n, t, k, and $\lambda = n-k$, considers two more integers $m \geq 0$ and $f \geq 1$, such that $m + f = k$ and $t = 2m + f - 1$ (or, equivalently, $t = 2k - f - 1$). The fault-tolerance properties of this algorithm are summarized in Table 1.

Table 1. k-set agreement: tolerates crash failures with $\lambda = n - k$ and $k = m + f$

The k-set agreement algorithm: fault-tolerance properties	
Total # of failures tolerated	$t = 2m + f - 1$
"λ-constrained" crash failures	$2m$
"Any time" crash failures	$f - 1$

More generally, the parameters m and f, where $k = m + f$, can be seen as parameters allowing the user to tune the type of crash failures that are dominant in the considered application context. At one extreme, the pair of values $\langle m, f \rangle = \langle 0, k \rangle$ maximizes the number of any time failures, and allows up to any time $k-1$ crash failures. At the other extreme, the pair $\langle m, f \rangle = \langle k - 1, 1 \rangle$ maximizes the number of λ-constrained failures: it allows up to $2k - 2$ λ-constrained failures and no any time failure.

Since $t = 2m + f - 1$ we can say that, intuitively, *one* any time failure "equals" *two* $(n - k)$-constrained failures. That is, it is possible to trade *one* *strong* (any time) failure for *two* *weak* (λ-constrained) failures and vice versa, as demonstrated in Table 2.

Table 2. k-set agreement: tradeoffs "λ-constrained/any time" crash failures, with $\lambda = n - k$

The k-set agreement algorithm: tradeoffs			
Total # of failures	$m = 0$	$m = \lfloor k/2 \rfloor$	$m = k - 1$
$t = 2m + f - 1$	$f = k$	$f = \lfloor k/2 \rfloor$	$f = 1$
$2m$ "λ-constrained" crash failures	0	k	$2k - 2$
$f - 1$ "any time" crash failures	$k - 1$	$\lfloor k/2 \rfloor - 1$	0

Interestingly, the particular instantiation $\langle m, f \rangle = \langle k - 1, 1 \rangle$ boils down to a specific case of the algorithm described in [20][1].

Additionally, as it will become clear in its description, Algorithm 1 presented in Sect. 4 sheds new light on a relation linking k-set agreement and ℓ-mutual exclusion.

3.2 Results Concerning M-Renaming

Considering a new name space of size $M = n + f$, the paper presents a general M-renaming algorithm that, in addition to the model and problem parameters n, t, and $\lambda = n - t - 1$, as previously, considers two integers $m \geq 0$ and $f \geq 0$, such that $t = m + f$. The fault-tolerance properties of this algorithm are summarized in Table 3.

Table 3. M-renaming: tolerated crash failures, with $\lambda = n - t - 1$

The $(n + f)$-renaming algorithm: fault-tolerance properties	
Total # of failures tolerated	$t = m + f$
"λ-constrained" crash failures	m
"Any time" crash failures	f

Similarly to the case of k-set agreement, the parameters m and f, where $t = m + f$, allows the user to tune the type of crash failures and (here) the size of the name space that are dominant in the considered application context. At one extreme, the pair of values $\langle m, f \rangle = \langle 0, t \rangle$ maximizes the number of any time failures (which is good) but also maximizes the size of the name space (which is bad). At the other extreme, the pair $\langle m, f \rangle = \langle t, 0 \rangle$ maximizes the number of λ-constrained failures and minimizes the size of the name space (which is good). This is demonstrated in Table 4.

---

[1] It is proved in [20] that for every two positive integers ℓ and k, there is a k-set agreement algorithm for n processes, using registers, that can tolerate $\ell + k - 2$ λ-constrained crash failures, where $\lambda = n - \ell$. So, for the special case where $\ell = k$, the algorithm can be tolerated $2k - 2$ $(n - k)$-constrained failures.

Table 4. M-renaming: tradeoffs "λ-constrained/any time" crash failures, with $\lambda = n - t - 1$

The $(n + f)$-renaming algorithm: tradeoffs			
Total # of failures	$m = 0$	$m = \lfloor k/2 \rfloor$	$m = t$
$t = m + f$	$f = t$	$f = \lfloor k/2 \rfloor$	$f = 0$
m "λ-constrained" crash failures	0	$\lfloor k/2 \rfloor$	t
f "any time" crash failures	t	$\lfloor k/2 \rfloor$	0
The size of name space	$n + t$	$n + \lfloor k/2 \rfloor$	n

4 k-Set Agreement: Algorithm ($k \geq 2$)

This section presents a k-set agreement algorithm that allows to circumvent the known impossibility result for solving k-set agreement in crash-prone asynchronous read/write systems where $t \geq k$ [6,13,18]. The algorithm considers the contention-related failure model, and assumes all correct processes participate. It is characterized by the following theorem.

Theorem 1. *For any $n \geq 1$, $n - 1 \geq t \geq 0$, $m \geq 0$ and $f \geq 1$ such that $t = 2m + f - 1$ and $k = m + f$, it is possible to solve k-set agreement for n processes in the presence of at most t crash failures, $2m$ of them being λ-constrained failures where $\lambda = n - k$, and $f - 1$ of them being any time failures.*

In the algorithm described below, it is assumed that the identity of a process p_i is its index i.

Shared Objects. The processes cooperate through the following objects.

- $PART[1..n]$: snapshot object, initialized to $[\mathsf{down}, \cdots, \mathsf{down}]$, used to indicate participation.
- DEC: atomic register initialized to $\bot$ (a value which cannot be proposed). It will contain values (one at a time) that can be decided.
- $MUTEX[1]$: one-shot deadlock-free f-mutex object.
- $MUTEX[2]$: one-shot deadlock-free m-mutex object.

For the special case where $m = 0$ and $f = k$, in the proposed algorithm no process will ever try to access the $MUTEX[2]$ object. Thus, there is no need to define the notion of a 0-mutex object.

Local Variables. Each process p_i manages the following local variables: $part_i$ is used to locally store a copy of the snapshot object $PART$; $count_i$ is a local counter; and $group_i$ a binary variable whose value belongs to $\{1, 2\}$.

Behavior of a Process p_i. Algorithm 1 describes the behavior of a process p_i. When it invokes propose(in_i) (where in_i is the value it proposes), p_i first indicates it is participating (line 1). Then it invokes the snapshot object until at least $n - t$ processes are participating (lines 2–4). When this occurs, p_i enters group 1 or

---

operation propose(in_i) **is**

(1) $PART$.write(up);
(2)   **repeat** $part_i \leftarrow PART$.snapshot();
(3) $count_i \leftarrow |\{x \text{ such that } part_i[x] = \text{up}\}|$;
(4)   **until** $count_i \geq n - t$ **end repeat**;
(5)   **if** $count_i \leq n - k$ **then** $group_i \leftarrow 2$ **else** $group_i \leftarrow 1$ **end if**;
(6)   launch in parallel the threads $T1$ and $T2$.
% Both threads and the operation terminate when p_i invokes return() (line 7 or 12).

thread $T1$ **is**
(7)   **loop forever if** $DEC \neq \bot$ **then** return(DEC) **end if end loop**.

thread $T2$ **is**
(8)   **if** $group_i = 1 \vee m > 0$ **then**
(9) $MUTEX[group_i]$.acquire();
(10)   **if** $DEC = \bot$ **then** $DEC \leftarrow in_i$ **end if**;
(11) $MUTEX[group_i]$.release();
(12)   return(DEC).
(13) **end if**;

Algorithm 1: k-SA despite up to $2m$ "$(n - k)$-constrained" and $f - 1$ "any time" failures

group 2 according to the value of its counter $count_i$ (line 5), and launches in parallel two threads $T1$ and $T2$ (line 6).

In the thread $T1$, p_i loop forever until DEC contains a proposed value. When this happens p_i decides it (line 7). The execution of return() at line 7 or 12 terminates the invocation of propose().

The thread $T2$ is the core of the algorithm. Process p_i tries to enter the critical section controlled by either the f-mutex or the m-mutex object $MUTEX[group_i]$ (line 9). If it succeeds and DEC has still its initial default value, p_i assigns it the value in_i it proposed (line 10). Finally, p_i releases the critical section (line 11), and decides (line 12). Let us remind that, as far as $MUTEX[1]$ (respectively, $MUTEX[2]$) is concerned, up to f (respectively, m) processes can simultaneously execute line 10.

Remark. The reader can check that the line 8 (together with line 13) and line 11 can be suppressed without compromising the correctness of the algorithm. This is a side-effect of task $T1$. For clarity, we nevertheless keep these lines.

5 k-Set Agreement: Proof

Lemma 1. *At most $n - k$ processes have a counter less or equal to $n - k$ when leaving the repeat loop (lines 2–4).*

Proof. Assume by contradiction that more than $n - k$ processes have their counter less or equal to $n - k$ when leaving the repeat loop (2–4). P being this set of processes, we have $|P| \geq n-k+1$. Moreover, let p_i be the last process of P that invokes $PART$.snapshot() (line 1). It follows from the atomicity of the write() and snapshot() operations on the object $PART$ that $count_i \geq |P| \geq n-k+1$, a contradiction.   □

Lemma 2. *In the presence of at most $t = 2m+f-1$ crash failures, $2m$ of them being $(n-k)$-constrained, if processes participate in $MUTEX[1]$, at most $f-1$ of them can fail.*

Proof. If a process p_i participates in $MUTEX[1]$ it follows from line 5 that $count_i > n-k$ when it exited the repeat loop (lines 2–4). Thus, the contention was at least $n-k+1$ when p_i exited the loop and, due to the definition of "$(n-k)$-constrained crash failures", there is no more such failures. As $t = 2m+f-1$, it follows that, if processes participate in $MUTEX[1]$, at most $f-1$ of them can fail.   □

Theorem 2 (Termination). *In the presence of at most $t = 2m+f-1$ crash failures, $2m$ of them being $(n-k)$-constrained, every correct process eventually terminates.*

Proof. Since there is at most t processes that may fail and participation is required, at least $n-t$ processes set their participating flag to up in the snapshot object $PART$ (line 1). Thus, no correct process remains stuck forever in the repeat loop (lines 2–4).

First, assume $m = 0$. By Lemma 1, at most $n-k$ processes have a counter less or equal to $n-k$ when they exit the repeat loop (lines 2–4). Thus, at most $n-k$ processes belong to group 2. If $m = 0$, there is $n-t = n-f+1$ correct processes and, since $k = f$, $n-f+1 > n-k$. So, among the processes participating in $MUTEX[1]$, at least one of them is correct and at most $f-1$ of them crash before returning from $MUTEX[1]$.release() (line 11). Due to the deadlock-freedom property of the one-shot f-mutex object $MUTEX[1]$, at least one correct process eventually enters its critical section and, if DEC has not already been written, writes its input into DEC. It then follows from task $T1$ that, if it does not terminate at line 11, every other correct process will decide and terminate.

Now, assume $m > 0$. There are two cases.

- If at least $y \geq f$ processes participate in $MUTEX[1]$, it follows from Lemma 2 that at most $f-1$ of them crash before returning from $MUTEX[1]$.release() (line 11), and consequently all other processes participating in $MUTEX[1]$ are correct. As $y > f-1$ and $f > 0$, there is at least one such correct process, say p_x. Due to the deadlock-freedom property of the one-shot f-mutex object $MUTEX[1]$, p_x eventually enters its critical section and, if DEC has not already been written, writes its input into DEC.
- Otherwise, less than f processes participate in $MUTEX[1]$. There are two sub-cases.

- If a correct process p_i participates in $MUTEX[1]$, it follows from this sub-case assumption and the deadlock-freedom property of the one-shot f-mutex object $MUTEX[1]$, that p_i eventually enters its critical section and, if $DEC = \perp$, writes its input in_x into this atomic register.
- Otherwise, no correct process participates in $MUTEX[1]$. By Lemma 1, at most $n - k$ processes have a counter less or equal to $n - k$ when they exit the repeat loop (lines 2–4). So at most $n - k$ processes participate in $MUTEX[2]$. Since no correct process participates in $MUTEX[1]$, all correct processes (they are at least $n-t$) participate in $MUTEX[2]$. Thus, at most $(n - k) - (n - t) = t - k = 2m + f - 1 - (m + f) = m - 1$ processes that participate in $MUTEX[2]$ fail. Hence, due to the deadlock-freedom property of the one-shot m-mutex object $MUTEX[2]$, at least one correct process enters its critical section and, if $DEC = \perp$, writes its input into DEC.

In both cases, every other correct process will decide and terminate.   □

Theorem 3 (Agreement and validity). *At most k different values are decided, and each of them is the input of some process.*

Proof. If a process decides (line 7 or line 12), it decides on the current value of DEC, which –due to the predicates of line 7 or line 10– has previously been set –at line 10– to the value proposed by a process. Due to the predicate and the assignment of DEC at line 10, and the fact that $MUTEX[1]$ is a f-mutex object, it follows that at most f processes assign a value to DEC in the critical section controlled by $MUTEX[1]$. Due to a similar argument, at most m processes assign a value to DEC in the critical section controlled by $MUTEX[2]$. Thus, at most $m + f = k$ different values can be written into DEC, and each of them is a proposed value.   □

As its proof involves neither the timing nor the number of failures, Theorem 3 gives rise to the following property (called *indulgence* [11,12]).

Corollary 1. *Whatever the time occurrence and the number of crash failures, the k-set agreement and validity properties are never violated.*

6 M-Renaming: Algorithm

This section presents a renaming algorithm that allows to circumvent the $(n+t)$ tight bound on the size of name space for renaming for infinitely many values of n. This algorithm considers the contention-related failure model, and assumes all correct processes participate. It is characterized by the following theorem.

Theorem 4. *For any $n \geq 1$, $n-1 \geq t \geq 0$, $m \geq 0$ and $f \geq 0$ such that $t = m+f$, it possible to solve $(n + f)$-renaming for n processes in the presence of at most t crash failures, m of them being λ-constrained failures where $\lambda = n - t - 1$, and f of them being any time failures.*

```
operation rename(id_i) is
(1)    PART.write(up);
(2)    repeat part_i ← PART.snapshot();
(3)           count_i ← |{x such that part_i[x] = up}|
(4)    until count_i ≥ n − t end repeat;
(5)    new_name_i ← RENAMING_f.rename(id_i);
(6)    return(new_name_i).
```

Algorithm 2: $(n + f)$-renaming despite up to m "$(n − t − 1)$-constrained" and f "any time" failures, where $t = m + f$

Shared Objects. The processes cooperate through the following objects.

- $PART[1..n]$: snapshot object, initialized to $[\textbf{down}, \cdots, \textbf{down}]$, used to indicate participation.
- $RENAMING_f$: $(n + f)$-renaming object which can tolerate up to f any time crash failures for a model where participation is not required. The fact that participation is not required means that a process that does not participate is *not* consider faulty. The object is not assumed to tolerate any additional λ-constrained failures. An example of such an algorithm is described in [5] (pages 359–360).

Local Variables. Each process p_i manages the following local variables: $part_i$ is used to locally store a copy of the snapshot object $PART$; $count_i$ is a local counter; id_i and new_name_i are used to store the original and new names, respectively.

Behavior of a Process p_i. Algorithm 2 describes the behavior of a process p_i. Every process p_i keeps on taking snapshots until it notices that $n − t$ processes (including itself) are participating. Then, the process invokes a rename operation of a $RENAMING_f$ object, stores the value of its new name in new_name_i, and returns this value.

7 M-Renaming: Proof

Lemma 3. *In the presence of at most $t = m + f$ crash failures, m of them being $(n − t − 1)$-constrained, if processes participate in $RENAMING_f$, at most f of them can fail.*

Proof. If a process p_i participates in $RENAMING_f$ it follows from line 4 that the predicate $count_i ≥ n − t$ is satisfied when it exited the repeat loop (lines 2–4). Thus, the contention was at least $n − t$ when p_i exited the loop and, due to the definition of "$(n − t − 1)$-constrained crash failures", there is no more such failures. As $t = m + f$, it follows that, if processes participate in $RENAMING_f$, at most f of them can fail.   □

Theorem 5. (Termination). *In the presence of at most $t = m + f$ crash failures, m of them being $(n-t-1)$-constrained, every correct process eventually terminates.*

Proof. Since there is at most t processes that may fail and participation is required, at least $n - t$ processes set their participating flag to up in the snapshot object $PART$ (line 1). Thus, no correct process remains stuck forever in the repeat loop (lines 2–4).

By Lemma 3, if processes participate in $RENAMING_f$, at most f of them can fail. Since, by definition, (1) $RENAMING_f$ can tolerate f any time failures, and (2) in $RENAMING_f$ participation is not required, it follows that every operation invoked by a correct processes on $RENAMING_f$ must return a value. Thus, every correct process eventually terminates.   □

Theorem 6. (Agreement and validity). *In the presence of at most $t = m+f$ crash failures, m of them being $(n-t-1)$-constrained, (1) no two processes decide on the same new name, and (2) the new names are in the range $[1..n + f]$.*

Proof. By Lemma 3, at most f processes can fail while executing $RENAMING_f$. Since, $RENAMING_f$ is an $(n + f)$-renaming object which can tolerate up to f crash failures for a model where participation is not required, any correct process that participates in $RENAMING_f$ must acquire a unique new name in the range $[1..n + f]$.   □

8   From M-Renaming to One-Shot Concurrent Objects

Let us consider any one-shot concurrent object OB, which provides a single operation op(), and tolerate up to x any time crash failures in a model where participation is not required.

This section presents an algorithm that transforms OB in an object OB' where, assuming all processes participate (i.e., invoke op()), allows to withstand additional λ-constrained crash failures. As in the previous sections, the transformation considers the parameters $n, t, \lambda = n-t-1, m \geq 0$, and $0 \leq f \leq x-1$. The fault-tolerance properties of the resulting object OB' are summarized in Table 5 (where, let us remind, x is the number of any time crash failures tolerated by the underlying object OB').

Table 5. Crash failures tolerated by OB', where $\lambda = n - t - 1$

Total # of failures tolerated	$t = m + f$
"λ-constrained" crash failures	m
"Any time" crash failures	$f \leq x - 1$

As before, the parameters m and f are parameters that allow the user to tune the type of crash failures that are dominant in the considered application context. At one extreme, the pair of values $\langle m, f \rangle = \langle t-x+1, x-1 \rangle$ maximizes the number of any time failures, and allows up to $x-1$ any time crash failures. At the other extreme, the pair $\langle m, f \rangle = \langle t, 0 \rangle$ maximizes the number of λ-constrained failures: it allows up to t λ-constrained failures and no any time failure. This is described in Table 6.

Table 6. Tradeoffs "λ-constrained/any time" crash failures ($\lambda = n - t - 1$)

Total # of failures	$t = m + f$		
m "λ-constrained" crash failures	$t - x + 1$	$t - \lfloor \frac{x}{2} \rfloor$	t
f "any time" crash failures	$x - 1$	$\lfloor \frac{x}{2} \rfloor$	0

Algorithm 3 transforms of OB into OB'. It is the same as Algorithm 2, which implements an M-renaming object coping with both λ-constrained failures and any time failures. The meaning of the underlying shared objects and local variables are the same as in Algorithm 2. In addition, res_i contains the result of the underlying invocation $OB.\mathsf{op}(in)$ (line 5), where in is the input parameter of $\mathsf{op}()$. The proof, which is the same as the one given in Sect. 7, is left to the reader.

```
operation op(in) is % applied to OB'
(1)    PART.write(up);
(2)    repeat parti ← PART.snapshot();
(3)            counti ← |{x such that parti[x] = up}|
(4)    until counti ≥ n − t end repeat;
(5)    resi ← OB.op(in);
(6)    return(resi).
```

Algorithm 3: Transformation of the operation op of a one-shot object tolerating up to m "$(n - t - 1)$-constrained" failures and f "any time" failures, where $t = m + f$

9   Conclusion

This paper addressed a process crash failure model in which some number of processes may crash only when process contention has not bypassed a predefined threshold λ, while another number of processes may crash at any time. It has been shown that this failure model allows impossibility results to be circumvented. To this end, the paper has presented algorithms building k-set agreement and renaming objects in such a model. So, it extends the set of possible executions in which k-set agreement and renaming can be solved despite asynchrony and process crashes. The proposed algorithms allow their users to tune them to specific failure-prone environments. This can be done by appropriately defining the pair of integers $\langle m, f \rangle$. As an example, considering k-set agreement, these parameters control the number of crashes allowed to occur before the contention threshold $\lambda = n - k$ is bypassed, namely $2m = 2(k - f)$, and the number of failures which can occur at any time, namely, $f - 1$. That is, it is possible to trade *one strong* "any time" failure for *two weak* "$(n - k)$-constrained" failures, and vice versa.

Finally, some issues remain challenging on the open problem side. More specifically, on the complexity/computability side of k-set agreement, it would be interesting to find out whether the upper bound we have proved on the number of failures $t = 2m + f - 1$ (where $2m$ failures are $(n - k)$-constrained and $f - 1$ failures are any time failures) is tight for $k \geq 2$. On the algorithm design side, as there is an algorithm (and a tight bound) for 1-agreement (see [20]), it would be interesting to find a more general algorithm, i.e., an algorithm which works for $k \geq 1$ (and not only for $k \geq 2$).

Acknowledgments. We thank Armando Castañeda for helpful discussions on the renaming problem. This work has been partially supported by the Franco-German DFG-ANR Project 40300781 DISCMAT (devoted to connections between mathematics and distributed computing), and the French ANR project ANR-16-CE40-0023-03 DESCARTES (devoted to layered and modular structures in distributed computing).

Last but not least, the authors also thank the referees for their constructive comments.

References

1. Afek, Y., Attiya, H., Dolev, D., Gafni, E., Merritt, M., Shavit, N.: Atomic snapshots of shared memory. J. ACM **40**(4), 873–890 (1993)
2. Afek, Y., Dolev, D., Gafni, E., Merritt, M., Shavit, S.: A bounded first-in, first-enabled solution to the ℓ-exclusion problem. ACM Trans. Program. Lang. Syst. **16**(3), 939–953 (1994)
3. Anderson, J.: Multi-writer composite registers. Distrib. Comput. **7**(4), 175–195 (1994)
4. Attiya, H., Bar-Noy, A., Dolev, D., Peleg, D., Reischuk, R.: Renaming in an asynchronous environment. J. ACM **37**(3), 524–548 (1990)
5. Attiya, H., Welch, J.L.: Distributed Computing: Fundamentals, Simulations and Advanced Topics, 2nd edn, p. 414. Wiley-Interscience, Hoboken (2004). ISBN 0-471-45324-2
6. Borowsky, E., Gafni, E.: Generalized FLP impossibility results for t-resilient asynchronous computations. In: Proceedings of 25th ACM Symposium on Theory of Computing (STOC 1993), pp. 91–100. ACM Press (1993)
7. Castañeda, A., Rajsbaum, S., Raynal, M.: The renaming problem in shared memory systems: an introduction. Comput. Sci. Rev. **5**, 229–251 (2011)
8. Chaudhuri, S.: More choices allow more faults: set consensus problems in totally asynchronous systems. Inf. Comput. **105**(1), 132–158 (1993)

9. Fischer, M.J., Lynch, N.A., Burns, J.E., Borodin, A.: Resource allocation with immunity to limited process failure (Preliminary Report). In: Proceedings of 20th IEEE Symposium on Foundations Of Computer Science (FOCS 1979), pp. 234–254. IEEE Press (1979)
10. Fischer, M.J., Lynch, N.A., Paterson, M.S.: Impossibility of distributed consensus with one faulty process. J. ACM **32**(2), 374–382 (1985)
11. Guerraoui, R.: Indulgent algorithms. In: Proceedings of 19th Annual ACM Symposium on Principles of Distributed Computing (PODC 2000), pp. 289–297. ACM Press (2000)
12. Guerraoui, R., Raynal, M.: The information structure of indulgent consensus. IEEE Trans. Comput. **53**(4), 453–466 (2004)
13. Herlihy, M.P., Shavit, N.: The topological structure of asynchronous computability. J. ACM **46**(6), 858–923 (1999)
14. Lamport, L.: The part-time parliament. ACM Trans. Comput. Syst. **16**(2), 133–169 (1998)
15. Loui, M., Abu-Amara, H.: Memory requirements for agreement among unreliable asynchronous processes. Adv. Comput. Res. **4**, 163–183 (1987)
16. Raynal, M.: Concurrent Programming: Algorithms, Principles and Foundations, p. 515. Springer, Heidelberg (2013). https://doi.org/10.1007/978-3-642-32027-9. ISBN 978-3-642-32026-2
17. Raynal, M.: Fault-tolerant message-passing distributed systems: an algorithmic approach, p. 550. Springer, Heidelberg (2018). https://doi.org/10.1007/978-3-319-94141-7. ISBN 978-3-319-94140-0
18. Saks, M., Zaharoglou, F.: Wait-free k-set agreement is impossible: the topology of public knowledge. SIAM J. Comput. **29**(5), 1449–1483 (2000)
19. Taubenfeld, G.: Synchronization Algorithms and Concurrent Programming, p. 423. Pearson Education/Prentice Hall, Upper Saddle River (2006). ISBN 0-131-97259-6
20. Taubenfeld, G.: Weak failures: definition, algorithms, and impossibility results. In: Proceedings of 6th International Conference on Networked Systems (NETYS 2018). LNCS, p. 15. Springer, Heidelberg (2018)

An Innovative Approach to Achieve Compositionality Efficiently Using Multi-version Object Based Transactional Systems

Chirag Juyal[1], Sandeep Kulkarni[2], Sweta Kumari[1], Sathya Peri[1], and Archit Somani[1(✉)]

[1] Department of Computer Science and Engineering,
IIT Hyderabad, Kandi, Telangana, India
{cs17mtech11014,cs15resch01004,sathya_p,cs15resch01001}@iith.ac.in
[2] Department of Computer Science, Michigan State University,
East Lansing, MI, USA
sandeep@cse.msu.edu

Abstract. The rise of multi-core systems has necessitated the need for concurrent programming. However, developing correct, efficient concurrent programs is notoriously difficult. Software Transactional Memory Systems (STMs) are a convenient programming interface for a programmer to access shared memory without worrying about concurrency issues. Another advantage of STMs is that they facilitate compositionality of concurrent programs with great ease. Different concurrent operations that need to be composed to form a single atomic unit is achieved by encapsulating them in a single transaction.

Most of the STMs proposed in the literature are based on read/write primitive operations on memory buffers. We denote them as *Read-Write STMs* or *RWSTMs*. On the other hand, there have been some STMs that have been proposed (transactional boosting and its variants) that work on higher level operations such as hash-table insert, delete, lookup, etc. We call them Object STMs or OSTMs.

It was observed in databases that storing multiple versions in RWSTMs provides greater concurrency. In this paper, we combine both these ideas for harnessing greater concurrency in STMs - multiple versions with objects semantics. We propose the notion of *Multi-version Object STMs* or *MVOSTMs*. Specifically, we introduce and implement *MVOSTM* for the hash-table object, denoted as *HTMVOSTM* and list object, *list-MVOSTM*. These objects export insert, delete and lookup methods within the transactional framework. We also show that both

A poster version of this work received **best poster award** in NETYS-2018. An initial version of this work was accepted as **work in progress** in AADDA workshop, *ICDCN* − 2018.

This research work is partially supported by NSF XPS 1533802 and IMPRINT India project 6918F.

Author sequence follows the lexical order of last names.

© Springer Nature Switzerland AG 2018
T. Izumi and P. Kuznetsov (Eds.): SSS 2018, LNCS 11201, pp. 284–300, 2018.
https://doi.org/10.1007/978-3-030-03232-6_19

these *MVOSTM*s satisfy opacity and ensure that transaction with lookup only methods do not abort if unbounded versions are used.

Experimental results show that *list-MVOSTM* outperform almost two to twenty fold speedup than existing state-of-the-art list based STMs (Trans-list, Boosting-list, NOrec-list, list-MVTO, and list-OSTM). Similarly, *HT-MVOSTM* shows a significant performance gain of almost two to nineteen times over the existing state-of-the-art hash-table based STMs (ESTM, RWSTMs, HT-MVTO, and HT-OSTM).

1   Introduction

The rise of multi-core systems has necessitated the need for concurrent programming. However, developing correct concurrent programs without compromising on efficiency is a big challenge. Software Transactional Memory Systems (STMs) are a convenient programming interface for a programmer to access shared memory without worrying about concurrency issues. Another advantage of STMs is that they facilitate compositionality of concurrent programs with great ease. Different concurrent operations that need to be composed to form a single atomic unit is achieved by encapsulating them in a single transaction. Next, we discuss different types of STMs considered in the literature and identify the need to develop multi-version object STMs proposed in this paper.

Read-Write STMs: Most of the STMs proposed in the literature (such as NOrec [1], ESTM [2]) are based on read/write operations on *transaction objects* or *t-objects*. We denote them as *Read Write STMs* or *RWSTMs*. These STMs typically export following methods: (1) *t_begin*: begins a transaction, (2) *t_read* (or *r*): reads from a t-object, (3) *t_write* (or *w*): writes to a t-object, (4) *tryC*: validates and tries to commit the transaction by writing values to the shared memory. If validation is successful, then it returns commit. Otherwise, it returns abort.

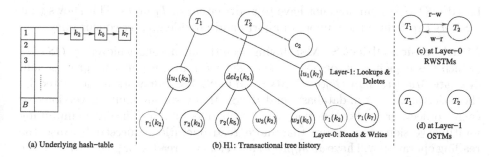

(a) Underlying hash–table   (b) H1: Transactional tree history

Fig. 1. Advantages of OSTMs over RWSTMs

Object STMs: Some STMs have been proposed that work on higher level operations such as hash-table. We call them *Object STMs* or *OSTMs*. It has been shown that *OSTM*s provide greater concurrency. The concept of Boosting by Herlihy et al. [3], the optimistic variant by Hassan et al. [4] and more recently *HT-OSTM* system by Peri et al. [5] are some examples that demonstrate the performance benefits achieved by *OSTM*s.

Benefit of *OTM*s over *RWTM*s: We now illustrate the advantage of *OSTM*s by considering a hash-table based STM system. We assume that the operations of the hash-table are insert (or *ins*), lookup (or *lu*) and delete (or *del*). Each hash-table consists of B buckets with the elements in each bucket arranged in the form of a linked-list. Figure 1(a) represents a hash-table with the first bucket containing keys $\langle k_2, k_5, k_7 \rangle$. Figure 1(b) shows the execution by two transaction T_1 and T_2 represented in the form of a tree. T_1 performs lookup operations on keys k_2 and k_7 while T_2 performs a delete on k_5. The delete on key k_5 generates read on the keys k_2, k_5 and writes the keys k_2, k_5 assuming that delete is performed similar to delete operation in lazy-list [6]. The lookup on k_2 generates read on k_2 while the lookup on k_7 generates read on k_2, k_7. Note that in this execution k_5 has already been deleted by the time lookup on k_7 is performed.

In this execution, we denote the read-write operations (leaves) as layer-0 and lu, del methods as layer-1. Consider the history (execution) at layer-0 (while ignoring higher-level operations), denoted as $H0$. It can be verified this history is not opaque [7]. This is because between the two reads of k_2 by T_1, T_2 writes to k_2. It can be seen that if history $H0$ is input to a *RWSTM*s one of the transactions between T_1 or T_2 would be aborted to ensure opacity [7]. The Fig. 1(c) shows the presence of a cycle in the conflict graph of $H0$.

Now, consider the history $H1$ at layer-1 consists of lu, and del methods, while ignoring the read/write operations since they do not overlap (referred to as pruning in [8, Chap. 6]). These methods work on distinct keys (k_2, k_5, and k_7). They do not overlap and are not conflicting. So, they can be re-ordered in either way. Thus, $H1$ is opaque [7] with equivalent serial history $T_1 T_2$ (or $T_2 T_1$) and the corresponding conflict graph shown in Fig. 1(d). Hence, a hash-table based *OSTM* system does not have to abort either of T_1 or T_2. This shows that *OSTM*s can reduce the number of aborts and provide greater concurrency.

Multi-version Object STMs: Having seen the advantage achieved by *OSTM*s (which was exploited in some works such as [3–5]), in this paper we propose and evaluate *Multi-version Object STMs* or *MVOSTMs*. Our work is motivated by the observation that in databases and *RWSTM*s by storing multiple versions for each t-object, greater concurrency can be obtained [9]. Specifically, maintaining multiple versions can ensure that more read operations succeed because the reading operation will have an appropriate version to read. Our goal is to evaluate the benefit of *MVOSTM*s over both multi-version *RWSTM*s as well as single version *OSTM*s.

Potential Benefit of *MVOSTM*s over *OSTM*s and Multi-version *RWSTM*s: We now illustrate the advantage of *MVOSTM*s as compared to single-version *OSTM*s (*SV-OSTM*s) using hash-table object having the same

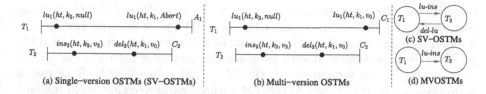

Fig. 2. Advantages of multi-version over single version $OSTM$

operations as discussed above: ins, lu, del. Figure 2(a) represents a history H with two concurrent transactions T_1 and T_2 operating on a hash-table ht. T_1 first tries to perform a lu on key k_2. But due to the absence of key k_2 in ht, it obtains a value of $null$. Then T_2 invokes ins method on the same key k_2 and inserts the value v_2 in ht. Then T_2 deletes the key k_1 from ht and returns v_0 implying that some other transaction had previously inserted v_0 into k_1. The second method of T_1 is lu on the key k_1. With this execution, any $SV\text{-}OSTM$ system has to return abort for T_1's lu operation to ensure correctness, i.e., opacity. Otherwise, if T_1 would have obtained a return value v_0 for k_1, then the history would not be opaque anymore. This is reflected by a cycle in the corresponding conflict graph between T_1 and T_2, as shown in Fig. 2(c). Thus to ensure opacity, $SV\text{-}OSTM$ system has to return abort for T_1's lookup on k_1.

In an $MVOSTM$ based on hash-table, denoted as $HT\text{-}MVOSTM$, whenever a transaction inserts or deletes a key k, a new version is created. Consider the above example with a $HT\text{-}MVOSTM$, as shown in Fig. 2(b). Even after T_2 deletes k_1, the previous value of v_0 is still retained. Thus, when T_1 invokes lu on k_1 after the delete on k_1 by T_2, $HT\text{-}MVOSTM$ return v_0 (as previous value). With this, the resulting history is opaque with equivalent serial history being T_1T_2. The corresponding conflict graph is shown in Fig. 2(d) does not have a cycle.

Thus, $MVOSTM$ reduces the number of aborts and achieve greater concurrency than $SV\text{-}OSTM$s while ensuring the compositionality. We believe that the benefit of $MVOSTM$ over multi-version $RWSTM$ is similar to $SV\text{-}OSTM$ over single-version $RWSTM$ as explained above.

$MVOSTM$ is a generic concept which can be applied to any data structure. In this paper, we have considered the list and hash-table based $MVOSTM$s, $list\text{-}MVOSTM$ and $HT\text{-}MVOSTM$ respectively. Experimental results of list-MVOSTM outperform almost two to twenty fold speedup than existing state-of-the-art STMs used to implement a list: Trans-list [10], Boosting-list [3], NOrec-list [1] and $SV\text{-}OSTM$ [5] under high contention. Similarly, $HT\text{-}MVOSTM$ shows significant performance gain almost two to nineteen times better than existing state-of-the-art STMs used to implement a hash-table: ESTM [2], NOrec [1] and $SV\text{-}OSTM$ [5]. To the best of our knowledge, this is the first work to explore the idea of using multiple versions in $OSTM$s to achieve greater concurrency.

$HT\text{-}MVOSTM$ and $list\text{-}MVOSTM$ use an unbounded number of versions for each key. To address this issue, we develop two variants for both hash-table and list data structures (or DS): (1) A garbage collection method in $MVOSTM$

to delete the unwanted versions of a key, denoted as *MVOSTM-GC*. Garbage collection gave a performance gain of 15% over *MVOSTM* without garbage collection in the best case. Thus, the overhead of garbage collection is less than the performance improvement due to improved memory usage. (2) Placing a limit of K on the number versions in *MVOSTM*, resulting in *KOSTM*. This gave a performance gain of 22% over *MVOSTM* without garbage collection in the best case.

Contributions of the Paper:

- We propose a new notion of multi-version objects based STM system, *MVOSTM*. Specifically develop it for list and hash-table objects, *list-MVOSTM* and *HT-MVOSTM* respectively.
- We show *list-MVOSTM* and *HT-MVOSTM* satisfy *opacity* [7], standard correctness-criterion for STMs.
- Our experiments show that both *list-MVOSTM* and *HT-MVOSTM* provides greater concurrency and reduces the number of aborts as compared to *SV-OSTMs*, single-version *RWSTMs* and, multi-version *RWSTMs*. We achieve this by maintaining multiple versions corresponding to each key.
- For efficient space utilization in *MVOSTM* with unbounded versions we develop *Garbage Collection* for *MVOSTM* (i.e. *MVOSTM-GC*) and bounded version *MVOSTM* (i.e. *KOSTM*).

2   Building System Model

The basic model we consider is adapted from Peri et al. [5]. We assume that our system consists of a finite set of P processors, accessed by a finite number of n threads that run in a completely asynchronous manner and communicate using shared objects. The threads communicate with each other by invoking higher-level methods on the shared objects and getting corresponding responses. Consequently, we make no assumption about the relative speeds of the threads. We also assume that none of these processors and threads fail or crash abruptly.

Events and Methods: We assume that the threads execute atomic *events* and the events by different threads are (1) read/write on shared/local memory objects, (2) method invocations (or *inv*) event and responses (or *rsp*) event on higher level shared-memory objects.

Within a transaction, a process can invoke layer-1 methods (or operations) on a *hash-table* t-object. A hash-table(ht) consists of multiple key-value pairs of the form $\langle k, v \rangle$. The keys and values are respectively from sets $\mathcal{K}$ and $\mathcal{V}$. The methods that a thread can invoke are: (1) t_begin_i: begins a transaction and returns a unique id to the invoking thread. (2) $t\_insert_i(ht, k, v)$: transaction T_i inserts a value v onto key k in ht. (3) $t\_delete_i(ht, k, v)$: transaction T_i deletes the key k from the hash-table ht and returns the current value v for T_i. If key k does not exist, it returns *null*. (4) $t\_lookup_i(ht, k, v)$: returns the current value v for key k in ht for T_i. Similar to t_delete, if the key k does not exist then t_lookup

returns *null*. (5) $tryC_i$: which tries to commit all the operations of T_i and (6) $tryA_i$: aborts T_i. We assume that each method consists of an *inv* and *rsp* event.

We denote *t_insert* and *t_delete* as *update* methods (or *upd_method*) since both of these change the underlying data structure. We denote *t_delete* and *t_lookup* as *return-value methods (or rv_method)* as these operations return values from *ht*. A method may return *ok* if successful or $\mathscr{A}$(abort) if it sees an inconsistent state of *ht*.

Transactions: Following the notations used in database multi-level transactions [8], we model a transaction as a two-level tree. The *layer-0* consist of read/write events and *layer-1* of the tree consists of methods invoked by a transaction.

Having informally explained a transaction, we formally define a transaction T as the tuple $\langle evts(T), <_T \rangle$. Here $evts(T)$ are all the read/write events at *layer-0* of the transaction. $<_T$ is a total order among all the events of the transaction.

We denote the first and last events of a transaction T_i as $T_i.firstEvt$ and $T_i.lastEvt$. Given any other read/write event rw in T_i, we assume that $T_i.firstEvt <_{T_i} rw <_{T_i} T_i.lastEvt$. All the methods of T_i are denoted as $methods(T_i)$.

Histories: A *history* is a sequence of events belonging to different transactions. The collection of events is denoted as $evts(H)$. Similar to a transaction, we denote a history H as tuple $\langle evts(H), <_H \rangle$ where all the events are totally ordered by $<_H$. The set of methods that are in H is denoted by $methods(H)$. A method m is *incomplete* if $inv(m)$ is in $evts(H)$ but not its corresponding response event. Otherwise, m is *complete* in H.

Coming to transactions in H, the set of transactions in H are denoted as $txns(H)$. The set of committed (resp., aborted) transactions in H is denoted by *committed(H)* (resp., *aborted(H)*). The set of *live* transactions in H are those which are neither committed nor aborted. On the other hand, the set of *terminated* transactions are those which have either committed or aborted.

We denote two histories H_1, H_2 as *equivalent* if their events are the same, i.e., $evts(H_1) = evts(H_2)$. A history H is qualified to be *well-formed* if: (1) all the methods of a transaction T_i in H are totally ordered, i.e. a transaction invokes a method only after it receives a response of the previous method invoked by it (2) T_i does not invoke any other method after it received an $\mathscr{A}$ response or after $tryC(ok)$ method. We only consider *well-formed* histories for *OSTM*.

A method m_{ij} (j^{th} method of a transaction T_i) in a history H is said to be *isolated* or *atomic* if for any other event e_{pqr} (r^{th} event of method m_{pq}) belonging to some other method m_{pq} of transaction T_p either e_{pqr} occurs before $inv(m_{ij})$ or after $rsp(m_{ij})$.

Sequential Histories: A history H is said to be *sequential* (term used in [11, 12]) if all the methods in it are complete and isolated. From now onwards, most of our discussion would relate to sequential histories.

Since in sequential histories all the methods are isolated, we treat each method as a whole without referring to its *inv* and *rsp* events. For a sequential history H, we construct the *completion* of H, denoted $\overline{H}$, by inserting $tryA_k(\mathscr{A})$

immediately after the last method of every transaction $T_k \in live(H)$. Since all the methods in a sequential history are complete, this definition only has to take care of completed transactions.

Real-Time Order and Serial Histories: Given a history H, $<_H$ orders all the events in H. For two complete methods m_{ij}, m_{pq} in $methods(H)$, we denote $m_{ij} \prec_H^{MR} m_{pq}$ if $rsp(m_{ij}) <_H inv(m_{pq})$. Here MR stands for method real-time order. It must be noted that all the methods of the same transaction are ordered. Similarly, for two transactions T_i, T_p in $term(H)$, we denote $(T_i \prec_H^{TR} T_p)$ if $(T_i.lastEvt <_H T_p.firstEvt)$. Here TR stands for transactional real-time order.

We define a history H as *serial* [13] or *t-sequential* [12] if all the transactions in H have terminated and can be totally ordered w.r.t $\prec_{TR}$, i.e. all the transactions execute one after the other without any interleaving. Intuitively, a history H is serial if all its transactions can be isolated. Formally, $\langle (H$ is serial$) \implies (\forall T_i \in txns(H) : (T_i \in term(H)) \wedge (\forall T_i, T_p \in txns(H) : (T_i \prec_H^{TR} T_p) \vee (T_p \prec_H^{TR} T_i)))\rangle$. Since all the methods within a transaction are ordered, a serial history is also sequential.

Legal Histories: A rv_method m_{ij} on key k is legal if it returns the value updated the latest committed transaction that updated key k. A history H is said to be legal, if all the rv_methods of H are legal. More details on legality are explained in the accompanying technical report [14].

Opacity: It is a *correctness-criteria* for STMs [7]. A sequential history H is said to be opaque if there exists a serial history S such that: (1) S is equivalent to $\overline{H}$, i.e., $evts(\overline{H}) = evts(S)$ (2) S is legal and (3) S respects the transactional real-time order of H, i.e., $\prec_H^{TR} \subseteq \prec_S^{TR}$.

3 *HT-MVOSTM* Design and Data Structure

HT-MVOSTM is a hash-table based *MVOSTM* that explores the idea of using multiple versions in *OSTM*s for hash-table object to achieve greater concurrency. The design of *HT-MVOSTM* is similar to *HT-OSTM* [5] consisting of B buckets. All the keys of the hash-table in the range $\mathcal{K}$ are statically allocated to one of these buckets.

Each bucket consists of linked-list of nodes along with two sentinel nodes *head* and *tail* with values $-\infty$ and $+\infty$ respectively. The structure of each node is as $\langle key, lock, marked, vl, nnext \rangle$. The *key* is a unique value from the set of all keys $\mathcal{K}$. All the nodes are stored in increasing order in each bucket as shown in Fig. 3(a), similar to any linked-list based concurrent set implementation [6,15]. In the rest of the document, we use the terms key and node interchangeably. To perform any operation on a key, the corresponding *lock* is acquired. *marked* is a boolean field which represents whether the key is deleted or not. The deletion is performed in a lazy manner similar to the concurrent linked-lists structure [6]. If the *marked* field is true then key corresponding to the node has been logically deleted; otherwise, it is present. The *vl* field of the node points to the version list (shown in Fig. 3(b)) which stores multiple versions corresponding to the key. The last field of the node is *nnext* which stores the address of the next node. It can be seen that the list of keys in a bucket is as an extension of *lazy-list* [6]. Given a node n in the linked-list of bucket B, we denote its fields as $n.key(k.key), n.lock(k.lock), n.marked(k.marked), n.vl(k.vl), n.nnext(k.nnext)$.

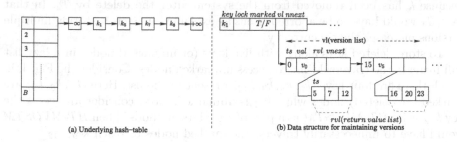

(a) Underlying hash–table

(b) Data structure for maintaining versions

Fig. 3. *HT-MVOSTM* design

The structure of each version in the *vl* of a key k is $\langle ts, val, rvl, vnext \rangle$ as shown in Fig. 3(b). The field *ts* denotes the unique timestamp of the version. In our algorithm, every transaction is assigned a unique timestamp when it begins which is also its *id*. Thus *ts* of this version is the timestamp of the transaction that created it. All the versions in the *vl* of k are sorted by *ts*. Since the timestamps are unique, we denote a version, *ver* of a node n with key k having *ts* j as $n.vl[j].ver$ or $k.vl[j].ver$. The corresponding fields in the version as $k.vl[j].ts, k.vl[j].val, k.vl[j].rvl, k.vl[j].vnext$.

The field *val* contains the value updated by an update transaction. If this version is created by an insert method $t\_insert_i(ht, k, v)$ by transaction T_i, then *val* will be v. On the other hand, if the method is $t\_delete_i(ht, k)$ with the return value v, then *val* will be *null*. In this case, as per the algorithm, the node of key k will also be marked. *HT-MVOSTM* algorithm does not immediately physically remove deleted keys from the hash-table. The need for this is explained below. Thus a rv_method (t_delete or t_lookup) on key k can return *null* when it does not find the key or encounters a *null* value for k.

The *rvl* field stands for *return value list* which is a list of all the transactions that executed rv_method on this version, i.e., those transactions which returned *val*. The field *vnext* points to the next available version of that key.

Number of versions in *vl* (the length of the list) as per *HT-MVOSTM* can be bounded or unbounded. It can be bounded by having a limit on the number of versions such as K. Whenever a new version *ver* is created and is about to be added to *vl*, the length of *vl* is checked. If the length becomes greater than K, the version with lowest *ts* (i.e., the oldest) is replaced with the new version *ver* and thus maintaining the length back to K. If the length is unbounded, then we need a garbage collection scheme to delete unwanted versions for efficiency.

Marked Nodes: *HT-MVOSTM* stores keys even after they have been deleted (nodes which have *marked* field as true). This is because some other concurrent transactions could read from a different version of this key and not the *null* value inserted by the deleting transaction. Consider for instance the transaction T_1 performing $t\_lookup(ht, k)$ as shown in Fig. 2(b). Due to the presence of previous version v_0, *HT-MVOSTM* could return this earlier version v_0 for $t\_lookup(ht, k)$ method. Whereas, it is not possible for *HT-OSTM* to return the version v_0 because k has been removed from the system after the delete by T_2. In that case, T_1 would have to be aborted. Thus as explained in Sect. 1, storing multiple versions increases the concurrency.

To store deleted keys along with live keys (or unmarked node) in a lazy-list will increase the traversal time to access unmarked nodes. Consider the Fig. 4, in which there are four keys $\langle k_5, k_8, k_9, k_{12}\rangle$ present in the list. Here $\langle k_5, k_8, k_9\rangle$ are marked (or deleted) nodes while k_{12} is unmarked. Now, consider an access the key k_{12} as by *HT-MVOSTM* as a part of one of its methods. Then *HT-MVOSTM* would have to unnecessarily traverse the marked nodes to reach key k_{12}.

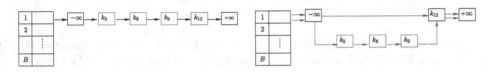

Fig. 4. Searching k_{12} over *lazy-list* (Color figure online)

Fig. 5. Searching k_{12} over *lazyrb-list* (Color figure online)

This motivated us to modify the lazy-list structure of nodes in each bucket to form a skip list based on red and blue links. We denote it as *red-blue lazy-list* or *lazyrb-list*. This idea was earlier explored by Peri et al. in developing *OSTM*s [5]. *lazyrb-list* consists of nodes with two links, red link (or RL) and blue link (or BL). The node which are not marked (or not deleted) are accessible from the head via BL. While all the nodes including the marked ones can be accessed from the head via RL. With this modification, let us consider the above example of accessing unmarked key k_{12}. It can be seen that k_{12} can be accessed much more quickly through BL as shown in Fig. 5. Using the idea of *lazyrb-list*, we have modified the structure of each node as $\langle key, lock, marked, vl, RL, BL\rangle$. Further, for a bucket B, we denote its linked-list as $B.lazyrb\text{-}list$.

4   Working of *HT-MVOSTM*

As explained in Sect. 2, *HT-MVOSTM* exports t_begin, t_insert, t_delete, t_lookup, $tryC$ methods. t_delete, t_lookup are rv_methods while t_insert, t_delete are upd_methods. We treat t_delete as both rv_method as well as upd_method. The rv_methods return the current value of the key. The upd_methods, update to the keys are first noted down in local log, $txLog$. Then in the $tryC$ method after validations of these updates are transferred to the shared memory. We now explain the working of rv_method and upd_method. Additional details including pseudocode is in the accompanying technical report [14].

t_begin(): A thread invokes a new transaction T_i using this method. This method returns a unique id to the invoking thread by incrementing an atomic counter. This unique id is also the timestamp of the transaction T_i. For convenience, we use the notation that i is the timestamp (or id) of the transaction T_i. The transaction T_i local log $txLog_i$ is initialized in this method.

rv_methods - $t\_delete_i(ht, k, v)$ and $t\_lookup_i(ht, k, v)$: Both these methods return the current value of key k. Algorithm 1 gives the high-level overview of these methods. First, the algorithm checks to see if the given key is already in the local log, $txLog$ of T_i (Line 2). If the key is already there then the current rv_method is not the first method on k and is a subsequent method of T_i on k. So, we can return the value of k from the $txLog_i$.

If the key is not present in the $txLog_i$, then *HT-MVOSTM* searches into shared memory. Specifically, it searches the bucket to which k belongs to. Every key in the range $\mathcal{K}$ is statically allocated to one of the B buckets. So the algorithms search for k in the corresponding bucket, say B_k to identify the appropriate location, i.e., identify the correct *predecessor* or *pred* and *current* or *curr* keys in the lazyrb-list of B_k without acquiring any locks similar to the search in lazy-list [6]. Since each key has two links, RL and BL, the algorithm identifies four node references: two *pred* and two *curr* according to red and blue links. They are stored in the form of an array with $preds[0]$ and $currs[1]$ corresponding to blue links; $preds[1]$ and $currs[0]$ corresponding to red links. If both $preds[1]$ and $currs[0]$ nodes are unmarked then the *pred, curr* nodes of both red and blue links will be the same, i.e., $preds[0] = preds[1]$ and $currs[0] = currs[1]$. Thus depending on the marking of *pred, curr* nodes, a total of two, three or four different nodes will be identified. Here, the search ensures that $preds[0].key \leq preds[1].key < k \leq currs[0].key \leq currs[1].key$.

Next, the re-entrant locks on all the *pred, curr* keys are acquired in increasing order to avoid the deadlock. Then all the *pred* and *curr* keys are validated by *rv_Validation()* in Line 7 as follows: (1) If *pred* and *curr* nodes of blue links are not marked, i.e., $(\neg preds[0].marked)$ && $(\neg currs[1].marked)$. (2) If the next links of both blue and red *pred* nodes point to the correct *curr* nodes: $(preds[0].BL = currs[1])$ && $(preds[1].RL = currs[0])$.

If any of these checks fail, then the algorithm retries to find the correct *pred* and *curr* keys. It can be seen that the validation check is similar to the validation in concurrent lazy-list [6].

Next, we check if k is in $B_k.lazyrb\text{-}list$. If k is not in B_k, then we create a new node for k as: $\langle key = k, lock = false, marked = false, vl = v, nnext = \phi \rangle$ and insert it into $B_k.lazyrb\text{-}list$ such that it is accessible only via RL since this node is marked (Line 14). This node will have a single version v as: $\langle ts = 0, val = null, rvl = i, vnext = \phi \rangle$. Here invoking transaction T_i is creating a version with timestamp 0 to ensure that rv_methods of other transactions will never abort. As we have explained in Fig. 2(b) of Sect. 1, even after T_2 deletes k_1, the previous value of v_0 is still retained. Thus, when T_1 invokes lu on k_1 after the delete on k_1 by T_2, *HT-MVOSTM* will return v_0 (as previous value). Hence, each rv_methods will find a version to read while maintaining the infinite version corresponding to each key k. In rvl, T_i adds the timestamp as i in it and $vnext$ is initialized to empty value. Since val is null and the n, this version and the node is not technically inserted into $B_k.lazyrb\text{-}list$.

If k is in $B_k.lazyrb\text{-}list$ then, k is the same as $currs[0]$ or $currs[1]$ or both. Let n be the node of k in $B_k.lazyrb\text{-}list$. We then find the version of n, ver_j which has the timestamp j such that j has the largest timestamp smaller than i (timestamp of T_i). Add i to ver_j's rvl (Line 22). Then release the locks, update the local log $txLog_i$ in Line 24 and return the value stored in $ver_j.val$ in Line 26).

Algorithm 1. rv_method: Could be either $t\_delete_i(ht, k, v)$ or $t\_lookup_i(ht, k, v)$ on key k that maps to bucket B_k.

```
 1: procedure rv_method_i(ht, k, v)
 2:     if (k ∈ txLog_i) then
 3:         Update the local log and return val.
 4:     else
 5:         Search in lazyrb-list to identify the preds[] and currs[] for k using BL and RL in bucket
        B_k.
 6:         Acquire the locks on preds[] and currs[] in increasing order.
 7:         if (!rv_Validation(preds[], currs[])) then
 8:             Release the locks and goto Line 5.
 9:         end if
10:         if (k ∉ B_k.lazyrb-list) then
11:             Create a new node n with key k as: ⟨ key = k, lock = false, marked = false, vl = v,
        nnext = ϕ⟩.
12:             /* The vl consists of a single element v with ts as i */
13:             Create the version v as: ⟨ts = 0, val = null, rvl = i, vnext = ϕ⟩.
14:             Insert n into B_k.lazyrb-list such that it is accessible only via RLs. /* n is marked */
15:             Release the locks; update the txLog_i with k.
16:             return null.
17:         end if
18:         Identify the version ver_j with ts = j such that j is the largest timestamp smaller than i.
19:         if (ver_j == null) then
20:             goto Line 11.
21:         end if
22:         Add i into the rvl of ver_j.
23:         retVal = ver_j.val.
24:         Release the locks; update the txLog_i with k and retVal.
25:     end if
26:     return retVal.
27: end procedure
```

---

upd_methods - t_insert and t_delete: Both the methods create a version corresponding to the key k. The actual effect of t_insert and t_delete in shared memory will take place in $tryC$. Algorithm 2 represents the high-level overview of $tryC$.

Initially, to avoid deadlocks, algorithm sorts all the *keys* in increasing order which are present in the local log, $txLog_i$. In $tryC$, $txLog_i$ consists of upd_methods (t_insert or t_delete) only. For all the upd_methods (opn_i) it searches the key k in the shared memory corresponding to the bucket B_k. It identifies the appropriate location ($pred$ and $curr$) of key k using BL and RL (Line 25) in the lazyrb-list of B_k without acquiring any locks similar to rv_method explained above.

Next, it acquires the re-entrant locks on all the *pred* and *curr* keys in increasing order. After that, all the *pred* and *curr* keys are validated by *tryC_Validation* in Line 27 as follows: (1) It does the *rv_Validation()* as explained above in the rv_method. (2) If key k exists in the $B_k.lazyrb\text{-}list$ and let n as a node of k. Then algorithm identifies the version of n, ver_j which has the timestamp j such that j has the largest timestamp smaller than i (timestamp of T_i). If any higher timestamp k of T_k than timestamp i of T_i exist in $ver_j.rvl$ then algorithm returns *Abort* in Line 28.

If all the above steps are true then each upd_methods exist in $txLog_i$ will take the effect in the shared memory after doing the *intraTransValidation()* in Line 33. If two *upd_methods* of the same transaction have at least one common shared node among its recorded *pred* and *curr* keys, then the previous *upd_method* effect may overwrite if the current *upd_method* of *pred* and *curr* keys are not updated according to the updates done by the previous *upd_method*. Thus to solve this we have *intraTransValidation()* that modifies the *pred* and *curr* keys of current operation based on the previous operation in Line 33.

Algorithm 2. *tryC(T_i)*: Validate the upd_methods of the transaction and then commit

---

28: **procedure** $tryC(T_i)$
29:     /*Operation name (*opn*) which could be either *t_insert* or *t_delete* */
30:     /*Sort the *keys* of $txLog_i$ in increasing order.*/
31:     **for all** ($opn_i \in txLog_i$) **do**
32:         **if** (($opn_i == t\_insert$) || ($opn_i == t\_delete$)) **then**
33:             Search in *lazyrb-list* to identify the *preds*[] and *currs*[] for k of opn_i using BL and RL in bucket B_k.
34:             Acquire the locks on *preds*[] and *currs*[] in increasing order.
35:             **if** (!*tryC_Validation()*) **then**
36:                 return *Abort*.
37:             **end if**
38:         **end if**
39:     **end for**
40:     **for all** ($opn_i \in txLog_i$) **do**
41:         *intraTransValidation()* modifies the *preds*[] and *currs*[] of current operation which would have been updated by the previous operation of the same transaction.
42:         **if** (($opn_i == t\_insert$) && ($k \notin B_k.lazyrb\text{-}list$)) **then**
43:             Create new node n with k as: ⟨ *key* = k, *lock* = false, *marked* = false, *vl* = v, *nnext* = ϕ ⟩.
44:             Create two versions v as: ⟨ *ts=i*, *val=v*, *rvl=φ*, *vnext=φ* ⟩.
45:             Insert node n into $B_k.lazyrb\text{-}list$ such that it is accessible via RL as well as BL /* lock sets *true* */.
46:         **else if** ($opn_i == t\_insert$) **then**
47:             Add the version v as: ⟨ *ts* = i, *val* = v, *rvl* = φ, *vnext* = φ ⟩ into $B_k.lazyrb\text{-}list$ such that it is accessible via RL as well as BL.
48:         **end if**
49:         **if** ($opn_i == t\_delete$) **then**
50:             Add the version i as: ⟨ *ts=i*, *val=null*, *rvl=φ*, *vnext=φ* ⟩ into $B_k.lazyrb\text{-}list$ such that it is accessible only via RL.
51:         **end if**
52:         Update the *preds*[] and *currs*[] of opn_i in $txLog_i$.
53:     **end for**
54:     Release the locks; return *Commit*.
55: **end procedure**

Next, we check if upd_method is *t_insert* and k is in $B_k.lazyrb\text{-}list$. If k is not in B_k, then create a new node n for k as: ⟨$key = k, lock = false, marked =$

$false, vl = v, nnext = \phi\rangle$. This node will have a single version v as: $\langle ts = i, val = v, rvl = \phi, vnext = \phi\rangle$. Here i is the timestamp of the transaction T_i invoking this method; rvl and $vnext$ are initialized to empty values. We set the val as v and insert n into $B_k.lazyrb\text{-}list$ such that it is accessible via RL as well as BL and set the lock field to be $true$ (Line 37). If k is in $B_k.lazyrb\text{-}list$ then, k is the same as $currs[0]$ or $currs[1]$ or both. Let n be the node of k in $B_k.lazyrb\text{-}list$. Then, we create the version v as: $\langle ts = i, val = v, rvl = \phi, vnext = \phi\rangle$ and insert the version into $B_k.lazyrb\text{-}list$ such that it is accessible via RL as well as BL (Line 39).

Subsequently, we check if upd_method is t_delete and k is in $B_k.lazyrb\text{-}list$. Let n be the node of k in $B_k.lazyrb\text{-}list$. Then create the version v as: $\langle ts = i, val = null, rvl = \phi, vnext = \phi\rangle$ and insert the version into $B_k.lazyrb\text{-}list$ such that it is accessible only via RL (Line 42).

Finally, at Line 44 it updates the $pred$ and $curr$ of opn_i in local log, $txLog_i$. At Line 46 releases the locks on all the $pred$ and $curr$ in increasing order of keys to avoid deadlocks and return $Commit$.

Now, we have the following properties about $HT\text{-}MVOSTM$.

Theorem 1. *Any history generated by $HT\text{-}MVOSTM$ is opaque.*

Theorem 2. *$HT\text{-}MVOSTM$ with unbounded versions ensures that $rv\_methods$ do not return abort.*

Theorem 2 gives us a nice property a transaction with t_lookup only methods will not abort.

5   Experimental Evaluation

In this section, we present our experimental results. We have two main goals in this section: (1) evaluating the benefit of multi-version object STMs over the single-version object STMs, and (2) evaluating the benefit of multi-version object STMs over multi-version read-write STMs. We use the $HT\text{-}MVOSTM$ described in Sect. 4 as well as the corresponding $list\text{-}MVOSTM$ which implements the list object. We also consider extensions of these multi-version object STMs to reduce the memory usage. Specifically, we consider a variant that implements garbage collection with unbounded versions and another variant where the number of versions never exceeds a given threshold K.

Experimental System: The Experimental system is a large-scale 2-socket Intel(R) Xeon(R) CPU E5-2690 v4 @ 2.60 GHz with 14 cores per socket and two hyper-threads (HTs) per core, for a total of 56 threads. Each core has a private 32 KB L1 cache and 256 KB L2 cache (which is shared among HTs on that core). All cores on a socket share a 35 MB L3 cache. The machine has 32 GB of RAM and runs Ubuntu 16.04.2 LTS. All code was compiled with the GNU C++ compiler (G++) 5.4.0 with the build target x86_64-Linux-gnu and compilation option -std=c++1x -O3.

STM Implementations: We have taken the implementation of NOrec-list [1], Boosting-list [3], Trans-list [10], ESTM [2], and RWSTM directly from the TLDS framework[1]. And the implementation of OSTM and MVTO published by Sathya Peri, one of the author of this paper. We implemented our algorithms in C++. Each STM algorithm first creates N-threads, each thread, in turn, spawns a transaction. Each transaction exports the following methods as follows: *t_begin*, *t_insert*, *t_lookup*, *t_delete* and *tryC*.

Methodology:[2] We have considered two types of workloads: ($W1$) Li - Lookup intensive (90% lookup, 8% insert and 2% delete) and ($W2$) Ui - Update intensive(10% lookup, 45% insert and 45% delete). The experiments are conducted by varying number of threads from 2 to 64 in power of 2, with 1000 keys randomly chosen. We assume that the hash-table of *HT-MVOSTM* has five buckets and each of the bucket (or list in case of *list-MVOSTM*) can have a maximum size of 1000 keys. Each transaction, in turn, executes 10 operations which include *t_lookup*, *t_delete* and *t_insert* operations. We take an average over 10 results as the final result for each experiment.

Results: Figure 6 shows *HT-MVOSTM* outperforms all the other algorithms (HT-MVTO, RWSTM, ESTM, HT-OSTM) by a factor of 2.6, 3.1, 3.8, 3.5 for workload type $W1$ and by a factor of 10, 19, 6, 2 for workload type $W2$ respectively. As shown in Fig. 6, List based MVOSTM (*list-MVOSTM*) performs even better compared with the existing state-of-the-art STMs (list-MVTO, NOrec-list, Boosting-list, Trans-list, list-OSTM) by a factor of 12, 24, 22, 20, 2.2 for workload type $W1$ and by a factor of 169, 35, 24, 28, 2 for workload type $W2$ respectively. As shown in Fig. 7 for both types of workloads, HT-MVOSTM and list-MVOSTM have the least number of aborts.

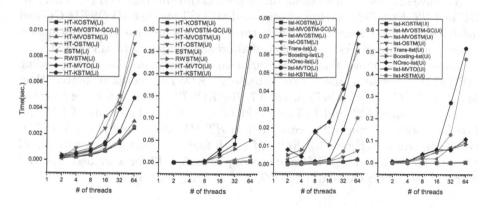

Fig. 6. Performance of *HT-MVOSTM* and *list-MVOSTM*

---

[1] https://ucf-cs.github.io/tlds/.
[2] Code is available here: https://github.com/PDCRL/MVOSTM.

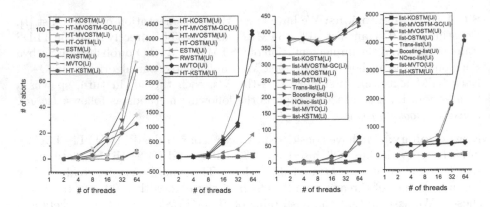

Fig. 7. Aborts of *HT-MVOSTM* and *list-MVOSTM*

MVOSTM-GC and KOSTM: For efficient memory utilization, we develop two variations of *MVOSTM*. The first, *MVOSTM-GC*, uses unbounded versions but performs garbage collection. **This is achieved by deleting non-latest versions whose timestamp is less than the timestamp of the least live transaction.** *MVOSTM-GC* gave a performance gain of 15% over *MVOSTM* without garbage collection in the best case. The second, *KOSTM*, keeps at most K versions by deleting the oldest version when $(K + 1)^{th}$ version is created by a current transaction. As *KOSTM* has limited number of versions while *MVOSTM-GC* can have infinite versions, the memory consumed by *KOSTM* is 21% less than *MVOSTM*. (Implementation details for both are in the technical report [14].)

We have integrated these variations in both hash-table based (*HT-MVOSTM-GC* and *HT-KOSTM*) and linked-list based MVOSTMs (*list-MVOSTM-GC* and *list-KOSTM*), we observed that these two variations increase the performance, concurrency and reduces the number of aborts as compared to MVOSTM.

Experiments show that these variations outperform the corresponding MVOSTMs. Between these two variations, *KOSTM* perform better than *MVOSTM-GC* as shown in Figs. 6 and 7. *HT-KOSTM* helps to achieve a performance speedup of 1.22 and 1.15 for workload type $W1$ and speedup of 1.15 and 1.08 for workload type $W2$ as compared to *HT-MVOSTM* and *HT-MVOSTM-GC* respectively. Whereas *list-KOSTM* (with four versions) gives a speedup of 1.1, 1.07 for workload type $W1$ and speedup of 1.25, 1.13 for workload type $W2$ over the *list-MVOSTM* and *list-MVOSTM-GC* respectively.

6   Conclusion and Future Work

Multi-core systems have become very common nowadays. Concurrent programming using multiple threads has become necessary to utilize all the cores present in the system effectively. But concurrent programming is usually challenging due to synchronization issues between the threads.

In the past few years, several STMs have been proposed which address these synchronization issues and provide greater concurrency. STMs hide the synchronization and communication difficulties among the multiple threads from the programmer while ensuring correctness and hence making programming easy. Another advantage of STMs is that they facilitate compositionality of concurrent programs with great ease. Different concurrent operations that need to be composed to form a single atomic unit is achieved by encapsulating them in a single transaction.

In literature, most of the STMs are *RWSTMs* which export read and write operations. To improve the performance, a few researchers have proposed *OSTMs* [3–5] which export higher level objects operation such as hash-table insert, delete etc. By leveraging the semantics of these higher level operations, these STMs provide greater concurrency. On the other hand, it has been observed in STMs and databases that by storing multiple versions for each t-object in case of *RWSTMs* provides greater concurrency [9,16].

This paper presents the notion of multi-version object STMs and compares their effectiveness with single version object STMs and multi-version read-write STMs. We find that multi-version object STM provides a significant benefit over both of these for different types of workloads. Specifically, we have evaluated the effectiveness of MVOSTM for the list and hash-table data structure as *list-MVOSTM* and *HT-MVOSTM*. Experimental results of *list-MVOSTM* provide almost two to twenty fold speedup over existing state-of-the-art list based STMs (Trans-list, Boosting-list, NOrec-list, list-MVTO, and list-OSTM). Similarly, *HT-MVOSTM* shows a significant performance gain of almost two to nineteen times better than existing state-of-the-art hash-table based STMs (ESTM, RWSTMs, HT-MVTO, and HT-OSTM).

HT-MVOSTM and *list-MVOSTM* and use unbounded number of versions for each key. To limit the number of versions, we develop two variants for both hash-table and list data-structures: (1) A garbage collection method in *MVOSTM* to delete the unwanted versions of a key, denoted as *MVOSTM-GC*. (2) Placing a limit of k on the number versions in *MVOSTM*, resulting in *KOSTM*. Both these variants gave a performance gain of over 15% over *MVOSTM*.

Acknowledgments. We are thankful to the anonymous reviewers for carefully reading the paper and providing us valuable suggestions.

References

1. Dalessandro, L., Spear, M.F., Scott, M.L.: NOrec: streamlining STM by abolishing ownership records. In: Govindarajan, R., Padua, D.A., Hall, M.W. (eds.) PPoPP, pp. 67–78. ACM (2010)
2. Felber, P., Gramoli, V., Guerraoui, R.: Elastic transactions. J. Parallel Distrib. Comput. **100**(C), 103–127 (2017)
3. Herlihy, M., Koskinen, E.: Transactional boosting: a methodology for highly-concurrent transactional objects. In: Proceedings of the 13th ACM SIGPLAN Symposium on Principles and Practice of Parallel Programming, PPoPP 2008, Salt Lake City, UT, USA, 20–23 February 2008, pp. 207–216 (2008)

4. Hassan, A., Palmieri, R., Ravindran, B.: Optimistic transactional boosting. In: PPoPP, pp. 387–388 (2014)
5. Peri, S., Singh, A., Somani, A.: Efficient means of Achieving Composability using Transactional Memory. In: NETYS 2018 (2018)
6. Heller, S., Herlihy, M., Luchangco, V., Moir, M., Scherer III, W.N., Shavit, N.: A lazy concurrent list-based set algorithm. Parallel Process. Lett. **17**(4), 411–424 (2007)
7. Guerraoui, R., Kapalka, M.: On the correctness of transactional memory. In: PPoPP, pp. 175–184. ACM (2008)
8. Weikum, G., Vossen, G.: Transactional Information Systems: Theory, Algorithms, and the Practice of Concurrency Control and Recovery. Morgan Kaufmann, London (2002)
9. Kumar, P., Peri, S., Vidyasankar, K.: A timestamp based multi-version STM algorithm. In: Chatterjee, M., Cao, J., Kothapalli, K., Rajsbaum, S. (eds.) ICDCN 2014. LNCS, vol. 8314, pp. 212–226. Springer, Heidelberg (2014). https://doi.org/10.1007/978-3-642-45249-9_14
10. Zhang, D., Dechev, D.: Lock-free transactions without rollbacks for linked data structures. In: SPAA 2016, pp. 325–336. ACM, New York (2016)
11. Kuznetsov, P., Peri, S.: Non-interference and local correctness in transactional memory. Theor. Comput. Sci. **688**, 103–116 (2017)
12. Kuznetsov, P., Ravi, S.: On the cost of concurrency in transactional memory. In: Fernàndez Anta, A., Lipari, G., Roy, M. (eds.) OPODIS 2011. LNCS, vol. 7109, pp. 112–127. Springer, Heidelberg (2011). https://doi.org/10.1007/978-3-642-25873-2_9
13. Papadimitriou, C.H.: The serializability of concurrent database updates. J. ACM **26**(4), 631–653 (1979)
14. Juyal, C., Kulkarni, S., Kumari, S., Peri, S., Somani, A.: An innovative approach for achieving composability in concurrent systems using multi-version object based STMs. CoRR abs/1712.09803 (2017)
15. Harris, T.L.: A pragmatic implementation of non-blocking linked-lists. In: Welch, J. (ed.) DISC 2001. LNCS, vol. 2180, pp. 300–314. Springer, Heidelberg (2001). https://doi.org/10.1007/3-540-45414-4_21
16. Perelman, D., Fan, R., Keidar, I.: On maintaining multiple versions in STM. In: PODC, pp. 16–25 (2010)

Ring Exploration with Myopic Luminous Robots

Fukuhito Ooshita[1]([✉]) and Sébastien Tixeuil[2]

[1] Nara Institute of Science and Technology,
Takayama 8916-5, Ikoma, Nara, Japan
f-oosita@is.naist.jp
[2] Sorbonne Université, CNRS, LIP6, 75005 Paris, France
Sebastien.Tixeuil@lip6.fr

Abstract. We investigate exploration algorithms for autonomous mobile robots evolving in uniform ring-shaped networks. Different from the usual Look-Compute-Move (LCM) model, we consider two characteristics: myopia and luminosity. Myopia means each robot has a limited visibility. We consider the weakest assumption for myopia: each robot can only observe its neighboring nodes. Luminosity means each robot maintains a non-volatile visible light. We consider the weakest assumption for luminosity: each robot can use only two colors for its light. The main interest of this paper is to clarify the impact of luminosity on exploration with myopic robots.

As a main contribution, we prove that (1) two and three robots are necessary and sufficient to achieve perpetual and terminating exploration, respectively, in the fully synchronous model, and (2) three and four robots are necessary and sufficient to achieve perpetual and terminating exploration, respectively, in the semi-synchronous and asynchronous models. These results clarify the power of lights for myopic robots since, without lights, five robots are necessary and sufficient to achieve terminating exploration in the fully synchronous model, and no terminating exploration algorithm exists in the semi-synchronous and asynchronous models.

We also show that, in the fully synchronous model (resp., the semi-synchronous and asynchronous models), the proposed perpetual exploration algorithm is universal, that is, the algorithm solves perpetual exploration from any solvable initial configuration with two (resp., three) robots and two colors. On the other hand, we show that, in the fully synchronous model (resp., the semi-synchronous and asynchronous models), no universal algorithm exists for terminating exploration, that is, no algorithm may solve terminating exploration from any solvable initial configuration with three (resp., four) robots and two colors.

Keywords: Autonomous mobile robots · Deterministic exploration
Discrete environments · Limited visibility · Visible light

© Springer Nature Switzerland AG 2018
T. Izumi and P. Kuznetsov (Eds.): SSS 2018, LNCS 11201, pp. 301–316, 2018.
https://doi.org/10.1007/978-3-030-03232-6_20

1   Introduction

1.1   Background and Motivation

Studies about cooperation of autonomous mobile robots have attracted a lot of attention recently in the field of Distributed Computing. The main goal of those works is to characterize the minimum capabilities of robots that permit to achieve a given task. Since the pioneering work of Suzuki and Yamashita [25], many results have been published in their Look-Compute-Move (LCM) model. In the LCM model, each robot repeats executing cycles of look, compute, and move phases. At the beginning of each cycle, the robot observes positions of other robots (look phase). According to its observation, the robot computes whether it moves somewhere or stays idle (compute phase). If the robot decides to move, it moves to the target position by the end of the cycle (move phase). To consider minimum capabilities, most studies assume that robots are identical (*i.e.*, robots execute the same algorithm and cannot be distinguished), oblivious (*i.e.*, robots have no memory of their past actions), and silent (*i.e.*, robots cannot communicate with other robots explicitly). Indeed, communication among robots is done only in an implicit way by observing positions of other robots and moving to a new position. Previous works considered problem solvability of LCM robots in continuous environments (*a.k.a.* two- or three-dimensional Euclidean space) [17,18,25], while others considered discrete environments (*a.k.a.* graph networks) [4,6,16,22,23].

In this paper, we focus on robots evolving in graph networks. The most fundamental tasks in graph networks are gathering and exploration. The goal of gathering is to make all robots meet at a non-predetermined single node. Gathering has been studied for rings [4,6,22,23], grids and trees [5]. Two types of exploration tasks have been well studied: perpetual exploration requires robots to visit nodes so that every node is visited infinitely many times by a robot, and terminating exploration requires robots to terminate after every node is visited by a robot at least once. For example, perpetual exploration has been studied for rings [1] and grids [2], and terminating exploration has been studied for rings [14,16], trees [15], grids [12], tori [13], and arbitrary networks [3].

All aforementioned works in graph networks make the assumption that each robot observes all other robots in the networks. That is, each robot has a sensor that can obtain a global snapshot. However, this powerful ability somewhat contradicts the principle of very weak mobile entities. For this reason, recent studies consider the more realistic case of myopic robots [8,10,19,20]. A myopic robot has limited visibility, *i.e.*, it can see nodes (and robots on them) only within a certain fixed distance ϕ. Datta et al. studied terminating exploration of rings for $\phi = 1$ [8] and $\phi = 2, 3$ [9]. Guilbault and Pelc studied gathering in bipartite graphs with $\phi = 1$ [19], and infinite lines with $\phi > 1$ [20]. Not surprisingly, in the weakest setting, *i.e.*, $\phi = 1$, robots can only achieve few tasks. It is shown [8] that, when $\phi = 1$ holds, five robots are necessary and sufficient to achieve terminating exploration in the fully synchronous (FSYNC) model. On the other hand, no terminating exploration algorithm exists in the semi-synchronous (SSYNC) and

Table 1. Ring exploration with myopic robots.

Reference	Exploration	Synchrony	ϕ	#colors	#robots	
					Necessary	Sufficient
[8]	Terminating	FSYNC	1	1	5	5
[8]	Terminating	SSYNC & ASYNC	1	1	Impossible	
[10]	Terminating	SSYNC & ASYNC	2	1	5	7
[10]	Terminating	SSYNC & ASYNC	3	1	5	5
This paper	Perpetual	FSYNC	1	2	2	2
This paper	Terminating	FSYNC	1	2	3	3
This paper	Perpetual	SSYNC & ASYNC	1	2	3	3
This paper	Terminating	SSYNC & ASYNC	1	2	4	4

asynchronous (ASYNC) models. Also, gathering [19] is possible when $\phi = 1$ only if robots initially form a star.

Since most results for myopic robots with $\phi = 1$ are negative, a natural question is which additional assumptions can improve task solvability. In this paper, we focus on a non-volatile visible light [7] as an additional assumption. A robot endowed with such a light is called a luminous robot. Each luminous robot is equipped with a light device that can emit a constant number of colors to other robots, a single color at a time. The light color is non-volatile, so it can be used as a constant-space memory. For non-myopic luminous robots, the power of lights is well understood [7,11,21]. For example, if each robot has a five colors light, the difference between the asynchronous model and the semi-synchronous model disappears [7]. However, to the best of our knowledge, the impact of lights on myopic robots has not been studied yet.

1.2 Our Contributions

We focus on ring exploration and the impact of lights on myopic robots with $\phi = 1$. We consider the weakest assumption for lights: each robot can use only two colors for its light. Table 1 summarizes our contributions and related works. Note that robots with no light are equivalent to robots with a single color light.

As a main contribution, we prove that *(i)* two and three robots are necessary and sufficient to achieve perpetual and terminating exploration, respectively, in the fully synchronous model, and *(ii)* three and four robots are necessary and sufficient to achieve perpetual and terminating exploration, respectively, in the semi-synchronous and asynchronous models. These results clarify the power of lights for myopic robots since, without lights, five robots are necessary and sufficient to achieve terminating exploration in the fully synchronous model, and no terminating exploration algorithm exists in the semi-synchronous and asynchronous models. Interestingly, even if robots can observe nodes up to distance three (*i.e.*, $\phi = 3$), five robots are required to achieve terminating exploration without light. This means that there exist some tasks that myopic luminous robots with small visibility can achieve, but that non-luminous robots with larger visibility cannot.

Similarly to previous works for myopic robots, all algorithms proposed in this paper assume some specific initial configurations because most configurations are not solvable. For example, when myopic robots are deployed so that no robot can observe other robots, they cannot achieve exploration. However, our perpetual exploration algorithms achieve the best possible property, that is, they are universal. This means that, in the fully synchronous model (resp., the semi-synchronous and asynchronous models), the proposed algorithm solves perpetual exploration from any solvable initial configuration with two (resp., three) robots and two colors. As for terminating exploration, we show that no universal algorithm exists. That is, in the fully synchronous model (resp., the semi-synchronous and asynchronous models), no algorithm may solve terminating exploration from any solvable initial configuration with three (resp., four) robots and two colors. Due to space limitation, all proofs are provided in the companion technical report [24].

2   Preliminaries

2.1   System Model

The system consists of n nodes and k mobile robots. The nodes $v_0, v_1, \ldots, v_{n-1}$ form an undirected and unoriented ring-shaped graph, where a link exists between v_i and v_{i+1}, for $i < n$, and between v_{n-1} and v_0. For simplicity we consider mathematical operations on node indices as operations modulo n. Neither nodes nor links have identifiers or labels, and consequently robots cannot distinguish nodes and links. Robots do not know n, the size of the ring. Robots occupy some nodes of the ring. The distance between two nodes is the number of links in a shortest path between the nodes. The distance between two robots a and b is the distance between two nodes occupied by a and b. Two robots a and b are neighbors if the distance between a and b is one. A set S of robots is *connected* if the induced subgraph of nodes occupied by the robots in S is connected; otherwise, S is disconnected.

Robots we consider have the following characteristics and capabilities. Robots are *identical*, that is, robots execute the same deterministic algorithm and cannot be distinguished based on their appearance (in particular, they do *not* have unique identifiers). Robots are *luminous*, that is, each robot has a light (or state) that is visible to itself and other robots. A robot can choose the color of its light from a discrete set Col. When the set Col is finite, we denote by κ the number of available colors (*i.e.*, $\kappa = |Col|$). Robots have no other persistent memory and cannot remember the history of past actions. Robots cannot communicate with other robots explicitly, however they can communicate implicitly by observing positions and colors of other robots (for collecting information), and by changing their color and moving (for sending information). Each robot r can observe positions and colors of robots within a fixed distance ϕ ($\phi > 0$) from its current position. Since robots are identical, they share the same ϕ. If $\phi = \infty$, robots can observe all other robots in the ring. If $\phi = 1$, robots are *myopic*, that is, they can only observe robots that are located at neighboring nodes.

Each robot executes an algorithm by repeating three-phases cycles: Look, Compute, and Move (L-C-M). During the *Look* phase, the robot observes positions and colors of robots within distance ϕ. During the *Compute* phase, the robot computes its next color and movement according to the observation in the Look phase. The robot may change its color at the end of the Compute phase. If the robot decides to move, it moves to a neighboring node during the *Move* phase. To model asynchrony of executions, we introduce the notion of *scheduler* that decides when each robot executes phases. When the scheduler makes robot r execute some phase, we say the scheduler activates the phase of r or simply activates r. We consider three types of synchronicity: the FSYNC (full-synchronous) model, the SSYNC (semi-synchronous) model, and the ASYNC (asynchronous) model. In the FSYNC model, the scheduler executes full cycles of all robots synchronously and concurrently. In the SSYNC model, the scheduler selects a non-empty subset of robots and executes full cycles of the selected robots synchronously and concurrently. In the ASYNC model, the scheduler executes cycles of robots asynchronously. Note that in the ASYNC model, a robot r can move based on an outdated view observed previously by r. Throughout the paper we assume that the scheduler is *fair*, that is, each robot is activated infinitely often. We consider the scheduler as an adversary. That is, we assume that the scheduler is omniscient (it knows robot positions, colors, algorithms, etc.), and tries to activate robots in such a way that they fail executing the task.

In the sequel, $M_i(t)$ denotes the multiset of colors of robots located in node v_i at instant t. If v_i is not occupied by any robot at t, then $M_i(t) = \emptyset$ holds, and v_i is *free* at instant t. Then, v_i is a *tower* at instant t if $|M_i(t)| \geq 2$. A *configuration* $C(t)$ of the system at instant t is defined as $C(t) = (M_0(t), M_1(t), \ldots, M_{n-1}(t))$. If t is clear from the context, we simply write $C = (M_0, M_1, \ldots, M_{n-1})$. If there exists an index x such that $M_{x+i} = M_{x-i}$ holds for any i, or if $M_{x+i} = M_{x-(i+1)}$ holds for any i (*i.e.*, there exists at least one axis of symmetry in the configuration), configuration C is called *symmetric*.

When a robot observes its environment, it gets a *view* up to distance ϕ. Consider a robot r on node v_i; then, r obtains two views: the forward view and the backward view. The forward and backward views of r are defined as $V_f = (c_r, M_{i-\phi}, \ldots, M_{i-1}, M_i, M_{i+1}, \ldots, M_{i+\phi})$, and $V_b = (c_r, M_{i+\phi}, \ldots, M_{i+1}, M_i, M_{i-1}, \ldots, M_{i-\phi})$, respectively, where c_r denotes r's color. Since we assume unoriented rings (where robots may not share the same notion of left and right), each robot cannot distinguish its forward view from its backward view. If the forward view and the backward view of r are identical, then r's view is *symmetric*. In this case, r cannot distinguish between the two directions when it moves, and the scheduler decides which direction r moves to. If r observes no other robot in its view, r is *isolated*.

2.2   Algorithm, Execution, Problem, and Exploration Problem

An algorithm is described as a set of rules. Each rule is represented in the following manner $<Label>:<Guard>::<Action>$. The guard $<Guard>$ is a possible
view obtained by a robot. If a forward or backward view of robot r matches a
guard in an algorithm, we say r is enabled. We also say the corresponding rule
$<Label>$ is enabled. If a robot is enabled, the robot may change its color and
move based on the corresponding action $<Action>$ during the Compute and
Move phases.

For an infinite sequence of configurations $E = C_0, C_1, \ldots, C_t, \ldots$, we say E is
an execution from initial configuration C_0 if, for any instant t, C_{t+1} is obtained
from C_t after some robots execute phases. We say C_i is the i-th configuration of
execution E.

A problem $\mathcal{P}$ is defined as a set of executions: An execution E solves $\mathcal{P}$ if
$E \in \mathcal{P}$ holds. An algorithm $\mathcal{A}$ solves problem $\mathcal{P}$ from initial configuration C_0 if
any execution from C_0 solves $\mathcal{P}$. We simply say an algorithm $\mathcal{A}$ solves problem
$\mathcal{P}$ if there exists an initial configuration C_0 such that $\mathcal{A}$ solves $\mathcal{P}$ from C_0. For
configuration C and problem $\mathcal{P}$, C is solvable for $\mathcal{P}$ if there exists an algorithm
(specific to C) that solves $\mathcal{P}$ from initial configuration C. Let $C_s(\mathcal{P})$ be a set of
all configurations solvable for $\mathcal{P}$. We say algorithm $\mathcal{A}$ is universal with respect
to problem $\mathcal{P}$ if $\mathcal{A}$ solves $\mathcal{P}$ from any initial configuration in $C_s(\mathcal{P})$. That is, a
universal algorithm solves $\mathcal{P}$ from any solvable initial configuration.

In this paper, we consider the perpetual exploration problem and terminating
exploration problem in case of $\phi = 1$.

Definition 1 (Perpetual exploration problem). *Perpetual exploration is
defined as a set of executions E such that every node is infinitely many times
visited by some robot in E.*

Definition 2 (Terminating exploration problem). *Terminating exploration is defined as a set of executions E such that 1) every node is visited
by at least one robot in E and 2) there exists a suffix of E such that no robots
are enabled.*

2.3   Descriptions

Let $C = (M_0, \ldots, M_{n-1})$ be a configuration. We say $C' = (M'_0, \ldots, M'_{n'-1})$ is
a sub-configuration of C if there exists x such that $M_{x+i} = M'_i$ holds for any i
$(0 \leq i \leq n' - 1)$. In this case, we say n' is the length of sub-configuration C'.
We sometimes describe a sub-configuration $C' = (M'_0, \ldots, M'_{n'-1})$ by listing all
colors in M'_i as the i-th column. That is, when $M'_i = \{c^i_1, \ldots, c^i_{|M'_i|}\}$ holds for
each i $(0 \leq i \leq n' - 1)$, we describe C' as follows:

$$
\begin{array}{cccc}
c^0_1 & c^1_1 & & c^{n'-1}_1 \\
c^0_2 & c^1_2 & & c^{n'-1}_2 \\
\vdots & \vdots & \cdots & \vdots \\
c^0_{|M'_0|} & c^1_{|M'_1|} & & c^{n'-1}_{|M'_{n'-1}|}
\end{array}
$$

When $M_i' = \emptyset$ holds, we write $\emptyset$ as the i-th column. If h free nodes exist successively, we sometimes write $\emptyset^h$ instead of writing h columns with $\emptyset$. For simplicity, when C' is a sub-configuration of C and all robots appear in C', we use C' instead of C to represent configuration C. We also use this description to represent views of robots.

Throughout the paper, we consider the case of $\phi = 1$. We describe a rule in an algorithm in the following manner:

$$\mathcal{R}_{rule} : \begin{array}{ccc} c_{-1,1} & c_{0,1} & c_{1,1} \\ c_{-1,2} & c_{0,2} & c_{1,2} \\ \vdots & \vdots & \vdots \\ c_{-1,m-1} & (c_{0,m_0}) & c_{1,m_1} \end{array} :: c_{new}, Movement$$

Notation $\mathcal{R}_{rule}$ is a label of the rule. The middle part represents a guard. This represents a view $V = (c_{0,m_0}, M_{-1}, M_0, M_1)$, where $M_i = \{c_{i,1}, \ldots, c_{i,m_i}\}$ holds for $i \in \{-1, 0, 1\}$. Intuitively, each column represents colors of robots on a single node and a color within parentheses represents its current color. If a forward or backward view of robot r is equal to V, r is enabled. In this case, r executes an action represented by c_{new}, $Movement$. Notation c_{new} represents a new color of the robot, and $Movement$ represents the movement. Notation $Movement$ can be $\perp$, $\leftarrow$, $\rightarrow$, or $\leftarrow \vee \rightarrow$: (1) $\perp$ implies a robot does not move, (2) $\leftarrow$ (resp., $\rightarrow$) implies a robot moves toward the node such that a set of robot colors is M_{-1} (resp., M_1), and (3) $\leftarrow \vee \rightarrow$ implies a robot moves toward one of two directions (the scheduler decides the direction). When the view V described in a guard is symmetric, $Movement$ should be either $\perp$ or $\leftarrow \vee \rightarrow$. As an example, consider the following rule.

$$\mathcal{R}_{ex} : \begin{array}{cc} & G \\ \emptyset & (W) \ G \end{array} :: G, \rightarrow$$

Robot r is enabled by $\mathcal{R}_{ex}$ if (1) the color of r is W, (2) the current node is occupied by two robots with colors G and W, (3) one neighboring node is occupied by no robot, and (4) another neighboring node is occupied by a robot with color G. If r is enabled by $\mathcal{R}_{ex}$, r changes its color to G and moves toward the node occupied by a robot with color G.

3 Full-Synchronous Robots

3.1 Perpetual Exploration

In this subsection, we provide a universal perpetual exploration algorithm for two robots with two colors in the FSYNC model. Note that, since one robot cannot achieve perpetual exploration clearly because the direction of its movement is decided by the scheduler, two robots are necessary to achieve perpetual exploration. A set of colors is $Col = \{G, W\}$. The algorithm is given in Algorithm 1. In the initial configuration, two robots with colors G and W stay at a

---

Algorithm 1. Fully-Synchronous Perpetual Exploration for $k = 2$

Initial configurations

$\frac{W}{G}$, GW and WG

Rules

0GW : $\emptyset$ (G) W :: G, $\leftarrow$ 0WG : $\emptyset$ (W) G :: W, $\rightarrow$

0T0 : $\frac{W}{\emptyset \, (G) \, \emptyset}$ :: G, $\leftarrow \vee \rightarrow$

---

single node or neighboring nodes. If the two robots stay at a single node (i.e., they form a tower), the robot with color G moves. When the two robots stay at neighboring nodes, the robot with color G moves in a direction away from the other robot, and the robot with color W moves toward the other robot. This implies two robots move in the same direction. Since they move synchronously, the views of the two robots are not changed. Hence, the two robots continue to move and achieve perpetual exploration. Clearly we have the following theorem.

Theorem 1. *In case of $\phi = 1$ and $k = 2$, Algorithm 1 solves perpetual explo-ration from initial configurations $\frac{W}{G}$, GW and WG for $n \geq 2$ in the FSYNC model.*

In addition, we can prove that other initial configurations are unsolvable. Hence, we have the following theorem.

Theorem 2. *In case of $\phi = 1$, $k = 2$, and $Col = \{G, W\}$, Algorithm 1 is uni-versal with respect to perpetual exploration for $n \geq 6$ in the FSYNC model.*

3.2   Terminating Exploration

In this subsection, we consider the terminating exploration problem in the SSYNC model. First, we prove that no algorithm solves terminating exploration for $k = 2$.

Theorem 3. *In case of $\phi = 1$ and $k = 2$, no algorithm solves terminating exploration in the FSYNC model. This holds even if robots can use an infinite number of colors.*

Next, we give a terminating exploration algorithm for three robots with two colors in case of $n \geq 3$. A set of colors is $Col = \{G, W\}$. The algorithm is given in Algorithm 2.

Executions of Algorithm 2 for $n \geq 5$ are given in Fig. 1. We consider three robots r_1, r_2, and r_3. In the figure, W_i (resp., G_i) represents robot r_i with color W (resp., G). Arrows represent that indicated robots are enabled. At configu-ration WWW, r_1 and r_3 are enabled by rule 0WW (Fig. 1(a)) and change their colors to G. At configuration GWG (Fig. 1(b)), robots r_1 and r_2 (*i.e.*, a pair of

---

Algorithm 2. Fully-Synchronous Terminating Exploration for $k = 3$

Initial configurations
  WWW, GWW, WWG, and GWG
Rules
  0GW : $\emptyset$ (G) W :: G, $\leftarrow$ 0WG : $\emptyset$ (W) G :: W, $\rightarrow$
  0WW : $\emptyset$ (W) W :: G, $\perp$ GWW :   G (W) W :: W, $\leftarrow$
  GWG :   G (W) G :: W, $\leftarrow \vee \rightarrow$

---

robots GW) and r_3 (*i.e.*, another robot G) move to the opposite directions by
rules 0GW and GWG. Note that, since the view of r_2 is symmetric at configuration GWG, the scheduler decides the direction of r_2. This implies that the next
configuration is GW$\emptyset\emptyset$G (Fig. 1(c)) or G$\emptyset\emptyset$WG. However, since the two configurations are symmetric to each other, robots move in the same manner after the
configuration. At configuration GWW (Fig. 1(d)), robots r_1 and r_2 move to the
opposite direction of r_3 by rules 0GW and GWW, and then the configuration
becomes one in Fig. 1(e). Note that, since configuration WWG is symmetric to
GWW, robots move in the same manner from configuration WWG. After configurations in Fig. 1(c)(e), robots r_1 and r_2 continue to move to the same direction
by rules 0GW and 0WG as explorers and r_3 remains to stay as a marker. After
explorers r_1 and r_2 explore the ring, they reach marker r_3 (Fig. 1(f)). After robot
r_2 moves, they terminate at a configuration in Fig. 1(g).

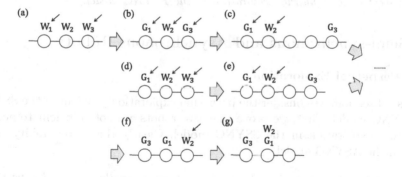

Fig. 1. Executions of Algorithm 2

We can easily verify that Algorithm 2 works for $n = 3$ or $n = 4$. Hence we
have the following theorem.

Theorem 4. *In case of $\phi = 1$ and $k = 3$, Algorithm 2 solves terminating exploration from initial configurations WWW, GWW, WWG, and GWG for $n \geq 3$ in
the FSYNC model.*

Note that we can construct another algorithm by swapping the roles of colors
G and W in Algorithm 2. Clearly this algorithm solves terminating exploration

Algorithm 3. Asynchronous Perpetual Exploration for $k = 3$

Initial configurations

WWG, WGG, GWW, GGW, $\dfrac{G \quad G}{W\,W}$, $\dfrac{G}{W\,W}$, $\dfrac{W}{G\,G}$, and $\dfrac{W}{G\,G}$.

Rules

0GW : $\emptyset\,(G)\,W :: G, \rightarrow$ 0WG : $\emptyset\,(W)\,G :: W, \rightarrow$

$0TW :$ $\dfrac{G}{\emptyset\,(W)\,W} :: G, \rightarrow$ $0TG :$ $\dfrac{W}{\emptyset\,(G)\,G} :: W, \leftarrow$

from configurations such that colors G and W are swapped from solvable configurations for Algorithm 2. This implies configurations GGG, WGG, GGW, and WGW are also solvable. Hence, we have the following lemma.

Lemma 1. *If $k = 3$ holds and a set of colors is $\{G, W\}$, configurations WWW, WWG, WGW, WGG, GWW, GWG, GGW, and GGG are solvable for terminating exploration in the FSYNC model.*

We can prove that there exists no universal algorithm with respect to terminating exploration for three robots with two colors. This validates the assumption that Algorithm 2 starts from some designated initial configuration.

Theorem 5. *In case of $\phi = 1$, $k = 3$, and $\kappa = 2$, no universal algorithm exists with respect to terminating exploration in the FSYNC model.*

4   Semi-synchronous and Asynchronous Robots

4.1   Perpetual Exploration

In this subsection, we consider the perpetual exploration problem in the SSYNC or ASYNC model. First, we prove that two robots are not sufficient to achieve perpetual exploration in the SSYNC model. Clearly this impossibility result holds in the ASYNC model.

Theorem 6. *In case of $\phi = 1$ and $k = 2$, no algorithm can solve perpetual exploration in the SSYNC model. This holds even if robots can use an infinite number of colors.*

Next, we give a universal perpetual exploration algorithm for three robots with two colors in the SSYNC and ASYNC models. We give a perpetual exploration algorithm by three robots with two colors in the ASYNC model, and we prove the algorithm is universal in the SSYNC and ASYNC models. A set of colors is $Col = \{G, W\}$. The algorithm is given in Algorithm 3.

Executions of Algorithm 3 for $n \geq 4$ are given in Fig. 2. Let us consider configuration WWG, and assume that r_1, r_2, and r_3 compose the configuration in this order (Fig. 2(a)). Here only r_3 is enabled with rule 0GW, and r_3 moves toward r_2. In a configuration in Fig. 2(b), only r_2 is enabled with rule $0TW$. If r_2 is activated, r_2 changes its color to G and moves toward r_1 (Fig. 2(c)). Note that, in the ASYNC model, after r_2 changes its color, some robots may observe the intermediate configuration before r_2 moves toward r_1. However, since no rule matches the intermediate configuration, robots do not move based on the configuration. After r_2 moves from Fig. 2(c) by rule $0TG$, the sub-configuration becomes WWG (Fig. 2(e)) but the robots change their positions from Fig. 2(a) to (e). Similarly, robots repeat the behavior from Fig. 2(a) to (e), and they achieve perpetual exploration. From configuration WGG in Fig. 2(d), r_1 moves by rule $0WG$ and becomes a configuration in Fig. 2(c). After that, they move similarly to the case from a configuration in Fig. 2(a). These executions include configurations

$$WWG, WGG, \frac{G}{WW}, \text{ and } \frac{W}{GG},$$

and consequently from these configurations robots can achieve perpetual exploration. Since remaining configurations

$$GWW, GGW, \frac{G}{WW}, \text{ and } \frac{W}{GG}$$

are symmetric to the above configurations, robots can also achieve perpetual exploration from the configurations. Therefore, we have the following theorem.

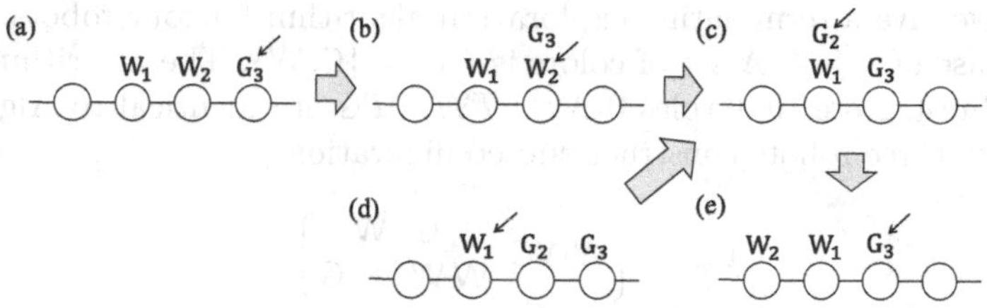

Fig. 2. Executions of Algorithm 3

Theorem 7. *In case of $\phi = 1$ and $k = 3$, Algorithm 3 solves perpetual exploration from initial configurations*

$$WWG, WGG, GWW, GGW, \frac{G}{WW}, \frac{G}{WW}, \frac{W}{GG}, \text{ and } \frac{W}{GG}$$

for $n \geq 3$ in the ASYNC model.

We can also show that other initial configurations are unsolvable for $n \geq 9$ in the SSYNC model. This implies Algorithm 3 is universal with respect to perpetual exploration for $n \geq 9$ in the SSYNC and ASYNC models.

Theorem 8. *In case of $\phi = 1$, $k = 3$, and $Col = \{G, W\}$, Algorithm 3 is universal with respect to perpetual exploration for $n \geq 9$ in the SSYNC and ASYNC models.*

Algorithm 4. Asynchronous Terminating Exploration for $k = 4$

Initial configurations
  WWGG, WWWG, WWGW, GGWW, GWWW, WGWW.
Rules
  0GW : $\emptyset$ (G) W :: G, $\rightarrow$ GGW : G (G) W :: G, $\rightarrow$

  0TW : $\dfrac{G}{\emptyset \,(W)\, W}$ :: G, $\rightarrow$ GTW : $\dfrac{G}{G \,(W)\, W}$ :: G, $\rightarrow$

  0TG : $\dfrac{W}{\emptyset \,(G)\, G}$ :: W, $\leftarrow$ 0WG : $\emptyset$ (W) G :: W, $\rightarrow$

4.2 Terminating Exploration

In this subsection, we consider the terminating exploration problem in the SSYNC and ASYNC model. First, we prove that three robots are not sufficient to achieve terminating exploration in the SSYNC model. Clearly this impossibility result holds in the ASYNC model.

Theorem 9. *In case of $\phi = 1$ and $k = 3$, no algorithm solves terminating exploration in the SSYNC model. This holds even if robots can use an infinite number of colors.*

Next, we give a terminating exploration algorithm for four robots with two colors in case of $n \geq 4$. A set of colors is $Col = \{G, W\}$. The algorithm is given in Algorithm 4. Note that rules 0GW, 0TW, 0TG are identical to Algorithm 3. Hence, once three robots construct sub-configurations

$$\mathcal{C}_{pe} = \left\{ WWG, \frac{G}{WW}, \frac{W}{GG} \right\},$$

they explore the ring as explorers similarly to Algorithm 3.

Executions of Algorithm 4 for $n \geq 5$ are given in Fig. 3. At configuration WWGG (Fig. 3(a)) only r_3 can move by rule GGW, and the configuration becomes one in Fig. 3(b) after it moves. Since r_1, r_2, and r_3 form a sub-configuration in $\mathcal{C}_{pe}$, they explore the ring as explorers. On the other hand, r_4 remains to stay as a marker. Hence, three explorer robots eventually join marker r_4 from the opposite direction (Fig. 3(c)). By considering all possible executions after a configuration in Fig. 3(c), we can observe that robots eventually terminate and thus Algorithm 4 solves terminating exploration from initial configuration WWGG (See the details in the full version [24]).

We consider other initial configurations WWWG and WWGW in Fig. 4. From initial configuration WWWG (Fig. 4(a)), robots eventually form configuration WWGG (Fig. 4(e)) and thus they can solve terminating exploration. From initial configuration WWGW (Fig. 4(f)), robots form a configuration in Fig. 4(g) and the configuration is the same as in Fig. 4(b). Hence, they can solve terminating exploration.

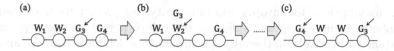

Fig. 3. An execution from WWGG of Algorithm 4

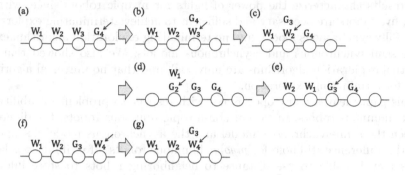

Fig. 4. Executions from WWWG and WWGW of Algorithm 4

Since configurations GGWW, GWWW, and WGWW are symmetric to WWGG, WWWG, and WWGW, respectively, we have the following theorem.

Theorem 10. *In case of* $\phi = 1$ *and* $k = 4$, *Algorithm 4 solves terminating exploration from initial configurations WWGG, WWWG, WWGW, GGWW, GWWW, and WGWW for* $n \geq 5$ *in the ASYNC model.*

Note that we can construct another algorithm by swapping the roles of colors G and W in Algorithm 4. Clearly this algorithm solves terminating exploration from configurations such that colors G and W are swapped from solvable configurations for Algorithm 4. This implies configurations GGGW, GGWG, WGGG, and GWGG are also solvable. Hence, we have the following lemma.

Lemma 2. *If* $k = 4$ *holds and a set of colors is* $\{G, W\}$, *configurations WWGG, WWWG, WWGW, GGWW, GWWW, WGWW, GGGW, GGWG, WGGG, and GWGG are solvable for terminating exploration in the ASYNC model.*

We also prove that there exists no universal algorithm with respect to terminating exploration for four robots with two colors. This validates the assumption that Algorithm 4 starts from some designated initial configuration.

Theorem 11. *In case of* $\phi = 1$, $k = 4$, *and* $\kappa = 2$, *no universal algorithm exists with respect to terminating exploration in the SSYNC and ASYNC models.*

5   Conclusions

In this paper, we investigated the possibility of exploration algorithms for myopic luminous robots evolving in uniform ring-shaped networks. Considering weakest possible assumptions for myopia and luminosity, we proved that: *(i)* two and three robots are necessary and sufficient to achieve perpetual and terminating exploration, respectively, in the fully synchronous model, and *(ii)* three and four robots are necessary and sufficient to achieve perpetual and terminating exploration, respectively, in the semi-synchronous and asynchronous models. These tight results characterize the power of lights for myopic robots since, without lights, five robots are necessary and sufficient to achieve terminating exploration in the fully synchronous model, and no terminating exploration algorithm exists in the semi-synchronous and asynchronous models. We also showed that our perpetual exploration algorithms are universal, and that no universal algorithm exists for terminating exploration.

This paper leaves many open issues with respect to problem solvability for myopic luminous robots. In case of non-myopic luminous robots, the difference between the semi-synchronous model and the asynchronous model disappears. Does this difference still hold for *myopic* luminous robots? If visibility ϕ is large, robots may be able to use distance to neighboring robots to store information instead of lights. Now, is there some relation between tasks achieved by myopic luminous robots with a large number of colors, and tasks achieved by non-luminous robots with large visibility? Is there a tradeoff between the visibility distance and the number of colors? It is also interesting to consider other tasks and topologies with myopic luminous robots.

Acknowledgements. This work was partially supported by a mobility scholarship of the author at Sorbonne University in the frame of the Erasmus Mundus Action 2 Project TEAM Technologies for Information and Communication Technologies, funded by the European Commission. This publication reflects the view only of the authors, and the Commission cannot be held responsible for any use which may be made of the information contained therein. This work was supported by Japan Science and Technology Agency (JST) SICORP and JSPS KAKENHI Grant Number 18K11167.

References

1. Blin, L., Milani, A., Potop-Butucaru, M., Tixeuil, S.: Exclusive perpetual ring exploration without chirality. In: Lynch, N.A., Shvartsman, A.A. (eds.) DISC 2010. LNCS, vol. 6343, pp. 312–327. Springer, Heidelberg (2010). https://doi.org/10.1007/978-3-642-15763-9_29
2. Bonnet, F., Milani, A., Potop-Butucaru, M., Tixeuil, S.: Asynchronous exclusive perpetual grid exploration without sense of direction. In: Fernàndez Anta, A., Lipari, G., Roy, M. (eds.) OPODIS 2011. LNCS, vol. 7109, pp. 251–265. Springer, Heidelberg (2011). https://doi.org/10.1007/978-3-642-25873-2_18
3. Chalopin, J., Flocchini, P., Mans, B., Santoro, N.: Network exploration by silent and oblivious robots. In: Thilikos, D.M. (ed.) WG 2010. LNCS, vol. 6410, pp. 208–219. Springer, Heidelberg (2010). https://doi.org/10.1007/978-3-642-16926-7_20
4. D'Angelo, G., Navarra, A., Nisse, N.: A unified approach for gathering and exclusive searching on rings under weak assumptions. Distrib. Comput. **30**(1), 17–48 (2017)

5. D'Angelo, G., Stefano, G.D., Klasing, R., Navarra, A.: Gathering of robots on anonymous grids and trees without multiplicity detection. Theor. Comput. Sci. **610**, 158–168 (2016)
6. D'Angelo, G., Stefano, G.D., Navarra, A.: Gathering on rings under the look-compute-move model. Distrib. Comput. **27**(4), 255–285 (2014)
7. Das, S., Flocchini, P., Prencipe, G., Santoro, N., Yamashita, M.: Autonomous mobile robots with lights. Theor. Comput. Sci. **609**, 171–184 (2016)
8. Datta, A.K., Lamani, A., Larmore, L.L., Petit, F.: Ring exploration by oblivious agents with local vision. In: IEEE 33rd International Conference on Distributed Computing Systems, pp. 347–356 (2013)
9. Datta, A.K., Lamani, A., Larmore, L.L., Petit, F.: Ring exploration by oblivious robots with vision limited to 2 or 3. In: Higashino, T., Katayama, Y., Masuzawa, T., Potop-Butucaru, M., Yamashita, M. (eds.) SSS 2013. LNCS, vol. 8255, pp. 363–366. Springer, Cham (2013). https://doi.org/10.1007/978-3-319-03089-0_31
10. Datta, A.K., Lamani, A., Larmore, L.L., Petit, F.: Enabling ring exploration with myopic oblivious robots. In: 2015 IEEE International Parallel and Distributed Processing Symposium Workshop, pp. 490–499 (2015)
11. D'Emidio, M., Frigioni, D., Navarra, A.: Characterizing the computational power of anonymous mobile robots. In: 36th IEEE International Conference on Distributed Computing Systems, pp. 293–302 (2016)
12. Devismes, S., Lamani, A., Petit, F., Raymond, P., Tixeuil, S.: Optimal grid exploration by asynchronous oblivious robots. In: Richa, A.W., Scheideler, C. (eds.) SSS 2012. LNCS, vol. 7596, pp. 64–76. Springer, Heidelberg (2012). https://doi.org/10.1007/978-3-642-33536-5_7
13. Devismes, S., Lamani, A., Petit, F., Tixeuil, S.: Optimal torus exploration by oblivious robots. In: Bouajjani, A., Fauconnier, H. (eds.) NETYS 2015. LNCS, vol. 9466, pp. 183–199. Springer, Cham (2015). https://doi.org/10.1007/978-3-319-26850-7_13
14. Devismes, S., Petit, F., Tixeuil, S.: Optimal probabilistic ring exploration by semi-synchronous oblivious robots. Theor. Comput. Sci. **498**, 10–27 (2013)
15. Flocchini, P., Ilcinkas, D., Pelc, A., Santoro, N.: Remembering without memory: tree exploration by asynchronous oblivious robots. Theor. Comput. Sci. **411**(14–15), 1583–1598 (2010)
16. Flocchini, P., Ilcinkas, D., Pelc, A., Santoro, N.: Computing without communicating: ring exploration by asynchronous oblivious robots. Algorithmica **65**(3), 562–583 (2013)
17. Flocchini, P., Prencipe, G., Santoro, N., Widmayer, P.: Gathering of asynchronous robots with limited visibility. Theor. Comput. Sci. **337**(1–3), 147–168 (2005)
18. Fujinaga, N., Yamauchi, Y., Ono, H., Kijima, S., Yamashita, M.: Pattern formation by oblivious asynchronous mobile robots. SIAM J. Comput. **44**(3), 740–785 (2015)
19. Guilbault, S., Pelc, A.: Gathering asynchronous oblivious agents with local vision in regular bipartite graphs. Theor. Comput. Sci. **509**, 86–96 (2013)
20. Guilbault, S., Pelc, A.: Gathering asynchronous oblivious agents with restricted vision in an infinite line. In: Higashino, T., Katayama, Y., Masuzawa, T., Potop-Butucaru, M., Yamashita, M. (eds.) SSS 2013. LNCS, vol. 8255, pp. 296–310. Springer, Cham (2013). https://doi.org/10.1007/978-3-319-03089-0_21
21. Heriban, A., Défago, X., Tixeuil, S.: Optimally gathering two robots. In: 19th International Conference on Distributed Computing and Networking, pp. 3:1–3:10 (2018)

22. Klasing, R., Kosowski, A., Navarra, A.: Taking advantage of symmetries: gathering of many asynchronous oblivious robots on a ring. Theor. Comput. Sci. **411**(34–36), 3235–3246 (2010)
23. Klasing, R., Markou, E., Pelc, A.: Gathering asynchronous oblivious mobile robots in a ring. Theor. Comput. Sci. **390**(1), 27–39 (2008)
24. Ooshita, F., Tixeuil, S.: Ring exploration with myopic luminous robots. CoRR abs/1805.03965 (2018). https://arxiv.org/abs/1805.03965
25. Suzuki, I., Yamashita, M.: Distributed anonymous mobile robots: formation of geometric patterns. SIAM J. Comput. **28**(4), 1347–1363 (1999)

Uniform Circle Formation for Swarms of Opaque Robots with Lights

Caterina Feletti[1], Carlo Mereghetti[2(✉)] [ID], and Beatrice Palano[1] [ID]

[1] Dipartimento di Informatica, Università degli Studi di Milano,
via Celoria 18, 20133 Milan, Italy
caterina.feletti@studenti.unimi.it, palano@di.unimi.it
[2] Dipartimento di Fisica "Aldo Pontremoli", Università degli Studi di Milano,
via Celoria 16, 20133 Milan, Italy
carlo.mereghetti@unimi.it

Abstract. The Uniform Circle Formation problem requires a swarm of mobile agents, arbitrarily positioned onto the plane, to move on the vertices of a regular polygon. Each agent, customarily called robot, acts through a sequence of look-compute-move cycles. The robots do not store past actions/system snapshots. They are anonymous and cannot be distinguished by their appearance and do not have a common coordinate system (origin and axis) and chirality. The system is fully synchronous in that all robots have a common clock/notion of time regulating cycles. From the literature, the Uniform Circle Formation problem is recently known to be solvable in a system where robots are punctiform or fat, but in both cases *transparent*: no robot obstructs the visibility of any other robot. Here, we solve the Uniform Circle Formation problem within a more realistic *opaque* robot system, i.e., robots may have obstructed visibility due to collinearities. Yet, our robots are assumed to be punctiform and *luminous*, i.e., equipped with a persistent light assuming different colors. This latter peculiarity represents the only way robots have to communicate. Our proposed algorithm uses a constant number of look-compute-move cycles as well as a constant number of colors.

Keywords: Autonomous mobile robots · Opaque robots
Uniform circle formation

1 Introduction

A well consolidated trend in the literature on distributed computing investigates models and algorithms for agent-based computing systems, having great relevance in several real-world applications. In these systems, a swarm of mobile computing entities, called *robots*, have to cooperate to solve a given problem by operating under several assumptions on robot capabilities and on the particular scenario. Of great importance are models where robots are autonomous, i.e. they act without a central control, and operate through a sequence of *look-compute-move* cycles in which each robot: (i) takes the snapshot of the system (*look*),

T. Izumi and P. Kuznetsov (Eds.): SSS 2018, LNCS 11201, pp. 317–332, 2018.
https://doi.org/10.1007/978-3-030-03232-6_21

(ii) executes a deterministic algorithm (*compute*), and *(iii)* travels to the computed destination, if any (*move*) [9,10,15].

Several modeling assumptions are considered, that can affect the computational power of the robots. E.g., robots may have distinct identifiers (yielding the ability of distinguish one robot from another) or, on the contrary, they may be anonymous. They may have a finite but persistent memory which is preserved from one look-compute-move cycle to the next. If no such memory exists, robots are said to be oblivious. A "compromise" between memory and obliviousness is represented by luminous robots, featuring a persistent light assuming different colors as a means of communication as well. Another step towards realistic models is to work with no point-like (punctiform model) but fat robots, where all robots are supposed to be solid discs on a plane with a certain radius. Moreover, they can be transparent, enabling a complete visibility of the system, or opaque. Yet, depending on the nature of the problem, robots can move either on the Euclidean plane, or on a graph which can either be known in advanced or not.

Concerning robot activation policy, three models are proposed in the literature: *fully synchronous*, where all robots execute their cycle synchronously, *semi synchronous*, where a subset of robots execute their cycle synchronously whereas the others remain idle, and *asynchronous*, where each robot acts asynchronously.

Several research efforts focus on very basic classes of geometric pattern formation problems to be solved within such distributed environments [21,22,24]. Robots might be required to meet in a certain specific location. This problem is known as Gathering. E.g., in [17], asynchronous robots move on the plane and have limited visibility. In [3], few fat asynchronous robots move on the plane. In [2], synchronous fat robots with limited visibility move on the plane. In [6], synchronous and asynchronous robots move on a ring and have to cope with malicious agents which can occupy positions. In the Uniform Circle Formation (UCF) problem, we ask robots to move to vertices of a regular polygon, the number of vertices—which can be known or not in advance—being exactly the number of robots in the system. In [8], an algorithm is proposed which asymptotically converges to a regular polygon. In [12], a semi-synchronous solution is given, starting from particular robot configurations. In [7], the authors solve UCF for asynchronous fat transparent robots. In [16], the problem is finally solved for the asynchronous case, with punctiform and transparent robots.

So far, we have mainly considered swarms of *transparent* robots. Nevertheless, several issues arise whenever *opaque* robots come into play. In this realm, the first natural problem to be tackled is Complete Visibility, where robots are required to displace on the plane so that each robot is visible to all others. Since obstructed visibility turns out to be a serious problem in robot systems, solutions in the literature are proposed for luminous robots, i.e., robots with persistent lights assuming different colors. The computational power of lights on swarms of robots is deeply investigated, e.g., in the seminal papers [4,5,13] for robots moving on the plane, and in [9,10] for robots on graphs. In [20], a $\mathcal{O}(\log N)$ time algorithm is presented, solving Complete Visibility by using $\mathcal{O}(1)$ colors in an asynchronous setting. For the semi-synchronous case, the problem is solved in [19] with a constant amount of time and colors. Finally, in [18] a $\mathcal{O}(1)$ time and $\mathcal{O}(1)$ colors algorithm is designed for the asynchronous setting. Recently, in [1] a fault-tolerant algorithm for Complete Visibility is exhibited.

1.1 Motivation and Contribution of the Paper

In this paper, we focus on the UCF problem which, as above recalled, consists of displacing robots on the vertices of a regular polygon. Such a problem received much attention from the literature for both theoretical and applicative reasons. From a practical point of view, a regular layout may preset several advantages for a distributed system. E.g., for a network of mobile agents, it may be convenient to regularly displace to facilitate communications, visibility and computations. Every agent is equidistant from its neighbors and it has the same view of the system: this guarantees a fair communication, where there are no evident differences in the energy spent in sending messages. Furthermore, this uniform pattern allows to implement distributed algorithms which guarantee a fair load balancing among the agents.

Our solution to UCF is based on [16]. However, we stress that a key point in their model is that each robot in the *look* phase *can see the whole system*. Precisely, robots are punctiform and *transparent*, i.e., no robot obstructs the visibility of any other robot. Such *full visibility* feature might not turn to be realistic, as above pointed out. Thus, *obstructed visibility* could represent a constraint making the model more interesting and realistic but, on the other hand, more difficult to manage. In this *opaque model*, if three robots are collinear, the middle robot obstructs the vision of the other two. Therefore, whenever a collinearity occurs, some robots may have a wrong perception of the real global number of agents in the system. Clearly, this pitfall turns out to be a severe limitation for solving our problem.

Here, we propose a solution to UCF in the *opaque* model [18,19], where we allow robots to communicate with a *light* able to assume different colors. Such a well studied functionality turns out to be a natural minimal enhancement for robots to solve several tasks (see, e.g., [4,5,9,10,13]). In particular, we exhibit and analyze an algorithm that solves the UCF problem in the fully synchronous setting with a constant number of cycles, and with a constant numbers of colors.

A Quick Outline of Our Algorithm for UCF. Our algorithms strategy presents a pre-computation phase where first complete visibility is reached by [19]. Next, robots move on their smallest enclosing circle (SEC) [23]. At this point, the original phase of the algorithm starts, where some reference points (pivot and angle robots) are fixed on the SEC, enabling the computation of the final destinations of the other robots. Such destinations are then reached by first moving robots within the SEC on some special chords. Finally, internal robots get back radially to the SEC, ending up in the regular polygon vertices. Along the whole process, deadlocks and collinearities are tackled and solved. Due to lack of space, some explaining material and proofs have been omitted.

2 Preliminaries: The Computational Model and the Problem

We give a quick overview of the distributed system we shall be dealing with, referring the reader to, e.g., [5,15] for a detailed exposition. Finally, we formally state the UCF problem.

Consider a finite set (swarm) of punctiform computational agents, called robots, which form a distributed system located in the plane $\mathbb{R}^2$. These robots are: *(i)* anonymous and indistinguishable: they do not share any own identifier, *(ii)* autonomous: there does not exist a central coordinator, *(iii)* homogeneous: they execute the same deterministic algorithm, *(iv)* oblivious: they do not remember any data about previous actions, *(v)* mobile: they can freely move on the plane, provided they never collide, *(vi)* rigid: they cannot be stopped before reaching the computed destination (i.e., no adversary can stop robot movement). The robots are equipped with sensory capabilities to determine the positions of other robots. Moreover, they are able to compute in finite time and infinite precision any algebraic function of points in the plane. In addiction, we assume the following limitations on robots: *(i)* they do not know how many they are, *(ii)* they are disoriented: no agreement among the individual coordinate systems, nor on unit distance and chirality (roughly speaking, clockwise direction), *(iii)* they are not transparent: collinearity causes obstructed visibility, this *opacity* feature being in sharp contrast with the transparent model in, e.g., [16].

Indeed these latter three inabilities introduce complications in algorithms design. E.g., due to opacity *(iii)* and lack of knowledge of robots number *(i)*, each robot may not be able to know whether or not some robots are hidden at any given time. Nevertheless, this lack of the knowledge of robots number makes the system easily scalable. Yet, the disorientation *(ii)* might result in robot collisions. To deal with these adversities, *we equip robots with a light displaying a certain number of different colors they can communicate through* (see, e.g., [4,5,9,10,13]). We emphasize that such a light is the only mean robots have to exchange information.

Let us formally describe how our robot swarms work. Let $\mathcal{R}$ be the finite set of all robots in the swarm, $|\mathcal{R}|$ being unknown by each robot. Let *Colors* be the finite set of colors the light of each robot can assume to communicate. At any instant t, a robot $r \in \mathcal{R}$ sits in a position $pos^t(r) \in \mathbb{R}^2$, and its light shines with a color $light^t(r) \in Colors$. For any $r, s \in \mathcal{R}$, we say that r sees s (formally, $r \trianglelefteq s$) if and only if either $r = s$ or there exists no third robot on the line segment joining r and s. Let $Vis^t(r) = \{s \in \mathcal{R} \mid r \trianglelefteq s\}$ be the set of all the robots visible by r at time t. It is clear that r has a *complete visibility* of the whole system $\mathcal{R}$ at time t whenever $Vis^t(r) = \mathcal{R}$. If $r \trianglelefteq s$, then r senses only the position and the light of s and no other information on s. For any $r \in \mathcal{R}$, we call *configuration* of r at instant t the pair $\phi_r^t = (pos^t(r), light^t(r))$. We call *snapshot* of r at time t the set $snapshot_r^t = \{\phi_s^t \mid s \in Vis^t(r)\}$.

Each robot r operates in *look-compute-move* cycles. Every cycle is executed in a single and atomic instant of time, and consists of these steps:

- **Look:** r obtains the instantaneous snapshot $snapshot_r^t$ according to its coordinate system.
- **Compute:** r runs a deterministic algorithm $\mathbb{A}$ which, by having $snapshot_r^t$ as input, computes the destination point of r and the (possibly) new color for the light of r. Formally, $\mathbb{A}(snapshot_r^t) = \phi_r^{t+1}$.
- **Move:** r sets its new color and moves straight toward the destination point above computed without being stopped (rigidity assumption).

In the *fully synchronous* model, all robots are activated at every round occurring at each time t. Since cycles are executed atomically, all robots terminate their cycle by the next round. Let $C_t = \{\phi_r^t \mid r \in \mathcal{R}\}$ be the *system configuration* at time t. We say that a system configuration is *valid* if there is no collision, i.e. for all distinct $r, s \in \mathcal{R}$, we have $pos^t(r) \neq pos^t(s)$. We stress that our model does not allow the trajectories of robots to cross in the move phase arising from C_t. Let C_0 be the *initial configuration*, where all robots in $\mathcal{R}$ are located in distinct positions on the plane, with lights off. Let $\mathcal{C}$ be the set of all the valid configurations. We define the relation $\vdash \subseteq \mathcal{C}^2$ such that $C' \vdash C''$ if and only if the configuration C'' is reachable from C' by executing a *look-compute-move* cycle. A *computation* on $\mathcal{R}$ is a sequence of valid configurations $C_0, \ldots, C_t, C_{t+1}, \ldots$ such that: (i) C_0 is an initial configuration, (ii) $C_t \vdash C_{t+1}$ for every $t \geq 0$. We say that the computation reaches a *terminal configuration* $C_{t_{end}}$ whenever $C_{t_{end}} = C_{t_{end}+1}$.

We are now ready to present the UCF problem we are to solve on fully synchronous swarms of opaque robots with lights. Let a fully synchronous swarm of n robots be in any given initial valid configuration C_0. The UCF problem asks the swarm to move from C_0 to a valid terminal configuration in which robots form a regular n-gon.

3   A Preliminary Step of Our Algorithm and Terminology

Clearly, in order to settle to vertices of a regular n-gon, any robot needs to know n. This may be achieved by first solving the Complete Visibility problem in our model. This problem asks all robots from any given initial system configuration to reach a terminal configuration where each robot is visible to all others. At this point, n can be clearly computed at a glance. Note however that n cannot be stored by the robots, and hence it will be somehow readily fixed in the topology of the swarm. A possible solution to the Complete Visibility problem moves robots to the vertices of their convex hull. To this aim, the algorithm in [19] fits our model, solving the Complete Visibility problem within a constant number of rounds and colors (i.e., not depending on the number of robots).

Next, each robot takes its snapshot (*look*), computes the *smallest enclosing circle* (SEC) e.g. by Welzl's algorithm [23] (*compute*), and eventually moves radially on the SEC (*move*). Clearly, such movements cannot collide, since each trajectory is radial to the same center. It might be the case that two robots (and, of course, no more than two) sit on the same radial trajectory. However, by computing distances from the two possible final destinations, they can easily choose to move in opposite directions and reach the two diametrically opposed locations. At the end of this preliminary phase, all robots lay on the SEC upon which the final regular n-gon will be formed. We stress that this SEC will not change along the whole algorithm execution, as the reader will be able to verify.

Let us now introduce some terminology useful in our algorithm design. Consider a set of n robots lying on their SEC, so they share mutual visibility. Call O the center of the SEC. Let p, q be two distinct robots on the SEC. They delimit two arcs $\widehat{pq}$ (clockwise, counterclockwise). We say that p and q are adjacent if there is at least one of the two arcs $\widehat{pq}$ where no other robot lies. We call *base angle* the angle $\alpha = \frac{2\pi}{n}$. Indeed, if the robots form a regular n-gon, each pair p, q of adjacent robots forms a base angle with the center of the SEC (i.e., $\widehat{pOq} = \alpha$).

Given p, q, r three distinct robots on the SEC, such that $\widehat{pOq} = \alpha = \widehat{qOr}$, we call (p, q, r) (or (r, q, p)) a *regular triple*. The middle robot q is said to be the *pivot*. Given a SEC, we define an equivalence relation among regular triples. We say that (p_1, p_2, p_3) and (p_4, p_5, p_6) are *concordant* if $\widehat{p_iOp_j} = k\alpha$ for some $k \geq 0$ and every $i, j \in \{1, \dots, 6\}$. As we will explain later, our strategy to collocate the robots on the vertices of a regular n-gon (inscribed in the SEC) starts by selecting particular regular triples. We will refer to them as *main regular triples* which will turn out to be concordant. The main regular triples will not move for the whole computation, while the other robots will move to form the regular n-gon.

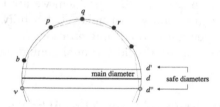

Fig. 1. The main diameter d and safe diameters d' and d'' for the regular triple (p, q, r). The black points are robots and b is the closest to the main diameter robot. The gray point ν is one of the two closest to the main diameter vertices of the regular polygon.

Given a regular triple (p, q, r), its *main diameter* is the SEC diameter d parallel to the chord $\overline{pr}$. Let b be one of the nearest robots to d and let $\ell(b, d)$ be the distance from b to d. Moreover, let ν be a closest but not belonging to d vertex of the regular polygon that has to be formed. Let consider two cases:

- **No robot on the main diameter, i.e., $\ell(b, d) > 0$:** Let d' and d'' be the two opposite chords parallel to d at distance $\min\{\ell(b, d), \ell(\nu, d)\}$ from d. We call d' and d'' *safe diameters* of (p, q, r). (See Fig. 1 below.)
- **One or two robots on the main diameter, i.e., $\ell(b, d) = 0$:** Let, e.g., e and e' be the robots on the endpoints of the main diameter, and let c be one of the robots nearest to d but not laying on d. We make e and e' go straight to the points on the SEC whose distance from d is $\frac{\min\{\ell(c,d), \ell(\nu,d)\}}{2}$; the direction of such movement can be arbitrarily chosen. Let d' and d'' be the two opposite

chords parallel to d at distance $\frac{\min \ell(c,d), \ell(\nu,d)}{2}$ from d and passing through e and e'. As above, we call d' and d'' *safe diameters* of (p, q, r).

Given four robots p, q, r, t such that both (p, q, r) and (q, r, t) are regular triples, we call (p, q, r, t) a regular 4-tuple, whose pivots are q and r. In this case, we call *main diameter* of (p, q, r, t) the diameter d parallel to the chord $\overline{pt}$. The safe diameters for the 4-tuple (p, q, r, t) are defined as above.

Let us consider two adjacent main regular triples (p_1, p_2, p_3) and (p_4, p_5, p_6) (no other triple lies on the SEC between them), and the shortest arc $\overparen{p_2 p_5}$. Similarly to safe diameters setting above explained, we may define a chord c laying between the shortest arc $\overparen{p_2 p_5}$ and the chord $\overline{p_2 p_5}$, parallel to this latter chord, and such that no robot or regular polygon vertex are on the SEC between c and $\overline{p_2 p_5}$. We call c *safe chord* of (p_1, p_2, p_3) and (p_4, p_5, p_6). (See Fig. 2 below.)

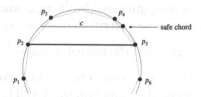

Fig. 2. The safe chord c for the two adjacent main regular triples (p_1, p_2, p_3) and (p_4, p_5, p_6). The region between c and the chord $\overline{p_2 p_5}$ does not contain robots or vertices of the regular polygon.

4   The Algorithm

We are now ready to outline our algorithm for solving the UCF problem on a *fully synchronous* swarm of opaque robots with lights. As stated at the beginning of Sect. 3, in a first phase all robots gain complete visibility of the swarm, and then move onto their SEC maintaining the knowledge of the exact number n of robots in the system. Let C_H be the swarm configuration at this point; without loss of generality, we assume robots lights having the same color. Clearly, all robots are again vertices of a convex hull. The resulting dynamic of the algorithm depends on the type of this convex hull, in particular on its degree of symmetry.

First of all, a special case occurs whenever the convex hull is *perfect* [11]. In this case, all robots lie on the edges of the associated regular n-gon (called *supporting polygon*, SP), two robots per edge. The goal of our algorithm for this particular configuration is to slide robots along the edges of the SP, until they reach the vertices of the SP. Notice that, given a perfect convex hull, the SP is unique and computable in a single round: each robot takes its snapshot (*look*), checks whether the system configuration forms a perfect convex hull and computes the SP (*compute*), eventually slides along the edge until it reaches the correct vertex (*move*). Notice that two robots on the same edge head in opposite directions, and therefore no collisions occur. We remark that a *biangular configuration*[1] is a special case of perfect convex hull. Also in [16], the perfect convex hull and the biangular configurations are dealt with as a special case at the beginning of their algorithm.

Summary of the Algorithm. Except for the perfect convex hull case, as above quoted, our distributed algorithm aims at finding the main regular triples in the configuration C_H as follows:

- Selects unambiguously some robots to be the pivots of the future main regular triples.
- Makes some robots move to form the main regular triples with the selected pivots. Indeed, these movement are not necessary if the main regular triples are already set. Once the main regular triples are formed, these robots will not move anymore.
- Makes the other robots compute their destination point (on the basis of the main regular triples) and move to form the regular polygon.

Our algorithm will be dealing with the following issues:

- Robots are oblivious. Once they make a move, they should be able to recover and recompute some essential information which will be necessary in the next cycles. In our algorithm, we encode such information by robots positions and colors.
- Obstructed visibility can cause deadlocks in particular configurations. To avoid them, we make use of safe diameters and chords above explained.
- In the *fully syncronous* model, an algorithm is efficient if it can fully exploit parallelism. Roughly speaking, if it makes the most of the robots move simultaneously during the same cycle, hence leading to quick executions. Our algorithm has to avoid situations yielding strictly sequential dynamics.

Let us now show cycle by cycle how our algorithm is implemented.

4.1   Cycle 1: Pivots Selection and Angle Setting

Starting from C_H, we select the main regular triples/4-tuples which will be the reference points for the movements of the other robots. In particular, we select the pivots and their adjacent robots which will form a base angle with the respective pivot. Once a main regular triple/4-tuple has been selected, it does not move anymore. As observed above, the dynamic of the algorithm depends on the degree of symmetry of C_H. We can distinguish between three cases: *asymmetry*, *symmetry with exactly one axis*, and *rotational symmetry*.

---

[1] A set of $n \geq 2$ robots forms a biangular configuration if robots lie on a circle C centered in O, and two non zero angles α, β exist such that for every pair r and p of robots consecutive on C, we have $\widehat{rOp} \in \{\alpha, \beta\}$ and α and β alternate clockwise [11].

Asymmetry. Consider the general case of asymmetry, where no symmetry axis can be found in C_H. In such a configuration, each robot r performs these phases:

- **Look-Compute:** The robot r unambiguously set the pivot robot p. Furthermore, r computes the positions a_1 and a_2 of the vertices which will be adjacent to the pivot p in the regular polygon.
- **Move:** If r is the pivot, then it does not move and sets its color as *pivot*. If r is the nearest adjacent robot to a_1 or a_2, it will form the main regular triple with p as pivot: r reaches this point (without collision) and sets its color as *angle*. Indeed, if two robots share the same distance from a_1 (or a_2), the algorithm chooses the robot which is nearer to p. Otherwise, r does nothing.

Symmetry with Exactly One Axis[2]. Consider now the case where exactly one axis of symmetry l exists in C_H. There are three cases:

ODD n. Consider the case where l passes through a robot, which will be the pivot p, and splits the opposite edge. The axis divides the convex hull into two symmetric halves, each with $\frac{n-1}{2}$ robots (except p). In such a configuration, each robot r performs:

- **Look-Compute:** r computes the axis of symmetry l and the positions a_1 and a_2 of the vertices which will be adjacent to the pivot p in the regular polygon.
- **Move:** If r belongs to l, it sets its color as *pivot*. If r is the nearest adjacent robot to a_1 or a_2, it sets its color as *angle* and moves to its nearest destination point a_1 or a_2. Indeed, if two robots share the same distance from a_1 (or a_2), the algorithm chooses the adjacent robot which is nearer to p. Otherwise, r does nothing.

EVEN n, TWO PIVOTS. Consider the case where l passes through two opposite robots, which will be the two pivots p and p'. The axis divides the convex hull into two symmetric halves, each with $\frac{n-2}{2}$ robots (except the two pivots). In such a configuration, each robot r performs:

- **Look-Compute:** r computes the axis of symmetry l and the positions a_1, a_2 and a_1', a_2' of the vertices which will be adjacent to the pivots p and p', respectively, in the regular polygon.
- **Move:** If r belongs to l, it sets its color as *pivot*. If r is the nearest adjacent robot to a_1, a_2, a_1' or a_2', it sets its color as *angle* and moves to its nearest destination point a_1, a_2, a_1' or a_2'. As before, if there are two robots sharing the same distance from their destination point, the algorithm chooses one robot unambiguously (e.g., by considering distances from l). Otherwise, r does nothing.

---

[2] Two or more symmetry axes imply a rotational symmetry, which is considered in the next case.

EVEN n, NO PIVOT. Let the case of l splitting two opposite edges. The axis divides the convex hull into two symmetric halves, each of them with $\frac{n}{2}$ robots. No robot lies on l. In such a configuration, each robot r performs:

- **Look-Compute:** r computes the axis of symmetry l and the positions $a_0, \ldots, a_3, a_0', \ldots, a_3'$ of the vertices which will be the nearest to l in the regular configuration. In particular, $\overline{a_1 a_2}$ and $\overline{a_1' a_2'}$ will be the two opposite edges splitted by l.
- **Move:** If r is the nearest robot to one of the computed positions, it sets its color as *pivot* if the nearest destination is a_1, a_2 or a_1', a_2', or as *angle* if the nearest destination is a_0, a_3 or a_0', a_3', and moves to such destination. As before, if two robots share the same distance from their destination point, the algorithm chooses one robot unambiguously. Otherwise, r does nothing.

Rotational Symmetry. Consider now the case of rotational symmetry. Let $r_0, \ldots, r_{n-1}$ be the sequence of robots consecutive on the SEC, ordered according to the minimum lexicographical angle-string[3]. If such string can be divided into k identical substrings up to rotation, the convex hull on the SEC can be divided into k identical sectors, each being the $\frac{2\pi}{k}$-rotation of the previous one. Let $P_i = \{r_j \mid j \equiv i \mod k\}$ be the class of symmetry which contains k robots sharing the same positions in the k different sectors. We can unambiguously choose a class of symmetry P (called *main class of symmetry*). The robots in P will be the *pivots*. We now show how to set k main regular triples in this k-angular configuration. Each robot r acts as follows:

- **Look-Compute:** r computes the main class of symmetry $P = \{p_1, \ldots, p_k\}$ and the positions $\{a_{j_0}, a_{j_1} \mid j \in \{1, \ldots, k\}\}$ of the vertices which will be the nearest to elements in P in the regular polygon.
- **Move:** If r belongs to P, it sets its color as *pivot*. If r is the nearest robot to some a_{i_0} or a_{i_1}, it sets its color as *angle* and moves to its nearest destination point a_{i_0} or a_{i_1}. If two robots share the same distance from their destination, we can unambiguously choose one robot as before. Otherwise, r does nothing.

4.2   Cycle 2: Preparing Safe Diameters Setting

Now that all the main regular triples or 4-tuples have been set, a cycle begins where we prepare for safe diameters setting possibly locating robots on the endpoints of the main diameter whenever such endpoints are vertices of the regular polygon to be formed. Clearly, if robots verify that the configuration already forms a regular polygon, the algorithm stops at this cycle. Let C be the configuration resulting at the end of the previous cycle. If C is a rotational symmetry, this cycle is skipped. Otherwise, C presents one or two main regular triples, or

---

[3] Given a sequence $r_0, \ldots, r_{n-1}$ of robots consecutive on the SEC, let $\alpha_i = \widehat{r_i O r_{i+1}}$ be the angle insisting on the edge $\overline{r_i r_{i+1}}$. The corresponding angle-string is $\alpha_0 \cdots \alpha_{n-1}$.

two main regular 4-tuples. So, as shown in Sect. 3, we can define the main diameter and the safe diameters. The main diameter d is unique and computable by each robot.

Then, we have two cases: *(i)* the endpoints of d are taken by robots, but the endpoints are not vertices of the regular polygon to be formed, or *(ii)* no robot lays on the endpoints of d, but the endpoints are vertices of the regular polygon. In both cases, we require robots to move. Thus, a robot r in this cycle performs:

- **Look-Compute:** If C is a rotational symmetry, the cycle is skipped. Otherwise, r computes the main diameter d.
  If r realizes to be in case *(i)*, it spots the nearest robot to d, say q, which does not belong to d. Clearly, if there are more robots which share the same minimal distance from r, there is always an unambiguous way to choose one of them. Then, r computes its destination point on the SEC toward q at distance one half of the distance between d and q.
  If r realizes to be in case *(ii)* and to be the robot that must move to an endpoint, it spots unambiguously the endpoint to reach, avoiding collisions.
- **Move:** If r is in case *(i)* or *(ii)*, it moves to the destination above computed. Otherwise, r does nothing.

4.3   Cycle 3: Fair Distribution on the Two Half-Disks

The aim of this cycle is to fairly distribute robots on the SEC. In case of rotational symmetry configurations, such a property is directly guaranteed by the nature of this kind of symmetry, and hence this cycle can be skipped. Instead, consider the cases where just one or two regular triples (or 4-tuples) have been selected, and consider their safe diameters d' and d''. Such diameters define a safe area (containing the main diameter), and they are the bases of two half-disks (which contain the pivots and the other robots). If there are n robots on the SEC, this cycle distributes robots as follows: if n is even, each half-disk will contain $\frac{n}{2}$ robots, otherwise the half-disk with the pivot will contain $\lceil \frac{n}{2} \rceil$ robots, while the other will keep the $\lfloor \frac{n}{2} \rfloor$ remaining robots. Such a fair distribution guarantees that in the following cycles, robot trajectories will not intersect and/or collide, since each half-disk is independent from the other, and all trajectories within an half-disk will be collision free.

Let us show how to reach this fair distribution from a configuration C, where safe diameters and half-disks are settled. We distinguish between two cases:

- If n is even, we want $\frac{n}{2}$ robots to be in each half-disk. Let H^+ be the half-disk which contains $\frac{n}{2} + k$ robots and H^- the half-disk which contains the other $\frac{n}{2} - k$ robots. Our strategy suitably chooses k robots in H^+ which have to migrate in H^- in such a way to avoid collisions among them and with the robots already in H^-.
- If n is odd, one robot is the unique pivot of the configuration, which will not move anymore. For the remaining $n - 1$ (even) robots, we act as above.

Choice of the k Migrating Robots. If k is even, our algorithm singles out from H^+ the $\frac{k}{2}$ robots nearest to the main diameter d starting from one end of d and the $\frac{k}{2}$ robots nearest to d starting from the opposite end. Otherwise, if k is odd, our algorithm spots $k-1$ (even) robots in H^+ as before. The k-th migrating robot can be unambiguously chosen among the remaining robots.

Migration. Our strategy is to migrate the selected robots on the arc of H^-, traveling perpendicularly to the main diameter d. This movement can be executed if and only if no robot lies in the destination points. Let $m_1, \ldots, m_k$ be the migrating robots in H^+, and $Q = \{q_1, \ldots, q_{\frac{n}{2}-k}\}$ be the set of the positions of robots in H^-. Given a migrating robot m_i, we call t_i its projection onto the arc of H^-, and let $T = \{t_1, \ldots, t_k\}$ be the set of such projections. If t_i is not taken by any robot in Q, then m_i reaches t_i by a straight trajectory. Otherwise, m_i computes the point $u \in Q \cup T \setminus \{t_i\}$ nearest to t_i. Let $\widehat{t_i u}$ be the length of the shortest arc joining u with t_i, and let t_i' be the point on the SEC satisfying $\widehat{t_i t_i'} = \frac{\widehat{t_i u}}{4}$. Then, m_i travels straight towards t_i' without colliding with any robot. Analyzing in detail the cycle, every robot r performs:

- **Look-Compute:** If the configuration is a rotational symmetry the cycle is skipped. Otherwise, if r is *pivot* or *angle*, it does nothing, else r computes the main diameter d and checks whether it is a migrant robot. If this is the case, it computes its destination point on H^- as seen above.
- **Move:** r reaches its destination point on H^-.

4.4   Cycle 4: Rappelling down on the Safe Diameters or Safe Chords

Summing up, this cycle starts from a configuration where: *(i)* all the robots lie on the SEC, so they know how many robots are involved in the regular polygon formation, *(ii)* there are $m \geq 1$ robots with color *pivot* (or $2m$ in case of main regular 4-tuples), *(iii)* there are at most $2m$ robots with color *angle*, *(iv)* there are m main regular triples colored as *angle-pivot-angle*, *(v)* all the other robots have no light on, *(vi)* all robots are equally distributed on m sectors, *(vii)* every robot on the SEC sees at least a main regular triple colored *angle-pivot-angle*. From now on, the m main regular triples will not move anymore, whereas the robots which are not yet in the right position will move within the SEC. Let us distinguish the following cases.

One or Two Main Regular Triples, or Two Main Regular 4-Tuples. Let us consider the case with only one main regular triple, or two main regular triples/4-tuples. Let d be their main diameter, which is unique as previously observed. Let d' and d'' be their safe diameters equidistant from d. In this cycle, every robot r performs (see Fig. 3 below):

- **Look-Compute:** If r is *pivot* or *angle*, it does nothing. Otherwise, r computes: the safe diameters d' and d'', its destination point t on the SEC, the point $t_\perp$, which is the projection of t on the safe diameter nearest to r.

– **Move:** r sets its color as *internal* and travels to $t_\perp$.

Three or More Main Regular Triples. Let us consider the case of $k \geq 3$ main regular triples. It is easy to see that this kind of configuration is a rotational symmetry. In this cycle, every robot r performs:

– **Look-Compute:** If r is *pivot* or *angle*, it does nothing. Otherwise, r computes: the nearest safe chord c (see Sect. 3), its destination point t on the SEC, the point $t_\perp$, which is the projection of t on c.
– **Move:** r sets its color as *internal* and travels to $t_\perp$.

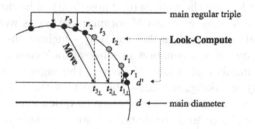

Fig. 3. Computing and collision free traveling towards the projections onto the safe diameter of robots final destinations.

4.5 Cycle 5: Reaching the SEC

At the end of the previous cycle, every robot which is not *pivot* or *angle* colored lies on a safe diameter or on a safe chord. Our strategy was to move the robots to a position which "contains" some information about its final destination point on the SEC. In this cycle, every robot r performs:

– **Look-Compute:** If r is *pivot* or *angle*, it does nothing. Otherwise, r is within the SEC on a safe chord or a safe diameter, and sees: *(i)* at least three robots on the SEC (*pivot* or *angle* colored) from which r can re-compute the SEC, or *(ii)* at least a pair of robots *pivot-angle* which defines the base angle. So, r computes: the original SEC upon which it has to travel to, the segment s (safe chord or safe diameter) where it currently lies on, its destination arc H, the projection point t of r on H.
– **Move:** r sets its color as *sec* and travels to t.

There may exist a different dynamic of this Cycle 5 in case of asymmetry (where only one pivot exists). In fact, some robots on the farthest from the pivot safe diameter may not see the main triple because of robots laying on the other safe diameter. So, this cycle must be repeated at most twice, one per safe diameter.

5   Conclusions and Future Work

In this paper, we design an algorithm solving the Uniform Circle Formation (UCF) problem, i.e., the problem of displacing on the plane a swarm of mobile robots such that each robot stands at the vertex of a regular polygon. Our robots autonomously operate through a sequence of look-compute-move cycles. They are anonymous, oblivious, and without any agreement on individual coordinate systems, unit distance and chirality. UCF has been recently solved in [16], for asynchronous systems of punctiform and *transparent* robots, i.e., no robot obstructs the visibility of any other robot. In contrast with such a transparency assumption, we considered a more realistic model where robots are punctiform and *opaque*, i.e., robots may have obstructed visibility due to collinearities. In addition, our robots feature the well-studied possibility of having persistent lights assuming different colors, as a means of communication as well.

Our proposed algorithm solves UCF for fully synchronous swarm of opaque robots with lights, by using a constant number of look-compute-move cycles as well as a constant number of colors. Moreover, the algorithm can fully exploit parallelism: roughly speaking, it makes the most of the robots move simultaneously during the same cycle, hence leading to quick executions. By suitable modifications to the algorithm here described, we were able to solve UCF *for the semi synchronous* setting, and the extension to the *asynchronous* case could be easily attained. Details may be found in [14].

Several directions for future researches may be explored. E.g., the constant number of colors in our solution is obtained by summing the constant number of colors needed to solve Complete Visibility [19] in the preliminary phase, plus the constant number of colors required by the rest of our own approach. A more careful integration between this two phases would certainly lead to lower the number of colors. Indeed, it would be interesting to establish the minimal number of colors needed to solve UCF in our setting. Moreover, it would be interesting to perform the same investigation on the number of colors and on the execution time for solving UCF on the semi synchronous and asynchronous settings. A starting point could be our algorithms in [14] which, as a preliminary phase, use the solution of Complete Visibility in the semi synchronous and asynchronous models [18, 19]. More generally, concerning the actual relevance of using lights for solving UCF, one may easily notice that a solution without light would imply a solution without light for Complete Visibility as well. To the best of our knowledge, this latter skill is still to be considered.

Another line of research could be the study and analysis of solutions of UCF for other models of robot swarms. For instance, it might be worth investigating the realistic case of fat opaque robots. A solution exists, for fat transparent robots [7]. Maybe, a first attempt could be performed by combining results and technique in [7] with the approach we presented in this paper.

Acknowledgements. The authors wish to thank the anonymous referees for valuable comments and remarks which helped improving the paper.

References

1. Aljohani, A., Sharma, G.: Complete visibility for mobile robots with lights tolerating faults. Int. J. Netw. Comput. **8**, 32–52 (2018)
2. Bolla, K., Kovacs, T., Fazekas, G.: Gathering of fat robots with limited visibility and without global navigation. In: Rutkowski, L., Korytkowski, M., Scherer, R., Tadeusiewicz, R., Zadeh, L.A., Zurada, J.M. (eds.) EC/SIDE -2012. LNCS, vol. 7269, pp. 30–38. Springer, Heidelberg (2012). https://doi.org/10.1007/978-3-642-29353-5_4
3. Czyzowicz, J., Gąsieniec, L., Pelc, A.: Gathering few fat mobile robots in the plane. Theor. Comput. Sci. **410**, 481–499 (2009)
4. Das, S., Flocchini, P., Prencipe, G., Santoro, N., Yamashita, M.: The power of lights: synchronizing asynchronous robots using visible bits. In: ICDCS 2012, pp. 506–515. IEEE (2012)
5. Das, D., Flocchini, P., Prencipe, G., Santoro, N., Yamashita, M.: Autonomous mobile robots with lights. Theor. Comput. Sci. **609**, 171–184 (2016)
6. Das, D., Focardi, R., Luccio, F.L., Markou, E., Squarcina, M.: Gathering of robots in a ring with mobile faults. Theor. Comput. Sci. (2018). https://doi.org/10.1016/j.tcs.2018.05.002
7. Datta, S., Dutta, A., Gan Chaudhuri, S., Mukhopadhyaya, K.: Circle formation by asynchronous transparent fat robots. In: Hota, C., Srimani, P.K. (eds.) ICDCIT 2013. LNCS, vol. 7753, pp. 195–207. Springer, Heidelberg (2013). https://doi.org/10.1007/978-3-642-36071-8_15
8. Défago, X., Konagaya, A.: Circle formation for oblivious anonymous mobile robots with no common sense of orientation. In: POMC 2002, pp. 97–104. ACM (2002)
9. D'Emidio, M., Frigioni, D., Navarra, A.: Synchronous robots vs asynchronous lights-enhanced robots on graphs. Electron. Notes Theor. Comput. Sci. **322**, 169–180 (2016)
10. D'Emidio, M., Frigioni, D., Navarra, A.: Characterizing the computational power of anonymous mobile robots. In: ICDCS 2016, pp. 293–302. IEEE (2016)
11. Dieudonné, Y., Petit, F.: Swing words to make circle formation quiescent. In: Prencipe, G., Zaks, S. (eds.) SIROCCO 2007. LNCS, vol. 4474, pp. 166–179. Springer, Heidelberg (2007). https://doi.org/10.1007/978-3-540-72951-8_14
12. Dieudonné, Y., Petit, F.: Squaring the circle with weak mobile robots. In: Hong, S.-H., Nagamochi, H., Fukunaga, T. (eds.) ISAAC 2008. LNCS, vol. 5369, pp. 354–365. Springer, Heidelberg (2008). https://doi.org/10.1007/978-3-540-92182-0_33
13. Di Luna, G.A., Flocchini, P., Gan Chaudhuri, S., Santoro, N., Viglietta, G.: Robots with lights: overcoming obstructed visibility without colliding. In: Felber, P., Garg, V. (eds.) SSS 2014. LNCS, vol. 8756, pp. 150–164. Springer, Cham (2014). https://doi.org/10.1007/978-3-319-11764-5_11
14. Feletti, C.: Regular polygon formation for swarms of robots. MSc thesis, Dipartimento di Informatica, Università degli Studi di Milano (2018). https://www.researchgate.net/profile/Caterina_Feletti/contributions
15. Flocchini, P., Prencipe, G., Santoro, N.: Distributed computing by oblivious mobile robots. Synth. Lect. Distrib. Comput. Theory **3**(2), 1–185 (2012)
16. Flocchini, P., Prencipe, G., Santoro, N., Viglietta, G.: Distributed computing by mobile robots: uniform circle formation. Distrib. Comput. **30**, 413–457 (2017)
17. Flocchini, P., Prencipe, G., Santoro, N., Widmayer, P.: Gathering of asynchronous robots with limited visibility. Theor. Comput. Sci. **337**, 147–168 (2005)

18. Sharma, G., Vaidyanathan, R., Trahan, J.L.: Constant-time complete visibility for asynchronous robots with lights. In: Spirakis, P., Tsigas, P. (eds.) SSS 2017. LNCS, vol. 10616, pp. 265–281. Springer, Cham (2017). https://doi.org/10.1007/978-3-319-69084-1_18

19. Sharma, G., Vaidyanathan, R., Trahan, J.L., Busch, C., Rai, S.: Complete visibility for robots with lights in $O(1)$ time. In: Bonakdarpour, B., Petit, F. (eds.) SSS 2016. LNCS, vol. 10083, pp. 327–345. Springer, Cham (2016). https://doi.org/10.1007/978-3-319-49259-9_26

20. Sharma, G., Vaidyanathan, R., Trahan, J.L., Busch, C., Rai, S.: $\mathcal{O}(\log N)$-time complete visibility for asynchronous robots with lights. In: IPDPS 2017, pp. 513–522. IEEE (2017)

21. Sugihara, K., Suzuki, I.: Distributed algorithms for formation of geometric patterns with many mobile robots. J. Robot. Syst. **13**, 127–139 (1996)

22. Suzuki, I., Yamashita, M.: Distributed anonymous mobile robots: formation of geometric patterns. SIAM J. Comput. **28**, 1347–1363 (1999)

23. Welzl, E.: Smallest enclosing disks (balls and ellipsoids). In: Maurer, H. (ed.) New Results and New Trends in Computer Science. LNCS, vol. 555, pp. 359–370. Springer, Heidelberg (1991). https://doi.org/10.1007/BFb0038202

24. Yamashita, M., Suzuki, I.: Characterizing geometric patterns formable by oblivious anonymous mobile robots. Theor. Comput. Sci. **411**, 2433–2453 (2010)

Arbitrary Pattern Formation
with Four Robots

Quentin Bramas[1]([✉]) [ID] and Sébastien Tixeuil[2]([✉])

[1] ICUBE, University of Strasbourg, CNRS, Strasbourg, France
bramas@unistra.fr
[2] Sorbonne Université, CNRS, Laboratoire d'Informatique de Paris 6, LIP6,
75005 Paris, France
Sebastien.Tixeuil@lip6.fr

Abstract. The pattern formation problem by autonomous mobile robots has been extensively studied and is at the core of oblivious mobile robots literature. However remaining cases involving few robots are still open. In this paper we propose a new geometric invariant that exists in any configuration with four robots. We then use this invariant to solve the pattern formation problem with four robots, with or without the common chirality assumption.

1 Introduction

We consider a set of mobile robots that move freely in a continuous 2-dimensional Euclidean space. Each robot repeats asynchronously Look-Compute-Move (LCM) cycles [7]. First, it *Looks* at its surroundings to obtain a snapshot containing the locations of all robots as points in the plane, with respect to its ego-centered coordinate system. Based on this visual information, the robot *Computes* a destination, and then *Moves* towards its destination. The robots are identical, anonymous and oblivious *i.e.*, the computed destination in each cycle depends only on the snapshot obtained in the current cycle (and not on the past history of execution). The snapshots obtained by the robots are not consistently oriented in any manner.

In this particularly weak model, it is interesting to characterize which additional assumptions are needed for the robots to cooperatively perform a given task. In this paper, we consider the pattern formation problem [7] in the most general asynchronous (ASYNC) model [4]. The robots start in an arbitrary initial configuration where no two robots occupy the same position, and are given the pattern to be formed as a set of coordinates in their own local coordinate system. An algorithm solves the pattern formation problem if within finite time the robots form the input pattern and remain stationary thereafter.

Related Work. The pattern formation problem has been extensively studied in the deterministic setting in the semi-synchronous model [7], and the set of deterministically formable patterns is well characterized [5]. An algorithm that

T. Izumi and P. Kuznetsov (Eds.): SSS 2018, LNCS 11201, pp. 333–348, 2018.
https://doi.org/10.1007/978-3-030-03232-6_22

solves all possible instances of the problem has been presented in the ASYNC model without a common coordinate system [4], but assuming robots share a common chirality (a proved necessary assumption) and that the number n of robots is greater than 4.

When the pattern to form is a regular n-gon, the problem has been solved without any additional assumptions when $n \neq 4$ [3]. Recently, a complex algorithm that uses several classes of configurations to form the square with 4 robots has been presented [6]. Finally, an algorithm that works with any number of robots with or without chirality that can form any pattern has been presented recently [2] but it assumes that the initial configuration is asymmetric.

Overall, the deterministic arbitrary pattern formation problem for four robots with arbitrary initial configuration remains open, with or without chirality.

Contribution. We consider the arbitrary pattern formation problem with four robots in the ASYNC model, with or without chirality.

We first define a new geometric invariant that exists in any quadrilateral, which we call H-segment. Geometric inveriants are very useful when creating algorithms for autonomous asynchronous mobile robots, as they enable persistent information over several execution cycles, and do not depend on what the other robots are doing (as long as their movements satisfy the geometric invariant). We believe this new invariant could be extended to configurations involving more robots, and thus be of independent interest.

Then, we present our algorithm that forms any target pattern from any solvable initial configuration (some patterns remain impossible to form due to symmetricity). Our algorithm works with or without the common chirality assumption (if robots do not share a common chirality, the set of solvable patterns is of course reduced). We use the H-segment invariant when the initial configuration is a quadrilateral. Our algorithm is defined using a set of phases, where each phase is associated with a geometric invariant. This way of describing an algorithm is inspired by the work of Cicerone et al. [2], but our use of geometric invariant can be viewed as an extension of their methodology to allow several robots to move together.

2   The Model

We consider a set of $n = 4$ robots on the two-dimensional Euclidean plane. The robots are anonymous and all execute the same algorithm.

Each time a robot is activated it starts a Look/Compute/Move cycle. After the *look* phase, a robot obtains a configuration P representing the positions of the robots in its local coordinate system. After an arbitrary delay, the robot *computes* a path to a destination. Then, it *moves* toward the destination following the previously computed path. The duration of the move phase, and the delay between two phases, are chosen by an adversary and can be arbitrary long. The adversary decides when robots are activated assuming a *fair* scheduling *i.e.*, in any configuration, all robots are activated within finite time. The adversary also controls the robots movement along their target path and can stop a robot before reaching its destination, but not before traveling at least a distance $\delta > 0$ (δ being unknown to the robots).

We say two set of points A and B are *similar*, denoted $A \approx B$, if B can be obtained from A by translation, scaling, rotation, and, if the robots are not chiral, symmetry. A *configuration* P is a set of positions of robots at a given time. Each robot that looks at this configuration may see different (but similar) set of points.

An *execution* of an algorithm is an infinite sequence $P(0), P(1), \ldots$ of configurations. A robot is *static* when it is not in the moving phase or if the robot has reached its destination. A configuration is static if all robots are static (note that this information is not known by the robots).

An algorithm ψ *forms a pattern* F if, for any execution $P(0), P(1), \ldots$, there exists a time t such that $P(t') \approx F$ for all $t' \geq t$. In the sequel, F denotes the pattern to form.

Symmetricity. The symmetricity of two dimensional robots configurations has been defined many times, usually by counting the number of rotations leaving the configuration invariant. This definition is well-suited when robots agree on a common chirality, but without chirality the configuration may also have an axis of symmetry. Recently the symmetricity of three-dimensional configurations has been defined formally in an elegant and general way [8–10]. We present here a short definition and how to apply it for two-dimensional configurations without chirality. For the complete definition, see the work of Yamauchi et al. [10]. We call a set of robots chiral if they all share the same chirality.

Given a configuration C, one can augment it by assigning an arbitrary coordinate system to each robot. We assume here that those arbitrary coordinate systems have the same chirality if the robots are chiral. A symmetry group of a configuration is a point group (a group of geometric symmetries) acting on the configuration augmented with arbitrary coordinate systems. The symmetricity of a configuration is the set of its symmetry groups. We can represent the symmetricity of a configuration just by giving the maximal symmetry groups of this configuration as it is clear that all the subgroups of a symmetry group of a configuration are also symmetry groups of this configuration.

In the two dimensional plane, there are only two kinds of symmetry groups, Cyclic groups of order k (C_k) and Dihedral groups of order $2k$ (D_k). For instance, the symmetricity of the square is $\{C_4, D_2\}$, or more precisely $\{C_1, C_2, C_4, D_1, D_2\}$. When a configuration C has a symmetricity $\{C_a, D_b\}$, we denote by $\rho(C) = a$ the rotational symmetricity, and $\Phi(C) = 2b$ the axial symmetricity (we write $\Phi(C) = 1$ if C has a symmetricity $\{C_{\rho(C)}\}$). If the robots have the same chirality, then $\Phi(C)$ is always 1.

It is well known [10] that forming a pattern F from an initial configuration C is possible only if $\rho(C)$ divides $\rho(F)$ and $\Phi(C)$ divides $\Phi(C)$ *i.e.*, if the symmetricy of C is a subset of the symmetricity of F, even if robots are fully synchronous and have memory.

Also, when robots are chiral, an algorithm exists in the two-dimensional plan for all solvable instances [5]. When robots are not chiral, there are some algorithms that solve partially this problem, for instance when C has symmetricity $\{C_1\}$ [2]. In this paper, we present an algorithm that works for all solvable instances, for configurations of four robots, with or without chirality.

4-robots Configurations. Four points form either a line, a triangle (if one point is strictly inside the triangle formed by the three others) or a quadrilateral. When four points form a quadrilateral, there is a unique way, up to rotation and mirroring, to order those points.

A quadrilateral is *orthodiagonal* when its two diagonals cross with right angles. A *kite* is an orthodiagonal quadrilateral such that one diagonal is the line bisector of the other. If the latter is longer than, or has the same length as, the former one, the kite is said to be a *long kite*. Table 1 presents the symmetricity of some 4-robots configurations.

Table 1. Symmetricity of several 4-robots configurations

Configuration C	$\rho(C)$	$\Phi(C)$
Square	4	4
Rectangle	2	4
Non-rectangle parallelogram	2	1
Rhombus	2	1
Isosceles trapezoid	1	2
Asymmetric quadrilateral	1	1
4 aligned robots (with central symmetry)	2	2
Triangle with a robot inside	1	1

3   The H-segment of a Quadrilateral

First we define the H-coordinates of a quadrilateral. Then, we define the H-segments of a quadrilateral and in which case one can be uniquely elected. Finally we present the properties of this H-segment and how it remains invariant.

3.1   The Construction of an H-segment

For simplicity we denote by $\{p_1, p_2\} \oplus \{p_3, p_4\}$ a partition in two sets $\{p_1, p_2\}$ and $\{p_3, p_4\}$ of a quadrilateral (p_1, p_2, p_3, p_4). The other possible partition is $\{p_2, p_3\} \oplus \{p_1, p_4\}$. The notation $\angle(a, b, c)$ denote then oriented angle at point b from a to c. The orientation is always clockwise if robots are chiral, or arbitrary otherwise (but it is always the same for a given robot). In particular, one can choose to orient the angles in the same way as the indexes of the quadrilateral. See Fig. 1 for an illustration of the following definition.

Definition 1 (The H-segment of a partition of four points). *Let* $\{p_1, p_2\} \bigoplus \{p_3, p_4\}$ *be a partition of a quadrilateral* (p_1, p_2, p_3, p_4). *The H-segment, if it exists, is the unique segment* $[b_1, b_2]$ *such that (i) among* $\angle(p_1, b_1, b_2)$ *and* $\angle(b_2, b_1, p_2)$, *one equals* $\frac{5\pi}{8}$ *and the other is congruent modulo* π *and (ii) the same is true with* $\angle(p_3, b_2, b_1)$ *and* $\angle(b_1, b_2, p_4)$.

Let c be the interesection of the two diagonals of the quadrilateral, then we show by construction that the H-segment is well-defined and exists if $\angle(p_1, c, p_2) < 3\pi/4$. Let $C_{1,2}$ be the circle pasing through p_1 and p_2 such that its center A verifies $\angle(p_2, A, p_1) = \frac{\pi}{2}$. In particular, A and c are on different sides of the line (p_1, p_2). Also, p_1 and p_2 divides $C_{1,2}$ into a long arc LC and a short arc SC that have the property that any point P on SC verifies $\angle(p_1, P, p_2) = \frac{3\pi}{4}$.

Let $h_{1,2}$ be the intersection of the segment bisector of $[p_1, p_2]$ with the longest arc of $C_{1,2}$. We construct $C_{3,4}$ and $h_{3,4}$ in the same way with p_3 and p_4. Let b_1, resp. b_2, be the intersection of the line $[h_{1,2}, h_{3,4}]$ with $C_{1,2}$ (other than $h_{1,2}$), resp. with $C_{3,4}$ (other than $h_{3,4}$). One can prove that b_2 is outside $C_{1,2}$ if $\angle(p_1, c, p_2) < \frac{3\pi}{4}$. Indeed, by continuity we have that, if b_2 is inside $C_{1,2}$, then the center c is inside $C_{1,2} \cap C_{3,4}$ and thus verifies $\angle(p_1, c, p_2) = \angle(p_3, c, p_4) \geq \frac{3\pi}{4}$.

By construction we have $\angle(p_1, h_{1,2}, p_2) = \frac{\pi}{4}$ and it can be shown that we have either $\angle(p_1, b_1, b_2) = \angle(b_2, b_1, p_2) = \frac{5\pi}{8}$, $\angle(p_1, b_1, b_2) = \angle(b_2, b_1, p_2) - \pi = \frac{5\pi}{8}$, or $\angle(p_1, b_1, b_2) - \pi = \angle(b_2, b_1, p_2) = \frac{5\pi}{8}$ depending on whether b_1 is in the shortest or the longest arc of $C_{1,2}$ delimited by p_1 and p_2. The same is true for p_3 and p_4 on the other side of the segment. b_1 are b_2 are unique as any such points should be located on $C_{1,2}$ and $C_{3,4}$ and the line passing through them should also pass through $h_{1,2}$ and $h_{3,4}$. See Fig. 1 for an illustration.

The construction is unique and depends only on the choice of the partition (and not on the way the indexes are chosen or on the orientation, as soon as the quadrilateral is convex). The fact that $\angle(p_1, c, p_2) < \frac{3\pi}{4}$ is a sufficient condition for the existence of a H-segment means that for any quadrilateral, there is at least one partition that have an H-segment. Indeed, among the two angles formed by the diagonals of a quadrilateral, at least one is smaller than, or equals to, $\frac{\pi}{2}$ (and thus to $\frac{3\pi}{4}$).

The following property is a direct consequence of the construction of the H-segment. Here (p_1, p_2, p_3, p_4) is a quadrilateral.

Proposition 1. *Let* $[b_1, b_2]$ *be the H-segment of a partition* $\{p_1, p_2\} \bigoplus \{p_3, p_4\}$ *and let* p'_1 *be a point in the line* (p_1, b_1). *If* (p'_1, p_2, p_3, p_4) *is still a convex quadrilateral, then* $[b_1, b_2]$ *is also the H-segment of the partition* $\{p'_1, p_2\} \bigoplus \{p_3, p_4\}$.

The previous property means that a H-segment is invariant by movement of a point toward one extremity of it (and even beyond it) as soon as the quadrilateral remains convex. A direct consequence is that if four robots agree on a partition, then they can move while keeping this H-segment invariant, to remember their previous destination for instance. Moreover, the length of the segment can be used as a unit distance that remains invariant.

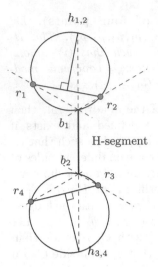

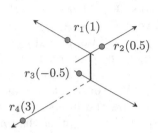

Fig. 1. Construction of the H-segment

Fig. 2. 4 robots on their H-axis associated with an H-segment. The H-coordinates of the four robots is the tuple $(-0.5, 3, 0.5, 1)$

3.2   The H-coordinates of Four Points

In a quadrilateral, given a H-segment and using the same notation as for its construction, the line (p_1, b_1) forms an axis where the zero is at b_1, the unit distance is the length of the H-segment, and the axis is directed so that a point p with positive coordinate satisfies $\angle(p, b_1, b_2) > \pi$. This axis is called the *H-axis* of p_1, and the coordinate of p_1 in its H-axis is called its *H-coordinate*. Let c_i be the H-coordinate of p_i, for $i \in \{1, \ldots, 4\}$. See Fig. 2 for an illustration.

The H-coordinates *associated* to an H-segment $\{p_1, p_2\} \bigoplus \{p_3, p_4\}$ is the smallest tuple (using the lexicographical order) among all the possible ordering of its coordinates, that respect the ordering of the vertices of the quadrilateral. In more details, H-segment is the smallest tuple between (c_1, c_2, c_3, c_4) and (c_3, c_4, c_1, c_2) if the robots are chiral, and the smallest tuple between (c_1, c_2, c_3, c_4), (c_3, c_4, c_1, c_2), (c_2, c_1, c_4, c_3), and (c_4, c_3, c_2, c_1) otherwise.

Definition 2. *The H-coordinates of a quadrilateral are the H-coordinates associated with the longest H-segment. If both H-segments have the same length, they are the smallest H-coordinates between the two.*

Theorem 1. *Two quadrilaterals are similar if and only if they have the same H-coordinates.*

Proof. Let Q and Q' be two similar quadrilaterals, and T be the transformation such that $Q' = T(Q)$. Since the construction of the H-segment does not depend on the coordinates system, the image of a longuest H-segment of Q by T is a longuest H-segment of Q'. The H-axes of Q are also transformed by T to the

H-axes of Q'. The length are multiplied by a constant number, but since the length of the longuest H-segment is used as a reference for the computation of the H-coordinates, the H-coordinates remain the same. For the converse, suppose that two quadrilaterals Q and Q' have the same H-coordinates, then let T be a transformation that transforms the H-segment associated to the H-coordinates of Q to the H-segment associated to the H-coordinates of Q' (one can choose an arbitrary H-segment if both H-segments are associate to the H-coordinates), and that associates the H-axis of the point with smallest (resp., the second, third, and fourth smallest) H-coordinate in Q to the H-axis of the point with the smallest (resp., second, third, and fourth smallest) H-coordinate in Q'. Then, since the transformation maintains angles and distance ratios, we have $T(Q) = Q'$.

3.3   The H-segment of a Non-orthodiagonal Quadrilateral

An easy way for all the robots to agree on a single H-segment is to only consider the longest one. One can prove the following property that indicates when we can discriminate the two H-segment using their distances.

Proposition 2. *The diagonals of a quadrilateral are perpendicular if and only if the two H-segments of the configuration have the same length.*

A quadrilateral that is not orthodiagonal is said to be a H-quadrilateral. The elected H-segment of a H-quadrilateral is the unique longest H-segment.

The following two properties are fundamental for the correctness of our algorithm, as they indicate that the elected H-segment of a H-quadrilateral is invariant by movements that either decrease a H-coordinate or that increase it assuming that the H-coordinates remains smaller than the H-coordinates of an existing quadrilateral.

Proposition 3. *Let C be a configuration, and s be one of its longuest H-segment. Let C' be the configuration after a robot moves on its H-axis in the direction that decreases its H-coordinate. Either s is the elected H-segment of C', or C' is not a quadrilateral.*

Proof. When a robot decreases its H-coordinate associated to a H-segment, the other H-segment gets shorter. Thus, after the robot's movement, s become the longuest H-segment, or remains the longuest if it was already the longuest in C.

Corollary 1. *Let Q and Q' be two quadrilaterals. Let $d = (d_1, d_2, d_3, d_4)$ be the H-coordinates of Q associated with an H-segment that is not necessarily the elected one, and $d' = (d'_1, d'_2, d'_3, d'_4)$ the H-segment of Q'. If $\forall i, d_i \leq d'_i$, then d is associated with the elected H-segment of Q.*

Proof. Q can be obtained from Q' by decreasing its H-coordinates and by Proposition 3, the elected H-segement remains the same.

3.4   The ε-square of a Segment

For a given ε, the ε-square of a segment $[a, b]$ is the square of size $\varepsilon \times ab$ centered at the middle of $[a, b]$ and that has two sides parallel to the (a, b) line.

A configuration of four robots is in a ε-square configuration if two robots are inside the ε-square of the segment formed by the two other robots.

Given two points p_1 and p_2, let $\xi > 0$. For any two points p_1' and p_2' such that the H-segment of the partition $\{p_1, p_1'\} \cup \{p_2, p_2'\}$ is of length $\xi \times p_1 p_2$, the sum of the H-coordinates of p_1 and p_2 is a constant that does not depends on the choice of p_1' and p_2'. Indeed, for any segment $[a, b]$ of length $\xi \times p_1 p_2$ such that $\angle(b, a, p_1) = \angle(a, b, p_2) = 5\pi/8$ we can use the law of cosines to compute the lengths $d(p_1, a)$ and $d(b, p_2)$ and show that it does not depend on the position of a and b. Moreover, for any set of four points having a H-segment of length l, the distance between two points is at least $\cos(2\pi/3) \times l$.

Combining those two claims, we have the following theorem.

Theorem 2. *For any real number $d > 0$, there exists $\varepsilon > 0$ small enough so that, if two robots robots are inside or on the ε-square of the two others, then all their H-coordinates are strictly greater than d.*

Indeed, the fact that two robots are close to one another means that the H-segment is also small compared to the distance between the two other robots. The latter means that the H-coordinates of those two robots are large.

In the remaining of the paper, ε is defined as in the previous theorem, using d as the maximum value among the H-coordinates of the pattern to form F (when F is a quadrilateral). This means that, if the H-coordinates of the configuration are smaller than the maximum H-coordinate of F, then the configuration is not an ε-square configuration.

4   4-Robot Pattern Formation Algorithm

In this section, we present our pattern formation algorithm. We first give an overview and then present in detail each move, followed by the proof of correctness.

4.1   Algorithm Overview

The algorithm is divided in several phases. Each phase corresponds a set of configurations and is associated with a geometric invariant that is used to ensure the robots have a persistent view of the configuration between two execution of their Look-Move-Compute cycles. The main phase of the algorithm is the one that is executed when the four robots form a quadrilateral. In this case we use the H-segment invariant to allow multiple robots to move simultaneously (which is necessary when the configuration is symmetric) while having persistent destination throughout the execution.

Then, there are two special phases. One if the configuration and the pattern are both long kites, and one if the configuration and the pattern are both lines.

In this case, the configuration remains a long kite, resp. a line, throughout the execution.

If the initial configuration is a long kite or a line, and the pattern to form is neither of that, then an ε-square configuration is formed to transition safely towards a quadrilateral so that the first phase can be executed.

Finally, when the pattern to form is a triangle, with a robot strictly inside it, then the goal is first to form a configuration whose convex hull is a triangle similar to the pattern. Then the robot in the middle can easily move towards the only remaining empty point of the pattern.

4.2   Algorithm Details

The algorithm consists of a set of phases. Each phase is a tuple containing a set of configurations, a geometric invariant, and a move. The move must preserve the geometric invariant, and when the robots reach a configuration from another phase, the robots must be static. This way of defining an algorithm for asynchronous robots is inspired by the work of Cicerone et al. [2], that helps decomposing the phases of an algorithm while ensuring that different phases are composable.

In the sequel a robot r also denotes its position in the plan.

Phases Definition. There are four main phases depending whether the configuration is (i) a triangle with angles a, b and $\pi - a - b$ ($T_{a,b}$), (ii) a line (L), (iii) a long kite (K), or (iv) another quadrilateral (H). Additionaly, there is a fifth phase used as a transition when the initial configuration is in $L \cup K$ and the target pattern F is in $H \cup T$. In some phase, we define two possible moves but only one applies at a time depending on the pattern. Usually, there is a move if the pattern can be reached directly, and another move if the goal is to reach another phase.

$\mathcal{F}$: This phase corresponds to the success of the algorithm. If the configuration is similar to the pattern, then, no move is executed.

$T_{a,b}$: **Configurations:** r_1 is inside the triangle formed by the 3 others. For simplicity, we consider that if $F \in T_{a,b}$, then the configuration where three robots form a triangle with angles a, b and $2\pi - a - b$ and the fourth robots is one an edge is also considered in $T_{a,b}$ (this is not the case for any other parameter a and b).
Invariant: The triangle convex hull.
Moves: If $F \in T_{a,b}$, move $m_{T \to F}$ to reach F.
Otherwise (in particular if $F \in T_{a',b'}$ with $(a,b) \neq (a',b')$), move $m_{T \to H}$ to reach H

L : **Configurations:** r_1 and r_2 are the two farthest robots and r_3 and r_4 are on $[r_1, r_2]$.
Invariant: Line $[r_1, r_2]$
Moves: If $F \in L$, move $m_{L \to F}$ to reach F.
Otherwise, move $m_{L \to \varepsilon\text{-}LB}$ to reach $\varepsilon - LB$

K : **Configurations:** r_1 and r_2 are the two farthest robots, and r_3 and r_4 are on the line bisector of $[r_1, r_2]$.

Invariant: Line $[r_1, r_2]$

Moves: If $F \in K$, move $m_{K \to F}$ to reach F.

Otherwise, move $m_{K \to \varepsilon\text{-}LB}$ to reach $\varepsilon - LB$

$\varepsilon - LB$: **Configurations:** r_1 and r_2 are the two farthest robots, and r_3 and r_4 are inside the ε-square, or on its boundary, except when the two robots are on two vertices of the ε-square.

Invariant: Line $[r_1, r_2]$

Moves: Move $m_{\varepsilon\text{-}LB \to H}$ to reach H

H : **Configurations:** the 4 robots are not in any previous configurations.

Invariant: The H-segment

Moves: If $F \in H \cup K \cup L$, move $m_{H \to F}$ to reach F.

Otherwise, move $m_{H \to T}$ to reach $T_{a,b}$ (if $F \in T_{a,b}$)

Moves Definition. We now describe the corresponding moves:

- move $m_{T \to F}$: The convex hull is a triangle that is similar to the convex hull of the pattern. By mapping the pattern to the current configuration so that both triangle coincide, we obtain the location of the fourth point of the pattern. The robot inside the triangle moves towards this point. If there are several such mappings (due to symmetry), and thus several possible destinations, we arbitrarily choose one of the closest.
- move $m_{T \to H}$: The robot inside the triangle formed by the three other robots moves towards one of the closest point on an edge of the triangle.
- move $m_{L \to F}$: The robots r_1 and r_2 are on the segment formed by the two farthest robots $[r_3, r_4]$ with $d(r_1, r_3) < d(r_2, r_3)$ (*i.e.*, robots are on the line in this order: r_3, r_1, r_2, and r_4). Similarly, in the pattern, two points f_1 and f_2 are located on the segment formed by the two other points f_3 and f_4 with $d(f_1, f_3) < d(f_2, f_3)$. Let $d_1 = d(r_1, r_3)$, $d_2 = d(r_2, r_4)$, $d_1' = d(f_1, f_3)$, $d_2' = d(f_2, f_4)$.

If the pattern has a center of symmetry, then $d_1' = d_2'$ and we command r_1 to move at distance d_1' from r_3, and r_2 to move at distance d_1' from r_4. If the other robot is in the trajectory, then we command to move half way through.

Otherwise, the pattern nor the configuration has a center of symmetry, and we can chose the indexes so that $d_1 < d_2$ and $d_1' < d_2'$. Then, we command r_1 to move at distance d_1' from r_3, except if r_2 is in its trajectory. Also, if $d_2' > d_1$, we command r_2 to move at distance d_2' from r_4.

- move $m_{L \to \varepsilon\text{-}LB}$: The robots r_1 and r_2 are on the segment formed by the two farthest robots $[r_3, r_4]$.

  Case 1: *If the symmetricity of the pattern F contains C_2 and D_1,* then the destinations of r_1 and r_2 are the two points at distance ε from the middle M of $[r_3, r_4]$ (on the different side of the segment). If both robots are on the same side of M, the robot closest to M first moves to its destination. If one robot is at distance less than ε to M, then it first moves towards its destination. Otherwise both robots can move towards their destination at the same time.

Case 2: *If the symmetricity of the pattern F does not contain C_2 nor D_1,* then the configuration has symmetricity $\{C_1\}$ (*i.e.*, no symmetry) and we can order the robots according to their distance to the extremities like in the previous move. Let d_1 and d_2 ($d_1 < d_2$) be defined as in the previous move. The destination of r_1 (resp., r_2), is the point at distance ε (resp., $\varepsilon/2$) from the middle M on the segment $[r_3, M]$ (resp., on the segment $[M, r_4]$). If r_2 already reached its destination, then r_1 moves towards its destination. If one robot is on the wrong side of M (it must be r_2), then it moves towards its destination and the other robot does not move. If one robot is at distance less than ε from the middle M (it must be r_2), then it moves towards its destination, and the other robot does not move. Ohterwise, r_2 moves towards its destination while r_1 does not move.

- move $m_{K \to F}$: The robots r_1 and r_2 are on the line bisector of the segment formed by the two farthest robots $[r_3, r_4]$. Let r_1 be at distance d_1 from the center and r_2 at distance d_2. If $d_1 = d_2$, the configuration as a rotational symmetry C_2, so has the target pattern. Thus, both robots move at distance d' from the center, where $d'/2$ is the distance of the shortest diagonal of pattern F.

Otherwise we assume that $d_1 < d_2$, and that in the pattern F, the two extremities of the shortest diagonal are at distance d'_1 and d'_2 (with $d'_1 < d'_2$) from the center. The destination of r_1 (resp., r_2) is the point at distance d'_1 (resp., d'_2) from the center. If $d_1 > d'_1$, then r_1 moves towards its destination, and r_2 does not move. If $d_2 < d'_2$, then r_2 moves towards its destination, and r_1 does not move. Otherwise both robots move towards their destination at the same time.

- move $m_{K \to \varepsilon\text{-}LB}$: The robots r_1 and r_2 are on the line bisector of the segment formed by the two farthest robots $[r_3, r_4]$. Let r_1 be at distance d_1 from the center, and r_2 be at distance d_2. If the symmetricity of the target pattern F contains C_2, then the destinations of r_1 and r_2 are the two points on the line bisector of $[r_2, r_4]$ at distance ε from the center (each robot and its destination are on the same half plane delimited by $[r_3, r_4]$). Both robots move towards their destination at the same time.

Otherwise, the configuration has no symmetry and we can assume $d_1 < d_2$. The destination of r_1 is the point on the line bisector of $[r_2, r_4]$ at distance $\varepsilon/2$ from the center, and the destination of r_2 is the point at distance ε from the center (each robot and its destination are on the same half plane delimited by $[r_3, r_4]$). If $d_1 < \varepsilon$, then r_1 moves towards its destination, and r_2 does not move. If $d_1 > \varepsilon/2$, only r_1 moves towards its destination. Otherwise r_1 and r_2 move towards their destination at the same time.

- move $m_{\varepsilon\text{-}LB \to H}$: r_1 and r_2 are in the ε-square of the segment $[r_3, r_4]$. Let M be the middle of $[r_3, r_4]$, and let V be the set containing the 4 vertices of the ε-square.

If r_1 is located at a point of V, then it does not move, and r_2 moves to the point in V, symmetric to r_1 by symmetry of axis $[r_3, r_4]$. Else, if $d(M, r_1) >$

$d(M, r_2)$, then r_1 moves towards the closest point in V, and r_2 does not move. Else, if r_2 is closer to the segment $[r_3, r_4]$ than r_1, then r_1 moves towards one of the closest point of V, and r_2 does not move. Otherwise, r_1 and r_2 are symmetric with respect to M, to the segment $[r_3, r_4]$ or to its line bisector. For all those cases, both robots move towards one of the closest point in V.

- move $m_{H \to F}$: Let $d = (d_1, d_2, d_3, d_4)$ be the H-coordinates of C, and $d' = (d'_1, d'_2, d'_3, d'_4)$ be the H-coordinates of F.
  If the pattern is a rectangle *i.e.*, all H-coordinates are equal to a number c, then we command each robot to move towards the point of coordinates c (a robot whose movement decreases its H-coordinate moves first).
  If the pattern has no symmetry, its H-coordinates can be ordered *min-first*, resp. *max-first*, if there is an ordering (d'_1, d'_2, d'_3, d'_4) such that d'_1 is strictly smaller, resp. strictly greater, than the other coordinates (strictly smaller, resp. greater, than d'_3 if the robots are chiral). We order the H-coordinates of the configuration in the same way as the pattern, and we denote (d_1, d_2, d_3, d_4). If it is not possible (for instance $(1, 2, 2, 2)$ cannot be ordered max-first), then a unique robot can be selected to move slightly to increase or decrease its H-coordinates so that the H-coordinates of the configuration are ordered in the same way as the pattern. With those ordered H-coordinates, each robot r_i moves towards the point of coordinate d'_i, while ensuring not to reach the coordinate of r_1, so that the H-coordinate of the configuration remains ordered in the same way during the whole phase. Also, the first robots commanded to move are the ones whose movement decrease their H-coordinate. Then, the other robots can move.
  If the pattern is symmetric, we do not reorder the H-coordinates, but if there exists an ordering (max-first, or min-first) for the configuration, then the robots' movements ensure that this ordereding is preserved (by not moving to the same H-coordinate as r_1.). If there exists no special ordering, then the configuration is also symmetric (with the same symmetry as the pattern), and can be partitioned into two groups of two robots. The robots in a group have the same coordinates and are assigned a destination with the same coordinates.
- move $m_{H \to T}$: Same as $m_{H \to F}$, but instead of forming F, the robots form F' whose convex hull is a triangle similar to the convex hull of F, and where the fourth robot is in the middle of one of the smallest edge (the first one in the clockwise order if there are many and the robots are chiral, or any if the triangle is equilateral).

Theorem 3. *Our algorithm forms any pattern F from any initial configuration I, if the symmetricity of I is a subset of the symmetricity of F.*

Proof. If the pattern and the initial configuration are both long kites, resp. lines, then phase K, resp. L, is executed to form the pattern.

If the pattern to form is not a long kite nor a line and the initial configuration is a long kite or a line, then phase K or L is executed to form a $\varepsilon\text{-}LB$ configuration. When phase $\varepsilon\text{-}LB$ is executed, a quadrilateral (not ε-square) is formed.

If the pattern to form is a triangle and the initial configuration is non-similar triangle, then phase $T_{a,b}$ is executed to form a quadrilateral.

When the configuration is a quadrilateral (not ε-square), and the pattern to form is a not a triangle, then phase H is executed to form the pattern.

When the configuration is a quadrilateral (not ε-square), and the pattern to form is a triangle, then a quadrilateral with a convex hull similar to the pattern is formed.

If the pattern to form is a triangle and the initial configuration is a similar triangle, then phase $T_{a,b}$ is executed to form the pattern.

4.3   Proof of Correctness

To prove the correctness of our algorithm, we prove for each phase that the geometric invariant remains invariant, and when the configuration of another phase is reached all the robots are static. Moreover, we prove that for all the phases, the symmetricity of the configuration remains a subset of the symmetricity of the pattern, *i.e.*, we do not create a symmetry that render the problem unsolvable. By proving so, we can assume inductively while executing a phase that the initial configuration is static and that the problem is solvable.

- move $m_{T \to F}$: The convex hull is a triangle that is similar to the convex hull of the pattern. One can match the pattern to the current configuration so that the robots forming the triangle are located at a point in F. The only robot inside the triangle moves to the last empty destination. If there are several possible ways to match the pattern (and thus several possible destinations for the robot inside the triangle), then moving to any of them will results in the pattern being formed. By choosing one of the closest one, we ensure that, after the robot is stopped during its movement and activated again, the same destination is chosen again so that it is reached in finite time.
  Invariant: During the whole movement, the convex hull is invariant as only the robot inside it is moving toward a point that is also inside it.
  Symmetry: There is no new symmetry as the convex hull is a triangle.
  When the robot reaches its destination, the configuration is similar to F, and no robot is moving.
- move $m_{T \to H}$: The robot inside the triangle convex hull moves toward the closest point on its edge.
  Invariant: Only the robot inside the convex hull moves, so the convex hull does not change during the movement.
  Symmetry: There is no new symmetry as the convex hull is a triangle.
  When the moving robot reaches its destination, the configuration is in H and no robots is moving.
- move $m_{L \to F}$: r_1 and r_2 are located on the line $[r_3, r_4]$.
  Invariant: The robots r_1 and r_2 are moving on $[r_3, r_4]$, so $[r_3, r_4]$ remains invariant.
  Symmetry: If the pattern has symmetry, then we are allowed to create new symmetry. We just need to avoid creating a point of multiplicity, which we

do by commanding the robots not to move at the same location as another robot. One can observe that there is no deadlock since their destinations are ordered on the segment in the same way as they are ordered.

If the pattern is asymetric, then $d(r_1, r_3) < d(r_2, r_4)$ is true during the whole phase. Indeed, r_2 moves only if $d'_2 > d_1$. In this case, since $d'_2 > d'_1$, then $d'_2 > d(r_1, r_3)$ remains true as soon as r_2 starts moving and until the end of the phase. When r_1 moves, either $d_1 > d'_1$, in this case $d(r_1, r_3)$ decreases and thus remains smaller than d_2, or $d_1 < d'_1$ but then we have $d_1 < d'_2$, r_2 can move and one can make the same observation as above.

When each robot reaches its destination, the pattern is formed, and no robot is moving.

– move $m_{L \to \varepsilon\text{-}LB}$: r_1 and r_2 are located on the line $[r_3, r_4]$.
  Invariant: The robots r_1 and r_2 are moving on $[r_3, r_4]$, so $[r_3, r_4]$ remains invariant.
  Symmetry: As in the previous move, symmetry might be created when the pattern itself contains symmetry. The proof is similar to the previous move. The only difference here is that we make sure that while robots are moving, the configuration remains in L, and does not ends up prematurely in $\varepsilon\text{-}LB$. To do so, we make sure that a robot that is at distance less than ϵ to the middle (there can be only one such robot, otherwise the inital configuration is already in $\varepsilon\text{-}LB$) moves first towards its destination before the other robot starts moving.
  At the end, when each robot has reached its destination, both robots are static and either both are at distance ε from the middle, or one is at distance ε and the other at distance $\varepsilon/2$.

– move $m_{K \to F}$:
  Invariant: The robots r_1 and r_2 are moving on the line bisector of $[r_3, r_4]$, ensuring $d(r_1, r_2) < d(r_3, r_4)$ so that $[r_3, r_4]$ remains invariant (the distance can be equal when the pattern is formed and it is a square).
  Symmetry: If the pattern is not symmetric, then we have to ensure that during the whole execution, the inequality $d_1 < d_2$ remains. If $d_1 > d'_1$, then r_1 moves towards the center and thus the inequality is preserved. If $d_2 < d'_2$, then r_2 moves away from the center, and thus the inequality is preserved. Otherwise, r_1 moves away from the center but stops at distance $d'_1 < d'_2 \le d_2$, thus the inequality is preserved.

– move $m_{K \to \varepsilon\text{-}LB}$:
  Invariant: The robots r_1 and r_2 are moving on the line bisector of $[r_3, r_4]$, ensuring $r_1 r_2 < r_3 r_4$ so that $[r_3, r_4]$ remains invariant.
  Symmetry: As before, we create symmetry only if the pattern is symmetric. Additionaly, if there is a robot at distance less than ε from the center, we command it to move first to ensure that we do not create configuration in $\varepsilon\text{-}LB$ while robots are moving.

– move $m_{\varepsilon\text{-}LB \to H}$:
  Invariant: The two farthest robots do not move so $[r_3, r_4]$ remains invariant.
  Symmetry: If the symmetricity of the configuration does not contain C_2 (no center of symmetry), resp. does not contain D_1 (no axis of symmetry

other than $[r_3, r_4]$), then the two robots are assigned vertices that are not symmetric with respect to the midde of $[r_3, r_4]$, resp. with respect to the line bisector of $[r_3, r_4]$. Indeed, in the first three cases of the move, only one robot is moving at a time and at the end of the phase, the two robots are symmetric with respect to $[r_3, r_4]$ *i.e.*, the configuration is asymetric. The last case of the move correspond either to the case where the two robots are symmetric with respect to $[r_3, r_4]$, then the obtained configuration is the same as before, or where there is a symmetry that might be preserved in the obtained configuration. In each case, the vertice selected by the robots are not the same because otherwise that would contradict with their symmetry.

– move $m_{H \to F}$: First, one can observe that if the quadrilateral is orthodiagonal, then an unique H-segment is elected when the first robot move. If there is no way to move a single robot, the there is axis of symmetry, and in this case symmetric robots select the H-segment so that they are in the same part of the associated partition.

One can also observe that if the quadrilateral is not orthodiagonal, then it is always possible to increase slightly the H-coordinate of a robot without creating an orthodiagonal quadrilateral, because the set of such H-coordinates is open. This is used when the pattern has a special order (max-first of min-first), and the H-coordinates of the current configuration cannot be ordered. If the quadrilateral is orthodiagonal, then the fact that the H-coordinates of the configuration do not have a special order implies that it is symmetric, and so the H-coordinates of the pattern do not have a special order neither. Finally, due to Theorem 2, no ε-square configuration can be created.

Invariant: The robots move on their H-lines while ensuring that the convex hull remains a quadrilateral. The elected H-segment remains the same because first, the robots decrease their H-coordinates (Proposition 3), and then, their H-coordinates are smaller than the H-coordinates of F (Corollary 1).

Symmetry: No unwanted symmetry is created because if the pattern asymetric, one of the robots has an H-coordinate that is greater or smaller than the other robots (or than the antidiagonal robot if robots are chiral).

When each robot has reached its destination, the target pattern and the current configuration have the same H-coordinates, *i.e.*, the pattern is formed (Theorem 1).

– move $m_{H \to T}$: This move has the same properties as the previous one, but when each robot has reached its destination, the configuration is in $T_{a,b}$ (such that $F \in T_{a,b}$).

5   Conclusion

We presented an algorithm to deterministically form arbitrary patterns with four robots in the most general execution model: ASYNC. This study complements existing protocols that assume more than four robots, and closes a long lasting open case.

An interesting question left for future work is to characterize the added benefits of randomization. It is known that when $n > 4$, a probabilistic approach can form *any* arbitrary pattern (even those with multiplicity points) [1]. However, the case of four probabilistic robots remains open.

References

1. Bramas, Q., Tixeuil, S.: Brief announcement: probabilistic asynchronous arbitrary pattern formation. In: Giakkoupis, G. (ed.) Proceedings of the 2016 ACM Symposium on Principles of Distributed Computing, PODC 2016, Chicago, IL, USA, 25–28 July 2016, pp. 443–445. ACM (2016). https://doi.org/10.1145/2933057.2933074
2. Cicerone, S., Di Stefano, G., Navarra, A.: Asynchronous arbitrary pattern formation: the effects of a rigorous approach. Distrib. Comput. 1–42 (2018). https://rd.springer.com/article/10.1007%2Fs00446-018-0325-7#citeas
3. Flocchini, P., Prencipe, G., Santoro, N., Viglietta, G.: Distributed computing by mobile robots: uniform circle formation. Distrib. Comput. **30**, 1–45 (2014)
4. Flocchini, P., Prencipe, G., Santoro, N., Widmayer, P.: Arbitrary pattern formation by asynchronous, anonymous, oblivious robots. Theor. Comput. Sci. **407**(1–3), 412–447 (2008). https://doi.org/10.1016/j.tcs.2008.07.026
5. Fujinaga, N., Yamauchi, Y., Ono, H., Kijima, S., Yamashita, M.: Pattern formation by oblivious asynchronous mobile robots. SIAM J. Comput. **44**(3), 740–785 (2015). https://doi.org/10.1137/140958682
6. Mamino, M., Viglietta, G.: Square formation by asynchronous oblivious robots. arXiv preprint arXiv:1605.06093 (2016)
7. Suzuki, I., Yamashita, M.: Distributed anonymous mobile robots: formation of geometric patterns. SIAM J. Comput. **28**(4), 1347–1363 (1999). https://doi.org/10.1137/S009753979628292X
8. Tomita, Y., Yamauchi, Y., Kijima, S., Yamashita, M.: Plane formation by synchronous mobile robots without chirality. In: Aspnes, J., Bessani, A., Felber, P., Leitão, J. (eds.) 21st International Conference on Principles of Distributed Systems, OPODIS 2017, Lisbon, Portugal, 18–20 December 2017. LIPIcs, vol. 95, pp. 13:1–13:17. Schloss Dagstuhl - Leibniz-Zentrum fuer Informatik (2017). https://doi.org/10.4230/LIPIcs.OPODIS.2017.13
9. Uehara, T., Yamauchi, Y., Kijima, S., Yamashita, M.: Plane formation by semi-synchronous robots in the three dimensional euclidean space. In: Bonakdarpour, B., Petit, F. (eds.) SSS 2016. LNCS, vol. 10083, pp. 383–398. Springer, Cham (2016). https://doi.org/10.1007/978-3-319-49259-9_30
10. Yamauchi, Y., Uehara, T., Kijima, S., Yamashita, M.: Plane formation by synchronous mobile robots in the three-dimensional euclidean space. J. ACM **64**(3), 16:1–16:43 (2017). https://doi.org/10.1145/3060272

Gracefully Degrading Gathering
in Dynamic Rings

Marjorie Bournat[✉], Swan Dubois, and Franck Petit

Sorbonne Université, CNRS, Inria, LIP6, 75005 Paris, France
{marjorie.bournat,swan.dubois,franck.petit}@lip6.fr

Abstract. Gracefully degrading algorithms [Biely et al., TCS 2018] are designed to circumvent impossibility results in dynamic systems by adapting themselves to the dynamics. Indeed, such an algorithm solves a given problem under some dynamics and, moreover, guarantees that a weaker (but related) problem is solved under a higher dynamics under which the original problem is impossible to solve. The underlying intuition is to solve the problem whenever possible but to provide some kind of quality of service if the dynamics become (unpredictably) higher.

In this paper, we apply for the first time this approach to robot networks. We focus on the fundamental problem of gathering a squad of autonomous robots on an unknown location of a dynamic ring. In this goal, we introduce a set of weaker variants of this problem. Motivated by a set of impossibility results related to the dynamics of the ring, we propose a gracefully degrading gathering algorithm.

Keywords: Gracefully degrading algorithm · Dynamic ring
Gathering

1 Introduction

The classical approach in distributed computing consists in, first, fixing a set of assumptions that captures the properties of the studied system (atomicity, synchrony, faults, communication modalities, etc.) and, then, focusing on the impact of these assumptions in terms of calculability and/or of complexity on a given problem. When coming to dynamic systems, it is natural to adopt the same approach. Many recent works focus on defining pertinent assumptions for capturing the dynamics of those systems [8,13,19]. When these assumptions become very weak, that is, when the system becomes highly dynamic, a somewhat frustrating but not very surprising conclusion emerge: many fundamental distributed problems are impossible at least, in their classical form [2,6,7].

To circumvent such impossibility results, Biely et al. recently introduced the *gracefully degrading* approach [2]. This approach relies on the definition of weaker

---

Work partly funded by Project ESTATE (Ref. ANR-16-CE25-0009-03), supported by French state funds managed by the ANR (Agence Nationale de la Recherche).

T. Izumi and P. Kuznetsov (Eds.): SSS 2018, LNCS 11201, pp. 349–364, 2018.
https://doi.org/10.1007/978-3-030-03232-6_23

but related variants of the considered problem. A gracefully degrading algorithm guarantees that it will solve simultaneously the original problem under some assumption of dynamics and each of its variants under some other (hopefully weaker) assumptions. As an example, Biely et al. provide a consensus algorithm that gracefully degrades to k-set agreement when the dynamics of the system increase. The underlying idea is to solve the problem in its strongest variant when connectivity conditions are sufficient but also to provide (at the opposite of a classical algorithm) some minimal quality of service described by the weaker variants of the problem when those conditions degrade.

Note that, although being applied to dynamic systems by Biely et al. for the first time, this natural idea is not a new one. Indeed, *indulgent* algorithms [1,14] provide similar graceful degradation of the problem to satisfy with respect to synchrony (not with respect to dynamics). *Speculation* [9,12] is a related, but somewhat orthogonal, concept. A speculative algorithm solves the problem under some assumptions and moreover provides stronger properties (typically better complexities) whenever conditions are better.

The goal of this paper is to apply graceful degradation to robot networks where a cohort of autonomous robots have to coordinate their actions in order to solve a global task. We focus on *gathering* in a *dynamic ring*. In this problem, starting from any initial position, robots must meet on an arbitrary location in a bounded time (that may depend on any parameter about the robots or the ring). Note that we can classically split this specification into a liveness property (all robots terminate in bounded time) and a safety property (all robots that terminate do so on the same node).

Related Works. Several models of dynamic graphs have been defined recently [8,15,19]. In this paper, we adopt the *evolving graph* model [19] in which a dynamic graph is simply a sequence of static graphs on a fixed set of nodes: each graph of this sequence contains the edges of the dynamic graph present at a given time. We also consider the hierarchy of dynamics assumptions introduced by Casteigts et al. [8]. The idea behind this hierarchy is to gather all dynamic graphs that share some temporal connectivity properties within classes. This allows us to compare the strength of these temporal connectivity properties based on the inclusion of classes between them. We are interested in the following classes: $\mathcal{COT}$ (*connected-over-time* graphs) where edges may appear and disappear without any recurrence nor periodicity assumption but guaranteeing that each node is infinitely often reachable from any other node; $\mathcal{RE}$ (*recurrent-edge* graphs) where any edge that appears at least once does so recurrently; $\mathcal{BRE}$ (*bounded-recurrent-edge* graphs) where any edge that appears at least once does so recurrently in a bounded time; $\mathcal{AC}$ (*always-connected* graphs) where the graph is connected at each instant; and $\mathcal{ST}$ (*static* graphs) where any edge that appears at least once is always present. Note that $\mathcal{ST} \subset \mathcal{BRE} \subset \mathcal{RE} \subset \mathcal{COT}$ and $\mathcal{ST} \subset \mathcal{AC} \subset \mathcal{COT}$ by definition.

In robot networks, the gathering problem was extensively studied in the context of static graphs, e.g., [10,11,18]. The main motivation of this vein of research is to characterize the initial positions of the robots allowing gathering in

Table 1. Summary of our results. The symbol — means that a stronger variant of the problem is already proved solvable under the dynamics assumption.

	$\mathbb{G}$	$\mathbb{G}_E$	$\mathbb{G}_W$	$\mathbb{G}_{EW}$
$\mathcal{COT}$	Impossible (Cor. 2 & 3)	Impossible (Cor. 1)	Impossible (Cor. 3)	Possible (Th. 2)
$\mathcal{AC}$	Impossible (Cor. 2)	Impossible (Th. 1)	Possible (Th. 3)	—
$\mathcal{RE}$	Impossible (Cor. 3)	Possible (Th. 4)	Impossible (Cor. 3)	—
$\mathcal{BRE}$	Possible (Th. 5)	—	—	—
$\mathcal{ST}$	Possible (Cor. 4)	—	—	—

each studied topology in function of the assumptions on the robots as identifiers, communication, vision range, memory, etc. On the other hand, few algorithms have been designed for robots evolving in dynamic graphs. The majority of them deals with the problem of exploration [3,4,16] (robots must visit each node of the graph at least once or infinitely often depending on the variant of the problem). In the most related work to ours [17], Di Luna et al. study the gathering problem in dynamic rings. They first note the impossibility of the problem in the $\mathcal{AC}$ class and consequently propose a weaker variant of the problem, the near-gathering: all robots must gather in finite time on two adjacent nodes. They characterize the impact of chirality (ability to agree on a common orientation) and cross-detection (ability to detect whenever a robot cross the same edge in the opposite direction) on the solvability of the problem. All their algorithms are designed for the $\mathcal{AC}$ class and are not gracefully degrading.

Contributions. By contrast with the work of Di Luna et al. [17], we keep unchanged the safety of the classical gathering problem (all robots that terminate do so on the same node) and, to circumvent impossibility results, we weaken only its liveness: at most one robot may not terminate or (not exclusively) all robots that terminate do so eventually (and not in a *bounded* time as in the classical specification). This choice is motivated by the approach of indulgent algorithms [1,14]: the safety captures the "essence" of the problem and should be preserved even in degraded variants of the problem. Namely, we obtain the four following variants of the gathering problem: $\mathbb{G}$ (*gathering*) all robots terminate on the same node in *bounded* time; $\mathbb{G}_E$ (*eventual gathering*) all robots terminate on the same node in *finite* time; $\mathbb{G}_W$ (*weak gathering*) all robots but (at most) one terminate on the same node in *bounded* time; and $\mathbb{G}_{EW}$ (*eventual weak gathering*) all robots but (at most) one terminate on the same node in *finite* time.

We present then a set of impossibility results, summarized in Table 1, for these specifications for different classes of dynamic rings. Motivated by these impossibility results, our main contribution is a gracefully degrading gathering algorithm. For each class of dynamic rings we consider, our algorithm solves the strongest possible of our variants of the gathering problem (see Table 1). This challenging property is obtained without any knowledge or detection of the dynamics by the robots that always execute the same algorithm. Our algorithm needs that robots have distincts identifiers, chirality, strong multiplicity detection (i.e. ability to count the number of colocated robots), memory (of size sublinear in the size of the ring and identifiers), and communication capacities but deals with (fully) anonymous ring. These assumptions (whose necessity is left as an open question here) are incomparable with those of Di Luna et al. [17] that assume anonymous but home-based robots (i.e. non fully anonymous rings). This algorithm brings two novelties with respect to the state-of-the-art: (i) it is the first gracefully degrading algorithm dedicated to robot networks; and (ii) it is the first algorithm solving (a weak variant of) the gathering problem in the class $\mathcal{COT}$ (the largest class guaranteeing an exploitable recurrent property).

Roadmap. The organization of the paper follows. Section 2 presents formally the model we consider. Section 3 sums up impossibility results while Sect. 4 presents our gracefully degrading algorithm. Section 5 concludes the paper.

2   Model

Dynamic Graphs. We consider the model of *evolving graphs* [19]. Time is discretized and mapped to $\mathbb{N}$. An evolving graph $\mathcal{G}$ is an ordered sequence $\{G_0, G_1, \ldots\}$ of subgraphs of a given static graph $G = (V, E)$ such that, for any $i \geq 0$, we call $G_i = (V, E_i)$ the snapshot of $\mathcal{G}$ at time i. Note that V is static and $|V|$ is denoted by n. We say that the edges of E_i are *present* in $\mathcal{G}$ at time i. G is the *footprint* of $\mathcal{G}$. The *underlying graph* of $\mathcal{G}$, denoted by $U_{\mathcal{G}}$, is the static graph gathering all edges that are present at least once in $\mathcal{G}$ (i.e. $U_{\mathcal{G}} = (V, E_{\mathcal{G}})$ with $E_{\mathcal{G}} = \bigcup_{i=0}^{\infty} E_i$). An *eventual missing edge* is an edge of E such that there exists a time after which this edge is never present in $\mathcal{G}$. A *recurrent edge* is an edge of E that is not eventually missing. The *eventual underlying graph* of $\mathcal{G}$, denoted $U_{\mathcal{G}}^{\omega}$, is the static graph gathering all recurrent edges of $\mathcal{G}$ (i.e. $U_{\mathcal{G}}^{\omega} = (V, E_{\mathcal{G}}^{\omega})$ where $E_{\mathcal{G}}^{\omega}$ is the set of recurrent edges of $\mathcal{G}$). We only consider graphs whose footprints are anonymous and unoriented rings of size $n \geq 4$. The class $\mathcal{COT}$ (connected-over-time) contains all evolving graphs such that their eventual underlying graph is connected (note that there is at most one eventual missing edge in any ring of class $\mathcal{COT}$). The class $\mathcal{RE}$ (recurrent-edges) gathers all evolving graphs whose footprint contains only recurrent edges. The class $\mathcal{BRE}$ (bounded-recurrent-edges) includes all evolving graphs in which there exists a $\delta \in \mathbb{N}$ such that each edge of the footprint appears at least once every δ units of time. The class $\mathcal{AC}$ (always-connected) collects all evolving graphs where the graph G_i is connected for any $i \in \mathbb{N}$. The class $\mathcal{ST}$ (static) encompasses all evolving graphs where the graph G_i is the footprint for any $i \in \mathbb{N}$.

Robots. We consider systems of $\mathcal{R} \geq 4$ autonomous mobile entities called robots moving in a discrete and dynamic environment modeled by an evolving graph $\mathcal{G} = \{(V, E_0), (V, E_1) \ldots\}$, V being a set of nodes representing the set of locations where robots may be, E_i being the set of bidirectional edges through which robots may move from a location to another one at time i. Each robot knows n and $\mathcal{R}$. Each robot r possesses a distinct (positive) integer identifier id_r strictly greater than 0. Initially, a robot only knows the value of its own identifier. Robots have a persistent memory so they can store local variables.

Each robot r is endowed with strong local multiplicity detection, meaning that it is able to count the exact number of robots that are co-located with it at any time t. When this number equals 1, the robot r is *isolated* at time t. By opposition, we define a *tower* T as a couple (S, θ), where S is a set of robots with $|S| > 1$ and $\theta = [t_s, t_e]$ is an interval of $\mathbb{N}$, such that all the robots of S are located at a same node at each instant of time t in θ and S or θ is maximal for this property. We say that the robots of S form the tower at time t_s and that they are involved in the tower between time t_s and t_e. Robots are able to communicate (by direct reading) the values of their variables to each others only when they are involved in the same tower.

Finally, all the robots have the same chirality, i.e. each robot is able to locally label the two ports of its current node with *left* and *right* consistently over the ring and time and all the robots agree on this labeling. Each robot r has a variable dir_r that stores the direction it currently *considers* (*right*, *left* or $\perp$).

Algorithms and Execution. The *state* of a robot at time t corresponds to the values of its local variables at time t. The *configuration* γ_t of the system at time t gathers the snapshot at time t of the evolving graph, the positions (i.e. the nodes where the robots are currently located) and the state of each robot at time t. The *view* of a robot r at time t is composed of the state of r at time t, the state of all robots involved in the same tower as r at time t if any, and of the following local functions: $ExistsEdge(dir, round)$, with $dir \in \{right, left\}$ and $round \in \{current, previous\}$ which indicates if there exists an adjacent edge to the location of r at time t and $t - 1$ respectively in the direction dir in G_t and in G_{t-1} respectively; $NodeMate()$ which gives the set of all the robots co-located with r (r is not included in this set); $NodeMateIds()$ which gives the set of all the identifiers of the robots co-located with r (excluded the one of r); and $HasMoved()$ which indicates if r has moved between time $t - 1$ and t (see below).

The *algorithm* of a robot is written in the form of an ordered set of guarded rules $(label)::guard \longrightarrow action$ where *label* is the name of the rule, *guard* is a predicate on the view of the robot, and *action* is a sequence of instructions modifying its state. Robots are uniform in the sense they share the same algorithm. Whenever a robot has at least one rule whose guard is true at time t, we say that this robot is *enabled* at time t. The local algorithm also specifies the initial value of each variable of the robot but cannot restrict its arbitrary initial position.

Given an evolving graph $\mathcal{G} = \{G_0, G_1, \ldots\}$ and an initial configuration γ_0, the *execution* σ in $\mathcal{G}$ starting from γ_0 of an algorithm is the maximal sequence $(\gamma_0, \gamma_1)(\gamma_1, \gamma_2)(\gamma_2, \gamma_3) \ldots$ where, for any $i \geq 0$, the configuration γ_{i+1} is the result of the execution of a synchronous round by all robots from γ_i that is composed of three atomic and synchronous phases: Look, Compute, Move. During the Look phase, each robot captures its view at time i. During the Compute phase, each enabled robot executes the *action* associated to the first rule of the algorithm whose *guard* is true in its view. In the case the direction dir_r of a robot r is in $\{right, left\}$, the Move phase consists of moving r in the direction it considers if there exists an adjacent edge in that direction to its current node, otherwise (i.e. the adjacent edge is missing) r is *stuck* and hence remains on its current node. In the case where its direction is $\perp$, the robot remains on its current node.

3   Impossibility Results

This section presents a set of impossibility results (refer to Table 1) showing that some variants of the gathering problem cannot be solved depending on the dynamics of the ring in which the robots evolve and hence motivating our gracefully degrading approach. First, we recall a result from Di Luna et al.. Note that differences between the considered models do not interfere with the proof.

Theorem 1 ([17]).   *There exists no deterministic algorithm that satisfies* $\mathbb{G}_E$ *in rings of* $\mathcal{AC}$ *with size 4 or more for 4 robots or more.*

Note that Di Luna et al. provide only informal arguments for this impossibility result while we provide in the companion report [5] its full formal proof. It is possible to derive some other impossibility results from Theorem 1. Indeed, the inclusion $\mathcal{AC} \subset \mathcal{COT}$ allows us to state that $\mathbb{G}_E$ is also impossible under $\mathcal{COT}$.

Corollary 1.   *There exists no deterministic algorithm that satisfies* $\mathbb{G}_E$ *in rings of* $\mathcal{COT}$ *with size 4 or more for 4 robots or more.*

From the very definitions of $\mathbb{G}$ and $\mathbb{G}_E$, it is straightforward to see that the impossibility of $\mathbb{G}_E$ under a given class implies the one of $\mathbb{G}$ under the same class.

Corollary 2.   *There exists no deterministic algorithm that satisfies* $\mathbb{G}$ *in rings of* $\mathcal{COT}$ *or* $\mathcal{AC}$ *with size 4 or more for 4 robots or more.*

Finally, impossibility results for bounded variants of the gathering problem (i.e. the impossibility of $\mathbb{G}$ under $\mathcal{RE}$ and of $\mathbb{G}_W$ under $\mathcal{COT}$ and $\mathcal{RE}$) are obtained as follows. The definition of $\mathcal{COT}$ and $\mathcal{RE}$ does not exclude the ability for all edges of the graph to be missing initially and for any arbitrary long time, hence preventing the gathering of robots for any arbitrary long time if they are initially scattered. This observation is sufficient to prove a contradiction with the existence of an algorithm solving $\mathbb{G}$ or $\mathbb{G}_W$ in these classes.

Corollary 3.   *There exists no deterministic algorithm that satisfies* $\mathbb{G}$ *or* $\mathbb{G}_W$ *in rings of* $\mathcal{COT}$ *or* $\mathcal{RE}$ *with size 4 or more for 4 robots or more.*

4   Gracefully Degrading Gathering

This section presents $\mathcal{GDG}$, our gracefully degrading gathering algorithm, that aims to solve different variants of the gathering under various dynamics (refer to Table 1). In the following, we informally describe our algorithm clarifying which variant of gathering is satisfied within which class of evolving graphs. Next, we present formally the algorithm and sketch its correctness proof.

Overwiew. Our algorithm has to overcome various difficulties. First, robots are evolving in an environment in which no node can be distinguished. So, the trivial algorithm in which the robots meet on a particular node is impossible. Moreover, since the footprint of the graph is a ring, (at most) one of the n edges may be an eventual missing edge. This is typically the case of classes $\mathcal{COT}$ and $\mathcal{AC}$. In that case, no robot is able to distinguish an eventual missing edge from a missing edge that will appear later in the execution. In particular, a robot stuck by a missing edge does not know whether it can wait for the missing edge to appear again or not. Finally, despite the fact that no robot is aware of which class of dynamic graphs robots are evolving in, the algorithm is required to meet at least the specification of the gathering according to the class of dynamic graphs in which it is executed or a better specification than this one.

The overall scheme of the algorithm consists in first detecting r_{min}, the robot having the minimum identifier so that the $\mathcal{R}$ robots eventually gather on its node (i.e., satisfying specification $\mathbb{G}_E$). Of course, depending on the particular evolving graph in which our algorithm is executed, $\mathbb{G}_E$ may not achieved. In class $\mathcal{COT}$ and the "worst" possible evolving graph, one can expect specification $\mathbb{G}_{EW}$ only, i.e., at least $\mathcal{R} - 1$ robots gathered.

The algorithm proceeds in four successive phases: M (for "am I the Min?"), K (for "min wait to be Known"), W (for "Walk"), and T (for "wait Termination"). Actually, again depending on the class of graphs and the evolving graph in which our algorithm is executed, we will see that the four phases are not necessarily all executed since the execution can be stopped prematurely, especially in case where $\mathbb{G}_E$ (or $\mathbb{G}$) is achieved. By contrast, they can also never be completed in some strong classes of dynamic graphs where the connectivity assumptions are weak (namely $\mathcal{AC}$ or $\mathcal{COT}$), solving $\mathbb{G}_{EW}$ (or $\mathbb{G}_W$) only.

Phase M. This phase leads each robot to know whether it possesses the minimum identifier. Initially every robot r considers the *right* direction. Then r moves to the *right* until it moves $4 * n * id_r$ steps on the right (where id_r is the identifier of r, and n is the size of the ring) or until it meets $\mathcal{R} - 2$ other robots such that its identifier is not the smaller one among these robots or until it meets a robot that knows the identifier of r_{min}. The first robot that succeeds to move $4 * n * id_r$ steps in the right direction is necessarily r_{min}. Depending on the class of graph, one eventual missing edge may exist, preventing r_{min} to move on the *right* direction during $4 * n * id_{r_{min}}$ steps.

However, in the case where there is an eventual missing edge at least $\mathcal{R} - 1$ robots succeed to be located on a same node. They are located either on the extremity of the eventual missing edge or on the extremity of a missing edge that is not eventually missing. The robot r_{min} is not necessarily located with these $\mathcal{R} - 1$ robots gathered. Note that the weak form of gathering ($\mathbb{G}_{EW}$) could be solved in that case. However, the $\mathcal{R} - 1$ robots gathered cannot stop their execution. Indeed, our algorithm aims at gathering the robots on the node occupied by r_{min}. However, r_{min} may not be part of the $\mathcal{R} - 1$ robots that gathered. Further, it is possible for $\mathcal{R} - 1$ robots to gather (without r_{min}) even when r_{min} succeeds in moving $4 * n * id_{r_{min}}$ steps to the right (i.e. even when

r_{min} stops to move because it completed Phase M). In that case, if the $\mathcal{R} - 1$ robots that gathered stop their execution, $\mathbb{G}_E$ cannot be solved in $\mathcal{RE}$, $\mathcal{BRE}$ and $\mathcal{ST}$ rings, as $\mathcal{GDG}$ should do. Note that, it is also possible for r_{min} to be part of the $\mathcal{R} - 1$ robots that gathered.

Recall that robots can communicate when they are both located in the same node. So, the $\mathcal{R} - 1$ robots may be aware of the identifier of the robot with the minimum identifier among them. Since it can or cannot be the actual r_{min}, let us call this robot *potentialMin*. Then, driven by *potentialMin*, a search phase starts during which the $\mathcal{R}-1$ robots try to visit all the nodes of the ring infinitely often in both directions by subtle round trips. Doing so, r_{min} eventually knows that it possesses the actual minimum identifier.

Phase K. The goal of the second phase consists in spreading the identifier of r_{min} among the other robots. The basic idea is that during this phase, r_{min} stops moving and waits until $\mathcal{R} - 3$ other robots join it on its node so that its identifier is known by at least $\mathcal{R} - 3$ other robots. The obvious question arises: "*Why waiting for $\mathcal{R} - 3$ extra robots only?*". A basic idea to gather could be that once r_{min} is aware that it possesses the minimum identifier, it can just stop to move and just wait for the other robots to eventually reach its location, just by moving toward the right direction. Actually, depending on the particular evolving graph considered one missing edge e may eventually appear, preventing robots from reaching r_{min} by moving toward the same direction only. That is why the gathering of the $\mathcal{R} - 2$ robots is eventually achieved by the same search phase as in Phase M (since the search phase permits to at least 3 robots to explore infinitely often the nodes of the ring until reaching a given node). However, by doing this, it is possible to have 2 robots stuck on each extremity of e. Further, these two robots cannot change the directions they consider since a robot is not able to distinguish an eventual missing edge from a missing edge that will appear again later. This is why during Phase K, r_{min} stops to move until $\mathcal{R} - 3$ other robots join it to form a tower of $\mathcal{R} - 2$ robots. In this way these $\mathcal{R} - 2$ robots start the third phase simultaneously.

Phase W. The third phase is a *walk* made by the tower of $\mathcal{R} - 2$ robots. The $\mathcal{R}-2$ robots are split into two distinct groups, *Head* and *Tail*. Head is the unique robot with the maximum identifier of the tower. Tail, composed of $\mathcal{R} - 3$ robots, is made of the other robots of the tower, led by r_{min}. Both move alternatively in the *right* direction during n steps such that between two movements of a given group the two groups are again located on a same node. This movement permits to prevent the two robots that do not belong to any of these two groups to be both stuck on different extremities of an eventual missing edge (if any) once this walk is finished. Since there exists at most one eventual missing edge, we are sure that if the robots that have executed the walk stop moving forever, then at least one robot can join them during the next and last phase.

As noted, it can exist an eventual missing edge, therefore, Head and Tail may not complete Phase W. Indeed, one of the two situations below may occur: (i) Head and Tail together form a tower of $\mathcal{R} - 2$ robots but an eventual missing edge on their right prevents them to complete Phase W; (ii) Head and Tail are

---

Algorithm 1. Predicates used in $\mathcal{GDG}$

MinDiscovery() $\equiv [state_r = potentialMin \wedge \exists r' \in NodeMate(), (state_{r'} = righter \wedge$
$\quad id_r < id_{r'})] \vee [\exists r' \in NodeMate(), idMin_{r'} = id_r] \vee [\exists r' \in NodeMate(), (state_{r'} \in$
$\quad \{dumbSearcher, potentialMin\} \wedge id_r < idPotentialMin_{r'})] \vee [rightSteps_r =$
$\quad 4 * id_r * n]$

$\mathbb{G_E}()$ $\equiv |NodeMate()| = \mathcal{R} - 1$

$\mathbb{G_{EW}}()$ $\equiv |NodeMate()| = \mathcal{R} - 2 \wedge \exists r' \in \{r\} \cup NodeMate(),$
$\quad state_{r'} \in \{minWaitingWalker, minTailWalker\}$

HeadWalkerWithoutWalkerMate() $\equiv state_r = headWalker \wedge$
$\quad ExistsEdge(left, previous) \wedge \neg HasMoved() \wedge NodeMateIds() \neq walkerMate_r$

LeftWalker() $\equiv state_r = leftWalker$

HeadOrTailWalkerEndDiscovery() $\equiv$
$\quad state_r \in \{headWalker, tailWalker, minTailWalker\} \wedge walkSteps_r = n$

HeadOrTailWalker() $\equiv state_r \in \{headWalker, tailWalker, minTailWalker\}$

AllButTwoWaitingWalker() $\equiv |NodeMate()| = \mathcal{R} - 3 \wedge \forall r' \in \{r\} \cup NodeMate(),$
$\quad state_{r'} \in \{waitingWalker, minWaitingWalker\}$

WaitingWalker() $\equiv state_r \in \{waitingWalker, minWaitingWalker\}$

PotentialMinOrSearcherWithMinWaiting(r') $\equiv state_r \in \{potentialMin,$
$\quad dumbSearcher, awareSearcher\} \wedge state_{r'} = minWaitingWalker$

RighterWithMinWaiting(r') $\equiv state_r = righter \wedge state_{r'} = minWaitingWalker$

NotWalkerWithHeadWalker(r') $\equiv state_r \in \{righter, potentialMin,$
$\quad dumbSearcher, awareSearcher\} \wedge state_{r'} = headWalker$

NotWalkerWithTailWalker(r') $\equiv state_r \in \{righter, potentialMin, dumbSearcher,$
$\quad awareSearcher\} \wedge state_{r'} = minTailWalker$

PotentialMinWithAwareSearcher(r') $\equiv$
$\quad state_r = potentialMin \wedge state_{r'} = awareSearcher$

AllButOneRighter() $\equiv$
$\quad |NodeMate()| = \mathcal{R} - 2 \wedge \forall r' \in \{r\} \cup NodeMate(), state_{r'} = righter$

RighterWithSearcher(r') $\equiv$
$\quad state_r = righter \wedge state_{r'} \in \{dumbSearcher, awareSearcher\}$

PotentialMinOrRighter() $\equiv state_r \in \{potentialMin, righter\}$

DumbSearcherMinRevelation() $\equiv state_r = dumbSearcher \wedge$
$\quad \exists r' \in NodeMate(), (state_{r'} = righter \wedge id_{r'} > idPotentialMin_r)$

DumbSearcherWithAwareSearcher(r') $\equiv$
$\quad state_r = dumbSearcher \wedge state_{r'} = awareSearcher$

Searcher() $\equiv state_r \in \{dumbSearcher, awareSearcher\}$

---

located on neighboring node and the edge between them is an eventual missing edge that prevents Head and Tail to continue to move alternatively.

Call u the node where Tail is stuck on an eventual missing edge. In the two situations described even if Phase W is not complete by both Head and Tail, either $\mathbb{G_E}$ or $\mathbb{G_{EW}}$ is solved. Indeed, in the first situation, necessarily at least one robot r succeeds to join u (either r considers the good direction to reach u or it meets a robot on the other extremity of the eventual missing edge that makes it change its direction, and hence makes it consider the good direction to reach u). In the second situation, necessarily at least two robots r and r' succeed to join u. This is done either because r and r' consider the good direction to reach

Algorithm 2. Functions used in $\mathcal{GDG}$

Function StopMoving()

  $dir_r := \perp$

Function MoveLeft()

  $dir_r := left$

Function BecomeLeftWalker()

  $(state_r, dir_r) := (leftWalker, \perp)$

Function Walk()

$$dir_r := \begin{cases} \perp & \text{if } (id_r = idHeadWalker_r \wedge walkerMate_r \neq NodeMateIds()) \vee \\ & \quad (id_r \neq idHeadWalker_r \wedge idHeadWalker_r \in NodeMateIds()) \\ right & \text{otherwise} \end{cases}$$

$walkSteps_r := walkSteps_r + 1$ if $dir_r = right \wedge ExistsEdge(right, current)$

Function InitiateWalk()

  $idHeadWalker_r := \textsc{max}(\{id_r\} \cup NodeMateIds())$

  $walkerMate_r := NodeMateIds()$

$$state_r := \begin{cases} headWalker & \text{if } id_r = idHeadWalker_r \\ minTailWalker & \text{if } state_r = minWaitingWalker \\ tailWalker & \text{otherwise} \end{cases}$$

Function BecomeWaitingWalker(r')

  $(state_r, idPotentialMin_r, idMin_r, dir_r) := (waitingWalker, id_{r'}, id_{r'}, \perp)$

Function BecomeMinWaitingWalker()

  $(state_r, idPotentialMin_r, idMin_r, dir_r) := (minWaitingWalker, id_r, id_r, \perp)$

Function BecomeAwareSearcher(r')

  $(state_r, dir_r) := (awareSearcher, right)$

$$(idPotentialMin_r, idMin_r) := \begin{cases} (idPotentialMin_{r'}, idPotentialMin_{r'}) \\ \quad \text{if } state_{r'} = dumbSearcher \\ (idMin_{r'}, idMin_{r'}) \\ \quad \text{otherwise} \end{cases}$$

Function BecomeTailWalker(r')

  $(state_r, idPotentialMin_r, idMin_r) := (tailWalker, idPotentialMin_{r'}, idMin_{r'})$

  $(idHeadWalker_r, walkerMate_r, walkSteps_r) :=$
    $(idHeadWalker_{r'}, walkerMate_{r'}, walkSteps_{r'})$

Function MoveRight()

  $dir_r := right$

  $rightSteps_r := rightSteps_r + 1$ if $ExistsEdge(dir, current)$

Function InitiateSearch()

  $idPotentialMin_r := \textsc{min}(\{id_r\} \cup NodeMateIds())$

$$state_r := \begin{cases} potentialMin & \text{if } id_r = idPotentialMin_r \\ dumbSearcher & \text{otherwise} \end{cases}$$

  $rightSteps_r := rightSteps_r + 1$ if $state_r = potentialMin \wedge ExistsEdge(dir, current)$

Function Search()

$$dir_r := \begin{cases} left & \text{if } |NodeMate()| \geq 1 \wedge id_r = \textsc{max}(\{id_r\} \cup NodeMateIds()) \\ right & \text{if } |NodeMate()| \geq 1 \wedge id_r \neq \textsc{max}(\{id_r\} \cup NodeMateIds()) \\ dir_r & \text{otherwise} \end{cases}$$

Algorithm 3. $\mathcal{GDG}$

Rules for Termination

   $\text{Term}_1 :: \mathbb{G}_E() \longrightarrow$ **terminate**

   $\text{Term}_2 :: \mathbb{G}_{EW}() \longrightarrow$ **terminate**

Rules for Phase T

   $\mathbf{T_1} :: LeftWalker() \longrightarrow$ MoveLeft()

   $\mathbf{T_2} :: HeadWalkerWithoutWalkerMate() \longrightarrow$ BecomeLeftWalker()

   $\mathbf{T_3} :: HeadOrTailWalkerEndDiscovery() \longrightarrow$ StopMoving()

Rules for Phase W

   $\mathbf{W_1} :: HeadOrTailWalker() \longrightarrow$ Walk()

Rules for Phase K

   $\mathbf{K_1} :: AllButTwoWaitingWalker() \longrightarrow$ InitiateWalk()

   $\mathbf{K_2} :: WaitingWalker() \longrightarrow$ StopMoving()

   $\mathbf{K_3} :: \exists r' \in NodeMate(), PotentialMinOrSearcherWithMinWaiting(r')$
      $\longrightarrow$ BecomeWaitingWalker(r')

   $\mathbf{K_4} :: \exists r' \in NodeMate(), RighterWithMinWaiting(r') \wedge$
      $ExistsEdge(right, current) \longrightarrow$ BecomeAwareSearcher(r')

Rules for Phase M

   $\mathbf{M_1} :: PotentialMinOrRighter() \wedge MinDiscovery()$
      $\longrightarrow$ BecomeMinWaitingWalker(r)

   $\mathbf{M_2} :: \exists r' \in NodeMate(), NotWalkerWithHeadWalker(r') \wedge$
      $ExistsEdge(right, current) \longrightarrow$ BecomeAwareSearcher(r')

   $\mathbf{M_3} :: \exists r' \in NodeMate(), NotWalkerWithHeadWalker(r')$
      $\longrightarrow$ BecomeAwareSearcher(r'); StopMoving()

   $\mathbf{M_4} :: \exists r' \in NodeMate(), NotWalkerWithTailWalker(r')$
      $\longrightarrow$ BecomeTailWalker(r'); Walk()

   $\mathbf{M_5} :: \exists r' \in NodeMate(), PotentialMinWithAwareSearcher(r')$
      $\longrightarrow$ BecomeAwareSearcher(r'); Search()

   $\mathbf{M_6} :: AllButOneRighter() \longrightarrow$ InitiateSearch()

   $\mathbf{M_7} :: \exists r' \in NodeMate(), RighterWithSearcher(r')$
      $\longrightarrow$ BecomeAwareSearcher(r'); Search()

   $\mathbf{M_8} :: PotentialMinOrRighter() \longrightarrow$ MoveRight()

   $\mathbf{M_9} :: DumbSearcherMinRevelation() \longrightarrow$ BecomeAwareSearcher(r); Search()

   $\mathbf{M_{10}} :: \exists r' \in NodeMate(), DumbSearcherWithAwareSearcher(r')$
      $\longrightarrow$ BecomeAwareSearcher(r'); Search()

   $\mathbf{M_{11}} :: Searcher() \longrightarrow$ Search()

---

u or because they reach the node where Head is located without Tail making them change their direction, and hence making them consider the good direction to reach u.

    Once a tower of $\mathcal{R} - 1$ robots including r_{min} is formed, $\mathbb{G}_{EW}$ is solved. Then, the latter robot tries to reach the tower to eventually solve $\mathbb{G}_E$ in favorable cases.

Phase T. The last phase starts once the robots of Head have completed Phase W. If it exists a time at which the robots of Tail complete Phase W, then Head and

Tail form a tower of $\mathcal{R} - 2$ robots and stop moving. As explained in the previous phase, Phase W ensures that at least one extra robot eventually joins the node where Head and Tail are located to form a tower of $\mathcal{R} - 1$ robots. Once a tower of $\mathcal{R} - 1$ robots including r_{min} is formed, $\mathbb{G}_{EW}$ is solved. Then, the latter robot tries to reach the tower to eventually solve $\mathbb{G}_E$ in favorable cases. In the case the robots of Tail never complete the phase W, then this implies that Head and Tail are located on neighboring node and that the edge between them is an eventual missing edge. As described in Phase W either $\mathbb{G}_{EW}$ or $\mathbb{G}_E$ is solved.

Algorithm. Before presenting formally our algorithm, we first describe the set of variables of each robot. We recall that each robot r knows $\mathcal{R}$, n and id_r as constants. In addition to the variable dir_r (initialized to $right$), each robot r possesses seven variables described below. Variable $state_r$ allows the robot r to know which phase of the algorithm it is performing and (partially) indicates which movement the robot has to execute. The possible values for this variable are $righter$, $dumbSearcher$, $awareSearcher$, $potentialMin$, $waitingWalker$, $minWaitingWalker$, $headWalker$, $tailWalker$, $minTailWalker$ and $leftWalker$. Initially, $state_r$ is equal to $righter$. Initialized with 0, $rightSteps_r$ counts the number of steps done by r in the $right$ direction when $state_r \in \{righter, potentialMin\}$. The next variable is $idPotentialMin_r$. Initially equals to -1, $idPotentialMin_r$ contains the identifier of the robot that possibly possesses the minimum identifier (a positive integer) of the system. This variable is especially set when $\mathcal{R} - 1$ $righter$ are located on a same node. In this case, the variable $idPotentialMin_r$ of each robot r that is involved in the tower of $\mathcal{R} - 1$ robots is set to the value of the minimum identifier possessed by these robots. The variable $idMin_r$ indicates the identifier of the robot that possesses the actual minimum identifier among all the robots of the system. This variable is initially set to -1. Let $walkerMate_r$ be the set of all the identifiers of the $\mathcal{R} - 2$ robots that initiate the Phase W. Initially this variable is set to $\emptyset$. The counter $walkSteps_r$, initially 0, maintains the number of steps done in the right direction while r performs the Phase W. Finally, the variable $idHeadWalker_r$ contains the identifier of the robot that plays the part of Head during the Phase W. Moreover, we assume the existence of a specific instruction: **terminate**. By executing this instruction, a robot stops executing the cycle Look-Compute-Move forever. To ease the writing of our algorithm, we define a set of predicates (presented in Algorithm 1) and functions (presented in Algorithm 2), that are used in our gracefully degrading algorithm $\mathcal{GDG}$. Recall that, during the Compute phase, only the first rule whose $guard$ is true in the view of an enabled robot is executed.

Sketch of Proof. Due to the lack of space, in this section we only sketch the correctness proof of Algorithm $\mathcal{GDG}$. The interested reader may find the complete proofs in the companion report [5]. More precisely, we present which instance of the gathering our algorithm solves depending on the dynamics of the ring in which it is executed. In the following, we consider in the order the classes $\mathcal{COT}$, $\mathcal{AC}$, $\mathcal{RE}$, $\mathcal{BRE}$ and $\mathcal{ST}$. For ease of reading, we abuse the various values of the variable $state$ to qualify the robots. For instance, if the current value of variable $state$ of a robot is $righter$, then we say that the robot is a $righter$ robot.

Theorem 2. *Algorithm $\mathcal{GDG}$ solves $\mathbb{G}_{EW}$ in $\mathcal{COT}$.*

Proof Outline. As the safety of $\mathbb{G}_{EW}$ directly follows from Rules **Term$_1$** and **Term$_2$**, we only focus on its liveness in the following. The proof is done by analyzing successively each phase of $\mathcal{GDG}$.

In Phase M, r_{min} is supposed to be able, in finite time, to know that it possesses the minimum identifier among all the robots of the system. In our algorithm, a robot is aware that it possesses the minimum identifier when it is either a $minWaitingWalker$ or a $minTailWalker$ robot. Let us call min a robot such that its variable $state$ is equal to one of these two values. To prove the correctness of this phase, we prove first that only r_{min} can become min and then that r_{min} effectively becomes min in finite time.

First note that, by the rules of $\mathcal{GDG}$, if a robot is located on the same node as a min, it stops to be in Phase M and hence cannot be min. By the rules of $\mathcal{GDG}$, a robot is necessarily a $minWaitingWalker$ before becoming a $minTail$-$Walker$. Moreover, only a $righter$ or a $potentialMin$ can become a $minWaiting$-$Walker$ (Rule **M$_1$**). Therefore, if a robot becomes min, then necessarily it considers the right direction from the beginning of the execution until it becomes min (Rule **M$_8$**). While executing the other phases of $\mathcal{GDG}$, a min can only consider either the $\bot$ or the right direction (refer to Rules **K$_2$**, **K$_1$**, **W$_1$**, and **T$_3$**). Besides, in the case a min robot r succeeds to execute all the phases of $\mathcal{GDG}$, it can only move from $4 * id_r * n + n$ steps in the right direction (refer to Rules **M$_1$**, **K$_2$**, **K$_1$**, **W$_1$**, and **T$_3$**). Moreover, because of the dynamism of the ring, two robots r' and r'' such that both $state_{r'}$ and $state_{r''}$ belong to $\{righter, potentialMin\}$, can have their variables $rightSteps$ such that $|rightSteps_{r'} - rightSteps_{r''}| \le n$. Besides, it takes one round for a robot to update its variable $state$ to min. Hence, since a $righter$ or a $potentialMin$ can be located with a robot r just the round before r becomes min, this $righter$ or $potentialMin$ can move again in the right direction during at most n steps without meeting the min. Hence, since for all $r \ne r_{min}$, $id_{r_{min}} < id_r$, we have $4 * id_{r_{min}} * n + n + n + n < 4 * id_r * n$. This implies that a robot r (with $r \ne r_{min}$) cannot become min thanks to the condition $rightSteps_r = 4 * id_r * n$ of the predicate $MinDiscovery()$ of Rule **M$_1$**. Finally, the other conditions of the predicate $MinDiscovery()$ of Rule **M$_1$** cannot be satisfied by another robot than r_{min}. Indeed, by the rules of $\mathcal{GDG}$, a $potentialMin$ (resp. a $dumbSearcher$) is a robot that is aware of the identifiers of $\mathcal{R} - 1$ robots (Rule **M$_6$**), and that possesses the minimum identifier among these $\mathcal{R}-1$ robots (resp. and that keeps in its variable $idPotentialMin$ the value of the smallest identifier among these $\mathcal{R} - 1$ robots). Therefore, the first (resp. the third) condition of the predicate $MinDiscovery()$ of Rule **M$_1$** is true only for r_{min}. Finally, when there is no min in the execution, an $awareSearcher$ (robot whose variable $idMin$ is different from -1) is a robot that is aware of all the identifiers of all the robots of the system (Rules **M$_5$**, **M$_7$**, **M$_9$**, and **M$_{10}$**) and that keeps in its variable $idMin$ the value of the minimum identifier among these robots. Thus, the second condition of the predicate $MinDiscovery()$ of Rule **M$_1$** is true only for r_{min}.

Then, we prove that r_{min} becomes min in finite time. First, note that as long as there is no min in the execution, r_{min} is either a $righter$ or a $potentialMin$. In the case where r_{min} succeeds to move in the right direction during $4*id_{r_{min}}*n$ steps, it becomes min (Rule $\mathbf{M_1}$). If r_{min} does not succeed to do so, then there exists an eventual missing edge, and necessarily $\mathcal{R} - 1$ $righter$ succeed to be located on the same node. From this time, they are $potentialMin$ and $dumb$-$Searcher$ in the execution. It is also possible to have $awareSearcher$ (Rules $\mathbf{M_5}$, $\mathbf{M_7}$, $\mathbf{M_9}$, and $\mathbf{M_{10}}$). As long as there is no min, $dumbSearcher$ and $awareSear$-$cher$ execute the function SEARCH at each time (Rules $\mathbf{M_9}$, $\mathbf{M_{10}}$, and $\mathbf{M_{11}}$), and the $potentialMin$ executes either Rule $\mathbf{M_8}$ or function SEARCH (Rule $\mathbf{M_5}$). By definition of SEARCH and of Rule $\mathbf{M_8}$, one robot succeeds to reach the node where r_{min} is stuck and to inform it that it has to become min.

Phase K is achieved when there are $\mathcal{R} - 3$ $waitingWalker$ robots located on the same node as r_{min}, while r_{min} is a $minWaitingWalker$. By the rules of $\mathcal{GDG}$, as long as this phase is not achieved, there are only $righter$, $potentialMin$, $dumbSearcher$, $awareSearcher$, $waitingWalker$, and $minWaitingWalker$. By Rules $\mathbf{K_3}$ and $\mathbf{K_2}$, all the $waitingWalker$ and $minWaitingWalker$ are located on a same node and do not move. By analyzing the movements of the other kind of robots, we prove that it exists a time t at which this phase is achieved and that there is at most one $righter$ in the execution from time t.

Similarly, **Phase** W **and Phase** T are proved by analyzing the movements of the robots. At the time when the Phase K is achieved, we can prove that the two robots r_1 and r_2 that are not on the same node as the min are such that $state_{r_1} \in$ {righter,potentialMin,awareSearcher,dumbSearcher} and $state_{r_2} \in$ {awareSearcher,dumbSearcher}. Moreover, once the Phase K is achieved, all the $waiting$-$Walker$ and $minWaitingWalker$ execute Rule $\mathbf{K_1}$. While executing this rule the robot with the maximum identifier among these robots becomes $headWalker$, the $minWaitingWalker$ becomes $minTailWalker$ and the other robots become $tailWalker$. Analyzing all the possible movements of these kind of robots we succeed to prove that whatever the position of an eventual missing edge, in finite time, either Rule $\mathbf{Term_1}$ or Rule $\mathbf{Term_2}$ is executed. Hence, either $\mathcal{R}$ robots terminate their execution (Rule $\mathbf{Term_1}$) or $\mathcal{R} - 1$ robots terminate their execution (Rule $\mathbf{Term_2}$) in finite time.   □

Once Theorem 2 proved, classes inclusions and a careful analysis of the robot movements allow us to deduce the following set of results.

Theorem 3. $\mathcal{GDG}$ *solves* $\mathbb{G}_W$ *in* $\mathcal{AC}$ *in* $O(id_{r_{min}} * n^2 + \mathcal{R} * n)$ *rounds.*

Theorem 4. $\mathcal{GDG}$ *solves* $\mathbb{G}_E$ *in* $\mathcal{RE}$.

Theorem 5. $\mathcal{GDG}$ *solves* $\mathbb{G}$ *in* $\mathcal{BRE}$ *in* $O(n * \delta * (id_{r_{min}} + \mathcal{R}))$ *rounds.*

Corollary 4. $\mathcal{GDG}$ *solves* $\mathbb{G}$ *in* $\mathcal{ST}$ *in* $O(n * (id_{r_{min}} + \mathcal{R}))$ *rounds.*

5   Conclusion

In this paper, we apply for the first time the gracefully degrading approach to robot networks. This approach consists in circumventing impossibility results in highly dynamic systems by providing algorithms that adapt themselves to the dynamics of the graph: they solve the problem under weak dynamics and only guarantee that some weaker but related problems are satisfied whenever the dynamics increases and makes the original problem impossible to solve.

Focusing on the classical problem of gathering a squad of autonomous robots, we introduce a set of weaker variants of this problem that preserves its safety (in the spirit of the indulgent approach that shares the same underlying idea). Motivated by a set of impossibility results, we propose a gracefully degrading gathering algorithm. We highlight that it is the first gracefully degrading algorithm dedicated to robot networks and the first algorithm focusing on the gathering in $\mathcal{COT}$, the class of dynamic graphs that exhibits the weakest recurrent connectivity.

A natural open question arises on the *optimality* of the graceful degradation we propose. Indeed, we prove that our algorithm provides for each class of dynamic graphs the best specification *among the ones we proposed*. We do not claim that another algorithm could not be able to satisfy stronger variants of the original gathering specification. Aside gathering in robot networks, defining a general form of *degradation optimality* seems to be a challenging future work.

References

1. Alistarh, D., Gilbert, S., Guerraoui, R., Travers, C.: Generating fast indulgent algorithms. TCS **51**(4), 404–424 (2012)
2. Biely, M., Robinson, P., Schmid, U., Schwarz, M., Winkler, K.: Gracefully degrading consensus and k-set agreement in directed dynamic networks. TCS **726**, 41–77 (2018)
3. Bournat, M., Datta, A.K., Dubois, S.: Self-stabilizing robots in highly dynamic environments. In: Bonakdarpour, B., Petit, F. (eds.) SSS 2016. LNCS, vol. 10083, pp. 54–69. Springer, Cham (2016). https://doi.org/10.1007/978-3-319-49259-9_5
4. Bournat, M., Dubois, S., Petit, F.: Computability of perpetual exploration in highly dynamic rings. In: ICDCS, pp. 794–804 (2017)
5. Bournat, M., Dubois, S., Petit, F.: Gracefully degrading gathering in dynamic rings. Technical report, arXiv:1805.05137 (2018)
6. Braud-Santoni, N., Dubois, S., Kaaouachi, M.-H., Petit, F.: The next 700 impossibility results in time-varying graphs. IJNC **6**(1), 27–41 (2016)
7. Casteigts, A., Flocchini, P., Mans, B., Santoro, N.: Shortest, fastest, and foremost broadcast in dynamic networks. IJFCS **26**(4), 499–522 (2015)
8. Casteigts, A., Flocchini, P., Quattrociocchi, W., Santoro, N.: Time-varying graphs and dynamic networks. IJPEDS **27**(5), 387–408 (2012)
9. Dubois, S., Guerraoui, R.: Introducing speculation in self-stabilization: an application to mutual exclusion. In: PODC, pp. 290–298 (2013)
10. Flocchini, P., Kranakis, E., Krizanc, D., Santoro, N., Sawchuk, C.: Multiple mobile agent rendezvous in a ring. In: Farach-Colton, M. (ed.) LATIN 2004. LNCS, vol. 2976, pp. 599–608. Springer, Heidelberg (2004). https://doi.org/10.1007/978-3-540-24698-5_62
11. Klasing, R., Markou, E., Pelc, A.: Gathering asynchronous oblivious mobile robots in a ring. In: Asano, T. (ed.) ISAAC 2006. LNCS, vol. 4288, pp. 744–753. Springer, Heidelberg (2006). https://doi.org/10.1007/11940128_74

12. Kotla, R., Alvisi, L., Dahlin, M., Clement, A., Wong, E.: Zyzzyva: speculative byzantine fault tolerance. TOCS **27**(4), 7:1–7:39 (2009)
13. Kuhn, F., Lynch, N., Oshman, R.: Distributed computation in dynamic networks. In: STOC, pp. 513–522 (2010)
14. Lamport, L.: The part-time parliament. TOCS **16**(2), 133–169 (1998)
15. Latapy, M., Viard, T., Magnien, C.: Stream graphs and link streams for the modeling of interactions over time. Technical report, arXiv:1710.04073 (2017)
16. Di Luna, G., Dobrev, S., Flocchini, P., Santoro, N.: Live exploration of dynamic rings. In: ICDCS, pp. 570–579 (2016)
17. Di Luna, G.A., Flocchini, P., Pagli, L., Prencipe, G., Santoro, N., Viglietta, G.: Gathering in dynamic rings. In: Das, S., Tixeuil, S. (eds.) SIROCCO 2017. LNCS, vol. 10641, pp. 339–355. Springer, Cham (2017). https://doi.org/10.1007/978-3-319-72050-0_20
18. Di Stefano, G., Navarra, A.: Optimal gathering of oblivious robots in anonymous graphs and its application on trees and rings. DC **30**(2), 75–86 (2017)
19. Xuan, B., Ferreira, A., Jarry, A.: Computing shortest, fastest, and foremost journeys in dynamic networks. IJFCS **14**(02), 267–285 (2003)

Concurrent Lock-Free Unbounded
Priority Queue with Mutable Priorities

Ivan Walulya[1]($\boxtimes$), Bapi Chatterjee[2], Ajoy K. Datta[3], Rashmi Niyolia[3],
and Philippas Tsigas[1]

[1] Department of CS&E, Chalmers University of Technology, Gothenburg, Sweden
{ivanw,tsigas}@chalmers.se
[2] IBM Research Lab, New Delhi, India
bhaskerchatterjee@gmail.com
[3] Department of CS, University of Nevada Las Vegas, Las Vegas, USA
Ajoy.Datta@unlv.edu, rashmi.niyolia@gmail.com

Abstract. The priority queue with DELETEMIN and INSERT operations is a classical interface for ordering items associated with priorities. Some important algorithms, such as Dijkstra's single-source-shortest-path, Adaptive Huffman Trees, etc. also require changing the priorities of items in the runtime. Existing lock-free priority queues do not directly support the dynamic mutation of the priorities. This paper presents the first concurrent lock-free unbounded binary heap that implements a priority queue with mutable priorities. The operations are provably linearizable. We also designed an optimized version of the algorithm by combining the concurrent operations that substantially improves the performance. For experimental evaluation, we implemented the algorithm in both C/C++ and Java. A number of micro-benchmarks show that our algorithm performs well in comparison to existing implementations.

Keywords: Heap · Lock-free · Linearizability · Concurrent heap
Priority-queue · Elimination

1 Introduction

A priority queue orders a set of items by a numerical cost – often called *priority* – associated with each item. In its most general form, a priority queue abstract data type (ADT) is defined by two operations – INSERT and DELETEMIN. An INSERT $(k, elem)$ inserts an item *elem* with priority k and a DELETEMIN () removes an item with the highest priority from the set of objects. Priority queues are widely used at operating system kernels as well as in user-space. Some well-known applications are discrete event simulations [10], graph search [20], operating systems schedulers [13], SAT solvers [5] and many others. Several of them, such as Dijkstra's single-source-shortest-path (SSSP) algorithm [7], Adaptive

© Springer Nature Switzerland AG 2018
T. Izumi and P. Kuznetsov (Eds.): SSS 2018, LNCS 11201, pp. 365–380, 2018.
https://doi.org/10.1007/978-3-030-03232-6_24

Huffman Trees [25], etc. require updating the priorities after inserting the items. In today's application settings, the underlying datasets grow immensely at run-time necessitating the employed data structure to be adaptable to size variations.

At the same time, the proliferation of multi-core systems have essentially mainstreamed the concurrent data structures. Concurrent data structure designs are evaluated on consistency (correctness) and progress guarantees in addition to scalability with increasing number of processing threads. The most common consistency framework used in concurrent settings is linearizability [16], which relates a concurrent execution on an object to its sequential specification. Linearizability requires that an operation appears to take effect instantaneously at a single linearization point between the operation's invocation and its response.

Consistency may be trivially achieved using mutual exclusion locks that serialize the access to the entire data structure, also called coarse-grained locking. However, it severely limits the concurrent operations. Even if the number of locks increase, i.e. fine-grained locking, they are still vulnerable to pitfalls such as deadlock, priority inversion and convoying. An alternative approach is lock-free implementation. In a lock-free concurrent data structure, at least one non-faulty processing thread is guaranteed to complete its operation in a finite number of steps. Effectively, lock-free data structures foster both scalability and progress guarantee. A stronger progress guarantee is wait-freedom, which ensures that all the non-faulty processes finish their operations in a finite number of steps. However, most often wait-freedom results in poor performance. Another approach to implement consistent concurrent data structure is using software transactional memory (STM) [22]. However, the performance of such implementations largely depends on the design of the STM. Unsurprisingly, using STM to design concurrent data structures has often resulted in unacceptable performance [8].

Thus, an efficient and scalable *unbounded* concurrent lock-free data structure implementing a *mutable priority queue*, i.e. one which offers updating priorities of items dynamically, is highly sought-after in a large number of applications.

Based on the employed data structure, a priority queue implementation can be categorized primarily as: (a) heap[1]-based, and (b) skip-list-based.

The previous attempts on heap-based concurrent priority queues have largely been blocking (lock-based) or impractical non-blocking designs. Hunt et al. [17] presented a fine-grained lock-based heap, which locks each node separately and operations release and re-acquire locks after each step in bubble-up to prevent deadlocks with concurrent bubble-down operations. Tamir et al. [24] extended the work of [17] by including operations, called CHANGEKEY, to update the priority of items. The focus of their work is on the CHANGEKEY operations, which they show that improves the overall performance of Dijkstra's SSSP algorithm.

The first attempt to implement a non-blocking concurrent heap was by Herlihy [15]. However, this wait-free algorithm required copying the entire heap making the implementation inherently sequential and of little practical interest. Barnes [3] proposed a wait-free algorithm to address the drawbacks of Herlihy. His definition of the wait-free property is different from the generally accepted

---

[1] In this work, by a heap we mean a binary heap.

definition. Additionally, no implementation of this algorithm exits. Israeli *et al.* presented a wait-free algorithm for heap-based priority queues [18] which utilizes atomic primitives[2] that are not implemented in existing hardware platforms.

Dragicive et al. [8] designed a lock-free heap that uses STM for concurrency control. Their design offered poor performance due to the overhead of the STM. We point out that all the previously available concurrent heaps are bounded to a fixed size allocated at the initialization. There are available works on skip-list-based concurrent priority queues – Shavit et al. [21], Tsigas *et al.* [23], etc. Alistarh *et al.* [1] proposed an approximate DELETEMIN operation in skip-lists. However, the skip-list-based implementations face difficulty to implement the algorithms that require mutable priorities at the runtime: observably, the overall performance of the algorithm degrades [24].

We present CoMPiQ - a Concurrent lock-free unbounded heap-based Mutable Priority Queue. The Table 1 summarily contrasts our contributions with the relevant existing works.

Table 1. Concurrent priority queues

Paper	Data Struc-ture	Progress Guarantee	Mutable Priority	Unbound	Practical Im-plementation
Herlihy [15]	Heap	Wait-free	No	No	No
Hunt et al. [17]	Heap	Lock-based	No	No	Scales poorly
Shavit *et al.* [21]	Skip-list	Lock-free	No	Yes	Yes
Tsigas *et al.* [23]	Skip-list	Lock-free	No	Yes	Yes
Dragicive et al. [8]	Heap	Lock-free	No	No	Scales poorly
Tamir *et al.* [24]	Heap	Lock-based	Yes	No	Yes
CoMPiQ	Heap	Lock-free	Yes	Yes	Yes

In the paper, first we present the system model and the sequential specification of the heap data structure (Sect. 2). Then, we describe the lock-free design of the heap in detail (Sect. 3). We present the proof of linearizability and lock-freedom of the concurrent operations (Sect. 4). We implemented the algorithm in both C/C++ and Java. We describe the micro-benchmarks that we used to evaluate the algorithm, wherein we also discuss the performance with respect to the design optimizations. Our experiments demonstrate that the presented algorithm performs well in comparison to the existing counterparts (Sect. 5).

2   Preliminaries

We consider an asynchronous shared memory system with a finite set of n *processing threads* $p_1, ..., p_n$ where n may exceed the number of physical processors. In addition to the atomic **read** and **write** instructions, the system supports *Compare-And-Swap* (**CAS**) atomic read-modify-write instructions. The

---

[2] SC2 which validates and writes to two disjoint memory locations atomically.

CAS($address, old, new$) instruction checks if the current value at a memory location ($address$) is equivalent to the given value old, and only if true, changes the value of $address$ to the new value (new) and returns TRUE; otherwise the memory location remains unchanged and the instruction returns FALSE.

The ADT *mutable priority queue* is defined by the following operations:

- INSERT($k, elem$): An INSERT($k, elem$) inserts an item $elem$ with priority k to the heap. We assume that k belongs to a totally ordered set. INSERT is typically a void procedure, however, we return a cross-reference to the insert item instance which can be used in the CHANGEKEY procedure[3]. In case there is an item $elem'$ available in the heap with the same priority k, the item $elem$ gets inserted and the two items $elem$ and $elem'$ can have arbitrary order by their indexes. Thus, the heap allows items with duplicate priority.
- DELETEMIN(): A DELETEMIN removes an item with highest priority from the heap and returns that item itself. DELETEMIN returns a special item EMPTY making no changes in the heap, if there are no items in the heap.
- CHANGEKEY(it, k_2): A CHANGEKEY(it, k_2) changes the heap so that an item $elem$ referenced by the iterator it, if existing in the heap, is placed at the priority k_2. It returns EMPTY if the item referenced by it was deleted from the priority queue.

In our work, a *heap* data structure implements a mutable priority queue. A heap is implemented by way of a *resizable array*. Thus, it contains items that allow for random access using a non-negative index. The array is considered virtually divided in *levels*. In the array, the *root* of the heap occupies the index 1 and is considered to be at the level 0. The *left* and the *right* children of the item at the index i are at the indexes $2i$ and $2i + 1$, respectively. We have considered a *minheap*, which means that the heap maintains the following *heap property*.

Heap Property: An item $elem_1$ with priority k_1 has higher priority than the item $elem_2$ with priority k_2, if $k_1 \leq k_2$. Thus, a parent always has a *smaller* priority compared to its children and the root has the highest priority. Moreover, no item exists at level l unless the level $l - 1$ is completely full.

To demonstrate the correctness of our concurrent heap design we verify the safety and liveness properties. The safety property that we use is *linearizability* [16], whereas, the liveness is proved as *lock-freedom* [14].

Lock-free Implementations utilizing CAS are prone to the ABA problem [19]: a thread P reads a value A from a shared memory location, a concurrent thread $\hat{P}$ changes the value to B and then $\hat{P}$ or another thread changes it back A; when P executes a CAS instruction on the location, it succeeds erroneously as if the location has not been changed since last read by P. Several memory management solutions have been proposed to address the ABA problem [11,19]. For ease of exposition, we assume the availability of a non-blocking memory management and garbage collection.

---

[3] In our implementation, the INSERT operations never returns a *null* or fails to make any change due to the reason of finding the heap *full*. The heap is never full as long as we have sufficient system memory available.

3   Algorithm

Our heap implementation utilizes the lock-free dynamic resizable arrays [6] as the underlying container, which offers both unbounded storage and lock-free progress guarantees. The ADT operations consist of a series of steps, such as modifying the size and then appending an item to the heap, or swapping the item at the root with the item at the bottom, or for that matter swapping any two items in case of a CHANGEKEY, followed by restoring the heap property. Each step comprises of at least one atomic primitive execution over a shared memory word. The procedures HEAPIFYUP and HEAPIFYDOWN restore the heap property.

In order to achieve lock-free synchronization on concurrent access, we apply the *cooperative technique* described by Barnes [2]. The main idea is to detach operations from the executing threads. A thread that wishes to execute an operation on a slot of the array, creates a description of the work that it needs to perform, and writes the descriptor on the slot: we call it *marking* the slot. The operation can be completed by any thread that encounters the descriptor, which comes handy to ensure lock-freedom if the thread that initiated the operation is delayed or crashes.

Please note that *marking is not locking* a slot. It can be thought as shutting the door of a slot after putting down the description of all that is to be done inside. Thus any concurrent thread instead of busy waiting at the door actually carries the description with itself and tries to finish the work initiated by another thread in case that thread could not finish in time.

In our design, we maintain a *global descriptor* which encapsulates the current size of the heap and allows atomic modification of the size value and the associated heap slots with a sequence of CAS instructions. Additionally, we use descriptor objects at the slots during HEAPIFYUP and HEAPIFYDOWN calls. The threads calling HEAPIFYUP or HEAPIFYDOWN synchronize by way of executing CAS at these descriptors.

```
1: type Heap {
2:     Slot *vdata[][];
3:     Info *hdescr;
4: }
5: OpType {HPUP, HPDOWN};

                        ▷ Heap initialized
6: Heap* heap ← ⟨vdata, ⟨1, null⟩⟩
```

```
1: type Info {
2:     bool pending;
3:     size_t size;
4:     size_t pos;
5:     OpType op;
6:     Elem *old, *new;
7:     Info *lup, *rup;
8: }
```

```
1: type Slot {
2:     Elem *elem;
3:     Info *info;
4: }
5: struct Elem {
6:     value_t key;
7:     T *item
8: }
```

(a)   (b)   (c)

Fig. 1. Type definitions for the heap structure, descriptors and initialization.

Data types and heap initialization are given in Fig. 1. The *Heap* structure holds pointers to the data storage arrays and a descriptor object, Fig. 1a - line 1 to 4. A descriptor object, Fig. 1b, maintains information about the state including the current size of the heap. Therefore, we initialize the heap with a dummy descriptor object with size 1, Fig. 1a - line 6. To store auxiliary data with the priorities, our design maintains the heap as an array of pointers to item nodes. Each slot in the heap has a pointer *elem* to an Elem and a pointer *info* to an Info object which records the *state* of the slot: *stable* or *transient* due to an update, Fig. 1c. An Info descriptor stores enough information, such that a thread encountering a slot in a transient state can help advance the operation.

3.1   Lock-Free ADT Operations

The mutable priority queue operations in the lock-free heap are shown by flow-charts in Figs. 2 and 4. The main procedures called by these operations are shown in Figs. 3, 5 and 6. The pseudo-codes of each of the operations, their subroutines, and detail descriptions thereof are presented in the extended version of the paper [26]. For ease of exposition, the flow-chart based presentation of the algorithm is recursive. However, our implementation is fully non recursive as presented in the pseudo-code in the [26].

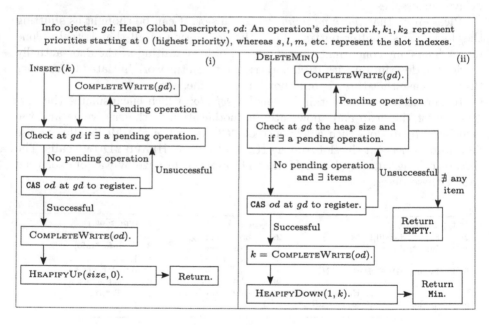

Fig. 2. INSERT and DELETEMIN operations in CoMPiQ.

The INSERT and DELETEMIN operations, Fig. 2(i) and (ii), start with an attempt to modify the size of the heap, this is achieved by *registering* the operation by way of executing a CAS to write its descriptor at the heap's global descriptor. That initiates the *preliminary phase* of the operation. The registered operation is considered pending until it is ready to call the procedures for

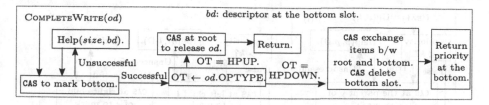

Fig. 3. COMPLETEWRITE procedure.

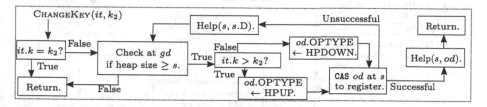

Fig. 4. CHANGEKEY operation in CoMPiQ.

restoring the heap property. The threads that encounter this operation, can help complete the preliminary phase.

The steps to complete the preliminary phase are taken in the procedure COMPLETEWRITE, see Fig. 3. COMPLETEWRITE first fixes the bottom of the heap and then depending upon the type of restoration required: HPUP or HPDOWN, release the root or bottom. This procedure helps in scaling the method because it releases one end of the heap as soon as the preliminary phase is completed. In case of DELETEMIN operation calling COMPLETEWRITE, it returns the priority of the bottom-most item in the heap.

A CHANGEKEY operation, Fig. 4, starts with checking the size of the heap at the global descriptor to verify if the item with the priority that it desires to change exists in the heap. Thereafter, it attempts to register itself by marking the slot of the item, and calls HEAPIFYUP or HEAPIFYDOWN as needed. If the marking fails, it helps the operation that would have marked the slot and thereafter reattempts marking.

In the Fig. 5, the procedures HEAPIFYUP and HEAPIFYDOWN are shown. They take two inputs: the index of the source slot where it starts and the priority of the destination. HEAPIFYUP keeps on exchanging the item with its parent up the heap until the destination priority is set at the slot such that heap property is restored. On the other hand, HEAPIFYDOWN traverses down the heap to do the same. To exchange the item of the current node with that of either the parent or a child, a CAS is used to first put a descriptor over there and thereafter exchange is done atomically. If CAS fails then HELP is called to first help the obstructing operation and then reattempt. The helping procedure ensures lock-freedom.

The HELP call is all about synchronization between concurrent HEAPIFYUP and HEAPIFYDOWN procedures. At a conflict, HEAPIFYDOWN is given priority. HEAPIFYUP allows the HEAPIFYDOWN to gain ownership of a child slot. This

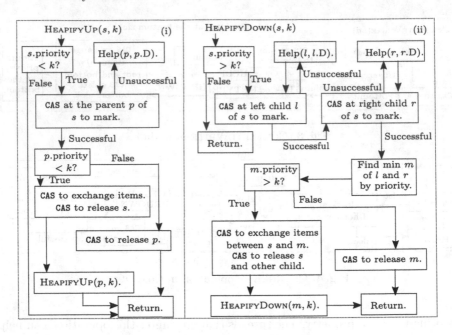

Fig. 5. HEAPIFYUP and HEAPIFYDOWN procedures.

is done by marking the slot with a so called flat descriptor that stores the old information as well. This information is carried by the descriptor at the heap slots, thereby other concurrent operations help accordingly. A HEAPIFYDOWN after completing its own task, restores the information of HEAPIFYUP if that existed at the slot previously.

Please note that, we compare the items at the slots according to their priorities. Moreover, the higher the value of a priority, the lower is the priority as per the min-heap property.

3.2 Design Optimizations

We add two optimizations: (1) "bit-reversal" to ensure that the consecutive INSERT operations traverse different subtrees up the heap to restore heap property [17]. (2) Elimination of INSERT by handing the items off to the concurrent DELETEMIN operations, instead of having the DELETEMIN uproot an item out of position from the end of the heap. An eliminated INSERT operation can return immediately without even attempting to register itself. Below a brief description of the elimination technique is given.

Elimination Optimization: We observe that the DELETEMIN operation lifts an item from the bottom slot in the heap and heapifesDown the heap, while as the INSERT operation appends an item to the end of the heap and heapifies Up the heap. Therefore, we can optimize by allowing the INSERT to hand-off its item to a concurrent DELETEMIN. Thus, the DELETEMIN takes an item from a pending INSERT instead of dislodging one from the end of the heap. Once an INSERT operation successfully hands-off its item, it returns without calling HEAPIFYUP.

We utilize elimination arrays as suggested by Hendlar et. al [12], with each INSERT operation having a dedicated slot in the array. The DELETEMIN operation traverses the array sequentially until it finds a pending INSERT or gets to the end of the array. If the DELETEMIN operation fails to eliminate a pending INSERT, it proceeds with displacing the last item in the heap, otherwise it continues with the item taken from the pending INSERT as described below.

After eliminating a pending INSERT operation (lifting its item from the elimination array), the DELETEMIN compares the lifted item to the item at the root of the heap. If the lifted item has a higher priority, the DELETEMIN returns the lifted item without having to call HEAPIFYDOWN. Otherwise, it proceeds to place the lifted item and returns the item previously at the root.

4   Correctness Proof

To prove linearizability, we define the *linearization point* of each ADT operation. We order the operations, which have *definitely returned*, according to their linearization points, thus obtaining a *sequential history* of execution. Thereby, it is shown that the *concurrent history* of execution of a finite number of ADT operations is *equivalent* to a sequential history. By induction, any concurrent execution is thus shown to be equivalent to a definite sequential history. Additionally, we need to show that each of the ADT operations necessarily brings the heap in a state that satisfies the heap property before its completion.

Proving lock-freedom requires that infinitely often some non-faulty processing thread will complete its operation in a finite number of steps regardless of the failed or delayed threads. To prove lock-freedom, we shall show that no operation *op busy-waits* (by holding locks, for example) when *obstructed* by a concurrent operation *op'* and goes to help *op'* to finish its operation. It may well be that *op* is repeatedly obstructed by concurrent operations op_i, $i \in \{1, 2, \ldots\}$ never letting it complete its own operation, however, by virtue of the same protocol it is proved that at least one non-faulty thread completes its operation in finite number of steps. Under the constraints of space, we sketch the two proofs here.

Theorem 1. *The ADT operations implemented by CoMPiQ are linearizable.*

Proof. The linearization points of the ADT operations are the following:

1. INSERT: An INSERT($k, elem$) operation begins with checking the global descriptor gd of the heap. If it finds that there is a pending concurrent operation, it goes to first help that by calling a COMPLETEWRITE(gd). Thus, an INSERT starts taking steps for itself only after the successful CAS that registers it. After that, INSERT calls COMPLETEWRITE to write its descriptor, and on completion, a HEAPIFYUP is called. The HEAPIFYUP finally makes the item *elem* part of the heap with the successful CAS. Thus for an INSERT operation

that successfully performs this CAS step, its linearization point is there. In case it gets helped by a concurrent operation the successful CAS that finally makes the item *elem* part of the heap is the linearization point. However, in either case the CAS of linearization point is performed before the completion of INSERT. For detail, see [26]. Clearly, the linearization point of an INSERT operation is between its invoke and return.

2. DELETEMIN: Depending on the return, there can be following cases:

   (a) DELETEMIN returns EMPTY: The linearization point is at the atomic read step where the DELETEMIN reads that the heap-size is 1 i.e. it contains a the dummy descriptor object.

   (b) DELETEMIN returns an item *elem*: In this case, where it registers itself by a successful CAS at gd, it is guaranteed that it will itself complete if not obstructed, or will get helped by a concurrent operation. Also, once the descriptor *od* is written, a concurrent INSERT or DELETEMIN operation treats the root of the binary heap as deleted. Thus, the return of the concurrent operation treats the DELETEMIN that successfully put the descriptor as if it had already returned. Therefore, the linearization point of a DELETEMIN in this case is at the step where it registers itself.

   Thus, the linearization point of a DELETEMIN is between invoke and return.

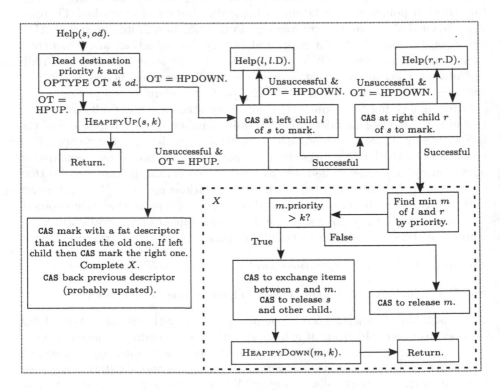

Fig. 6. HELP procedure in CoMPiQ.

3. CHANGEKEY: Similar to an INSERT, a CHANGEKEY terminates after its item is relocated from one slot to another by way of calling a HEAPIFYUP or a HEAPIFYDOWN. The CAS where the item will be visible to every operation with its modified priority is the linearization point of a CHANGEKEY operation. When a CHANGEKEY returns without making any changes in the heap, its linearization point is at the atomic **read** step where it reads the size of the heap.

Furthermore, it can be observably determined that no operation returns before the heap property is restored by calling either a HEAPIFYUP or a HEAPIFYDOWN procedure. Any write on a shared memory word in the algorithm happens by way of only a CAS. A dummy descriptor at the root ensures that no null pointer is dereferenced. Clearly, the heap invariant is maintained across the linearization points of the ADT operations.   □

Theorem 2. *The ADT operations implemented by CoMPiQ are lock-free.*

Proof. We can observe in the algorithm that a concurrent write at any shared word happens only using a CAS. Further, if op_1 and op_2 are any two concurrent operations, at no point after the failure of a CAS, op_1 or op_2 repeats the same CAS step without helping the other operation. This methodology ensures that at least one of the processes do finish its operation in a finite number of steps.   □

5   Evaluation

In this section, we present an evaluation of our lock-free heap using micro-benchmarks and a parallelized implementation of Dijkstra's SSSP algorithm described in [24]. For the micro-benchmark, we compare the *heap-based* concurrent priority queue implementations described below:

1. **CoMPiQ:** Our implementation of a lock-free heap as described in Sect. 3 with elimination optimization.
2. **LB-Heap:** A fine grained locking implementation by Hunt et. al. [17]. Releases locks and re-aquires them on each iteration of the heapifyup operation to prevent deadlocks with concurrent heapifydown operation.
3. **Champ:** Modification of LB-Heap to remove redundant unlock and lock operations. Deadlocks are prevented using tryLock() in the heapifyup and only releasing already acquired locks if a subsequent tryLock() fails. We received Java code from the authors, reimplemented it in C/C++ and included the exponential back-off and bit-reversal scheme [17] to reduce contention.
4. **STL-Heap:** The C++ STL std::priority_queue<T> made thread-safe with a single global lock (coarse-grained locking). We experimented with multiple lock synchronization primitives, however the mutex was the best performing.

Methodology: We performed our evaluations on a dual-socket server with a 3.4 GHz Intel E5-2687W-v2 having 16 physcores (32 hardware threads by hyper-threading), 16 GB of RAM, running Ubuntu 13.04 Linux. All the algorithms in

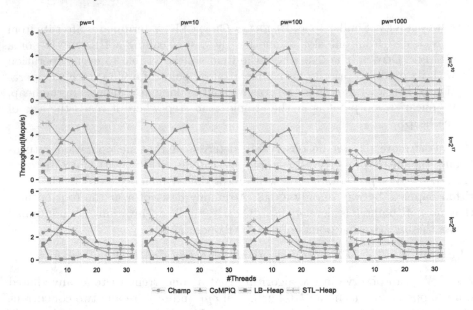

Fig. 7. Throughput `Insert/DeleteMin` operations executed uniformly and randomly independent on the heap implementations as we vary the number of threads and parallel-work (pw) in CPU cycles. K represents the initial number of items in the heap.

the micro-benchmark were implemented in C/C++, compiled with gcc version 4.9.2, -O3 and run as part of the ASCYLIB library [4]. Additionally, we pin software threads onto hardware cores so as to leverage CPU affinity within sockets. We utilize SSMEM [4] with epoch-based garbage collection [9].

We measured throughput as Million operations per second (Mops/s), while varying the number of threads, initial heap size and contention (parallel-work: work performed by threads outside accessing the heap). We do not expect the concurrent heap to be repeatedly accessed by threads without work in between so we simulate this work by varying parallel-work(pw), thus giving a more realistic evaluation than just stress testing. The lower the parallel-work, the more contention experienced by threads accessing the heap. We varied the number of items in the heap before starting the measurements with ($k \in \{2^{10}, 2^{17}, 2^{20}\}$). Operations on the heap are randomly chosen with a distribution of 50% Insert and 50% DeleteMin operations. Priorities for inserted items where selected uniformly at random from the range of all 64-bit integers. Each experiment run for 5 seconds, we present the average over 6 runs for each parameter configuration.

Throughput: Figure 7 presents measured throughput in Million operations per second (Mops/s) as we vary the contention in parallel-work (pw) in CPU cycles and the number of threads. We present three sets of graphs for three initial sizes of the heap ($k \in \{2^{10}, 2^{17}, 2^{20}\}$), this is to show the effect of heap size on the execution time of the operations.

The figure shows that with small initial size 2^{10} (row 1, Fig. 7), at low thread contention, the single lock implementation STL-Heap outperforms other implementations. This attributed to the low overheads incurred by STL-Heap using mutual exclusion, and high overheads on both the multi-lock LB-Heap, Champ and lock-free CoMPiQ. Similar observation about the single-lock implementation was made in previous works [17,23].

Champ optimizes on the heapifyup operation of LB-Heap by removing redundant unlock and re-lock operations in uncontended cases, however, in case of contention, failure to acquire a lock, results in releasing locks held, and an attempt to reacquire them. On modern architectures with private caches, a process that releases a lock has a much higher probability of reacquiring the lock if it attempts to acquire the lock immediately. Thus, an implementation of Champ was showing similar performance figures as LB-Heap. We modified the implementation by adding exponential back-off between releasing a lock, and attempts to re-acquire the same lock. This is the major reason for the performance differences between Champ and LB-Heap.

As we increase the number of threads, contention for the lock increases and performance deteriorates. We observe that the lock-free algorithm with elimination(CoMPiQ), scales up as we increase the thread count. Elimination increases the concurrency exploited by the operations as an INSERT completes without contending for the global descriptor or creating contention within the heap with HEAPIFYUP operations. All implementations degrade in performance as we deploy more than 16 threads due to communication overheads across sockets. We still observe that CoMPiQ offers better throughput on multi-socket executions.

As we increase the initial size of the heap (height of the heap), "bit-reversal" allows for more concurrency, and thus reducing the impact of synchronization overhead on the performance. In this regard, we see that for heap size 2^{20} the performance of the single-lock implementation drops significantly relative to other implementations with increasing thread count. The CoMPiQ performs best with increased opportunities for concurrency and reduced contention on the heap.

Increasing parallel work ($pw \in \{1, 10, 100, 1000\}$) affects the lock-based implementations more than the lock-free implementations because the concurrency overheads no longer dominate performance, but concurrency. Thus, CoMPiQ still outperforms other implementations.

Discussion: Key observations are that – the heap is an inherently sequential data structure and even the most efficient implementation is still outperformed significantly by a single thread executing on a sequential heap for low levels of parallel-work. However, as the parallel work increases, the benefit of increasing concurrency becomes more significant. Additionally, bit-reversal offers more opportunities for disjoint-access allowing better exploitation of concurrency on larger size heaps to offset synchronization overheads. This is less significant in smaller heaps as successive Insert operations conflict on the paths to the root. The root and the size variable create a severe bottleneck in both blocking and non-blocking implementations, as all operations have to modify the size variable, while all DeleteMin operations modify the size and also block the root for

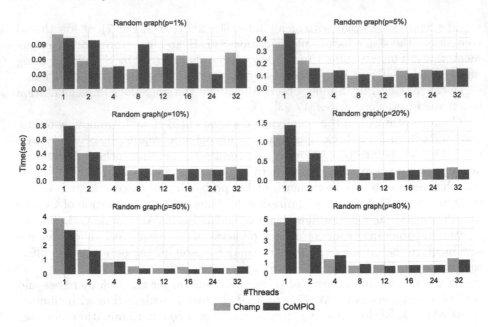

Fig. 8. Runtimes for parallel Dijkstra's SSSP for different random graphs

exclusive access. CoMPiQ uses elimination to reduce on the contention at the bottleneck, thus resulting in better performance.

Parallel SSSP: One important application of priority queues that utilizes the changeKey operation is the Dijkstra's SSSP algorithm. To evaluate the performance of **CoMPiQ**, we implemented CoMPiQ as part of the benchmark suite received from [24] which included a parallel implementation Dijkstra's algorithm and **Champ** which is the only other implementation that supports changeKey operation. The parallel Dijkstra's SSSP algorithm availed in the benchmark relies heavily on locks to ensure correctness, with this in mind, we plugged in our implementation without modifying the parallel SSP algorithm for fair comparison. A more optimistic parallel implementation of Dijkstra's SSSP algorithm is left as future work. In the benchmark, running time is measured over several input graphs and number of execution threads. Each input graph is generated with 10,000 vertices, with edges occurring independently randomly with some probability p and a random weight in the range [1–100]. The parallel Dijkstra's SSSP algorithm and the evaluated priority queues are implemented in Java.

Figure 8 shows that the **CoMPiQ** performs comparably with **Champ**. This implies that overheads incurred to ensure lock-freedom do not degrade performance of CoMPiQ when used in parallel applications. Note that node locks are used in this parallelization, thus, as pointed out earlier, we anticipate significant performance improvements with a more optimistic parallelization, that uses atomics to update node weights. We only considered implementations that support the changeKey operation. Please refer to [24] for an evaluation involving skiplist-based priority queues that do not support `changeKey`.

6   Conclusion

In this paper, we presented a novel algorithm for an array-based unbounded concurrent lock-free heap. The heap implements a priority queue interface with the additional facility of changing the priority of an item in the runtime. Our work contributes to many important applications, which use the priority queue ADT and need to modify the priority of the items dynamically, in a definitive way. Our micro-benchmark based experiments demonstrated that our algorithm performs well in comparison to similar existing algorithms that use locks.

With array-based implementations, it is trivial to represent a d-ary heap, however, implementation of a concurrent multi-way heap creates new challenges. The multi-way heaps lower the traversal cost by reducing the height of the tree, but increase the synchronization overhead as an operation attempts to determine the priorities of all the d-children. The techniques introduced in this article may be useful in implementing non-blocking versions of the heap-ordered d-ary heaps.

References

1. Alistarh, D., Kopinsky, J., Li, J., Shavit, N.: The spraylist: a scalable relaxed priority queue. In: ACM SIGPLAN Notices, vol. 50, pp. 11–20. ACM (2015)
2. Barnes, G.: A method for implementing lock-free shared-data structures. In: 5th SPAA, pp. 261–270 (1993)
3. Barnes, G.: Wait-free Algoritzms for Heaps. Department of Computer Science and Engineering, University of Washington (1994)
4. David, T., Guerraoui, R., Trigonakis, V.: Asynchronized concurrency: The secret to scaling concurrent search data structures. In: 20th ASPLOS, pp. 631–644 (2015)
5. de Moura, L., Bjørner, N.: Z3: an efficient SMT solver. In: Ramakrishnan, C.R., Rehof, J. (eds.) TACAS 2008. LNCS, vol. 4963, pp. 337–340. Springer, Heidelberg (2008). https://doi.org/10.1007/978-3-540-78800-3_24
6. Dechev, D., Pirkelbauer, P., Stroustrup, B.: Lock-free dynamically resizable arrays. In: Shvartsman, M.M.A.A. (ed.) OPODIS 2006. LNCS, vol. 4305, pp. 142–156. Springer, Heidelberg (2006). https://doi.org/10.1007/11945529_11
7. Dijkstra, E.W.: A note on two problems in connexion with graphs. Numer. Math. 1(1), 269–271 (1959)
8. Dragicevic, K., Bauer, D.: Optimization techniques for concurrent STM-based implementations: a concurrent binary heap as a case study. In: 23rd IPDPS, pp. 1–8 (2009)
9. Fraser, K.: Practical lock-freedom. Ph.D. thesis, University of Cambridge (2004)
10. Fujimoto, R.M.: Parallel discrete event simulation. Commun. ACM 33(10), 30–53 (1990)
11. Gidenstam, A., Papatriantafilou, M., Sundell, H., Tsigas, P.: Efficient and reliable lock-free memory reclamation based on reference counting. IEEE Trans. Parallel Distrib. Syst. 20(8), 1173–1187 (2009)

12. Hendler, D., Shavit, N., Yerushalmi, L.: A scalable lock-free stack algorithm. In: 16th SPAA, SPAA 2004, pp. 206–215 (2004)
13. Henry, G.J.: The unix system: the fair share scheduler. AT&T Bell Lab. Tech. J. **63**(8), 1845–1857 (1984)
14. Herlihy, M.: Wait-free synchronization. ACM TOPLAS **13**(1), 124–149 (1991)
15. Herlihy, M.: A methodology for implementing highly concurrent data objects. ACM Trans. Program. Lang. Syst. **15**(5), 745–770 (1993)
16. Herlihy, M.P., Wing, J.M.: Linearizability: a correctness condition for concurrent objects. ACM TOPLAS **12**(3), 463–492 (1990)
17. Hunt, G.C., Michael, M.M., Parthasarathy, S., Scott, M.L.: An efficient algorithm for concurrent priority queue heaps. Inf. Process. Lett. **60**(3), 151–157 (1996)
18. Israeli, A., Rappoport, L.: Efficient wait-free implementation of a concurrent priority queue. In: Schiper, A. (ed.) WDAG 1993. LNCS, vol. 725, pp. 1–17. Springer, Heidelberg (1993). https://doi.org/10.1007/3-540-57271-6_23
19. Michael, M.M.: Hazard pointers: safe memory reclamation for lock-free objects. IEEE Trans. Parallel Distrib. Syst. **15**(6), 491–504 (2004)
20. Prim, R.C.: Shortest connection networks and some generalizations. Bell Labs Tech. J. **36**(6), 1389–1401 (1957)
21. Shavit, N., Lotan, I.: Skiplist-based concurrent priority queues. In: 14th IPDPS, pp. 263–268. IEEE (2000)
22. Shavit, N., Touitou, D.: Software transactional memory. Distrib. Comput. **10**(2), 99–116 (1997)
23. Sundell, H., Tsigas, P.: Fast and lock-free concurrent priority queues for multi-thread systems. J. Parallel Distrib. Comput. **65**(5), 609–627 (2005)
24. Tamir, O., Morrison, A., Rinetzky, N.: A heap-based concurrent priority queue with mutable priorities for faster parallel algorithms. In: 19th OPODIS (2016)
25. Vitter, J.S.: Design and analysis of dynamic huffman codes. J. ACM (JACM) **34**(4), 825–845 (1987)
26. Walulya, I., Chatterjee, B., Datta, A.K., Niyoliya, R., Tsigas, P.: Concurrent lock-free unbounded priority queue with mutable priorities. Technical report, 2018:06, ISNN 1652–926X, Department of Computer Science and Engineering, Chalmers University of Technology (2018)

Brief Announcement: Deterministic Leader Election in Self-organizing Particle Systems

Rida A. Bazzi[✉] and Joseph L. Briones

Arizona State University, Tempe, AZ, USA
bazzi@asu.edu

Abstract. We consider the leader election problem in the geometric Amoebot model in which nodes have no unique identifiers and only share a common local sense of direction. Unlike other works, we consider the deterministic leader election problem for general connected systems. We propose a new deterministic leader election protocol that always succeeds in finding 1, 2, 3, or 6 leaders. We show that if the protocol does not elect a unique leader, deterministic leader election impossible for the system.

1 Introduction

Leader election is a fundamental problem that has been studied in both shared memory and message passing system models. It is a prototypical symmetry breaking problem [7]. The goal of leader election is to identify a unique member of the system as the leader. In anonymous systems, the requirement is for one unique member to self-identify as a leader and for other members to agree that a leader has been self-identified.

In this paper, we are interested in leader election in self-organizing particle systems, specifically the well studied Amoebot Model [3]. In this model, particles occupy cells in a hexagonal grid. They have finite memory, can communicate with adjacent particles, and can expand into unoccupied adjacent cells. The system of particles is assumed to be initially connected because there is no way to achieve coordination between different connected components without additional system assumptions [6]. Electing a leader can facilitate solving problems such as shape-formation [8], object coating [5] and system compression [1].

Leader election in the Amoebot model has been studied in the general case without restrictions on the connectedness of the system [2,4], but those solutions are probabilistic. The only deterministic solution for leader election is that of Di Luna et al. [8] who use deterministic leader election to solve the deterministic shape formation problem. While technically involved, their solution assumes that the particle system is simply connected which means that the unoccupied cells form a connected component. Their solution takes advantage of the fact that the shape has no holes. It starts with an initial *erosion* phase in which particles on the *corners* of the system eliminate themselves as candidate leaders. This

T. Izumi and P. Kuznetsov (Eds.): SSS 2018, LNCS 11201, pp. 381–386, 2018.
https://doi.org/10.1007/978-3-030-03232-6_25

phase ends with a unique leader or 2 or 3 candidate leaders. If there are 2 or 3 candidate leaders left, they form trees containing other particles in the system and compare these trees to each other to break the symmetry. If the trees are identical, it follows that the particle system has symmetry that makes deterministic leader election impossible. The approach of Di Luna et al. does not work in a system with holes because erosion does not work in the general case. The work of Di Luna et al. assumes no shared local sense of direction (chirality), but, once candidate leaders have been identified, achieves a common chirality using particle movement to beak symmetry.

The main contribution of this paper is a solution to the deterministic leader election problem in general connected systems. To overcome the limitation of the earlier work, we come up with a novel approach to determine a small number of leaders (1, 2, 3, or 6) on the unique outer boundary of the system. After the candidate leaders are determined, the solution proceeds as in [8]. Candidate leaders grow trees that are then compared to break symmetry. If breaking symmetry is not possible, then, like [8] we establish constructively that deterministic leader election is not possible. Unlike [8] in which candidate leaders are adjacent, in our setting, coordinating candidate leaders requires more care.

2   System Model

We consider the geometric Amoebot model [3] in which anonymous particles with finite memory occupy cells within a hexagonal lattice. Particles have the same chirality. Particles can occupy one cell (contracted) or two cells (expanded) and no cell can be occupied by more than one particle. Since our leader election algorithm does not involve any expansion, each particle has six ports ordered clockwise from port 0 through port 5, one port on each of the adjacent cells. The ports are used to communicate with other particles in adjoining cells and to sense if an adjacent cell is occupied by another particle or is empty. A communication edge between two particles consists of a pair of corresponding ports. For example, between cells A and B in Fig. 1, port 3 of A and port 4 of B form a communication edge between A and B. Two adjacent particles know the port numbers that form the edge between them. Particles communicate by writing to their local memory and reading the local memory of adjacent particles. This allows for a simple message passing between particles. We assume the particle system to be connected.

In the solution, we introduce six virtual nodes for each cell, one node per port. These nodes are represented in Fig. 1 by black dots at the vertices of the cells occupied by the particle. Port i is on the edge between node $i - 1 \mod 6$ and node i. Nodes execute steps when they are activated by the scheduler which we assume to be completely asynchronous.

3   Leader Election

The algorithm has two main phases. In the first phase, a small number of candidate leaders are selected on the outer boundary of the system and in the second phase further reduction of this number is attempted. If the algorithm does not elect a unique leader in the second phase, the system must have symmetry that prevents deterministic leader election.

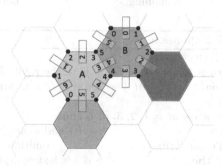

Fig. 1. Particle system surrounded by unoccupied cells

In the first phase, the algorithm starts by running separate instances of a *boundary leader election* algorithm on all the boundaries of the system (a node is on a boundary if it is adjacent to an empty cell). An instance of a boundary leader election algorithm is designed to work correctly if the participants in the election consist of all nodes of a boundary. On the inner boundaries, if any, it is guaranteed that no leader is elected. On the unique outer boundary, 1, 2, 3, or 6 candidate leaders are selected. Each leader also has what we call a *stretch*, a sequence of contiguous nodes, associated with it. If there is a unique leader, the algorithm terminates, but if there are multiple leaders, this means that the outer boundary has symmetry that prevents the deterministic election of a unique leader. This initial phase is the more involved phase and is done in a sequence of phases that are not strictly synchronized. Having a small number of leaders that can communicate around the outer boundary allows us to use the tree comparison approach of [8] in the second phase.

If at the end of the first phase there are multiple candidate leaders, each particle with a leader node tries to recruit as many particles as it can to form a tree with the particle itself as the root of the tree. This is the same as the approach of [8]. After all particles in the systems have joined a tree, each root compares its tree to the tree of the root to its *right* on the outer border according to an order relation. Every candidate leader then shares the results of these comparisons will all other candidate leaders on the boundary. If the results of all these comparison are equality, then there is symmetry in the system and deterministic leader election is not possible. If the result of one of the comparisons

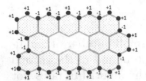 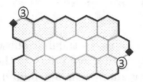 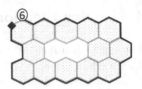

Fig. 2. Vertex labeling and initialization of stretches.

Fig. 3. Intermediate step with two stretches remaining.

Fig. 4. Final configuration. Termination detected.

Algorithm 1. Stretch Expansion

1: **function** ATTEMPTEXPANSION()
2:    ▷ s and s' are two adjacent stretches. s' is to the right of s.
3:    **if** $s.count > s'.count \wedge (s.count + s'.count \leq 6 \wedge s.count > 0)$ **then**
4:        MERGE(s, s')
5:    **else if** $s.count = s'.count = 1, 2, 3,$ or 6 **then**
6:        **if** $s \equiv s'$ **then**   ▷ if s and s' are lexicographically equal
7:            DETECTTERMINATION()   ▷ initiate termination detection
8:        **else if** $s > s'$ **then**   ▷ if s is lexicographically greater than s'
9:            MERGE(s, s')

---

is inequality, then one or more candidate leaders are eliminated and the process is repeated with the remaining roots. This is repeated a constant number of times until either there is one unique remaining leader or there are multiple leaders who are all tied in the tree comparison. If there is a unique leader, we are done, otherwise, there is symmetry that prevents deterministic leader election. In what follows, we describe some of the details of the first phase.

The first phases starts by having each particle sense its surrounding to determine if one or more cells around it are unoccupied. A particle can be on more than one border, but each node can be on at most one border. When a particle has identified itself as part of the outer border and its successors and predecessors have been initialized, the particle labels its nodes with a unary label which is +1 for border nodes that belong to only one particle and −1 for border nodes that are shared between adjacent particles. This is illustrated in Fig. 2.

After labeling each node on the outer border, stretches attempt to expand to eliminate possible leaders. The leftmost node in a stretch is considered the leader (or head) of the stretch. The rightmost node in a stretch is called the tail of a stretch. Within a stretch, each node has a predecessor pointer and a successor pointer. The leader of the stretch maintains a counter which is equal to the sum of the unary labels of the nodes in the stretch. The counter value never exceeds the value 6. Initially, all nodes on the outer border are considered independent stretches, of size 1, with a respective counter equal to their unary label. All nodes are initialized to be both the head and tail of their stretch. Figures 3 and 4 illustrate stretches.

Algorithm 2. Termination Detection

```
1: function DETECTTERMINATION(s)
2:     terminate ← true
3:     for i ← 1, k/s.count do                                    ▷ k = 6/s.count
4:         s' ← s
5:         for j ← 1, i − 1 do
6:             s' ← s'.left                          ▷ Rotate to the stretch left of s'
7:             terminate ← (terminate ∧ (s'.count ≡ s.count))
8:         s' ← s'.left
9:         terminate ← (terminate ∧ (s'.count = s.count)) ∧ s' ≡ s
10:    return terminate
```

Stretches can expand by merging with adjacent stretches. When two stretches merge, the leader of the stretch on the left (s in Algorithm 1) becomes the leader of the resulting stretch and its new count is the sum of its old count and the count of the stretch being merged into. A merge is allowed only if the sum of the two counts is less than or equal to 6. We avoid deadlocks by placing an order relationship based on the count and lexicographic comparison between stretches. We require that the stretch s on the left has a positive count and either its count is larger than that of the stretch s' on the right (s') or the two counts are equal, but the sequence of unary labels of s is lexicographically larger than that of s'.

Finally, to detect termination, a stretch attempts to establish that the whole border on which it resides is covered with k identical stretches that have the same positive count ($k = 1, 2, 3$, or 6).

References

1. Cannon, S., Daymude, J.J., Randall, D., Richa, A.W.: A Markov chain algorithm for compression in self-organizing particle systems. In: Proceedings of the 2016 ACM Symposium on Principles of Distributed Computing, pp. 279–288. ACM (2016)
2. Daymude, J.J., Gmyr, R., Richa, A.W., Scheideler, C., Strothmann, T.: Improved leader election for self-organizing programmable matter. In: Fernández Anta, A., Jurdzinski, T., Mosteiro, M.A., Zhang, Y. (eds.) ALGOSENSORS 2017. LNCS, vol. 10718, pp. 127–140. Springer, Cham (2017). https://doi.org/10.1007/978-3-319-72751-6_10
3. Derakhshandeh, Z., Dolev, S., Gmyr, R., Richa, A.W., Scheideler, C., Strothmann, T.: Brief announcement: amoebot-a new model for programmable matter. In: Proceedings of the 26th ACM Symposium on Parallelism in Algorithms and Architectures, pp. 220–222. ACM (2014)
4. Derakhshandeh, Z., Gmyr, R., Richa, A.W., Scheideler, C., Strothmann, T.: An algorithmic framework for shape formation problems in self-organizing particle systems. In: Proceedings of the Second Annual International Conference on Nanoscale Computing and Communication, p. 21. ACM (2015)
5. Derakhshandeh, Z., Gmyr, R., Richa, A.W., Scheideler, C., Strothmann, T.: Universal coating for programmable matter. Theor. Comput. Sci. **671**, 56–68 (2017)

6. Flocchini, P., Prencipe, G., Santoro, N., Widmayer, P.: Arbitrary pattern formation by asynchronous, anonymous, oblivious robots. Theor. Comput. Sci. **407**(1–3), 412–447 (2008)
7. Itai, A., Rodeh, M.: Symmetry breaking in distributed networks. Inf. Comput. **88**(1), 60–87 (1990)
8. Di Luna, G.A., Flocchini, P., Santoro, N., Viglietta, G., Yamauchi, Y.: Shape formation by programmable particles. In: 21st International Conference on Principles of Distributed Systems, OPODIS 2017, Lisbon, Portugal, 18–20 December 2017, pp. 31:1–31:16 (2017)

Brief Announcement: Time Efficient Self-stabilizing Stable Marriage

Joffroy Beauquier[1], Thibault Bernard[2], Janna Burman[1],
Shay Kutten[3], and Marie Laveau[1(✉)]

[1] LRI, Université Paris-Sud, CNRS, Université Paris-Saclay,
Bat 650, Rue Noetzlin, 91190 Gif-sur-Yvette, Orsay, France
`laveau@lri.fr`
[2] LI-PaRAD, Université de Versailles, Université Paris-Saclay, Versailles, France
[3] Technion - Israel Institute of Technology, Haifa, Israel

Abstract. "Stable marriage" refers to a particular matching with constraints having a wide variety of applications in different domains (two-sided markets, Cloud computing, college admissions, etc.). Most of the studies on this problem performed up to now were for centralized and synchronous settings assuming initialization. We consider a distributed and asynchronous context, without initialization (*i.e.*, in a self-stabilizing manner, tolerating any transient fault) and with some confidentiality requirements. The single already known self-stabilizing solution in Laveau et al. (SSS' 2017), based on Ackerman et al.'s algorithm (SICOMP' 2011), stabilizes in $O(n^4)$ *moves* (activation of a single node). We improve on this previous result considerably by presenting a solution with $O(n^2)$ steps, relying on the idea of Gale and Shapley's algorithm (AMM 1962), which takes also $O(n^2)$ moves, but in a centralized synchronous context. Moreover it is not self-sabilizing solution and a corruption cannot be repaired locally, as noticed by Knuth (1976).

1 Introduction

We are interested in a matching problem on complete bipartite graphs which was originally called stable marriage by Gale and Shapley [9]. The aim is to match nodes of two different sets without *blocking pairs* (see the definition later). Gale and Shapley proposed the first algorithm [9] (GSA) that is centralized and proceeds in synchronous rounds, alternating proposals (by women) and acceptances (by men). Intuitively speaking the algorithm avoids blocking pairs by gradually improving the quality of the matchings ("better match" dynamics). As noticed by Knuth in [11], GSA requires an initial configuration in which no node is matched, meaning that it is not *self-stabilizing* [7]. A self-stabilizing solution was proposed in [12]. It is distributed, correct in an asynchronous context and

---

The full version of the paper is available in [6].

This work was supported in part by grants from Digiteo France and by the Israeli ministry of Science and Technology.

T. Izumi and P. Kuznetsov (Eds.): SSS 2018, LNCS 11201, pp. 387–392, 2018.
https://doi.org/10.1007/978-3-030-03232-6_26

guarantees confidentiality of the preferences. Its complexity is $O(n^4)$ moves, in contrast to that of GSA, $O(n^2)$, although with different assumptions.

The solution proposed here improves the complexity of [12] under the same assumptions (distributed, self-stabilizing, asynchronous, confidential), providing a complexity of $O(n^2)$ moves. The new algorithm is based on a different approach than that of [12]. While the solution in [12] of $O(n^4)$ moves is inspired by a two-phase algorithm due to Ackerman et al. [1], the proposed solution relies on GSA. Making GSA self-stabilizing without augmenting its complexity is challenging, because GSA is inherently not self-stabilizing [11]. As we wanted to keep the "better match" dynamics of GSA because it ensures a good complexity, we are naturally led to detect locally the blocking pairs and to repair them globally, since no local repair is possible. More technically, the solution follows a scheme proposed in [2], and formalized in [5] for the asynchronous model. It relies on two modules. First, a detection module checks locally and perpetually the correctness of the configuration. If a problem is detected, the module triggers a reset reinitializing the system. We use a self-stabilizing reset (e.g., [3,4]) having particular properties defined in [5]. It is propagated on a spanning tree of height 2 that is constructed over the given bipartite graph (this construction requires no assumptions). This first module stabilizes in $O(n^2)$ moves. Then, a second module builds a stable marriage from the reinitialized system such that neither a blocking pair is created during the process, nor the reset is triggered again. For this latter module, we develop an algorithm, Async-GSA, solving an asynchronous stable marriage.

Regarding the optimally of the solution, it has been proven in [10] that the communication complexity [13] of the stable marriage problem is $\Omega(n^2)$ bits. This result implies an $\Omega(n^2/\log(n))$ bound in moves in our model (assuming constant size communication registers). Thus, the algorithm proposed here can be considered as near optimal. Nevertheless, we believe that a more careful analysis can provide a better $\Omega(n^2)$ lower bound for the model here.

Preliminaries. We consider a distributed system represented by a complete bipartite graph $K_{n,n}$ (one set of women and one of men). Each node u has a unique identifier and a different *priority* for each node v in the other set (denoted $priority(u,v)$), between 1 (the most preferred) and n.

The goal is (1) to match (marry) the women and the men together such that everyone is matched and (2) that there is no pair (w,m) of a woman and a man that are not matched to each other, but by their priorities they prefer each other over their current matches. When there are no such pairs, called *blocking pairs*, the set of marriages is said *stable*.

We adopt the link-register communication model (*cf.* [8]). Each process is associated with a set of atomic registers, each of a size of $O(1)$ bits. A process can write in its registers and can read any register of a neighbor. The *state* of a node is the vector of the values of its internal variables and its registers. A *configuration* is the vector of the states of all nodes. A distributed algorithm is described by a finite set of *guarded rules* per node. In a configuration, the *distributed unfair scheduler* selects a non-empty subset of nodes with *enabled* rules (having their guards to true). Then, per such node, it chooses one of such enabled rules (according to predefined priorities) and atomically executes the corresponding actions. An execution of the actions of one rule (of a particular node) is called a *move*.

A distributed algorithm solves the stable marriage problem in a *self-stabilizing* way if it solves it for any possible initial configuration. Even if the variables of all nodes have been corrupted once, *i.e.*, by transient failures (producing an arbitrary configuration), the algorithm reaches a *terminal* configuration (not changing any more in the execution), in which there is a stable marriage. The time complexity of an algorithm is evaluated in terms of the maximum number of moves until a terminal configuration, starting from an arbitrary one.

2   Self-stabilizing Stable Marriage in $O(n^2)$ Moves

It was proven in [5] that if an initialized solution satisfies some specific properties, it can be transformed into a self-stabilizing one. For the transformation to be correct, the non self-stabilizing algorithm has to be *locally checkable* [2] satisfying Definition 1 below (adapted to our case). Then, nodes can locally detect if a configuration is incorrect. Correct configurations are those reached by an execution of the given non-self-stabilizing algorithm starting from a correct configuration, C_{init} in our case. Once an incorrect configuration is locally detected, a global reset is launched, setting each variable to a predefined value (defined by C_{init}). Then the algorithm behaves as if it has been started from a correct configuration and reaches a terminal configuration with a stable marriage.

Thus, the issue is to design a locally checkable solution. We design such an algorithm Async-GSA. It is described below shortly. Then, we prove that it is locally checkable (according to Definition 1), by constructing the predicate (named $LP_{m,w}$) that will be checked locally and periodically by each man m, in the final self-stabilizing solution.

In Async-GSA each woman makes proposals to men in the order of her preference list starting (in C_{init}) from the most preferred neighbor (these actions are implemented by a guarded rule **Propose**). Men reply by accepting or refusing each proposal (using rules **Accept** or **Refuse**, resp.). If a man receives several proposals, he accepts the most preferred one and refuses the others. If he is already married but receives a better proposal, he accepts the proposal and cancels (still by **Refuse**) the previous marriage. If a man accepts a proposal, the proposing woman accepts as well (using **Confirm** rule). Otherwise, if he refuses (or cancels), she shifts to the next element in her preference list (rule **Refusal_Management**) and thus makes a new proposal (rule **Propose** again). The complete formal description and proof of Async-GSA is given in [6].

Theorem 1. *From C_{init}, after at most $O(n^2)$ moves, a terminal configuration with a stable marriage is reached.*

In Definition 1 below, $LP_{m,w}$ is a predicate on the internal variables and registers of m and also on the registers of w (that can be read by m) in a solution Alg. Also, Π is a global predicate on configurations.

Definition 1 ([2], [5]). *[Local Checkability adapted to our model] A solution* Alg *to a problem is locally checkable for Π iff the following conditions hold.*

1. *There exists a set $\mathcal{L}$ of local predicates $LP_{m,w}$, for each man m and each woman w, such that $\Pi = \bigwedge\limits_{\forall(m,w)\in E} LP_{m,w}$.*
2. *There exists a configuration of* Alg *satisfying Π.*
3. *Each $LP_{m,w}$ is such that if C is a configuration satisfying $LP_{m,w}$ then the next configuration C' in the execution also satisfies $LP_{m,w}$.*

The local predicate $LP_{m,w}$ that we construct for proving the local checkability of Async-GSA is of the following form. $LP_{m,w} \equiv (P^0_{m,w} \vee P^{Propose}_{m,w} \vee P^{Refuse}_{m,w} \vee P^{Accept}_{m,w} \vee P^{Confirm}_{m,w} \vee P^{R\_M}_{m,w}) \wedge \neg P^{BP}_{m,w}$

$P^0_{m,w}$ is a predicate satisfied by local states of nodes in Asynch-GSA in a configuration where no proposal/refusal/acceptance has been made on (w,m) and in all configurations reached from it as long as no rule has been applied on (m,w). Notice that C_{init} satisfies $P^0_{m,w}$, thus satisfying point 2 of Definition 1. Each of the five next predicates is related to one of the rules of the solution. Indeed, $P^{Propose}_{m,w}$ is the predicate satisfied in a local state in a configuration where a proposal has been made by woman w. Proposals are made in a configuration satisfying $P^0_{m,w}$ using rule **Propose**. In the same manner, $P^{Refuse}_{m,w}$, $P^{Accept}_{m,w}$, $P^{Confirm}_{m,w}$ and $P^{R\_M}_{m,w}$ describe local states that can be reached after a particular rule of the algorithm. The last predicate is for detecting a blocking pair. A complete description of these predicates is in the full paper. Roughly, $LP_{m,w}$ is designed to check whether the edge (m, w) is a blocking pair. For that, w communicates to m whether it prefers m to its current spouse. With this information, m is able to detect a blocking pair but also an inconsistency in the variables. Notice that the exchange of information between w and m is limited and respects the privacy: preference lists are not communicated.

Theorem 2. *Let $\Pi = \bigwedge\limits_{\forall(m,w)\in E} LP_{m,w}$.* Async-GSA *is locally checkable for Π.*

Composition and Analysis. Let us now speak of the composite algorithm, including the three modules- the reset, Async-GSA and the checking. First, using identifiers and the structural properties of the bipartite graph, a rooted spanning tree of depth 2 (used by the reset) can be easily constructed, stabilizing in $O(n^2)$ moves (see details in [6]). Then, in the worst case, an execution is divided in three parts: an initial part in which a reset (propagated on a tree) is enabled (its rules) but not triggered, a second part during which a reset is performed and a third part, which corresponds to an execution with the correct initialization (of Async-GSA). We discuss upper bounds for each of these parts. Assume that the rules of a node are activated according to the following priorities: first the spanning tree construction, second the rules involved in the reset, then the rules of local checking and at the end, the rules of Async-GSA.

For the last part, Theorem 1 gives the $O(n^2)$ moves upper bound. Now, consider the first part. There are some incoherent nodes or nodes involved in a blocking pair in the starting configuration. The other nodes simply execute rules of `Async-GSA`. The longest execution segment of this part is obtained when the unfair scheduler chooses to ignore the incorrect nodes (from executing the rules of the inconsistency detection). This may take at most $O(n^2)$ moves, until no woman could make a new proposition, as the end of her preference list is reached. Then, an incorrect node is activated, triggering a reset. The task of building a partial stable marriage takes $O(n^2)$, still from Theorem 1.

For the reset part, we adopt the algorithm from [3]. This algorithm proceeds in "waves" (of broadcast and convergecast) propagated over a tree and coordinated by the root. Such a reset can be decomposed into three subparts: (a) a reset request launched towards the root, (b) a "freezing" wave from the root to the leaves, initializing the `Async-GSA` variables (following by a feedback to the root), and then c) an "unfreezing" wave from the root to all the nodes, launching the `Async-GSA`. Since the waves are diffused on the tree, each wave takes $O(n)$ moves. Furthermore, the reset has a delay of $O(n)$ moves before being operational since reset variables can be incoherent. Finally, even if each node launches a reset simultaneously, that takes less than $n \times O(n) = O(n^2)$ moves. After a reset has been accomplished, variables are set to their initial values and `Async-GSA` can start. This justifies the overall complexity of $O(n^2)$ moves.

References

1. Ackermann, H., Goldberg, P.W., Mirrokni, V.S., Röglin, H., Vöcking, B.: Uncoordinated two-sided matching markets. SIAM J. Comput. **40**, 92–106 (2011)
2. Afek, Y., Kutten, S., Yung, M.: Memory-efficient self stabilizing protocols for general networks. In: van Leeuwen, J., Santoro, N. (eds.) WDAG 1990. LNCS, vol. 486, pp. 15–28. Springer, Heidelberg (1991). https://doi.org/10.1007/3-540-54099-7_2
3. Arora, A., Gouda, M.: Distributed reset. IEEE Trans. Comp. **43**, 1026–1038 (1994)
4. Awerbuch, B., Patt-Shamir, B., Varghese, G.: Self-stabilization by local checking and correction. In: Proceedings of 32nd Annual Symposium of Foundations of Computer Science (1991)
5. Awerbuch, B., Patt-Shamir, B., Varghese, G., Dolev, S.: Self-stabilization by local checking and global reset. In: Tel, G., Vitányi, P. (eds.) WDAG 1994. LNCS, vol. 857, pp. 326–339. Springer, Heidelberg (1994). https://doi.org/10.1007/BFb0020443
6. Beauquier, J., Bernard, T., Burman, J., Kutten, S., Laveau, M.: Time efficient self-stabilizing stable marriage. Technical report (2018). https://hal.inria.fr/hal-01266028
7. Dijkstra, E.W.: Self-stabilizing systems in spite of distributed control. CACM **17**, 643–644 (1974)
8. Dolev, S., Israeli, A., Moran, S.: Self-stabilization of dynamic systems assuming only read/write atomicity. Distrib. Comput. **7**(1), 3–16 (1993)
9. Gale, D., Shapley, L.S.: College admissions and the stability of marriage. The American Mathematical Monthly (1962)
10. Gonczarowski, Y.A., Nisan, N., Ostrovsky, R., Rosenbaum, W.: A stable marriage requires communication. In: SODA 2015 (2015)

11. Knuth, D.E.: Mariages stables et leurs relations avec d'autres problemes combinatoires. Les Presses de l'Université de Montréal (1976)
12. Laveau, M., Manoussakis, G., Beauquier, J., Bernard, T., Burman, J., Cohen, J., Pilard, L.: Self-stabilizing distributed stable marriage. In: Spirakis, P., Tsigas, P. (eds.) SSS 2017. LNCS, vol. 10616, pp. 46–61. Springer, Cham (2017). https://doi. org/10.1007/978-3-319-69084-1_4
13. Yao, A.C.-C.: Some complexity questions related to distributive computing (preliminary report). In: STOC 1979. ACM (1979)

Brief Announcement: Feasibility of Weak Gathering in Connected-over-Time Dynamic Rings

Fukuhito Ooshita[1(✉)] and Ajoy K. Datta[2]

[1] Graduate School of Science and Technology,
Nara Institute of Science and Technology,
Takayama 8916-5, Ikoma, Nara 630-0192, Japan
f-oosita@is.naist.jp

[2] Department of Computer Science, University of Nevada, Las Vegas, USA

1 Introduction

Background and Motivation. The *gathering problem* is a fundamental problem for cooperation of mobile agents (or simply, agents). The problem requires multiple mobile agents initially located at different nodes to eventually meet at a single node. The problem is called the *rendezvous problem* for the case of two agents. Mobile agents may be software programs that can autonomously move in a distributed system, or robots that can move in a real world. By solving the gathering problem, agents can share information previously collected by each mobile agent, or divide and assign tasks to agents.

The gathering and rendezvous problems have been extensively studied with various assumptions [5]. However, most works assume the network is *static*. That is, the network topology does not change during execution of the algorithm. On the other hand, frequent topology changes are not anomaly in some networks such as a mobile ad-hoc network and a transportation network. For this reason, *dynamic* networks, where the network topology may change over time, have received a lot of attention recently [3].

A few gathering algorithms have been proposed for dynamic networks. Di Luna et al. [4] studied *1-interval-connected* (dynamic) rings, in which at most one edge is missing at each time unit. They prove that it is impossible to make all agents meet at a single node, and so they provide algorithms to achieve a *weak gathering* such that all agents meet at a single node or gather at two neighboring nodes. As a less-restricted model, Bournat et al. [1] have studied a *connected-over-time* (dynamic) ring recently. The only constraint of connected-over-time rings is that any node is infinitely often reachable from any other node. Different from [4], Bournat et al. provide a gathering algorithm such that all agents but at most one agents meet at a single node. In this paper, we follow the definition of weak gathering in [4] and study the feasibility of weak gathering in connected-over-time rings.

This work was supported by Japan Science and Technology Agency (JST) SICORP and JSPS KAKENHI Grant Number 18K11167.

T. Izumi and P. Kuznetsov (Eds.): SSS 2018, LNCS 11201, pp. 393–397, 2018.
https://doi.org/10.1007/978-3-030-03232-6_27

Our Contributions. In this paper, we study the gathering problem in connected-over-time rings with n nodes, and clarify conditions to realize a gathering algorithm. We consider k synchronous agents and assume that they have unique identifiers and know neither n nor k. We aim to achieve a *weak gathering* in [4] such that all agents meet at a single node or gather at two neighboring nodes.

First, we prove that there exists no gathering algorithm (1) when agents cannot leave information at nodes, (2) when agents and nodes have arbitrary initial states, or (3) when all agents should terminate. The third impossibility contrasts with an algorithm for 1-interval-connected rings [4], which realizes termination on the assumption that agents have no identifiers and leave marks at their starting nodes. From these impossibility results, we should consider stronger conditions to develop a gathering algorithm.

Second, we propose a gathering algorithm such that (1) agents can use whiteboards, (2) agents and nodes have designated initial states (with arbitrary initial positions), and (3) agents may not terminate. From the above impossibility results, the assumptions of our algorithm are weakest. Our algorithm guarantees that, if every edge appears infinitely often, agents meet at a single node and terminate. Otherwise (i.e., if one edge disappears forever), agents may gather at two end nodes of a missing edge and continue to move toward the missing edge.

2 Preliminaries

In this paper, we extend the model in [4] to connected-over-time rings [1], which is based on *evolving graphs* introduced in [2]. An evolving graph $\mathcal{G}$ is a sequence of graphs $\mathcal{G} = G_0, G_1, \ldots$ such that, for any $i \geq 0$, $G_i = (V, E_i)$ is a subgraph of a given graph $G = (V, E)$. Graph G_i represents the topology at time i, i.e., edge e is present at time i if and only if $e \in E_i$ holds. The *underlying graph* of $\mathcal{G}$, denoted by $U_{\mathcal{G}}$, is a graph composed of all edges that are present at least once in $\mathcal{G}$, i.e., $U_{\mathcal{G}} = (V, E_{\mathcal{G}})$ where $E_{\mathcal{G}} = \cup_{i=0}^{\infty} E_i$. Edge e is *eventually missing* if there exists i' such that $e \notin E_i$ holds for any $i \geq i'$. An *eventual underlying graph* of $\mathcal{G}$, denoted by $U_{\mathcal{G}}^e$, is a graph composed of all edges that are not eventually missing. An evolving graph $\mathcal{G}$ is a *connected-over-time* ring if and only if its underlying graph $U_{\mathcal{G}}$ is a ring and its eventual underlying graph $U_{\mathcal{G}}^e$ is connected. This means each node is infinitely often reachable from any other node. Note that, in connected-over-time rings, at most one edge is eventually missing.

We assume that agents start their actions from arbitrary nodes (multiple agents may stay at a single node initially). Each agent a is assigned a unique identifier, denoted by $a.id$. Agents know neither the number of nodes n nor the number of agents k. Agents execute synchronous rounds, each of which consists of *Look*, *Compute*, and *Move* phases. Consider an agent a at node v. During the Look phase, a obtains the snapshot of local states. That is, a obtains states of v and all agents at v. Agent a does not obtain whether edges incident to v are present in G_i or not. During the Compute phase, a executes the algorithm based on the snapshot obtained in the Look phase. If a decides to move, it tries to move during the Move phase. If the link from v to the destination appears in this round, a succeeds to move. Otherwise, a remains to stay at v.

In this paper, we say agents achieve a (weak) gathering if both of the following conditions hold: (1) all agents gather at a single node or at two neighboring nodes, and (2) no agent changes its position after that.

3   Impossibility Results

In this section, we give three impossibility results. We show the following theorems on the assumption that all agents agree on the direction of the ring. That is, these theorems hold even if agents have a sense of direction.

Theorem 1. *If agents cannot leave any information at nodes, no algorithm with designated initial states solves gathering without termination.*

Theorem 2. *Even if agents can use whiteboards at nodes, no algorithm with arbitrary initial states solves gathering without termination. This holds even if agents know n and k.*

Theorem 3. *Even if agents can use whiteboards at nodes, no algorithm with designated initial states solves gathering with termination. This holds even if agents know n and k.*

Proof (Sketch). For contradiction, assume that there exists such an algorithm $\mathcal{A}$. If the adversary continues to remove an edge between two agents a_1 and a_2, these two agents cannot meet and hence terminate at two neighboring nodes v_1 and v_2. We define v_0, v_3, and v_4 as nodes such that v_0, v_1, v_2, v_3, and v_4 are five successive nodes.

Let r_1 (resp., r_2) be the last round during which some agents join v_1 (resp., v_2). Without loss of generality, we assume $r_1 \le r_2$. After the r_2-th round, all agents eventually terminate without moving to other nodes. This implies that agents in v_1 will eventually terminate as long as no other agent visits v_1.

On the other hand, we can show that the adversary removes (v_1, v_2) in the r_2-th round. This implies that some agent a_3 stays at v_3 in the $(r_2 - 1)$-th round and moves to v_2 during the r_2-th round.

Now we change the behavior of the adversary so that the adversary removes edges (v_2, v_3) and (v_3, v_4) additionally after the r_2-th round. This implies that a_3 cannot join v_2 in the r_2-th round. In this case, a_3 remains to stay at v_3, while agents in v_1 will eventually terminate. After agents in v_1 terminate, the adversary removes only an edge through which a_3 decides to move. Since agents continue to stay at v_1 and v_3, $\mathcal{A}$ cannot achieve a gathering. This is a contradiction.   □

4   A Gathering Algorithm

In this section, we propose an algorithm to complement the impossibility results presented in the previous section. The algorithm solves gathering without termination on the assumption that agents can use whiteboards at nodes and they start from designated initial configurations.

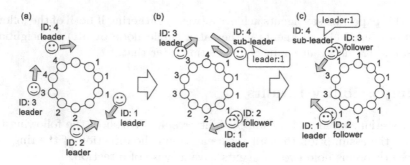

Fig. 1. The basic behaviors of the algorithm.

States of Agents. The algorithm works based on leader election. In the algorithm, a_i has variable $a_i.state \in \{\texttt{leader}, \texttt{sub-leader}, \texttt{follower}\}$. We say agent a_i is a leader, a sub-leader, or a follower depending on $a_i.state$. Each leader or sub-leader agent a_i maintains the leader ID in variable $a_i.leader$. If a_i is a leader, $a_i.leader = a_i.id$ holds. If a_i is a sub-leader, $a_i.leader = a_j.id \neq a_i.id$ holds for some agent a_j. In this case, we say a_i is a sub-leader of a_j.

When two leader or sub-leader agents a_i and a_j meet, they compare leader IDs $a_i.leader$ and $a_j.leader$. When the leader IDs are different, agents execute a leader election. Without loss of generality, we assume $a_i.leader < a_j.leader$ holds. In this case, a_j becomes a follower of a_i. That is, a_j sets $a_j.state = \texttt{follower}$ and $a_j.follow = a_i.id$, where variable $a_j.follow$ stores the ID of the agent that a_j follows. After a_j becomes a follower of a_i, a_j just moves together with a_i. Note that, since a_j can observe the states of all agents at the current node, a_j can observe the decision of a_i and move together. If a_i terminates, a_j also terminates. If a_i becomes a follower of some agent a_ℓ, a_j also becomes a follower of a_ℓ.

Behaviors of Leaders and Sub-leaders. In the following, we explain the behaviors of leaders and sub-leaders. To simplify the explanation, we assume that two agents never cross via an edge in the opposite directions at the same time. This assumption can be removed but due to limitation of space we omit the details.

Initially, all agents are leaders, that is, $a_i.state = \texttt{leader}$ and $a_i.leader = a_i.id$ hold for any agent a_i. Each leader tries to traverse a ring and during the movement, it writes its leader ID to whiteboards. That is, each leader a_i sets $v.leader = a_i.leader$ for every visited node v, where $v.leader$ is a variable on the whiteboard of node v. Figure 1(a) shows a configuration after a few rounds. The number near node v represents the value of $v.leader$.

If leader a_i finds a smaller leader ID at node v (i.e., $v.leader < a_i.leader$ holds), a_i becomes a sub-leader and records the leader ID (see the agent with ID 4 in Fig. 1(b)). That is, a_i sets $a_i.state = \texttt{sub-leader}$ and $a_i.leader = v.leader$. After that, a_i moves in the opposite direction. Similar to the leaders, sub-leader a_i writes its leader ID to whiteboards during the movement.

If multiple leaders or sub-leaders with different leader IDs meet, they execute leader election as described before (see agents with IDs 1 and 2 in Fig. 1(b)). As a result, the agent with the minimum leader ID remains as a leader or a sub-leader and other agents become followers of the remaining leader or sub-leader.

Consider the case that a sub-leader and a leader with the same leader ID meet (consider configurations after Fig. 1(c)). This happens only when the leader ID is the minimum among all agents. In addition, all other agents have become followers of the leader or the sub-leader. This implies that all agents stay at the same node in this case. Hence, the leader and the sub-leader terminate with their followers and achieve the gathering.

If all agents meet the agent a_{min} with the minimum ID before they visit some node v with $v.leader = a_{min}.id$, there exists no sub-leader of a_{min}. In this case, a_{min} traverses the ring without meeting a sub-leader of a_{min}. That is, a_{min} visits node v with $v.leader = a_{min}.id$. In this case, since all other agents have become followers of a_{min}, a_{min} terminates with its followers and achieves the gathering.

From these behaviors, all agents keep moving before they terminate by achieving the gathering. This implies that, if there exists an eventually missing edge and agents do not meet at a single node, all agents stay at two end nodes of the eventually missing edge and try to move toward the edge. Hence, they have achieved the (weak) gathering.

References

1. Bournat, M., Dubois, S., Petit, F.: Gracefully degrading gathering in dynamic rings. In: Proceedings of 20th International Symposium on Stabilization, Safety, and Security of Distributed Systems (2018)
2. Bui-Xuan, B., Ferreira, A., Jarry, A.: Computing shortest, fastest, and foremost journeys in dynamic networks. Int. J. Found. Comput. Sci. **14**(2), 267–285 (2003)
3. Casteigts, A., Flocchini, P., Quattrociocchi, W., Santoro, N.: Time-varying graphs and dynamic networks. IJPEDS **27**(5), 387–408 (2012)
4. Di Luna, G.A., Flocchini, P., Pagli, L., Prencipe, G., Santoro, N., Viglietta, G.: Gathering in dynamic rings. In: Das, S., Tixeuil, S. (eds.) SIROCCO 2017. LNCS, vol. 10641, pp. 339–355. Springer, Cham (2017). https://doi.org/10.1007/978-3-319-72050-0_20
5. Pelc, A.: Deterministic rendezvous in networks: a comprehensive survey. Networks **59**, 331–347 (2012)

Brief Announcement: Optimal Self-stabilizing Mobile Byzantine-Tolerant Regular Register with Bounded Timestamps

Silvia Bonomi[1(✉)], Antonella Del Pozzo[1,2], Maria Potop-Butucaru[2], and Sébastien Tixeuil[2]

[1] Sapienza Università di Roma, Via Ariosto 25, 00185 Roma, Italy
{bonomi,delpozzo}@diag.uniroma1.it
[2] Sorbonne Université, CNRS, Laboratoire d'Informatique de Paris 6,
75005 Paris, France
{maria.potop-butucaru,sebastien.tixeuil}@lip6.fr

Abstract. This paper investigates on the implementation of a self-stabilizing regular register emulated by n servers that is tolerant to both *mobile Byzantine agents*, and *transient failures* in a round-free synchronous model. Differently from existing Mobile Byzantine tolerant register implementation, this paper considers a more powerful adversary where (i) the message delay (i.e., δ) and the period of mobile Byzantine agents movement (i.e., Δ) are completely decoupled and (ii) servers are not aware of their state i.e., they do not know if they have been corrupted or not by a mobile Byzantine agent.

We claim the existence of an optimal protocol that tolerates *(i)* any number of transient failures, and *(ii)* up to f Mobile Byzantine agents.

1 Introduction

Byzantine fault tolerance is a fundamental building block in distributed systems as Byzantine failures include all possible faults, attacks, virus infections and arbitrary behaviors that can occur in practice (even unforeseen ones). Such bad behaviors have been typically abstracted by assuming an upper bound f on the number of Byzantine failures in the system. However, such assumption has two main limitations: (i) it is not suited for long lasting executions and (ii) it does not consider the fact that compromised processes/servers may be restored as infections may be blocked and confined or rejuvenation mechanisms can be put in place [22] making the set of faulty processes changing along time.

Mobile Byzantine Failure (MBF) models have been recently introduced to integrate those concerns. Failures are represented by Byzantine agents that are managed by an omniscient adversary that "moves" them from a host process to another and when an agent is in some process it is able to corrupt it in an unforeseen manner. Models investigated so far in the context of Mobile Byzantine

T. Izumi and P. Kuznetsov (Eds.): SSS 2018, LNCS 11201, pp. 398–403, 2018.
https://doi.org/10.1007/978-3-030-03232-6_28

Failures consider mostly *round-based* computations, and can be classified, according to Byzantine mobility constraints, in *(i)* constrained mobility [11] where agents may only move from one host to another when protocol messages are sent (similarly to how viruses would propagate), and *(ii)* unconstrained mobility [2,4,14,18–20] where agents may move independently of protocol messages.

A first step toward decoupling algorithm rounds from Mobile Byzantine movement is due to Bonomi *et al.* [8]. In their solution to the regular register implementation, Mobile Byzantine movements are synchronised, but the period of movement is independent to that of algorithm rounds.

Concerning *self-stabilization* [12,13], it is a versatile technique to recover from *any number of Byzantine participants*, provided that their malicious actions only spread a *finite* amount of *time*. In more details, starting from an arbitrary global state (that may have been caused by Byzantine participants), a self-stabilizing protocol ensures that problem specification is satisfied again in finite time, without external intervention.

Register Emulation. Traditional solutions to build a Byzantine tolerant storage service (*a.k.a.* register emulation) can be divided into two categories: *replicated state machines* [21], and *Byzantine quorum systems* [3,15–17]. Both approaches are based on the idea that the current state of the storage is replicated among processes, and the main difference lies in the number of replicas that are simultaneously involved in the state maintenance protocol. Recently, several works investigated the emulation of self-stabilizing or pseudo-stabilizing Byzantine tolerant SWMR or MWMR registers [1,6,9]. All these works do not consider the complex case of Mobile Byzantine Failures.

To the best of our knowledge, the problem of tolerating both *arbitrary transient failures and Mobile Byzantine Failures* has been considered recently only in round-based synchronous systems [5]. The authors propose optimal *unbounded* self-stabilizing atomic register implementations for *round-based synchronous* systems under the four Mobile Byzantine models described in [2,4,14,20].

Our Contribution. The main contribution of this paper is proving the existence of a protocol $\mathcal{P}_{reg}$ emulating a regular register in a distributed system where both arbitrary transient failures and Mobile Byzantine Failures can occur.

2 System Model

We consider a distributed system composed of an arbitrary large set of client processes $\mathcal{C}$ and a set of n server processes $\mathcal{S} = \{s_1, s_2 \ldots s_n\}$. Each process in the distributed system is identified by a unique identifier. Servers run a distributed protocol emulating a shared memory abstraction and such protocol is totally transparent to clients.

Communication Model and Time Assumption. Processes communicate through message passing. In particular, we assume that: *(i)* each client $c_i \in C$ can communicate with every server through a broadcast() primitive, *(ii)* each server can communicate with every other server through a broadcast() primitive, and *(iii)* each server can communicate with a particular client through a send() unicast primitive. We assume that communications are authenticated and reliable. We assume that if a process sends a message m at time t then it is delivered by time $t + \delta$. Moreover, we assume that δ is known to every process. Any process is provided with a physical clock, *i.e.*, non corruptible.

Failure Model. An arbitrary number of clients may crash while servers are affected by *Mobile Byzantine Failures* i.e., failures are represented by Byzantine agents that are controlled by a powerful external adversary "moving" them from a server to another. We assume that, at any time t, at most f mobile Byzantine agents are in system. In this work we consider the Δ-synchronized and Cured Unaware Model, i.e. $(\Delta S, CUM)$ MBF model, introduced in [8] that is suited for round-free computations[1].

As in the case of round-based MBF models [2,4,11,14,20], we assume that any process has access to a tamper-proof memory storing the correct protocol code.

Let us stress that during the system life time at any time t, at most f servers can be controlled by Byzantine agents, but all servers may be affected by a Byzantine agent.

Processes may also suffer from *transient* failures, *i.e.*, local variables of any process (clients and servers) can be arbitrarily modified [13]. It is nevertheless assumed that transient failures are quiescent, *i.e.*, there exists a time τ_{no_tr} (which is unknown to the processes) after which no new transient failures happens.

3 Self-stabilizing Regular Register Specification

A register is a shared variable accessed by a set of processes, *i.e.* clients, through two operations, namely read() and write(). The Self-Stabilizing Single-Writer/Multi-Reader (SWMR) register is specified as follow:

- ss − Termination: Any operation invoked on the register by a non-crashed process eventually terminates.
- ss − Validity: There exists a time t_{stab} such that each read() operation invoked at time $t > t_{stab}$ returns the last value written before its invocation, or a value written by a write() operation concurrent with it.

---

[1] The $(\Delta S, CUM)$ model abstracts distributed systems subjected to proactive rejuvenation [22] where processes have no self-diagnosis capability.

4   Optimal Self-stabilizing MBFT Regular Register

This Section provides the main claim of the paper and its informal proof.

Theorem 1. *Let n be the number of servers emulating the register and let f be the number of Byzantine agents in the $(\Delta S, CUM)$ round-free Mobile Byzantine Failure model. Let δ be the upper bound on the communication latencies in the synchronous system.*

If (i) $n \geq 6f + 1$ for $\Delta = 2\delta$ and (ii) $n \geq 8f + 1$ for $\Delta = \delta$, then there exists an optimal protocol $\mathcal{P}_{reg}$ implementing a Self-Stabilizing SWMR Regular Register in the $(\Delta S, CUM)$ round-free Mobile Byzantine Failure model.

Due to the lack of space, the protocol $\mathcal{P}_{reg}$ proving the claim is detailed in the complete version of this work [7].

The basic ingredients of protocol $\mathcal{P}_{reg}$ to solve issues coming from the $(\Delta S, CUM)$ model and from transient failures are the following:

– Concerning the $(\Delta S, CUM)$ assumption, the protocol needs to handle processes that have been affected by a Byzantine agent and are not aware about that. This is done by implementing a mechanism that keep separated "trusted" values from *untrusted* ones whenever processes need to collect information from the others (e.g., during a read() operation). Trusted values are basically values acquired directly from clients or acknowledged by "enough" processes while untrusted ones are those stored locally that can be compromised. This requires to keep track of the last three written values and to use multiple data structures managed trough time-windows.
– Concerning the management of transient failures, $\mathcal{P}_{reg}$ is able to stabilise by using bounded timestamps from the $\mathcal{Z}_{13}$ domain.

Finally, $\mathcal{P}_{reg}$ is optimal as it matches lower bounds proved in [10].

5   Concluding Remarks

This paper investigated on the existence of a self-stabilizing regular register emulation in a distributed system where both transient failures and Mobile Byzantine Failures can occur, and where messages and Byzantine agent movements are decoupled.

An interesting future research direction is to study upper and lower bounds for *(i)* memory, and *(ii)* convergence time complexity of self-stabilizing register emulations tolerating Mobile Byzantine Failures.

Acknowledgements. This work was performed within Project ESTATE (Ref. ANR-16-CE25-0009-03), supported by French state funds managed by the ANR (Agence Nationale de la Recherche). This work has been also partially supported by the INOCS Sapienza Ateneo 2017 Project (protocol number RM11715C816CE4CB).

References

1. Alon, N., Attiya, H., Dolev, S., Dubois, S., Potop-Butucaru, M., Tixeuil, S.: Practically stabilizing SWMR atomic memory in message-passing systems. J. Comput. Syst. Sci. **81**, 692–701 (2015)
2. Banu, N., Souissi, S., Izumi, T., Wada, K.: An improved Byzantine agreement algorithm for synchronous systems with mobile faults. Int. J. Comput. Appl. **43**(22), 1–7 (2012)
3. Bazzi, R.A.: Synchronous Byzantine quorum systems. Distrib. Comput. **13**(1), 45–52 (2000)
4. Bonnet, F., Défago, X., Nguyen, T.D., Potop-Butucaru, M.: Tight bound on mobile Byzantine agreement. In: Kuhn, F. (ed.) DISC 2014. LNCS, vol. 8784, pp. 76–90. Springer, Heidelberg (2014). https://doi.org/10.1007/978-3-662-45174-8_6
5. Bonomi, S., Del Pozzo, A., Potop-Butucaru, M.: Optimal self-stabilizing synchronous mobile Byzantine-tolerant atomic register. Theor. Comput. Sci. **709**, 64–79 (2018)
6. Bonomi, S., Dolev, S., Potop-Butucaru, M., Raynal, M.: Stabilizing server-based storage in Byzantine asynchronous message-passing systems. In: Proceedings of the ACM Symposium on Principles of Distributed Computing (PODC 2015) (2015)
7. Bonomi, S., Del Pozzo, A., Potop-Butucaru, M., Tixeuil, S.: Self-stabilizing mobile Byzantine-tolerant regular register with bounded timestamp. Research report. http://arxiv.org/abs/1609.02694
8. Bonomi, S., Del Pozzo, A., Potop-Butucaru, M., Tixeuil, S.: Optimal mobile Byzantine fault tolerant distributed storage. In: Proceedings of the ACM International Conference on Principles of Distributed Computing (ACM PODC 2016), Chicago, USA. ACM Press, July 2016
9. Bonomi, S., Potop-Butucaru, M., Tixeuil, S.: Byzantine tolerant storage. In: Proceedings of the International Conference on Parallel and Distributed Processing Systems (IEEE IPDPS 2015) (2015)
10. Bonomi, S., Del Pozzo, A., Potop-Butucaru, M., Tixeuil, S.: Optimal storage under unsynchronized mobile Byzantine faults. In: 36th IEEE Symposium on Reliable Distributed Systems, SRDS 2017, Hong Kong, 26–29 September 2017
11. Buhrman, H., Garay, J.A., Hoepman, J.-H.: Optimal resiliency against mobile faults. In: Proceedings of the 25th International Symposium on Fault-Tolerant Computing (FTCS 1995), pp. 83–88 (1995)
12. Dijkstra, E.W.: Self-stabilizing systems in spite of distributed control. CACM **17**(11), 643–644 (1974)
13. Dolev, S.: Self-Stabilization. MIT Press, Cambridge (2000)
14. Garay, J.A.: Reaching (and maintaining) agreement in the presence of mobile faults. In: Tel, G., Vitányi, P. (eds.) WDAG 1994. LNCS, vol. 857, pp. 253–264. Springer, Heidelberg (1994). https://doi.org/10.1007/BFb0020438
15. Malkhi, D., Reiter, M.: Byzantine quorum systems. Distrib. Comput. **11**(4), 203–213 (1998)
16. Martin, J.-P., Alvisi, L., Dahlin, M.: Minimal Byzantine storage. In: Malkhi, D. (ed.) DISC 2002. LNCS, vol. 2508, pp. 311–325. Springer, Heidelberg (2002). https://doi.org/10.1007/3-540-36108-1_21
17. Martin, J.-P., Alvisi, L., Dahlin, M.: Small Byzantine quorum systems. In: 2002 Proceedings of International Conference on Dependable Systems and Networks. DSN 2002, pp. 374–383. IEEE (2002)

18. Ostrovsky, R., Yung, M.: How to withstand mobile virus attacks (extended abstract). In: Proceedings of the 10th Annual ACM Symposium on Principles of Distributed Computing (PODC 1991), pp. 51–59 (1991)
19. Reischuk, R.: A new solution for the Byzantine generals problem. Inf. Control **64**(1–3), 23–42 (1985)
20. Sasaki, T., Yamauchi, Y., Kijima, S., Yamashita, M.: Mobile Byzantine agreement on arbitrary network. In: Baldoni, R., Nisse, N., van Steen, M. (eds.) OPODIS 2013. LNCS, vol. 8304, pp. 236–250. Springer, Cham (2013). https://doi.org/10.1007/978-3-319-03850-6_17
21. Schneider, F.B.: Implementing fault-tolerant services using the state machine approach: a tutorial. ACM Comput. Surv. **22**(4), 299–319 (1990)
22. Sousa, P., Bessani, A.N., Correia, M., Neves, N.F., Verissimo, P.: Highly available intrusion-tolerant services with proactive-reactive recovery. IEEE Trans. Parallel Distrib. Syst. **4**, 452–465 (2009)

Brief Announcement Continuous *vs.* Discrete Asynchronous Moves: A Certified Approach for Mobile Robots

Thibaut Balabonski[1], Pierre Courtieu[2], Robin Pelle[1], Lionel Rieg[3], Sébastien Tixeuil[4,5], and Xavier Urbain[6(✉)]

[1] LRI, CNRS UMR 8623, Université Paris-Sud, Université Paris-Saclay, Paris, France
[2] CÉDRIC – Conservatoire National des Arts et Métiers, Paris, France
[3] Yale University, New Haven, CT, USA
[4] Sorbonne Université, CNRS, Laboratoire d'Informatique de Paris 6, LIP6, 75005 Paris, France
[5] Institut Universitaire de France, Paris, France
[6] Université Claude Bernard Lyon-1, LIRIS CNRS UMR 5205, Université de Lyon, Lyon, France
Xavier.Urbain@lri.fr

Networks of mobile robots captured the attention of the distributed computing community, as they promise new application (rescue, exploration, surveillance) in potentially harmful environments. Originally introduced in 1999 by Suzuki and Yamashita [27], the model has been refined since by many authors while growing in popularity (see [20] for a comprehensive textbook). From a theoretical point of view, the interest lies in characterising, for each of these various refinements, the exact conditions under which a particular task can be solved or not.

In the model we consider, all robots are anonymous and operate using the same embedded program through repeated Look-Compute-Move cycles. In each cycle, a robot first "looks" at its environment and obtains a snapshot containing some information about the locations of all robots, expressed in the robot's own self-centred coordinate system, whose scale and orientation might not be consistent with the other robot's coordinate systems. Then the robot "computes" a destination, still in its own coordinate system, based only on the snapshot it just obtained. Finally the robot "moves" towards the computed destination.

The general model is agnostic to the shape of the space where the robots operate, which can be the real line, a two dimensional Euclidean space, a discrete space (*a.k.a.* a graph), or even another space with a more intricate topology. To date, two independent lines of research focused on *(i)* continuous Euclidean spaces, and *(ii)* graphs, studying different sets of problems and using distinct algorithmic techniques.

1 Continuous *vs.* Discrete Spaces

The core problem to solve in the context of mobile robot networks that operate in bidimensional continuous spaces is *pattern formation*, where robots starting from

© Springer Nature Switzerland AG 2018
T. Izumi and P. Kuznetsov (Eds.): SSS 2018, LNCS 11201, pp. 404–408, 2018.
https://doi.org/10.1007/978-3-030-03232-6_29

distinct initial positions have to form a given geometric pattern. Arbitrary patterns can be formed when robots have memory [27] or common knowledge [21], otherwise only a subset of patterns can be achieved. Forming a point as the target pattern is known as *gathering* [27], where robots have to meet at a single point in space in finite time, not known beforehand. The problem is generally impossible to solve [25] unless the setting is fully synchronous [3] or robots are endowed with multiplicity detection [10]. Recently, researchers considered tridimensional Euclidean spaces [28], where robots must solve *plane formation*, that is, land on a common plane (not determined beforehand) in finite time. In the context of robots operating on graphs, typical problems are *terminating exploration* [16,19], where robots must explore all nodes of a given graph and then stop moving forever, *exclusive perpetual exploration* [7,14], where robots must explore all nodes of a graph forever without ever colliding, *exclusive searching* [6,13], where robots must capture an intruder in the graph without colliding, and *gathering* [8,14,22,23], where robots must meet at a given node in finite time.

Although some of the studied problems overlap (*e.g.* gathering), the algorithmic techniques that enable solving problems are substantially different. On the one hand, robots operating in continuous spaces may typically use fractional distance moves to another robot, or non-straight moves in order to make the algorithm progress, two options that are not possible in the discrete model. On the other hand, in the asynchronous continuous setting, a robot may be seen by another robot as it is moving, hence at some arbitrary position between its source and destination point within a cycle, something that is impossible to observe in the discrete setting. Indeed, all aforementioned works for robots on graph consider that their moves are atomic, even in the ASYNC setting, which may seem unrealistic to a practitioner.

2   Related Works

Designing and proving mobile robot protocols is notoriously difficult. Formal methods encompass a long-lasting path of research that is meant to overcome errors of human origin. Unsurprisingly, this mechanised approach to protocol correctness was successively used in the context of mobile robots.

In the discrete setting, model-checking proved useful to find bugs (usually in the ASYNC setting) in existing literature [5,17,18] and formally check the correctness of published algorithms [5,15]. Automatic program synthesis [9,24] can be used to obtain automatically algorithms that are "correct-by-design". However, those approaches are limited to small instances with few robots. Generalising to an arbitrary number of robots with similar approaches is doubtful as Sangnier *et al.* [26] proved that safety and reachability problems become undecidable in the parameterised case.

When robots move freely in a continuous bidimensional Euclidean space, to the best of our knowledge the only formal framework available is the Pactole framework.[1] Pactole enabled the use of higher-order logic to certify impossibility results [1,4,11] as well as certifying the correctness of algorithms [3,12], possibly for an arbitrary number of robots (hence in a scalable manner). Pactole was recently extended by Balabonski *et al.* [4] to handle discrete spaces as well as continuous spaces, thanks to its modular design. However, to this paper, Pactole only allowed one to express specifications and proofs with the FSYNC and SSYNC models.

3　Our Contribution

In this brief announcement, we explore the possibility of establishing a first bridge between the continuous movements and observation vs. discrete movements and observation in the context of autonomous mobile robots. Our position is that the continuous model reflects well the physicality of robots operating in some environment, while the discrete model reflects well the digital nature of autonomous robots, whose sensors and computing capabilities are inherently finite. For this purpose, we consider that robots make continuous, non atomic moves, but only sense in a discrete manner the position of robots. Our approach is certified using the Coq proof assistant and the Pactole framework.

In more details, our full paper [2] first extends the Pactole framework to handle the ASYNC model, preserving its modularity by keeping the operating space and the robots algorithm both abstract. This permits to retain the same formal framework for both continuous and discrete spaces, and the possibility for mobile robots to be faulty (even possibly malicious *a.k.a. Byzantine*). Then, as an application of the new framework, we formally prove in the full paper [2] the equivalence between atomic moves in a discrete space (the classical model for robots operating on graphs) and non-atomic moves in a continuous unidimensional space *when robot vision sensors are discrete* (that is, robots are only able to see another robot on a node when they perform the Look phase, but robots can move anywhere between two adjacent nodes), irrespective of the problem being solved. Our effort consolidates the integration between the model, the problem specification, and its proof that is advocated by the Pactole framework.

Pactole and the formal developments of this work are available at http://pactole.lri.fr.

References

1. Auger, C., Bouzid, Z., Courtieu, P., Tixeuil, S., Urbain, X.: Certified impossibility results for Byzantine-tolerant mobile robots. In: Higashino, T., Katayama, Y., Masuzawa, T., Potop-Butucaru, M., Yamashita, M. (eds.) SSS 2013. LNCS, vol. 8255, pp. 178–190. Springer, Cham (2013). https://doi.org/10.1007/978-3-319-03089-0_13
2. Balabonski, T., Courtieu, P., Pelle, R., Rieg, L., Tixeuil, S., Urbain, X.: Continuous vs. discrete asynchronous moves: a certified approach for mobile robots. Research report, Sorbonne Université, CNRS, Laboratoire d'Informatique de Paris 6, LIP6, Paris, France (2018)

---

[1] http://pactole.lri.fr.

3. Balabonski, T., Delga, A., Rieg, L., Tixeuil, S., Urbain, X.: Synchronous gathering without multiplicity detection: a certified algorithm. In: Bonakdarpour, B., Petit, F. (eds.) SSS 2016. LNCS, vol. 10083, pp. 7–19. Springer, Cham (2016). https://doi.org/10.1007/978-3-319-49259-9_2

4. Balabonski, T., Pelle, R., Rieg, L., Tixeuil, S.: A foundational framework for certified impossibility results with mobile robots on graphs. In: Proceedings of International Conference on Distributed Computing and Networking, Varanasi, India, January 2018

5. Bérard, B., Lafourcade, P., Millet, L., Potop-Butucaru, M., Thierry-Mieg, Y., Tixeuil, S.: Formal verification of mobile robot protocols. Distrib. Comput. **29**(6), 459–487 (2016)

6. Blin, L., Burman, J., Nisse, N.: Exclusive graph searching. Algorithmica **77**(3), 942–969 (2017)

7. Blin, L., Milani, A., Potop-Butucaru, M., Tixeuil, S.: Exclusive perpetual ring exploration without chirality. In: Lynch, N.A., Shvartsman, A.A. (eds.) DISC 2010. LNCS, vol. 6343, pp. 312–327. Springer, Heidelberg (2010). https://doi.org/10.1007/978-3-642-15763-9_29

8. Bonnet, F., Potop-Butucaru, M., Tixeuil, S.: Asynchronous gathering in rings with 4 robots. In: Mitton, N., Loscri, V., Mouradian, A. (eds.) ADHOC-NOW 2016. LNCS, vol. 9724, pp. 311–324. Springer, Cham (2016). https://doi.org/10.1007/978-3-319-40509-4_22

9. Bonnet, F., Défago, X., Petit, F., Potop-Butucaru, M., Tixeuil, S.: Discovering and assessing fine-grained metrics in robot networks protocols. In: 33rd IEEE International Symposium on Reliable Distributed Systems Workshops, SRDS Workshops 2014, 6–9 October 2014, Nara, Japan, pp. 50–59. IEEE (2014)

10. Cieliebak, M., Flocchini, P., Prencipe, G., Santoro, N.: Distributed computing by mobile robots: gathering. SIAM J. Comput. **41**(4), 829–879 (2012)

11. Courtieu, P., Rieg, L., Tixeuil, S., Urbain, X.: Impossibility of gathering, a certification. Inf. Process. Lett. **115**, 447–452 (2015)

12. Courtieu, P., Rieg, L., Tixeuil, S., Urbain, X.: Certified universal gathering in $\mathbb{R}^2$ for oblivious mobile robots. In: Gavoille, C., Ilcinkas, D. (eds.) DISC 2016. LNCS, vol. 9888, pp. 187–200. Springer, Heidelberg (2016). https://doi.org/10.1007/978-3-662-53426-7_14

13. D'Angelo, G., Navarra, A., Nisse, N.: A unified approach for gathering and exclusive searching on rings under weak assumptions. Distrib. Comput. **30**(1), 17–48 (2017)

14. D'Angelo, G., Di Stefano, G., Navarra, A., Nisse, N., Suchan, K.: Computing on rings by oblivious robots: a unified approach for different tasks. Algorithmica **72**(4), 1055–1096 (2015)

15. Devismes, S., Lamani, A., Petit, F., Raymond, P., Tixeuil, S.: Optimal grid exploration by asynchronous oblivious robots. In: Richa, A.W., Scheideler, C. (eds.) SSS 2012. LNCS, vol. 7596, pp. 64–76. Springer, Heidelberg (2012). https://doi.org/10.1007/978-3-642-33536-5_7

16. Devismes, S., Petit, F., Tixeuil, S.: Optimal probabilistic ring exploration by semi-synchronous oblivious robots. Theor. Comput. Sci. **498**, 10–27 (2013)

17. Doan, H.T.T., Bonnet, F., Ogata, K.: Model checking of a mobile robots perpetual exploration algorithm. In: Liu, S., Duan, Z., Tian, C., Nagoya, F. (eds.) SOFL+MSVL 2016. LNCS, vol. 10189, pp. 201–219. Springer, Cham (2017). https://doi.org/10.1007/978-3-319-57708-1_12

18. Doan, H.T.T., Bonnet, F., Ogata, K.: Model checking of robot gathering. In: Aspnes, J., Felber, P. (eds.) Principles of Distributed Systems - 21th International Conference (OPODIS 2017), Leibniz International Proceedings in Informatics (LIPIcs), Lisbon, Portugal. Schloss Dagstuhl-Leibniz-Zentrum fuer Informatik, December 2017

19. Flocchini, P., Ilcinkas, D., Pelc, A., Santoro, N.: Computing without communicating: ring exploration by asynchronous oblivious robots. Algorithmica **65**(3), 562–583 (2013)

20. Flocchini, P., Prencipe, G., Santoro, N.: Distributed Computing by Oblivious Mobile Robots. Synthesis Lectures on Distributed Computing Theory. Morgan & Claypool Publishers, San Rafael (2012)

21. Flocchini, P., Prencipe, G., Santoro, N., Widmayer, P.: Arbitrary pattern formation by asynchronous, anonymous, oblivious robots. Theor. Comput. Sci. **407**(1–3), 412–447 (2008)

22. Kamei, S., Lamani, A., Ooshita, F., Tixeuil, S.: Asynchronous mobile robot gathering from symmetric configurations without global multiplicity detection. In: Kosowski, A., Yamashita, M. (eds.) SIROCCO 2011. LNCS, vol. 6796, pp. 150–161. Springer, Heidelberg (2011). https://doi.org/10.1007/978-3-642-22212-2_14

23. Kamei, S., Lamani, A., Ooshita, F., Tixeuil, S.: Gathering an even number of robots in an odd ring without global multiplicity detection. In: Rovan, B., Sassone, V., Widmayer, P. (eds.) MFCS 2012. LNCS, vol. 7464, pp. 542–553. Springer, Heidelberg (2012). https://doi.org/10.1007/978-3-642-32589-2_48

24. Millet, L., Potop-Butucaru, M., Sznajder, N., Tixeuil, S.: On the synthesis of mobile robots algorithms: the case of ring gathering. In: Felber, P., Garg, V. (eds.) SSS 2014. LNCS, vol. 8756, pp. 237–251. Springer, Cham (2014). https://doi.org/10.1007/978-3-319-11764-5_17

25. Prencipe, G.: Impossibility of gathering by a set of autonomous mobile robots. Theor. Comput. Sci. **384**(2–3), 222–231 (2007)

26. Sangnier, A., Sznajder, N., Potop-Butucaru, M., Tixeuil, S.: Parameterized verification of algorithms for oblivious robots on a ring. In: Formal Methods in Computer Aided Design, Vienna, Austria (2017)

27. Suzuki, I., Yamashita, M.: Distributed anonymous mobile robots: formation of geometric patterns. SIAM J. Comput. **28**(4), 1347–1363 (1999)

28. Yamauchi, Y., Uehara, T., Kijima, S., Yamashita, M.: Plane formation by synchronous mobile robots in the three-dimensional Euclidean space. J. ACM **64**(3), 16:1–16:43 (2017)

Author Index

Altisen, Karine 186

Balabonski, Thibaut 404
Baldoni, Roberto 139
Bazzi, Rida A. 381
Bazzi, Rida 254
Beauquier, Joffroy 387
Bernard, Thibault 387
Bonomi, Silvia 139, 170, 398
Bournat, Marjorie 349
Bramas, Quentin 333
Briones, Joseph L. 381
Bultel, Xavier 111
Burman, Janna 387
Busch, Costas 221

Chatterjee, Bapi 365
Cohen, Johanne 80
Courtieu, Pierre 404

Datta, Ajoy K. 365, 393
Del Pozzo, Antonella 398
Devismes, Stéphane 186
Doi, Keisuke 96
Dolev, Shlomi 139
Dreier, Jannik 111
Dubois, Swan 349
Dumas, Jean-Guillaume 111
Durand, Anaïs 186, 269

Farina, Giovanni 170
Feldmann, Michael 16
Feletti, Caterina 317

Gąsieniec, Leszek 126
Götte, Thorsten 50

Herlihy, Maurice 221, 254

Juyal, Chirag 284

Kijima, Shuji 96, 126
Knollmann, Till 1
Kolb, Christina 16
Kulkarni, Sandeep 284
Kumari, Sweta 284
Kunne, Stephan 80
Kutten, Shay 387

Lafourcade, Pascal 111
Laveau, Marie 387

Mereghetti, Carlo 317
Michail, Othon 154
Min, Jie 126
Miyahara, Daiki 111
Mizuki, Takaaki 111

Nagao, Atsuki 111
Niyolia, Rashmi 365

Ooshita, Fukuhito 301, 393

Palano, Beatrice 317
Pelle, Robin 404
Peri, Sathya 284
Petit, Franck 349
Pilard, Laurence 80
Potop-Butucaru, Maria 398
Poudel, Pavan 32

Rai, Shishir 221
Raynal, Michel 139, 269
Rieg, Lionel 404

Sasaki, Tatsuya 111
Scheideler, Christian 1, 16, 50, 239
Setzer, Alexander 50, 239
Shaer, Amitay 139
Sharma, Gokarna 32, 203, 221
Shinagawa, Kazumasa 111
Somani, Archit 284

Sone, Hideaki   111
Spirakis, Paul G.   154

Taubenfeld, Gadi   269
Theofilatos, Michail   154
Tixeuil, Sébastien   170, 301, 333, 398, 404
Trahan, Jerry L.   203
Tsigas, Philippas   365
Turau, Volker   65

Urbain, Xavier   404

Vaidyanathan, Ramachandran   203

Walulya, Ivan   365

Yamashita, Masafumi   96
Yamauchi, Yukiko   96

Printed in the United States
By Bookmasters